LAGRANGE COUNTY LIBRARY

LAGRANGE COUNTY PUBLIC LIBRARY
LGR   B WE   91487
West   H.G. Wells :   aspects of a life

3 0477 0005 8013 8

OFFICIAL DISCARD

D1380572

BOOKS BY ANTHONY WEST

D. H. Lawrence
The Vintage
Another Kind
Heritage
Principles and Persuasions
The Trend Is Up
David Rees, Among Others
John Piper
H. G. Wells: Aspects of a Life

H. G. WELLS

Aspects of a Life

LAGRANGE COUNTY LIBRARY

H. G. WELLS

Aspects of a Life

Anthony West

Random House   New York

Copyright © 1984 by Anthony West

All rights reserved under International and Pan-American Copyright Conventions.
Published in the United States by Random House, Inc., New York, and
simultaneously in Canada by Random House of Canada Limited, Toronto.

Grateful acknowledgment is made to the Executors of the Estate
of H.G. Wells for permission to quote from his works.

Library of Congress Cataloging in Publication Data

West, Anthony, 1914–
H.G. Wells: aspects of a life.

Includes index.
1. Wells, H. G. (Herbert George), 1866–1946—
Biography. 2. Novelists, English—20th century—
Biography. I. Title.
PR5776.W46   1984   823'.912   83-2074
ISBN 0-394-53196-5

Manufactured in the United States of America

24689753

FIRST EDITION

LAGRANGE COUNTY LIBRARY

For Olivia

14.14

5/84

Acknowledgements

I am deeply indebted to G. P. Wells and to Amber Blanco White for information about my father fundamental to the interpretation of his character and behaviour offered in this book. Frank Wells, E. S. P. Haynes, Odette Keun, and Moura Budberg, all made contributions only slightly less vital to my understanding of him before they died. My mother, Rebecca West, Dorothy Richardson, and Edward Pease, the former secretary of the Fabian Society, were helpful to me in a rather different way. Mary Ceibert, of the Rare Book Room in the Library of the University of Illinois Library at Champaign-Urbana was unfailingly courteous and efficient in meeting my demands for help in finding my way about the Wells Archive.

Fisher's Island, 1983   A.P.W.

H. G. WELLS

Aspects of a Life

Chapter I

... he was now concealing beneath the lively surface of activities with which Mr. Direck was now
familiar, a very extensive system of distresses arising out of the latest, the eighth of these
digressional adventures . . .

—Mr. Britling Sees It Through

WHILE I WAS BEING BORN, IN THE FIRST
few minutes of August 5, 1914, my
father was not close at hand to give my mother his comfort and
support. He was elsewhere, and his attention was concentrated on
another matter. In those very minutes the youthful Harold Nicolson
was walking across St. James's Park in London. He was on his way
from the British Foreign Office to the German Embassy in Carlton
House Terrace, and he was carrying with him the passports of the
ambassador and the embassy staff. The British government's ultimatum to the German government had expired at midnight, and since
that moment the two countries had been at war. My father, who was
H. G. Wells, was putting the finishing touches to an article in which
he discussed the meaning of this catastrophe, an article which was to
be the first in a series of twelve that he had already placed with *The
Daily Chronicle* in England, and which he hoped to sell to an American
syndicate.

My father had not been taken by surprise by the outbreak of the war.
He was one of a number of people who had seen it coming for several
years, and he had been giving it more and more thought as he had
watched it spreading out of the Balkans, dragging one great power

3

after another into it, since the end of June. He did not believe that it could have been avoided, and he did not want to believe that it would be futile. He hoped that it would do more than teach the Germans that aggression did not pay, and that its probable cost and its certain horrors would bring the age of competing nationalisms to an end. It was not just the Germany of the Junkers and of Bismarck's expansionist foreign policy that he wished to see broken—he longed to see the entirety of the old royalist military establishment hustled off the European stage. He was not narrowly anti-German, he detested the whole cast of befurred and befeathered, breastplated and helmeted crown princes, grand dukes, archdukes, and princelings who stood for Europe's divisions, and hoped that the war would mean the end of them all.

As my father worked away at his article in the stillness of the warm summer's night his mind ran on ahead of the hour. When the war was over there would be a chance to create a new European order. The victors and the defeated would have to get together to set up a League of Nations. One of its functions would be to provide a forum in which an open diplomacy could be carried on; it would be an international parliament. Another of its functions would be the organization of an international peace-keeping force. If such a body were to be kept in being on a permanent basis, aggressive war might become a thing of the past. A blow struck at one nation would be an assault on the world community, and aggression would become a loser's game. If men set their minds to it when the fighting ended, there might never have to be another war between the nations.

My father realised that he had found the perfect title for the article that he had just finished. He wrote it down, and liked it: "The War That Will End War." He turned out the lights in his study and went upstairs to bed. He was in Easton Glebe, the roomy and pleasant old rectory of a tiny hamlet near Great Dunmow in the Essex countryside northeast of London in which he had been living with his wife Jane and his two sons since 1912. My mother was just about a hundred miles away, across the breadth of East Anglia, in furnished lodgings at Hunstanton in Norfolk. A sister and a friend were with her. She was not married to anyone, and she was just beginning to realize how awkwardly she was situated.

My mother was nineteen years of age and twenty-six years younger than my father when she first met him in 1912. She had begun by wanting to be an actress, and in that phase she had changed her name

4

from Cicily Fairfield to Rebecca West. This was an act of homage to Henrik Ibsen, by whose *Rosmersholm* she had been powerfully affected. She was a young provincial, of mixed Scots and Northern Irish origin, who had been brought up in Edinburgh. When she met my father she had been living in London's Hampstead Garden Suburb with her mother and her two sisters for just under four years. She had been a student at RADA, the Royal Academy of Dramatic Art, for a couple of them, and she had done some touring, but she was in the process of discarding her theatrical for literary ambitions. These were considerable. A photograph taken not long after my father had come into her life shows her standing defiantly beside a bust of Dante. The photograph suggests that she intended the comparison to be made, and was serving notice on the literary world that it would soon have to reckon with her as a major figure.

My mother made her start as a writer by reviewing books for a radical feminist weekly called *The Freewoman,* whose slightly kooky editor thought of the vote as a secondary issue. For this offbeat magazine she wrote a slating of my father's novel *Marriage,* in which she took issue with his ideas about women. It was a lively piece of work which aroused his curiosity and amused Jane Wells, with the result that she was invited to come and spend a weekend with them at Easton Glebe.

Exactly what happened after that visit is not clear to me, but it is evident that my mother took the initiative. The originals of the letters that she wrote to my father before their affair had properly begun have not survived, but the copies of them that she rather remarkably made and kept leave no room for doubt about that. Although their tone is that of a Russian novel that has been passed through the mind of a Woody Allen character, they are not lightly to be dismissed. They make it plain that she was determined to be involved, and monumentally so, with my father. She was urging a *grand amour* upon him, the sort of thing from which the substance of romantic biographies of great and famous persons are made.

My father's replies to these letters—at first simply backing off, and then stating, with a candor that can only have been intended to be deterrent, the extremely limited extent to which he was willing to make himself available—leave his position in no doubt. If it was to be anything at all, their affair was not to be serious—it was to be light, and she was always to remember that it was a matter of two people finding each other physically attractive and coming together to couple for coupling's sake. And it was not to last. My father was explicit about that. When he finally wrote to her to say, in almost so many words, "Oh, all right then, if you insist . . ." he spelt it out: she was to understand that his horizon for the affair, the location for its conceptual vanishing point, was never to be thought of as lying further off than his next change of mood. It was to be all in fun, or it was not to be at all. He would do his best not to hurt her, but she was to understand that as soon as he began to find their little adventure boring or tiresome he would drop her. And that would be the end of it.

When my father proposed to have this affair on these temptingly easy terms he had no idea that my mother was one of the more gifted members of her generation, or that she would in due course be respected as a woman with an intelligence as great as his own, and an even livelier and sharper wit. These things were not as yet discernible. She was at that time deeply involved in a post-adolescent crisis of unusual severity, and self-enclosed to a remarkable degree. When they met to become lovers she did not strike him as the brilliantly amusing talker and the wonderful companion that she had it in her to be. Their meetings were, indeed, clouded by a certain awkwardness. She had come on in the role of the wholly liberated woman, and had overplayed the part. My father had found her affected, silly, and pretentious. He broke off the affair by letter, and killed the correspondence with a chilly rebuke when she protested. She had his sympathy, but until she was prepared to take a light relationship lightly it would have to be goodbye.

They did not see each other again until she had reviewed another of his novels. This time it was *The Passionate Friends.* In her critique she made the observation that there could be circumstances in which it was appropriate to take sex casually, and "to think no more hardly of two lovers who part soon than we do of spring for leaving the earth at the coming of June." This suggested to him that she might be closer to an acceptance of the ground rules that he laid down for his affairs than he had thought, and he decided that if she was still inclined he would give her another try.

There is something a little ominous in the fact that it was her criticism of this particular novel that revived his interest in her. Whatever it may amount to as literature, it has to be a haunting book for anyone who knows the detail of my father's life. When he wrote it he was working a grief out of his system. He had loved Amber Reeves, the young woman who bore him a daughter on the last day of 1909, as fully as he was capable of loving anyone, and it was the pain of losing her that gave him the substance of this novel.

Amber Reeves had been the embodiment of my father's ideal of what a liberated woman should be. Her kindly and well-meaning parents had held advanced views. They had brought her up to believe that she should consult her conscience rather than her knowledge of the conventions whenever she had to make a choice between one course of conduct and another. She had grown up to be a lively-minded, outgoing, generous, and courageous being, just as they had hoped. But she was also headstrong, as her mother had been before her, and, as is often the case with very clever young people, she grew up to find her elders more interesting company than members of her own generation. She first got to know my father as a friend of her parents, and became his friend while she was still in her late teens. She came to know him better after she had become a student at Cambridge and was beginning to think of herself as a young woman. When she found that she wanted him, and became aware that he was attracted to her, she consulted her conscience, which told her that it did not matter that she was just over twenty and he was almost forty, and that it would not be wrong for her to become his mistress. She knew of physical desire as a healthy and natural thing, and she saw no reason to flinch away from it when she experienced it. She delighted in my father as a companion, and she found him an adorable lover. She was neither frightened nor upset when it became apparent to her, after they had been lovers for some time, that she was going to have a baby.

It was, once again, a matter of her upbringing. Ever since her childhood she had been hearing her mother and her mother's friends talking of the new woman and the new woman's right to live her life as she chose. She felt that, conventions or no conventions, she should be free to become an unmarried mother if she wanted to. When her parents learned of her condition and of what she planned to do they were appalled. They had never meant their daughter to confuse principle with practice, or dreamed that she might actually *do* what they had wanted her to feel *free* to do. She stood by her literal reading of what she had taken to be their principles. Heartbroken and bewildered, they became furiously angry with my father for, as they saw it, cynically taking advantage of their daughter's unworldliness. She ran

7

away to France with him, to distance herself from the ugly squabbling and the pressure, and to give her parents time to recover from the shock.

My father settled Amber Reeves into a gawky little holiday villa in Le Touquet. Living with him among strangers in a foreign country, she made discoveries about him and about herself. He wanted her to run the house and to look after him. She had never given the art of running houses a thought, and had no wish to learn it. He couldn't endure her almost sacrilegious indifference to his creature comforts. He was soon darting back across the Channel for days at a time to take refuge from her casualness with Jane Wells, who knew how to look after him so beautifully, and who managed his literary and financial affairs so efficiently. Amber Reeves came to a full understanding of those absences one night while she was spending some unpleasant hours lying at the foot of the villa's steep staircase. My father was in England with Jane, and she was alone. She had taken a fall down the staircase while making her way to the bathroom in the dark. When she had tried to get up, a stabbing pain in her back had told her to stay where she was. So she lay there, wondering how badly she was hurt, and if the baby was going to be all right, until the daily woman came in the morning. As the hours had passed she had begun to realise that she knew Jane Wells almost as well as she knew my father, and that she understood much more about that relationship than she had been admitting to herself. They were an ideally matched pair: just as Jane Wells was a woman who, for whatever reason, needed a husband who could be counted upon to be unfaithful to her with one woman after another, so he was a man who had to have a woman at the center of his life who would condone his endless infidelities, and cherish and support him between the absences in which he would be gone in pursuit of other women. Amber had no desire to upset Jane Wells's applecart; she didn't in the least want to take part in their game, much less to break it up. And in her loneliness she had also realised, as she hadn't before, how profoundly conventional and unadventurous her professedly liberal and advanced parents really were, how horridly she had shaken them, and how fond of them she was. She had no wish to ride roughshod over their feelings.

When my father got back to Le Touquet he was in a bad mood. It was tiresome running to and fro across the Channel all the time. He told Amber so. She told him that the whole thing was, indeed, becoming quite impossible. He asked her what, in that case, she wanted to do. She told him that she had no idea. She didn't see how she could go on with him, and she didn't see how she could give him up. He snapped at her, telling her that she was being childish and unrealistic. They argued round and round the issue until they had worked up a quarrel. In a cold fury he told her that if she couldn't go through with what she had let herself in for, she had better take the obvious way out and get herself married to young Rivers Blanco White, who was always dangling about after her. She was amazed by this suggestion. Was my father asking her to marry a man for whom she felt nothing in particular just to get them out of a passing social difficulty? He would be recommending prostitution to her next! He exploded. She was a fool. She was a *damned* fool. She didn't understand anything.

My father went back to England that same day, leaving her to follow him, or not, as she chose. She didn't have that many options. She sent Rivers Blanco White a telegram asking him to meet her at Newhaven, and packed her bags for the homeward journey. She couldn't, for the moment, think of anything else to do. She didn't know for certain that she could count on Blanco White. He was a young lawyer, very little older than she was herself. He had asked her to marry him not long before, and he had been very gentlemanly when she had refused him. He had told her that his feelings for her weren't going to change, and that if she ever was to find herself in any kind of trouble, she was to turn to him because there was nothing he would not do for her. But that, surely, was just what was said on such occasions. Could anybody, when it came to it, be that noble?

On the Channel packet she walked to and fro asking herself what she would have to say to Blanco White if he should be there, at Newhaven. The first thing that she would have to tell him, in honour bound, was that she still didn't love him; the second, that she was with child by another man; the third, that she wanted very much to keep that child. Her doubts overwhelmed her. It occurred to her that there was something she could do that wouldn't drag poor Rivers into her mess . . .

A young steward, who had been keeping an eye on her agitated movements for some time, read her face and forestalled her action by grabbing her arm and hustling her off to lock her into an empty cabin. He came back a few moments later with the great English universal panacea, a nice cup of hot tea. While she was drinking it he made some trivial observation to the effect that nothing, no matter what, could be that bad, which somehow reached her and seemed immensely reassuring. And in the outcome, things were not that bad. Rivers Blanco White was waiting for her at Newhaven, behind the barriers at the far end of the customs shed, and he proved to be as good as his word. He made Amber Reeves his wife at the end of July so that she could face the remaining five months of her pregnancy with a secure claim to be a married woman.

Amber Reeves's parents were delighted. They thought that their daughter had come to her senses at last, and that she had broken with my father. They were outraged when they learned that he was paying the rent of the attractive little cottage at Woldingham in Surrey in which the young couple had set up house, and that he was spending a great deal of his time there with the knowledge of their new son-in-law. Amber Reeves's father took this discovery especially hard. He felt that a deliberate effort to deceive him had been made, and he became even angrier with his daughter and my father than he had been in the first place. He took to ranting about them as "Wells and his paramour," and, in a complicatedly miserable frame of mind, began telling anyone who was willing to listen all about what seemed to him their shameless and abominable proceedings.

William Pember Reeves's fury was that of a man who feels that he has been betrayed by a friend. As a members of the Fabian Society, he and his wife had become friendly with Jane Wells and my father at the time when he was making his attempt to wrest control of that society from its established leaders. My father had tried to organise a revolt of younger members of this socialist society against the coterie of older men and women who dominated its executive committee. I will deal with that venture later in my story, for the moment it is sufficient to say that the Old Guard had not been pleased when their control of their plaything was challenged, and they had been disconcerted by the narrow margin by which they had won their victory. They were left in embittered possession, and although my father resigned after his defeat, they pursued him with their malice because he had left a legacy of active internal opposition behind him. The two leaders of the Old Guard, Beatrice and Sidney Webb, detested him with a special fervour.

Sidney Webb hated my father for two reasons: he envied him for having an ability to appeal to other people's emotions that he notably lacked, and he felt threatened by the strength of the very mixed feelings that my father aroused in his wife. Beatrice Webb disliked my father for the second of these reasons. She did not like to be troubled by emotions that she could neither explain nor control. The tensions between the Webbs and my father were further complicated by the very great deal that he had in common with Sidney Webb. They were both little men of undistinguished appearance, and they were neither of them strong. The one essential in which they differed to a marked extent was that while Sidney Webb was virtually sexless, and as unresponsive to most women as he was unattractive to them, my father was precisely the reverse. In this Beatrice Webb was far more like my father than like her husband, but although she was a sensuous woman she had deliberately repressed her sexuality at an early stage in her career when she found herself being swept off her feet by a man, Joseph Chamberlain, who stood for everything in politics and ideas that she most disliked. She had found the experience a highly disagreeable one, and had decided never to let such a thing happen to her again. The effort of constantly curbing her instincts had cost her a great deal in the long run, and by 1909 she was beginning to develop many of the traits that are traditionally attributed to aging spinsters. By the greatest of bad luck it was these two people, whose feelings about my father were so heavily influenced by resentment and envy, to whom Pember Reeves first turned to pour out the story of the terrible wrong that that bounder Wells had done to him.

Beatrice Webb's response to his complaint was as violent as it was eccentric. She began by treating the matter as if it were public business and my father a shady employer who had been caught in contravention of the Factories and Small Workshops Act. She decided that Amber Reeves had been his passive and incompetent victim and that she must be saved from herself by group action. She told her sister Kitty how she intended to proceed with the rescue operation: "We will make a real effort to get a hold over her and prevent the rot going further." The reply she got startled her: it was to the effect that unless she knew for certain that something truly awful was going on, it just wasn't her business—Amber and my father had the right to be left alone to live their private lives privately. Beatrice saw that this was a line of argument that might appeal to many of the Fabians and set out to undermine its basis by giving the widest possible circulation to her story that the liaison had been a sordid intrigue in which a lecherous married man had exploited the innocence of an inexperienced and badly brought up girl. She began writing poison-pen letters to such members of the Fabian Society as had daughters of between fifteen and twenty, advising them to keep their girls out of my father's way.

11

My father's friend Sydney Olivier, whose four daughters figure in the biographies of Rupert Brooke and David Garnett, and in many memoirs of the period, was one of the Fabians who was so warned. Beatrice Webb's remarkable circular reached him one morning as he was taking his breakfast face to face with my father, who had been his guest overnight. "Here's something that'll make you laugh, Wells," he said, handing it across the table. My father was not amused, and presently wrote a furious letter to the Webbs. The ferocity of its language frightened Sidney Webb, who had been scared stiff by an earlier brush with my father in this region, and who had not realised how far his wife had gone. He warned her of the risks she was running by putting her libels on paper and signing her name to them. She drew in her horns somewhat after that, and from then on left the actual mudslinging to her personal secretary, W. A. Colegate. A veteran of the Fabian Society's internal power struggle, Colegate was a smooth careerist who was to end up as a director on the board of Brunner Mond and a Conservative Member of Parliament. He already knew better than to put pen to paper in such a situation. The attack on my father's reputation continued with a sharpened intensity, and with even more damaging effect, as a whispering campaign.

As the scandal, fed by Pember Reeves's distressed outpourings and Colegate's nastinesses, gained momentum, Beatrice Webb began to entertain some doubts as to the propriety of her part in working it up. To justify her conduct she took to concocting more and more extravagant accounts of the dreadful fate that would be sure to overtake Amber Reeves if she were left to mind her own business. She could see, she told her friends, "poor little Amber in the gutter, consorting in her despair with some other man, doomed to sink deeper into the mire with every fresh adventure." When she was not cooking up such self-serving fantasies she was wobbling. One day she would tell Amber Reeves that she had "a genuine desire to see H. G. W. saved from a big smash," and on the next she would be telling someone else that she couldn't bear the thought that he might find some way out of the scrape he was in without punishment.

At this point George Bernard Shaw, who was, at any rate ostensibly, on friendly terms with all the parties to this increasingly bitter row, decided to put his oar in. He thought that Beatrice Webb was going out of her mind with the excitement of it all, and he was determined to bring her down to earth before it was too late. He began by congratulating her, in the hope that it would make her do so, for having had the good sense to try to get Pember Reeves and Colegate to shut up. Having done that, he went on to tell her that her dark views of Amber Reeves's future prospects and my father's conduct were unrealistic and absurd. The worst that she could afford to say of their arrangement, he told her, was that it was a questionable social experiment.

Under the pressure of Shaw's knockabout common sense Beatrice Webb slowly and reluctantly started to climb down. But she threw out some odd observations as she did so. Sexual irregularity, she argued, necessarily involved deceit and secrecy. It was this that made any divergence from conventional morality so sordid and lowering. That was why, she told her sister Kitty, upright minds were careful not to experiment except in the usual way. She did not enlarge upon this arcane hint, and her sister took it to mean that Beatrice was of the opinion that married upright minds should have recourse to prostitutes when they felt the need for relief from the constraints of the marriage bond. She was incapable of clear or consistent thinking at the time because she was in shock. Shaw had shaken her profoundly by telling her that her mental picture of Amber Reeves's seduction was all wrong. The only thing that he could see that was at all astonishing in the real story was that my father had been able to hold out against such an attractive and determined assailant for as long as the year in which he had kept up his resistance. It had, of course, been weak of him to give in, but then, he was notoriously weak in that department, and it was idle to treat weakness as wickedness. What was more, it might even be dangerous to enrage my father further by treating him as wicked. He was no fool, and he knew that the Webbs had been turning a blind eye on innumerable irregularities in the private lives of the Fabians for years. They had winked at overt lesbianism, at covert and overt homosexuality, and at countless special arrangements under which wives covered for husbands and husbands for wives. If the Webbs went on exploiting their knowledge of Wells's private life, he could be counted on to hit back where it would hurt them most—he had a sitting duck ready to hand in the person of that old Tom Cat Bland, who was as active amorously inside the Society as he was out of it, and who had been boasting of his conquests for years. The only possible consequence of a further airing of the dirty bed linen of the Fabians would be the reinstatement of the lunatic-fringe image of the organisation that they had spent the past twenty years tearing down. Was that what they wanted?

Shaw's cold douche put a damper on Beatrice Webb's enthusiasm for her vendetta, and the scandal ceased to be a Fabian operation against my father in the early part of October 1909. But by then it no longer needed either feeding or direction. It had acquired a life of its own, and was spreading on the wings of the common fund of gossip. Even Shaw, despite his professions of amity for all concerned, was making a good story out of it. He developed a splendid set piece about an occasion on which a still unenlightened Pember Reeves had nearly caught my father in the act of spending a companionable evening with Amber and her husband in the small sitting room of the Woldingham cottage. My father had been hustled into concealment behind the curtains of a bow window as Pember Reeves stood at the front door asking the maid if there was anyone at home. And there, behind those curtains, with his feet tucked up on the window seat, my father had been forced to stay for the rest of the evening, listening as his one-time friend brought the conversation back, time and time again, to the subject of his blackguardly lack of any moral sense. Shaw gave me a performance of this number when I went to see him at Ayot St. Lawrence in 1948, and the high polish on it convinced me that it was something that he had run through a great many times before and relished as much as ever after nearly forty years. As he told it, the story was as good as a play. It might, indeed, have been something that he had invented himself.

He may well have done just that. But even if slanderers like Cole-gate and compulsive gossips like Shaw had been silenced overnight, nothing could have saved my father from the disaster that he was about to bring down upon his own head. He had written a novel, and even though every friend of his who had read it had begged him not to publish it on the ground that its effect on the scandal would be like that of pouring gasoline on a fire, nothing could persuade him to hold back its publication.

It must be hard for any modern reader who comes on *Ann Veronica* unprepared to understand what all the fuss was about. In broadest outline, the novel deals with the taming of a young idealist who thinks of herself as a New Woman and sets out to live in accordance with her principles. My father brings her cleanly honesty up against the grubby realities of English middle-class existence as they were in those days. She finds, painfully, that the time has not yet arrived in which the freedoms that she had thought of as part of her birthright can be exercised. She begins by challenging every convention and ends very ordinarily married. She is last seen living, as she puts it, "hedged about with discretions—and all this furniture." And there is not, as the novel's most vehement detractor had to admit, a coarse word or an explicitly erotic passage in it.

It was not, of course, what *Ann Veronica* actually was that mattered at the time. My father's novel was attacked because it could be read in the light of the scandal as a self-serving justification of his own scandalous behaviour. It was vulnerable from this angle because there couldn't be any doubt about Ann Veronica herself; she was only too clearly drawn from life. She used turns of phrase familiar to everyone who knew Amber Reeves, spoke in her voice, and behaved as she behaved. It was this quality of recognisability in its heroine that made the novel a deadly weapon in the hands of one of my father's most dangerous enemies.

This enemy was John St. Loe Strachey, then the editor of *The Spectator* and a leader of something that called itself The National Social Purity Crusade. Strachey had been keeping a sharp eye on my father for the three years which had passed since the publication of *In the Days of the Comet.* He had seen this novel as a straight piece of propaganda for unlimited promiscuity and a dangerous threat to the family, the state, and ultimately to civilisation itself. When he reviewed *Ann Veronica* in mid-November he began by saying that it had long been one of *The Spectator*'s house rules that it should never give the advertisement of scandal to any book, and especially to any novel, that seemed in its essence to be depraved and likely to injure its readers. But there had to be exceptions to every rule, and the publication of a book that he could only call poisonous provided an exception to this one. The loathing and indignation that *Ann Veronica* inspired in Strachey was due to the effect that it was likely to have in undermining the sense of continence and self-control in the individual that was essential to a sound and healthy State. The book was based on the negation of woman's purity and of man's good faith in the relations of sex. It taught that there was no such thing as a woman's honour, and that when sexual temptation was strong enough, the tempted person was not only justified in yielding but even entitled to take pride in doing so. It taught, in fact, that if an animal lust was only sufficiently strong, it was to be obeyed. Self-sacrifice was a dream, and self-restraint a delusion, according to my father, in the muddy world of whose imaginings such things had no place. The community of his ideals was one of scuffling stoats and ferrets, unenlightened by any ray of duty or abnegation.

So much for the warm-up; after that Strachey got down to his real business. He added a paragraph in which he established the point that the heroine of the novel had been unchaste in such a way as to entail a sacrifice of her purity of mind and body. He then pointed out the correspondences between the facts of the hero's biography and what was known of my father's, so establishing the point that the novel was to some extent autobiography and suggesting that the heroine could well have had a model among its author's acquaintances. He followed this up by doing the real damage. Having said that there would be those who might be seduced into moderating the harshness of their condemnation of Ann Veronica's vices because she had a great deal of charm and even goodness in her make-up, he recalled the smart put-down with which Dr. Johnson had silenced Jamie Boswell when he spoke up for the character of a married woman of their acquaintance who had taken a lover. "My dear sir," the great humbug had said, "never accustom your mind to mingle virtue and vice. The woman's a whore, and there's an end on't."

Strachey's review intensified the public scandal. My father soon found himself being ostracised by a disagreeably large proportion of the inhabitants of his social and professional worlds. Henry James avoided him for a time, and he was even made a victim of the ultimate social sanction of the period. He was forced, by some exceedingly nasty verbal bullyragging, to resign from his London club.

But these were only minor inconveniences; what truly mattered was that the review hurt Amber Reeves. When the diatribe appeared she was not surprised by it, but she was deeply wounded by the fact that it was my father's recklessness that had exposed her to its sadistic jeerings. She minded the publication of the novel even more than the review because it had so much in it that could only add to the distress of people who had already been hurt badly enough by her actions. She was near breaking point. She had been under heavy stress ever since she had discovered that she was pregnant, and she was no longer borne up by the excitement of being gallantly rebellious. She was feeling the physical strains of carrying her child and of sustaining her defiant attitude. She was in a lowered state, and she was suffering. Rivers Blanco White, who was more in love with her than ever, saw it with pain, and with anger.

Blanco White was a lawyer, and he had seen the deeper malice behind Strachey's venomous attack. It had been intended to demonstrate the book's potential as the foundation for a libel suit. Blanco White did not, however, entertain the idea of punishing my father in the way that Strachey would have liked him to, by taking him into court. He developed a strategy of his own. A court could only award damages after an injury had been proved, a process that would put the matter of the scandal into the public domain. He had no desire either to see Amber's story in the newspapers or to ruin my father. He wanted, quite simply, to eliminate my father from Amber's life and his own. His leverage was very strong. As the English law of libel then stood, an allegation of premarital unchastity made against a married woman was considered to be as damaging a libel as could be made, and it was thought to be as damaging to the husband as to the wife. There was almost no limit to the damages that Blanco White was likely to collect if the matter did go to court, and Strachey's clear statement of the view that any normally composed jury would be likely to take of Ann Veronica's conduct if it were to be described to them by hostile counsel left little doubt that he would collect. Any possibility that the question of identification would be a problem had been removed when Blanco White secured a number of depositions from people who had read the book and recognised Ann Veronica as a portrait of his wife. He presented my father's lawyers with a case that they could not possibly defend. They were relieved when Blanco White proposed an alternative to court proceedings. He would not take things any further if my father would sign an undertaking by which he would be bound not to see Amber Reeves, or to attempt to hold any communication with her whatever, for a term of years. There was nothing he could do and, a month before Amber's child was born, he signed the covenant. Shaw told him not long after that he had signed away nothing, for, since Amber was volatile and he was inconstancy itself, their liaison could not have lasted anyway. But this was cold comfort for my father, whose intuitions had began to tell him that his defeat had been even more complete than the terms of the undertaking might suggest. He had failed Amber, and failed himself.

In her review of *The Passionate Friends,* the novel that my father almost immediately squeezed out of his intensely disagreeable experience, my mother took him to task for allowing his lovers to give up their ship too easily, and for justifying their surrender. He wasn't, she told him, being true to himself in having them knuckle under so readily, he was being pusillanimous in his effort to conform to the common tameness. He nullified the virtue in his being what he was, the prophet of a new order of candour and honesty, by putting his hero up to mouth tactful deprecations of rash defiances of convention after he'd been whipped into line, by seeming to tolerate his heroine's weaknesses and flinchings, and by seeming, in the end, to prefer the slow collective wisdom of the social flock to the quick instinctive knowledge of the flesh-and-blood individual. In effect, she challenged him to rally to the device that he had once flaunted on Ann Veronica's banner: "Once you begin with love you have to see it through."

From behind the printed words my father felt that he heard the echo of the voice of an unbroken Amber Reeves. The timbre of youth was there, the passion and the intensity. He began to see my mother again, and this time he was bowled over.

My mother was, of course, already her sufficiently remarkable self, and the stimulation that he got from her lively company accounted for a great deal of his enchantment, but overwhelmingly the point of her was that she was young and promising. She was the embodiment of that audience of younger people that had, only a few years before, seemed to be in the hollow of his hand. It had fallen away from him when the scandal had made him disreputable. By her eagerness for him, and her evident determination to have a place in his life, she made him feel that he was, after all, still not yet on the shelf, that he still counted and might have a future. He turned to her, as to a fountain of youth, whenever he felt in need of revitalisation. He fed —there is no other word for it—on her immense, and still virtually untapped, store of promise. She gave him back his confidence in his continued ability to create. His dependence upon her increased every time that they met. It was still growing when, just three intoxicating months after the renewal of their affair, in the first few days of 1914, an uncertainty in her mind became a certainty, and it became necessary for her to tell him that she was expecting a child.

Chapter II

Mr. Britling had got into it very much as he had got
into the ditch on the morning before his smash. He
hadn't thought the affair out and he hadn't looked
carefully enough. And it kept on developing in just
the ways that he would rather that it didn't.

—Mr. Britling Sees It Through

RATHER EARLY IN THE COURSE OF MY mother's pregnancy—just about as soon as he had come to realise that there was no chance at all of his being able to talk her into an abortion—my father managed to persuade himself to believe that it need not change anything between them. Once it was all over they would be able to take up their game of being free spirits and the best of good companions and go on with it as before. He ignored the problems that he was going to be faced with as he retraced the route that he had travelled so disastrously with Amber Reeves, managing to throw the dust into his own eyes by concentrating on one of them to the exclusion of all others. He told himself that the business with Amber had gone so terribly wrong because far too many people had known about it: everything would be all right this time if the coming event was to be kept as far as was possible a secret, known only to their very closest friends and a few relatives. My mother consequently found herself being pushed through a series of weirdly complicated manoeuvres in the opening weeks of January 1914. They required numerous and sudden changes of address, the use of assumed names, and frequent resort to stratagems that seemed to belong to the world of Feydeau's farces—journeys made to identical destinations on different trains or by alternate routes. The comedy reached its highest level when my father was visiting Russia. He wrote to my mother from St. Petersburg giving her detailed instructions for a move to Llandudno in Wales, a resort that he had chosen as the ideal place for her accouchement on the ground that it had remarkably good rail connections with Bournemouth, a seaside town on the English south coast that could easily be reached from London at any time of the day. In the end he dropped Llandudno in favour of what was, if anything, an even stranger location, Hunstanton, in Norfolk.

My birthplace was then, and is still, an almost recklessly unpretentious seaside resort with a northwestern exposure. Its principal attraction is a dwarfish pier which runs out into the Wash, a vast expanse of shallow water often spoken of as an arm of the North Sea which is more easily recognisable as an extension of the Lincolnshire and Cambridgeshire fens. Its recommendation to my father can only have been that it was so far off the socially beaten track, so desperately without conventional allure, that nobody having any claim to be anybody—in the Edwardian sense of that term—was likely to be encountered there in conceivable circumstances. Once my mother was safely installed in Hunstanton she was very unlikely to be seen by any friend or acquaintance who might read the outward signs of her condition and start rumours. My father pushed his caution to extreme lengths. With an anticipated delivery date no closer than the end of July, he had completed my mother's disappearance from her usual haunts and got her into covert at Hunstanton by the last week in February. She spent March, April, May, June, and July there, making herself as comfortable as she could in the rawly ugly and somewhat poky late-Victorian villa called Brig-y-Don, in which a Mrs. Crown let furnished rooms. While my mother made what she could of her exile my father got on with his life and visited her when his other engagements permitted.

My father did not exactly neglect my mother during this period of waiting, and he did his best to make up for the brevity and irregularity of his appearances at Brig-y-Don by writing a great many letters to her. In these he said, again and again, that everything was going to be all right, that she was to trust him and to look forward to the happier time that would surely come after her baby had been born. They would then have a house of their own, and he would be able to come to her whenever he wished, to stay for as long as he pleased.

In due course she would have her place at the center of his life. She was not to know that he was at the same time giving his wife the most absolute assurances that the central role in his life was hers, and always would be.

Amy Catherine Wells, or Jane, as my father preferred to call her, had known all about his affair with my mother from its very beginning. In the later stages of the crisis in her marriage generated by his affair with Amber Reeves she had made a bargain with her husband: so long as he did not attempt to keep them a secret from her, and provided that he undertook not to have them with women she didn't like, he could have as many affairs as he wished. She had sized my mother up as an affected little goose who was unlikely to constitute any sort of threat to her marriage when she was brought to Easton Glebe in the autumn of 1912, and she raised no objection when the affair first began. She saw no reason to change her view when it was renewed in 1913, or when she was told that my mother was pregnant. She had my father's word for it that the affair was still no more than an episode so far as he was concerned. She felt able to offer a large measure of sympathy to a young girl who had let her instinct for the dramatic run away with her. She had come to know my father very well indeed, better than anyone else was ever to know him, and she consequently knew just what my mother had let herself in for. She pitied her as she had pitied Amber Reeves when her troubles began.

Although the outrageous way in which my father was lying to my mother during her pregnancy cannot be excused, it is easy enough to explain. In the situation in which he found himself in 1914 he needed both women. He had to have Jane as the balance wheel of his existence, but he needed my mother just as much as a species of tonic, sovereign against his sense that he was aging and losing touch.

Although 1914 had begun well for him he was to suffer a series of setbacks in the course of the year. He had been given a warm welcome by Alexander Tyrkhov and his literary friends when he made his trip to Russia in Maurice Baring's company in late January and early February, but the encouragement that he got from the admiration of these cultivated and intelligent people was soon cancelled out. Not long after his return to England, Henry James published an article in *The Times Literary Supplement* in which he wrote of my father patronisingly as a member of the younger generation, discussing his work along with that of Hugh Walpole and D. H. Lawrence, men who were then still raw beginners and his juniors by more than fifteen years.

James brought my father's work forward as an awful warning. His novels were to be taken as a demonstration of the evil effect that a political commitment to democratic ideas was likely to have upon a writer's style. The decline in the interest and quality of his once fascinating writing, James argued, was to be taken as a sign of the times, an indicator of the general collapse of literary and artistic standards that was to be expected as more and more people succumbed to democratic notions.

My father did not enjoy being written off as a precursor of a new age of barbarism in this way, and his unhappiness about it was not modified by his nagging consciousness that his most recent offering had fallen very flat indeed. A large part of his early success as a writer had been due to what was, until about 1910, his possession of an almost uncanny sense of the timely. He had attached one book after another to some topic that the course of events was about to make important and interesting to large numbers of readers. This gift seemed, for the moment, to have deserted him utterly. *The World Set Free* was grotesquely untimely in context of the events of 1914. In the summer and winter of the previous year, when he was writing it, he must have been one of the very few people in the world thinking seriously, or at all, about the horrors that atomic warfare might bring into it. As 1914 rolled on, and the threat that a civil war might spread out of Ulster and into England gave way to the certainty that there was going to be a great European conflict before the end of the summer, the sheer irrelevance of the subject became startling. And it was not only that, the way in which my father had expressed his concern might have been designed to justify Henry James's attack. Once he had been detached from the book by its publication, and could take an objective view of it, he could see all the mistakes that he had made. On page after page he was lecturing to his readers over the heads of his silent and inactive characters. And when those puppets occasionally were allowed to get a word in edgewise they were only permitted to speak in his own preaching voice.

A resounding public failure is a hard thing for anyone to have to live with at any age, but it hits those who have to endure such misfortune with a special force if they have to face it in their late forties after they have become used to success. My father was to be forty-eight that September, and as the extent of his unlucky book's failure became apparent to him, his spirits sank into his boots. In his early days as a writer he had often been bracketed with Dickens, on account of the bounce and vitality in his work. Now more and more people were following the lead impishly offered them by Max Beerbohm—who began linking his name with that of Thomas Hardy—who was twenty-six years his senior. My father's morale was at a very low ebb indeed by the end of June when the shot fired at Sarajevo started all Europe on its sickening slide into a general war.

I don't think that it is unfair to my father to say that he found a welcome relief from his private tensions in the excitement of the enormous and threatening public event. It may be objected that nobody was thinking of the coming war in those terms then, but he certainly was. On the day on which Archduke Francis Ferdinand was assassinated, he went over to see his neighbour R. D. Blumenfeld, the expatriate American newspaperman who was editing *The Daily Express,* and they argued about what was going to happen. Blumenfeld thought that there would be a war, but not a big one. My father told him that it would set the world alight. Blumenfeld told him that he couldn't see why the world should fight over the act of a lunatic. My father had put himself in the position of a Cassandra; he'd been predicting the big war as far back as 1908, when *The New York World* had asked him to write an article on what the next thirty years might hold for New Yorkers. He had responded with a warning. Europe was arming for war, and war might very well come. If it did, it would be a general war, and because America's prosperity was tied up with Europe's it could impoverish them both. It could be that, instead of going resistlessly onward, Atlantic civilisation was going to have a setback. And by that he hadn't meant that Americans might have to pay for a big European war with a couple of decades of depression; he meant that they might find themselves in a ruined world, learning how to re-create a civilisation from somewhere near scratch. And here, it seemed to him, even if men like Blumenfeld wouldn't see it, the big war was. He decided that it was up to him to open their eyes to the perils and the opportunities that it could bring. He set out to do the job in a mood of buoyancy, almost of exhilaration, and had the first of his series of twelve articles on the subject ready for the press the day after England came into the war.

His mood didn't last. He found that he quite simply wasn't wanted. There was nothing that he could helpfully do, and the soldiers were not much interested by the ideas that had begun bubbling up in his mind. They were professionals, and they did not want suggestions about the way they should be doing their jobs from a speculator in

ideas whose sole claim on their attention was that he had written a
rather jolly little book called *Floor Games* adapting the Kriegspiel that
was played at staff colleges for nursery use. They sniffed at the qualifications of a man whose only military experience was with toy soldiers
and toy guns.

And then, after the battle of the Marne had been fought, and as the
shaken armies were settling down to the dismal grind of trench warfare after First Ypres had petered out in deadlock, he had the bad luck
to be caught up in a last flicker of nastiness left over from the Oscar
Wilde affair: a suit for libel brought against Lord Alfred Douglas by
Robert Ross. My father went into the witness box to testify to Robert
Ross's good character one cheerless day in November, and was given
a rough time, as a declared advocate of free love, by Lord Alfred's
counsel. It carried him back to the days of old St. Loe Strachey's hue
and cry against *Ann Veronica,* and he came away from the sooty and
spiky Gothic law-courts building in the Strand feeling battered and
out of it all. In those darkening days his need for the tonic effect of
my mother's company became very pressing. But when he turned to
her now he found that their relationship had assumed a new character.

My father had been elated when my mother's long vigil beside The
Wash had come to an end. Things had gone very well. No one had
found them out. There had been no talk. And it was unlikely that there
would be any. The outbreak of the war had given people other things
to think about. This time everything was going to be all right, and he
wasn't in danger of being forced to give up his young mistress and his
child. His jubilation found an outlet in cheerful letters to the few
friends in the know. He told one of them that he was overjoyed to have
"a manchild" from my mother, and he said the same thing to her, in
letters in which he addressed her as his "dear little mate."

But my father's enthusiasm for his paternity was apt to be greater
when he was parted from my mother than when he was with her.
There are not many things in nature whose interests and energies are
more completely pre-empted than those of a nursing mother, and
there are possibly even fewer with a greater capacity for making their
presences felt than a very young baby. Every time that my father came
to see my mother after that coincidentally fateful day in August he was
given further cause to realise that he no longer had an exclusive claim
on the person and the attention of the high-spirited and fiercely
independent loner who had so determinedly set out to become his
mistress.

My mother had, as a matter of fact, ceased to exist in that character. Her life style had changed, and my father could never find her alone. She had become the mistress of an establishment, and there were always people about her. There was a nurse, there was a maid, and sometimes a second maid. There was a cook, and there was, as often as not, a companion or friend in the role of chaperone. There had to be, even at that late date, to save her from a further fatal loss of respectability: a woman living on her own, without a husband, and with a young child in the house, would have been assumed to be disreputable unless there was another woman of her own class in the menage. My mother had been brought up in Edinburgh, the town that is to the middle classes of Scotland what Rome is to the devout Roman Catholic, and she had been educated at one of its most rigidly orthodox schools, George Watson's Academy for Young Ladies. After her delivery had taken place, the values of upbringing had reasserted their authority. It occurred to her, as it had not in the absence of a baby, that her gesture of rebellion might be misunderstood, and that it might not be clear to the world at large that she was, although an unmarried mother, still every inch a George Watson's girl and respectability itself. It was to make this point that she kept herself in such state.

But in surrounding herself with staff, my mother was taking on more than she knew. She had not had much experience with domestic servants until then, and she did not realise how much tactful handling would be involved. Above all, she had no idea how cruelly ornery they might become were they to take against her for any reason. She thought of them, naïvely, as simple, good-hearted people who would be helpful, friendly, and loyal for as long as she needed them and was able to pay the going rates. She was startled to find how few of them were like that, a discovery that she made the hard way, because she had what amounted to a positive knack for picking embittered, resentful, and profoundly disaffected members of the profession when she was hiring help. Time and time again her choice fell on women who were unwillingly in service and who were eager to compensate themselves for what their circumstances compelled them to put up with by taking down an employer who had any sort of an exploitable weak point. My mother, green as grass, manifestly unmarried, and with a baby on her hands, was just what was needed to bring out the worst in them. The consequence was that whenever my father came to see her, the chances were that he would find her small empire either in the throes of some new crisis of demoralisation or on its brink. It might be that the cook had been accusing the maids of lascivious carryings-on, or that the maids were accusing the cook of drinking, or that someone had been caught pilfering from the larder or dipping into the housekeeping money—or merely that some order or request had been made in the wrong tone to the wrong person. And when my mother tried to take the firm line that was called for, the boot was put in. She was told that hers was not a house that any decent girl should be asked to work in, that there were women who had the right to order other women about, and others who didn't, and that nobody with self-respect could be expected to stay where things weren't right— dark sayings that called for a week's pay in lieu of notice, and instant departures.

My father would arrive to find the air electric with the makings of a scene, or jangling with the vibrations of its aftermath. Bags would have been hurriedly packed, someone would have disappeared, and the surviving servants would be poker-faced and evasive. My mother would be walking up and down in the sitting room trying to calm herself in a way that was calculated to increase her agitation. She paced to and fro like a caged animal, turning quickly when she found herself facing a wall, or blocked by a piece of furniture, to pace off in the opposite direction until another obstacle made her turn again. As she walked up and down she rubbed her left wrist and thumb so rapidly and so vigorously with her right hand that she sometimes broke the skin over the radius and the lower part of her thumb. When my father came to her as she was working off one of these fits of exasperation she would round on him to tell him that he had put her in an intolerable position, and that he had to do something about it. He had to pacify her and wheedle her into a better humour. It was not what he had come for.

My father had indeed blundered. He had not given any thought to the problem of how and where my mother was to live after her delivery until much too late. He had then improvised a temporary solution to it that took little into account but his own personal convenience, and started her off very much on the wrong foot. He had brought her down from Hunstanton and installed her in a rented house in an obscure hamlet called Quinbury which was, if not exactly on his own front doorstep, at least at no great distance from the back entrance to his home in Essex. A cross-country journey of ten miles or so by relatively unfrequented country lanes would take him from one house to the other. He would be able to get over to see her almost every day.

But when that much has been said for Quinbury, one has come to an end of its virtues. The actual house, standing a short way down a dirt road that went nowhere, at a distance of about a quarter of a mile from the tiny cluster of farm workers' cottages and the small public house making up the hamlet, was a piece of Victorian brutalism, utterly lacking in charm. It had been built as part of a set of foolishly costly farm buildings at the beginning of the eighteen-seventies and had the air of being an assemblage of afterthoughts. It looks bleak from outside, and inside it is uncomfortable and gloomy. It is hard not to suspect that it has been an unlucky place for its tenants, and that it must have broken a good many of them in its day.

My mother moved into this inauspicious dwelling at the beginning of September 1914, when I was just over a month old. As the days began to shorten and the first rains of winter began to fall, the dirt approach road, poached by the comings and goings of the farm animals, turned into a sea of mud. The bad weather brought out the spot's other shortcomings: Quinbury had no shop, and the nearest village, a mile and a half off, was not much of a place to go marketing. Some roundsmen came to the door once or twice a week, but they didn't offer much, and if my mother wanted to buy anything of any quality she would have to hire the tub trap kept by the landlord of the public house to take her five miles to the nearest shopping center. If she wanted to catch a train to London, that would mean hiring the same vehicle to get her to the branch-line station at Standen two and a half miles away. The landlord's fat cob was no longer young and its trot was hardly faster than its walk, so that riding behind it was something of a torment. Such trifles have a cumulative effect, and it wasn't long before my mother began to feel that she was being very badly treated indeed.

My mother's situation deteriorated rapidly when she fired a housekeeper who had been caught taking money from her reserve of petty cash. The angry woman did some talking at the public house before she left. The Quinbury cottagers had already developed their suspicions of the young woman who had suddenly come out of nowhere to live in the gaunt farmhouse with her new baby, and who was visited in and out of season by a gentleman who was here one minute and gone the next. She *said* he was her Mr. West, and that he was a busy journalist up to London, but there were those who said he was a Mr. Something Else who had a wife and two boys over Dunmow way.

The robustly realistic local moral tradition allowed for both an easy tolerance of a slip, and for the frankly loose behaviour of a woman who wasn't of the marrying kind, but there was no mercy for those who pretended to be virtuous when they weren't. The front that my mother was keeping up in the Quinbury farmhouse was deeply offensive to the cottagers. Once they knew for certain the she wasn't Mrs. West—or Mrs. Anybody—and that her Mr. West was really Mr. Wells, she found herself the target of the dumb insolence and poker-faced derision that is the downtrodden countryman's traditional answer to the smart townee's shams and pretences.

As a stranger in the middle of a hostile countryside my mother soon began to find her position more than uncomfortable. And because she was suffering from the usual postpartum slump, her thoughts took a darker turn than they might otherwise have done. She allowed herself to suspect that my father might have chosen the godforsaken hole that he dropped her into deliberately—either to cut her off from her younger friends and her future, or, under the pressure of some incomprehensible psychological necessity, to force her to act out the role of the disgraced and ill-treated heroine of some Victorian novelette. But whatever he had in mind he certainly wasn't keeping any of the promises he had made to her in Hunstanton. She was no nearer the centre of his life than she had ever been. She was living a hole-in-corner existence on its outer margin. She told him that Quinbury wouldn't do, even as a temporary makeshift. She must have something more like the house of their own that he had promised her. He was to make it possible for her to live, proudly and openly, as if she really was his wife. If she wasn't to take over Jane Wells's position altogether, she was at least to be given parity with her when it came to the quality of her accommodation, and she was to be supported on a scale that would enable her to live just as well. She was not going to put up with anything less than that.

My father did his best to persuade her to stick it out at Quinbury for a little while longer. His excuse was that the upheavals and confusions caused by the outbreak of the war were making it difficult for him to find the time for a search for the perfect house. But he found somewhere else for her to live very quickly indeed when she told him that she had solved her problem. She had, she said, made a tentative arrangement to move in with Violet Hunt in South Lodge. It would be wonderful to be back in London again, and she had such happy memories of South Lodge.

South Lodge was one of those marvellous suburban houses with grounds, that can still be found quite close to central London. For some years before the war it had been the headquarters from which Violet Hunt's lover Ford Madox Ford had run *The English Review* and his campaign to put new life into English letters. As editor of that magazine, Ford, who already knew almost everybody of note in the English literary world, had been able to play the part of the kindly and enthusiastic uncle to a whole generation of literary newcomers. He made a point of inviting every young or youngish writer who showed any sign of promise to South Lodge, pressing them to come to the lunches, the lavish old fashioned teas, the tennis parties, and the jolly crowded evenings that Violet Hunt laid on for him. The tone of Ford's South Lodge years is caught by his anecdote of an incident that took place in the Pall Mall Restaurant. Maurice Baring came in and was hailed by my father from a table at which he was seated with Ford, Chesterton, and Belloc. "Come on over," my father said, "here's Fordie telling us he's found another genius." Ford's new find turned out to be the then still unheard-of D. H. Lawrence.

Ford had spotted my mother as a somebody-to-be in her *Freewoman* days, and he had then taken her up as a promising recruit for the group of South Lodge regulars he liked to call *les jeunes.* She had fitted instantly into a company that included Compton Mackenzie, Wyndham Lewis, Ezra Pound, and a number of his American discoveries. Pound and his friends had made the place a home from home—so much so that Violet Hunt's parrot could be counted upon to start screaming "Ezra! Ezra!" in imitation of her welcoming cry whenever he appeared. Wyndham Lewis was then rather more the painter than the writer, and he had done over two of the downstairs rooms in South Lodge in the decorative idiom of his Vorticist movement, giving, by so doing, literary England its first glimpses of the angular motifs of hard-edged abstract painting. This foretaste of things to come that wasn't made any less striking by its association with the Pre-Raphaelite family portraits that had come Violet Hunt's way as the niece of Holman Hunt. She was herself, in a sense, a Pre-Raphaelite icon. When she was a girl she had modeled for Burne-Jones, and had been immortalised as the lovely and bewildered virgin in "King Cophetua and the Beggar Maid," a picture that was for many years among the best known and most popular of the later Pre-Raphaelite paintings. South Lodge had its link with the literary side of the movement, too. When Ford was about to move in with her there Violet Hunt had prepared a study for him dominated by the imposing mass of the very desk on which Christina Rossetti had written her *Goblin Market.*

One can see why, after a year of Hunstanton and Quinbury, South Lodge appealed to my mother. And on the face of it, the proposition that she should find shelter there looks reasonable enough. Ford was away in the army. Violet and my mother were on good terms. What more natural than that a woman who found herself lonely in a suddenly emptied house should think of sharing it with a friend? And what more natural than that my mother should be attracted by the prospect of moving into a place with which she had such entirely pleasant associations? For her it was simply a matter of returning to the place where above all others in London she had been given a warm welcome at the start of her career. Going back there would be a step towards returning herself to circulation. It would be easy for her to renew her literary contacts from South Lodge, and once she was settled with Violet she would be well on her way toward taking up her professional life where it had been broken off.

My father did not see the proposal in quite that light. The move had a theatrical quality in his eyes. He saw the actress in my mother taking over, and thought of her as planning to step out into stage center, shameful bundle and all, to make herself maximally visible to a packed house. Everybody in London who was anybody knew Violet, and if there was any more compulsive and irresponsibly inventive gossip in the literary swim than Ford himself, she was most certainly it. She loved gossip passionately, and she was as unable to refrain from asking personal questions as she was from passing on the answers. If my mother wanted to advertise the reasons for her prolonged absence from the London scene, moving into South Lodge with Violet and a baby would be her best way of doing it. She would not be able to keep any secrets once she was living there, and what was more she would be associating herself with someone who had already been the subject of a public scandal.

Ford was a sweet man in many ways who was also a fool, and a stubborn one. Back in 1909 when his wife Elsie refused him a divorce after he had run away with Violet Hunt, he had decided to show her how little he cared by carrying on just as if he was legally married to his new woman. Violet Hunt had supported him in this by calling herself Mrs. Ford. My father, to Ford's fury, had warned her not to do this. As he was then in the thick of the troubles that he had brought on himself by mishandling his affair with Amber Reeves, Violet had laughed at him for offering her the benefit of his superior wisdom. She wasn't to be persuaded that a case for libel could be made out against anyone who applied the legally recognised name of a married woman to her husband's mistress. She remained unconvinced of it until Ford's lawful wife had collected damages and costs from *The Daily Mirror* and *The Throne,* and apologies and costs from *The Lady.* The court proceedings against *The Throne* had been presided over by Mr. Justice Avory with a peculiarly vindictive bloody-mindedness, and counsel for Ford's wife had been allowed the widest latitude in introducing evidence detrimental to Violet Hunt. As she wasn't a party to the suit, which was technically a matter of Ford's wife versus the paper, she wasn't entitled to be represented by counsel, and the allegations against her character and reputation went into the newspaper reports unchallenged. By the time that the two-day hearing was over, her reputation had been destroyed, and she found that a great many of the people she had thought of as her friends had dropped her. Ford took her abroad for six months in the hope that the whole thing would blow over, but although his bohemian friends rallied round to welcome her back to South Lodge when they returned, the doors of the respectable were only slowly reopened to her many years later, and then with reserve. In 1915 she was still very generally considered a woman of ill repute.

It can be seen that my father wasn't being altogether unreasonable when he told my mother that, as an unmarried woman with a newish baby, she wouldn't be doing herself any good by moving into South Lodge with Violet Hunt. He persuaded her to see his side of the argument at the time, but she was not altogether convinced. The suspicion that he was trying to keep her away from her peers and the young friends she had made at South Lodge remained dormant in her mind. It was to grow there and to become a fixed sense of grievance as the relationship deteriorated.

After her release from Quinbury my mother became involved in a series of moves and changes of retinue that my father found purely exasperating. She spent two months in the raffish Riviera Hotel by the river at Maidenhead and then found a large, straggling, and effectively unnegotiable Edwardian house at Hatch End on the northwestern outskirts of London. It looked more genteel than Quinbury, but it was still a brute of a place to run and things soon started to go wrong there. My mother was once again always in the middle of a debacle or a drama when my father came to see her, and this time he attributed

31

her troubles to an old friend of hers called Wilma Meikle, who had joined her household as companion-housekeeper. He decided that Wilma was an incompetent muddler and a troublemaker, and urged my mother to get rid of her. If she were only gone, everything would be well. But she stayed. Her manner, when she was ineffectually ordering them about, enraged the servants, and her dispiriting and discontented presence at mealtimes and in the evenings, when my father wanted to have my mother to himself, enraged him. By the beginning of 1916 things were coming close to breaking point. My mother wrote dismally to tell an old friend that she was hardly ever allowed to see my father, to whom she referred with heavy irony and capitals as "The Great Man," and that when she did see him it was as likely as not to be in public and among strangers. She was, she said, in a most miserable state, and losing heart. She was possessed by a terrifying sense that she was growing old and that there were no more peacocks and sunsets in the world.

My father knew that she was thinking along these lines, but he found it hard to take her complaints as seriously as she wished him to. He still thought Wilma was the problem, and told my mother that she had to go. My mother took refuge from this ultimatum in flight. She was in lodgings beside the sea on the south coast for most of May 1916, then at the Riviera Hotel again for a while, and after that at Whitby in Yorkshire. She was there for most of August and September, while my father was being given a conducted tour of the battle zones in France and Italy. When he came back they had a long weekend together at a secret retreat downstream from Maidenhead at Bray. He wouldn't, he couldn't, go to Hatch End to face more of those stultifying evenings with Wilma. He told her so. She wrote sadly to him to say how much she hated being separated from him. Did he realise that he'd only seen her twice since his return from France?

My father replied with his old refrain. The conditions under which they were meeting were really a very severe test of his love for her. She should think of some scheme for putting her household in order. She ought to make it a place where she could work, and where she could work, too, when he was with her. She should, for a start, get rid of Wilma.

My mother did her best. She moved out of the unmanageable house at Hatch End, away from the busy triviality of the northwestern sector of the commuter belt, and into southern Essex. She found herself something much more compact and agreeable to her at Leigh-on-Sea on the north shore of the Thames Estuary, just short of Southend, and about forty minutes' run from London's Fenchurch Street Station.

The house my mother had moved to was a charming one in the suburban British idiom. It looked out over the wide expanse of the estuary from a position set back from the crest of a line of bluffs that ran parallel to the shoreline. They were steep enough and just high enough to prevent any noise from the commuter trains that ran on the single-line branch railroad below them from reaching the house. Less than five minutes from it a flight of steps led down to a station where the London trains stopped. From the new house it was as easy for my mother to run up to meet my father at his *pied-à-terre* in Claverton Street in Pimlico as it was for him to drive over to her from Dunmow by way of Chelmsford.

On top of everything else, Leigh was the sort of place my father liked. Beyond the little station, authentic working fishing boats were drawn up on the shingle strand among the tarred wooden sheds in which the fishermen boiled up the winkles from Leigh Sands and Marsh End Flats that East Enders still considered a delicacy in those days. To the west there were miles of good walking along the earthen dikes that kept the high tides out of the saltings on Leigh Marsh and Hadley Marsh, across Benfleet Creek from a Canvey Island then innocent of tank farms. My mother loved walking, and liked such places just as much as my father did. They had some pleasant days together walking the sea walls together at Leigh between March 1917 and the beginning of the summer. But then the tensions between them started to build up again.

The trouble started in the usual way. My mother's reduced establishment was thrown into the familiar state of disarray when one servant left because she was jealous of another who had given in her notice in order to get married. My father found it impossible to make head or tail of my mother's account of what had happened or why, and in his exasperation made the mistake of reviving a long-standing project of his for the reform of her household. Three years earlier, back in my mother's Quinbury days, he had decided that her inability to keep her people happy was a product of her lack of experience in such matters. He'd asked Jane if she could help out by finding some older woman at the end of her career as an upper servant who might come to work for my mother for six months or a year as a kind of housekeeper-instructor.

Jane, who was always inclined to be helpful in such matters (she had

33

provided Amber Reeves with her layette when it appeared that nobody else was going to do so), made enquiries round and about her
part of the county and presently found Auntie North. Auntie North
had begun life as a nursemaid in a large gentry house, had been cook
there for a while, and had ended as to sole empress of the
housekeeper's room. Her former employers spoke well of her, but my
mother had not warmed to the idea of taking her on. She had held out
against the proposal until her departure from Quinbury had led to the
shelving of the idea.

Why my mother weakened when my father revived his project for
bringing in Auntie North in the summer of 1917 is not clear to me,
but in the event her original determination to have nothing to do with
the lady proved to have been fully justified. She was one of those
trusted old family servants who win the privilege of speaking their
minds over the years, and come to identify themselves with their
employers. She knew that she was a servant well enough, but she also
had it firmly in her head that she was a gentry servant who belonged
with the gentry. She was astonished and exceedingly put out when she
found herself in a middle-class establishment where there was neither
a housekeeper's room nor a servant's hall. A fish out of water, she
decided that her place in my mother's house was in the sitting room,
and that she would be fulfilling her functions well enough if she made
acidly critical comments whenever the occasion for criticism arose. In
very short order she decided that my mother was nobody in particular
and no better than she ought to be into the bargain. Since she took
no trouble to keep her opinions to herself, she soon brought my
mother's household to yet another crisis. When my father next arrived, shortly after my mother had brought it halfway to an end by
putting Auntie North and the cook out of doors, he was genuinely
surprised to find that she was furiously angry with him. He had, after
all, only been doing his best to be helpful.

My father did not realise for some time that this farcical episode had
opened my mother's eyes to aspects of her situation that she had until
then been able to ignore. At the start of her affair with my father, his
compact with Jane had been explained to her, but she had not fully
understood the implications of what she had been told. There had
been nothing in her previous experience that could have alerted her
to the marching strength that a married couple capable of making
such an arrangement would be likely to possess. It was only after she
had been bruised by her brief passage with Auntie North that she

began to understand what she might be up against. The incident put her on notice of the fact that her pregnancy and the birth of her child had changed nothing. She might have mortgaged her future to its pursuit and given it years of her life, but her affair with my father was still nothing more than a small thing on the outer margin of his marriage. She saw, without any kind of pleasure, that she had put herself in a position that made it easy for Jane to patronise her. And now that it was much too late she also saw that when my father had been telling her how things were between him and his wife at the beginning of her affair with him, he had been telling her that there were no circumstances in which she could expect to become anything more to him than Jane's second fiddle.

That was painful enough, but she saw, too, that Jane had known as much. Jane had known that she would have nothing to fear from any woman who would be willing to take my father on under the terms of their agreement. She intended to be my father's lawful wedded wife until death should them part, and she was not about to tolerate, even on the furthest fringes of the relationship, the presence of a rival she would have to think of as worthy of her respect. She was not a sensuous woman, and she had never been able to understand the feelings of either men or women who allowed their physical appetites to rule their behaviour. She consequently found it impossible to respect any woman who would be willing to humble herself before her in order to obtain licence to bed with her husband. She even took a certain cynical pleasure in finding out how far my father's women were willing to go in this direction. Often, by making considered gestures of amiability and sympathy toward them, indicating that she was unrattled, and that she had no hard feelings, she lured them into opening correspondences with her. The letters they wrote to her she kept, annotated. She put nothing ill-natured or even impolite in their margins, managing to give much more effective expression of her feelings of derision and contempt by taking up a hard lead pencil to draw attention to every false note and obvious insincerity by faintly underlining a phrase here and there, or putting a ghostly exclamation point beside it. She was a woman who put many men and some women who did not know her very well in mind of a Dresden China shepherdess, but, as Beatrice Webb had recognised in a clairvoyant moment early in their acquaintance, there was an element of steel in her make-up. She was, when it came to the defense of what she considered to be her own vital interests, a very tough cookie indeed, and nonetheless formidable for having a lively sense of fun. She had found my father's suggestion that she might be doing my mother a kindness by producing an experienced old servant to teach her all that she needed to know about household management a wildly funny one when it first came up. It seemed even more preposterous when it came up for the second time nearly three years later.

Had my mother laughed in my father's face when he offered her Auntie North for a second time she might have shaken Jane, but she was still too green to know that she could not afford to listen to the suggestion, let alone give it serious consideration. And then, having made the blunder of letting the cranky old woman into her house, she compounded her error. She did not have enough experience to know that such mistakes are not to be retrieved by taking retaliatory action, and must be thought of as mistakes and put behind one. My mother unhappily, then as later, held an image of herself in her mind as a bonneted, claymore-wielding highland laddie who would stand his ground giving blow for blow in no matter how tight a corner. She felt that she had been offered a provocatively tendered reminder of her status as second fiddle, and she responded as if she had been offered a challenge. She would show Jane what she was made of—that she was a principal, not a bit player, and that she meant to be the lead in any show in which she took part. The woman who had dared to patronise her was to be made to step down in her favour. My father was to divorce Jane so that he could marry her. She was going to fight on, until there was no room for doubt as to who was the central figure in his life.

Jane was able to take this development in her stride as soon as she became aware of it. She did not believe in hacking about with broadswords, or even in raising her voice. She gave a few lunches, and had tea with various friends and acquaintances. She gave it out that she was a little disappointed in my mother, who had shocked her, rather, by not playing the game. She told her intimates that she had done nothing to spoil my mother's affair with her husband, and that she had, on the contrary, been as understanding and kind about the whole thing as she could in reason have been expected to be. And now my mother was proposing to repay her for her tolerance by forcing her to agree to a divorce. She was sure that my father wouldn't dream of such a thing if it were to be left to him, but my mother was so very young, and so very attractive, and my father did have this weakness for younger women. He was under very great pressure.

The word that my mother was behaving badly and doing her best to break up my father's marriage in a way that could only be very hard on his nice little wife began to spread—as it was intended to. And, as it was also intended to, it presently reached my mother. She responded, predictably, by hitting back. In her anger she began to think and speak of Jane as a vindictive hypocrite, and she made no secret of her belief that my father was indeed under an obligation to her to divorce his wife and to marry her. She began to urge my father to recognise the existence of this obligation, and to prepare to honour it. When Jane heard that my mother was doing this, she was able to retire gracefully from the unequal struggle. There was no need for her to say or do anything more. All she had to do after that was to smile gently and look just a little bit martyred before changing the subject whenever her friends brought it up. She could safely leave it to my mother, who had not called herself Rebecca West for nothing, to do herself any damage that the situation might require. Her own position was a very strong one, and her young adversary could only injure herself, and aggravate my father, if she tried to attack it.

Jane Wells was not being overconfident. She had done a great deal for my father since their marriage and she had accumulated a huge credit balance with him. She had decided very early on that she was not going to let anything that her remarkable husband might do rattle her. He was the answer to her necessities, and she was going to be the answer to his, whatever they might prove to be. A photograph of the two of them taken in the middle 'nineties tells most of the story. It shows them in a boat on the river. He is at the oars, very much in charge, and she is looking at him from the seat in the stern. He is the thin young man of those years, with the wonderfully clear blue eyes and the birdlike alertness, all nerves, insecurity, push, and uncertain brilliance, going up in the world like a rocket. She is much the older in spirit, and she is considering him guardedly, with tenderness and wonder. What on earth is this extraordinary creature who has got her going to do next? It is the expression that one might expect to see on the face of a mother whose child is turning out to be a prodigy, and who is wondering how far her darling is to go.

My father had tried Jane very hard over the years, but she had never lost her nerve. When he had required her to leave the house looking out over the English Channel at Sandgate that he had built for her in the days of their first prosperity, and to move to Church Row in Hampstead so that he could the more easily carry on his affair with

Amber Reeves, she had done what he asked of her without hesitation. And when he had consoled himself for the loss of Amber Reeves by starting another affair, this time with Katherine Mansfield's cousin Mary Beauchamp, she hadn't been fazed by that either. She was amused by Mary Beauchamp and she enjoyed her company, but she had been a little worried when a restlessness induced by that affair had led my father to plan a world tour that would have taken him away from them both for over a year. She hadn't liked the idea of that at all. Her two boys were eleven and seven then, and they needed him. Her answer to this problem couldn't, in the long run, have turned out better. She had found a house that offered him the chance of a fresh start in a new setting, The Old Rectory at Little Easton in Essex. Something about it—a Georgian solidity and spaciousness— had spoken to him. They had taken it on a short lease, and when that ran out in the spring of 1914, they had renewed it for a much longer term, one that would justify the extensive program of renovations and alterations that they both felt to be needed if the house was to be made as agreeable to live in as it was to look at. A new lease was signed, and the alterations were put in hand in the early summer. As Jane went over the plans for the proposed works with my father and the architect Randall Wells, she knew that a long future was built into them, and that she had nothing to worry about. The child that was going to be born up there in the depths of darkest Norfolk wasn't going to change anything.

But as it happened, the new house, Easton Glebe as they were presently to call it, was to give Jane her first and only twinges of anxiety about my mother. The execution of the improvements, which called for the installation of several bathrooms, the modernisation of the kitchens, the addition of three bedrooms for the servants, and a very handsome bow window to the dining room, was barely begun when the war broke out in August, and dragged on interminably afterwards. The plumbing gave particular difficulty. What there had been in the early-eighteenth-century house had been largely a matter of Victorian improvisations, some of them of a startlingly primitive character, and the modernisation seemed to demand endless tearings down and pullings about that filled the house with dust and grit. My father, through much of 1915, was less often in his new home than he was away from it.

Jane had her moment of doubt that year. Her two boys had started going to boarding school, and she was lonely. Did my father, after all, really want to leave her? She put it to him, and he instantly reassured her, after his fashion. He'd been, he admitted, irritable and impatient over the past several months, but she didn't, he thought, fully understand what a torment to him it was to have to work in a house that was all promise of future comfort failing to realise itself. He hated unfinished projects. He hated having things out of place. He hated hammerings, and flapping tarpaulins. He wanted things settled. He wanted his home to be a place to live in, to have people to. He couldn't bear home while it was a noisy, unsympathetic muddle. And then there was the other issue: when he was at Easton for more than a few days at a stretch he got into a state of irritability . . . the brute fact was that he had urgent physical needs that she couldn't meet. He was affectionate and all that, and he truly loved his family, but he had this simpler need for the thing itself. He had to have it when the hunger came upon him, to steady his nerves and leave his mind free for really important things. He loved her very deeply. She was the bone of his bone and the flesh of his flesh, and she had been the making of him. He could never leave her.

Jane breathed again. He was only telling her what she already knew, but it was, all the same, a relief to have it said once more. Their ancient pact was renewed, and secure in the knowledge that he still needed her to be unfaithful to as badly as ever, she was freed to give her mind to the really important business of getting the house and the garden put to rights. She began to pour all her energies into the task, and to perform miracles. By the late summer, Easton had become the perfect place for my father to work and play in, and had taken on the character it was to keep for a decade.

Those months were important to them for another reason. By the middle of 1915 my father had written himself out of the slump that he had been in since the failure of *The World Set Free* in 1914. His self-confidence had come flooding back, and he could see his way ahead. He no longer needed reassurance and certification of his identity: he was H. G. Wells, and he was writing a new book. All he wanted was time to work on the one hand, and stimulating relaxation on the other. He had no use at all for fuss and bother. Against Jane and Easton Glebe my mother didn't have a chance.

Chapter III

Of course, one knows that real literature is something that has to do with leisure and cultivated people and books and shaded lamps and all that sort of thing. But Hallery wants to drag in not only cathedrals and sanctuaries, but sky-signs and hoardings. . . . He wants literature to embrace whatever is in or whatever changes the mind of the race, except purely personal particulars.

—Boon

M Y FATHER CAME TO A TURNING POINT in his career in 1914. A few months after *The World Set Free* had fallen flat, *The Wife of Sir Isaac Harman* came out and met with a tepid reception. His heart had never been in the book, and he had never been able to persuade himself that its immediate successor, *Bealby,* had ever, the money apart, been worth finishing. He was told it was charming by people who wanted to console him for the two failures that preceded it, but he knew that it was namby-pamby stuff. And *The Research Magnificent,* to which he had, off and on, given two years of work, was still sullenly defying him. More and more often, as he fought to get it moving and to bring some life into it, he found himself facing the fundamental question: What on earth am I trying to do?

Since he was so entirely what he was, there could be only one answer to this question—the solution to his problem clearly lay in writing another book. This one would be about a popular novelist who had lost his faith in his calling in the face of the mounting horror of a great war. It couldn't be anything heavy, or it would make him choke, as he had choked on *The Research Magnificent;* he was too stale to have any luck with another effort of that kind. He would have to try something in a different vein altogether if he was to get the release he was hoping for. He was in the habit of refreshing himself with play when he felt used up, and he presently found himself taking up a running family joke about an imaginary writer called George Boon.

George Boon was my father's caricature of himself, a short, mercurial outsider with a tendency to plumpness whose sudden and immense success had made him a figure in a literary world to which he didn't quite belong. My father had invented him in the middle of his Sandgate years, when he had found himself living within easy cycling distance of Henry James's Lamb House, over on the other side of Romney Marsh. An acquaintance had developed, and Boon had come into being to relieve some of the tensions generated by the awful weight of that looming literary presence.

My father's relationship with Henry James has been substantially misrepresented in biographies of both men. The American writer Leon Edel has allowed himself to say that the two were excellent friends for a time. They were never friends, and for a simple reason: James's feelings about my father were very much those that Balaam must have had about his ass after it had spoken to him. He recognised that my father was a phenomenon, but he could not bring himself to think of him as an equal. He patronised my father relentlessly, and he did it in the most offensive possible way. He made it quite apparent to my father that he was assuming that he would be too thick to know what was being done to him. In the early stages of their acquaintanceship James rapidly became a figure of fun to both my father and Jane, partly because of the serenity of his self-reverence, the great vice in which he was encouraged by his sister, Alice, and partly because of the persistence of his missionary efforts to persuade my father to rise to the levels of dignity and decorum required of him by his newly won social position. James made it very clear to him that it was his duty not to let literature down. My father was a gifted mimic, and nothing delighted him more than to duplicate the fantastically overelaborated verbal pagodas in which James would express his astonishment over such things as the fact that poor, unhappy George Gissing, who had been born so meanly and obscurely into the ranks of the lower middle class—and in the north, at that—had been able to speak French well, with an almost excessive perfection of accent, or that there were people of education and refinement who were all the same able to believe that the irredeemably provincial lout, William the Player, had written the plays and the poems.

41

But the James joke had soured in the end. The older man had written to my father too many times to shower him with oily praise as a preliminary to telling him that his latest book had proved, yet again, that he didn't begin to know what he was doing. He played this obscurely motivated game once too often when he wrote to my father to say, apropos *The Passionate Friends,* that there was, quite simply, no way in which he could be taken seriously as a writer:

> I find myself absolutely unable, and still more unwilling, to approach you . . . in any projected light of criticism, in any judging, or concluding, or comparing, in fact in any aesthetic or "literary" relation at all . . .

For one writer to address another privately for the sole apparent purpose of letting him know that, while his writing has a sort of claim to interest as a manifestation of his personality, it is otherwise absolutely worthless, is to ask for trouble. And James's offence was all the greater because his letter caught my father in a mood of acute self-doubt. He took up his pen to relieve his feelings, and let James know, in intentionally abrasive language, just how useless and impertinent he found criticism from a colleague so clearly incapable of either comprehending or sympathising with aims and intentions other than his own. And he included a brusque hint that James was presuming in taking a master-to-pupil line with a fellow writer who had never invited him to do so, and who might, since he had managed to find publishers for thirty-odd not entirely unsuccessful novels, be considered to have found his own path.

James, who liked to surround himself with toadies and who was consequently used to having his boots licked, found my father's sarcasm irritating. Feelings that had been lurking in his bosom since 1912 were rekindled. In that year James had joined forces with Edmund Gosse, a genteel sub-academic critic whose highest literary ambitions were ultimately to be fulfilled by his appointment as Librarian to The House of Lords, in an effort to persuade my father to become a member of the Academic Committee of The Royal Society of Literature. The two men were well-intentioned. They were meaning to help my father to re-establish his respectability after the scandal he had been through, and they were much affronted by his instant refusal to have anything to do with the proposal. In dismissing it, my father had told James that he had no use for academies, and that he didn't believe that the arts could profitably be institutionalised, adding that if he ever were to consider joining a society of Literature, it certainly wouldn't be a royal one. James had been cut to the quick. He told Gosse that my father's reply to their invitation had revealed to him the extent to which he "wouldn't at all do among us." And he had gone on to equate my father's refusal to join his pompier organisation with a conscious decision to cut himself off from literature itself. Given the further affront of my father's refusal to submit to his critical authority in the matter of *The Passionate Friends,* James decided that the time had come for this young upstart from below stairs to be taught a lesson. He proceeded in due season to the insufferable dismissal in *The Times Literary Supplement* that I have already mentioned. A particular phrase that James applied to my father's writing, *incorrigible levity,* gave him special offence. It was too much to be accused of that by the man who, on his own admission, had given up a full year of his life to an effort, productive of *The Awkward Age,* to beat Gyp, the titled French lady who successfully wrote one mediocre drawing-room novel after another, at her own silly game.

I find it easy to enter into my father's feelings of outrage. Whatever else he had been doing since he wrote *Love and Mr. Lewisham* fifteen years earlier, he had at least tried to come to grips with those things in his life that bore most pressingly and most urgently upon him. He had thought that the particular matters he had dealt with should be pursued in public because he was sure that they, or concerns very like them, were the substance of the lives of large numbers of the men and women he saw in pain about him. In all his books he had been asking himself and his readers what he had thought to be vital questions. Why were their lives so cramped and confined? Why were their days filled with so much moral and physical ugliness? Why were the sexual relationships that should be a source of joy to them so often squalid and demeaning? Why were conventions tolerated that deformed so many people's lives? Were there not better ways to live? Could that constant probing, that search for the heart of what *mattered,* what truly *meant,* in so many ordinary lives, however inartistically conducted, possibly be less serious as an enterprise than giving oneself up, year in and year out, to the production of highly polished and exquisitely finished objets d'art to be savoured by the privileged and refined in their leisure moments?

The more my father thought of them the more intolerable James's papal pretensions seemed to him. The old fat cat could not rest content with his absolute freedom to do his own precious thing—he had to foreclose on all other forms of the novel, and to insist upon a literature limited to the single intention that he was prepared to recognise: the achievement of aesthetic experience for its own sake. All novelists were to be compelled to write the Jamesian novel in the Jamesian way. He was trying to function as if he was an Academy all on his own—laying down rules that stipulated what might or might not be done with the novel, and threatening all those who wanted to go on exploiting its infinite variety of form and approach with a kind of excommunication. In his irritation it came to my father that George Boon's doubts about what he was doing with his time could best be encapsulated as a review of his own doubts about the culture of the drawing rooms and weekend house parties, of the college high tables, and of the West End clubs, of which Henry James was the ultimate fine flower. Through Boon he could have a go at the whole crowd that had talked up the idea of a British Academy—the men like the perpetual chairman of literary dinners, Lord Reay, who had never written anything, like the living Sir Walter Raleigh; like "old Q," Sir Arthur Quiller-Couch, like Professor Saintsbury of the cellar book, and, of course, like Edmund Gosse, the gentleman's outfitter of literary culture.

My father gave the resulting attack on elitist letters, a pioneer effort in that field, the form of a memorial volume. George Boon has died, and a certain Reginald Bliss, a refined amateur who has known him without understanding him in his later years, has become his literary executor. His thought is that he will be able to write a polished essay recalling George Boon, the good companion, that will serve as an introduction to his literary remains. He has high hopes of these, since Boon has led him to suppose that he has been working on a comprehensive review of the present state of literary culture for several years. To his dismay he finds that this magnum opus does not exist, and that it never has existed. Boon has discussed it with his friends, but he has never written a line of it. Bliss finds a few incomprehensible notes, but that is all. He is driven in the end to attempt to recover as much of it as he can by sifting his memories of Boon's conversations with his friends. What emerges from his struggles is a wonderfully funny collection of skits and parodies clustered round a satire upon W. H. Mallock's *The New Republic,* a literary oddity which is in essence an attack by an ultraconservative Anglo-Catholic on the ideas of the liberal-theologian Benjamin Jowett, who had been master of Balliol when my father was a small boy.

My father despised Mallock's general ideas, but he had a good deal of sympathy with his loathing for Jowett, which had much in common with his own distaste for Henry James. As Mallock's deathbed conversion to Roman Catholicism was later to show (he was still alive when *Boon* was written), he was committed to a belief that the foundations of the culture that he valued rested on an acceptance of the Christian faith. He believed as Pascal had believed, and he detested Jowett as the type of the trendy liberal Christian theologian who waters the faith down to a point at which it loses all its substance. In *The New Republic* Mallock's caricature of Jowett preaches at an interfaith service that begins with the recitation of a passage from the Koran, passes through a version of Anglican morning prayer from which the Creed has been excised and ends with a short prayer of St. Francis Xavier's. In the sermon which forms part of this performance, the pseudo-Jowett makes it clear that he is proposing a Christian belief that does not require acceptance of any particular thing. It centers upon a quotation from some words of Christ's which do not appear in any of the gospels, but which are to be found in the works of Clement of Alexandria, who did not believe in his divinity:

> The Lord being asked when his Kingdom should come, said "When two shall be one, and that which is without as that which is within, and the male with the female—neither male nor female."

Mallock saw the death of Christianity as a credible faith in this sort of thing, and my father was impressed by the similarity between his outraged reaction to Jowett's religious attudinisings and his own response to James's aestheticism. He felt that James's trivialisation of the matter of literature, and the frivolity of his abuse of the higher claims of art to justify his immersion in the minutiae of the transactions between idle members of a privileged class, was on a par with Jowett's perversion of the virtue and primitive strength of the Christian ethos, and something that could very well bring about the death of literature as a social force. The Jamesian rules laying down the proper concerns of writing would, if they were applied even half as rigidly as he wished them to be, produce a body of literature meaning so little to the vast majority of people that it would not carry any weight with them at all. It would be a playtime thing, a game of private references to be played by cultists.

This view may seem to be an extreme one, but my father had attempted, as few of James's latter-day admirers in English departments have had the opportunity to do, to discuss serious subjects with him. The experience had convinced him that James did not know what seriousness was. To make this point, he produced the superb and bitterly resented parody of a typical Jamesian novel that forms the core of *Boon* and is the clew to it. It goes directly to my father's two main points of objection to his adversary's writing: that it does not say anything very clearly, and that it does not say very much—the points made in Hardy's muted observation that James had developed a "ponderously warm manner of saying nothing in infinite sentences." My father addresses them by way of *The Spoils of Poynton,* the novelette that had stayed in his mind as the prime example of James's trivialising tendency from the time when he had first read it in 1897, and recognised it as the gross and wilful enfeeblement of a theme—concerned with the passion for acquisition—lifted from Balzac.

To bring this parody off, my father had first to solve a technical problem: he had to invent an overwhelmingly pointless story that would have a point that could not be missed. He found his answer in the story of the misadventure that befalls a Mr. Blandish, a man of more than adequate means and of no occupation, who spends a great deal of time trying to find something in his house that isn't any longer there. He is one of those idle people who fill in their time by going shopping, a pastime that he dignifies by saying that he is collecting antiques. He has acquired, over the years, a houseful of fine things, and he is now in pursuit of somewhere to put them, the antique-lover's ultimate piece—the perfect, time-mellowed country house, the antique that one can get into and become a part of. Mr. Blandish eventually finds just what he thinks he is looking for, only to learn when he has taken possession of it, and it of him, that he has bought a strange and vaguely threatening *something* with it. What that may be he can't for the life of him make out. His efforts to identify it are prolonged because, being a James character, he is barred from making a direct enquiry from anybody who might possibly be able to help him. He is condemned by his cruel literary destiny to pursue that *something* from hint to hint through a thick web of interminable conversations with a series of persons who cannot make direct statements about anything, and who cannot be told what poor Mr. Blandish's problem is. The solution to it is found in the end to lie in the realm of allegory: when Mr. Blandish bought the house it contained, walled up in the cellars, a large stock of the wine of life. When he learns this it is far too late for the knowledge to do him any good, someone else has been beforehand with him in making the discovery, and has consumed every drop of the precious fluid. There is none left for Mr. Blandish. All that he will ever know is that there was once something worthwhile in the place.

What my father is saying in this parody, and throughout *Boon,* is that life and living comprise the overwhelmingly important and interesting whole of which art and connoisseurship are among the contributing, but lesser, parts. Insofar as *Boon* was my father's direct response to James's spiteful and ungenerous attack on him and his work in *The Times Literary Supplement,* it may be said to have malice behind it, but in the making the riposte became his considered rejection, once and for all, of the elitist values of the English literary establishment.

With *Boon* finished, and his attitudes defined, my father felt that a great load had been lifted from his spirit. His block had been blown away, like the cork from a champagne bottle, and a new novel—*Mr. Britling Sees It Through*—was soon absorbing his energies and attention. By the time that *Boon* had been through the presses and was ready for distribution it was very much finished business so far as he was concerned. Distanced from him by print and hard covers, it seemed to him to be no more than a legitimately hard-nosed contribution to the continuing debate about first principles that is the life and health of the literary profession. As for its handling of James, the old man had taken his whack at him, and could expect to be given a taste of his own medicine now and again. The publishers let him have his complimentary copies of the book in June 1915, and a few days after they arrived my father dropped one off in the porter's box at James's club in the West End. He said that there was no urgency about getting it to Mr. James, it could wait until he came in.

I have seen it suggested that the fact that my father left no note for James with the book when he put it into the club porter's hands indicates that he had a bad conscience about its irreverent treatment of The Master. But the truth is that by this time he felt that he owed very little even in the way of formal courtesies to a man who had been talking very freely about him behind his back for some years. James loved telling stories, and he loved polishing the stories that he told. Since the great Fabian row there had been no end to the circulation of gossip about my father, and since the affair of The Royal Society of Literature James had shown no hesitation about joining in the game. It is an unwritten rule of polite society that no holds should be barred when it comes to running down people who *won't do,* or who are *not the right sort,* and some of the stories that James had been telling had been very unpleasant indeed. My father was, consequently, genuinely astonished when James, with whom he had had very little contact for some time, wrote to him early in July to protest against the savaging that he felt that he had been given in *Boon,* as if it had come on him out of a clear sky and had not been earned. This revelation—that James was entirely unaware of his own increasingly offensive and provocative behaviour—gave my father his first hint that the older man had begun the slide into the senility that was soon to allow him to believe that he was the Emperor Napoleon and resident in the Tuileries. After making discreet enquiries as to James's condition, and learning that he was indeed breaking up, my father sent the letter of objection an evasive answer. In it he told James that *Boon* was not to be taken all that seriously: the parody that had hurt James was a *jeu d'esprit* that had been written, oh, years ago. He'd found a rough version of it while turning over some old papers, and had seen something in it that was expressive of a thought about the novel as such that had been on his mind, and he'd worked it up as a diversion; it was the first relief he'd found from his obsession with the increasing horribleness of the war in quite some time. When he'd done with it he felt that it made its point. James should try to forget the whole thing, it really had no importance.

That my father hadn't cringed and apologised infuriated James, who was always morbidly sensitive to parody. He replied with the stately but incomprehensible rebuke that his admirers have been printing and reprinting in awe ever since. It is said to have crushed my father, but the truth is that he took it for the confused utterance of a very sick man and found it pathetic. He was wholly unimpressed by the famous declaration of faith with which it approaches its close: "It is art that makes life, makes interest, makes importance . . . and I know of no substitute whatever for the force and beauty of its process." My father was able to admire the sonorities of this declaration, but the more he thought about it the less it seemed to mean. In his reply he mildly hinted that it seemed to him that it might not in fact have *any* meaning ("I don't clearly understand your concluding phrases") and brought the exchange to a close.

There are those who have insisted that my father did not defend himself more vigorously on this occasion because he knew in his heart that James was in the right, and that his own position, and his conduct, had both been indefensible. But the simple truth is that he had learned how rapidly James's condition was deteriorating by the time that he received his second letter, and that he had been unwilling to add to a dying man's confusion and distress. James was, indeed, far gone at the time, and on the brink of losing touch with reality altogether. He received no more visitors after his powers of speech deserted him in October, and from December onwards he was in a state in which he did not know who or where he was for long periods. He died in the following February.

I have given this much attention to the questions of what my father was thinking about while he was writing *Boon,* and of what the precise nature of his relationship with James truly was, for two reasons. The most persuasive of them is that he once spoke of *Boon* as the most self-revealing thing that he ever wrote. Second to this comes my belief that an understanding of these matters throws a great deal of light on the extent of his incompatibility with my mother. Her first published book, which appeared shortly after the publication of *Boon,* was a critical study of James's fiction. She took exception in it to some of James's more unendurable mannerisms, but she made rather more of her endorsement of his claims for the overriding importance of art and the artist in the universal scheme. In doing so, she stated her view that the artist-as-writer was no mere mortal making up a story, and reasoning and discriminating as he did so; as she saw it, he was something more in the nature of a dervish souping himself up for use as the instrument of a higher power. She propounded the view, for which my father had no use at all, that

> the artist at the moment of creation must be like the saint awaiting the embrace of God, scourging appetite out of him, shrinking from sensation as though it were a sin, deleting self, and lifting his consciousness like an empty cup to receive the heavenly draught . . .

My father saw this sort of thing as an exercise in the abuse of language in the interest of self-regard and self-importance, and, detesting it sufficiently on general grounds, found it doubly exasperating as the utterance of an intimate friend. Had my mother wished to drive a wedge between them, she could hardly have hit on a better way of doing it than by publishing this particular book at that particular moment.

Their relationship was soon exposed to other strains. Not long after my mother had moved from Hatch End to Leigh-on-Sea the consequences of radical improvements in German bomber design began to make themselves felt. A new four-engined Gotha made the bombing of London a practical proposition. It was well within the capacity of these machines to fly across the North Sea and, after making a landfall on the Essex coast, to follow the north shore of the Thames estuary through to the capital before returning home. Their first daylight raids, which produced something close to panic in the East End of London, were presently followed by night attacks. The German fliers had learned that for several nights on each side of full moon it was as easy to come in along the line of the estuary by moonlight as it was by day. Flying over Essex and looking south, the pilots could easily see where the darkened landmass ended and the moonlit water began. Keeping track of just where they were on their line of route with the primitive navigational devices then in use was another matter, however, and it fairly often happened that the fliers were misled by the sudden narrowing of the estuary between Canvey Island and Tilbury into thinking that they had come to the beginnings of London. They would then drop their bombs into the salt marshes between Southend and Tilbury and turn for home. As luck would have it, my father was visiting my mother on a couple of these occasions, and he did not enjoy the experience. They were both, reasonably enough, afraid. But while my mother's way of dealing with her fears was Celtic and declamatory, my father preferred to conceal his emotions. This difference in approach became very marked on the second occasion on which they found themselves within earshot of exploding bombs. My mother's moans of *"God, oh, God!"* every time another Gotha droned by overhead simply revolted him. He felt that it was all part of a performance. She always, it seemed to him, wanted to work things up for more than they were worth, and to make the most of every chance to hog stage center. He, of course, was not in the least like that.

My father kept his resentment to himself at the time, but it grew on him and passed out of his control while he was driving back to Easton Glebe on the following day. Soon after he had reached his comforta-

ble and beautifully managed home he sat down to write to my mother
to let her know exactly what turn his thoughts were taking. The events
of the night had made him wonder why he was keeping the thing
between them going, and even if he felt any love for her at all. He
suspected that he was clinging to an illusion. At the start of their affair
he had made up his mind to believe that she was a woman of courage
and determination who was going to be his love mate and his happiness mate in private, who was going to succeed gallantly in her own
person in public, and who was going to make a great history with him.
But it hadn't been like that; their past several years had been an utterly
disagreeable affair of unending fusses with servants and nonentities
played out over a ground base of her cantankerous mother's nagging
disapproval. The atmosphere in her various homes had always been
made poisonous for him by alien presences, and loving her had come
to mean domination by a succession of base, limited, timid, comic,
and plain ugly spirits. Between her entourage and her family their
joint life had been destroyed. There was nothing left but the few
afternoons and nights that they snatched from the wreckage by going
to the one place where they could count on being alone together;
those wretched rooms in Claverton Street where they lived out of
their suitcases. He didn't *blame* her for any of it, but there it was. She
lived too much in the world's regard, worrying about what people who
didn't matter a damn might be thinking of her, and letting her appre-
hensions about what they *might* be thinking dominate her actions. She
hadn't got it in her to make the best of things. It was in her nature
to darken her world, and to close off every chance of happiness that
came her way with dismal forebodings. He could see that it was going
to be the same for as long as he went on with her. There was really
no point in what they were doing.

How my mother actually replied to this tremendous blast I have no
idea, but my father's response to her presently unavailable rejoinder
suggests that she met it by agreeing to a cooling-off period in which
they would both be able to think things out—it was relaxed and almost
cosy. He told her that if he was not to go on being her lover, he was
going to carry on in the role of a loving brother. He was glad that the
air had been cleared. Her letter had made it plain to him that she was
as uncertain about what the final state of their relationship was going
to be as he was—all he, on his part, could be sure of was that he was
done with love for good. Lust, excitement, and the pretty-pretty might
still get a hold on him from time to time, but love was out. He wasn't

going to go in for any more emotional commitments; he was going to make the World State his mistress, and love that.

And there, with the unsayable and the unforgivable said, and with all bets called off, the thing should have ended. But that is not what happened. My mother was still as determined as ever to oust Jane Wells from her position, and she could hardly do that without renewing the relationship as an active affair. In spite of my father's clear warning that he wasn't to be had on other than his own terms, it was renewed in a matter of weeks. My mother took up her loser's hand once again, to play the game on as doggedly as ever.

Chapter IV

But my going away becoming customary must have
impressed Helen as the supreme outrage. Because,
you see, it was not that I went away to see to tiresome, necessary things; that might have been forgiven. But I went away to things because they were
more important to me. She was incidental and they
were essential! It was incredible. Could anything be
more important than the service of personality
and the mood of love?

—THE WORLD OF WILLIAM CLISSOLD

BY 1917 IT WAS FAR TOO LATE FOR MY
mother to challenge Jane Wells's
possession of the central position in my father's life with even the
faintest hope of success. He identified Jane with Easton Glebe, and
since the difficult days of endlessly uncompleted alterations in the
winter of 1914–1915 the Glebe had come into its own. It was providing him with perfect working conditions and an abundance of the sort
of free and easy, rather romping social life that he enjoyed most. It
was no great distance from London, and Jane had made it an attractive
place to come to.

The typical Easton weekend had taken on an established form as a
complete relief from wartime tension and grimness. It offered wildly
played outdoor team games, long argumentative walks through the
deer park belonging to the raffish and agreeable Lady Warwick which
surrounded the house, and evenings that could be given up to more
talk, or to dancing, or hotly contested games of racing demon, or to
charades so elaborately worked out and dressed up as to tremble on
the brink of amateur theatricals. Above all, they featured stunning
mixtures of people: established writers, journalists, actors, politicians,
painters, scientists, and academics, and quantities of the young—

beginners in all those fields who were still, war or no war, full of go, fresh ideas, and laughter. Some of the young were the almost grown-up children of old friends, and some were the suddenly grown-up children of strangers who had, overnight, been transformed into officers of the infantry regiments training in the neighbourhood. A tide of visitors recommended either by their vivacity or their talents swept into the house every Friday, to sweep out again after an early breakfast on Monday morning. The routine cheerfulness of these affairs never became a curse to my father, because Jane Wells had got together with the architect responsible for altering the Glebe to arrange things so that whenever he wanted to get away from the chatter and the bustle it was easy for him to put a couple of doors between him and the crowd and to get on with his work undisturbed. During the week the whole machine turned round his needs. He had never been so well looked after in his life.

All this was made possible by the success of *Mr. Britling Sees It Through.* It had come just in time. At the beginning of 1914 my father had just about £20,000 to his name, and could count himself well off. But by the autumn of 1915 the combination of his reduced earnings with the costs of doing up the Glebe and providing for my mother had run the total of his savings and cash in hand down to something slightly less than £5,000. If he was not yet in actual trouble at that point, he was not far from it. And then *Mr. Britling* was published, and began to sell, and sell. In its first eighteen months it brought him in £50,000, a sum equal to about $275,000 at the prevailing rate of exchange, when both the pound and the dollar had eight to ten times their present purchasing power. He had crossed a boundary, and was not to be drawn back over it again.

As my father had prospered, so had his partnership with Jane. She had bloomed as she saw his pleasure in Easton Glebe growing, and as she bloomed he found more pleasure than ever in her buoyancy, her tart jokes, her inner strength, and her immense tact. She was always there when she was wanted and never underfoot when she was not; he had come to appreciate and admire that something in her that was entirely her own and held back. He liked what she had done for him, and he liked what she had done for their two boys. They had come on well. At fifteen, Gip was developing a quick and mordant humour of his own and an unfrightened attack upon the business of living. Frank, who looked as much like Jane as Gip resembled my father, was coming along too, and beginning to show signs that he had

COURTESY OF MARTIN J. WELLS

My father in heaven, as a freshman at the
Normal School in South Kensington taking the
great Thomas Henry Huxley's course
in Elementary Biology.

UNIVERSITY OF ILLINOIS AT URBANA-CHAMPAIGN

Sarah Wells as mistress of the housekeeper's room at
Uppark in the middle eighties—as sure as ever that her
youngest boy is tempting providence by trying to rise
above his true station in life.

UNIVERSITY OF ILLINOIS AT URBANA-CHAMPAIGN

My father's cousin and first wife, Isabel Mary Wells, not
long after their marriage in June 1891.

UNIVERSITY OF ILLINOIS AT URBANA-CHAMPAIGN

Amy Catherine Robbins as she was in December 1892,
when Isabel Wells told my father that his pupil had
fallen in love with him, and that he would have to
choose between them.

UNIVERSITY OF ILLINOIS AT URBANA-CHAMPAIGN

My father and Amy Catherine mounting up for a spin on the
Humber tandem bicycle of unusual design that he had made
to his special order in 1894.

My father was as fond of rowing as he was of cycling; he is
seen here at the oars of a rented wherry, Amy Catherine has
the tiller lines.

UNIVERSITY OF ILLINOIS AT URBANA-CHAMPAIGN

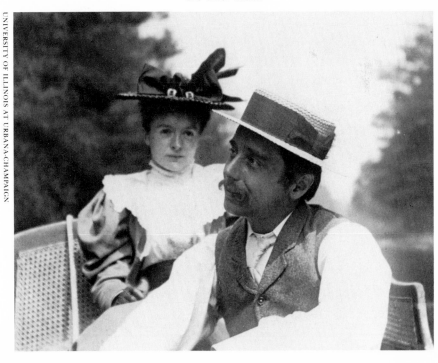

UNIVERSITY OF ILLINOIS AT URBANA-CHAMPAIGN

My father in his first dinner jacket; it was run up for him overnight in January 1895 after Harry Cust had offered him the job of dramatic critic on *The Pall Mall Gazette* at short notice.

PICTORIAL PARADE

Oscar Wilde in his glory in 1885, the year in which he
did my father the favour of persuading Frank Harris
that his essay, "The Universe Rigid," deserved a place in
The Fortnightly Review. Wilde's *An Ideal Husband* was the
first play my father saw as a dramatic critic.

AUTHOR'S PRIVATE COLLECTION

W.E. Henley as the roistering hearty he affected to be because he hated being pitied as the cripple the rough-and-ready surgery of his boyhood days had made of him. He launched my father by showing him how to turn the idea for *The Time Machine* into a book.

something approaching his mother's understanding of him. There was, for instance, a difficult moment in which my father fell for a grotesque theory about the classical Greek runners. On the strength of an examination of the Greek painted pottery in the British Museum he had concluded that these athletes had been taught to tame their instincts to the point at which they were able to run in a way that involved swinging their arms and legs together, right arm with right leg, and left arm with left leg. He insisted that Gip should learn the art of the Greek runners so as to make a clean sweep at the Oundle School sports. It was Frank who handled this delicate matter. He learned how to move in the manner indicated, and then taught the art to Gip, to Lady Warwick's nimble and pretty daughter Mercy, and to one or two others of the regular weekenders at the Glebe. When all his pupils had become really fluent in the exercise he staged a demonstrate on the front lawn of the Glebe which, with only a hint of balletic parody in its later stages, laid the theory to rest forever without even a moment of overt obstruction or defiance.

That story may suggest that my father was foolish about games, but while he did like to believe that he was a better tennis player than was in fact the case, this is not generally true, and he was able to hold his own wherever quickness and cunning could make up for lack of strength and bulk. He even invented one very good game that was peculiar to Easton Glebe, a form of volleyball played in the old barn. When Jane Wells first saw the place, her eye was caught by a rather decrepit barn-cum-byre with a squalidly rundown cattle yard behind it, standing not far from the northwest corner of the house. As soon as time and funds became available she waved her magic wand over it, and, having transformed the yard into an attractive sunken garden with a small plunge pool at its center, converted the barn into a superb ballroom and playroom by putting in French windows and a hardwood floor. I think that dancing, and getting the noisier activities of the young out of the main house, were the motives that were uppermost in her mind when she embarked on this program, and I don't believe that my father was more than dimly aware of what she was about until the work was finished. But as soon as he took in the nature of the barn's changed state he saw that Jane had produced a heaven-sent answer to the problem of the wet weekends that ruled out all the outdoor games that had become part of the Easton tradition. He eyed the grid of heavy beams, purlins, and braces that held up the mass of the old thatched roof and seemed to rule out any ball game other than

Ping-Pong, and had an immediate inspiration: volleyball with all that hoary woodwork to complicate it could be a lot of fun. And very good fun it was, all the more enjoyable in the circumstances prevailing at the Glebe because those low-slung beams evened things out between the young and strong and the old and cagey.

The years that saw the Glebe coming into its own were those in which I was forming my first impressions of my father. They were odd, partly because I was not supposed to know what the relationship was, and partly because he had by then given up all pretence that he was sharing in the routine of my mother's existence. The house at Leigh-on-Sea was less than ever the home of their own that he had promised her in 1914. It was the place where she would be waiting when he dropped by to pick her up, or from which he would call her away whenever he wanted to have her with him. As far as I was concerned, he was the usually genial and friendly man who came by in a motorcar from time to time to carry my Aunty Panther off or to bring her back. There might be a day, a couple of days, a week, a week or two, even a month, between his appearances. Sometimes it would be a little different. She would go off by herself, and after however long it was, he would bring her back in his exciting machine.

The phrase that I have just dropped into this narrative, "My Aunty Panther," was, though I wasn't aware of it, one more bone of contention between them. I had been brought up from the beginnings of my conscious awareness of such things to think and speak of my mother as my aunt. My father had always been against this on realistic rather than other grounds. Back in the Quinbury days he had told my mother that any nurse or ordinarily observant servant with the usual number of eyes in her head would only have to see us together to realise what we were to each other, and that the ploy would be bound to create more difficulties for her than it could possibly remove. He had been unable to turn her from the idea at the outset, and could not get her to change her mind later, even after she had been through her endless troubles with her servants in 1915 and 1916. He told her again and again that these troubles had their origin in the fact that she started out with them on a false basis, but she would not listen to him. He, after all, had begun the deceptions by calling himself "Mr. West," and he was still insisting that I should not know that he was my father. I was allowed to call him *Wellsie,* but expressly forbidden to speak to him or of him as *father, papa,* or *daddy.* On his side he never let drop a word that might have told me that I had any special claim on his interest or good will, even though he made that interest evident enough while he was about—so much so that the warming memory of his presences buoyed me up through his absences. Expressions, gestures, tones of voice, and touchings, must have told me what the truth of these matters was often enough—but I did not have it spelt out to me to be sure of until nearly ten years later. In 1917, so far as I was consciously aware, my father was simply an endlessly fascinating man who, without apparent rhyme or reason, blew into my life and out of it again whenever he felt like doing so. It was a matter of distress to me, nonetheless, when I came to realise, in the course of 1918, that his visits were becoming few and far between.

Later in her life my mother was to give a great deal of time and energy to the concoction and dissemination of evidence supporting her view that my father didn't really know what he was about in the years in which their relationship was coming apart. She gave this idea its first airing in a letter she wrote to a friend in March 1923. In it she says that she has led an appalling life for the past five years. Their horrors—the word is hers—have been partly due to difficulties arising from the nature of the relationship, and partly to an increasing nervous instability on his part. This has, she goes on, led to long periods, beginning with fits of almost maniacal rage, in which he has been almost childish in his dependence upon her. She had spent two months with him in Spain in the previous year in which he had been in a normal state for only ten of the sixty days. She had stuck to him through those five years, partly for his own sake and mainly for mine —but really a lot for his sake because he had, to an extent that nobody quite realised, not a soul on earth to look after him. But now she's beginning to feel more and more strongly that she can't go on. She can't, for one thing, go on spending most of her time sick-nursing while she tries to keep an eye on me *and* get on with her writing—and she could assure him that she wasn't getting any adequate financial recompense for the trouble she was being put to . . . and so on, passionately and at length.

The tone and substance of this letter may come as a surprise to those who have read my mother's published work, but it is typical of a great deal of what she wrote. Like George Sand before her, she thought of her life history as something that could easily be improved by editing, and like George Sand again, she realised that if her biographers were to portray her to her liking, she would have to provide them with suitable material to work upon. She consequently devoted a great deal of time and no inconsiderable part of her creative energy to building a dossier that would win her a good posthumous press and ensure that a future generation would see her in the right light. Before she was out of her twenties she had begun to plant the documentation for an ideal biography on a variety of correspondents, and she was to go on doing so for the rest of her life. She may not have written as many letters as George Sand in her day, but she usually wrote at much greater length than the mistress of Nohant when she was addressing posterity. Her caches of letters to the future are rich in examples that run on from seven to seventeen and sometimes even to twenty pages, and they are riveting mixtures of wit, acute observation, sharply intelligent commentary, and a wild paranoia. Their strangeness, and the cruelty of many of the caricatures of her contemporaries that they contain, as well as the freedom with which they approach the truth, make it seem highly unlikely that her executors will make them generally available for a long time to come.

But while their secrets may be kept for a while, hints of their style and content are to be derived from a parallel source. Not long after my father's death my mother came to the tardy realisation that she would have to worry about his biographers as well as her own if she was to make sure that posterity took her view of the rights and wrongs of their affair. She was, consequently, busy throughout the fifties with the production of a body of source material documenting her side of the story of their relationship and her view of his character. With this to back up her statements she began, from the middle of the sixties onwards, to play a steadily increasing role as a source in the developing field of Wells studies. The quality of the evidence that she produced in abundance for her interlocutors has always seemed dubious to me, less because of the inherent defects of the supporting archive, which is a rag bag of such things as memoranda drawn up, for reasons not explained, thirty to forty years after the events to which they relate, drafts of letters of which no other record remains, and typed extracts from diaries whose originals cannot be produced; but much more because they abound in those little, entirely unverifiable, extra touches of detail that the confirmed fabulist cannot resist putting in to dress up the naked whopper. I will give an example of the sort of thing I mean, taken from an American authority's account of my mother's hard times at Quinbury in 1914. I have described the difficulties she had with her staff while she was in that unhappy house, and I don't question the reality either of her difficulties or of her unhappiness in those days. But that the following, in which it seems to me that the American has caught the tone and fall of my mother's voice very precisely, has anything but the most tenuous claim to relate to the world of experience is something that I cannot believe: "There was the cook, for example, who came into the dining room one night and began to pour out obscene tales about the nurse and the housemaid in the blotted speech of undecided consonants that comes to the mad. Rebecca discovered that she had lost her sweetheart, and her three brothers, in the war." Those obscene tales, on top of the madness, and the sweetheart, and the three brothers, convince me that my mother is piling it on.

In another passage from the same source as the above my father and mother run into trouble on a visit to Italy. Soon after they have checked into a hotel in Amalfi they run into a "drunken old Major of fiercely Tory principles" who finds out who they are and behaves in a most objectionable way." Their embarrassment is much increased shortly thereafter when "an English acquaintance of Wells's" turns up. My father's reaction to this is a crazy one, to ease his discomfiture at being caught in a scandalous situation by an acquaintance, he makes a point of being outrageously rude to my mother in front of him. The whole hotel sees what is going on: "Rebecca was so distressed and humiliated as to be touched by the smallest favours. In after years she remembered with gratitude how an ironmonger, a capable person later to become Mayor of Croydon, who could talk entertainingly about the local ironwork, went out of his way with his sister to accompany Wells and herself to the ruins of Paestum. But this display of kindness and others like it were of no avail, because Wells would not accept them. As soon as people began to behave cordially he found them bores."

My father's pocket diary for 1921 gives another impression of this Italian excursion. The English acquaintance who ran into them in the hotel was Sir Maurice Hankey, the permanent secretary to the British Cabinet. He joined them for a walk a couple of days after his arrival. They went on to Rome from Amalfi, and while there, saw a good deal of Reggie Turner, an amusing man who had been a friend of Oscar Wilde's. From Rome they went on to Florence, where they lunched with Ettie and Willie Desborough, perhaps the grandest of my father's friends in high society, and spent some extremely pleasant hours with George Orioli, the most generous and good-humoured of publishers. The record shows, I think, that the Italy to which my father took my mother that year was a part of his world as it was part of hers, and nothing like the gothick dreamland infested by anonymous bogeymen that she was to invent.

Her story, as told by the American author, goes on at the level of the Paestum adventure. My father made a visit to the United States that autumn and stayed there until the end of the year. He did not go straight home to England when it was over, sailing instead from New York to Gibraltar, where he had arranged to meet my mother. The plan was that they were to spend a couple of months together in Spain before returning to London by way of Paris. The venture was, it appears, doomed from the start. My father stumbled ashore in the shadow of the Rock, at once exhausted by the rigors of his lecture tour in America, and dangerously exalted by the adulation with which he had been received there. My mother had hardly settled him into an hotel in Algeciras before she found herself being put through a grisly repetition of her hateful experiences of the previous spring in Amalfi. The usual anonymous witnesses to her humiliations came thronging forward to offer her assistance: "The proprietor of the Hotel Maria Christina came to me and told me that if I had not the fare to get home he and his wife would give it me and they would get me a passage on a boat and smuggle me over to Gibraltar. In Seville the English Chaplain and his wife asked if they could not wire my relatives in England to come and fetch me."

These kindly interventions on behalf of a mere child of twenty-eight did not, however, inspire her to shake off her dreadful bondage, and she went on to be treated still more appallingly in Madrid and in Paris. Some of his behaviour in each of these places was so wildly extravagant that she had to believe that he was actually out of his mind. He seemed to her to be wholly out of touch with reality. And yet, when Arnold Bennett, who was level-headed if anyone ever was, ran into him in the street the day after his return to England he noticed nothing wrong. He even put his opinion down on paper. When he wrote a note to Hugh Walpole from his club within an hour of the encounter he put in a line to say that "Wells is back and in the greatest form."

Though I fear that the reader may well be feeling that he has had quite enough of this theme, I must stick with it until we get to the point at which my father definitely passed across the boundary between sanity and madness. It came in August 1922 as a fitting sequel to those melancholy Spanish and French episodes of February and

March, though just where it happened it is impossible to say. My father went down to Cornwall in his car to find my mother at The Ship Inn in Porlock, where she was staying with a group of friends of her own age or close to it. The party at The Ship Inn consisted of G. B. Stern, a novelist who was celebrating her first big commercial success; her husband Geoffrey Holdsworth, who was suffering from a bad case of what used to be called shell shock in those days; my formidable Aunt Letitia, my mother's blond and blue-eyed sister, opposite in all things, and rival; her lawyer friend Dicky O'Sullivan, who wished to be her lover; a young woman who had been hired to look after me; and myself. My father had come down to see my mother, and he soon saw that he wasn't going to have more than a few minutes out of the long weekend alone with her if he was to hang around Porlock as part of this crowd. He accordingly took her off into the blue for three days. I have to be this vague, because when she was telling the story to her American interviewer in the early seventies she professed to have no idea where they went. My bet would be that he knew of a comfortable and pleasant place to stay in those parts, and that he took her there, but that wouldn't have made the sort of story she was in the mood to tell. She has him driving off at a venture, and then:

"Finally we settled for the night in the middle of a barren moor, near a place which I think was called Box. This was kept by a man who was obviously going out of his mind and who lived there alone with his despairing daughter. I think that this man had bought the inn on [*sic*] some sort of gratuity he got at the end of a term in the Colonial service. Anyway nobody was coming to the inn, which seemed natural enough as there was not a soul in sight. The nearest village was miles away. Someone else arrived, a commercial traveller, and H. G. and the landlord, and the commercial traveller played some three-handed game of cards for the whole day, and the daughter and I sat in the kitchen and she wept and we did the household chores together."

I cannot believe a word of this, any more than I can believe in the cat that died of machine-gun bullets, or in those entertaining chats about the local ironwork with the future mayor at Paestum, or in the agitated concern of the English chaplain in Seville. And I am least impressed by these figments when the particular American scholar that I have been quoting all along offers the letter that my mother wrote to her old friend and mentor S. K. Ratcliffe (and which is quoted above on page 128) as unshakable documentation for their genuineness. The boot is on the other foot; they are inventions intended to support the allegations made in that letter of March 21, 1923, and their marvellous combination of complete unverifiability with patness to the purpose stamps them for what they are.

But in the end it is the bare fact of its date that does in the credibility of this letter. The five-year period of which it speaks takes one back to March 1918, and the record of what my father was doing in the real world, as opposed to that of my mother's fantasy, between these two dates cannot be reconciled with the claim that he was a used-up man at this stage in his career.

In the spring of 1918 my father unexpectedly found himself involved in the war machine. Since 1916 he had been spending much of his time with such people as Gilbert Murray, H. N. Brailsford, J. A. Spender, J. L. Garvin, Henry Wickham Steed, and Leonard Woolf, as a member of committees working either for a declaration of Allied war aims or to win support for the idea of a League of Nations. These solemnly conducted get-togethers had produced a wealth of position papers, circulatable memoranda, and earnestly composed pamphlets, but they had not led to any noticeable movement of public opinion. In the depressing atmosphere of the bleak winter of 1917–1918 my father had lost much of his faith in the utility of his work in this field. He felt that the only people he was reaching were those members of the liberal intelligentsia who were already sympathetic to the proposals he was supporting. He was consequently delighted when, shortly after Lord Beaverbrook's appointment to be Minister of Information in February 1918, he was asked to join the staff at Crewe House as chairman of the Policy Committee for Propaganda in Enemy Countries. It seemed as if the break he had been waiting for had come at last.

My father took a very short ride in this pumpkin coach. His brief tenure of the resoundingly titled office is often held against him as an indication of his lack of mental discipline, and of his constitutional inability to work in harness with his peers. He started work at Crewe House in May 1918, and resigned his illusory chairmanship in July. But his conduct was not as capricious as it may seem to have been at first sight. His opening move on taking up the post had been to offer his director the draft of a paper outlining his conception of the only potentially successful policy that the agency could adopt. It would, he argued, be a waste of time to attempt to incite the nationals of the enemy countries to repudiate their military leaders and their governments without first giving them a clear idea of the sort of peace that they could then expect. He followed this up with suggestions, based on his eighteen months of committee work, for the sort of assurances that the Allies would have to give the enemy populations to achieve the desired result. This paper was passed on by the Director of Enemy Propaganda to the Foreign Office, with the result that my father was presently summoned to attend a conference with Sir William Tyrrell at that ministry.

When he went to this conference my father was naïve enough to suppose that he had been called in to discuss the contents of his paper, and he had briefed himself for an exchange of views. But Sir William, who was an old Foreign Office hand, had not the smallest intention of getting into an argy-bargy with anyone. While my father sat looking at him he delivered himself of a homily which disregarded the paper at issue and its contents entirely in favour of a vaguely pro-French discourse on the course of Franco-German relations over the previous seventy-five years, and assumed his listener's complete ignorance of the subject. When he had done with that he rose, and after massaging my father with a few moments of general conversation, indicated that the meeting was over.

My father came away from this encounter with some doubt in his mind as to why it had been arranged, but on thinking the whole thing over, he realised that there had been an actual something embedded in the soft soap offered him in its last few moments: an obscurely worded hint to the effect that The Propaganda in Enemy Countries Committee should not consider that its hands were tied in any way. It was free to recommend anything it thought the enemy populations might swallow about the general character of the peace settlement the victorious Allies might make. The committee need not consult the Foreign Office as to the details of anything that might be said; it might, in fact, be better if the Foreign Office knew nothing about that sort of thing.

A light then began to dawn for my father, who had not previously thought to investigate the precise standing of the institution for which he was working. Crewe House, he presently learned, was an ad hoc creation that had been conjured up by Lloyd George for the ultimate purpose of keeping its Director, Lord Northcliffe, occupied and out of trouble. Northcliffe was then the owner of *The Times, The Daily Mail,* and *The Evening News,* and he could be a considerable nuisance to the government when he felt so inclined. The post of Director of Enemy Propaganda had been invented in order to make Northcliffe feel like a part of the government, in the hope that the feeling might make him inclined to support it, but the organisation over which he presided had no legal standing as a government agency. Its actions could not bind the government to anything, and its statements could be disowned at the government's convenience. While wishing to keep Northcliffe happy and occupied, Lloyd George had not intended for one moment to make him any more powerful than he already was. My father had been brought into the Crewe House scheme in much the way in which titled nonentities were at one time invited to join the boards of city companies—to lend them the appearance of respectability. The job he had been given was to make promises to the enemy peoples, particularly the Germans, that the government had no intention of honouring.

As soon as my father understood the real nature of the organisation that Beaverbrook had brought him into, the fatuity of his job became apparent to him. While he was urging the German people to trust in the good will of the Allies, his director's newspapers were whipping up the spirit of a pogrom. Day in and day out the Northcliffe papers were announcing that when the Germans were beaten they would be given a lesson they would never forget. The peace settlement, when it came, would be made along the lines implicit in the Roman slogan "Woe to the vanquished." My father wrote to his Director at the end of June to tell him that while his organisation and his papers went on speaking in two voices, neither would be credible. Northcliffe replied huffily, telling him that he wasn't about to discuss the policies of his papers with anybody. My father resigned as soon after this exchange had taken place as he reasonably could. A wild idea had come to him. He had something much better to do than telling incredible lies to the Germans. He had to get down to the business of writing a popular history of the human race, a biologist's history of the species that would give the idea of the unity of humankind a substance it lacked, and provide the emotional foundation that could give the concept of a League of Nations more than a purely intellectual appeal. It might even start something that would, in the end, make the creation of a world state or a world federation a practical proposition.

My father was roughing out a prospectus for his *Outline of History* between mid-July and the end of September 1918. While the broken-backed war dragged on toward its close he was reading voraciously and gathering together the group of friends and acquaintances who were to be his advisors and consultants during the execution of the huge project: Ray Lankester, Gilbert Murray, Denison Ross, Ernest Barker, Philip Guedalla, and Harry Johnston. By October he had a scheme on paper that was substantial enough to serve as the basis for contracts with publishers in England and the United States. With that solid ground under his feet he could move on to the business of organising a research team and drafting a skeleton for the actual book. Work on the text began in the early days of 1919, and the first version was finished by the end of the year. It met with criticism from specialists in various periods that called for substantial revisions, and by the time these had been made, and a short version had been prepared for publication in 1922, my father had written just over three quarters of a million words with the fine-nibbed Waterman fountain pens that he always used.

But *The Outline* was not all that my father managed to produce between March 1918 and the end of 1923. In that period he wrote the second half of the novel *Joan and Peter,* and wrote and published the following novels, collections of articles, and pamphlets: *The Undying Fire* (a novel), *British Nationalism and the League, The Idea of a League of Nations,* and *The Way to a League of Nations* (pamphlets) in 1919; *Russia in the Shadows* (collected articles revised and extended), 1920; *The Salvaging of Civilisation* (collected articles), *The New Teaching of History* (pamphlet), *Washington and the Hope of Peace* (collected articles revised and extended), 1921; *The Secret Places of the Heart* (a novel), The *World, Its Debts, & Rich Men* (pamphlet), 1922; and *Men Like Gods* (a novel). This list represents a considerable workload by itself, and makes it quite clear that the claim made in my mother's letter to S. K. Ratcliffe —that in those years her relationship with my father was requiring her to spend most of her time sick-nursing him—cannot be true.

The obvious explanation for that letter is not far to seek. From the very beginning *The Outline* affected my father's life profoundly. Its immediate consequence was to concentrate his existence on Easton Glebe and to draw him closer than ever to Jane. She had for many years been acting as his comptroller, and as soon as he had thrown up his Crewe House job he had to ask her if she would go along with his plan to take a plunge on this enormous project. She gave it her enthusiastic endorsement, and made herself a working partner in the scheme by acting as one of his research assistants until it had been completed. Something of the spirit of the early years of the marriage, in which they had been good companions embarking on the great Balzacian adventure of making it against the odds, returned, and the

Glebe became a hive of dedicated industry. Some of the men who came to the house to work on the project—notably Philip Guedalla and Frank Horrabin—were never to forget the happy atmosphere that they found there, or the inspiring example presented by my father's total commitment. The house and the work being done there were all-important to him, and he did not like to waste a minute away from the place while the text remained incomplete.

But that was only the beginning. The success of *The Outline* changed the character of my father's life. It completed the transformation of his financial affairs initiated by the impressive sales of *Mr. Britling*, making him a rich man and an exile from Bohemia. It also brought him into a personal relationship with Lord Beaverbrook, and Beaverbrook introduced him to a new world in which he was able to see himself with a fresh eye, as someone with an importance that was not related to the literary value of his writing. The nature of his frequentations underwent a change. A vignette, in which my father and Jane may be seen in this newly penetrated realm, is to be found in the memories of William Gerhardie. Beaverbrook had invited this Anglo-Russian novelist to dinner to meet the Wellses, and he was the first guest to arrive on the appointed night. Not knowing what to expect, but imagining that the evening would probably be a literary one, Gerhardie became more and more astonished as their successive arrivals showed that he was to spend the evening with His Royal Highness the Aga Khan, Admiral of the Fleet the Earl Beatty, and Reginald McKenna, a former Home Secretary and Chancellor of the Exchequer who had gone on from politics to become chairman of the Midland Bank. The Wellses finally arrived just as Gerhardie was beginning to suppose that he must have come on the wrong night, but while their appearance eased his mind on that point, he was left wondering what exactly my father was doing in such company.

The answer to his unuttered question is to be found in *The Autocracy of Mr. Parham,* a satirical novel written some ten years later, in which my father gives a somewhat wry account of the exhilarating and seductive experience involved in being taken up by Beaverbrook. In this light-heartedly entertaining work he caricatures himself as Mr. Parham, and shows at once just what he thought he was doing when he allowed himself to become a regular at Beaverbrook's Stornoway House dinners, and how fond he had become of that oddly beguiling monster by the time that they came to the parting of their ways. The group assembled for the dinner attended by Gerhardie was typical of the company that Beaverbrook kept, and my father cultivated Beaver-brook for that reason. He did not want to meet such people because they were celebrities, but because most of them were either the people responsible for making important decisions, or insiders so placed in the social scheme as to be able to influence those people. And it was not the perennial fascination of the corridors of power and the inside track that led him into this pursuit; it was a passionate belief in two propositions that he wished these people to accept. In the course of 1918 he had become convinced that it would be a disaster for Europe, and possibly for the world at large, if the foreign offices of the Allied Powers were to make their traditional hostility to anything revolution-ary the basis of their approach to the new regime in Russia; and that it might be an even greater misfortune if a League of Nations was to be created at the end of the war that could be seen to be a mere League of Victors pursuing narrowly national interests. By the end of the year it was perfectly clear to him that the victorious Allies were determined to try to bring down the Soviet regime by force of arms, and that the peace treaty when it came would create an instrument for punishing the defeated, and the Russians, tailored to French para-noia. This double defeat for causes that my father had espoused told him that Winston Churchill had been right when he had told him, back in 1900, after the publication of *Anticipations,* that he had been wrong to denigrate politicians. Churchill had gone on to argue that politicians had a useful social function as propagandists for new con-ceptions of what could and should be done by governments. It was not wise for a man of his views who wished to bring about social reforms to ignore them. His chances of getting what he wanted by making a direct appeal to public opinion were small. It was the men the public had elected to govern them who had to be won over if tangible results were to be achieved with any rapidity. Once the men in power had been convinced of the virtues of a new idea it was an easy matter for them to get the public to take it up.

In the light of hindsight, my father's decision to try to do his bit towards bringing about a reversal of the British Government's poli-cies in the matters of Russia and the League by breathing in the ears of Beaverbrook and Beaverbrook's cronies may appear to have been naïve. But when the 'twenties began, Beaverbrook was still a wholly credible power behind the scenes in British politics. He had played an important part in the manoeuvres that had put the incompetent As-quith out of office and made David Lloyd George Prime Minister in his place in 1916, and he was the close friend and confidant of the Conservative leader Bonar Law, who looked to be the certain successor to Lloyd George as soon as the time came to replace the wartime coalition with a party government. He had still to be undone by the sudden death, in 1923, of Bonar Law, which made Stanley Baldwin, who had no use for him, leader of the Conservatives; and he had not yet been guyed into absurdity by the cartoonist David Low and his imitators, a ten-year process that only bore its full fruit after 1930. My father had every reason to think that he was getting close to the center of things when he entered the enchanter's circle.

In 1920 a burning issue that was being discussed at the Stornoway House dinners was that of interventionism, which had been resurrected by the outbreak of war between Poland and Russia in January. Churchill and a great many of his followers in the parliamentary party thought that the Polish move into the Ukraine to give armed assistance to the Ukrainian Separatists under Petlyura had created a favourable opportunity for a renewed effort to bring down the Soviet regime. When my father argued the case against this view he felt that he did not have much knowledge to put behind his words. His Russian impressions of 1914 were badly out of date, and he had never been in any of the East European countries. He decided to fill in the gaps in his knowledge as soon as he could, and within a few weeks of the beginning of the new war he was on his way to Czechoslovakia.

When my father arrived in Prague toward the end of June he found the city in an edgy mood. The war had begun well for the Russians, and it seemed that they could not put a foot wrong while they were clearing the Polish forces out of the Ukraine. The news of the day was of another big Russian victory; rumours were spreading that the Red Army would be driving straight on to Warsaw, and that it would be Czechoslovakia's turn next. The only Czechs who seemed to be unperturbed were the ex-soldiers who had fought their way across Russia to Siberia and back again during the civil war as members of the Czechoslovak Legion, and Masaryk, the new country's first president. My father saw a good deal of him, since, on Karel Čapek's advice, the President was going out of his way to be attentive to him. They had a number of long talks together. Masaryk told him, among other things, that the Russian victories in the Ukraine were more a sign of Polish weakness than of Russian strength. He assured my father that conditions were unimaginably bad inside Russia, and that the odds were that the Bolshevik regime would be unable to survive the winter. Masaryk was certain that the Red Army would disintegrate as soon as it suffered its first serious defeat, an event that he expected to take place very soon after the war moved out of Russian territory and onto Polish soil. However good the Red Army might be when it was motivated by the defence of the homeland, it would not be up to exporting the revolution; half its power would be gone as soon as it became a foreign army fighting on an alien soil. In Russia itself the only thing that the Soviets had going for them was that no plausible alternative to their regime was in sight.

My father passed this optimistic assessment of Poland's chances on to Beaverbrook and his friends on his return to London towards the end of July. His words rang hollow in his mouth, because the Russians had won a second major victory on the northern front on July 7th, and were clearly driving on in the direction of the Polish capital. The more belligerent Communist leaders were already talking of sweeping on beyond Warsaw to link up with the comrades in Germany. There was talk of the possibility of setting up revolutionary regimes in both Poland and Germany before the end of the year. Masaryk seemed to have had the whole thing wrong. And then, in the third week in August, General Weygand, and a large staff, and a great many train-loads of arms, ammunition, and supplies, transformed the situation. An adequately equipped Polish army first stopped the Russians dead within a few kilometers of Warsaw, and then defeated them so decisively that their forces simply dissolved.

This dramatic turnabout created a new peril. Winston Churchill and his followers saw the outcome in Poland as the fullest possible justification for the interventionist policy. As they saw it, the Polish recovery had been a function of the help they had been given by the French. The time had clearly come for Britain to join France in the renewal of the great anti-Bolshevik crusade. The Churchillian gift for the larger view came very much to the fore: with the main body of the Red Army wiped off the board at the gates of Warsaw, there was nothing to prevent an internationally supplied White Army from driving through the Ukraine to link up with the remains of Petlyura's forces near Kiev. They would then drive on to make contact with the armies of General Wrangel, which were still in being, and in possession of the Donets coal field and the Crimea. If this were done—and it *could* be done—the Cossacks *could* rise again, the country *could* catch fire, and the revolutionary regime *could* fall.

Masaryk had foreseen that these temptations would arise. When he had told my father that he was not really afraid of what the Red Army might do in Poland, he went on to say what it was that he really dreaded. It was the fear of a Russian collapse that made him sweat in the dark hours of the night. He believed that if the civil war was to be cranked up again, anarchy might rot through Europe from east to west, and that there could be the beginning of another Hundred Years' War, with bandit armies fighting endlessly across the map, looting and pillaging. He was sure that the paranoia of desperation was what lay behind Russian belligerence, and that what the whole region wanted above everything else was money to finance reconstruction, and time in which to put it to work.

When my father put Masaryk's case against intervention to Beaverbrook and his hard-headed friends in business and banking they admitted that it made sense, given his view of the facts. But how could they be sure that Masaryk's assessment of the situation was correct? Were conditions in Russia really that bad? Wrangel's people, and the French, insisted that things could be turned round, and a new regime installed, without shedding too much blood, or spending too much money, in quite a short time—say, eighteen months.

In August my father had a second letter from Gorky, who had already written to him to assure him that Lenin and his associates were not the fiends in human shape that their enemies made out. This time Gorky had written to ask him to do Russia a favour. His request seemed to my father to throw a flood of light on the realities of the Russian situation, and to confirm the worst of Masaryk's suspicions. My father took Gorky's letter to Beaverbrook and showed it to him. Gorky had asked my father to organise a private relief mission. The winter was not far off. Food shortages in the Petrograd area were already so acute that it was plain to see that rations were going to be cut, and cut again, before it was over. That had to mean that a good many older people would starve. Some of Russia's leading scientists, such as Pavlov, were no longer young, and the war had made heavy inroads into the ranks of the younger men who would be their replacements in the ordinary course of events. There was a real danger that the scientific community was about to suffer almost irreparable damage. This could be prevented if these notables could be given extra fats and sugar to supplement their rations. The quantities needed to make a significant difference to their chances of survival wouldn't have to be very great. Two or three hundred pounds of such things as lard, butter, and sugar, and a proportion of things that didn't involve any cooking, like butterscotch and chocolate, would do the trick. The handling of such a consignment might appear to present difficulties, but it could all be packed in three or four cases of a hundred to a hundred and fifty pounds dead weight; a traveller could bring it to Petrograd with his luggage as personal effects. Did my father know anyone who might be able to make the trip and bring in these desperately needed supplies?

As Beaverbrook was reading the letter he took in the point: it reflected a situation that had to be very bad indeed. The idea for a series of circulation-building articles for *The Sunday Express* then leapt into his mind: *Wells Goes to Russia.* The man was on the crest of a wave. The fortnightly parts in which his *Outline of History* was appearing were selling at the rate of a hundred thousand copies an issue. His name would sell the paper. "Why don't you go yourself?" he asked. My father left for Russia on September 15.

He had last been there in the spring of 1914, when the shrewd and perceptive Russophile Maurice Baring had been his guide. Baring had fallen in love with the country and its people and in the early years of the century, and as far back as 1906, when the dust of the disturbances of the previous year was still settling, had predicted the coming of a second, and much more serious, revolutionary outbreak within a decade. While he was introducing my father to the beauties of St. Petersburg as it was in 1914, he had made much of the huge gap that had, even then, opened up between the monarchy and the people. In the light of Baring's commentaries my father had seen the most beautiful of northern cities as something in the nature of a dazzling arrangement of theatrical scenery, a skin of pretence erected in front of the stark and forbidding structure of the theatre itself. But he had not been able to share Baring's dread of the day when the flats that had been set up for the last act of the czarist tragedy would be struck. His sympathies had been for the lower orders, whose lot would, he believed, be exalted when the great day of revision finally came. He had been staying with my mother at the detested Claverton Street apartment when the news that the last of the czars had been forced to abdicate reached London in March 1917. His immediate reaction to this event had been to hurry to her side. He had burst in on her with the excited words "It's begun . . ." He saw it as the beginning of a universal revolt. The men at the front were going to stop serving the guns and go home, the interminable war was going to come to an end, and the crowns were going to be torn off the heads of all the kings who still cumbered the ground. He was still as hopeful when Guchkov and Miliukov, the right-wingers in the Provisional Government, were put out in favour of Kerensky, in May. My father had written joyfully to Gorky at that time to wish him and his friends success in their "struggle to liberate mankind, the German people included, from the net of aggressive monarchy, and to establish international good will on a basis of international justice and respect." It excited him that St. Petersburg had played a leading role in making this glorious new departure: the city by the Neva, rather than Moscow, had been the city of the revolution.

Even though he had over two hundred and fifty pounds of edible fats and sugar in his baggage, and knew that these things were badly needed up ahead, he half expected to find his destination transformed and its people electrified, as he had found Prague and its people electrified, by the coming of the new times.

But it was not St. Petersburg to which he was returning. He was on his way to Petrograd, the empty city foreseen in the curse put on her husband's creation by the wife of Peter the Great. The doors and windows of half its buildings had been boarded up, and their peeling and neglected façades looked diseased. A heavy quiet brooded over the town and nothing was being made in its factories. The port was virtually at a standstill, and the railroad yards on its outskirts were silent parks of useless rolling stock and dead locomotives that had been run until they were beyond repair, cannibalised for spare parts, and abandoned on the tracks. There was hardly any traffic on the streets. Droshkys and private cars had vanished altogether, carts and trucks were few and far between, and decrepit street cars, crammed to overflowing, whined by uncertainly at long intervals. The lively St. Petersburg crowd had melted away, and the few gaunt people to be encountered on the streets were either in shabby uniforms or in rags. My father heard no laughter and saw no one smile as he walked the almost deserted pavements. Most of the men and women he passed stood in queues, grey-skinned and expressionless, either outside government offices from which vouchers were issued for all the necessities of life or outside the food and clothing stores at which those vouchers could be exchanged for commodities, if any were available. Everything that had been the life of St. Petersburg had come to an end, and nothing that might bring half-emptied Petrograd to life had yet begun. My father was horrified by the slow pace at which people moved about, by the even slower pace at which things were being done, and by the general state of numbed apathy that prevailed. The whole city had been living with hunger for three years and now famine was coming. All its inhabitants knew what that would mean. Thousands of them would not live through the winter. By the time spring came, they would have died of starvation and exposure.

My father was staying with Gorky in the enormous Kronversky Avenue apartment that he had been able to make by punching a door through into a second set of rooms. There he found himself living in the middle of an heterogeneous population made up partly of old friends of Gorky's from the worlds of literature and the arts, and partly of people previously unknown to him who were temporarily homeless or avoiding the attentions of the police. One of the permanent residents was a former Grand Duke and patron of the arts named Gabriel Romanov, who occupied a single room with his wife and their little dog. Others in the same category were Gorky's first wife, Ekatarina Peshkova, and his second, Marya Andreeva. The poet Khodasevich came and went unpredictably, as did Tatlin, the constructivist; but Khodasevich's niece and the young woman who was Tatlin's mistress were there all the time. A crowd of others, among them Zamiatin, a writer who was one of my father's more vocal Russian admirers, came and went, sometimes staying for a few hours and sometimes for the night. My father, feeling rather lonely among all these new faces, and not at all sure of what to make of its richly confused group life, clung for moral support to the only one of the apartment's fixtures, Gorky and Marya Andreeva apart, he had ever met before. This was the Countess Benckendorff, the former Moura Zakrevskaya. He had first known her as an elegant debutante in 1914, when she had been rich and able to help herself to anything that money could buy. Now she possessed the clothes she stood up in, and a spare set of underclothing. She had just become Gorky's secretary and mistress, even though he knew, because she had warned him of it, that she had been planted on him as a police spy by Zinoviev, who hated him.

Part—though only a small part—of Moura's complicated story has been told in the book called *Memoirs of a British Agent,* in which Bruce Lockhart tells the story of his adventures as First Secretary to the British Embassy in Petrograd during the revolution. When my father renewed his acquaintance with her in 1920 she was still in the nightmarish situation that had arisen from that involvement. The GPU had released her from prison, where she was being held as an accomplice in Lockhart's espionage activities, on condition that she would serve that organisation as an informer. She had then been planted in Gorky's entourage. She had found her position intolerable from the start, and had soon felt compelled to warn Gorky of her connection with the police. Gorky admired her for having the courage to be straightforward with him in the circumstances, and made himself her protector. He used his considerable influence with Lenin to get the heat taken off her. Her situation remained precarious, however, since Zinoviev, who was in effect Lenin's viceroy in the Petrograd region, looked upon her as a defector from this point on, and included her in his detestation of Gorky and all his works. The GPU was no longer putting pressure on her, but made sure she knew that she was under constant surveillance. Her irrepressible wit and bubbling good humour, and the coolness with which she handled herself under this pressure, made an ineffacable impression on my father. His liking for her was powerfully re-enforced by the fact that she was an extremely attractive woman, with few inhibitions, a passionate nature, and great intelligence. It was inevitable that he should fall for her.

Gorky unwittingly furthered this development. He managed to persuade a number of the leading Bolsheviks, who were then much more open to foreign contacts than was to be the case later on, that my father was someone who might be listened to in England and the United States, and that since the regime was going to need every foreign friend it could make, they should go out of their way to win his good will. He was consequently the subject of an extremely effective stroking operation. Even Zinoviev, who was in principle opposed to the policy of soft-soaping the foreign bourgeois left, had a long and ostensibly friendly talk with him. At the end of this meeting he flatteringly arranged for my father to give an address to the Petrograd Soviet. Zinoviev then had to leave for Germany, where he was to attend the Halle Conference at which the Communist International was founded, and at which he ferociously denounced the thesis that there could be any profit in cooperation between the working-class left and the bourgeois left of western Europe. Before he left for Halle he handed my father over to Chicherin, then the leading Bolshevik diplomat and second only to Kamenev in his influence on Soviet foreign policy. Chicherin shared Zinoviev's views, and had an especially poor view of the British left, which had not been willing to help him when the British government had tossed him in jail for the offense of presenting his credentials as Russian

Ambassador to the Court of St. James's at the Foreign Office. He was, however, a man with a feline wit who could be very charming when he wished to be so. He bottled up his feelings when he met my father, making himself very agreeable, and promising to arrange for him to meet Lenin. He then called Lenin by telephone and persuaded him to invite my father to come and see him in Moscow. When that had been done he got in touch with Moura's controller in the GPU and suggested that she should make the trip with my father as his guide and interpreter.

In the course of the few days that they spent together in Moscow, Moura established a hold on my father's affections that was to prove unbreakable. He had loved every moment that he had been able to spend alone with her, and he hated to part from her when the time came for him to return to England. The pain of leaving her so soon after he had found her was all the greater because there seemed so very little ground for hope that he would ever see her again. Their hours together had been stolen. He knew when he embarked on the affair that Gorky was as fascinated and delighted by her as he was, and that he had become dependent upon her. He knew also that she was under a tremendous obligation to Gorky, and devoted to him. She had told my father, while they were in Moscow, and he had accepted the fact, that she would not be able to think of leaving Gorky for anyone else until he had given her clear signs that he had done with her. But my father could not reason himself out of his intoxication with her, and however little future his passion might seem to have, he went home with it burning in him.

Of my father's meeting with Lenin there is much that can be said, but the salient fact about it is that no stenographer was present. Lenin was proud of his command of English, and there was not even an interpreter in the room. There is a choice of accounts of how the interview went. One was written by my father, who was present, almost immediately after it took place. The other was produced by Leon Trotsky. He was not present, or even in Moscow, at the time, and his account was not written until more than three years later, after Lenin's death. It was then produced to order, when someone drew his attention to the chapter in my father's book *Russia in the Shadows* which is entitled "The Dreamer in the Kremlin." It may, or it may not, be significant that Trotsky had nothing to say about the interview as such that could not have been derived from that source. He has nothing further to contribute. All that he has to add is what he alleges that

75

Lenin said to him about the interview when no one else was present
. . .

In justice to Trotsky, it should be remembered that in 1924, when he at last got his account of the meeting down on paper, he was frantic with frustration and anxiety. He had been decisively outmanœuvred by Stalin in the party power struggle that followed Lenin's demise and he was standing on a trap with the Georgian's greased rope around his neck. He had lost, once and for all, the great doctrinal battle between the partisans of the *world revolution now* thesis and those who felt that *revolution in one country* was the winning ticket. His defeat had left Trotsky with a bilious loathing of a wide variety of real and fancied enemies, among them, rather weirdly, a miscellaneous group of persons, all of them quite unknown to him, who had been organised in his mind into the membership of a coherent and Machiavellian anti-revolutionary and pro-parliamentary English left. He had denounced this monster of his own creation in a venomous little pamphlet entitled *Whither Britain?* that first appeared, I believe, in 1923. This contained a great deal of the rant that is Trotsky's unmistakable signature:

> Together with theological literature Fabianism is perhaps the most useless, and in any case the most boring form of verbal creation. . . . The cheaply optimistic Victorian epoch in which it seemed that tomorrow would be a little better than today, and the day after tomorrow still better than tomorrow, found its most finished expression in the Webbs, Snowden, Macdonald, and other Fabians . . . these arrogant and ranting poltroons . . . systematically poison the Labour movement, befog the consciousness of the proletariat and paralyse its will. . . . At any cost these self-satisfied pedants, these gabbling eclectics, these sentimental careerists, these upstart liveried lackeys of the bourgeoisie must be shown in their natural form to the workers. To reveal them as they are will mean their hopeless discrediting.

And so forth, and so, shrilly, on. On first sight of this diatribe I thought that it was rather scholarly of Trotsky to have heard of Snowden as early as 1923, but on looking into the matter, I found that the whole of *Whither Britain?* almost certainly owes its existence to the fact that Philip Snowden's wife had been in Georgia in 1921, and had reported on her return to England that none of the Georgians she had encountered had been Communists, and that none of them had wanted Georgia to become a part of the Russian motherland. Be that as it may, it seems clear to me that when Trotsky wrote his little piece asserting that Lenin had reacted to his mention of my father's name by crying out "Ugh! What a narrow petty bourgeois! Ugh! What a Philistine!" he was merely having a go at "showing him in his natural form to the workers," or lying for a purpose, as was his custom. Inventing convenient sayings discreditable to enemies and rivals for attribution to Lenin became something in the nature of a cottage industry in inner party circles during the testing time in which Stalin was inching his way to the top of the greasy pole, and Trotsky was as fertile in this field of creative fiction as any of them. It seems to me to be highly unlikely that Lenin ever said anything whatever to Trotsky about either my father or the meeting, and almost certain that the two dismissive ejaculations quoted above, and so often elsewhere, with so much relish, are pure fabrications.

But whatever Lenin may or may not have said about my father, *his* feelings about the Russian leader are not in doubt. He took to Lenin, liking him for his courage, openness, and determination. He believed every word of it when Lenin said that it was his purpose to make a new kind of society, better and more humane than anything that had ever existed, out of the shattered ruins of the czarist state. But he also found Lenin pitiful. He did not believe that the Russian leader realised how bad his situation was, or how unlikely it was that his hopes for the transformation of Russia would be fulfilled. Knowing how short of food and fuel the larger Russian cities were, and how close the new regime had come to collapse because it had no answers to the problems created by those and other shortages, and by the virtually complete breakdown of the national railroad network, he was taken aback at the start of the interview when Lenin told him that he was relying on a vast, and manifestly enormously demanding, scheme for rural and urban electrification to get the country out of its present difficulties. White power, generated in huge hydroelectrical plants, and a national grid of power lines were to be the answers to the problems of fuel supply and distribution. My father felt that he was being made privy to pipe dreams rather than being given a sketch of what Lenin really thought that he might be able to do. He tentatively threw out the observation that it didn't appear to him that the regime had either the time or the resources that such a program called for —where, for instance, was Russia going to find the army of technicians, toolmakers, machinists, electricians, engineers, draftsmen, and designers that would be needed to carry it out? And what about the formidable educational deficit that seemed to be involved? A work force that hadn't been educated up to the level of his plans surely wasn't going to collaborate either willingly or effectively in their execution; the men wouldn't be able to understand what they were being asked to do, or why they were being asked to do it. What was Lenin going to try to do about that in the very short time that he had in hand?

Lenin replied by outlining a stupendous crash program for popular education that was to begin with a rapid conquest of the problem of adult illiteracy and was to be as comprehensive in its scope as the scheme for national electrification. My father had been shown schools in Petrograd which had been as short of pens, pencils, paper, and even blackboard chalk as they were of textbooks, so that this made him blink. He had gathered that there was very little left of the old czarist educational system, and that the regime would be starting again from somewhere very close to scratch when it actually got down to business. He could not help wondering if Lenin had any idea of the scale of the effort his plans for universal education would call for. To find out, he embarked on an outline sketch of the fifteen- to twenty-year period of phased expansion that the English school system had been going through while he was growing up. Would Lenin's people be moving ahead step by step in the same way? Or had he thought of some other way of producing trained teachers in phase with the expansion of the student body? How did he mean to do it?

It was Lenin's turn to blink. Could this Englishman, whose intelligence and sympathetic outlook had been vouched for by Gorky, be urging the merits of gradualism and evolutionary reform upon him, just as if there had been no revolution? Didn't he realise that the reformist game was played out, and that revolution demanded revolutionary solutions to its problems? The conversation faltered for a moment, and then became one of the hammer-and-tongs arguments that Lenin had so much enjoyed having with Radek's English friend, Arthur Ransome, back in 1919. Lenin explained that revolution had made the whole nation a school. In the Red Army, for instance, the literate in each platoon became the teachers of the illiterate, and had to be the same in the factories and on the farms. Revolution meant release from the constraints of bourgeois formalism.

Lenin spoke with certainty, and with an attractive fluency and vivacity of which no trace is to be found in his leaden and mendacious writings. What he said moved my father, though it failed altogether to make him believe that the proposed improvisations could bring about the desired results. But for all that, Lenin was the Communist leader, and the Communists were the only people left in the country with the determination to act in unison in the face of the great social collapse that threatened to overwhelm it. His leadership, and their cohesion and sense of purpose, had put them in possession of the wreckage created by the incapacity and folly of their rivals, and there was no one else. My father saw that the state of things was even worse than Masaryk had thought, and that the chances were anything but remote that his nightmare might become reality. The worst had yet to happen, but it very easily might. My father returned to England with a strengthened conviction that the greatest threat posed by Russia lay in the possibility not that the Bolsheviks might consolidate their position, but that they might fail to do so. If they could not rule, nobody could, and the country would renew its slide into further depths of barbarism and anarchy. The answer to the looming threat could not be military intervention; it had to be relief, trade, and loans.

Gorky had a great deal to do with the shaping of my father's opinions. The developing ambiguities in the Russian writer's situation escaped him altogether in those early days, and he took Gorky for an unimpeachable source. In many ways he was. There is, for instance, no doubt of the genuineness of Gorky's experience with the "wandering children," a thing that made a tremendous impression upon my father. Nineteen-twenty was the third year in which these children had been a major social problem. They were the wild creatures who had been cast adrift when their families and communities had been torn apart or obliterated by war, revolution, and civil war. Gorky had been asked to take part in framing a program for their reclamation and rehabilitation; and to find out what the problem was he had made an exploratory visit to one of the hostels that had been set up for their benefit in Petrograd. Unaware that the institution he was visiting was in fact a jail, he had attempted to get a friendly dialogue going by asking the assembled inmates what they would like him to do for them. They had responded by howling him down and mobbing him. He had been tumbled down a staircase and stripped of most of his clothing before the staff could rescue him. What had appalled Gorky had been that all the inmates had been girls, none of them older than fifteen. The majority of them were either pregnant or had already produced children, and all had been living by prostitution, thieving, and possibly murder, for two years or more. When the revolution had begun they had been between ten and twelve years old . . . Gorky's horror of the debasement that these children had undergone was very great. It had been difficult for him to speak of what had happened; he had nerved himself to do so, and when he came to it he had begun to sweat and his hands had clenched.

My father had experienced a similar horror when Gorky was proudly showing him over the various thinly disguised soup kitchens and warming places for intellectuals and members of the intelligentsia that had been set up at his urging by the Petrograd Soviet under the rather grandiose titles of The House of Science, The House of Art, and The House of Writers. There he encountered a certain number of people who were still functioning resolutely in spite of the disintegration of their worlds of association and meaning, but he was more impressed by the others, who had disintegrated with them. They were alive, but they had given up on themselves and on the possibility of a future, and had become what were later to be known to the world of the Nazi concentration camps as Moslems: living dead who had surrendered before time to the negation of all their hopes. They had been intelligent and creative people with names and reputations, but they had been broken. This social debris, along with the lost children that Gorky had told him of, became for him emblematic of the high cost of the Russian collapse: it was impoverishing the present and the future. Come what might, that trend had to be reversed.

When my father got back to England towards the end of October, he immediately began to propagate these ideas, and soon found himself embroiled with Winston Churchill. Their arguments, begun at a variety of friendly dining-room tables, in Stornoway House and elsewhere, presently widened in scope. My father found himself one of a group of people taking part in a general attack on the subservience of the English Foreign Office to the Quai d'Orsay. The main thrust of English policy throughout 1919 and 1920 had been directed toward the achievement of two objectives, both chosen by the French. The first, designed to consummate the military defeat of Germany by ruining its economy, was that of securing 132 billion gold marks from the Germans as reparations for wartime losses. The second, intended to bring about the collapse of the Russian regime, was to secure the diplomatic and economic isolation of Russia inside a *cordon sanitaire* of client states linked to France by a web of economic and military pacts.

Both policies were conceived on the nebulous foundation of a worst-case scenario, according to which France would be attacked as soon as Germany had achieved an economic recovery by an unbeatable combination of German industrial strength and technical mastery with Russia's inexhaustible manpower. The French right-wing politicians saw Communism as a highly infectious social disease to which the Germans were especially likely to succumb. Men like Clemenceau and Poincaré felt that it was only by ruining Germany and putting Russia into rigid quarantine that the formation of a Communist super-state extending from the Friesian shore to Vladivostock could be prevented. They believed that once such an entity had come into being, there could be no holding the lid down on the world revolution that Trotsky was announcing as a forthcoming attraction in almost every speech he made.

My father was sure that this scenario was more or less precisely back to front. He believed that the ruin of Germany would bring them the peacetime equivalent of the wartime disaster that had made the Russian revolution a revolution instead of a constitutional upheaval. The plans that the French were making for the containment of Russia were simply a recipe for the destruction of Europe. From the winter of 1920 onwards he was doing all that he could to build public and private opposition to further British support for these fatal designs, and to bring about their replacement by others more likely to get Europe back to work. He spoke, in season and out, for a long-term policy of recognising Russia's government and bringing that country back into the community of nations; of scaling down reparations to a point at which they might become commensurate with Germany's ability to pay them out of current earnings; and of effective disarmament.

My father was not alone in reaching his conclusion that these were the right policies for the times, nor had he thought more profoundly about them than many of those who joined him in urging them upon the politicians and the public. But he had a firm grasp of the main issues, and a vivid sense of what the immediate consequences of following the wrong line would be, and he had an exceptional gift for dealing with such matters in the common tongue used by the mass of ordinary people.

In the light of hindsight it is easy to underestimate my father's skill and effectiveness as a populariser and a propagandist; much of what he was saying in the early twenties has since become commonplace because his advocacy won it widespread acceptance. But he was not thought to be dealing with commonplaces at the time. When *The Sunday Express* began to run the articles Beaverbrook had commissioned before he set out for Russia, the paper's circulation went up by 80,000 copies, and the increase held, just as the sales of *The Outline* in fortnightly parts had held, until the last article in the series appeared. The success of the articles led to their almost immediate reissue as the substance of *Russia in the Shadows,* the book that Trotsky was to dislike so much later on. When Beaverbrook saw it he decided to give the lemon another squeeze. He gave the book to Winston Churchill for review and at the same time invited my father to reply to his criticism. When Winston's slating and my father's counterblast appeared in *The Daily Express,* its circulation jumped just as that of *The Sunday Express* had done.

This convincing proof that my father had made himself a name that sold papers with *The Outline of History* put him very close to the top of the journalistic tree, and when Lord Northcliffe wanted him to cover the Washington Conference on Naval Disarmament for the features syndicate that was his newest plaything at the end of the following year, he offered him what was then a staggering £10,000 to do it. His arrival in that field was coincident with an enormous enlargement of his reputation as a writer outside the literary world. In its various hard-cover versions his *Outline of History* sold more than two million copies in England and the United States, and as many more in translation elsewhere. This success created a market for cheap reprints of the novels that he had written in the 'nineties and in the first years of the nineteen-hundreds, published in paperback by Ernest Benn and in hard covers by Nelson's in their Library of Modern Classics, they racked up sales of nearly three million copies in England alone. All this activity tempted a number of foreign publishers to give his books a run in translation in countries in which he had never been published before. Between 1918 and 1923 he became a world figure whose name was known wherever books were printed and newspapers were sold.

I find it very hard to accept the hero of this success story, with his wide-ranging interests, his energetic pursuit of his goals, and his record of accomplishment, as the half-mad Wells of that bizarre letter addressed to S. K. Ratcliffe by my mother. I think it is self-evident that whatever might have been happening to his career as a novelist in those five years, they saw my father transforming himself into a busy, productive, and increasingly self-confident publicist who was, in the main, creditably and profitably employed. The riddle remains: how is that letter to be explained? I said earlier that the explanation is not far to seek, and that the first place to look for the clue to it is in my mother's insistence on the point that my father's preparations for his trip to Czechoslovakia in 1920 had an abnormally inflating effect upon his ego. There is a coincidence here.

In May 1920 my father ran into a woman who seemed to be the perfect material for one of those casual affairs licensed by his understanding with Jane. She was a New York parlour radical, a friend or acquaintance of many such people as Big Bill Haywood, John Reed, Emma Goldman, and Mabel Dodge. She had made a name for herself in the circles in which they moved by running a paper of her own called *The Woman Rebel,* and had become more widely known for standing trial and serving a prison term for advocating the unrestricted sale of contraceptives in defiance of federal law banning the dissemination of birth-control information. Liberated in the modern sense, she was on the loose in England for a summer's lease, nerving herself to take, after a three-year delay, the legal steps that would end an unsatisfactory marriage by divorce. When it is added that Margaret Sanger was also a pretty woman, grey-eyed, auburn-haired, trimly built, and fairly overflowing with high spirits and physical energy, it will be seen why my father jumped at the chance of having an affair with her. No complications could possibly come of a frolic with her. She knew what she was about, she already had her passage back to the United States, and she had her American life to get on with when she returned. There seemed no way in which the thing could get out of hand.

But Margaret Sanger was not a woman to be taken lightly. She possessed a species of radiant common sense, and she had a developed sense of humour. She was as quick-witted as my father was, and as devoid of self-reverence. He was delighted to find himself dealing with a woman who had her feet so firmly planted on solid ground, and who was in the habit of setting herself attainable goals. Before he knew it they had become friends as well as lovers, and by the time that she had to go back to the United States, at the end of October, they both knew that their parting was not to be the end of their affair.

If this instance stood by itself, I would not care to risk suggesting that my mother's observation about the inflating effect that my father's preparations for his visit to Prague had upon his ego was in fact a coded reference to the beginning of his long-lasting relationship with Margaret Sanger. But it is noticeable that my father's "outra-geous" performances at Amalfi in January 1921, where he was so astonishingly unresponsive to the overtures from that future mayor of Croydon, and so "awful" to my mother with so little reason, were staged soon after his return from Russia with the glow of his intoxica-tion with Moura Zakrevskaya-Benckendorff very visibly upon him. The bizarre repetitions of those Amalfi scenes that were presently staged in the Hotel Maria Christina at Algeciras took place just a year later, on my father's return from the visit to the United States, in the course of which his light-hearted affair with Margaret Sanger trans-formed itself into the lasting relationship that was only to be broken off by his death.

I have to find these correlations suggestive. They tell me that my mother's accounts of my father's demented behaviour, however sharply detailed and however plausible in their *trompe l'oeil* literalness, are expressive of her states of feeling rather than descriptions of actual sublunary occurrences. They appear to me to be artifacts, manufactured to stand in the place of perceptions of an intolerable reality. This wasn't, I feel almost certain, any simple matter of her objection to the infidelities that my father so frequently and so reck-lessly embarked upon but much more a question of something more objectionable, that they implied, and which was very much harder to bear. What that something was presents itself with dazzling clarity in her account of the very odd, the almost preternaturally improbable, episode that is said to have taken place at the Inn on the barren moor in the late summer of 1922. This appears to me to be a beautifully organised allegory designed to express the outraged feelings of a woman who has been relegated to the background of a man's inter-ests.

There is another pointer towards an identification of this something in the account of the life that my father was living in the early twenties that my mother developed in the late sixties, and which has shown up in the more recent biographies. It is said to explain the dreadful state of physical and mental exhaustion that had overtaken my father by 1923–1924, and consists of a harrowing picture of the routine that had undone him. "He went round and round like a rat in a maze," one biographer was told, and he was given a weekly programme that consisted of "a feverish weekend at Easton Glebe, Monday to Tuesday at the London flat, two days with me, two days in London again, and back to Easton." I find this *perpetuum mobile* like an invention from one of M. R. James's ghost stories—it seems to me to have an unaccountable extra presence in the shape of an eighth day sliding around in it. But however many days the week that it envisages may contain I can't persuade it to yield up more than two days in seven or two days in eight of my father's time to my mother. And, sadly, I can't ignore the evidence to the point presented by my father's pocket diaries. They don't show that he was allowing her a regular ration of his time through this period, and they do make it perfectly clear that he was giving her less and less of it. To put it brutally, what my mother was living in the years leading up to the March day in 1923 on which she wrote that letter to S. K. Ratcliffe wasn't an appalling life with my father, but one that was, appalling or no, being lived very largely without him. Whatever she may have wished that particular correspondent to believe, the dismal truth was not that the relationship had become one that required her to spend most of her time sick-nursing, but that it quite simply didn't require much of her time. It had never done that, and I think that what must have made those five years so hard for her to endure was, to be precise, the pains he was taking, as they went by, to make it absolutely clear to her that there were no circumstances conceivable to him in which it was ever going to.

Chapter V

She became obsessed by the idea that I must marry her, and then "everything would be different."

It was only too plain to me that nothing would be different. We parted again with some heat and bitterness and had a second inconclusive reconciliation. . . .

. . . And then, filled with wrath, not so much with her as with myself, I set myself, sullenly and steadily, to break those humiliating and intolerable bonds.

I told her that now at last we had come to the end of our relationship.

—THE WORLD OF WILLIAM CLISSOLD

BEFORE HE SET OUT FOR RUSSIA IN the autumn of 1920 my father had begun a new novel, *The Secret Places of the Heart,* that drew very directly on his experiences of the spring. He hadn't, however, had time to get well into it before Gorky's appeal came to him, to shake him out of his routines. It wasn't until the latter part of the following year that he came back to it. He then polished it off, rather more rapidly than he should have, and had it ready for publication in 1922. It is not among his best works, but despite all its defects, it remains a book that no one who undertakes a biography of my father can afford to ignore.

The hero of *The Secret Places of the Heart* is a public man whose private life is in a mess. His marriage is in a bad way, since his career has taken a great deal from him that should have gone into it. His wife has become accustomed to finding what happiness and satisfaction she can in an interior life in which he plays no part. All she asks of him is that he will keep up the appearance of being a devoted husband; as long as he does that, he is free to do as he pleases. He has a mistress called Martin Leeds, but that relationship also is beginning to sour on him. This emancipated but romantic young woman thinks of sexual intercourse as the final seal put upon an absolute commitment to a partnership in which deceptions and infidelities can have no place. When the book opens, Sir Richmond Hardy—as my father is calling himself on this occasion—is hamstrung by indecision. He knows that he should break out of his emotionally sterile marriage in order to honour his obligations to Martin Leeds, but when it comes to it he just doesn't want to do that. Much as he likes her, fond of her as he is, he feels that she wants much more from him than he has to give.

In the hope that a change of scene taking him away from both women will help him to make up his mind one way or the other, he takes off on a motor tour of the West of England in the company of his medical advisor. He means to talk the thing out as they go. There is a nice piece of self-caricature here: they talk and talk and talk as they roll along—Sir Richmond at the wheel, of course—and occasionally, though not often, the professional man gets a word in edgewise. The therapy has hardly begun by the time they get to Stonehenge, and there, among those ancient relics, Sir Richmond picks up a young American woman who is exploring the English countryside with a female friend. The medical man sees what is coming, tries to dissuade Sir Richmond from the irrelevant adventure, and leaves in a huff when his advice is turned down.

The affair that provides the core of the book then gets going. It would be very banal indeed if it were not being treated as if a partly dried-out alcoholic's return to the bottle were in question. The American visitor is an amorist's dream come true. She thinks that sex is a thing to be enjoyed for its own sake, without sin and without shame, whenever inclination and opportunity combine to make it possible. She feels that the act commits her to nothing, and that it leaves whoever it is that she has chosen as her playmate for the hour or the day under no greater obligation to her than can be discharged by keeping in touch and letting her have a newsy letter now and again. I don't think that there is any room for doubt but that this is my father's portrait of Margaret Sanger as he first perceived her, and before he had come to know her properly. His motive for dredging up his wholly mistaken reading of her estimable character is made evident as the affair proceeds. He is writing a study of the language of self-deception. Both parties are to lie their way through the episode.

Although Sir Richmond knows that the woman he is chatting up is a bird of passage who has no intention of remaining in England for more than a couple of weeks, he calls her his dear wife and mate when he kisses her for the first time. They have been together for a full week by then, and have a full week more to look forward to. A few lines further on Sir Richmond tells himself, and with solemnity, that he is in love with her, more in love than he has ever been. When they next face each other they both know that they are headed for bed. So he says that he loves her with all his heart, and she tells him that she loves him with all hers. They then have their week of motoring from place to place, sightseeing, eating meals in hotel dining rooms, and bedding down in hotel bedrooms. The most must be made of it. It has, he assures her on their last night together, been the best thing in all his life; he adds that she is his heart's desire, his priestess of life, and the embodiment of his idea of divinity. The next place that they get to is Exeter, where he puts her on board a train that will take her off to Southampton and the boat home, and that is it.

It is tempting, since my father was notoriously inept when it came to writing love scenes, to put Sir Richmond's resolute debasement of the language of courtship down to an accident of birth. But I find support for my belief that my father knew just what he was doing on this occasion in the dashingly conceived and executed surprise that follows the American visitor's departure. When Sir Richmond has watched her train pulling out of Exeter Station he suddenly finds himself at loose ends. He has several days left to him before he is expected back at his office, and he hasn't a thing to do:

> He went outside the station and stared at his motor car. He had to go somewhere. Of course! down to Cornwall to Martin's cottage. He had to go down to her to be kind and comforting. . . . He had always for some inexplicable cause treated Martin badly. Nagged her and blamed her and threatened her. That must stop now. No shadow of this affair must lie on Martin . . . and Martin must never have any suspicion of any of this. . . . Martin! Old friend! Eight days were still left . . . eight days of golden kindness. He would distress Martin by no clumsy confession. he would just make her happy as she loved to be made happy . . .

Candor could hardly be carried further. My father has drawn a ruthlessly honest picture of his procedures, and of himself. Sir Richmond is as unable to meet any serious emotional demand that may be made upon him as he is incapable of dealing honestly with his women, and he is under a compulsion to trivialise every relationship from which such a demand might arise. His dive at the American Visitor is, for a man in his situation, a decision for trivialisation; and his next project, for spending what remains of his holiday in hood-winking his mistress, is its confirmation. He is to make his relationship with her a carbon copy of what he has with his wife. He is to run Martin Leeds as a second woman to leave, to be unfaithful to, and to go back to, to buy a meaningless absolution with meaningless reassurances. By thinking of her in that role he finds it possible to feel quite fond of her.

Had my father broken off *The Secret Places of the Heart* at that point, he would have had a telling piece of work in the acidly ironic vein that he was attempting. But he went on from that adequate climax to the anticlimax that I have already described as ludicrous. It must seem so to any reader who comes to it without a key, and I am not sure that a knowledge of the foundations in reality upon which its characters are built is enough to clear it of a certain fruity absurdity. What happens is that my father first butchers himself in the person of Sir Richmond, and then, when he has laid himself out stiff and stark, brings Martin Leeds onto the stage to mourn for him. She has been an offstage presence up to this point, and the reader has been given no hint that might lead him to expect her to come on as a character on ticket of leave from a Lyceum melodrama. She has been given a sexually ambiguous name, and has been described as having the face of a sensitive youth rather than the face of a woman, but the perform-ance she gives over and around Sir Richmond's still open coffin in the embarrassed but understanding presence of the medical man we last saw back at Stonehenge can only be called full-bosomed.

> She held out her hands towards the doctor. "What am I to do now with the rest of my life? Who is there to laugh with me now and jest?
>
> "I don't complain of him. I don't blame him. He did his best —to be kind . . .
>
> "But all my days now I shall mourn for him and long for him . . ."
>
> She turned back to the coffin. Suddenly she lost every ves-tige of self-control. She sank down on her knees beside the trestle. "Why have you left me?" she cried.

"Oh! Speak to me, my darling! Speak to me, I tell you! Speak to me!"

It was a storm of passion, monstrously childish and dreadful. She beat her hands upon the coffin. She wept loudly and fiercely as a child does . . .

When discussing the book in the early seventies, my mother said that she had always found this passage, and the entire novel, exceedingly funny. She added that my maternal grandmother, the redoubtable Mrs. Fairfield, who normally thought of her daughter's association with my father as a tragic matter, was reduced to hopeless (sic) laughter when she read it. She went on to say that my father was very much annoyed when she told him of the old lady's reaction. I am inclined to think that if my father had ever been given this information, it would have been more likely to astonish than to annoy him. He was not used to being told that his books had been read by people in my grandmother's situation. After ailing for some time, she had become acutely ill in June 1921, and had died on August 9 of that year. As I have already said, this novel was not set up in type and published until the spring of 1922.

This incautious invention of my mother's makes me doubt that she ever found this novel all that funny. My belief is that it was that final scene, at once absurd and acute, that she objected to: it makes the point that Martin Leeds is so entirely an actress that a performance is her answer to everything, even a confrontation with her lover's corpse. Her posturings are, however, in sharp contrast to her possession of genuine insight. She is well aware of the realities of the situation: Sir Richmond dead is out of reach, and has been all along. Her performance comes to an end with a statement which, although entirely false as *speech,* is entirely true as to content: "Sometimes, I think, he loved me. But it is hard to tell . . . he could be intensely kind, and yet he didn't seem to care for you. There was a sort of dishonesty in his kindness. He would not let you have the bitter truth. He would not say that he did not love you . . ." My father was not to be forgiven, ever, for giving her these lines.

The offence given by *The Secret Places of the Heart* was compounded by a number of letters written to my mother in the course of 1922–1923. These show that my father was trying to get her to choose between two courses at that time. She was either to break with him or to make the most of their relationship on his terms. This did not mean that he wanted things to go on between them on an unchanged footing. She was to mend her ways. He didn't approve of them. She spent too much of her time with the wrong sort of people. She owed it to herself and her career to frequent her equals in talent and ability more than she was doing. And she was frittering away too much of her precious gift on turning out too many entertainingly astringent book reviews. It was all one with him as to whether she went on with him or not, but it did matter that she wasn't getting on with her real business of making herself a considerable writer.

It has been suggested that it was grossly impertinent of my father, as "a tired and sick man on the brink of old age," to take this governess line with a young genius whose literary position was already established. But in fact, my father, at fifty-six, was on the crest of his wave, and my mother had still a long way to go. She had proved herself as a book reviewer, but Henry James's friends had effectively killed her little book about the master's work; she had written a sentimental novelette in *The Return of the Soldier,* and although her major effort, *The Judge,* had then, and still has, its admirers, it was more widely seen as an ill-advised attempt to beat Dostoevsky at his own game, and had fallen flat. My father was to a large extent justified in speaking of it as a "sprawl of a book with a faked hero and a faked climax" and as "an aimless waste of her powers." While he was savaging this novel he told her why he was pitching into it so ferociously. He had tried, he said, to let her down lightly, but he felt that if they were to go on together, she had to know what he thought of what she was doing. They couldn't have suppressed opinions of each other's work: the irritation of that sort of withholding would destroy any sort of mental community they might have; with them there had to be a complete understanding or there could be nothing. And he was wondering more and more if the basis for a complete understanding was there.

The line of argument proposed makes me feel that he was working for a breach with these letters. Their tone becomes more provocative throughout the winter of 1922–1923. He tells her again and again that, yes, he does love her, after his fashion, and, yes, he does admire a great many of her qualities, but then, there is the overriding fact of their incompatibility in the realms of character, aim, and outlook. He doesn't want what she wants, and she doesn't want what he wants. In the end it is as simple as that.

How my mother answered him isn't altogether clear, since her side of this prolonged exchange isn't for the time being available. But judging from the number of times that he feels obliged to explain why he doesn't feel that there would be an end to all their disputations if he were to divorce Jane in order to marry her, and why he has no intention of doing the one thing or the other, it is fairly easy to make an educated guess at the general line she was taking. Her persistence with this old theme drove him to a sudden explosion of bitterness that found its outlet on a curiously significant date—March 21, 1923. He didn't think, he then wrote, it fair of her to turn on him with her growing mania about the injustice he was doing her by not murdering Jane. She had gone on with that grievance and he was tired of it. He regretted very bitterly ever having met her, but he had done everything he could to make something tolerable of the relationship once it had come into being. He didn't feel that he could have done more. It was her business to forget all about the scandals that it might give rise to, and to go off to America to have the success there that he was sure would be hers.

Whatever else may be said about this letter, the one thing beyond question is that it was written on the same day as the communication from my mother addressed to S. K. Ratcliffe that I have referred to so often before. It is worth comparing its content with the final paragraph of my mother's letter:

> I have tried to leave H. G. innumerable times, but never without his following me and asking me to come back. I have as a matter of fact left him at the moment but I am dreading another attempt to get me to come back. It is also, as I have a steady monogamous nature, and would have been the most wifely wife on earth, extremely difficult not to take the job again. My only hope therefore of getting and keeping clear is to go to America!

My father was not, as a matter of fact, about to make any such attempt. His next move was to put forward a proposal for the regularisation of their finances; to put it crassly, he tried to buy her off. He suggested that his responsibilities to her would be properly discharged if he were to bind himself to pay her £500 a year until such time as she should marry, and to undertake the full costs of my keep and education until I had graduated from a university. My mother seems to have found this a mingy offer, and to have let him know it.

Judging from the answer that her letter provoked, she also seems to have reminded him of all the humiliating and degrading experiences that she believed she had been let in for by her involvement with him, and to have rounded out the bill of particulars by telling him yet again that the only thing he could honorably do to compensate her adequately for all that she had been called upon to endure would be to divorce Jane and marry her.

This inane return to square one exasperated my father beyond measure. But he contained his reaction, and started all over again. He was precise about his feelings. He didn't believe that they could make a marriage work, because he didn't see how any two people could make a go of a union that began with so much resentment and hostility. He reminded her of what had been said at their last meeting. She had told him, face to face, that she wanted no more of the relationship. He had told her that he felt the same way. She had said that she did not want to see him again, ever; and he had told her that he had no wish to have her back. He very much regretted an enormous failure and the loss of ten years out of their lives. She obviously had the makings of a successful life ahead of her, and she was young enough to recover easily from any wounds that she might have suffered while they were forcing themselves to play at being in love against the grain of their inclinations. All he could honestly say to her was that he didn't love her and didn't feel the slightest stirrings of jealousy where she was concerned. He felt the very greatest admiration for her, and he was full of friendly feelings for her. Couldn't they agree to part, like reasonable human beings, on those terms?

But it was no use. This statement of the case only produced another tirade, and a further demand for Jane's head upon a charger. My father tried a new line in reply to it. He tried to explain just why he didn't think my mother would like being in Jane's place if she ever found herself there. He told her of all the many things that his wife did for him, and to how great an extent what she did involved putting his career and his interests ahead of her own. Did my mother really want to start doing all that? She had never shown any signs of wanting to do so, and he didn't think that, given her ambitions and temperament, she would enjoy it. Wouldn't it be more sensible, since they had come so close to breaking point, to drop the idea that they could ever make a married couple in the sense that he and Jane were a couple? Wouldn't it be better to face the fact that they weren't such a couple, hadn't ever been such a couple, and couldn't possibly be.

And so they hassled on, as spring ended and summer began. At that point, in June 1923, a young Austrian woman called Hedwig Verena Gatternigg made a brief but extremely disturbing reappearance in my father's life. He had enjoyed a brief passage with her in the previous autumn. It had been one of those episodes, void of any emotional content, that had been coming his way at the rate of three or four a year ever since 1900, the year in which he had first publicly expressed the opinion that sexual intercourse, now that reliable contraceptive devices were readily available, could be looked upon as a pleasant social pastime in a class with golf or cards. The surge of gossip that had been generated by John St. Loe Strachey's effort to finish him off as a writer at the end of the first decade of the century had spread the word of his availability for light affairs even more widely, and his ambiguous reputation made him a magnet for "nice" women and girls who were in the mood for mildly adventurous experiments in the use of their newly gained freedoms. After 1911 he was almost constantly being homed in on by some new candidate for such civilities. Most of the women who offered themselves to him on these terms came and went without bother or fuss after having filled in his "awkward hour" —the time between five and seven in the afternoon, three or four times, but there were those, like Hedwig Verena, who wanted more, and came back to get it. My father had been quite taken by her the year before, by her light build, her delicate features, her darkly lustrous hair, and her big brown eyes with their curling lashes, but when he saw her again in 1923 he didn't at all care for the glint of determination he detected in them. He backed off and did all he could to convince her that his very full schedule left him no time for what she had in mind, and he leapt at the out she gave him when she began to ask him to help her get started as a journalist. Eager to keep her at arm's length and fully occupied, he professed every willingness to help and gave her the names of numbers of people she could profitably interview. They would certainly find time to see her if she presented them with the letters of introduction that he would be only too pleased to give her.

These tactics would have been reasonable enough if my father had not made the capital blunder of including my mother's name on the list of eminent and promising writers that Hedwig Verena was to seek out. It is not possible to be sure of what went on in that young woman's mind, but it is more than likely that this error suggested the scenario for the little drama that she eventually staged with herself in the leading role. By 1923, gossip had made the liaison between my parents a matter of common knowledge among watchers of literary celebrities, and as a journalist Hedwig Verena would have seen the potential value in a news story about a young woman's suicide attempt in the flat of a well-known novelist following a confrontation with his mistress earlier in the day. That would cause a stir, and she would be at the center of it. One of the big Sundays might buy her story . . . "Why I Did It" . . . "The Wells I Knew". . . That sort of thing.

Hedwig Verena, armed with my father's letter of introduction, turned up on my mother's doorstep in Kensington late in the morning of June 20 and asked if she could come in. My mother saw her, and after they had talked for three quarters of an hour Hedwig Verena took herself off. What she did with the rest of the day I don't know, but she reappeared that evening at the door of my father's apartment in Westminster. The maid who answered the bell told her that my father couldn't see her, as he was dressing to go out to a formal dinner, but Hedwig Verena insisted that it was a matter of urgency that could not wait. She must see Mr. Wells as soon as possible. She was shown into his study, where he joined her in a mood of considerable irritation as soon as he had put on his evening clothes. He had barely begun to scold her for bothering him at such an inconvenient hour when she produced a cutthroat razor from the pocket of her coat, waved it in his face, and told him that she would kill herself with it if he went on being so unkind to her. He did not believe that she meant what she was saying, and after making a brief and apparently effective attempt to calm her down, left her sitting in a chair while he went to get the hall porter to help him to deal with the situation. He had made a mistake. When he came back with the porter he found Hedwig Verena walking about the room in a dazed way with the razor in her hand. It was covered with blood and so was her coat. She had a number of wounds on her throat and wrists.

The porter was the only practical person present. A former sergeant major, he had somewhere learned what to do when it was a case of a woman with a razor. It had to be taken from her. He knew a trick that made it a relatively easy thing to do. He did it. With her talisman lost, Hedwig Verena had no more sense of being in control of the situation. There was so much, so very much, more blood about than she had been prepared for, and more and more of it seemed to be welling out of her. She keeled over in a faint, and the thought that had no doubt made her do so passed to my father. Could she have overdone it and really cut into an artery? This thought was almost immediately cancelled by another, one that can be roughly summarised as *God! When the papers get their teeth into this!* When the porter had rolled the unconscious woman over onto her back as a preliminary to applying some rough-and-ready first aid, her coat had fallen open and it had become apparent that she had nothing on under it but a night-dress.

As the remainder of the evening and the early part of the night were consumed in the wearisome husbandry of this kind of event, in calling the doctor, in doing what could be done to staunch the flow of blood, in getting an ambulance, in calling the police, and in doing all that had to be gone through as the consequences of calling upon them, all in the shadow of his uncertainty as to whether the woman might actually be going to die, and as to just how long it would be before the reporters from the dailies and the evenings could be expected to get onto the story, my father had plenty of time to give an admiring thought or two to the completeness of the job that had been done on him.

His mind may also, though I can't say for certain that it did, have gone back to 1912 in the course of that night, to the time when my mother had threatened him with suicide. The situations had been very much the same. He had drifted lazily into a little walk-out, and it had come to an end. There had been a complete break, and then after several months the young woman had wanted to start things up again. He hadn't wanted that to happen, and when he told her so, she had written him a very bitter letter that started out with a threat: if she didn't hear from him in the course of the next few days, she was going to do something final, it would probably be a matter of putting a bullet through her head. She had gone on to tell him—he supposed in an effort to get him to take her seriously—that she had actually already attempted suicide twice on his account. He hadn't found it possible to believe her, any more than he had found it possible to believe the long story about an incident in Spain, in which she was said to have wounded herself with a revolver, that she had previously told him . . . and then there had been a silly business in the drawing room of his flat, when she had flopped around on his carpet simulating convulsions, that had impressed him even less. The postscript that she had added to one of her letters threatening suicide had been, in its way, a classic: "If I live, write to me now and then . . ." The absurdity of the line had made it easy for him to turn her down: "How can I be your friend to this accompaniment? I don't see that I can be of any use or help to you at all. You have my entire sympathy—but until we can meet on a reasonable basis, goodbye."

What would have happened to him then, had my mother responded to that brusque refusal to take her threats seriously by carrying them out, as Hedwig Verena, damn her, appeared to have done? And how was she going to take it when she learned that she was involved, however marginally, in this grisly second go-round of that burlesque incident in their past?

My mother seems to have taken the mini-drama calmly enough initially, and to have found no objections to cooperating in the strategy devised by my father's attorney, E. S. P. Haynes, in the course of that night and the following morning; one of keeping stiff upper lips, and of giving outsiders no hint that anything out of the ordinary might be going on. My father had called him in as soon as he saw that it was a matter for the police, and things were well in hand by the following morning. The police had agreed that nothing should be said to the newspapers unless it became absolutely necessary; and as soon as it had been made certain that Hedwig Verena's life was not in danger she had been whisked out of the Charing Cross Hospital's emergency ward and transferred to a private room in the Westminster Infirmary in another borough. By midmorning the administrations of both institutions had been alerted to the desirability of discretion, and all concerned had been instructed not to discuss the patient or condition with any outsider.

Haynes was at pains to arrange all this because time was vital. Although the prospect of an ugly scandal triggered by "revelations" brought out in evidence at an inquest had been laid to rest by the discovery that none of Hedwig Verena's wounds were more than skin-deep, another danger, represented by the reporters of the metropolitan dailies and their editors, still had to be faced. Should any reporter get hold of the story of what had happened in my father's apartment that night before Haynes could get to the one agency capable of putting a stop on it, the Newspaper Owner's Association, there would be no containing the scandal.

Word that something worth investigating might have happened during the night in Whitehall Court reached Fleet Street late in the morning of June 21, and during the afternoon a reporter from the now defunct *Evening Star* managed to put together the broad outline of the story. He had his piece ready in time to catch the Late Night

Final edition. The paper was being sold on the streets when my father, behaving, on Haynes's advice, as if nothing out of the ordinary was troubling him, took my mother out to have dinner with him at The Ivy in St. Martin's Lane, and on to a theatre afterwards. Three of the dailies, *The Daily Express, The Daily News,* and *The Daily Herald,* had picked up the story by the following morning, but by midday, when the racing editions of the evenings came out, only *The Star* was carrying it—and all that that paper ran was a brief report emphasising Hedwig Verena's satisfactory condition, and leaving my father out of it. In the course of the morning my mother had been to see her useful acquaintance Lord Riddell, owner of *The News of the World* and Chairman of the Newspaper Owner's Association, and my father had been to see Beaverbrook. By noon these powerful personages had made the necessary calls to their fellow members of the association, asking them to drop the story "as a personal favour," and it had been killed. That was, so far as the press and the public were concerned, the end of the Gatternigg affair. June 22 was a Friday, and the weather was perfect. It was strawberry time. The coming of the weekend simply obliterated the little remaining public interest in the matter.

As for the participants, my father went down to Easton Glebe on Friday night to see Jane for the first time since this little storm had burst round him forty-eight hours earlier. She had been out of it all for a simple reason. She had not gone up to town with her husband that week because her older boy, George Philip, was due to receive his Bachelor of Arts Degree in the Senate House at Cambridge that Tuesday. It had been arranged between them that Gip would drive over to Easton after the public ceremonies to be the host at a private celebration and dance. Five of his Cambridge friends were to be put up at the Glebe, and of those, two had been invited to stay on over the Wednesday night. The celebration was to be on a rather larger scale than the number of house guests might suggest, since Gip had a great many friends in the neighbourhood who were expected to come in for the supper and the dancing. Frank and a contingent of his friends were also to be on the scene. Jane had stayed in the country that week partly because her son wanted her to be at his party, and partly because she wanted to be on hand to see that all the housekeeping arrangements that would ensure its success were properly carried out. She was a good deal of a perfectionist in such matters.

If her reasons for not being present in the Whitehall Court apartment when Hedwig Verena staged her poor little drama are unexceptionable, her behaviour after the event is also beyond criticism. When my father telephoned her on the Wednesday night to let her know what had happened, and to warn her that the reporters might be after her in the morning, it was already too late for her to make any sudden rush up to town to rally to his side. On Thursday morning she was told that Haynes was against her making a move that might be picked on as a sign of agitation in my father's circle, and my father was due to return to Easton on the Friday. Jane went up to London with my father when the weekend was over, on Monday, June 25, and spent the rest of the week there with him, fulfilling various longstanding social engagements in a routine fashion. They dined, for instance, with Trotsky's *bête noire* Philip Snowden, the Labour Party leader who was to be England's first Socialist Chancellor of the Exchequer, and his wife at the House of Commons on Thursday, June 28. My mother was in Germany by that time, having left for Marienbad on the 25th in accordance with a plan she had made some weeks earlier. There was nothing to keep her in London.

As for poor Hedwig Verena, she had been transferred from the rather stark Westminster Infirmary to a private nursing home, where she remained, at my father's expense, for several weeks, until she was considered rather more than fit to face the ordeal of returning to her home and her devoted parents. Jane, as the family paymaster, paid the nursing-home bills and saw that Hedwig Verena had all the necessities and small comforts that she might require. It seemed obvious to all concerned that Jane couldn't very well preside over Hedwig Verena's recovery in person, so the office of finding out what that young woman's needs and fancies were, and of keeping the Wellses apprised of her progress, was very kindly undertaken, without any dubious motive or intent whatever, by Jane Wells's impulsive, wildly tactless, but essentially good-hearted American acquaintance Nancy Astor.

It may seem that I have said altogether too much about this three-day crisis in my father's life, and the very insignificant affair from which it arose. But accounts of the matter based on information supplied by my mother that are at once very largely untrue and highly misleading have now found their way into three biographies so far. In the most unpleasant of them, Jane is said to have been in my father's flat when Hedwig Verena staged her suicide attempt—if that is what it was—and to have been the first person to come upon her after the event. My mother's version of the story implied that Jane cleared out as soon after making her discovery as she could, leaving my father to face the music alone. He is said to have gone into a blue funk on finding himself abandoned, and to have pleaded with my mother to give him the support that his wife had denied him. He is also alleged to have used my mother for his own protection throughout the incident, selfishly disregarding the risks that he was asking her to run. The worst of these, once the danger that she might be called upon to give evidence at the inquest on Hedwig Verena had passed, was that resulting from her exposure to the Iago-like malignancy of Nancy Astor, who is said to have hovered around the poor girl's sickbed in the hope of being able to "employ her crusading weapons" in an attack on my mother's reputation if she could manage to worm any nastiness of a damaging character out of the helpless patient. At the end of the episode, according to her account, my mother was left with the feeling that my father was "really insane with selfishness." She decided that she had suffered enough and that the time had come for her to break every tie linking her to him and to Jane. She had to do it, however much my father might resist the inevitable. When she sailed for America toward the end of October that year she meant the necessary separation to be the instrument of the relationship's death.

Or so my mother insists. The record shows that my father joined her at the Hotel Klinger in Marienbad on July 19, and that he stayed there with her until the 27th. They were both back in England in August, and in that month and in September spent several weekends together at Eastbourne and Swanage. In the second half of September and in the first part of October they were dining out and going to theatres together in London. Everything seemed to be going on as usual—and as usual they were getting on very well when they were together and quarrelling afresh as soon as they parted. The bone of contention was still marriage, but the discussion had taken on a new form. My mother had come up with the proposition that if my father wasn't going to divorce Jane in order to marry her, the least he could do in common decency would be to pay her an allowance of £3,000 a year instead. I am not sure what this Balzacian suggestion implied, but the issue is academic, as my mother failed to carry her point. She settled for £5,000 down, and an undertaking that my father would meet all my educational costs.

All this does rather suggest that something in the nature of a final settlement was being reached, but the letters that my father wrote to my mother after her departure for America don't suggest that there had been anything in the nature of a clean break. The first letter that he had from her after she had crossed the Atlantic evidently gave him precisely the contrary impression. Something in it must have led him to suppose that she still hoped to keep things going, since it provoked him to dissuasions. If, he told her, there was any prospect of her prolonging her American tour, she would be well advised to do that. He wasn't at all well, and he was going to have to take things quietly for a bit—in some warm climate. With her lively and impatient character she wasn't going to be suitable company for him to keep—and if she were to tag along, she would be bored to death, and she'd bore him—from the time that she didn't get up in the morning until the time when she didn't come home from the hotel dance at night. He didn't want to even try the experiment. He couldn't see any reason for not being frank about his feelings. She was much too alive and discursively jolly to stand being tethered to him any longer, and he was too much wrapped up in himself to stand any more of her bright, irrelevant activities. They must follow their destinies, and their destinies were diverging. There was no reason why they shouldn't still be very loving—provided that they didn't see too much of each other.

It might be supposed that a letter flinging the door open in this fashion would have come as a godsend to a woman who was determined to escape from its writer's clutches at all costs. The natural course would have been to answer it by return, accepting its conclusions with relief, and rejoicing at the happy ending to a period of stress that it signaled. But the letter went unanswered, and my father didn't hear from her again until he had written her, to tell her with some irritation, that he had just run into Robert and Sylvia Lynd, who had tactfully let him know that they had heard that she was in America to escape from him. Why in heaven's name, he asked her, did she have to manufacture a drama out of their parting now, when it would have been so easy to have a decent and friendly break back in the spring?

The text of my mother's answer to this mild rebuke is, again, not for the moment available, but my father's response to it gives every indication that it contained a renewed statement of her case for their going on. In it he says that he thinks of her as the same dear and wonderful a person as ever, but that he doesn't exactly look forward to meeting her again. He'd been bored to death when they were together in Marienbad, and bored again when they'd been dragging about London during the autumn. She'd been planning to go to America alone for a year at least, and there she was, in the United States without him, and enjoying herself. Why not face the facts? And then, incredibly enough, he feels obliged—it can only have been by something in her letter—to go back over the stale issue of their impossible marriage all over again. Why, he asked her plaintively, did she have to bring Jane into it whenever they were discussing their situation? Jane hadn't done her out of anything. Couldn't she see that they would have ended up at odds even if they had been married ten times over? What difference could the existence or nonexistence of a marriage contract make to their present situation? Time had made it plain that she liked people of a kind that he had no use for, and that she enjoyed doing things with them that he had no wish to do. The common ground between them was gone. It was idle to say that they wouldn't have come to breaking point if they had been married at some time in the past—marriage would have done nothing to alter the case.

I think that it is clear from all this that the Gatternigg affair has been blown up out of all proportion to its original significance over forty years after the event in order to conceal the unpalatable essence of the situation as it had really been while the major relationship had been dismally coming to its end. It is not very hard to construct a scenario for what actually took place. All the available evidence suggests that the main events of my father's insufficiently private life between 1920 and 1922 had given my mother more than sufficient grounds for reaching the conclusion that even if his marriage with Jane were to break up for any reason, it was highly unlikely that she would be the beneficiary from its dissolution. She would seem, however, to have been determined not to come to terms with what she had to recognise as the facts of the case, and to have hung in there pitching until, during the winter of 1922–1923, she finally had to face the meaning of his constantly repeated declarations that their partnership hadn't worked out for him, and that he was tired of it. She then appears to have elected for a program that would give her another chance of winning him over on the one hand, and on the other, the appearance of taking the initiative in breaking things up. She would have one last go at making him feel that they should go on together during the spring and summer, and if that failed, she would go off to the United States in the autumn, after telling all her intimate friends that she had been forced to make the trip as the only way open to her of getting away from my frantically possessive father. The affair would thus seem to have ended on her terms.

The only flaw in this program became apparent to my mother when she had the letter from my father in which he spoke of his encounter with the Lynds. Its text will have made it obvious to her that he had told them his side of the story, and made it clear to them that he had lost all interest in keeping the affair going. He wouldn't go back to her on any terms, even if he could set them. This reflection made her mindful of the large number of friends they had in common. Goodness alone knew how many of them might not have heard both sides of the story already? And there were worse possibilities. My father was a good friend of Arnold Bennett's. Arnold Bennett was a great admirer of Jane Wells, and, as everybody knew, he kept a journal. It was his aspiration to be another Goncourt—that was part of his frantic effort to purge himself of his provincialism and his Englishness—just like that pathetic involvement with the awful Frenchwoman he had so stupidly married—by assuming the airs of a French literary man. Everything that Arnold could pick up went down in that wretched journal. Suppose that my father had discussed the affair with Arnold, man to man! What might he not have told him? If he had said that the end of the affair had come to him as a relief, that would have been just the sort of thing that Arnold would have gobbled up for his odious record. And my father could have said the same thing to other, even more malicious people. The story of how things had ended between them that she had planted with such care might not stand up, even over the short run.

The gross inflation of the importance of the Gatternigg affair that has been a feature of recent biographical studies of my father, and its strange transformation into a drama in which my mother figures as a principal rather than as the barely involved accessory to the action of the actual record, are clearly products of some such chain of thought as is outlined here. The calculation would be that if the storm in that small teacup were worked up until it could be presented as an outrage characteristic of my father's recklessly selfish and utterly inconsiderate way of behaving, it might be made to look like an altogether plausible last straw—one of those incidents that any normally worldly person would be able to accept as a member of the class of explosively divisive happenings that cause men and women to think *Enough!* and walk out on their lovers or husbands after years and even decades of toleration. It may be accepted as an event of that kind by the outsider, but I, for one, cannot believe that it was anything as simple and as manifestly unimportant as Hedwig Verena's brief passage through the outer margins of my father's life that brought the long drawn out game that he had played with my mother over the years to an end. From its beginning the course of the affair had been set by psychological imperatives working on both parties that were deeply rooted in their earliest experiences.

What those imperatives might be was something that remained a mystery, in my father's case, until after his death, when I first came to appreciate the very unusual character of the web of relationships in which he had been involved from 1924 until the early thirties. Through most of this period—from 1926 onward—he was on terms of friendly enmity with my mother. Although he could not stand to be with her, and did not like what she was doing or the company she kept, he insisted that he bitterly regretted losing her, and that he had always truly loved her, and still did. What had happened to him with Amber Reeves had happened all over again. Once he was sure that he had lost her, and that the loss was irreversible, he was able to give his feelings for her uninhibited expression. He was just as certain that he was in love with Margaret Sanger, who, holidays apart, was living her American life three thousand five hundred miles away from him on the other side of the Atlantic, and even more certain that he loved Moura Zakrevskaya-Benckendorff, who had been transformed by a fleeting marriage into the Baroness Budberg, and who was now living with Gorky in the Villa Sorrito in Sorrento in Italy. Margaret Sanger had married a very rich and very tolerant man who was more than willing to let her do anything that she thought might make her happy, and Gorky was more dependent upon Moura than he had ever been. There was not the slightest danger that either woman would come after my father to ask anything of him. Jane, who had never done that, was still at Easton Glebe, as companionable, good-humoured, patient, endlessly tolerant, and quietly efficient as ever. Because she was always there when he wanted her to be, and never in his way when he didn't need her, he failed to notice that this central relationship was changing.

Jane was in fact quietly withdrawing herself from life. She was allowing my father's secretaries to take over more and more of her functions as manager of his affairs and controller of his finances, and she was spending more and more of her time thinking her own thoughts all by herself and away from Easton Glebe in a tiny flat in Bloomsbury which she jealously preserved as her own entirely private place. My father was nonetheless sure that she was still his Rock of

Gibraltar, and that his life revolved around her, just as it had always done. He resolutely closed his mind to the fact that he was spending most of his time in Provence, where he was living with Odette Keun, the tempestuous daughter of a Dutch father and a Greek mother who had been brought up in Constantinople. This new relationship had an interesting feature built into it; it was an offshore affair that could not be pursued in the United Kingdom. This curious characteristic arose from the fact that Odette Keun had been black-listed by the British Military Authorities at the time of the British intervention in the Russian Civil War. She had then been a journalist writing for various French papers of the left, and she had written things that the British Military Authorities did not like about what was being done in the oil republics in the Caucasus. She was expelled from the region under suspicion of left-wing sympathies, and was consequently unable to get an entry visa for Britain for several years. This meant that my father could only cohabit with her when he was abroad. He did not find this quite such a nuisance as she did. It gave him a tactical advantage. If, for any reason, he wished to get away from her for a time, he had only to say that the necessities of his professional life required him to go to England for a while. He liked living with her, but he could not stand more than a certain amount of her.

My father had been living with Odette Keun for two years when he brought out *The World of William Clissold,* the strangest of his novels. One of the elements contributing to its strangeness is the portrait of Odette Keun that it contains. She appears close to the end of its second volume, soon after its hero has broken with a determinedly egotistical actress who is only too recognisably my mother. My father calls Odette Clementina, and arranges for her to be picked up in Paris by the hero when he is taking an evening stroll down the Champs Elysées. The circumstances make it quite plain that after having been something very like a kept woman, Clementina is on the brink of becoming something very like a streetwalker. As Odette Keun was presently to become rather fond of saying, it was a thing that only a writer with very odd feelings about women could do to a woman he was still living with. But odd as this is, it is not the strangest thing in the novel: That is the decease, shortly before my mother makes her entry into the story, of a character called Sirrie—who begins as someone quite different and then slowly turns into Jane Wells. In the novel she has tuberculosis, but the description of her death, with the hero stubbornly declining to recognise how ill she really is, and how certainly and inevitably she is dying, is uncannily like the death that Jane Wells was to die from cancer just about a year after the publication of the book.

Chapter VI

If she was pseudo-oriental and addicted to every extremity of emotional exaggeration, he had a heart as cold as it was light.

—APROPOS OF DOLORES

M Y FATHER DID NOT MEET ODETTE Keun for the first time either by chance or in the Champs Elysées. He met her by arrangement in Geneva after an exchange of letters. The correspondence originated, though remotely, in her deportation from Constantinople. When she returned to that city from the Georgian Republic the British Military Authorities picked her up and, with no nonsense about due process or legality, immediately shipped her off to the Crimea. That should have been the end of her, but she managed to wangle her way across Russia to Moscow, and eventually back to France. There she settled down in the village of Maganosc near Grasse and wrote a short book about her experiences. When it appeared, under the title *Sous Lénine,* she sent a copy to my father with a covering note in which she said how much she admired his work, and what an inspiration he had always been to her. He liked her letter and the book, and when he was called upon to review it he gave it a favorable notice. She wrote to thank him for it, and he replied. The correspondence that sprang up between them soon grew warm in tone, and before long she had told him something of her history. She was the child of marriage between a Dutchman in his native country's Consular Service and a Greek lady who had been brought up as a member of the Phanariot community in Turkish Constantinople. They had met as a consequence of being posted to that least European of Europe's cities. They had given their daughter a curiously modern and progressive upbringing, largely by inadvertence, because neither felt able to inflict the conventions of their own background upon the child of the other. As a result Odette found herself very much adrift when, at eighteen, she was sent to complete her education at a university in a then primly conformist Holland. She took refuge from the very un-Greek ethos into which she had been plunged by throwing herself into the arms of the Roman Catholic Church. She followed up on her conversion by becoming a postulant in a Dominican Convent. She might very well have gone further, and taken the vows that would have made her a nun, had she not been outraged to learn that some historians believed that St. Dominic had played an ugly role in the extirpation of the Albigensian heresy. As she was then in the third year of her novitiate, the strength of her sympathy with the Albigensians told her that she could have no true vocation, and she had jumped over the wall in order to rededicate herself to the radical-socialist cause. She had based herself in Paris for a while, but while officially living there she had spent a great deal of her time in parts of Algeria and Morocco that were only nominally under French control. She travelled these regions with a medically qualified lover and a mobile dispensary, issuing drugs to the women in the villages and teaching them how to use them to protect their children from the minor but crippling ailments, such as trachoma, that were endemic among them. As she did this admirable work she told the villagers, male and female, that the French had no right to be in their country unless they were going to bring them similar or even better medical services on a regular basis. The French colonial administration came to look upon her as a considerable nuisance, and in due course she was expelled from French North Africa.

Her troubles with the British Military Authorities in Constantinople in 1919–1920 were of a somewhat similar kind. The articles that she had written for publication in France had put heavy stress on the way in which the Allied Powers and the Bolsheviks were putting their interests in oil from the Baku field ahead of the best interests of the Georgian people. She had been especially outraged by the irresponsibility shown by the Allies in persuading the Georgians to expose themselves to Russian vengeance by setting up an independent Georgian Republic while knowing perfectly well that they would be unable to give the new country adequate military support. This story had come to an especially nasty end. When, in the inevitable course of events, the Georgian Republic collapsed, there was one of those evacuations. The ministers of the Nationalist and anti-Soviet government, their aides, and their families were assigned places in the three rear coaches of what was clearly going to be the last train that the British would be able to get out of Tiflis and down to the coast. These coaches were uncoupled just before the train pulled out, and the wretched Georgian politicians and their families were left behind to take their chances with the Russian forces that were already entering the farther outskirts of the town. This episode had moved Odette to a fury of indignation and contempt.

She was, to tell the truth, an earnest and idealistic woman of the crusading humanitarian type. But her profound seriousness was masked, almost completely, by a rather childish desire to shock, and by a degree of sexual exhibitionism. She liked to make the most of her freedom from bourgeois inhibitions at all times, but most of all when she was in stuffy company. It was this weakness that was in the end to bring about her undoing with my father. It led her to contrive a first meeting with him that left him with an ineffaceable impression that she was just another young intellectual out for some sexual fun with a celebrity. She had planned the encounter so that when he came to her room in the Genevan hotel to introduce himself to her he would find her naked and in the dark. She wiped out whatever chance she may have had of living down this initial blunder by making a good story of it and telling it on suitably inappropriate occasions. She told it to me, for instance, in my father's presence, and to his evident dismay, before I had known her for a full twenty-four hours. I was fourteen, very uncertain of my sexual identity, and as shockable as only an insecure adolescent can be. My father was at the wheel of his handsome Voisin at the time, and fully occupied with the business of driving us up the road that runs out of the back of Nice, through Vence, and on to Grasse. Odette was sitting in the front of the car beside my father, twisting herself around in the bucket seat so that she could face me as I sat in the back. She was putting me at my ease, I think, showing me how open and free she could be, and letting me know that I wasn't to be frightened of her, when she let this shocker drop into the flow of her prattle.

Odette liked to bring off these surprises, but she preferred to work with an audience. I was the victim of one of her set-piece provocations a few days later when Elizabeth Russell and the Aga Khan, who was staying at St. Jean de Cap Ferrat with Somerset Maugham, came over to lunch. During the meal Odette turned the conversation to the part that incest has played in the breeding of bloodstock, and developed the topic over my father's protests. He suspected that it might be booby-trapped, and he was quite right. I suddenly became aware that Odette, who was given to dramatic gesticulations, was pointing at me with an outflung arm.

"Look!" she cried. "Loooook! Anthonee is blushing. He is really blushing! Can it be that you know nothing of these theeengs, that you are still a virgin?"

"Odette!" screamed my father. "You're going too far. I won't have it, you've got to behave . . ." "Oh, Pidou, Pidou," Odette screamed right back, "you are such a prude for all your fine talk." She turned for support to the Aga Khan. "Are the English not an extraordinary people—so prudish in public, so nice so very nice—and so lubricious in private!"

The Aga Khan gave me a speculative look and began to say something wise about the horrifying effect of the hatred of the body that was built into the protestant version of the Christian religion. The conversation moved on.

The subject of my sexual development was not forgotten, however, and Odette brought it up again later on. This time we were driving up into the mountains behind Grasse on our way to have lunch at Thorenc. The road was narrow and steeply cambered, and there were innumerable blind corners as it twisted and turned on its way up into the lavender-growing country. The crop from those sweetly scented upland fields was being harvested just then, and every five minutes or so we would meet yet another truck destined for one of the scent factories down in Grasse below us barrelling down the long incline with a load of lavender as big as a haystack roped onto its back. The steep camber made their drivers favour the middle of the road and we seemed to meet them as often as not just as we were coming to a blind corner. Odette was sitting beside my father as usual, and, as usual, was sitting corkscrewed into her seat so that she could keep me from getting bored or feeling left out of it by talking to me. She kept up her flow, and my father, intent on survival, pressed down on the horn button every time the road ahead twisted round a bend and out of sight.

My uncertainty as to my sexual identity had by this time become apparent to her. She was anxious to know how far things had gone. Was there, she asked me, much homosexuality among the boys at my school? Had any advances been made to me? Did I not have some special friend? Had I not ever found myself entertaining some more complicated feeling than simple friendship for one of my older companions? Did any of my London girl friends ever come down to see me in term time? Did I not, perhaps, have some older woman friend who could visit me . . . "Odette," cried my father at this point, "will you, for heaven's sake, drop it! Leave the boy alone. Oh! Damnation!" Another lavender-laden truck was bearing down on us. Its horn blared. Our horn blared back. Clenched fists appeared in the cab window of the oncoming truck. They were being shaken. "An older woman," Odette was shrieking, "can play a very important role in the life of a boy of a certain age. She can do for him something that no little miss, all gaucherie, and inexperience, and self-regard, can ever do. If you wish to be happy in your love life, you should start off with an older woman who knows what she is about in a hard, hard, bed. She will put you on the right path, and bring an end to all your confusions and hesitations, believe me."

The full impact of these tirades is lost without Odette's accent. She said *"eef"* for "if," and *"eem"* for "him," and *"oldare wooman"* for "older woman." It was a very exaggerated French accent as formalised for use in English farces. There were times when the pattern of mispronunciation involved drove my father frantic. This was one of them. He pulled the car over onto the dusty shoulder of the road and stopped. "I've got a bone to pick with you, Odette," he said and climbed out. Odette leapt out on her side of the machine and ran round it to face him. She was delighted, there was going to be a scene! They both began to swing their arms about and shout, so that it soon became clear to me why my father had found it wise to stop the car before initiating their discussion. I couldn't hear all that they were saying, but the words that reached me were enough to give me the drift. My father was saying that she had no business putting ideas into the head of a child, and she was insisting that I wasn't a child, that I was growing up, that I was soon going to be a man, that I was in trouble, that I couldn't look a woman in the eye or speak to one, that I'd spent so much of my time with women in a woman's household that I wasn't too sure which sex I belonged to, that it looked to her as if I could have been given the idea that there was something wrong with being a man, that I was utterly unprepared for life because he'd never done a thing for me that a man should do for his sons, and that he'd be letting me down miserably if he didn't do all he could to get me out of the mess she thought I was getting into. At about that point my father grabbed Odette by the arm and marched her up the road until they were altogether out of earshot.

I sat watching them from the hot shadow in the back of the Voisin, looking through the windshield, across the curved top of the bonnet, and past the falcon on the radiator cap that made a V for Voisin with its wings. Odette was thin, almost scrawny, sunburned to a gypsy nutbrown. Her hair was very black, perhaps dyed. She was taller than my father by a head. He was short and stout, with the build of a teddy bear. He was wearing a panama hat, a relic of Edwardian chic rationalised by the fact that his blue eyes couldn't deal with the midday glare of the Provençal sun unshielded. He had on a white shirt that had been made for him, and silk shantung trousers. She was wearing a white tennis dress, a coloured scarf, and a dozen bangles on her forearms. They flashed in the sunlight as she gesticulated at him. She bent down towards him to shake the index finger of her right hand under his nose. He threw up his hands in expostulation. They both gave way to a *fou rire,* throwing back their heads as the laughter burst from them. They came back to the car arm in arm.

"We have these little tiffs," my father said, "they're hell to go through, but when they're over they're over—you mustn't let them upset you. Now let's get on to Thorenc . . . ." Odette gave me a friendly wink. I did my best to smile back, but I was miserable, and sure that they were both mad.

I have interpolated this piece of autobiography because I think that it shows how easy Odette's style made it for people who didn't know her well to misread her. I was made miserable by this episode because it seemed to me that she had dragged the secret troubles that I hadn't been able to tell a soul about into the open for the sheer hell of it— and in front of my father, the one person in the world I was least anxious to discuss them with. I took it that she could only have done this because she disliked me or felt contempt for me. How far her concern for me went at that time only became known to me years later, when I learned that she had found that my father believed that he had made adequate financial provision for me by settling a sum on me that would give me an income, when I reached the age of twenty-one, of around £100 a year. As soon as Odette had discovered this, she had embarked on a campaign of verbal harassment, jeering at him mercilessly and persistently for his pathological meanness, until he had promised to beef up the trust to a point that would bring the income to slightly more than five times that amount.

My gratitude to Odette on this score isn't in any way diminished by my certainty that there was more to this disinterested act than a desire to do me a service. It was, in the end, her feelings for my father that provided the spur. She had a high opinion of him and she wished him to live up to it. She had fallen in love with the best of him as she had found it in his work, and when she came to know him she wanted him to live at the level of that best all the time. She could not bear him to be mean, small, or deceitful, and she did her best to save him from the temptation to be copious, glib, and superficial to which his great journalistic success and his fame had exposed him. It was because of the way in which she had staged their first encounter that he was never able to recognise that her assaults upon him, when she seemed to be nagging for nagging's sake, were the products of a genuine devotion. As time went on, he found her increasingly strenuous and consistently ill-conceived efforts to save him from himself harder and harder to take. Their breakup would have come much sooner than it did if Odette had not been, under all the rattle and clatter and the wildness, a very good manager and organiser. When my father was with her everything that could be done for him was done perfectly and without any fuss. He was as well catered for and ministered to when he was with her as when he was at Easton with Jane. And before his considerable irritations with her had built up to an unendurable point, the long-established center of his life vanished. Jane died, and Easton Glebe became an empty shell. This was a departure from the agreed game plan that my father had altogether failed to foresee. In his script Jane was always to be dependably there in the home he had made for her; and wherever he had been and whatever he might have been doing, she was to receive him with understanding, forgiveness, tolerance, and pride on his return. And there it shockingly was. She had broken out of the role, and he was left with no one to confess to and to be absolved by when his latest break-out was over. He was at a loss, until he conceived the extraordinary idea of carrying on as usual with Odette in the part that Jane had played for so long.

When Jane began to die, in the first few months of 1927, my father took refuge from the fact in denial. He did not wish to know that he was being left. His son Frank, the younger of Jane's two boys, who was closer to her than any other mortal at this time, warned him that she was showing every sign of being in serious trouble when he saw how exhausted she had become in the course of the family's relaxed and less than usually demanding Christmas festivities at the end of 1926. My father ignored this warning. He told Frank that it was natural for a woman of Jane's age to tire easily when faced with that sort of thing. He would not admit that his wife was dying until an astonishingly late stage in her long illness.

Some part of his obliviousness to the fact that his wife was quietly and undemonstratively failing can be assigned to his preoccupations. He was again involved in a monstrous project, putting together a work that was to do for biology what *The Outline of History* had done for that subject. *The Science of Life* was intended to give ordinary, moderately educated people who had missed out on a scientific education a grasp of biology that would enable them to recognise their place in the natural order as readily as the readers of *The Outline* had been enabled to locate themselves and their societies in the grandiose sweep of the evolutionary time scheme. The project was a demanding one, and in order to get the job done—it involved giving a succinct account of all that was known of living things and life processes—within a reasonable period my father was driving his collaborators (the great Thomas Henry Huxley's grandson Julian and his own older son, George Philip) mercilessly. Julian Huxley has recorded that he had to give up all other work while *The Science of Life* was in the making in order to keep up the cracking pace insisted on by my father, and Gip also found himself fully extended. My father drove his helpers by setting the pace. While he was keeping stimulatingly ahead of them he was also working on his own account, giving the idea of what he was later to call *The Open Conspiracy* its final form, and writing a weekly article on current topics for Beaverbrook's papers. In February 1927 he also found the time to prepare the text of the address that he had been invited to make to the Sorbonne in mid-March.

My father had felt honoured by this invitation, and he thought it would be appropriate if Jane, who had done so much to help him build his reputation over the years, should share in the glory of the event. He also had the notion that it might do her some good to be feted in Paris for a few days. She had been a bit down in the mouth since Christmas if Frank was to be believed. It would draw her out of herself . . . So my father had Odette put him on the train at Cannes on March 13, and was in Paris waiting for his wife to arrive when she came over from England on the following day. They were in the city together, being run off their feet, until March 19, when he took her back across the Channel. They went straight through London to Easton Glebe. My father had delivered his address, called "Democracy Under Revision," on the 15th, and after that it had been a round of festivities, topped off by a big dinner given for them by André Maurois on the 18th. My father was not surprised by the state of exhaustion to which Jane had been reduced by the time they were back at Easton. She had been put through it. But he was sure that a few days' rest would put her right. She would, he was confident, be in fine fettle again by April 20, the date that had been set for Gip's marriage to Marjorie Craig, the rather austere young Scotswoman who had been his superefficient secretary for just over a year. He was quite unaware that Jane was now having mild but disquietingly persistent bouts of pain. No one else was aware of it either, because Jane herself was saying nothing about them, or about the fact that they were showing a tendency to become more severe. She told no one, not even Frank, about this development. She did not wish anything to cast a shadow on the forthcoming wedding.

My father's Sorbonne presentation was not at all bad, and received the final accolade of being published by Leonard and Virginia Woolf at the Hogarth Press later in the year. If anything, it reads more convincingly today than it did then. It now seems far-sighted in its expression of faith in the proposition that Democracy has a future, and not, as it did at the time, blind to the historic drift indicated by the rise of Fascism. However jolly the twenties may now be made to look by those who see them in terms of the Charleston, nifty runabouts with rumble seats, Scottie and Zelda and Ernest, Art Deco, and the efflorescence that produced such as Joyce and Proust, and Picasso and Matisse, they were then greyly experienced as years of contraction, narrowing through a time of putsches, abortive revolutions, savage reprisals, and military usurpations, all taking place against a grim background of economic confusion and social breakdown. My father had the acumen to tell his Sorbonne audience that it was not living through the start of a new authoritarian or totalitarian age but enduring a time of troubles marking the transition from one democratic epoch to another. He felt that something had gone very wrong with the adversary parliamentary democracy of the era that was coming to an end, because its characteristic features of government and opposition, ins and outs, led almost inevitably to polarisation and confrontation. It bred such labels as Whig and Tory, Radicals and

Conservatives, Labor and Capital, Left and Right, Them and Us. Under the norms of parliamentary democracy, the first concern of any incoming government or administration was as likely as not to be the annulment or reversal of the largest possible part of its predecessor's policies and programs. With that task accomplished, it would then get down to the enactment of "positive" programs less concerned with the common good than with the establishment of its own tenuous identity.

My father's belief was that the revitalisation of democracy could be achieved by a shift from adversary to consensual politics. He felt that the first step in this direction was electoral reform, holding that proportional representation and the single transferable vote would bring in government by coalition and break up the party system. He thought that when that happened the energy that had traditionally gone into the maintenance of the distinctions between parties, and into conflicts of the Tweedledum and Tweedledee variety, would be channeled into a search for common ground, and into collaborative efforts to achieve genuinely worthwhile legislative aims.

My father didn't, however, believe that electoral reform could do the job by itself. He didn't believe that any form of democracy could survive over the long haul while the greater part of the voting mass remained marginally literate and effectively innumerate. His thinking in these matters was very English, and the electorate that he knew best was largely composed of people whose education had come to a dead stop just as soon as they had been given the skills required to punch time clocks and fill in betting slips. He looked on the uneducated voter as a natural bribe eater, an elector whose vote would always be on sale to the first comer who offered him a penny off the price of a pint of beer or tuppence a quarter off the price of tea. My father managed to put his case against the uneducated voter in "Democracy Under Revision" so strongly as to raise the suspicion that he was thinking in terms of narrowing the franchise by stripping the masses of their votes. He was not doing this, but he was advocating what struck many believers in whole-hog democracy as just about as wrong in principle. He was arguing that the time had come for the educated to save democracy from itself by becoming a political force. The intelligentsia of the world was appealed to. Its members were to commit themselves *en masse* to the creation of a liberal-humanitarian consensus based on the scientific outlook with the same devotion and ardor that the members of Mussolini's Fascisti, Chiang Kai-shek's Kuomintang, and the

Russian Communist Party committed themselves to the given ideologies. The enterprise he was proposing was not, he asserted, a futile one. What these various authoritarian groups had done was to take over whole countries, with populations of a great many millions when they had marching strengths of only a few hundred thousand. With these examples of what highly motivated minorities had been able to do before them, why should the liberal and the humane hang back? They should come together to pursue their common goals. What was there to prevent a drive for social and economic world unity from succeeding if the educated minority in every country—that was to say, all of mankind that mattered—got behind it?

Many have seen the cloven hoof of the closet Fascist Beast in that last almost defiantly elitist phrase, "all of mankind that matters," and while I must confess that it does rather lack the authentically democratic ring, I think that it was innocently used. My father was not proposing a takeover by jack-booted thought-controllers, or, indeed, any kind of authoritarianism. He had something more like the working of yeast in the body of a loaf in mind—it was to be a matter of permeation, influence, and persuasion. There was to be no coup, no seizure of power, no dictation or coercion. *The Open Conspirators,* as he was later to call them, were simply to be *there* wherever and whenever policies were to be framed and decisions made. They were to be routinely present in the political parties, in the agencies of national and local governments, on the boards of the public companies and the great multinational corporations, in banking, in the professional organisations, and in the trades unions. They were to be inescapable, and they were to speak in the cause of reason and the common good. Rationality was to come in like an irresistible tide.

All this must have seemed purely visionary at the time, and I imagine that it is the sort of thing that Lord Beaverbrook had in mind when he told me, some twenty-two years and a big war later, that my father's trouble was that he had led a very sheltered life, and had never had to learn what had to be done to get men to work together in business and in politics. It was, nonetheless, an international consensus of educated opinion that first brought the United Nations and then the European Economic Community into being after the Fascists had been beaten into the ground. It is the same nebulous force that has kept these supranational organisations alive ever since. I am convinced that my father played an honourable and useful part in creating that force by going against the grain of the history of his times and producing the body of writing in the twenties and thirties of which "Democracy Under Revision" is typical. He has been jeered at for peddling a characteristically modern and fatuous optimism in these years, but he was in fact being rather old-fashioned. He was restating, in the language of a later age, a leading idea of Swift's: "God hath given the bulk of mankind a capacity to understand reason when it is fairly offered, and by reason they would easily be governed, if it were left to their choice." My father was—I would say "courageously"—working his eighteenth-century field piece in a dark hour when he made his Sorbonne presentation, and looking forward over the heads of the marching masses of Fascisti and storm troopers to a time when adversary democracy might give way to a democracy of reason fairly offered. I believe that his French audience understood this, and realised that he was exhorting them to hold firm to a belief in reason in face of the temptations of the hour, but I cannot imagine what Jane Wells thought of it as she sat there holding on tight and letting no sign of her sense that she was in the worst kind of trouble escape her.

After their return from Paris my father stayed at Easton Glebe, taking things pretty quietly, until the end of the month. He then went back to his normal English routine, weekending at Easton after spending Monday midday to Friday teatime at Whitehall Court. He stuck to this steady round, and to his belief that there was nothing very much the matter with his wife, until the day after Gip's marriage on April 20. He then went over to France to rejoin Odette. He left Paris on April 21 and drove south by easy stages, making stops at Vichy, Le Puy, and Avignon. He reached Grasse on April 26.

While my father was making this leisurely journey Frank Wells was becoming more and more uneasy about his mother's condition. Once the wedding had taken place she was no longer about to keep up the front that she had been presenting to the world. Frank had again warned my father that there was something terribly wrong with her just after Gip had gone off on his honeymoon, telling him bluntly that she was in a much worse state than she was admitting to. He had begged my father to make her see a specialist, and to stay with her until she had done so, but the warning and the appeal had been brushed aside. My father took the line that what Jane was going through was something that was common enough. People grew old without knowing it, and suddenly became conscious of what had happened to them. They were shaken, naturally enough, by their discov-

COURTESY OF THE BBC HULTON PICTURE LIBRARY

Clement Shorter took my father up soon after Henley
had launched him. He knew that half of making a living
as a writer was a matter of knowing the right people in
the editorial offices, and he very kindly saw to it that my
father rapidly came to know most of them.

COURTESY OF THE MARY EVANS PICTURE LIBRARY

George Gissing was only a little less clean-cut and
wide-open than this when my father first met him among
the members of Shorter's literary dining club, the
Omar Khayyam, in 1896.

CULVER PICTURES

My father in 1895 or 1896. He is wearing one of the new
pure-wool suits, designed by the health crank Dr. Jaeger,
that Max Beerbohm was soon to make fun of as the
outward sign of the true progressive.

UNIVERSITY OF ILLINOIS AT URBANA-CHAMPAIGN

Gissing is already a sick man when this photograph
was taken in 1901; he will die in 1903. My father
will be horrified by what he learns of his friend's
secrets after his death.

UNIVERSITY OF ILLINOIS AT URBANA-CHAMPAIGN

Henley's end was almost as disconcerting to my father as Gissing's. After the loss of a much loved daughter, his façade of toughness collapsed. He began to frequent mediums in the hope of getting through to her on the other side, started drinking heavily, and was soon pitifully gone.

UNIVERSITY OF ILLINOIS AT URBANA-CHAMPAIGN

In 1900 my father moves into the new house designed for him
by the distinguished architect Charles Voysey. It looks out over
the English Channel from the top of the bluffs at the
Shoreham end of the Folkstone Leas.

The transformation of Amy Catherine into Jane Wells is
completed in the new house; she will hardly ever be called by
any other name in the next twenty-seven years. Her
two sons are born here in 1901 and 1903.

COURTESY OF MARTIN J. WELLS

COURTESY OF MARTIN J. WELLS

Sarah Neal visits with my father not long before her
death in 1905. Building is, for her, the ultimate
extravagance. She is more convinced than ever that my
father is riding for a fall.

UNIVERSITY OF ILLINOIS AT URBANA-CHAMPAIGN

Sarah Wells photographed by my father in 1905 as she
lies laid out for burial.

UNIVERSITY OF ILLINOIS AT URBANA-CHAMPAIGN

ery, and tried to postpone the day of reckoning with the truth by professing to be ill. Jane would soon come to terms with her situation, and when she had done that there would be no more talk of illness. She would get her second wind, so to speak, and then she would take up her life again with her old spirit. She had a great many years in her yet.

On this cheerful note my father took his departure, leaving his twenty-four-year-old son in charge of the developing situation. It fell to Frank to get his mother to a specialist, and then to deal with the sequel to that consultation. Sir Hugh Rigby was the titled medical grandee called in to give the second opinion in this case, and he had no doubt that Jane was already beyond aid. His weight was more than usually necessary on this occasion. As soon as the original specialist had given his verdict, Frank, feeling exceedingly lonely and a good way out of his depth, wrote to my father to tell him that the circumstances called for his immediate return to Easton. But this letter arrived at its destination when my father had been in the south for no more than a couple of days. He did not wish to leave so soon. He temporised, writing to Frank to tell him that he did not believe things could be as bad as all that. It was easy to be misled by x-ray photographs. It could all be a false alarm. He would wait for a second opinion before he changed his plans—he would be back in England by the end of May anyway as things stood . . . That my father's plans called for him to return to England by way of Geneva, where Margaret Sanger was to be spending part of the month as a participant in a World Population Conference, may have been a factor in shaping this tepid response. But however that may have been he made no move to leave Grasse until Frank wrote to him again, this time telling him what the unchallengeable Sir Hugh Rigby had said. That left him with no alternative but to face the reality of the situation. His wife was dying.

He had this bad news on May 10, and left for London late the following day. Before he went down to Cannes to get aboard the *Train Bleu,* he wrote to Margaret Sanger to let her know that he wouldn't after all, be meeting her in Switzerland. His little wife, he told her, was dying of cancer and he wished to spend such time as she still might have at her side. He evidently felt a shade uneasy to be telling her this from an address that placed him over a thousand miles from the object of his concern, and did his best to explain the point away by saying that Jane's illness had "come upon us all very suddenly. . . . I left her in London not three weeks ago, smiling and alert, but looking a little tired. . . ."

The curse that lies upon all quick-minded people with a vivid imagination now descended upon my father. He had, though unwillingly, accepted the facts. His wife had cancer and was going to die. But cancer, which can possess its victims so suddenly, can also be languid in the consummation of its conquests. The woman lived on through what remained of May, through June, through July, through August . . . she was not in the end to go until the evening of October 6. My father became impatient with this dismal prolongation of a process that was already completed in his mind. He began to show it by running up to town for a day or two now and then. Nothing could be more reasonable than that. Life, after all, must go on. The big outline of biology was clamouring for attention, and the work was falling behind. He was soon forced to spend the middle of every week in the London flat as a regular thing. And then, when he had demonstrated that his wife could safely be left for two or three days at a stretch, he extended his range and took to nipping across the channel to meet Odette a couple of times every month. And when he was at Easton he did his best to bully the life there into a simulated normality. Julian Huxley and G. P. Wells were summoned to the house to press on with work on *The Science of Life* just as if things were as they had been in the days when *The Outline of History* was in the making. Counterfeits of the old cheerful weekend parties with boisterous games, charades, and racing demon, were staged regardless of the emotional cost. Julian Huxley, who was made to bear a part of it, felt the mounting strain. So did Arnold Bennett when he came over with Dorothy Cheston Bennett for an unhappy farewell visit during a weekend that left two entries in my father's pocket diary: "Jane down for the last time. We watch the fire together" and "Jane much worse." Bennett, who was very fond of Jane, didn't like the hectic party atmosphere in the crowded house and noted sourly that "H.G. likes a lot of people to distract him." Bennett also noted, without pleasure, that my father's acceptance of Jane's death had by this time reached a stage at which he had found it possible to prepare the draft of an oration to be delivered at her funeral and was capable of asking him to approach a suitable person to deliver it. My father's choice had fallen upon a man called Page, who was known to have a full and mellow voice, but who had no other claim to distinction, and had played no part at all in Jane's life or his own.

Bennett had gone home, deeply depressed, on the Sunday evening, leaving my father free to start work on the twentieth in the series of syndicated articles he was writing for Beaverbrook. It was a far-sighted piece on the importance of having a coherent world energy policy. Begun on the Monday, the article went out on time by the morning post on Tuesday. The long-drawn-out death watch was now coming to an end, and its final stages are recorded by sparse entries in the pocket diary: "September 28. We watch the shadows on the wall. October 2. Another fall in strength. October 4. Last Days. October 6. Jane dies at 6.30. . . . October 10. Cremation. October 11. Twentyfirst article done." My father went up to London on the 16th, and left London for Paris on the morning of the 18th.

Those who did not know my father may be tempted to suppose that his behaviour during this unhappy summer showed that he was in an almost indecent hurry to get on with his new life. That would be a mistake. It was his old life that he wished to get on with, and it was during this summer that he decided that things would go on as before with Odette in Jane's place. There was no chance that this program would work out, but he was quite unaware of that. This was partly, as I have said, because he had a fundamentally wrong idea of her, and partly because he misunderstood her willingness to play second fiddle to Jane during her lifetime. He took it for a parallel to his wife's tolerance of his *passades.* He did not realise that Odette's willingness to go along with that arrangement was based on a formal admission of the claims of ancient acquaintance. She was at heart a conventional woman, and she felt that she had no right to supplant someone who had meant so much to my father for so long, and who had done so much for him so well. But it was one thing for Odette to let him go whenever he wished to be with a woman to whom he owed a great deal, but with whom he had ceased to have an active sexual relationship, and another one altogether to agree to his leaving her to her own devices for as long as he felt inclined whenever he came across a new woman he fancied and who was willing to have an affair with him. She could, just, condone his having light affairs while she remained the vital centre of his physical life, but she had no intention of submitting to the arrangement he was proposing. This struck him as a maddening piece of inconsistency on her part. What right had she to become so demanding and possessive, virtually overnight, after letting him come and go as he pleased for years? He was exasperated by the sheer unreasonableness of her complete change of front. She became in-

creasingly impatient with his obtuse failure of perception—why could
he not see her as she truly was?

The tension between them was building steadily through their last
six years, and although it was relieved from time to time by bouts of
the kind of farcical rowing that I have already described, it finally
reached a level that had to produce an explosion. The fuse was lit by
Gorky's response to events that had been taking place in Russia. In
his pleasant retreat at Sorrento, Gorky became aware that the persecution of his fellow writers in his homeland had moved on from the
malignant harassment of suspect individuals to something more like
a pogrom aimed at the destruction of the whole class of pre-revolu-
tionary literati. Every voice that did not simply echo that of the party
was being silenced. Aleksey Maximovitch began to feel that he was
living the life of a deserter, and that he had failed in his duty by going
abroad and abandoning his post as the recognised intermediary between the writers and the regime. He felt that he had to go back, to
see if he could become under Stalin what he had been in the days of
Lenin. He might save at least a few survivors of the old avant-garde
from exile and the camps. His own great enemy Zinoviev had lost out
in the bitter power struggle that had followed Lenin's death and been
formally expelled from the party in 1926. With that man gone, and
with his own officially recognised position in the party's scheme of
things, as father of Russian socialist realism and godfather of Soviet
literature, he might have a chance to gain Stalin's ear. Gorky went
back briefly in 1928, and finally, after testing the temperature of the
water two or three times more, packed up all his books and papers,
and left for Russia with his son, his daughter-in-law, and his two
granddaughters in May 1933.

Moura Budberg, as she was now known, the Baroness, did not go
back to Russia with Gorky. He had told her from the first that although
he was almost certain that his internal and international standing
would make it possible for him to live in Russia, he didn't believe that
the mantle of his name would be enough to protect her if she accompanied him. The risk was one that he couldn't ask her to take, and he'd
feel easier in his mind if she stayed outside. The Baroness Budberg
came to London while Gorky was in Russia in the autumn of 1931, and
saw my father. All the feelings she had aroused in him in 1920 were
reawakened by this encounter, and he began writing to her after she
had returned to Sorrento. In his letters he urged her to make her
home in England if Gorky should stick to his plans for repatriating

himself. He also told her how very much she had always meant to him. She answered his letters in a way that made it quite plain that she was still as interested in him as she had ever been.

Odette managed to get her hands on some of Moura Budberg's letters to my father in the latter part of 1932. She judged from their tone that he was embarking on a new and serious affair. She made a tremendous row. My father quieted the storm temporarily by telling her that nothing that need upset her was going on—it was a simple matter of two old friends getting in touch with each other for old time's sake. Odette was not wholly convinced, and she told him so. But she did not pursue the matter. My father's reaction to her inaction was characteristic. He decided that since she now knew of his interest in Moura Budberg and was living with it, he would in future keep her informed of what was happening as it happened, or even in advance of the event—just as he had kept Jane abreast of his adventures and plans. There would, he foolishly thought, be no more misunderstandings and no more furies that way. It was in the late spring of 1933 that he told Odette what he would be doing for the next several weeks. He had arranged to meet Moura Budberg in Dubrovnik, where the International PEN Club would be holding its annual conference, and when that was over, he would be taking a holiday in Austria with her. Then, after Moura had gone back to her new home in England, he would be returning to Grasse, where he would expect to find Odette waiting for him.

My father was very much taken aback by the way in which this straightforward announcement was received. He was used to Odette's explosions, and he had learned how to let even her most violent exhibitions blow themselves out. But this time she was not putting on a show. She was telling him, with a precision that told him that she had already consulted a lawyer, just what would happen if he did go off to Dubrovnik with this other woman. He might afterwards come back to their house at Grasse, but it would not be to stay. It would be to remove his things. He had, as he had told her often enough, built the house for her—and he had given her a deed that assured her of lifetime possession of the property. The house was hers, and no one else's, for as long as she should remain alive. This point had the quality of news for my father. He seems to have managed to persuade himself at some stage that if he were to break with Odette for any reason, she would be honour bound to let him have it back. His feelings on this issue were so strong that they leaked into the biography written forty years later by Norman and Jeanne MacKenzie, and led them to conclude the chapter that they devote to this section of his life with a truly splendid piece of bathos: "It had been a hard decision to leave the house he had built for himself. But on May 22 H.G. walked through his olive grove for the last time and went down to Cannes to catch the train for Trieste. 'It needed an effort,' he wrote a year later, 'but once more the liberating influence was the stronger.' " But that was not quite how it had been. He had been sent packing. Odette had thrown him out.

Chapter VII

I wish I was not sixty; . . . I wish there was an
inexhaustible supply of nervous energy between
myself and the phase of irritation. . . . Perhaps I
have fifteen years still left, or it may be twenty.
Much may be done in such a ration of time, with a
flying start and good fortune.

—THE WORLD OF WILLIAM CLISSOLD

THERE IS NO DENYING THAT MY FA-
ther was getting a bad press from
the early thirties onwards, and that he was having difficulty in placing
some of his work towards the end of the decade. I believe that this is
because he fell out with the intellectual left in those years. The main
thrust of his writing, from the later twenties onwards, had to be
intolerable to those who wanted to play the Communist card against
the rising power of Fascism. My father had put himself out on a limb
by declaring himself an anti-Marxist socialist committed to the view
that the rigidity of Marxist dogma made it useless as a tool for ap-
prehending the realities of a world of evolution and growth. He was
particularly firm in holding to his thesis that there could be no future
for a working-class party that thought of itself as having interests
diametrically opposed to those of the rest of the community. To stick
with that concept meant sticking to the politics of class war, and that
had to be as destructive and as wasteful of human potential as any
other kind of warfare. It could only lead into a dead end, for socialism, and for human progress. But what put him altogether beyond the
pale in the eyes of the left was a sentence that had appeared in his
novel of 1926, *The World of William Clissold:* "I shall look to America

rather than Moscow for the first installments of the real revolution."

The real revolution of this line was not to be concerned with replacing one set of privileged persons with another, or with paying off old scores. It was not to be a matter of the poor giving the rich what-for, or anything of the kind. Its aim was to bring the men of good will in all classes together to work for the creation of a just and prosperous society of free men, humane laws, and wide tolerances, and it had been in progress since 1776.

My father's decision to plump for the United States as the likely scene for the opening stages of the consensual revolution of his dreams was bold for the time. In the twenties most Europeans still saw America through a veil of resentments generated by the hard line on war debts insisted upon by the Congress, its wanton sabotage of the infant League of Nations, and its brassy claim to have won the war in which it had barely taken part. The America of the founding fathers, the magnificent Constitution, and Lincoln was almost forgotten in those years of bitterness. It was hard for outsiders looking westwards to see anything but the weird country mocked by Mencken—the land of Warren Gamaliel Harding and the Kitchen Cabinet, of Coolidge in his Indian war bonnet and stiff collar, of insanely high tariff barriers and suddenly illiberal immigration quotas, of the Scopes trial, of Sacco and Vanzetti, of Aimee Semple McPherson, and, to all appearances, of a more wildly exaggerated nationalism and a noisier commercialism than the world had so far seen. My father had not been unshaken by the efflorescence of postwar America. He had gone through a phase of intense irritation with things American in 1919–1920, when the Republicans were savagely clobbering Woodrow Wilson's peace treaty. He had relieved his feelings about the triumph of the isolationists by putting a one-hemisphere map of the world on the cover of the last of the twenty-six fortnightly parts in which *The Outline of History* had appeared: over a caption dramatically announcing "The Next Stage," it had shown the Euro-Asian land mass, Africa, and Australia with the stirring legend THE UNITED STATES OF THE WORLD boldly lettered across the space between Paris and Peiping. America was not visible. It was round at the back, on its own and out of things, where the Congress had elected to put it for the shabbiest of reasons.

But in spite of the antics of its Bible thumpers and its boobocracy, my father was unable to stay mad at the United States for long. He knew that its creative energy and its commitment to the principles of the Constitution were still there, and as soon as he got to Washington to cover the naval disarmament conference in 1922 he was able to see that the high seriousness was still there too, and that the nonsenses that were making the headlines were merely the outward signs of something akin to an adolescent crisis. The phase of American history in which farming had been the life of the Republic was coming to an end, and it was entering on its maturity as an industrial society with an international role. It was not quite ready to consciously assume the function of world leadership, but as the leading society in the fields of industrial organization and the application of technological innovation it was already shaping the future course of social history as effectively as it had in the days when the ideas expressed so clearly in the literature of its revolution had swept round the world to bring one historical era to an end, and to set the tone of its successor.

My father took the view, I believe correctly, that the industrialised Republic was an even more potent agency for the promotion of social progress than it had been when its influence was predominantly ideological. The logic of industrial development in a country that was perennially short of labour had done away with the proletariat of Marxist dogma. A fully industrialised society dependent for its prosperity on the efficient use of its machines and its energy supply simply could not afford the luxury of a poverty-stricken underclass made up of slow-witted illiterates. It was self-evident that men and women who had been crippled mentally and physically in childhood could not be contributors, either as producers or consumers, to the common wealth. Common sense had put American business on the side of social progress. Its need for workers worth employing had put it behind the idea of an educated people and free education, just as its need for customers had made it see the point of paying better than subsistence wages. In spite of the evil reputation of the American employer, it was in his workshops that the lesson was learned that long hours worked in squalid conditions were less profitable for all concerned than a shorter day in clean, well-lit, and well-ventilated plants. Some American businesses began badly, and remained bad sectionally, supported by a native tradition of resistance to regulation and control, but by the turn of the century, as my father saw it, the national tide was running irresistibly away from exploitation in the direction of a society of community of interest. It seemed to him that the Republic's first great social achievement, the destruction of the sort of social structure that recognises a fundamental division between the categories of rulers and the ruled, was being followed by another in which the barriers between employers and the employed were being broken down.

When my father first saw this society of the American Revolution, in 1906, he was impressed by the extent to which it was under threat, from the greed of its entrepreneurial class on the one hand, and from the influx of European proletarians on the other. He saw the underclass of a disastrous future pouring in through Ellis Island, and feared the worst. But over the years he came to recognise the strength given to the society by the bone and muscle of the Constitution and the Supreme Court, and by the passionate desire for Americanisation on the part of the overwhelming majority of the immigrant mass. Its members had, he realised, gone to America not only to earn money, but even more to become members of a reasonably governed free society. That the America of Harding, Coolidge, and Hoover fell far short of their ideal, and considerably short of the native American ideal, was beside the point. However defective the current performance might be, the aspirations declared in the documents that constituted the charter of the Republic remained in the record as its goals. It was a committed society. And in 1931–1933, as it reeled under the impact of the kind of economic disaster that led inevitably to coups d'état and military dictatorships in European experience, it remained loyal to its basic principles. The American answer to the conditions that gave Hitler power in Germany was Franklin Delano Roosevelt and the New Deal.

My father's personal response to the developing situation in those years was to attempt to use his position as a publicist with a worldwide audience to counter the drift of both the left and the right towards a simplistic totalitarianism. It reflected his belief that the life of a free society is dependent on a continuing debate on its principles, immediate goals, and ultimate aims. Early in 1932 he sat down at his desk in Odette Keun's house outside Grasse to draft a memorandum defining the terms of what he felt might be a workable liberal consensus to which all those who believed in the concept of a free society would be able to subscribe. It stated in broad outline an alternative social ideal to that proposed by the totalitarians, and suggested a route to it based on the progressive expansion of the public sector in industry and finance, the creation of a world monetary system, international control of the arms traffic, massive educational programs, and the adoption of a world bill of rights guaranteeing freedom of speech, information, publication, and movement. When he had

worked out this positive conspectus of what he was *for*—he felt that
it would be much more useful than a purely negative announcement
of his hostility to Fascism—he circulated his paper, sending it to a
large number of public figures in Europe and America who seemed
to him to possess influence equal to or greater than his own. He
hoped in this way to initiate an international discussion of democratic
principle from which an anti-Fascist common ground might emerge.
In this he was, for the time being, disappointed. He did not get the
response he hoped for, and no general debate took place. He saw, too
late, that his approach had been wrong. He had emphasised the positive to the extent of virtually excluding the negative. The recipients
of his paper took it that he was unrealistically ignoring the reality of
the Fascist menace. This was not the case. He was, as usual, taking the
long view. He had quite correctly seen that Fascism was an episode,
and a minor one, in the time of troubles that the world would have
to pass through before a new and more soundly conceived world
order could come into being from the wreckage of the old order of
nation states. He felt that the most pressing order of business for the
immediate future was to make the generality of men realise that it was
in their power to take charge of the drift of history, and to limit the
extent of the coming troubles and their duration by working for
definite aims. He was looking ahead, beyond the struggle with the
nationalist dictatorships that was then in the making, and seeing that
the real issue of the time would prove to be a choice between following the Russian or the American way.

There are those who attribute the pattern of my father's thinking
throughout the early thirties to his having been "insulated from the
impact of the depression" by his wealth and his isolation in Provence.
Had he been nearer the heart of things, they tell one, he would have
realised that the stock market crash of 1929 had put paid to his dream
both of an American future and to that of an evolutionary process by
which the great corporations would outgrow the nation states which
had produced them and become multinational institutions powerful
enough to erode sovereignties, and so, by creating a global economic
community, lay the foundations for a world state. Because he had
been too much "involved in the social life of the Riviera smart set"
he had failed to notice that the depression had shipwrecked the super-
businesses that he had naïvely mistaken for the wave of the future. It
is less pleasingly said today that it was only my father's vanity that kept
him from taking up the totalitarian cause in the early thirties. The

allegation is that he had an affinity with both the Communists and the Fascists, and if I understand these critics correctly, their belief is that he would have thrown in his lot with one or the other group if he hadn't had a swollen-headed feeling that it was their place to come courting him rather than his to go over to them. The next step from there was to indicate that, as the author of *The Shape of Things to Come*, my father was one of the creators of the spirit of Munich. According to this thesis the fantasia in question, which first saw the light in 1933 and was very soon afterwards made into a film, with my father's active and enthralled participation, has to be considered as one of the many factors which created public support for the policy of appeasement because it featured a massive air attack on London, shrewdly previsioned as taking place in 1940. The fact is that the book, and like it the film, has the character of one of the awful warnings that my father was fond of producing. Its clearly expressed message can be summed up as: Watch out! This is the sort of thing you will more than likely be in for if you don't take a stand against Fascism now. It has been said that the film was intended as an antiwar tract, but this is the last thing that my father would have been able to produce at any time. He was particularily impatient with the pacifist case just then, when each day that passed made the necessity for fighting and defeating the Fascist powers more obvious. His sentiment was that a stand had to be taken and the war fought sooner rather than later, since the free societies might become indistinguishable from the totalitarian ones if they were to become involved in the rigors of a fight for survival in the last ditch. In spite of the clarity of his intentions, his critics contend that he wanted to see the world plunged into a long, destructive period of war and anarchy, from which a puritan tyranny of technicians and scientists would emerge, because he was peeved with it for not listening to his own preachings. The thesis is that he wrote *The Shape of Things to Come* to punish his time for making him feel futile and insignificant.

Oddly enough, it was just then, in 1933, that the most didactic and from the literary point of view the least successful of all my father's books was playing a fateful role in human affairs. In 1932, while he was circulating the unlucky position paper setting out his conception of what a plausible declaration of anti-Fascist principle should contain, a Berlin publisher chose to bring out a translation of his long-forgotten novel of 1914, the unlucky *World Set Free*. No rivers were set on fire by this exhumation, but a year after it took place, a copy of the book fell into the hands of the then up-and-coming physicist Leo Szilard. He had realised not long before just how a theoretically possible chain reaction releasing the energy locked up in the nucleus of the atom might be achieved in practice, and in the course of 1932–1933 had come within sight of a patentable procedure. He was therefore astonished by the book's first chapter, in which he was introduced to a young physicist called Holsten whose work was bringing him to this very point—and in the year 1933. While Szilard was delighted by this favourable omen for his own success he was more seriously impressed by my father's script for the sequel to Holsten's achievement. The invented physicist had been a scientist of the old school who believed in the open publication of his results as a duty he owed to the scientific community. He had published, as his faith called upon him to do, and publication had led to a world-wide atomic war, vividly described. Szilard considered this scenario in the light of his knowledge of what was going on in Germany, and when he presently found himself in a position to take out his patent he was ready with a plan. "Knowing what this would mean," he wrote later, "—and I knew it because I had read H. G. Wells—I did not want this patent to become public. The only way to keep it from becoming public was to assign it to the Government. So I assigned it to the British Admiralty."

There may, of course, be some people capable of believing that the world would be very much the same today even if the Fascist war machine had been able to arm itself with atomic weapons before it was broken, and they will probably dismiss this as a trivial matter. I am not able to do so, and bearing in mind Speer's remark that the Nazis had been too much occupied with their war to have time to show the world how far they had it in them to go in the way of wickedness, I feel very glad indeed that my father had written *The World Set Free* and that it was there to be read by Szilard at that particular juncture.

But there is a great deal more than this one exceedingly fortunate hit to justify both my father's belief that he was a usefully influential man and his dogged persistence in writing his particular brand of socially functional, if aesthetically inexcusable, book. He has a solid claim to importance as the individual who, from 1914 onwards, preached the doctrine of the desirability and feasibility of creating supranational world authorities with planning and police powers to a widening constituency. It has been argued that his relentless advocacy of this cause had cost him the greater part of his standing with the general public, and not just that of the intellectual left by the middle thirties. They argue that his persistence in playing the same old tune had by then forced most people to write him off as an aging man who had run out of fresh ideas. This conveys what was also the received opinion of the literary world, but it ignores the fact that the over- whelming majority of mankind ignores literary values when it comes to considering ideas. While my father was unquestionably boring the minority he was doing as much as any man then living to create the climate of opinion in the middle ground that was to make the creation of the United Nations and the establishment of the European Eco- nomic Community an inevitable part of the peacemaking process at the end of World War II. Those who feel, as I do, that these institu- tions are among the most promising of mankind's sociopolitical crea- tions of any age will have difficulty in accepting the idea that my father was an artist *manqué* who wasted his time and diminished his stature by labouring on through the last third of his life in this particular vineyard.

But however large or small his constituency may have been in those years there is no hint of slowing up or of weakness about that most characteristically Wellsian of his performances of the early thirties, an account of which he rightly made the climax of his autobiography. In that book, which is half novel and half what its title claims it to be, he set out to describe the mental adventures of a man born in provincial obscurity in 1866 who lived in his own person the thrilling experience of the opening up of the modern mind. He begins with a description of the very humble home into which he was born, as the late and unwanted child of a pair of upper servants turned shopkeepers, and ends it with a joyous celebration of his arrival at the heart of things. This presents him with a problem. How is he to convince his readers that he has really made it into that larger sphere? He is more than a little disingenuous when he comes to presenting his solution to it, and suggests that the very remarkable thing that he managed to do was the product of an idle whim: "In the spring of 1934 I took it in- to my head to see and compare President Franklin Roosevelt and Mr. Stalin. . . . " Having decided to do that, my father got to see the President of the United States in May and the Russian chief of state in July.

My father's account of the episode is a very compact and skilful piece of writing. In its few pages he gives sharply etched impressions of the rich diversity of opinion he encountered in America, of the openness of its expression, and of the receptivity of the society. He deals brilliantly with the diversity of the Presidential styles of the four men who had, at different times, received him in the White House: Theodore Roosevelt, Harding, Hoover, and Franklin Delano Roosevelt. He had been doubtful of FDR's staying power at the time of his election, but when he met that inexhaustibly curious, quick-minded, and alertly intelligent man he was entirely convinced by him, and by the spirit of his Administration. He contrasts the flexibility and openness of the regime, and the continuous growth of its leader's mind, with the rigidity of the dead conformism that ruled in Russia, and in the Kremlin more than anywhere else. The most effective of these Russian pages are those in which he describes the horrifying deterioration that had overtaken Gorky since his return from Italy. My father found him in a pitiable state. All the hopes with which he had gone home in 1928 had been disappointed, and his position had become one of hideous ambiguity. He was perpetually on view as Stalin's favorite writer and the regime's hero of culture. But even though streets, avenues, squares, parade grounds, primary schools, clinics, housing developments, and even whole towns, were being named for him all over Russia, he was living in fear, poised so precariously on the razor's edge between favour and disfavour that he no longer dared to utter a word in any of the foreign languages in which he had once been fluent for fear of giving colour to the accusation that he was courting the international bourgeoisie. It was not simply that he was afraid, he was constantly making disavowals, through the leaden-tongued interpreters who filtered all his utterances, of precisely those ideas of personal and intellectual freedom in which he had formerly believed most passionately.

These pages are moving as my father's lament for a lost friend, but they are also stirring as a proudly free man's scathing indictment of the wasteland of fear and sycophancy that the country of the revolution had become under Stalin. When he compared what he saw in the Russia of 1934 with what he had seen in the famine-stricken country that he visited in Lenin's day, he had to admit the reality of the achievements of the Stalin years. But in the light of what living in the Georgian's cold shadow had done to Gorky, and could be seen to be doing to a whole generation of younger intellectuals and academics, he could only view the regime as a joyless one, devoid of the promise of an even tolerable future. When he had spoken with Stalin he made no bones about saying what the two encounters had taught him. He had been right in 1926. It was Roosevelt's Administration that had provided him with the vision of a truly modern government in action. The future lay there, in Washington. The Russian way led to a dead end.

The trenchant pages that bring my father's autobiography to close do not stand alone. They are supported by the verbatim record of his exchange with Stalin. There is no doubt about what was said on this occasion. Everything that passed between the two men was written down at the time by a Comrade Umansky of the Soviet foreign service. He had to be present as an interpreter because, unlike Lenin, Stalin spoke no English. In spite of this language difficulty the meeting had none of the qualities of the polite brushoff that men of power usually give to irrelevant but unavoidable celebrities who press themselves into their schedules. My father went into the Kremlin half expecting such treatment, supposing that he would be lucky to spend as much as half an hour with the great man. But when he suggested that he was wearing out his welcome at the end of his first forty minutes, Stalin told him that he had two hours and twenty minutes still to go. My father made full use of this generous allotment, and showed, I think, a great deal of courage in doing so. He was not, of course, in any kind of physical danger while he was face to face with the tyrant. But when it comes to it, the ability to talk freely and easily to powerful men of blood is not given to everyone. As Stalin sat impassively before him, toying with one of his famous pipes, my father nerved himself to do what he had to do, and managed it. He told Stalin that he should, in the best interests of mankind, abandon two of his policies—the stifling of dissent, and the institutionalisation of class war. He told Stalin that they had already done Russia a great deal of harm, and that they would do it still greater damage if they were taken further. It was not merely a question of the loss and misery that was being inflicted upon the Russian people, appalling though that aspect of the matter was. It was more seriously a question of the effect that the brutalities inseparable from the execution of these policies were having upon opinion throughout the world, and in particular upon opinion in the United States. The last point was of special importance for mankind, since the United States and the USSR, as the world's leading industrial power and its only potential equal, were clearly destined to emerge as superpowers within the next twenty to thirty years. Inside that period they would both become far stronger, economically and militarily, than any of the European or Asiatic nation states that had been recognised as great powers under the old order. As both countries were dedicated to the same long-term goals—the elimination of ignorance, want, and injustice from their societies—and as their chosen means to their common end, industrialisation, had a social logic of its own that was clearly impelling them in the same general direction, there should be nothing to prevent their becoming allies and collaborators. They would soon be in a position to exploit a unique historical opportunity if they could but recognise the extent of their common ground and aim at convergence rather than confrontation. Once the obstacles standing in the way of their cooperation had been removed, it would be in the power of the two countries to lay the foundations for a global commonwealth in which national divisions and old enmities could be expected to wither away. They could establish something that might, by a natural evolutionary process, become a world state in the fullness of time. It would be nothing less than tragic if this opportunity were to be lost because the Russian leadership proved to be too rigid to take the necessary first steps in the direction of convergence. The United States had shown the way. It was no longer a capitalist society in the primitive sense. The actions of Roosevelt's Administration, and the massive support that they had been given by the American public, showed that the Republic had swung over to the idea of governmental orchestration of the economy. The mood in Washington was unlikely ever to swing back towards the state of affairs in which the Federal government had been little more than a cypher. A real revolution had taken place. If the Russians were to show their flexibility by abandoning their dogmatic hostility to the concepts of individual rights and intellectual freedom, along with their stubborn loyalty to the outworn theory of class war, a brilliant prospect for all mankind might open before them.

My father developed his thesis step by step, and Comrade Stalin declined to consider it in the same way, politely giving his reasons. He relied for the most part on the medieval technique of the appeal to authority, and only occasionally referred to his own experience of the real world. In both cases my father was disconcerted by his replies, since it appeared that Stalin's experience invariably confirmed the theses of the authorities to whom he habitually appealed, Marx, Engels and Lenin. As the interview went on, he began to suspect that this was a probable source of Stalin's strength as the leader of the Communist Party: he could be counted upon never to trouble the membership with the challenge of an original idea, or even to require them to re-examine, and if necessary to discard, any doctrine that had ever figured in the Marxist-Leninist canon. His arguments were circular. The stifling of dissent, for example, could not do Russia any harm, since what was being stifled was criticism of Marxist-Leninism and therefore subjective and biased. Criticism and debate were, of course, necessary, but the restatement of exploded errors was not what was wanted. What *was* needed was objective Marxist-Leninist criticism founded on correct theses. Such criticism could only come from within the party. In the same way it was impossible that the class war should inflict any damage upon Russia because its only victims were the tools and agents of the international bourgeoisie who were enemies of the Russian people. My father was in error when he said that the majority of its victims fell into social categories that Russia had special need of if the norms of the Five-Year Plan were to be fulfilled: Stalin was sure of this because he had found that these people, scientists, engineers, and technical specialists, members of the so-called technical intelligentsia, had been among the most stubborn opponents of socialist reconstruction. Salaried employees for the most part, they were not really a class at all, they were mere lackeys of the propertied interests, and *necessarily* enemies of the working class. As for cooperation with the United States, no compromise or working arrangement with the pluto-democracies of the west was possible for the USSR. Roosevelt was *necessarily* a lackey of the propertied classes. There was no way for him to be anything else until they had been dispossessed of their property. Ownership meant control, and while the capitalists continued to be the owners of the means of production in the United States, there could be no talk of common ground shared by that country and the USSR. Roosevelt's New Deal was a fraud designed to hoodwink the exploited masses of rightless American proletarians. When the United States had been through the revolutionary process, which *necessarily* involved the dispossession of the capitalist class, and only then could there be any prospect of convergence and collaboration.

My father came away from this meeting with mixed feelings. He had wanted to be told that his dream of a Russo-American rapprochement was something more than that, but he had always known in his heart that the Soviet commitment to the sterilities of Marxist dogma ruled it out as a possibility. It was a disappointment to have it dismissed with finality by the man who could speak with more real authority on the question than any other. But the negative outcome of the meeting did not make it futile. My father's plea for a Russo-American rapprochement had been turned down in unambiguous terms. He was able to admire the forthright honesty with which Stalin had exploded the idea. This was important, as the left-wing parties in the surviving democracies in Europe and throughout the world were still deluding themselves with the thought that the USSR was fundamentally on their side. By putting the question of a partnership with the Americans to the Russian leader, my father had persuaded him to reveal the extent to which this idea was a delusion. The Soviet state was interested in the survival of Soviet Communism and nothing else. The price of Russian support against the threat from Fascism was to be the abandonment of anything resembling the concept of an open society, and an irreversible commitment to the Soviet brand of totalitarianism. As this was not what the spokesmen for the Communist parties outside the USSR were giving the left and left-of-centre parties in their various countries to understand, Stalin's very candid disclosure had its value. My father's feeling that it should be put into the public record at the earliest possible moment led him to arrange for publication of the official Russian transcript of the exchange in the then still reputable political and literary weekly *The New Statesman* as soon as he was out of Russia. With that done he turned aside from his direct route homewards in order to spend a month in Estonia with Moura Budberg.

For reasons that I shall later explain, my father thought that he had little hope of enjoying this prearranged encounter. He was consequently all the more pleased to have settled matters with *The New Statesman* before he set out for Tallin. Whatever might be waiting for him there, he could still look forward to the wide-ranging debate on fundamentals that he felt sure that publication of the exchange would provoke. With it in the record, in Stalin's very own words, that there was nothing to hope for from the Russians, those who wanted to go on living in open societies would have to see that the time really had come when they would have to organise themselves for the coming struggle against Fascism. They wouldn't have a chance of winning the fight if they didn't know what they were fighting *for*. This time he was throwing something into the ring that, unlike his earlier memorandum, they weren't going to be able to ignore, and there was a very good chance that a plausible set of war aims might come out of it all. In this expectation my father was to be cruelly disappointed, because the editor of *The New Statesman* was Kingsley Martin.

It would not be altogether fair to describe this very characteristic English left-wing intellectual as one of those middle-class fellow travellers whose sincerest hope was to be able to keep travelling without ever having to arrive. Although he had no principles, his behaviour derived a certain consistency from his being, by temperament and habit, an opposition man. He would have been against any establishment, no matter what its political complexion, and he was unquestionably pro-Russian in the thirties, less because he believed in Marxism than because he saw espousal of the Soviet cause as the easiest way to get up the noses of the members of the predominantly anti-Soviet English establishment. He was embarrassed when he read the transcript, because he had been one of the most vocal of those advocating a policy of snuggling up to Stalin as the only possible answer to the developing Fascist threat. It was open to him to ask my father to place his offering somewhere else, but that would have been an affront to his conscience, which was that of a committed journalist. He had undertaken to build the minuscule circulation of *The New Statesman* when he was a candidate for its editorship, and he knew that "Wells Talks with Stalin" would sell extra copies. But he did not like what he was being compelled to do. His solution to the problem was in line with the streak of treachery that was a conspicuous element in his make-up—he liked nothing better than to build up the confidence of a friend while preparing to do him a mischief behind his back. While telling my father how delighted he was to be able to publish the text of the interview, and what a big thing it was going to be for the magazine, he quietly arranged for George Bernard Shaw to write a commentary on the discussion, to be run in the issue following that in which it was to appear.

Although Kingsley Martin was a consistently foolish man, he was a long way from being stupid. He knew just what he was doing when he made this plan. He had understood the relationship between Shaw and my father since he had seen him clowning at Jane Wells's funeral. It was of a kind that is more noticeable, even if it is not any commoner, among schoolboys than it is among adults, and was that which obtains between bully and favourite victim. Rather early in their acquaintance, which had begun in the nineties, Shaw had recognised an ideal subject in my father. He saw that he had to deal with a man who could be deeply wounded by anyone who laughed at him when he was trying to be serious. Shaw was a coldly cruel man by nature, and once he had learned how my father could be hurt he cultivated him in order to be able to indulge himself in the pleasure. He often went to extravagant lengths to satisfy his appetite. As soon, for instance, as he set eyes on the first of the fortnightly parts in which *The Outline of History* made its original appearance, he saw the full extent to which my father had invested himself in it. Within hours of his receiving it, Shaw's copy of that issue was in the post and on its way to my father, scrawled all over with derisive comments, and with crude drawings parodying the illustrations. A number of later issues in the twenty-six-part press run were given similar treatment and sent on in the same way. Although some of Shaw's gibes were undeniably funny, the effect of this sustained exercise in malicious jeering is still chilling—and not only because it was carried on under the mask of friendship.

The same pressing need to do whatever he could to destroy a fellow creature's confidence in himself and his abilities appears in the letters that Shaw wrote to my father at the end of 1906 and the beginning of the following year. They are written in the persona of a friend offering a man who has taken on a task for which he is not quite prepared the benefit of his wisdom and experience. My father was challenging the Webbs for the leadership of the Fabian Society at the time, and he was under the necessity of swinging a number of public meetings to his side if he was to bring it off. Shaw, who was in fact supporting the efforts of the Webbs to keep things in the Society as they were, offered him advice on how the campaign should be run, and gave him tips on how he should conduct himself as a speaker. On the eve of the final and crucial meeting, Shaw wrote to tell him that he hadn't done too well so far. He had to face it that he wasn't a very effective speaker. He would have to remember that his somewhat thin voice was apt to become squeaky when he tried to sound forceful. But he shouldn't, on the other hand, *mumble,* as he often did. And then he must, he simply had to, drop some of his platform mannerisms— they could only remind his auditors that he had once served behind the counter of a draper's shop. He had, for instance, a trick of pausing and leaning forward with his weight on his hands when he wanted to give the next thing he was going to say a special emphasis. It was not the effective device he seemed to think it. It made people flinch for fear that his next words might turn out to be "And the next article, modom?" He must be sure never to let himself do that again.

Softened up by this brilliantly conceived psychological assault my father went to the crucial meeting miserably self-conscious and set up to choke. He made a muddle of his speech, fell into a confusion that allowed Shaw to take the meeting over, and the vote went for the Webbs.

It took my father a long time to decide whether these performances of Shaw's, and the many others like them, were to be attributed to malice or to a defective sensibility. He came down for the former motivation after Jane Wells's funeral. My father had quite enough on his conscience on that particular afternoon to make the ritual hard to endure, and Shaw's outrages came very close to making it unbearable for him. There was no open quarrel, but my father never again thought of Shaw without loathing. With all this between the two men, it is not surprising that my father feared the worst when he learned that Kingsley Martin had invited Shaw to write a commentary on his wholly serious exchange with Stalin. When he saw what Shaw had actually written he exploded with anger . . . and replied, as Kingsley Martin had counted on his doing, while he was still angry.

And so the debate, from which my father had hoped that so much might come, opened, not with a consideration of the fuller implications of what Stalin had so bluntly and unambiguously told him, but as a further instalment of the old, tired Shaw-Wells harlequinade in which my father was destined to take the pratfalls while Shaw made play with his slapstick. As soon as he cooled down, my father saw what had happened. He had been tricked out of his discussion of the realities of Soviet policy and into a vulgar barney with Shaw on the subject of his own standing. Had he or hadn't he *trotted* into the Kremlin? Had he been boorish and impertinent when he urged Stalin to give up the folly of class war? His great moment, in which he had spoken up for common sense and humanity against a Byzantine obliquity and cruelty, had been trivialised beyond redemption.

And in the event, my father's dismay was fully justified because Shaw had opened the debate with such an inane piece of fooling no one took it seriously. It dwindled rapidly into an in-house correspondence reflecting the views of the *New Statesman*'s regular readership and very little else. My father had some relief from his very great disappointment when Kingsley Martin published the whole thing, the text of the exchange, Shaw's commentary upon it, and the resulting correspondence, as a pamphlet. But there was only a little comfort in having the record set out in a form that left no doubt as to the nature of Shaw's duplicity. Not many people would see the pamphlet, and the course of events was making the issue a trifling one. Over the next few years the scene was dominated by the dismal spectacle of the liberal and left-wing parliamentary parties in the surviving democracies falling one after another for the cynical Soviet hoax called The United

Front Against Fascism. While that farce was being staged in the west by the Comintern, Stalin, within the USSR, was going steadily on with the sickening business of having one and three-quarter millions of his fellow Russians shot as class enemies and agents of the international bourgeoisie.

Soon after Kingsley Martin had brought off this neat journalistic feat, my father fell victim to another editorial coup. The operator this time was the barrel-shaped owner-editor of *Time and Tide,* Lady Rhondda, the wealthy and extremely tough daughter of a coal owner who had made his millions out of the pits in the Rhondda valley. She had irritated my father a good deal in the course of 1929, when she had, he felt, played too active a role in encouraging my mother to embark upon a series of complicated legal moves designed to make her my sole legal guardian and to eliminate him from my life. In his vexation with her he had allowed himself a tiny poke at her in his next book—a passing reference to *"Wear and Tear,* the ladies' paper." This led to a certain amount of sniping to and fro, and to a steady increase in resentment on Lady Rhondda's part. Like many tough people, she was also heavy-handed, and for a while my father's quickness enabled him to score all the points. But when my father's autobiography came out she saw that she had been given a wonderful opportunity to get a bit of her own back. She had met Odette Keun, who had by this time made her peace with the British authorities and was able to visit England, and had discussed my father with her. She had the brilliant idea of assigning the book to Odette for review. Odette jumped at this chance to relieve her feelings, and produced an analysis of my father's flaws as a writer and a man, which ran in three parts published in successive issues of *Time and Tide* in the course of October 1934.

Odette, as was to be expected, made the most of her free hand. She aired all her grievances, and with some art gave an account of my father's relationship with his public over the years in terms of her experience of him as a lover. He was, she said, in his writing what he was in everything else, like a child playing a game, or an actor reading a part. He was never committed beyond the current performance, and he never intended to deliver in real life. She explored the defects of temperament and character that led to his "ultimate and irrevocable failure to be great," and deplored his self-indulgence, his instability, and his vanity. And she explained why it was that the only thing that anyone who trusted in him could count upon would be a let-down. This was because, she said, he had no conviction of reality about either humanity or the individual. He was enclosed within himself, and utterly unaware of others.

My father was not as deeply wounded by these tirades as Odette may have hoped, but he was extremely angry with Lady Rhondda for printing them. He shrugged them off by saying that he had heard a good deal of that sort of thing in the course of his last year or two with Odette, and that he had been expecting something of the kind ever since they broke up. His indifference was not altogether affected, and he found it possible to laugh when Amber Reeves presently told him of a scene that had been staged in her little house in Downshire Hill at about this time. Amber had gone to answer a ring of her doorbell and had found Odette, heavily veiled and dramatically costumed, on her front doorstep. It turned out that she was quite literally dressed to kill. She had in the end produced a small nickel-plated revolver and suggested that, as the two women who had been most grossly wronged by my father, they should go to his house in Regent's Park together in order to shoot him.

"And then she let you take the pistol away from her," said my father.

"How on earth did you know that?" Amber had asked, and he had laughed and said that he knew Odette.

Amber Reeves had indeed had no trouble at all in talking Odette out of her project, explaining to her that the British police had little understanding of either *crimes passionels* or unlicensed firearms. She had persuaded her to hand the elegant little weapon over, and later in the day she had taken it to the police station up at the top end of the street where she had turned it in with the story that she had found it while out walking on Hampstead Heath. "And to think that she has the nerve to call me a comedian," my father said when Amber had completed her account of this episode.

But although he took it lightly enough at the time, he repaid Odette in her own coin three years later, trading one fantasy killing for another when he murdered her by proxy as the ebullient woman around whom his novel *Apropos of Dolores* turns. But he was mellowing, and his retaliation for her low blow, however she may have felt about it, is genial rather than spiteful.

There are those who would insist that my father spent the twelve years that were left to him when he was done with the first two volumes of his *Experiment in Autobiography* in vain regret. He is said to have been haunted by his awareness that even though his essential message was becoming more timely and more urgent by the hour, fewer and fewer people were reading him. That he didn't enjoy aging at a moment in which things in general were going terribly wrong is not to be denied, but I think that the dark tone of most of his later work had a more immediate origin in his personal experience. His faith in reason received a challenge that he found himself at a loss to deal with.

I have already recorded that when my father left Russia after having had his interview with Stalin he went to spend a month in Estonia with Moura Budberg. Her plans for this visit had been idyllic: they were to be off by themselves for thirty days in a lakeside summer cottage that Moura had known since her girlhood, enjoying the tranquil pleasures of a setting very much like that in which they had first met in 1914. But in the event, the meeting was to have the flavour of a confrontation.

Moura had not gone into Russia with my father. She had told him that it would be impossible for her to go there with him. Her situation was, she had said, still very much what it had been back in 1920, and even though her arch-enemy Zinoviev was now in bad trouble himself, and no longer to be feared, there were still apparatchiks in the NKVD who looked upon her as a piece of unfinished business. If she were rash enough to put herself within their reach, she might be arrested at any time and dealt with summarily as a previously condemned fugitive. She would be in luck if it ended with her being sent to a labour camp; it was more likely that she would be shot out of hand as soon as her identity had been established. My father took it for granted that she was telling the truth and naturally enough agreed with her when she said that she could not go to Moscow with him. He consequently took another companion along on the trip, my Russian-speaking half-brother George Philip, who was then thirty-three years old.

Arriving in the country under the aegis of its Foreign Minister, Litvinov, my father was made much of by the Soviet authorities on each side of his Kremlin interview. They intelligently gave him a number of parties that were plausibly literary, informal, and convivial. At them he met and talked with a representative sample of those native writers of the day who had managed to find some way or other of coming to terms with the Soviet machine and remaining in production. It included, very much to my father's surprise, a considerable number of men and women who had no hesitation in introducing themselves to him in front of whoever it might be as dear friends of Moura's. He was never given as much as a hint by any of them that she might be under a cloud or in any way dangerous to know. His feeling became one of bewilderment and shock when he realised, and had it confirmed to him by Gip, who could keep his end up in a Russian conversation, that these friends of Moura's were talking of her as someone with whom they were frequently in touch. They saw her whenever she came to Moscow. It hadn't been long since her last visit, and they expected to be seeing her again soon. Discussing each new discovery as they made it, and putting the pieces of the jigsaw puzzle together one by one, Gip and my father presently had a clear picture. Moura had been in Moscow not just once since 1931, but several times. She was visiting Russia annually, and sometimes getting there at intervals of as little as three months. All that she had told my father about her situation *vis-à-vis* the Russian authorities had to be untrue. She was crossing the Soviet frontiers all the time, and circulating with impunity when on Russian soil. There was only one circumstance in which anyone with her record could move between the two worlds and within Russia as openly as she was doing: her movements had to be made with the knowledge and consent of the secret police. She had to be a Russian agent in good standing.

As soon as he came within sight of this conclusion my father was compelled to consider its implications. The most obvious of them had to be that she had been planted on him just as she had been planted upon Gorky. She would almost certainly have been under the orders of her controller when she came to seek him out in England after Gorky had decided to go home. Her employers would have wanted to outfit her with some plausible motive for moving from Sorrento to London. It came to him with a sickening thrust that the piece of candour with which she had won Gorky's absolute confidence could have been nothing more than an astutely concocted double bluff in which she had been coached. *Yes, yes,* Gorky must have been counted on to say to anyone who tried to denounce her to him as a police spy, *I have known all about that for a long time. She has been absolutely frank with me from the very beginning. She warned me why she had been placed in my household. We are friends in the truest sense.* And her trick of laying all the cards on the table had been played on him just as it had been played on Gorky. When she had told him exactly what her position was when they were briefly in Moscow together in 1920, he had been tremendously moved by the frankness and courage with which she had made the admission. She had somehow managed to make her humiliating confession into an absolutely convincing display of integrity.

But when my father at last came face to face with Moura in Estonia, the hardest thing for him to deal with was that she could still work that magic. Spy or no, Moura was Moura, and in spite of all that he had learned about her double dealing, her physical and emotional holds upon him were as strong as ever. Had she been anyone else she might have alienated him by offering him denials or excuses. But that was not her way. She admitted to the truth of every count in his indictment. She had never once been in control of her life since the Germans had caught her spying for the Russian military authorities and sentenced her to death in 1916. From then she had done what the realities of each new situation had required of her. What had happened to her had been no more and no less than what happens to people during revolutions and after them. Not to do what has to be done at such times is to elect not to survive.

My father tried to make Moura concede that there were things that could not be done in any circumstances—things so utterly ignoble that it would be preferable to die than to live with the knowledge that one had been a party to them. Moura had laughed at him when he said so, and told him that as a biologist he had to know that survival was the first law of life. For the species, yes, my father told her, but for the conscious human individual, no. She looked at him across a wide gulf, but forgave him his unwillingness to take her point. He had never known what it was to be absolutely helpless. What she had learned above everything else from what she had been through was that until one had been so badly damaged physically as to be beyond repair, one more day of life was worth whatever it might cost. Anything might happen in the course of another twenty-four hours. Here she was, with him, and they would soon be back in England. She had paid the going price for those things. He would be foolish to press her to say what it had been, even more foolish to try to guess at it. There was, in her view, nothing to be gained by raking over dead ashes, and she was not about to let him force her to relive episodes that she was doing her best to put behind her. If he wanted to go on being her lover, he would have to take her on her own terms, the first of which was that all her skeletons should stay in the dark in the cupboards in which she had put them. If he wanted plain dealing and nothing held back, he would have to look for some other woman.

Long before they left Estonia it had become apparent to my father that he would indeed have to break with Moura if he was to prevent his private life from becoming an ongoing refutation of all that he publicly stood for. What was truly appalling to him about this realisation was that it was as clear to him that he couldn't even contemplate actually doing such a thing—no matter what Moura might have done, no matter what she might still be doing, it was quite simply not a possibility that he should give her up.

I don't think that the effect that this discovery had upon my father can be overrated. My half-brother George Philip is a uniquely competent witness in that domain. He had come to understand my father very well in the years after Jane's death, but while they were in Moscow a genuine rapport had been established between them. Gratitude had something to do with it: my father's feeling was that had his oldest son not been there to see him through it, the experience that Moura's obliquity had let him in for might well have been a knockdown blow. But a more solid basis for their coming together was provided by their similarities in looks, temperament, and outlook, and by the fact that Gip had become the biologist that my father had once aspired to be. Whatever those things add up to, it remains true that after Gip had supported my father through that Moscow ordeal he was more completely in his confidence, and more in tune with his thinking, than any other man had ever been, or ever would be. I have it from him that he is convinced that despite all outward appearances to the contrary, my father was bothered to the end of his days by his inability to come up with a rationale for the continuance of his relationship with Moura. It distressed him almost beyond measure to have to admit to himself that his reason had no voice at all in determining so vital a matter as the nature of his principal association.

No word of my father's Moscow discoveries ever became public property, and when the liaison was given a form of social recognition in 1935, the occasion was assumed to be an unclouded one. The company that assembled to do them honour at a dinner given at the Quo Vadis restaurant in Soho included Maurice Baring, who had introduced them to each other in 1914, Violet Hunt, Max Beerbohm, Lady Lavery, Lady Cunard, Enid Bagnold, Harold Nicolson, David Low, and many others of the success-and-somebody London set. Moura was generally perceived at that time as a great beauty who had just passed her prime, and I was among those who saw her in that light. I find the photographs that insist that she was a plain woman who dressed dowdily so many inexplicable mysteries, and cannot forget my first breath-taking sight of her as she sat talking to my father in the garden at Easton Glebe one day in 1931. Her fatalism enabled her to radiate an immensely reassuring serenity, and her good humour made her a comfortable rather than a disturbing presence: I always looked forward eagerly to my next meeting with her, and remember my last with pleasure. I believed unquestioningly in her *bona fides,* and had never a doubt but that without her warmth, affection, and calm stoicism behind him, my father would have been a gloomier and more pessimistic man in the years that lay between his seventieth birthday and his death. Whenever I saw them together I felt sure that they were truly happy.

In the last good years before he began to die my father was as easy to misread as Moura was: he was open and genial as he had never been before, and he took an innocent pleasure in his contentment and well being. He had formed his personal style in the first ten years of the century, and he came through the late thirties and into the forties in the guise of an Edwardian big shot, neatly tailored and well-hatted, with homburgs with braided brims in wintertime and spotless Panamas in the height of summer. He wore beautifully made shoes on his tiny feet; and his wallets, of dark-blue leather, and such accessories as his gold cigar cutter, were the best that money could buy, though not the most expensive. He was a good deal over the weight that a man of his height should have been carrying, but he never appeared to be fat. His buoyant carriage, and something compact in his appearance, made him look light rather than heavy. David Low saw him as someone who was always on tiptoe, poised for takeoff, and his caricatures almost always caught his air of alertness and vitality. It was difficult to remember his age, and I never thought of him as being old until he came back from Australia at the beginning of 1939, when he was in his seventy-third year.

While much of my father's energy was at this time consumed in the simple business of living an active and amusing life, and as much again in producing the five full-length novels, the three novellas, and the eight political tracts varying from pamphlet to book length that he managed to complete and publish between 1935 and the end of 1940, the greater part of it was burned away in the search that I have already mentioned, for the final achievement that would go into the record as the essence of what he had stood for throughout his career. He thought for a time that he had found it in a project for creating a new world encyclopedia, a compendium of the entirety of human knowl-

147

edge, but he saw before too long that the technology for the storage and retrieval systems that such a thing would require was still lacking, and that its time had not yet come. In the end he found what he was looking for without knowing it: the solution to the problem presented itself to him as something that common sense required him to do.

When the long awaited war between Fascism and the democracies at last broke out in September 1939, my father was in Stockholm, where he had gone to give an address to a meeting of the PEN Club that did not, in the event, take place. On his return to England three weeks later, he found that a correspondence on the subject of war aims had sprung up in *The Times*. He jumped into it, and, after writing one letter to that newspaper couched in what he soon saw to be a vague rhetoric, almost immediately followed it up with another in more concrete terms. In his second letter he set out a rough draft for a modernised version of the Bill of Rights embodied in the Constitution of the United States. The War, he suggested, would be worth fighting if it was to end with a declaration by the victors that these were the inalienable rights of all men.

This second letter might have been no more than a damp squib fizzing off momentarily in the gathering darkness if the proposal that it contained had not struck a responsive chord in the mind of the science correspondent of *The Daily Herald,* Ritchie Calder. He persuaded his editor to give the issue of a universal bill of rights one full page in every month for as long as it might take to give the concept a negotiable form. This offer does not now seem to have been overly generous, but it at least promised the certainty of a continuity of debate—a thing that the then rabidly conservative editors of *The Times* had declined to provide, on the grounds that the idea of a bill of rights had to be some kind of socialist trap. With that continuity assured, it was possible to recruit a drafting committee whose members could reasonably be asked to attend meetings and devote time to the project.

My father was originally to have been both the chairman of the drafting committee and the editor of the *Herald*'s Rights of Man page. But when, a few days before the committee's first meeting, a vitriolic article appeared there over his signature in which he gave full vent to his feelings about the fact that Neville Chamberlain and Lord Halifax, the chief architects of the policy of appeasement, were remaining in office to prosecute the war, threats of resignations induced him to step down in favour of someone with a cooler head and less obvious political affiliations. The member chosen to replace him as the committee's chairman, though not as editor of the page, was a lawyer and former Lord Chancellor, Lord Sankey, so that what my father was campaigning for from then on, and what the committee at length produced, has gone into the record as *The Sankey Declaration of the Rights of Man.* But after this shaky beginning it was my father more than anyone else, even the indefatigable Ritchie Calder, who drove the committee on, keeping it at work and the public debate alive. He felt an overwhelming need to get a substantial document, one that would seem neither tentative nor specifically western on paper and on record before the strange period of inaction that had followed the rapid gobbling up of Poland should come to an end. He felt reasonably certain that the renewal of the fighting, when it came, would very quickly push matters of principle off into the background in favor of the more vital interest of survival from day to day. And he was worried, too, by signs of demoralisation on the part of some of the members of the committee (it included, in addition to my father and Lord Sankey, Lord Horder, Sir Norman Angell, Miss Margaret Bondfield, Sir Richard Gregory, Mrs. Barbara Wootton, Sir John Boyd Orr, Francis Williams, and Ritchie Calder) who began to feel that they were building a sand castle in the face of a rising tide. As the reader is unlikely to have heard anything of the well-thought-out and even impressive document that was finally brought into being, he may suppose that the feelings of these doubters, and the anxieties of my father's insomniac nights, were justified in the end. But that is not the case. The committee was truly representative of the British middle ground of opinion, and the debate in the pages of *The Daily Herald* drew in a wide range of people who addressed themselves to the issues constructively and at a high level of seriousness. Something well worth while had emerged from the welter of argument for this and that specific point, and before the so-called phoney war came to an end, my father got his document: an unambiguous statement of a particular thing that the ordinarily reasonable Englishman thought his country ought to be fighting to establish as part of the common law of the nations.

And that is what it was, thrillingly enough, taken for all over the world. The preliminary discussions and the text of the Declaration were extensively reported and commented upon in at least twenty-nine countries, among them Italy and Germany. Mussolini's *Popolo d'Italia,* rather surprisingly, ran the text of the Declaration on its front

page, and the German State radio, possibly less so, attacked it in a
series of broadcasts put out at the rate of one every night for a week.
But while it had its resonance throughout the western world, it set up
much more important reverberations outside the parish boundaries
of the Atlantic and Mediterranean societies. My father had been struck
by Sun Yat-sen's failure to win the Chinese people to support the new
constitution of 1911, and he had always felt that this disaster could
be attributed mainly to the Chinese leader's reliance on the political
language of western democracy. He reached a constituency of students and educated men, but he failed to move the Chinese people.
With that debacle in mind, my father insisted on rejecting the translations of the Declaration prepared for use in the eastern countries by
various members of the London School of Oriental Studies in favour
of vernacular versions of the text produced by working journalists
from the countries concerned who were in the business of com-
municating with popular audiences. As my father was also known to
be pressing to have the liquidation of the European colonial systems
recognised as a secondary war aim at that time, these vernacular texts
were well received by radicals and nationalist students in India and in
the Southeast Asian countries. These threshings and winnowings of
fundamental democratic ideas did not die down when the dramatic
successes of the German offensives of the spring and early summer
of 1940 drove such matters from the minds of most Europeans. They
were pursued with renewed vigour wherever the evident collapse of
the old European order was seen to be creating hopes of imminent
liberation. The idea of a codification of human rights seemed more
rather than less important to the intellectuals in the colonial territories who knew that they would soon have to decide what kinds of
society they were going to create for themselves when the war ended.
And so it came about that the work of what had seemed for a time to
be one of the phoney war's more fatuous drawing-room committees
did not end when the German bombs rained down on Rotterdam. Its
true conclusion came much later, when an overwhelming third-world
sentiment in favour of such a thing compelled the victorious Allies to
incorporate a Declaration of Human Rights in the Charter of the
United Nations. But by then my father was dead.

Towards the end of the thirties he had seemed to be indestructible.
He had learned to live with his diabetes, and the diet that his complaint forced upon him had led to a marked improvement in his
general health. When he set out for Australia in the summer of 1938

he was looking unusually well and was in good spirits. He had been asked to go there to deliver an address at the meeting for the Australian and New Zealand Association for the Advancement of Science, and it had pleased him to find that he was still being taken seriously in such circles. It had always irked him that he was considered not quite respectable by the English scientific community. Disaster overtook him on what was to have been his last day in the Australian capital. Because he was unaware of the peculiarities of Canberra's rather special climate, he had gone to sleep close to an open window, with no more than a linen sheet over him. During the night the temperature, which had been in the upper eighties when he went to bed, had dropped to below freezing point. By the time that the cold woke him he was already chilled through and through, and by the following evening he was down with viral pneumonia. He was seventy-three, and this lowering complaint hit him hard. He was not fit to face the journey home until after the new year, and when he reached England he looked as if he still had a long way to go before he would be fully recovered.

His remaining reserves were exhausted in the summer of 1940, when he undertook an extended lecture tour in the United States. At that point Americans in general were not eager to be drawn into another European war, and as he was offering them a presentation in which he told them that it was their fight, and that they ought to get into it in order to take it over, he ran into some open hostility and more indifference. As my father's argument in favour of an early American takeover of the Allied leadership was based on the thesis that the French and British establishments then in charge were fighting less to defeat the Nazis than to put the clock back to the Europe of Nations of 1914, he was even less popular with the British Embassy in Washington than he was in the isolationist heartland. To counter the effect of his appearances, the British ambassador initiated a whispering campaign against him that added somewhat to his difficulties. On top of it all, it was the year in which Wendell Willkie challenged FDR, and he had a hard time competing with the presidential election for public attention. Those who were fond of him were shocked by the state he was in when he returned to London. He was worn and emaciated, and his hands had become those of a very old man. He no longer filled his clothes, which hung on him like reach-me-downs. He had undergone an abrupt diminishing and no longer had the physical presence of an important man. A number of his younger admirers who came to see him at this time, either because they were troubled by the course that the war seemed to be taking or because they were disturbed by what had happened to them in the services, were upset when they found themselves face to face with a man who was obviously a survivor from the past. My father was as well aware of his deterioration as anyone, and he did not enjoy the progressive stages of his decline. The diabetes that he had been able to keep in check for many years by dieting now took a graver turn, and he began to be attacked by a variety of systemic disorders to which it had opened the door. A progressive breakdown of liver function was paced by the development of a cancer that presently proved to be malignant.

He was not a man to deceive, and he was told what his situation was, and what his prospects were. Initially he accommodated himself to the facts of his case with courage and a certain gloomy dignity, but then his disease played him false. A remission gave him an unlooked-for reprieve that undid him. When the term that had been set upon his chances of survival had passed, leaving him feeling better than he had done for months, he became certain that there had been a mistaken diagnosis. Liver trouble, nasty, but of a kind that had never killed anybody, had been confused with cancer. He was in no danger of dying, and might live on for ten years or more.

When the remission ended, as capriciously as it had begun, he knew that there had been no mistake and that this time he was for it. Many who find themselves in this situation can deal with it without despairing, feeling that they have lived their lives and done what they had it in them to do. My father was denied that comfort by his pervading sense that he had not quite managed to put the capstone on his career. His final statement had not been made.

For part of the time in which my father lay dying in his coldly elegant house looking out over Regent's Park I was working as a sub-editor in the newsroom of the British Broadcasting Corporation in Broadcasting House, and living in the mews flat down at the end of his back garden, a place that he called "Mr. Mumford's" and which had many things in it that I had first seen at Easton Glebe. While this arrangement lasted I would look in to see him almost every day. I would come in and find him sitting with a light rug over his knees, dozing at what had been his worktable, or, on sunny days, basking in the presence of a variety of potted plants in a big armchair that had been put out for him on the glassed-in balcony at the back of the house. We were sharing silences rather than talking by then. He was already extremely weak, and he had developed a habit of husbanding his energies through long drowsy periods in which he seemed almost comatose. When he wished to give his full attention to something or somebody he seemed to come back to the surface as if from a great depth. I would sit with him for a few minutes, for half an hour, for an hour, in the hope of catching his interest and drawing him back. I wanted to have his full attention for just as long as it would take me to clear his mind of an impression—I do not care, even now, to think too much about who had put it into his mind or why—that I had been got hold of by members of a pro-Nazi conspiracy who had somehow or other entrenched themselves in Broadcasting House. These people were, he had been told, blackmailing me in some way and forcing me into some mysteriously discreditable line of conduct for some arcane ulterior purpose, the nature of which I have never been able to discover. This nightmare cobweb of lies had fallen between me and my father while the flying-bomb attack on London was at its height, and it remained upon our faces through all the time that the assault lasted, through the more dreamlike time of the big V-2 rockets, and on after that, until the war had receded into the Pacific to leave London in shocked and stunned silence.

At first my father had seemed to be too ill to be troubled with the necessary explanations and reassurances. Then he had his remission, and it seemed wrong to break in on his euphoria with such stuff. After that, when he had learned that he had no hope after all, it became obvious that the moment for clarifications was never going to come. Sitting beside him one day, at once close to and utterly remote from him, and thinking him asleep, I fell into a passion of misery and buried my face in my hands. How long my spasm of pain lasted I have no way of knowing, but when its intensity slackened I suddenly felt that I was being watched. I looked up to find my father's blue eyes fixed on me with the light of his full intelligence in them. We stared at each other for an instant, until he said faintly, "I just don't understand you . . ." with that light fading from his eyes as he spoke. He had turned himself off, as it were, and had withdrawn into that absence in which he waited for his coming death. The last chance of communication had gone, and there was not to be another.

My father died on the afternoon of the thirteenth of August 1946, a few weeks before reaching his eightieth birthday. His body was cremated three days later, and rather more than a year after that I chartered a boat named the *Deirdre,* owned by Captain Miller of Poole in Dorset. My half-brother George Philip Wells came down from London bringing the ashes with him, and we went out to scatter them on the sea at a point we had picked out on a line between Alum Bay on the Isle of Wight and St. Alban's Head on the Dorset shore. That was our intention. But when the *Deirdre* cleared the narrow mouth of Poole Harbour we found that the wind coming up the Solent from the South West beyond St. Alban's Head was freshening. The tide was just turning and beginning to run out into the face of the wind. A wind blowing over a contrary tide is a recipe for short steep seas, and the *Deirdre* was soon pitching nastily.

The idea of burying my father at sea had come to my half-brother during the memorial service at the crematorium. A passage from the last chapter of his novel *Tono-Bungay,* "Night and the Open Sea," had then been read with telling effect, and while listening to its description of the book's narrator taking his newly launched torpedo-boat de-stroyer down the Thames and out into the North Sea to run its speed trials, my half-brother had thought, yes, that will be it, that will be the right thing to do. "We make and pass," the passage concludes by saying. "We are all things that make and pass, striving upon a hidden mission, out to the open sea."

The idea had seemed romantic and suitable when it was put to me, and I had been for it. But its defects soon became clear in that condi-tion of wind and tide. My half-brother and I both became quiet and thoughtful. Captain Miller became entirely expressionless as he kept his boat bunting into the waves. We could all see that as soon as we were out of the shelter of Purbeck Island and in the open Solent things were going to be a lot wetter and much more uncomfortable. While we were still abeam of the two chalk stacks called Old Harry and Old Harry's Wife that stand below the white cliffs between Swanage and Studland, my father's ashes went into the sea. The wind took them off as a long veil that struck the very pale green water with a hiss. The *Deirdre* wallowed as Captain Miller put her about, and I had a moment of agony. He was really gone now, and I was never, ever going to get that stupid business about blackmail and the pro-Nazi conspirators in the BBC straightened out with him. I was surprised by the intense bitterness this thought aroused in me, and by the discov-ery that I could feel so strongly about the matter when he was no longer in a position to care about anything at all.

Chapter VIII

> . . . it was, I know, only the accepted code of virtue
> and discretion that prevented her destroying her
> marriage certificate and me, and so making a clean
> sweep of her matrimonial humiliation. I suppose I
> must inherit something of the moral stupidity that
> could enable her to make a holocaust of every little
> personal thing she had of him. There must have
> been presents made by him as a lover, for example
> —books with kindly inscriptions, letters perhaps, a
> flattened flower, a ring, or suchlike gage. She kept
> her wedding ring of course, but all the
> others she destroyed.
>
> —Tono-Bungay

To understand my father and his
personal history one must look
back beyond his origins to those of his parents. Things that had
happened to them before he was born had made them the people he
knew, and what he saw them do and heard them say to each other left
him marked for life.

My grandfather, Joseph Wells, was born in Kent in 1827, in a
cottage that belonged to the Penshurst Place estate. His father, who
was also named Joseph Wells, had also been born on the estate, and
had worked in the Penshurst gardens all his life. He had made a start
as a gardener's boy at the age of twelve, and had climbed steadily up
to the top of that particular tree. He became head gardener soon after
his employer, Philip Shelley Sidney, had become the first Baron De
L'Isle in 1835. His promotion had put him into the head gardener's
cottage, a comfortable small house standing at the southeastern corner of the collegiate spread of late-medieval, Tudor, and sixteenth-
and eighteenth-century buildings that together constitute the great
house. It was here, across the kitchen and stable courts from the main
buildings, that my grandfather grew up with his older brothers,

Charles-Edward, Henry, Edward, and William, and his sisters, Lucy, Elizabeth, and Hannah.

There were advantages and disadvantages to being brought up as part of such an establishment. It cast a shadow, but it also gave protection. I am sure that if anyone had ever asked my great-grandfather what he thought of his employers, he would have replied that the Sydneys had always been very good to him, and that they were people who could be counted upon to do the right thing by their tenants, their property, and their employees. This is not to say that he would have been unaware that the estate had been entangled in chancery suits at the time of his birth, and that the house had then been falling into ruin. And he would also have had his own ideas about the rights and wrongs of a man being made a peer of the realm as a reward for marrying a daughter of the King's mistress, and about the severity of the sanctions that were likely to fall on any cottager who showed signs of not knowing his place. But the evidence of his long career shows that at some early stage he had considered his chances and decided on a policy of making the most of what Penshurst had to offer and of never being seen to quarrel with his bread and butter. And at the end of his day he would have felt that he had done the right thing for his family by toeing the line. As head gardener he was a figure in the society of the place, ranking only slightly lower than the steward and the housekeeper in the hierarchy of the hundred or so indoor and outdoor servants making up the household, and he was "looked up to" for a great many miles round about. He had bettered himself by raising his standing from that of estate labourer to that of upper servant, and by so doing had been able to give his older children winning chances of consolidating the gains he had made, or of further bettering themselves. He had started some of them on the next stage of the upward climb by helping them to move on into the fringes of independence as shopkeepers and tenant farmers. I am sure he felt that he was also doing well by the youngest of his boys when, having taught him all he knew in the Penshurst gardens, he found him a place as an under-gardener on a nearby property that that had become famous in gardening circles.

According to the account of this matter that appears in my father's autobiography, my grandfather's first employer, the owner of a property called Redleaf that marches with the Penshurst estate on its northwestern boundary, was a kindly older man of liberal and aesthetic tastes who took a fatherly interest in his new employee. My father's story is that the master lent his man books on botany and gardening so that he could study them in his spare time and improve himself. He goes on to say that my grandfather took these friendly gestures to mean that the owner of Redleaf was intending to do something for him if he showed signs of profiting from his studies, and that he came, later on, to feel that his employer's death in 1847 had lost him the chance of a start in life that would have changed everything for him.

The truth is rather different. The owner of Redleaf was a certain William Wells, a self-made man who had been known as "Tiger" Wells when he had been the hard-driving master of an East Indiaman at the start of his career. The nickname stayed with him when he went on from ship's captain to become a shipowner in business on his own account, and it followed him into Kent when he retired and settled down to live the life of a man of property and an art patron. His reputation as a rough customer was kept alive by the savagery with which he would rebuke tourists who came to his door to ask permission to see his gardens or his picture collection without first writing for leave to do so. His gardens were famous. With the aid of his extremely talented head gardener he had made what was then called an "American" garden, a thing inspired by the sketches and reports of the botanists who were exploring the Pacific Northwest of the United States. It was the first exotic wilderness garden to be created in England, and its unusual layout, and the number and variety of recent introductions from Asia and the Americas growing in it, began to attract widespread attention in the eighteen-twenties. It was put on the gardening map once and for all in 1839, when it was given the accolade of a very full description in Loudon's pioneering publication *The Gardener's Magazine.* Among the other things that Loudon records in his account of the place is that William Wells, the proprietor, had a head gardener named Joseph Wells. The details given make it quite clear that this was not my great-grandfather. The Joseph Wells in question had become head gardener at Redleaf some twelve years before my great-grandfather reached a similar eminence at Penshurst. However confusing it may be, what happened in 1843 was that the Joseph Wells who was head gardener at Penshurst put his son Joseph Wells into a place as under-gardener to William Wells's head man Joseph Wells. The romantic, and slightly ambiguous, story of the old employer's fatherly interest in his young namesake's future has to go.

The story of my grandfather's start in life seems to have been rather a sad one. My great-grandfather had put his son to work at Redleaf because it was a launching pad from the professional point of view. Its Joseph Wells was a gardener of distinction. His wilderness garden was not his only innovation. He had set another, more lasting fashion by exploiting an outcropping of Kentish ragstone on the property to make the first modern Alpine rock garden. He is also credited with having raised the first dwarf dahlias. He was obviously an able man with a good deal to teach, and if my grandfather had come away from Redleaf knowing half of what was to be learned there, he would have been off to a very good start indeed. But he was not of the stuff from which Victorian success stories were made. My father records his most vivid and readily available recollection of his Redleaf days. It has nothing to do with gardening, or of the man he was working with: ". . . in the summer, directly the day's work was over, my father would run, he told me once, a mile and more at top speed to the pitch at Penshurst to snatch half an hour at cricket before twilight made the ball invisible. . . ." However ready one may be to sympathise with the impatience of youth—my grandfather was at Redleaf from his sixteenth to his nineteenth years—it is a clock-watcher's memory. He didn't have his heart in the profession that his father had chosen for him. And, as is the way with the young, he believed that he had all the time in the world ahead of him. He would get down to the work and the studying and show them all what he was made of next year, or the year after. It escaped him that William Wells was failing until, suddenly, his employer was dead, the property was up for sale, and Joseph Wells, who was in his seventies, was retiring. There was no more time in hand, and the opportunity for getting in on the ground floor of the new gardening had gone.

This check seems to have meant a great deal to my grandfather. The year in which he found himself out of a job for the first time was the worst in a decade of increasingly acute depression known to social history as the Hungry Forties. The harvest failed and there was hunger in the cities. My grandfather later told my father that his chances had seemed so poor that winter as to make him think seriously of making a fresh start overseas. As two and a half million men and women left the country for just that reason during the decade, the probability is that my grandfather was having real difficulty in finding himself a job that had anything worthwhile to offer. But this makes it all the harder to understand what happened, again and again, when he was lucky enough to find himself a place. The line of work he was in, it should be remembered, was one in which personal references were all-important. Gardeners were *in service,* and anyone who hoped to work as a servant had to be able to produce references from former employers testifying to their competence, ability to live with other servants, sobriety, honesty, cleanliness, and reliability. When it came to an interview an applicant for a place could count on being asked how long he had stayed with his previous employer and why he had left him. Any candidate who showed up with a fistful of unenthusiastic or evasive recommendations, and a record of short stays and inexplicable movings on would be rejected automatically. But knowing that, my grandfather had walked into and out of at least three, and possibly four, places between the summer of 1847 and that of 1851. Then he was at Uppark in Sussex from June 1851 to May 1853, and at Shuckburgh Park in Warwickshire from April 1854 to August 1855. This record may only mean that my grandfather was feeling young and restless in these years, or that he was unlucky with his employers, but it does rather strongly suggest that he was looking for trouble. The story of his marriage begins during his stay at Uppark, and its opening chapters make it seem that he was by this time deeply committed to a compulsive search for personal disaster that had passed quite beyond his control.

My grandfather's arrival at such a very odd box as Uppark then was is consistent with such a search. The widowed Lady Fetherstonehaugh who lived there with her unmarried sister Frances Bullock was not one of the gentry. She had been the daughter of one of her husband's outdoor servants, the man who had been Sir Harry Fetherstonehaugh's poultry keeper, and ranger in charge of his deer park. As plain Mary Anne Bullock, Lady Fetherstonehaugh had been working for Sir Harry as a dairymaid when his eye first fell upon her. She was then eighteen, and he was in his seventy-first year. Sir Harry had always liked young women, and when he was in his thirties he had briefly had a promising young fifteen-year-old called Emmy Lyon in keeping. She had later become Lord Nelson's Emma Hamilton. A freethinker, womaniser, and hard-riding gentleman jockey in his day, Sir Harry had become something of a recluse after quarreling with the prince regent over the settlement of a wager. Sir Harry felt that he had been cheated by the prince, and was so outraged that he broke off all contact with his circle and the life he had been living. One morning, several years after he had withdrawn from society, he passed by the door of the model dairy in which Mary Anne Bullock was floating cream, looked in, saw her beautiful arms, liked her pleasant country face, and fancied her. He had paused for a word.

Whatever Sir Harry's original intentions may have been, the eventual outcome of the encounter was unexpected. Sir Harry courted Mary Anne Bullock, sent her into France for a year to learn polite manners and deportment, and married her on her return. By that time she was twenty and he was seventy-two. No good might have been foreseen as the result of this leap over class lines and a generation gap, but Sir Harry's young wife proved to be all that he had hoped, and perhaps rather more than that. The apparently mismatched pair lived happily together until he slid quietly out of this world and into the next in 1846, some months after he had reached the age of ninety-two.

Uppark stands by itself on high ground in the middle of an oddly out-of-the-way and empty piece of country walled off from the populous valley of the river Rother by the steep rise of the Harting Downs. Lady Fetherstonehaugh had been cold-shouldered by most of the county families while her husband was alive, and once Sir Harry was gone, very few of the gentry thought it worth their while to face the steep hills between them and the socially dubious household inhabiting the austerely beautiful house. It consisted of the ex-dairymaid and her younger sister, Miss Sutherland the chaperone, and the ambiguous steward, Mr. Weaver, who had been Sir Harry's valet, and who may, or again may not, have been an illegitimate child of some passage in his raffish years. When my grandfather found that he had become a member of this oddly constituted and physically isolated little society he must have realised that he was getting very near the end of the line so far as his gardening career was concerned. Even if he were to succeed in parting from Lady Fetherstonehaugh on good terms, a reference from such a source, however glowing, would hardly recommend him to a worthwhile place. It would be more than likely to do him harm, by raising the question of how it had come about that he had fallen so far and so fast after making a start at Penshurst and Redleaf. And at this point, when he had well and truly cornered himself, and had every reason to think hard before he made his next move, he walked off the job and got himself engaged to my grandmother while he was still unemployed.

Sarah Neal, who was some six years older than my grandfather, had started work at Uppark as Frances Bullock's lady's maid just under a year before my grandfather was taken on as head gardener by Mr.

Weaver. It was not a place that my grandmother had wanted to accept, and she put off her decision to go into it for as long as she possibly could, but once she had taken it she loved it. She found a friend in Fanny Bullock, and she hated to give in her notice when the shadow of the coming trouble that was to overwhelm her family forced her to do so in April 1853. It was some consolation to her that she did not have to go very far, no further than the next valley where her father, George Neal, kept the New Inn at Midhurst.

George Neal had called his daughter home because her mother had come to need night-and-day nursing. She had been ill for some time, but she had taken a turn for the worse on being told of the death of a sister. When my grandmother reached The New Inn she found that her mother was just as seriously ill as she had been told, but she was more concerned by her father's strange looks and incomprehensible behaviour. After a day or two, in which she came to realise that her mother was in fact dying, my grandmother decided that her father's distraught manner could be put down to feelings natural enough in the circumstances. She was consequently taken utterly by surprise when her father had a seizure and died within the space of a few hours at the end of August. Her mother at first seemed to be unmoved by the event, but on the day following her husband's funeral she went out of her mind. My grandmother was hit all the harder by her mother's transformation into a violently hostile stranger because of the situation in which she found herself. Her father was over his ears in debt when he died and as soon as they heard of his end, his creditors descended on the New Inn *en masse* in order to stake out their various claims upon his assets. My grandmother had to fend them off as best she could while making the funeral arrangements, looking after the mad woman, and caring for her twelve-year-old younger brother.

George Neal had been an easygoing, idle, and expansively sanguine man with a fixed habit of living beyond his means. This had been disastrously re-enforced in 1833 when he came into a legacy just large enough to give him a dangerous illusion that he was a man of substance who could afford to run into debt. Under this spell he had kept the Fountains Inn at Chichester in a lavish and gentlemanly way for seven years. He had then moved on to the New Inn at Midhurst, where in thirteen years he had never managed to get on top of the load of debt that he had brought with him. The strain of living with the knowledge that time was running out on him, and that he might be imprisoned by his creditors at any minute, accounted for the tense and distracted behaviour that had frightened my grandmother so much when she returned home from Uppark. They had also provided the substance of her mother's ravings after his death. The mad woman had equated her husband's burial with his imprisonment, and, considering her daughter to be the responsible party, had deluged her with abuse and attacked her a number of times for being so cruel as to have sent him away to be locked up.

My grandmother had a very sad and miserable time of it until her mother recovered her sanity, but while that brought her some relief, the ending of Mrs. Neal's tirades didn't mean that her physical condition was in any way improved. My grandmother now had to keep a deathwatch at her mother's bedside. She was also given a little respite at this point. Her father's creditors, however tough they may have been over the long haul, were not viciously inclined; and when they saw how things were, they backed off to wait until Mrs. Neal was also dead. They may have been a mite put out when she lasted through September and October and on into November, since they went into action with a certain brusque callousness as soon as the lady was gone, telling the solicitor acting for George Neal's pitiful estate that they could wait no longer for the winding-up. He gave my grandmother the bad news immediately after the funeral. I imagine that he found her difficult as well as embarrassing to deal with, since she still had no idea of the realities of her position. She was clinging to the idea that she might be able to persuade the landlords of the New Inn to let her take over her father's lease. When the lawyer told her that this was not a possibility, she told him that it *had* to be arranged so that she could give her brother a home until he was old enough to earn his own living. In an effort to jolt her into an understanding of what her chances were, the lawyer then let her know that she was technically a pauper, and that, strictly speaking, she had no claim to any of her father's or mother's possessions, even the most intimate. Everything in the New Inn, down to the last knickknack in the private parlour, belonged legally to the men who had been holding her father's notes for years. When, even then, my grandmother fought against admitting that her home was gone, she was braced by a harshly worded threat. If she hadn't the money to keep her brother elsewhere, he could be admitted to the Midhurst workhouse as a pauper. The following morning the agent for the brewers who owned the Inn came around to tell her that she was to be off the premises within twenty-four hours so that a new tenant could move in. Her world disintegrated. She had lost her father and mother, and her home, and she was alone in the world with nowhere to go, and with a boy who was not yet thirteen on her hands.

My grandfather had been addressing my grandmother as "My own, my dearest Sarah" since the end of 1852, but they were not officially engaged when she left Uppark in April 1853. My grandfather threw up his job there a month after she had gone, and made it the first business of his unemployment to follow her to the New Inn to settle this issue. When their understanding had been given formal recognition and blessed by George Neal, he had gone up into Gloucestershire to stay with his farmer brother Charles-Edward at Minsterworth while he looked for a new place. He hadn't found one, and was still out of work when word reached him of the appalling way that things were going with his intended. He hurried south to lend her what support he could. They were married seventeen days after her mother's death, on November 22, 1853. The difficulties of getting a special license in a hurry made it necessary for them to be joined together in an unfamiliar setting, at St. Stephen's, Coleman Street, in the City of London, among strangers. The improvised event did not come up to my grandmother's expectations of what a wedding should be. There had been "no preparation," she had been dressed in full mourning, not in bridal white, and she had not had a bridesmaid.

Between November 22, 1853, and January 1, 1854, my grandmother was engaged in a task that did not augur very well for this marriage. The product of her strange activity is now lodged in the Rare Book Room of the library of the University of Illinois at Champaign-Urbana, where it is described as her diary. This is not exactly what it is, though its second part, entered up in an old desk diary printed for use in the year 1835 certainly is a genuine day-to-day record of her life from January 1, 1854 onwards. What makes it unlike most diaries is that the entry for that day is not by any means the first in the volume. It comes after forty-seven pages of carefully edited extracts from earlier diaries covering the years 1845 through 1853. The original diaries from which these extracts were made have not survived, and it is legitimate to assume that they were destroyed when my grandmother had finished gutting them. There is, of course, nothing sinister in this procedure as such—a newly married woman might have a variety of reasons for wishing to suppress things that she had unguardedly committed to her private journals before she knew who

her husband was to be. But there is something a little special about
the edited version of my grandmother's selection from her premarital
diaries, it does not contain a single reference to my grandfather that
even suggests that she had ever had any regard for him at all. The only
hint at the nature of her feelings for the man who had just become
her husband that creeps into it is a highly ambiguous one that is
related to her father's death: The night he died he kissed me and his
last words were "Do not cry my child. I know you will have *one* who
will be good and kind to you!!!" It is, of course, arguable that these
three shriek marks need not mean anything very much, but the remainder of the document shows that it was my grandmother's habit
to put three of these signs in the place of a full stop at the end of
accounts of things said or done by my grandfather or his sisters that
struck her as especially outrageous or unfeeling. I am convinced that
they stand there to make some such comment as "How wrong poor
father was!" The entries that follow January I, 1854, lend support to
this reading. The remainder of the diary is less a record of day to day
events than an indictment. In it my grandmother sets down the origin
and the development of each and every one of her outstanding grievances against her husband, and grimly celebrates the anniversary of
the offence as it comes round. The nearest thing to an appreciative
reference to the poor man that I can remember finding in its pages
is one that says that she has had a happy day because he did her the
kindness of going to church with her. Collectively the entries make it
clear that she does not like him, that she cannot think of herself as his
partner, and that she looks on the marriage as a trap in which she has
been caught. And time does not improve matters. "Ten years tonight," she writes on August 31, 1863, "my poor father died from that
sad moment new troubles began for me and up to this time continue."

Six months later her oldest child, the much-loved girl named
Frances for Fanny Bullock, and always called Possy, died, and she was
given another anniversary to keep. "One year today my darling ill,"
she wrote on January 10, 1865. "But Oh! I ought to rejoice my sweet
girl in her innocence is removed from a world of sorrow. What happiness have I known as a wife? Morose unpleasant treatment spend
night after night alone my children in bed and I left to work work is
what woman is destined for man's slave." Her resentment of my
grandfather's behaviour wells up to drown the pain of her loss as
quickly in the case of her daughter as in that of her father. And the
theme is constant: all she has to endure has a single cause, her involve-

ment with my grandfather. He has failed her in all things, and she has nothing to thank him for. The document as a whole makes it plain that this marriage was already on the rocks in its fortieth day, and that my grandmother was determined to keep it there.

My grandfather was not actually unemployed at the time that the marriage took place—he had found a job of sorts at Trentham in Staffordshire, but it was almost worse than nothing as it didn't provide living quarters for a married man. My grandparents consequently parted within a few hours of the ceremony, and while he went back up into the Midlands she was left to make the rounds of his relatives in the south. The couple had to live apart until April. My grandfather then found himself something that seemed ideal, the Shuckburgh place, where he was to be head gardener with ten men under him. He was to have twenty-five shillings a week, a good wage for the period, and occupancy of what my grandmother was to look back on as "a pretty cottage with a dear little garden." My grandfather's new employer was the only drawback. He was a hard drinker and a bully, whose wife and children lived in constant fear of what he might do in his next bout of violent ill temper. He was notorious for his quarrels with his people, and my grandfather had his first set-to with him within a month of his arrival. That he was able to stay on there for as long as he did is testimony to some residual spark of decency in his apoplectic employer's make-up. My grandmother was visibly pregnant by the late autumn of 1854 and the child came in January. The baby girl won the family a few more months of grudging consideration, but my grandfather was given his marching orders in July, and in August he had to go.

Sarah Wells, as she now was, spent September 1855 doing the rounds of her husband's relatives once again while he travelled about, unsuccessfully offering himself and his deterrent record to the cold-eyed scrutiny of a succession of possible employers. In October, when it must have been quite clear to him that he had come to the end of the line so far as his gardening career was concerned, a cousin, a certain George Wells, offered him a proposition. He could have a home of his own, with a nice little business to finance it, for no more than fifty pounds down and the reversion to the first hundred pounds of any capital sum that he might inherit from his father. For that he was to have the leasehold of the business premises, consisting of the shop and upper part known as Atlas House, at 47 High Street, Bromley, along with the stock and good will of the retail china shop that his cousin had been running there. With winter closing in, his small reserve of cash running low, and his family's patience showing signs of strain, my grandfather was bound to find this proposal irresistible. On October 23, 1855, he moved into Atlas House with his wife and his baby daughter.

"And so they were caught," says my father in his autobiography as he comes to this point. He seems to be following my grandmother's diaries when he goes on to put forward the view that George Wells had seen the green in my grandfather's eye and had saddled him with a hopeless business that he had no other way of unloading and was longing to get off his hands. He piles on the agony, and makes the new departure even harder on my grandmother than it actually was. "My mother," he says, "with one infant in arms moved into 47 High Street in time to bring my eldest brother into the world there." Since the older of his two brothers was not in fact born until 1857, this must be considered an odd way of putting it. The mistake points, I think, to a subliminal awareness on his part that my grandfather was doing my grandmother some kind of mischief at this time that involved a more or less brutal exploitation of her vulnerability as a woman, or, if not that, as the particular kind of woman that she was.

My grandmother seems to have made up her mind that she was going to be a lady's maid rather early in life. Some of my father's biographers have suggested that she had been "schooled to be a lady" and that she was disappointed and hurt when circumstances forced her to go into service, but this is a mistake that comes of noting that she spent three years at Miss Riley's school in Chichester without asking too many questions about the kind of school it was, or considering the meaning of what she did when she was through there. Miss Riley's was not a school that young ladies went to; its pupils were the daughters of local tradesmen who were going to have to earn a living if they didn't get married. My grandmother went on from Miss Riley's to be an apprentice, first to a dressmaker and then to a hairdresser. As the daughter of a man who kept a public house, and not a particularly elegant one, she belonged to precisely the class of socially indeterminate betwixt-and-betweeners from which lady's maids usually came. The job was one that no girl from a labourer's cottage or unskilled workman's home could hope to fill successfully; it needed a multitude of skills that simply weren't to be learned on the wrong side of the poverty line. The lady's maid was expected to be ready to wait on her lady from the time of her first waking in the morning until she went to bed at night, no matter how late that might be. She had to be at hand to dress, undress, and re-dress her lady, and to do and re-do her hair just as often as her social program called upon her to change her costume. And when she wasn't actually waiting on her lady, the lady's maid had to look after her clothes, mending and altering them as required; to make, mend, and wash her underclothes; to trim, retrim, and sometimes make her hats; to make up such face creams and lotions as she might need; and to do much else besides in the way of ironing, pressing, and cleaning. However unattractive the degree of servitude involved may seem from the contemporary point of view, the job had one very great attraction for such a person as my grandmother. The girl who got it participated to an astonishing extent in the life of her lady, and vicariously lived an upper-class existence as long as she held it. The lady's maid spent most of her day in the attractive and comfortable world above stairs, and if she could hold her end up in light conversation without presuming, she would often be treated as a companion by a kindly mistress, both when she was at home and when she was travelling. Her real moments of glory came when she took her place in a carriage with her mistress, or when she sat down in her lady's dressing room to wait for her to come to bed—no other servant but the housekeeper could sit for as long as an instant in the presence of her employer in public or in any one of the family rooms above stairs.

But in the end it was a possible future that made the post worthwhile. If she could win and keep the confidence of her lady, the lady's maid had good chances of becoming the housekeeper in due season. That promotion would make her manageress of the whole household, and her mistress' deputy in all matters concerning the practical side of running the establishment. The lady's maid had no lien on the housekeeper's room, the keys of the store cupboards and the linen rooms, and she lacked the power to hire and fire female staff, but promotions from the one level to the other took place often enough to give her a reasonable expectation of the succession. And when it came to her turn to retire she could, if she had managed to make the upward move, count on the enjoyment of a small pension and a rent-free estate cottage until she died. The career, rewarding enough to draw a great many who, like my grandmother, had limited ambitions and a need for a rock to cling to, had only one string attached to it: the woman who wanted to succeed in it had to turn her back on the world of love and marriage; the lady's maid could not, as a rule, expect to have a life of her own.

It might be going too far to say that my grandmother had never been one of the marrying kind, but it does rather look as if she had formed a resolution to do without that sort of thing at about the time that she went to Uppark. It was a resolve that many ordinarily constituted young men and women were coming to under the pressure of circumstances in those hard times. Forty out of every hundred British women between the ages of twenty and forty were then unmarried, and three million of both sexes who were members of this age group were in the same condition—a formidable figure in relation to a total population of a little more than eighteen million. My grandmother will have felt the force of the most cogent of the arguments for avoiding marriage that were obviously in so many of these people's minds, that to be poor and to have children was to be wretched most of all, and she would also, I think, have found support for thinking so in her own inclinations. A number of the edited entries from her early diaries suggest that something in her upbringing had left her with a predisposition to mistrust men, and that her first brush with a man had left her with unpleasant memories. Even if she hadn't had a dislike for the mechanical aspects of sex, she had very much disliked finding herself in a position in which she had to trust a man.

And then, as she turned thirty, she fell in love with Uppark. Before she went there she had been in two beginner's posts with families belonging to the minor gentry, but although she had done well in them, and had been liked and generously treated by her employers, her experiences in those places hadn't given her any clear idea of what being an upper servant in a great house was going to be like. She must have felt that she was entering a new world when she got to Uppark, one beyond petty economies and free from all uncertainty, in which she would lack for nothing, and be cooked for, waited upon, and splendidly housed for as long as she was able to give satisfaction.

When I say "splendidly housed" it may seem that I am introducing a somewhat unlikely consideration, but I am quite certain that it was one that carried weight with the girl from the New Inn. Uppark was originally built, regardless of expense, by an exceedingly rich man at a time, 1685–1690, before lightness had come in as an architectural virtue, and when evident weight and substance was still appreciated as an element in the grand style. Its meanest features—as, for instance, the back stairs that my grandmother had to climb every day in her comings and goings between the downstairs offices and her mistress's bedroom and dressing room on the first floor—consequently have a degree of solidity and strength that seems positively Roman. Even in her comparatively tiny dormer-window attic bedroom my grandmother would have felt that she was being nobly sheltered. And, as the edited portion of her diary shows, and was meant to show, she was not only happy to be working in that splendid setting, she also positively loved the sense of position she was given by doing so. When she accompanied her ladies to the few great houses in the county in which they were received, she was made welcome in their housekeeper's rooms as an upper servant in good standing, as a below-stairs somebody. "Visited Lord Leconfield's early in the summer of '52 quite among old friends there," she wrote contentedly in her diary. And she revelled in such small treats as her carriage rides with Fanny Bullock, and their visit to London to see all the wonders of the Great Exhibition in Paxton's amazing Crystal Palace. She was happier and more certain of a future than she had ever been before; she had a delightful place, and a kind mistress who was fast becoming a real friend. She could see a way, and an attractive one, clear before her. And then my grandfather came along, and having momentarily wakened something in her more powerful than her reason or her prejudices, caught her off balance while she was shattered by the loss of her parents, and married her before she could recover it.

Therein lies the first great cause of the passion of resentment that produced that fearful diary. My grandmother never forgave my grandfather for breaking down her prudent resolve and separating her from the freemasonry and security of the upper servants' world in which she had been so happy. She dreamed night and day of getting back to it, and, strange to say, her dream at last came true. She was thirty-three in 1855 when her first child, her daughter Frances, was born. Her two older boys, Frank and Fred, followed in 1857 and 1862. My father was born in the autumn of 1866, two years after the death of the girl she had loved so much. It was fourteen years after that, just as soon as she could in decency do it, that she pitched my father out into the working world by apprenticing him to a draper, and walked out on her husband in order to go back into service.

In the normal course of events, a former lady's maid aged fifty-eight who had been out of employment for twenty-five years would have found it next to impossible to find anything better than a mediocre

place as a housekeeper-companion to a widow in reduced circumstances, or cook-housekeeper to some rundown old bachelor or wid-
ower. My grandmother had, however, managed to contrive a special
destiny for herself. She had kept in touch with her lady, Frances
Bullock, all through her lost years in Atlas House. Her frequent letters
and occasional visits to Uppark had kept her old mistress's affection
for her alive. Lady Fetherstonehaugh had died in 1875, leaving her
sister in sole possession of the house and the estate, and when the
sitting housekeeper died in her turn five years later, Fanny Bullock
was distressed by the thought that she might soon find herself living
with nothing but strangers about her. Not liking the prospect, she
looked into the past for a replacement, and first to the woman she had
thought of for so many years as her devoted Sarah Neal. I am sure that
my grandmother saw this as an answer to her prayers. It was indeed
an extraordinary thing: she was being given a chance to go back to the
far-off point in her life at which she had made her one great, catastrophic error to start all over again, just as if she had never set eyes
on my grandfather, or let her passions overrule her common sense.
It seemed like a special dispensation. She was to be delivered, miracu-
lously, from the consequences of her foolish marriage. My father, who
was one of those consequences, did not share her pleasure in this
development, and did not intend to be disposed of all that easily.

Chapter IX

"Hole!" said Mr. Polly, and then for a change, and
with greatly increased emphasis: *"Ole!"* He paused,
and then broke out with one of his private and
peculiar idioms. "Oh! Beastly Silly Wheeze
of a Hole!"

—THE HISTORY OF MR. POLLY

I AM NOT AT ALL SURE WHAT THE
home that my father lost when my
grandmother made her escape back into her past was really like. In
the second chapter of his *Experiment in Autobiography*, in the section
headed "Origins. I. 47 High Street, Bromley, Kent" he takes us on
a guided tour of the premises. For a long time we don't meet anybody.
We creep up and down the uncarpeted stairs, examine the horrid
underground kitchen, look in at the inconveniently located coal bun-
ker, pass out into the back yard, where we are shown the smelly and
otherwise unattractive earth closet, all without encountering a living
soul. But as we were peering over the party wall down at the far end
of the back yard, we come on someone at last. It's not a member of
the family, though; it's Mr. Covell, the butcher, and he's bloodily
about the business of slaughtering his weekly tally of pigs, sheep, and
horned cattle. We haven't, however, been brought here to learn anything about Mr. Covell. My father is showing us that we can catch a
glimpse, over there, beyond the butcher's slaughterhouse, of Bromley's ancient church and graveyard. As we crane our necks in its
direction my father tells us that the body of his short-lived sister
Frances lies buried among those mossy tombs and tilted gravestones.

We turn back toward the house, and are immediately rewarded with the sight of a living member of the family. We catch a glimpse of my grandfather as he checks over his stock of red glazed earthenware crocks in the covered way between Number 47 and the premises next door, occupied by Mr. Munday, the haberdasher. We aren't allowed to watch my grandfather at his work for long, or even told his name for that matter. We are whirled about instead to be given one of the strangest introductions to a mother that is to be found in any English autobiography. We get to her by a roundabout route. My father draws our attention to the other side of Number 47, and shows us the extension that Mr. Cooper, the tailor, has added onto the back of his shop. It is, he tells us, a workshop, and in it Mr. Cooper's men cut out and make up the suits, jackets, and trousers ordered by his customers. The trouble is that its windows overlook the cinder path leading from Number 47's back door to the earth closet down at the far end of the yard. It was, we are told, always a matter of concern to my grandmother that she could never be sure that Mr. Cooper's men and boys were not spying on her comings and goings along this path. One such thought leads to another, and our attention is now directed to the small flower bed beside the earth closet—nothing would grow in that sad piece of soil we learn, because so many of the local cats used it as their lavatory. With gardening brought up in this sidelong way, my father goes on to tell us that my grandfather was a gardener of some determination, and to prove it he shows us a vine covering a large part of the back of Number 47. It has been made to prosper even though it was unpromisingly planted in a hole punched through a stretch of brick paving close to the back door.

We go back indoors again, to learn how miserably underfurnished the house is, and with what rotten old secondhand stuff. And then, suddenly, my father is telling us that his parents had slept in separate rooms from as far back as he can remember, and that he believes that these sleeping arrangements constituted a substitute for a birth control technique. He drops that subject to say that he has two older brothers, and goes on to talk of cockroaches. His recollection is that there were so many of these insects in Number 47 that the premises generally smelt either of the rank odor that they give off when they are crushed, or of the paraffin oil with which my grandfather used to drench the skirting boards and the wooden floors in the hope of getting them to go elsewhere. My father ends his digression with the sour observation that every part of the house had given off its own distinctive smell. This information somehow clears the air, and he announces that he has finished with the surroundings into which he was born, and that the time has come for him to say something about his father and mother. He will try to let us know what sort of people they were, and how it was that they had come to be in this squalid hole. He will even tell us their names.

In spite of the vividness of my father's evocation of the horrors of Atlas House there is something about their presentation that suggests to me that his description may well be subjective rather than objective, and that the picture he gives may be more closely related to his mother's feelings about the place than to its physical properties. Old photographs tell me that the building was one of a group of structures characteristic of English small-town High Street architecture—each with its two full storeys and an attic floor above its ground-floor shop. They appear to have been given a misleadingly Victorian look by late-nineteenth-century restylings of their shop fronts, but their general appearance makes it almost certain that they belong to the very large class of similar English buildings originally put up in the sixteenth and seventeenth centuries and modernised between 1770 and 1840. They were then given new façades of stock brick, or subjected to alterations of a more formidable nature involving the reconstruction of the entire front part of the building. Atlas House and its neighbours look to me to have been given the more drastic treatment, and left with a set of late-Georgian rooms opening onto the street and screening the much older timber-framed structure behind them. My father's description of it makes it sound as if it had been a slum house in a bad way when it was his home, but the probability is that it was then what it had always been, a solidly built tradesman's house that anyone who was even halfway happy would have found a pleasant enough dwelling. My grandmother, however, never gave it a chance. Her diaries show that she had hated Atlas House from the moment in which she first set eyes on it, and that in her first days under its roof she had made up her mind that George Wells had tricked them into buying him out just before his business foundered into bankruptcy. The tone of her accounts of the dingy and uncared-for state of the rooms in which she was to live, and the poor quality of the rundown inventory, leaves no doubt about that. It tells me that she felt sure my grandfather's impetuous plunge was about to make her repeat all that she had been forced to endure at The New Inn after her father's death. She was to be stripped of everything all over again, and to be turned out onto the street in the end with nowhere to go but to the workhouse.

The prospects for the modest retail china store that my grandfather had taken over were not really that bad. Its location was good. The times were getting better, and Bromley was a growing town. It had four thousand inhabitants in '51, five thousand five hundred in '61, and ten thousand six hundred in '71. Allowing for the slower tempo of those days, it could be said that my grandparents had taken over the venture at the start of a boom. Those who know Bromley today may feel that it was then a threatened place, on the brink of being overwhelmed by London's suburban sprawl. But that was something that came a great deal later, and this threat was not apparent in the fifties. The railroad that came through from London in 1861 to make commuting a possibility seemed far from threatening, particularly from the point of view of a local retailer. John Murray's *Handbook to the Environs of London* was able to speak well of the place in the middle seventies.

> Bromley stands on high ground in the midst of a richly wooded and picturesque country; is reputed healthy, has good seats, is easy of access, and consequently much in favour with city merchants for whom comfortable villas have been built on every available site. The town itself has a quiet air of conscious respectability. The approach to it from the railway station is between the tall walls of well timbered domains some of which are however being broken and built over.

All the available information confirms this genial report, and suggests that there was nothing whatever to prevent a live wire from making a go of it at Atlas House, selling necessities to the new households that were pouring into the neighbourhood. That this view of Number 47 High Street as a commercial proposition isn't perversely contradictory of my father's grimmer assessment of its possibilities is shown, I think, by the time scheme for my grandfather's failure. Great as his talent for contriving disaster for himself and for his dependents undoubtedly was, it took him no less than thirty-one years to run the business into the ground. Having taken Atlas House over in October 1855, he wasn't finally sold up and put out until May 1887. The shop, or so it seems to me, must have put up a dogged resistance to his quite determined mismanagement.

It is fairly easy to see where my grandfather went wrong. He had gone into a trade that he knew nothing about, and his one hope of success lay in giving his enterprise all his attention and most of his time until he was on top of it. He was underfinanced, and he could not afford either to waste a penny or to make a single false move until he had built up a cash reserve. But he had an expansive nature, and he didn't have the temperament to discipline himself to the practice of ruthless economies and to hard work. He began to describe himself as a Master China Dealer before he had learned the rudiments of the game, and he dropped easily into the habit of using charm as a substitute for capital. He had an attractive personality, and it was easy for him to talk up extensions of credit. The story of his business career was consequently to be one of slowly accumulating trouble of his own making.

And then there was the game of cricket. While queering his gardening chances in his Redleaf days, he had laid the foundations of a career as a professional player. He was good enough to be a star player for the West Kent Cricket Club throughout his first decade in Bromley, and at the start of the sixties his deadly slow spinners won him a place as a bowler on the county side. He was then in his physical prime, and capable of doing great execution among batsmen when the wicket was right. His moment of glory came one day in June 1862, when he won a place in the record books as the first bowler to take four wickets with four successive balls in a county match. This feat made him a local celebrity, and gave him a reputation that qualified him for the coaching job at Norwich Grammar School that was to yield him a steady income in the later sixties and most of the seventies. It was a job that took him away from home and from the shop for the greater part of every summer, from early May until the end of July.

My grandmother's hatred for my grandfather's cricket playing ran second to her hatred for Atlas House and the shop until the year in which he performed the bowling feat that made him a local celebrity. After that, cricket was given first place among her detestations. His day of glory on the cricket field in the high summer of 1862 was paid for later in the year. By Christmas time things were so bad between the pair of them that my grandfather left home on December 24 and went up into Gloucestershire to spend the remainder of the holiday with his brother Charles-Edward. My grandmother devoted one of her more scathing diary entries to that outrage, but there was worse to come. In the following summer my grandfather decided to exploit his fame as a cricket player by making the shop an outlet for sporting goods as well as for china. This upset my mother for two reasons. The first was that she knew that there was no money on hand to finance the new departure. He could only be branching out by going further into debt. She was quite right. My grandfather was on friendly terms with a cousin named John Duke who made cricket bats and balls at Penshurst, and it had been easy to talk him into letting him have all he wanted for nothing down. The new debt frightened my grandmother because she knew that her husband was following the dangerous tactic of rolling his debts. He was holding off his most pressing creditors with payments on account while letting the less demanding wait. She saw, with horror, that his way of life was becoming more and more like her father's. The second cause for her anger was that the new line of business brought cricketers into the shop. She had always hated being called away from her household chores to sell china in her husband's cricketing absences, and she positively loathed being summoned by the shop bell jangling on its coiled spring to talk of bats and balls and gloves with cricketers. Her diary entry for August 29, 1863, is almost incoherent with outrage, my grandfather had been away all day playing in an end-of-season match at the county side's home ground:

> J. W. last day of the season at Chiselhurst What a life! This cricket making me a slave. We cannot afford to keep a servant and this high awkward house to keep clean mind working and nurse three children attend to the shop nearly every day and do all the needle work. Still I am not appreciated!!! What can man expect of woman.

It may seem unlikely that things can have become any worse than this, but they very soon did. One day in 1864 Frances Wells went to tea with the children of Mr. Munday in the house next door. She came home excited and happy, was taken ill in the night, and presently died of what was then called inflammation of the bowels. My father inclined to the view that it was a burst appendix that killed her, but my poor grandmother was always sure that the Mundays had let her eat something that was not quite right at that tea party, and that she had died of food poisoning. My grandmother blamed them for the death and never spoke to them again. The loss of her adored "Possy" gave her a demoralising feeling that the one thing that her marriage had brought her that was worth having had been taken away, and in her grief she took a desperate gamble. She resumed sexual relations with my grandfather in the hope that God would take pity on her and give her another girl. He didn't, and there she was with a new baby, another male, at the age of forty-three.

After that, life in Atlas House took on the appalling character evoked by my grandmother's record of the household's Easter holiday disaster of 1867. My grandfather had asked two of his young cousins over from Penshurst for the whole week. There was a misunderstanding; they thought that they had been asked for the days of Easter only.

> April 16: Expected visitors all day did not come. 17th: Ann did not come or write. 18th: Arrived this morning. Had to get beefsteaks for dinner and so much fuss. 19th: Good Friday. Ann and Eugenia went to Bickley Church came to dinner had a fuss to get them all a fish dinner. Ann behaved today extremely heartlessly. I never can forget it. After dinner I made a fire upstairs and carried tea up and waited on them all day could not get to my church and towards E she spoke of my poor dear loved Fanny so unkind that I told her plainly my friend cruel hard hearted woman to speak of my loved one that is gone so unkind. I did not mind what I said. 20th: After tea I had more trouble with my husbands friends than it is possible to relate—proud haughty set they treat me like their servant . . .

My father was to spend the first fourteen years of his existence in this rancorous atmosphere. In the ordinary course of events my grandmother would be going about the business of running the house tight-lipped, alertly accumulating fresh grievances like so many green stamps, biding her time until she has enough of them on hand to be exchanged for an outburst of rage and hostility. Every so often it would come to an old-fashioned barney, and the neighbours would hear my grandfather furiously trying to shout her down as she had her say out. While she was building up for such an explosion, she would find some ongoing relief in a species of domestic sabotage. Would-be purchasers of cricket gear who came into the shop when she had been left in charge of it would have to leave empty-handed, baffled by her inability to find anything that they might have come for that wasn't in plain view, or to put a price on it if it were. Family meals came to table botched and burned, and when my grandfather did choose to spend an evening at home, it was apt to be blighted by her resort to a frosty mutism. She even managed to make her needlework carry her messages of outrage. This may sound like a purely fantastic notion, but the fact remains that, after recording that my grandmother had been apprenticed to a dressmaker for four years, and that for a further ten years she had been in situations that required her to be an accomplished needlewoman, my father goes on to say that she made his clothes so badly, and mended them so clumsily, that he became an object of derision when he wore them to school.

Her efforts to make someone pay for her sufferings had the long-term effect of increasing them: the more she raged at her husband for neglecting her and his business for the sake of his beloved cricket, the more he stayed away from home. And the more he stayed away from home the more he needed the ready cash that his cricketing brought in. And the more time he spent on the cricket field the less he had to give to his business and his wife. It was the year after that Easter holiday explosion that he took the Norwich coaching job that was to keep him away from Bromley for three months of every summer for most of the next decade. And it was at about the same time that he developed a settled habit of spending most of his evenings when he was in Bromley either in the snug bar of The Duke's Head over the way from Atlas House, or a little farther up the street at The Bell.

If my father is to be believed, my grandfather's frequentation of The Bell did him no harm in the long run. He claimed that it did him a great deal of good in a rather peculiar and roundabout way. One day in 1874, when he was eight, his two older brothers took him to watch a cricket match. While they were playing about in the neighbourhood of the beer tent they ran into the just-grown-up son of the landlord of The Bell, who recognized them as sons of one of his father's regulars and ventured on a familiarity. He grabbed my father and began to play a game with him, tossing him up in the air, higher and higher, and asking him "Whose little kid are you?" each time he launched him into the void. On his last throw he missed his victim, who fell onto a tent peg and broke his tibia. What my father said of this accident in 1933 was that he would probably have died an early death as a worn-out shop assistant if it hadn't been for that broken bone. He had just discovered the joys of reading to himself, and it had transformed his outlook upon life. He was sure that if he hadn't been laid up for what remained of that summer, his parents would almost certainly have seen what was happening and taken steps to break him of this unsuitable habit before it got a real hold on him. But as things fell out, he was given all the books he could wish for to make it up to him for being immobilised. And so it was the fumble by the son of the landlord of The Bell that set him on the road to becoming a literary man.

The story is plausible enough, but I'm far from sure that it *is* the story. My father drops his account of the accident and its sequel into his narrative between two curious passages, the first concerned with his mother, and the second with the beginnings of his interest in sex. The first can be described as a bold attempt to rewrite his mother. In it he says that he doesn't think that she was acutely unhappy. He believes that she took refuge from reality in a world of innocent reverie when she sat down to her sewing every evening. As she plied her needle she comforted herself with a string of petty agreeable fictions. She imagined pleasant encounters that hadn't taken place and weren't likely to, and she had warm and cosy thoughts about her children, of how "dear Bertie" was doing so well at school, and how "dear Frankie" and "dear Freddie" were doing even better at work . . . He is talking of those solitary evenings of brooding that produced the corrosive bitterness of the diary entries. This fantasy about my grandmother's fantasies ends in heaven, my father sends her there to dream of meeting her beloved "Possy" again in some celestial garden as an unchanged and eternal child. The second topic comes up as he is talking about the books he was given to read while his leg was mending. There were some bound volumes of *Punch* among them, and, if he is to believed, the political cartoons in these are what set him off. Linley Sambourne's sexy personifications of the nations as Britannia, Erin, Columbia, La France, and so on, did the trick. "I became woman-conscious from those days onward," he says.

It may well have been so, but it is hard to believe that it is mere accident that accounts for my father's leap from this statement to a weirdly defensive passage in which he takes issue with the ideas of "the masters of psycho-analysis." What they say, he argues, may be true of Austrian Jews and Levantines, and yet not true of the English or the Irish. He can't, he says, find any trace of a mother fixation or an Oedipus complex, or any of that stuff, in his make-up, and he goes on, almost defiantly, to assert that his mother's kisses were significant acts, and that they were expressions, not caresses. He concludes with the breath-taking claim that as a small boy he found no more sexual significance about his always decent and seemly mother than he did about the chairs and sofa in the parlour. He then reverts defiantly to the topic of his goddesses, and this time he adds to his list of safe love objects the plaster casts of Greek statuary that were to be found educationally clustered in the museum section of the Crystal Palace, over the hill from Bromley in nearby Sydenham, in the days of his youth. Yes, truly, he insists, it was those cold, unmoving, casts; those drawings, those groupings of inked lines on paper pages; those arbitrary signs for the real thing, that gave him his first consciousness of women as things in some important way unlike the parlour furniture. Having to do with creatures of flesh and blood like, and yet unlike, himself had nothing to do with it.

I did not realise how very odd this claim was when I first came across the passage soon after my father's autobiography came out. Its strangeness only became apparent to me when I belatedly made the discovery that he had said it all before in his novel of 1922, *The Secret Places of the Heart.* The relationship between the equivalent passages in the two books is so close as to make it reasonably certain that a piece of what had been fiction had become fact in the decade after its invention.

My father can only have made this prolonged effort to convince himself that those unlikely white goddesses had meant so much to him because he didn't want to have to come to grips with the less negotiable anxieties that had really been plaguing him at that time. It is not difficult to see what they were. The son of the landlord of The Bell had really put him on the spot with his question: Whose little kid was he, his father's or his mother's? And he had been asked it on the occasion of one of his earlier ventures onto his father's turf, when he was being initiated by his older brothers into the secrets of that world of manly fellowship that his mother so evidently loathed and despised. The landlord's son, known to him to be a friend of his father's, had been asking him to take sides. The probability is that he had been trying to blurt out his father's name when he was dropped, and then down he came, and his leg broke. It must have seemed as if he had been punished for wanting to be his father's boy. My guess is that he had already realised, from the reserve with which his mother treated him, that he had betrayed her in that region. She had been disappointed when he turned out to be a boy. She can't have been able to conceal it from him that to please her he should have been a girl.

I don't feel that it is anachronistic to raise the issue of sexual identification in the context of my father's childhood. It is not good enough to say that the Victorian English were simply unaware of such conceptions because they lived in a pre-Freudian era. It was not necessary for them to have the related problems defined to them in Freudian terms to be troubled by them—and in this case their liability to be bothered was exacerbated by social custom. The earliest photograph of my father that I know of shows him, not long before his fourth birthday, dressed in a frock with an off-the-shoulder neckline, short puffed quarter-length sleeves, and a three-quarter-length skirt running to about two and a half yards on the hemline. This was in no way odd in 1869. In those days, boys under five were thought of as belonging in the woman's world of the nursery, and as only potentially masculine. They would begin to move out of the nursery when they were past their fourth birthday, and changes in their costume would give expression to their changing status. In a family in which things were going wrong between husband and wife in such a way that the children had to be aware of it, this complicated the matter of sexual identification for obvious reasons. A small boy who was fond of his mother, and who had good reason to fear his father, was more than likely to feel that he was being disloyal to her when he put on the uniform of maleness and moved out of her world. The women would feel it, too, that their boys were being taken from them and made to join the enemy camp, and would not hide their bitterness from their sons. My father had been brought up in an atmosphere that was itself a criticism of my grandfather, and he will have been subjected in and out of season to hints and barbed references to the head of the household's shortcomings. He was taught from the start to think of him as someone disastrously inept who was failing to function as a man in some rather important way. This view of Joseph Wells would first have been challenged when my father's brothers let him know that they had discovered that their old man was a personality of note outside Atlas House. The boys' discovery of their father's standing in the sporting world accelerated the switch from the shop to cricket as the focus of complaint in my grandmother's diaries. What hurt was not that he had performed a feat that made him a figure among the cricketers, but that he had become a glorious model to his boys. Frank and Fred would have seen their father being made welcome in a world of good-natured fellowship as a man possessing an abundance of virtue, and if they didn't tell their younger brother in so many words that their father's outdoor world was a good deal more interesting and much more fun than that inhabited by their mother, they will certainly have let him know that he was missing a lot that they were enjoying, and that he would go on doing so as long as he was content to be a "mamma's boy." And when he at last got to the cricket field, to find that he had an identity waiting for him there as "Wells the bowler's little chap," and that people around the scorer's box and the beer tent were inclined to be friendly and jolly with him on that account, he was very soon punished for his wicked disloyalty with a broken leg.

It is possible to wonder if the brash and overconfident young lout who tossed my father up in the air that day really did ask him that singularily pertinent question. But it doesn't in the end matter whether or no my father carried those exact words in his head for the fifty-eight years between the time that he thought he heard them and the time that he set them down in 1932–1933. The point, for me at any rate, is that he was moved to attach them to the remembered incident after that lapse of time. This tells me that the question, in one form or another, had been weighing on him at the time of the accident, that he had been terribly torn between being his mother's boy or his father's, and made to feel appallingly guilty by the inescapable fact that his physical development was hustling him on to what could only be a masculine future.

A pleasant photograph of 1876 seems to make a nonsense of this notion. It shows my father as he sits in a photographer's fancy studio chair, not even pretending to be interested in the album that lies open on the occasional table in front of him. He has a pertly and confidently boyish air, and looks full of bounce and cheek. His Zouave jacket may seem a little ambiguous to a modern eye, but the style was then military and thought to be smartly masculine. Altogether, in his bearing and in his dress, he projects a properly manly appearance. The photograph matches with what he says of his life at this time in his autobiography—that he was happier than he had been for years, and happier than he was to be for a good long time to come. The change in him had come about because as soon as his broken leg had mended he had begun to attend Bromley Academy, the little private school at the other end of the High Street where a Scotsman named Thomas Morley was doing what he could for a student body of between twenty-five and thirty-five boys between the ages of seven and fourteen.

My two uncles, Frank and Fred, had already passed through Morley's hands without noticeable benefit when the photograph of my

UNIVERSITY OF ILLINOIS AT URBANA-CHAMPAIGN

Jane Wells and her two boys: George Philip, dark and
very like his father; and Frank Richard, fair and
as like his mother. The year is 1907.

AUTHOR'S PRIVATE COLLECTION

Amber Reeves and her family in 1908. She is
at the end of the line to the right of her
mother, Maude Reeves.

UNIVERSITY OF ILLINOIS AT URBANA-CHAMPAIGN

Amber, now Amber Blanco White, and her daughter
Anna-Jane.

COURTESY OF MARTIN J. WELLS

Joseph Wells in his last years. He died five
years after Sarah, in 1910. My father's *History of Mr. Polly*,
published in that year, is in part an affectionate
tribute to his spirit.

PICTORIAL PARADE

George Bernard Shaw

COURTESY OF THE BBC HULTON PICTURE LIBRARY

Hubert Bland

FABIAN ENEMIES

Belfort Bax

COURTESY OF THE BBC HULTON PICTURE LIBRARY

COURTESY OF THE OLIVIER FAMILY

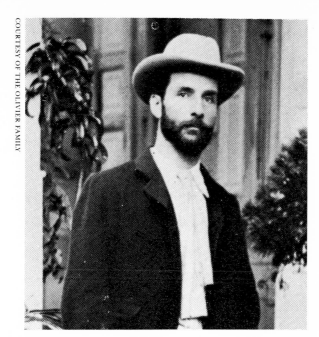

Sydney Olivier

FABIAN ALLIES

Graham Wallas

AUTHOR'S PRIVATE COLLECTION

COURTESY OF THE BBC HULTON PICTURE LIBRARY

The young Ramsay MacDonald, who, like my father and Graham Wallas, was shocked by what the Webbs had done with the Hutchinson fund.

father in his Zouave jacket was taken. Frank had moved on from the school, to become an articled apprentice to a draper, at the end of '71; and Fred had vanished from the scene, bound for a similar servitude, early in '76. His translation had left my father very much on top of the heap at the Academy, for although neither Frank nor Fred had made any particular impression on him, Morley had already spotted my father as one of the brightest and most promising pupils who had ever come his way, and was pushing him along as fast as he could go.

Being the apple of Morley's eye was one thing, and friendship was another. With Fred gone from the school, my father found himself in possession of a private life for the first time. A world of companionship and interest unclouded by family tensions and sibling rivalry suddenly opened before him, and in it he had the luck to find a real friend, a lively-minded young man named Sidney Bowkett who went on to achieve a measure of success as a journeyman playwright and who gave him the foundation for the character called Chitterlow in *Kipps.* Bowkett was my father's inseparable companion until the end of his Bromley days, and his friend for another twenty-five years after that. The photograph of '76 shows my father radiant with the discovery of this world, and with something that Morley had shown him.

In his rather back-handed tribute to Morley in his autobiography my father doesn't altogether concede that he was handed a script for the early part of his career at Bromley Academy. He contents himself with a rather lukewarm defence of middle-class values, and thanks Morley for inculcating them in him. He doesn't mention the most important thing that Morley did for him: provide him with what for the moment appeared to be the solution to his central problem. It doesn't matter too much just how Morley saw my father as succeeding, the point was that as an indubitable male Morley was able to put before my father a program for an authentically male way of making it that could not, as he saw thing, possibly be objectionable to his mother. I doubt if my father stated the case to himself in these terms, or anything like them, when he was a boy of ten. But I am quite sure he recognised that the path Morley was opening to him would be "all right," as any route modelled on any of his father's procedures clearly wouldn't be. That, I'm sure, was something that he was entirely conscious of—and that picture shows him, or so it seems to me, positively rejoicing in the notion that he was swimming with a flowing tide for the first time in his young life.

In 1876 my father had the better part of four years at Bromley

Academy still before him. By the beginning of 1880, when he was approaching his fourteenth birthday and was almost done with it, he had accomplished all that Morley had hoped from him and rather more. He had sopped up everything that the little school had to offer him like a sponge, and when he took his final examinations he won distinctions in more than half a dozen subjects. The key to the chance of a good start in life that Morley had shown him how to cut was in his hands. The examinations he had sat for were organised by an association of private-school operators which had a nationwide membership, and in one of his subjects my father had come out equal first on a list of candidates coming from all over England. If he had done nothing else, he had demonstrated that he was a natural for further schooling. The thought would have been in his mind. There had been difficulty with his school fees during his last year at the Academy, and Morley had shown his belief in my father by waiving them. Morley, beyond any question, will have told him that it would be a great pity if he didn't find some way of getting further education, and will have discussed ways and means with him. I suspect that at some time during his last year at the Academy, Morley told him about one chance that was open to him, he could become a pupil teacher in the state school system. Pupil teachers were a new element in the table of organisation of the National Schools. They were young people of between fourteen and eighteen years of age who had been through the elementary schools. They were taken on to teach the lower forms in such schools on terms that gave them a bare living wage and certain amount of free time in which to study. After four years of that they would, if they had minded their books in their free time, have qualified for two years at a teacher training college from which they would either go straight into salaried teaching in the service of the Board of Education, or, if their examination results justified it, up to a university.

I know that I am disregarding the account of this matter given by my father in his autobiography, where it is said that he learned about the possibility of becoming a pupil teacher from his distant, and engagingly disreputable, maternal cousin Alfred Williams sometime after he left Morley's Academy. However presumptuous this may seem, I am sticking to it, because I find it hard to believe that my father would have been as outraged as he was by what happened to him next if he hadn't known that the opportunity was open to him. In July 1880 he found that his mother was leaving his father to go back to become housekeeper at Uppark, and that he had been bound as an apprentice to a firm of drapers in Windsor, Rodgers and Denyer of the High Street. The door that he had opened for himself by all his hard work at Morley's Academy was to be slammed in his face.

Chapter X

I have said that a cardinal stroke of good fortune
was the breaking of my leg when I was seven years
old. Another almost as important was the breaking
of my father's leg in 1877, which made the dissolution of our home inevitable.

... Now if this had not happened, I have no doubt
I should have followed in the steps of Frank and
Freddy and gone on living at home under my
mother's care, while I went daily to some shop, to
which I was bound apprentice. This would have
seemed so natural and necessary that I should not
have resisted. I should have served my time and
never had an idea of getting away from the shop
until it was too late. But the dislocation that now
occurred closed this easy path to frustration.

—Experiment in Autobiography

Had my father been an only child,
or a youngster with younger rather
than older brothers, he might not have realised what was happening
to him when he was delivered into the hands of those Windsor drapers. But both his brothers were his seniors, and by 1880 they were well
into the mill for which this kind of apprenticeship was the hopper.
Frank had been sickened by what he had seen of a counter-jumper's
life while serving out his four-year stint as a draper's dogsbody. His
passion was for machinery and he had a natural gift for understanding
such things as gear trains. With his engineering potential going to
waste he was miserably unhappy. Frederick had no objections to the
draper's trade as such, but at the end of his apprenticeship he was
learning that he had been put into an overcrowded calling. He was
finding it hard to get a place, and beginning to notice that while
employers were in the habit of asking their men to be *keen* and to show
signs of being *determined to get on,* they offered them very limited
opportunities for doing so; Juniors became Seniors after years behind
the counter, but very few Seniors ever went on to become floor walkers or buyers. And even on a senior's wages there was very little hope
of saving enough to make a start on one's own.

I don't suppose that my uncles will have told my father just what it was that bothered them about their line of work, by way of giving him fair warning, but he will have gathered what was happening to them by listening to their talk, and he will have been struck, unpleasantly, by the way in which the two cheerful boys he had grown up with were being dulled and reduced. He will have seen them becoming less lively and less confident. And as soon as he found himself being broken into the routine of endless days indoors in a trap similar to the traps in which they had been tamed and blunted, he will have recognised why they had changed, and how he might change if he submitted to this fate. He reproduced the letter that he wrote to his mother at the end of his first week with Rodgers and Denyer in his autobiography, and as it has been quoted elsewhere I shan't offer it again here, with its harrowing account of a working day that began at seven-thirty in the morning and ended at eight-thirty in the evening, and of a life without privacy, or comfort, or promise. The Improvers and the Juniors whose lot he was being forced to share slept four to a room, ate in company in a canteen in the cellar, to which the daylight never penetrated, and had two hours out of the twenty-four to call their own —between eight-thirty and ten-thirty at the end of the day. It was then that they had their only chance of getting a breath of fresh air or of taking any exercise. They couldn't make use of the full time because the lights were turned out on them at ten-thirty. If they left it to the last minute to come in, they would have to undress and get to bed in the dark. When the lights went out, the shop doors were locked, and they weren't reopened for latecomers.

The tone of my father's letter becomes increasingly bitter as it goes on, and his handwriting gets uglier in phase with the growth of his indignation, finally breaking down into a splatter of furious alterations and scratchings-out as a craven "I like the place fairly well . . ." is obliterated and transformed into a franker "I don't like this place much . . ." But the letter's real jolt lies in the style of its ending. The letter starts off, as might be expected, with "My dear Mother" but it ends "Yours, H. G. Wells." Later on, when he had put the dismal business of selling yard goods over the counter behind him forever and he was in a fair way to getting his teacher's diploma and his B.Sc., he would be able to sign himself "your most loving son, Bertie," but that would not be for another ten years of unrelenting battle.

My father made his first move prematurely. He decided to show the world that he wasn't cut out to be a draper's assistant, and he made a considerable success of doing so. When he had been with them for just over two months his employers took the very unusual course of cancelling his articles on the ground of his entire unsuitability to the trade. There was some talk of his having to face a charge of lifting money from the till, but his "uncle" Tom Pennicott of Surly Hall up the river saved him from that and took him in until something else could be found for him. Pennicott, who was a second cousin of my grandmother's on her mother's side, had a distant cousin of his own named Alfred Williams who was taking over one of the Board of Education's new Elementary Schools at Wookey down in Somerset, and when he wrote to say that he would be willing to take my father on as a pupil teacher it seemed like an answer to prayer.

But Alfred Williams, alas, was not straight goods. He had obtained his headmastership, for which he had no real qualifications, by snowing the board with forged certificates and references. His frauds caught up with him at the end of November 1880, and he was fired early in December. My father, who had been a pupil teacher for just over sixty days, made his way back to Surly Hall on foot, and after stopping there for a week or two went on to Uppark to join his mother for Christmas.

It is customary for my father's biographers to take a break at this point in order to describe my father's delighted discovery of the riches of Uppark. But my father's initial visit to Uppark began on December 20, 1880, and ended on January 15, 1881. I don't think that the bewildered and disturbed boy of fourteen and a half who had got himself into such a mess at Windsor, and who had been visited with such a hideous disappointment at Wookey immediately afterwards, finding himself in the wholly unfamiliar setting of the servants quarters of a great house, could, in the short time available, have calmed himself sufficiently to settle down to anything much in the way of a constructive exploitation of its cultural resources. His discovery of Uppark, I am sure, came later, after he had won the first part of his battle for an education, and after he had learned what to look for in that splendid library. But in 1880 my father still had a long way to go before he was in shape to make anything of what Uppark had to offer. He still had his most frustrating and exasperating experiences of the now-you-see-it now-you-don't variety ahead of him.

On January 15 he left Uppark and went over to Midhurst, where another apprenticeship was waiting for him—this time he was to be in servitude to a Mr. Samuel Cowap, a chemist who was to give him a training that would qualify him as a pharmacist. Almost as soon as he had moved into Cowap's house as a boarder and been shown the layout of the dispensary it became clear that there was going to be a hitch. My father had no Latin, a language that he had to know if he was to read and write labels and make up prescriptions. My father's spirits sank, but Mr. Cowap rose to the occasion. He'd taken a liking to my father, and to give him a chance he'd arranged for him to go to the local grammar school for an hour every evening to be taught Latin there by its headmaster.

In this way Horace Byatt came into my father's life. Byatt had just come south from Burslem in the Midlands, where another writer to be, Arnold Bennett, had been one of his star pupils, to take part in the resurrection of Midhurst Grammar School, an ancient foundation that had died in the sixties and had just been brought back to life. The school had a student body of thirty-two, and Byatt was struggling to push it over the hump and give it academic respectability. Bright pupils were of special interest to him, partly because their examination results would build the reputation of the school, and partly because they would give him a chance to increase his income. His opportunity arose from a characteristically British and Victorian response to the discovery that English schools in general were falling behind those of France and Germany in the teaching of scientific subjects. The Board of Education lacked the power to order the teaching of new subjects, so it sought to remedy the deficiency by offering headmasters with university degrees an inducement to take a gamble out of school hours. They were advised that if they would hold evening classes in their own selection from any of thirty extracurricular subjects they would be awarded capitation fees on a sliding scale for every attending student who got a pass mark or better when sitting for the Board's examinations. The fees, which rose to a top figure of four pounds per subject taught, don't look very handsome by modern standards, but they allowed a headmaster with a gift for cramming to add as much as a third to his annual income.

Byatt was just the man to jump at such a lure, but like Morley before him in my father's life, he had a passionate belief in the value of education, and he meant to play fair by his students. They were taught their subjects, not merely trained to jump through hoops likely to be held up by the examiners. They benefited as much as he profited. As soon as my father's rapid progress with Latin had shown Byatt how responsive he was to coaching, he realised that he could give the boy a great deal more than the chemist could. He would profit, but the boy would make a much greater profit.

On February 23, 1881, after he had been an apprentice pharmacist for a little over a month, my father moved out of Mr. Cowap's friendly home and into Horace Byatt's. On the following day he became a full-time pupil at the Midhurst Grammar School. I suspect that these two kindly men of good will had entered into a private conspiracy to do the right thing by this astonishingly promising boy, in the belief that they would be able to bring his mother round to their arrangement as soon as she had been given time to take in all the advantages it held for him. They didn't, however, know my grandmother; faced with the apparent *fait accompli* of the resumption of her son's education, she did some conspiring of her own. She told Frances Bullock how much she was worried by the problem of getting her youngest boy, who had been given ideas above his station by undesirable associates, a good start in life. She was given leave to enlist the aid of Sir William King, the Uppark estate manager, who was sure to be able to find a solution to it. Reverting to her obsession, my grandmother told Sir William that she wanted to see my father selling yard goods, and he obligingly arranged for her to have her way.

In May 1881 my father was brusquely pulled out of Horace Byatt's clutches—I am sure that my grandmother saw it in that way—and packed off to undergo a month's trial preliminary to his being bound apprentice to Edwin Hyde, owner of the Southsea Drapery Emporium in the Kings Road, Southsea. He went like a lamb because Sir William had been warned that he might repeat his Windsor performance and had provided against that. He had arranged the terms of my father's new engagement so that he was delivered into Hyde's hands knowing that he could break away from him only by inflicting a loss upon his mother equivalent to a year of her earnings. At fifteen he had no answer to this kind of blackmail, and for the next two very long years he endured what was for him the unendurable, working the thirteen-hour days of the six-day weeks that the Emporium required of him, and making pathetic efforts to keep up with his studies in his free time before lights out in the Emporium's stuffy dormitories.

For most of his first year in the Southsea shop I believe that my father was in a semi-paralysed mental state, numbed by his disappointment at finding himself thrown in mid-stride just when he had thought he was off to a flying start, and overwhelmed by his knowledge of how fast his chances were withering away. Each new day

brought him a little closer to the age at which the pupil-teacher gate
to the profession he longed to follow would be closed against him
once and for all. It also made him a little older, and a little more
familiar with the realities. By 1883 my father was no longer frightened
of the fifty pound forfeit his mother would have to pay if his articles
were to be cancelled. However great the sum might seem in relation
to a week's or a year's pay, it had to be recognised as trifling when it
was set off against the difference between the probable lifetime earnings of an educated man and an uneducated one, the figure for the
loss that he was being called upon to shoulder. He began to bombard
my grandmother with letters asking her the vital questions with brutal
urgency: Was it really worth saving fifty pounds now at the price of
guaranteeing him a rotten lifetime? Did she realise that he would be
powerless to help her in her old age on a shop assistant's miserable
wages? He began using his Sundays and Bank Holidays to get together the information needed to back up his case. He sought out his
brother Frank, who was in a wretched place in Godalming, to squeeze
from him a realistic picture of what his own prospects as a shop
assistant would be. And he made his way to Midhurst to see Horace
Byatt to find out from him if there was still, now that his hopes of
becoming a pupil teacher had finally gone, any way at all that he could
make a late entry into teaching. Could he, for instance, have a place
under Byatt as an usher?

Byatt was cool at first, and then responsive to a limited extent. If
my father was willing to work for him without pay for six months to
a year while he caught up on his lost two years of schooling, and if
he was able to pass a stiff examination at the end of that time, he could
have a post as an assistant master at Midhurst Grammar School. It was
half a loaf, and a pretty hard and dry one at that, but it was bread, and
what my father wanted more than anything else in life. He liked Byatt,
and the look of Byatt's adventure. The number of pupils in the re-
created school had gone up from thirty-two to sixty, and Byatt had
lately taken on two youths like himself as assistant masters. If he could
get out of Hyde's shop to join forces with Byatt, he would have more
than a mere chance of finishing his education—he could come out of
it with the gloss on him of a young trier who had taken part in the
making of what would be, to all intents and purposes, a new school.
He could see himself rising to a headmastership by the time he was
thirty-five . . .

My father went into the figures of Byatt's proposition with one of the young assistant masters, and began to bombard my grandmother with them. He could get full board, with laundry included, for ten shillings a week by sharing digs with young Harris, the assistant master. He would need ten pounds in his first year for clothes and sundries. And that would be it. He would need thirty-five pounds in all, over and above the money that had been thrown away on Hyde, to see him started on a professional career. It might seem like a great deal:

> But then, when the start is made there is every prospect of rising to a good position in the world, while in my present trade I am a draper's assistant throughout life. But I must begin at once. If I start at all I must start next September.

June slipped away, and a fever rose in him. In his tense and frustrated state my father got himself into a stand-up row with Hyde one Saturday evening, and broke out of the shop just after dawn the following morning. He walked the seventeen miles to Uppark to have things out with my grandmother. He couldn't move her, and in the afternoon he walked back to Southsea defeated. He knew what he was up against now. His mother wanted him to live and die as a shop assistant. She would fight him every inch of the way to prevent his escape from that fate.

July was almost gone, and he had a bare six weeks left. He was desperate, and his letters to Uppark show it. He raged at my grandmother for being so obtuse. He went so far as to hint at suicide, and at worse things that might disgrace the family.

My father's behaviour at this point seems overwrought to anyone who has been brought up in the modern world, but I feel that it is unjust to talk of him, as some of his biographers have done, as childishly trying to get his own way by resorting to temper tantrums. It wasn't just a matter of wanting to have his own way, it was the much graver one of not wanting to be thrown aside and wasted. The episode lies on the far side of almost a century of social change, most of it for the better. However liberal that vanished order may have been in rewarding the successful, it had no pity on those who fell behind in the struggle to get on. My father was in real danger of being trapped in the worst of all of its social niches, that of the white-collar worker who had to keep up the appearances of gentility while earning a day-labourer's wage. A shop assistant had no security of employment and no prospect of a pension or any form of retirement benefits. He lived in dread of being given his notice at the end of the week. He knew that he would be as good as finished before he'd begun if he gave way and accepted the role that had been assigned to him.

My father's physique has to be taken into account here, too. He was a skinny youth, well below the average height, and although he had very great energy, he had no strength, and no reserves. He had learned, humiliatingly, at Rodgers and Denyers and at the Southsea Emporium that he was a misfit so far as the drapery trade was concerned, and that his physical traits were going to count against him more rather than less as time went on. He was the sort that employers were never going to like the look of, ever. He would have seen floor walkers eyeing him with distaste, and he would have seen older versions of himself, weedy and shambling, cringing when they were exposed to the same unappreciative glares. These partly worn-out men, penny-pinching to build up some reserve against the evil day when they failed to please in their last crib, were what his brothers were becoming, were what he would surely become if his mother had her way.

My father was saved from the fate my grandmother had chosen for him by Horace Byatt. Just as my father was about to abandon hope, Byatt told him that the job was his—he was to have twenty pounds for his first year, and forty pounds a year after that. Faced with these figures, my grandmother could not hold out, and gave way, though reluctantly. She could not really believe that her son was capable of making a wise choice of career. He had been nicely taken in by Tom Pennicott's friend. She would wait and see.

My father had one last exasperation to endure. The statutes of the ancient foundation that Byatt had taken over and reanimated had been resurrected with it, and one of them provided that all its teachers had to be communicants of the Church of England. My father demurred, hinting at his unbelief by saying that he found certain of the church's Thirty-Nine Articles hard to accept, but Byatt explained to him that things were as they were, and that there was no way around the terms of the statute. My father would have to be confirmed and pay homage to my grandmother's God—just as if he believed in him —if he wanted to become a member of the staff of Midhurst Grammar School. He went through the motions with the best grace he could muster, but the humiliation of being required to profess a faith to which he could not in any sense subscribe stayed with him for the rest of his life. He felt that he had been forced to take part in a dishonorable charade.

It was at this point in his career that my father showed the first real signs of being somewhat out of the ordinary run of brightly eager and gifted boys. Once at Midhurst, he settled down easily to a routine of days spent in teaching Byatt's junior forms and evenings working as a pupil, sometimes the only one, in Byatt's extracurricular courses on the foundation subjects of the sciences. There was a division of labor: my father gutted the textbooks and Byatt coached him in the art of writing answers to examination questions that would make the most of his knowledge. They worked together in perfect harmony from September 1883 through the winter and on into May 1884. My father then sat for what was to have been the first set of the Board of Education examinations through which he would learn his keep. He did very well in them, and more than satisfied Byatt's expectations by winning several of the advanced passes that brought in the maximum capitation fee. That was reward enough, but neither Byatt nor my father had realised that there could be more to come. The Board's scheme for promoting the teaching of scientific subjects was linked to a less well publicised one designed to encourage students to train as science teachers by awarding scholarships to the Normal School of Science in South Kensington, a branch of the University of London, to men who scored high marks in its examinations. The first my father knew of all this was when a letter from South Kensington came to him through the mail letting him know that he had qualified for the scholarship, and inviting him to complete the enclosed form of application for an award. He hastened to fill it out and to return it, and a few days later he was pouring out the great news to Byatt. He was to have a place at the Normal School. He was to have a maintenance grant of a guinea a week. He was to read biology under no less a person than Darwin's old lieutenant, the great Professor Huxley himself. He was to enroll at the Normal School in September.

This was the first that Byatt had heard of the scholarship, and he had a moment of bitterness. He was hurt to find that the application had gone in, as he put it, behind his back. He let my father know what he thought, and there was tension in the air for a day or two—but when Byatt had given himself time to remember my father's youth and eagerness and inexperience he forgave him for a moment of thoughtlessness and let him go with his blessing. Just one year after he had gone to Midhurst to join Byatt's expanding staff he moved on to South Kensington to see what he could make of the greater opportunity that he had won for himself.

My grandmother did not care for this new development; as soon as she heard that her son had won the scholarship and would be leaving Midhurst to go to the Normal School, she despaired. It gave her one more proof that her boy did not know his own mind and was incapable of sticking at anything; it was only a year since he had been moving heaven and earth to get himself settled into his position with Mr. Byatt, and now here he was set on something else. To let my father know how she felt she refused to ask Frances Bullock if she could have him with her at Uppark for the summer. He went to Atlas House to spend what remained of June, and July, and August with my grandfather. He had nowhere else to go.

Chapter XI

He was quite sure that he had failed in this last examination. He knew that any career as a scientific man was now closed to him for ever. And he remembered now how he had come along this very road to that great building for the first time in his life, and all the hopes and resolves that had swelled within him as he had drawn near. That dream of incessant unswerving work! . . . "Yes," he said, speaking aloud to himself; "yes—*that's* all over. . . . Everything's over."

—LOVE AND MR. LEWISHAM

MY FATHER DEALS WITH THE SUMMER he spent with my grandfather in 1884 in his autobiography, but he comes to it by way of his older brother's then recent death in 1933, and gives it evasive handling. When he went back to Bromley to stay with my grandfather that summer he had found the older man living out a grown-up child's dream, getting up when he liked, going to bed when he liked, shutting up the shop whenever he felt inclined to go wherever he fancied. He had revived his interest in clock making and clock mending, and partially dismantled clock motions, cannibalised for parts or waiting for repair, lay about in the kitchen and in the parlour, among the remains of old meals. No longer able to play cricket, he justified frequent closures of the shop for the sake of the playing fields round and about Bromley by taking along a pedlar's bag full of batting gloves, wicket keepers gauntlets, bats, pads, and balls. He could pretend that his long days spent with the players round the pavilions and in the beer tents were all in the way of drumming up trade. He was still pretending, even though the end of the shop was now only three years off.

If my grandfather had been just any other dirty, flabby aged man with a habit of taking one or two beers too many whenever the opportunity offered, my father would, I imagine, have been purely disgusted with him. But Joseph Wells had enormous charm, and he could gather himself to use it whenever he wanted to. He knew that he had lost my father at that point, and he set out to win him back. He pulled himself together and took his son on a number of country rambles in the neighbourhood and down Penshurst way that he was to remember for the rest of his life. He knew that my grandfather was doing his best to charm him, and I think that he was even then subliminally aware that there would be some kind of danger in letting himself be charmed. In his later life, when he saw what had happened to my uncle Frank, I think that my father saw clearly enough how lethal that display of charm could have been to him. My grandfather charmed Frank into accepting his way of life as model for his own behaviour, so much so that he became a rerun for the old man. The bright lad with a bent for mechanics who had been mishandled by Morley because he had no use for books, and who had been dulled and broken in the drapery trade, had at last become an itinerant clock mender and watch pedlar, a happily useless man who earned pin money at his trade and had his living from my father. He, too, ended by acting out a child's dream, endlessly cycling through the leafy lanes of southeast England, doing what he liked and returning to his lair when he felt inclined. When I was younger it used to seem to me that he had found a rather agreeable way of living, and I found it hard to understand why my father had been genuinely horrified to see his much loved older brother turning into a replica of my grandfather. The word "horrified" may suggest an irrational overreaction, since it is easy for those who have only encountered them at second hand in print to look on the pair as a couple of rather jolly dropouts who made quite a success out of being failures. But since he had been ten years old my father had known just how absolute my grandfather's failure had been, and to what lengths it had taken him.

The moment of his revelation is described in a passage that is dropped without warning into the hymn of hate for Atlas House with which he opens his autobiography, it is just added to the list of the horrors of the place that his father was one day found lying in its back yard after suffering an accident that left him crippled for life. Details of the accident are given, but on examination they turn out to be improbable. While he was alone in the house and my father and grandmother were in church one Sunday in October 1877 my grandfather had taken the opportunity to climb up a rickety erection made by setting the garden ladder up on a bench so that he could prune the grape vine that covered the back of the house. That a man who had been trained as professional gardener would set out to do such a job in such a manner or that a man with the physical *savoir-faire* required of a professional cricketer would trust himself to such a structure, seems so unlikely as to be impossible. The autobiography account of the event, written in 1932–1934, raises the suspicion that my father knew this, and the fictionalised account given in *The New Machiavelli*, a novel written twenty years closer to the accident, in 1910–1911, very close to the time of my grandfather's death, makes it quite clear that he thought it was a failed attempt at suicide. The point is underlined by the fact that the "accident" is fatal in the novel, where the mother and son come back from church to find a dead man lying in the back yard. The word suicide, though spelt out by the circumstances, isn't actually used in the novel, but what makes it permissible to interpolate it into a reading of the text is the existence of *The History of Mr. Polly*, a comedy written at roughly the same time as *The New Machiavelli*. This tells the story of a man who makes a considerable success of the most absolute failure by surviving an attempted suicide. Though society was firm in denying him the chance to do anything he wanted to do while he was alive, once Mr. Polly has disappeared and dwindled into a ghost he is able to do just what he likes and to live happily ever after. As one of the things he has been released from by his failed suicide is marriage to an overdemanding and constantly nagging wife who wants him to smarten up and turn himself into something he doesn't have it in him to be, it isn't possible for me to doubt that my father got his inspiration for the book from his memories of the summer he spent with my liberated grandfather in Bromley, or that the book's ultimate foundation was his conviction that the accident of 1877 had really been an attempt at suicide. What he had seen in the summer of 1884 was his father serenely enjoying the happiness that had come to him as his reward for giving up on himself after he had been driven to the end of his tether. My grandfather's very great charm made it a beguiling spectacle, and I think that it frightened my father to realise that there was something in him that was strongly tempted by the example.

My father was not in a very joyous frame of mind when he went up to London at the end of that summer to become a student at the Normal School. He knew that he was doing something to which his mother was utterly opposed, and which had no meaning to his father. He was absolutely on his own, and unsupported either by their pride in his achievement or by their encouragement. If he succeeded at the school, he would only be compounding his original offence of having got there by proving them wrong, and if he failed, he would be doing the same thing by proving them right. He had pleased nobody by making his point that he was fit for further education. My grandmother, after all, had been drumming it into his head for the past four years that all he had to do to please her was to take it from her that all he was good for was an ignominious servitude; and for the past three months my grandfather had been giving him a very clear set of signals conveying the message that there could be great deal of comfort in failing and having done with it. I won't say that he set out for South Kensington feeling that he was under an obligation to fail there, but I think that the shadow of that notion was rather strongly present in the back of his mind. This may seem unlikely to those who have been brought up to believe in my father as a ruthless self-improver and go-getter. But it may appear to be rather more plausible than it does at first sight when consideration is given to the fix he had engineered for himself ten years from the date of his first arrival in London. His performance between the autumn of 1884 and the late summer of 1894 should be compared with my grandfather's track record for the period between his sixteenth and twenty-sixth years.

The reader will recall that it was in the dead of winter in 1853 that my grandfather, out of a job and as good as unemployable in his chosen profession, elected to improve his chances by getting married to a woman who was even worse off than he was himself. My father had gone my grandfather one better by getting himself married to a girl with whom he had nothing whatever in common a month after he had turned twenty-four, when he was, if anything, in a rather worse position.

When my father went off to London he wasn't faced with the problem of finding lodgings, it had been solved for him by my grandmother, who had been much worried by the possibility that he might fall into bad company if he were to choose his own living quarters. She knew that the daughter of a very old friend of hers took in lodgers at her home in Westbourne Park and arranged for him to board with her, certain that the daughter would take after the well-conducted, churchgoing and sober woman she had known. The daughter had, however, gone to the bad, and my father found himself living in a *louche* atmosphere in which the constant "goings on" gave rise to an endless succession of rows in which a great deal was spelt out that my father would have preferred to know nothing of. One of the customs of the house was that its inmates should go pub-crawling *en bande* on Saturday nights, and much of the trouble in which it simmered perpetually rose out of the boozy gropings and tumblings that were the usual aftermath of these excursions. My father didn't care for this setup, but didn't know quite how to get out of it until a friend of my grandfather's, a woman named Janie Gall who worked in the dress department at Derry and Toms in Kensington High Street, and who had been asked to keep an eye on him, came to the rescue. She saw that he was unhappy, found out why, and immediately arranged for him to move from Westbourne Park to the Euston Road, where his aunt by marriage, a certain Mary Wells, kept lodgings.

Mary Wells was the widow of my grandfather's brother William. She had a daughter, Isabel, to whom my father was presently married. There is nothing out of the way in the marriage of cousins, and since my father lodged contentedly with his aunt for the rest of his days as a student at the Normal School, this one might seem to be the most natural of events. So it may well have been, since contiguity is almost all in these matters. It bothers me a little, nonetheless, that, having had his tremendous battle with my grandmother to get out of the drapery trade, he should have made it his first independent act as an adult to marry the daughter of a man who had been a draper, who had failed in the profession, and who had died in the workhouse. It could have been no more than a coincidence, but it looks odd.

The circumstances in which the marriage took place were ominous. My father blew his great opportunity for getting a university degree as a grant-aided student, and was dropped at the end of his third year. He had managed it by diffusing his interests. He had given up too much of the time that he should have put into studying his assignments to following his own lines of reading in unrelated fields, predominantly literary and artistic, and by allowing himself to let his unsatisfied hunger for sexual experience prey on his mind. His wrought-up state made him aggressive and foolish, and he had been defiant and provocative in his dealings with teachers on whose good will he was largely dependent. When the question of the renewal of his grant came up at the end of his third year some of them were anxious to see the last of a student they had come to look on as a disruptive nuisance.

With his grant gone, my father found that he had limited options. He could either throw in the towel so far as attempting to get a degree was concerned and make a late entry into some trade as an untrained beginner, or he could try to save something from the wreck by continuing to work for his B.Sc. on his own while scratching what he could get in the way of a living from teaching. Without any very clear idea of the difficulties that he would have to face, he elected to follow the second course. He was doing his best to make a go of it from the summer of 1887 until the late autumn of 1889, and finding the effort very taxing indeed. He had been underfed all through the three-year stretch during which he had been living on his guinea-a-week grant, and he now paid the penalty for having run down his reserves. He would get into a new job as a teacher, work himself into the ground for a few months, and then collapse. His situation improved towards the end of 1889 when he took the intermediate examination for his B.Sc. and came away with second-class honours in zoology. He followed that up by winning his teacher's diploma with numerous distinctions. This made him fully qualified, and soon brought him a handsome offer from William Briggs, a pioneer in the field of correspondence schools. Briggs had spotted his name and the list of his distinctions in the published results of the diploma examination, and had been impressed. He wrote to offer him an immediate two pounds a week if he would take over the biology courses offered by his grandly named University Correspondence College, and promised him that if he won honours with his B.Sc. when he sat for the finals, he could count on four pounds for a week of thirty coaching hours preparing candidates for their university entrance examinations at his tutorial college down by the Strand.

My father was jubilant, buoyed up by his sense that he was fulfilling all the ambitions that he had formed while he was working under Byatt in Midhurst. He was on the track again. His mood, now that he had a good job in hand, and a better one in prospect, endured, and gave him the self-confidence to write to my grandmother at last, apologising for all the worry and anxiety he had caused her over the years, and signing himself once again as "your most loving son." He won his B.Sc. with first class honours in zoology, and Briggs proved better than his word. My father found himself bringing home six pounds a week for teaching fifty hours at the Tutorial College. This may not look good to a contemporary eye, but my father's feelings about what Briggs was paying him have to be related to the fact that at that time experienced male shop assistants were working an eighty-hour week and getting less than thirty shillings for it. He was already earning four times that amount and he was doing more than drawing his wages. He made himself a money spinner when he wrote a biology textbook for the use of Briggs's students, and he acquired a second source of regular income when he undertook the editorship of Briggs's paper, *The University Correspondent.* In addition to these things there were the oncers and the occasionals: he mopped up twenty pounds in prize money when he sat for the Fellowship Examination of the College of Preceptors, and he picked up fifty pounds in twelve months by writing briefs on topical subjects for *The Educational Times.*

But if it seemed for the moment as if my father had found a solution to the problem of getting by, he was not yet out of his cycle of new job, overwork, physical collapse, and return to scraping. He had a warning breakdown right at the start of 1890, just as he was about to sit for the finals for his B.Sc., and this was followed by something more serious soon after the new year. It began, as usual, with convincing hemorrhages, and when these had pulled him down he fell an easy victim to a bout of influenza that brought him in sight of death. He had to admit that his condition was serious, and that he could not go on driving himself as relentlessly as he had been doing. In the summer of that year he wrote to my grandfather in this new mood, telling him in broad outline of the state he was in, and hinting that he was beginning to wonder if he was ever going to be in a position to get married. But with the coming of the brisker autumn weather he began to feel better, and he took up his routine where he had left it off. Briggs radiated confidence in him, and he found it possible to believe in himself again. On the last day of October he married his cousin Isabel, and during November he started to play house with her in a villa with a little garden in suburban Wandsworth, within easy commuting distance of Briggs's centre of operations at Red Lion Square, in Holborn.

For the next eighteen months my father was under steadily mounting stress. He had married the wrong woman. His cousin was sweet-natured and had the best of intentions, but she did not have a lively mind and she had nothing in common with the statuesque but hot-blooded creatures who figured in her inexperienced husband's fantasy life. When those stately neo-Greek persons from the Crystal Palace and the pages of *Punch* came alive to pleasure him they knew exactly what was wanted from them, and they were always ready. They needed no courting and no foreplay. My father was badly rattled when he found that he had no idea how to rouse his unawakened wife's sexual appetite, and was even more shaken when he discovered that she did not particularily want to have it aroused. She was well content to minimise the role in marriage of an element that she thought of as not quite nice. He might have been even more disturbed if he had realised then, as he was to later, that what he had done was to complicate his already difficult position as a man with uncertain health by constructing for himself a duplicate of my grandfather's marriage of incompatibilities with my grandmother.

My father's perplexities, and his distress, were greatly increased, quite soon after his marriage, when he had what he describes in his autobiography as an adventure. It took place in the house in Wandsworth. Mary Wells, who had come to live with the young couple, was out on a shopping expedition: Isabel had gone up into the West End to deliver some of her retouched negatives to the Regent Street photographers who had been her employers before her marriage, and the only people left in the house were my father, working away in his ground-floor study and a young woman who was upstairs in Isabel's attic workroom. She was there because she was Isabel's pupil. She was learning the art of retouching negatives from her, and in her mentor's absence she did not have quite enough to do. Her mind turned to my father, and to certain thoughts that she had allowed to enter her head. She knew that Mary Wells took shopping seriously. She knew how long the trip from Wandsworth to Regent Street and back would take. The coast was as clear as it would ever be. She went downstairs and joined my father in his study. She said she had been thinking of making some tea, and asked him if he cared for a cup? It was revealed to him by some instinct that she had not been thinking of making tea. The act was swiftly and agreeably accomplished, to the entire satisfaction of both parties if one is to believe the account of the transaction written by my father just over forty years later. "It was," he then observed, and I think that he betrays some uncertainty in doing so, "the most natural thing in the world." And he goes on to say that this chance became the foundation of a policy. After the event had taken place he embarked on what he calls an enterprising promiscuity. Although his love for Isabel wasn't, he asserted, dead, he meant to get in all the minor and incidental love adventures that he could . . .

This is, I think, my father's gloss on his memory of the way things went. I do not believe that he had any such clear-cut picture of the course of events at the time, and I am quite sure that it did not then seem at all natural to him that he should, on the one hand, be quite unable to establish a happy sexual relationship with the woman to whom he felt emotionally committed, and on the other highly successful when it came to pleasing women and girls who meant nothing very much to him. If it had seemed as natural as all that, it does not seem likely that the situation would have bothered him as much as it evidently did.

While my father was getting used to the idea that he was to look outside his marriage for sexual pleasure, the general situation of his family was undergoing a sharp deterioration. My grandfather had hit bottom a little earlier, in 1887, when he was put out of Atlas House and sold up after letting himself falling unconscionably far behind with the rent. Stripped of his last pretensions to being an independent businessman, and of most of his worldly goods, he had then moved away from Bromley to set himself up in a cottage at Nyewood, a tiny hamlet south of Rogate in Sussex, where he was within sight of Harting Down and the Uppark beech hangers. My grandmother paid his rent. Soon after he had settled in there he was joined by my uncle Frank, and the pair lived there together in companionable squalor for the next few years. The household, redolent of shag tobacco, gun oil, and beer, and noisy with the ticking of Frank's clocks, was nothing like self-supporting, and it was very soon in trouble when my grandmother's Indian summer in Uppark came to an ugly end. She lost her hearing, and as is the case with so many people who suddenly find themselves enclosed by this affliction, she soon became crotchety and difficult. Her employer, who was herself failing, had already become impatient with her, and now began to find her exasperating. My grandmother was given her warning notice in the latter part of November 1892. She was to go at the end of two months, and she was to have a year and a half's pay for a golden handshake. This was a liberal arrangement for the time, and my grandmother was not very much upset by it, thinking of herself as she did as housekeeper at a great house who had demonstrated her competence over the years by the mere fact of being the unchallenged possessor of the housekeeper's room and the keys. But when she looked about for other employment, she was quickly disillusioned. By the start of the New Year she had come to realise that she was old, deaf, and useless; that she had become unemployable; and that the hundred pounds that she had been given to pay her off was in all probability the last money she would ever earn. Understandably, she panicked, and clung to her place in the Uppark household. It took heavy pressure to get her to leave at last, nearly three weeks after her notice had run out.

My father claims in his autobiography to have foreseen this catastrophe, but if he did so, he had made no plans for the contingency. His reactions to it bear all the earmarks of improvisation. He took the frightened old lady—she was now an elderly seventy—into his Wandsworth home for a few days, and then passed her on to make what she could of life with my grandfather and my uncle Frank in that very small cottage at Nyewood. I am not sure just how small it actually was, since the only detailed description of it that I have been able to find, in which it is said to have had only three rooms, occurs in a facetious letter written by my father to his old friend Elizabeth Healey in the early part of 1888. He was writing for effect, and making the most of old Joseph Wells's unreconstructed ways. Whether or no the cottage was actually as small as all that, it still must have been very hard for my grandmother to take kindly to being asked to live at close quarters with a man she had never altogether cared for, thirteen years after she had escaped from him to live as the mistress of the housekeeper's room in the solidly splendid great house just down the road and over the crest of Harting Down. The servants who had once minded her laughed and jeered at her so unkindly in her last weeks there, when they knew that she had fallen irretrievably out of Miss Fetherstonehaugh's favor, it would be unbearable if they were to hear that she was living so close to them, and in such a fashion. They might walk over to crow over her in her fallen state.

It does not surprise me to find that my father writes apologetically of his treatment of my grandmother at this time when he gets to it in the autobiography. He has, he says, the impression that he was hasty, harsh, and stupid in his handling of the crisis, and uncouthly regardless of the humiliations he was visiting on his family as their problems crowded in upon him. He felt, looking back on it, that he had been particularily hard on my uncle Frederick.

No sooner had my father packed my grandmother off to Nyewood than he found Fred on his doorstep. Fred had been fired from what had seemed like a very good job in Wokingham in a disillusioning fashion that had shattered his morale. He had been given to understand that he had won his employer's confidence there and that he had real prospects of taking over the business in the fullness of time—but his real function had been to keep a place warm that his employer's son was to have as soon as he was old enough. That day had arrived, and my uncle had been put out on the street at short notice. He'd been nicely taken in, and had been mocked for it. Fred's morale revived quickly under my father's roof. He began to show fight. He wasn't without resources. He'd saved. He had a little nest egg. He had nearly a hundred pounds. He could make a fresh start, on his own. He could move into a little shop. If he could find the right location—and if my father could give him a little help with stocking up, a couple of hundred perhaps. He had an expression on his face as he mentioned this sum that my father was coming to recognise.

They were all beginning to depend on him whenever there was a crisis. My father found that although he was earning more than ever, he wasn't getting much benefit from his increased income. About a third of what he was bringing home was going to his family. Once he had found himself in Briggs's good books, he had made a resolution to keep fifty pounds on hand at all times as catastrophe insurance. The amount would give him a year's leeway, if he cut back hard and went into really cheap lodgings. Now he found that he was having difficulty keeping a float of more than five pounds in his bank account. That was no margin at all for a married man with a mother-in-law, parents, and two unlucky brothers to support. He was up against it again. He worked on under this increasing strain until one night in May 1893 when he broke. He was making his way down to the Charing Cross Underground Station, where he was to catch a train back to Wandsworth after working late at the Tutorial College, when he was seized by a fit of coughing that stopped him in his tracks. Within seconds he was being nauseated by the taste of his own blood. He managed to get himself onto his train, and during the ride home the attack passed off. But it was renewed at three o'clock on the following morning, and this time the hemorrhage was massive. Blood was welling up into his mouth in terrifying quantities. A doctor was called in, and for a few hours it was touch and go. But while he was out of danger before dawn, and well enough to take solid food again at the end of a week, it was quite clear to him that he was very seriously ill indeed and that his teaching days were over.

My father's first reaction to this blow was a healthy but not especially likable use of his instinct for self-preservation. He got my uncle Fred off his back with a brusque display of almost Napoleonic ruthlessness. My uncle was still boarding in the Wandsworth villa, and it soon occurred to my father that he was spending far too much of the time that he should have been out looking for a new place sitting at his bedside, either playing draughts or chess with him or, even less constructively, outlining in a discursive way a variety of nebulous schemes for setting himself up in business. In some of these he was to have my uncle Frank as a partner, in others not, but in all of them he was to need more capital than he had at his disposal, and in every case my father was looked upon as the source from which the deficiency was to be made up. While he was being introduced to his brother's dream world by way of these explanations it also became clear to him, from the monotonous way in which the board games came out in his favor, that poor Fred was nowhere near as bright as he had thought him in his younger days. The four years of seniority and experience that had once meant so much had ceased to count; he had caught his brother up, and had left him behind. Fred was, or had become, a dullard who did not even believe in his own dreams. My father began to scan the want ads in the papers that my uncle was looking over with a lacklustre eye, and he soon saw one that looked like the very thing, there was a vacancy for an experienced shop assistant in South Africa.

My father's own account of the little family drama that followed can hardly be bettered, either as self-revelation or as a narrative.

> [Fred] was honest, sober, decent and pleasant, he was trustworthy to the superlative degree and he lacked the sort of push, smartness and self assertion needed to make any sort of business success in England. In the colonies shop assistants do not run as straight or as steadily as they are compelled to do at home, they feel the breath of opportunity and the lure of personal freedom, so that out there his assets of steadiness and trustworthiness would be a precious commodity, and therefore I determined he must go. I had to overbear a strong sentimental resistance on the part of my mother, but Freddy was greatly sustained by my agreement with him, and in a week or so the engagement was made and the adventurer was buying his outfit and packing for the Cape. . . . With Freddy thus provided for and having undertaken to carry a share of the expenses of Nyewoods so soon as his first money came in, my mind was liberated to go into details of my own problem.

The words in the above, "Freddy was greatly sustained by my agreement with him," refer to the unhappy truth—that my uncle did not really want to go off to South Africa and would just as soon have stayed at home. He was in fact bullied into going.

My father's statement that poor Freddy's deportation liberated his mind to go into the details of his own problem is also one that needs interpretation, particularily since it is followed up by an assertion: that he had a solution to it in mind. This suggests that he thought things out and came to the conclusion that the best thing for him to do was to try to make a living as a writer, working his own hours at home. He gives up some three pages to ingenious special pleading for regarding this decision as a reasonable one, but I am unable to believe that he made the decision as a decision, or that he made it on the grounds given. He did not, in fact, have any options. There were very few things that he could do, taking his physical condition into account. His only resource other than his proven ability as a teacher, was a knack for writing what were then known as "chatty pars," readable half- and quarter-column fillers for trade journals and newspapers. How far he had then developed this capacity it would be difficult to say. As the editor of Briggs's *University Correspondent* he had been giving himself an inside track, and when he submitted contributions to the *Educational Times* he was offering them to a friend who was a colleague on Briggs's teaching staff. It is true that he had written an essay called "The Rediscovery of the Unique" in 1887 that had nothing to do with his professional speciality and which had found its way, after much rewriting, into the pages of the *Fortnightly Review* in July 1891, but this success had been no more than a flash in the pan. It had indeed led to a notable fiasco. When he had tried to follow it up he had found himself quite unable to tell an indignant Frank Harris, the then editor of the *Fortnightly,* what his second submission, an essay entitled "The Universe Rigid," was supposed to be *about.* As he stumbled out of Harris' office, feeling disconcerted and ashamed of his inadequate performance, he heard the formidable little adventurer cursing behind him: "Gahd! How I've been let in!"

My father had really had no experience of selling original work in the open market until he read J. M. Barrie's *When a Man's Single* in the course of a convalescent fortnight spent in lodgings at Eastbourne in early June 1893. One of Barrie's characters had developed a foolproof formula for writing a salable short piece for the newspapers, and Barrie had said just what it was. Within hours of reading the passage my father had made his first trial of the formula, and the next day had sent a fair copy off to *The Pall Mall Gazette* in London. By return mail he had a letter of acceptance with a request for more such short pieces. The paper had just been bought by William Waldorf Astor, who had given his newly appointed editor, Harry Cust, orders to liven up the paper, and to keep an eye open for new writers with a light touch. Cust thought that my father's trial piece, "On the Art of Staying at the Seaside," was exactly what he wanted. My father began to churn out shorts written to Barrie's formula as fast as he could dream up notions to pin them to. When the paper sent him a cheque early in November, settling for his October contributions, he was delighted to see that he had earned nearly fifteen pounds in the month. He wrote jubilantly to his exiled brother to tell him of this triumph: "Not bad is it? But this may be a lucky month. However I am not drawing on savings, thank goodness, and I am keeping indoors, and I think pulling round steadily." That was the full extent to which he was in possession of the solution to his problem—he was just breaking even as he lived from hand to mouth. He was still an invalid, and he was in no shape to assume further responsibilities; he obviously had to watch his step for some time to come.

My father did not do the obvious thing. In August of 1893, buoyed up by his success with *The Pall Mall Gazette* he had moved out of the villa in Wandsworth and into a slightly larger house close to the North Downs at Sutton in Surrey, in those days relatively untouched by suburban sprawl. The move was reasonable enough. The state of my father's lungs made it wise for him to go where he could breathe something more like country air for a time. He seemed to be settling down to the terms of his new life with a certain realism. But between Christmas and the New Year, at the end of 1893, he walked out of the house in Sutton, leaving his wife and her desolated mother behind him. He never went back.

My father did not move to a neighbourhood that anyone could have recommended to a man with lung trouble, he found lodgings in a rundown quarter in northwest London, on the frontier between Euston and Camden Town. Once an attractive area of Regency and early-Victorian developments, it had been badly hit by railroad blight when the two main lines to the north had been blasted through it in mid-century. When my father went there in '93 it had been going downhill for forty years, and was still deteriorating. Its special character was set by the load of soft-coal soot that the prevailing winds brought over from the West End to be mixed with the more acid exhaust smoke from passing locomotives. As soon as he had established himself in these dismal surroundings my father was joined by a young woman called Amy Catherine Robbins who had been a member of one of his classes at the Tutorial College. They were living together as man and wife.

Elizabeth Healey, who saw Amy Catherine Robbins for the first time in the early part of 1893, said that she was then one of the prettiest girls that she had ever seen. She was tiny and very delicately made, even smaller than my father, and endowed with pale golden-blond hair, dark-brown eyes, a flawless peaches-and-cream complexion, and a perfect figure. She had joined my father's classes as an aspirant for the B.Sc. in September 1892, and had made an indelible impression upon him when, after missing a few sessions in October, she had returned in deep mourning. She was, in accordance with the still rigid convention, wearing black from head to toe to mourn for her father, who had just died in circumstances that were ambiguous, but which were strongly suggestive of suicide. None of the witnesses at the inquest had been able to say what precisely had happened. All that could be said for certain was that he had been found dead on the line between the platforms of Putney Station, after having either fallen or thrown himself in front of a passing train. His affairs had not been going well for some time, and his wife and daughter were left in reduced circumstances. There was the house in Putney in which they were living, and very little else.

The marked resemblance between my grandmother's situation at the time when my grandfather rushed her into marriage and that of Amy Catherine Robbins when my father swept her into what was to be a lifetime relationship, for her, and, for him, his most enduring involvement, may, perhaps, be purely coincidental. Possibly all that really counted was that she was very attractive, and that she was capable of being interested in what interested him, and that she was there. It so happened that she was assigned to one of his classes, it so happened that it was his last class of the day, and it so happened that when they left the Tutorial College and turned their backs on Red Lion Square they both walked down to the Charing Cross Underground Station to catch a train on the District Line that would let him off at Wandsworth and carry her on to Putney. Between the College and the Underground Station one of the new teashops of the Aerated Bread Company offered its temptations. These were newly established institutions, the not overly benevolent Victorian God's gift to the youth of the lower-middle classes. An innocent place of rendezvous, they provided the perfect answer to the problem facing a young man with very little money who had nowhere to go when he wanted to sit and talk with a respectable girl. No nice girl could afford to be seen entering or leaving a young man's digs, and public houses were out of the question, so that between the front parlour of the girl's home, and walks, late Victorian London offered very little to couples who were getting to know each other until the ABC tearooms came along. In them you could sit, warm and dry, and socially safe, for as long as you liked if you had the price of two cups of tea and an order of buns. What harm could there be in turning aside to snatch a few minutes' talk in such a place on the way down to catch the train back to Wandsworth?

My father was already a marvellous talker. Some of the men who had been his fellow students at the Normal School in South Kensington and who had lost touch with him soon afterwards could still recall the pleasures of hearing him playing with ideas thirty or forty years later. He talked his way into the center of Miss Robbins's life very quickly, and she was one of the first people to come to the Wandsworth house to wish him well when he was able to receive visitors after his collapse of May 1893. It may possibly have been then that Isabel picked up some vibration of interest emanating from her successor-to-be that led her to favour the move from Wandsworth to Sutton that followed in August. Be that as it may, my father was still unconscious of what had befallen him at that late date, and managed to remain so until the middle of December. Isabel then braced him with the realities of the developing situation at the end of a high-risk weekend that had been set up by Miss Robbins. She had persuaded her mother—who cannot have had any notion of what was taking shape—to ask my father and his wife to stay from Friday night to Monday morning in their Putney house. What was in her mind there is no way of knowing, but in the course of the weekend Isabel's suspicions became knowledge. As soon as she had my father back at home in Sutton she told him that, whether he had intended it to happen or not, Miss Robbins had fallen in love with him, and that he would have to give up this dangerous association if he wanted his marriage to survive. My father took rather less than ten days to make up his mind as to what he should do, and when he sat down to his Christmas dinner with Isabel and her mother he was already packed up to leave.

When my father left Sutton on the 27th of December, 1893, he was taking with him heavier burdens than his trunk and his books, he was now financially responsible for two households, the one he had just left and the one at Nyewood, and for Miss Robbins. And he was faced with the possibility that he might soon have Fred back on his hands. Ill feeling between Boers and Englanders was growing, and my scared and homesick uncle was showing signs of giving up on South Africa. At the same time a shadow of anxiety was infecting my father with doubts about himself: divorces were not taken lightly in those days, and he couldn't be sure that editors would still want his articles once he had had his name in the papers as the guilty party in a divorce case. This does something to explain why, despite his eagerness to get his new life with Amy Catherine off to a good start, he did all he could to persuade Isabel to postpone the legal proceedings for as long as possible. He had a burden of another kind to deal with in the person of poor Mrs. Robbins, who had never fully recovered from the ugly shock given her by the manner of her husband's death. She took my father's seduction of her daughter—she could not think of the matter in any other terms—as yet another blow of the same order. Her daughter assured her that she knew what she was about, but she was sure that her child did not, and that she was courting ruin. In her desperation Mrs. Robbins sent as many of her friends and acquaintances as she could talk into doing so to call upon my father in his Mornington Place lair, all of them instructed to appeal to his better nature and to beg him to send his innocent victim home to her mother before she suffered the irretrievable degradation of being "named" in court as a home-wrecker and an adultress. Mrs. Robbins' agitation was briefly eased when Amy Catherine, appalled by the effect that the incessant appeals to his better nature were having upon my father's temper, agreed to go back to Putney. But it was soon raised to new levels of intensity when her daughter told her that she had only returned for as many days as it would take to calm her down, and that as soon as she had accomplished her mission she would be rejoining my father for good. She was simply not going to be blackmailed into giving him up. Her display of determination paid off, and she was able to get back to Mornington Place sooner than she had expected.

It seems, at this point, as if all the necessary arrangements had been made for the waters to close over my father's head. With all that he had undertaken there was no way that he could survive as the sort of low-grade journalistic hack he had become. As soon as he showed signs of tiring, and his work began to lose its freshness, he would be done for, he would go into the dark as a member of the great regiment of the unlucky.

His fate seemed inevitable. But just at that juncture Harry Cust produced a new opening for him. Cust felt that my father was writing beneath his proper level for *The Pall Mall Gazette,* and that he had better things in him than the formula pieces he was churning out. He needed saving from his talent for making the odd guinea. Cust had a word with Lewis Hind, the literary editor of *The Gazette*'s weekly supplement, *The Pall Mall Budget,* and later introduced my father to him as someone who might make an ideal contributor to his pages. Hind liked him, and asked him if he would care to try his hand at fiction of a special kind. He provided my father with another formula, he was looking for single sitting shorts with a scientific flavour, and he would pay five guineas for anything in that line that was printable.

It was the story of the Barrie formula all over again, my father got it right at his first try, delighting Hind with a very characteristic period piece called "The Stolen Bacillus." The realm of endeavour into which Hind had drawn him was not so far from the domain of hack work to which the Barrie formula had given him the key, but in it he was at least called upon to use his imagination, and to give it free rein. Hind saw that it was a very active imagination, and a very fertile one, and soon felt that my father had much more in him than the rather bitty pieces to which the limitations imposed by the format of *The Pall Mall Budget* were necessarily confining him. There was no saying what he might not be able to do for anyone who could give him his head. So Lewis Hind passed my father on to W. E. Henley at *The National Observer,* and his hour came, to be made or spoiled.

Henley, who had provided Robert Louis Stevenson with a physical model for Long John Silver, the pirate captain in *Treasure Island,* was a burly giant of a man who had been crippled by primitive surgery in his youth, when a painful organic disease had attacked his feet. He had grown up with a determination never to be pitied, and had made himself the brilliant editor whose essences were captured forever in an unforgettable portrait by William Nicholson. While he was a sucker for Kipling's resounding vulgarities on the one hand, he was also the man to appreciate Yeats, and to say snap to Conrad after reading a single page of "The Nigger of the Narcissus," the marvellous thing that they were running as a serial . . .

When my father was summoned to Henley's office for the first time, he was for the moment short of fresh ideas. Knowing that he would have to have an answer ready if the editor of *The National Observer* should ask him what he was likely to be offering in the near future, and that it had better be something serious, he took a quick look over his file of trial pieces written before Frank Harris had scared him off seriousness. His one useful find was the idea of the time traveller that had lost itself in an inept presentation in the *Science Schools Journal.* He killed off the pretentiously named Dr. Nebo Gipfel, and the poorly organised story in which he had figured, and worked up the raw idea of *The Time Machine* until he had the subject in talkable form. When he presently met Henley he liked him, and found him easy to talk to. The ideas poured out. Henley was familiar with many of them as abstractions, but this was different. The tiny, almost birdlike man in front of him talked of the past and future of the planet, and of the entire solar system, as if all of it, from beginning to end, was part of his own experience. He took Henley millions of years into the future to show him a world that had almost ceased to revolve dying under a cooling sun.

Henley had his doubts. It was not that he recognised that this particular idea was a mistake, generated by the errors of pre-nuclear physics, but because, as his poems testified, he was by temperament disinclined to accept inevitabilities. His line was that he was the master of his fate and the captain of his soul. But he could not resist the scope and sweep of my father's vision of those last days, he had never come across anything so clearly imagined and felt as that faraway end. He told my father what his rates were, and said that he would give him space for ten articles. It would be up to my father to do what he could with his opportunity.

My father did not make very good use of his great chance for reasons that are easy enough to understand. Mrs. Robbins made very heavy weather of her daughter's determination to stay with my father, and made her ruin, as she saw it, the pretext for the release of all the feelings of uncomprehending distress that she had been bottling up since she had been hit by the ambiguities of her husband's death. She quite simply broke up, and spent so much time weeping that she was altogether incapable of looking after herself for a while. Since there was no one else to carry it, the burden of her care fell on the young couple. The house in Putney was let on a long lease, and Mrs. Robbins moved into more commodious new lodgings found by my father in the Mornington Road. Although she was now living with him, she was still far from reconciled to the arrangements that her daughter had made, and she made her disapproval and her grief manifest, in season and out of it. The strain created by her disapproving presence and her constant demonstrations told on my father's work and on Amy Catherine's health. By midsummer of 1894 she had lost so much weight and was looking so drawn and pale that her doctor felt that she might be threatened with trouble of the kind that had produced my father's collapse of the previous year. A move to the country was insisted upon as urgent and essential. By the end of July the whole ménage was installed in furnished rooms in an ugly but comfortable villa in Sevenoaks, and there the roof fell in on my father.

The first blow came when *The Pall Mall Gazette* returned a batch of occasional pieces as being too slackly written to be publishable. Then Astor, having decided that he was going to close down the unprofitable *Pall Mall Budget,* had ordered Hind to stop buying new material. And on top of that the owners of *The National Observer* sold it over Henley's head, and the new management fired him. His successor began a rigorous housecleaning by cutting Henley's losses on the time-traveling project. My father had delivered seven of the ten projected articles and the new man could see nothing in them. They were indeed poor stuff, showing only too plainly how much else he had on his mind. They were didactic and lifeless, and utterly without the sparkle and glitter that had fascinated Henley when my father was talking up the project. He was told not to bother to deliver any more of the proposed articles with a coldness that made it clear to him that he could forget about *The National Observer* as a market. He had not foreseen this sudden drop in his earnings when he moved out of town, and he now felt that he was in a very tight corner indeed, one that was not made any more tolerable by the behaviour of Mrs. Robbins. She was being as difficult as ever, and she had added to her tactics of harassment the device of retiring to her room to take her meals whenever she had been upset by anything that reminded her of the irregularity of her daughter's situation. The consequence of this was a catastrophic falling-out between my father and the landlady, who suddenly proposed to charge an extra sixpence for all meals served to Mrs. Robbins in her upstairs bedroom. I don't doubt but that in resisting this surcharge my father, who was already alarmed by the rate at which his outgoings were beginning to exceed his earnings, visited some of his anger with Mrs. Robbins upon the landlady. However that may have been, he certainly made an enemy of her. In due course he paid the full price for doing so. She began to go through his incoming letters, and soon learned from them that her tenants were an unmarried couple who were also the parties to the wrong side of a divorce action. My father found himself fighting a defensive war on two fronts.

It was at this point that the resilient and generous Henley came to the rescue. Dead as the editor of *The National Observer,* he was due to rise again as editor of *The New Review* the following January. He had to tell my father that the Time Traveller articles had gone all wrong, but he still believed in the project. He thought he knew what the trouble was—my father had written *about* time travelling in his articles, he hadn't taken his readers time-travelling with him. If he would give the subject another try, using a different approach, all would be well. The thing to do was to invent a sympathetic character who could go off to explore the past and the future in person, and take the reader along with him. Henley was sure that it could be done, and that my father was the man to do it—so sure that he was ready to promise him a hundred pounds down for the serial rights to the still-unwritten work, and to give him an undertaking that it would be run in *The New Review* at the earliest possible date. Henley went even further out onto this limb. He talked up the project to William Heinemann so convincingly as to persuade that hardheaded publisher to offer my father an advance of fifty pounds, starting royalties of fifteen percent and a guarantee of a first printing of ten thousand copies, for the hardcover rights.

Inspired by these astonishing displays of confidence in his ability to deliver the goods he had put in his shop window, my father settled down in the middle of the crossfire of aggravations put up by Mrs. Robbins and the termagant landlady to write what was to be his first novel. He wrote under pressure and against the clock, and in September, when he was in sight of his ending, he became exhausted and doubts started nagging at him. He sent a copy of the opening chapters to Henley, along with a note asking him if he was working on the right lines, and if it was worth his while to put more time and effort into the book. Henley's answer gave him the lift he needed: "Rather! . . . It is so full of invention & the invention is so wonderful, so running over . . . it must certainly make your reputation."

Henley's enthusiasm was just what was wanted to get my father out of his finishing slump and to carry him on, as soon as he was done with *The Time Machine,* into *The Wonderful Visit.* And while he was settling into his second novel the idea for a third came to him. It was a growth from a feeling of horror that had been planted in his mind in his

Westbourne Grove days, one day when he had found himself being jostled and hustled along with the tipsy, sweaty, crowds of Londoners who were taking the day off to go to the annual summer fair on Hampstead Heath, one of the great low-life carnivals on Victorian London's calendar. The memory of that experience suddenly took charge of his imagination, and in a few leisure hours it was transformed into a roughly sketched outline for *The Island of Dr. Moreau*. My father was started at last; between them, Cust, Hind, and Henley had found him his metier, and had made a novelist of him.

My father's situation was transformed in the next few months. Henley's *New Review* began to run *The Time Machine* as a serial in April; Dent snapped up *The Wonderful Visit* early in May, and by the end of that month Methuen had agreed to take *The Island of Dr. Moreau*. In June a collection of his old *Pall Mall* pieces was issued in book form as *Select Conversations with an Uncle,* and *The Time Machine* appeared in hard covers. *The Wonderful Visit* came out in September, by which time a collection of the stories he had written for Hind, *The Stolen Bacillus and Other Incidents,* was being readied for distribution in November.

Henley was delighted to see my father's career taking off in this way, but concerned for him, and his future. *The Wonderful Visit* was given an enthusiastic reception by the reviewers, and Henley took the opportunity to give him some advice when he wrote him a congratulatory letter about the book and its reception. There were, he said, brains in *The Wonderful Visit,* any amount of them—"brains & character & humour." But my father should take care. He had a unique talent, that much was certain, and had managed to produce three books inside a year. That was magnificent. And yet it had to be faced, books that could be turned out that fast couldn't be literature. Henley hastened to assure my father that he wasn't losing confidence in him— he believed in his powers of invention as strongly as ever. It was just that he didn't want to see those powers played out by overuse. He was sure that my father, whatever he did with his gift, had a future as a writer. But he wanted that future to be a brilliant one, not that of a man whose work had been made commonplace by overexposure. Oh, yes, indeed, he admired more than ever the way in which my father could pour his wonderful stuff out, so copiously, so easily. But he still had to say what needed, urgently, to be said: "You could also do better—far better; & and to begin with, you must begin by taking yourself more seriously."

Henley's letter, written on September 5, 1895, marked a turning point in my father's career that was to be at least as important to it as his arrival, self-liberated, on the doorstep of the Normal School in South Kensington ten years earlier. He had known that his life had been changed by the success of *The Time Machine,* but he believed that it had come to him as the more or less accidental consequence of his doing, quite simply, what had presented itself to him as the only possible thing to do next. His conception of the novel had been that of a larger, and more rewarding, something to be attached to an idea in accordance with the Barrie formula for producing a saleable short piece. He had gone on to write *The Wonderful Visit* in just that way. His attention had been drawn to a remark, attributed to Ruskin, to the effect that if an English sportsman came across an angel his first impulse would be to shoot it. My father had heard the bang, seen the gorgeous wings crumple, and heard the marvellous body landing with a thump on the damp British turf; and he had taken it from there, arriving at his novel by that process. Henley had brought it home to him that there should be more to writing than letting one fancy lead on to another. He would have to make his work more than a mere exuberant outpouring if the name he had made for himself so easily was to last and to stand for more than the brand name of a new sauce or soap. He was to think about what he was doing, and by making his writing considerable he was to reopen the door to the world of importance and influence that he believed to have been closed against him forever by his dismal personal failure at South Kensington. That disaster still loomed very largely in the back of his mind. His hero and model was still T. H. Huxley, the presiding god of the Normal School in his days there, and the height of his aspiration was to become one of the world's great teachers. His two most keenly felt literary admirations testify to this, they were for Swift and Voltaire, writers who had written less for writing's sake than to make other men ask themselves what they were doing with their lives, with the object of improving the quality of life for all mankind. Henley may have made a novelist of my father, but he had not given him literary ambitions.

Chapter XII

But while I was fearless of theology I must confess
it was comparatively late before I faced and dared
to probe the secrecies of sex. . . . I had an instinctive
perception that it would be a large and difficult
thing in my life, but my early training was all in the
direction of regarding it as an irrelevant thing, as
something disconnected from all the broad signifi-
cances of life, as hostile and disgraceful in its quality. The world was never so emasculated in
thought, I suppose, as it was in the Victorian time.

—THE NEW MACHIAVELLI

T HE YEAR OF MY FATHER'S ARRIVAL
on the literary scene was that in
which Oscar Wilde was overwhelmed with disaster, an event which
cast a shadow on his relationship with Henley. Henley exulted in
Wilde's downfall, and noisily claimed to have had a hand in bringing
it about. He always contended that it was a review of *The Picture of
Dorian Gray* that he had run in *The Scots Observer* back in his Edinburgh
days that had marked the beginning of the end for his enemy.

When that novel had been about to come out in the early summer
of 1890, a review copy had been sent to *The Scots Observer* in the
ordinary way of business. Henley had glanced through it, and seeing
that it was concerned with the world of high society, had assigned it
for notice to one of his London contributors, a man called Charles
Whibley who was thought to be at home in that milieu. Whibley,
however, knew less of polite society than he did of its underside, the
night world of the heavy swells, the gambling houses, and the smarter
brothels. In that domain he had picked up some of the earliest rumors
of Wilde's frequentations of male prostitutes and homosexual hang-
outs. He made full use of his knowledge when he sat down to write
his review. "Why go grubbing in muck heaps?" he asked, and went

on from there to say that the novel had a medico-legal rather than a literary interest. It was, he concluded, as false to art as it was to morality, because it nowhere made the point that its author preferred a life of cleanliness, health, and sanity to courses of unnatural iniquity.

Where Whibley was worldly and malicious, Henley was naïve. He had not read Wilde's book, and on the strength of his quick glance through it, had formed the notion that Dorian Gray's sins had been those of most West End clubmen of Whibley's stamp—matters of buying women like commodities when sex was wanted, of gingering up routine performances with a certain amount of kinky cruelty, and of being callous and insensitive after the fact. He accordingly ran the review as it had been written, without giving a second thought to what the phrase "unnatural iniquity" might be taken to imply. He did, however, do something else. *The Scots Observer* had a house rule that forbade the appearance of any contributor's signature more than once in a single issue. Whibley already had a piece in the running order when his review of Wilde's novel came in. Henley accordingly followed his normal procedure, took Whibley's name off the review, and ran it over the single initial "H."

Wilde knew nothing of all this, and when he saw that he had been attacked viciously by "H" in Henley's paper, assumed that he had been savaged by its editor. Wilde was unacquainted with Henley at that time, but he was aware that he was ugly and a cripple. In his anger he remembered Thersites the Railer, the lame man in Homer who had been the ugliest of the Greeks to fight at Troy. Thersites had been jealous of Achilles, and had vented his envious spite against the hero by accusing him of being inspired by an unnatural lust when he had mourned for the Queen of the Amazons after killing her in battle. When Wilde wrote to *The Scots Observer* to object to the tone of its review of his novel, he made a passing reference to the author of the offending piece as "a Thersites." Henley, who knew his Homer, took the point and returned the blow. He ran Wilde's letter in the issue that was then making up with a rejoinder of his own immediately below it. It was, he said, arguable that the artist had a right to be as nasty as he pleased whenever he felt so inclined, but given that the privilege existed, it was one that he could only exercise at his peril . . . and by the next post he wrote to Whibley to tell him that if he wanted to have another go at Wilde he was welcome to all the space he might require. Whibley jumped at this chance, and the censorious tone of his renewed assault drew the dramatic critic William Archer, the translator and passionate admirer of Ibsen, into the correspondence. Archer noted that Whibley's line of attack on Wilde was just about the same as that taken by the more philistine denigrators of his idol, and went on to say that the proposition that the artist who felt impelled to deal with the uglier side of life must himself be an ugly fellow was indefensible. Life was as it was, and the artist had to deal with things as they were. The correspondence took fire at this stage, and realised every struggling editor's dream by becoming a controversy that attracted widespread attention.

Henley was at first delighted to see the sales of his paper increasing, but the venom in some of the letters that came in to support Whibley's attack on Wilde soon made him suspect that something was going on that he did not understand. He wrote at last to another of his more worldly acquaintances to ask for enlightenment: "What," he inquired, "is this 'dreadful scandal' about Oscar Wilde?" When he had his answer he fell into an inexplicable frenzy of outrage from which he emerged with the determination to do everything he could that might damage his enemy.

At about this time Wilde came across a recently published collection of Henley's literary essays that contained a declaration of his critical principles. It was Henley's thesis that no artist could achieve real excellence unless his work was directed toward a morally worthy end. It appeared to Wilde that what Henley was saying was that the artist should be working to win a wider acceptance for the prevailing liberal-humanitarian consensus as to what was right and proper. This struck him as a vulgarly utilitarian conception, and moved him to derision. He waited for his moment, and as soon as the correspondence in *The Scots Observer* showed its first signs of flagging, he moved in on it to finish it off with one of those effortless displays of teasing that had made him a popular favorite. He began with a restatement of his own, possibly sincere, belief that the artist could do no wrong in submitting to the necessities of the subject that had claimed him, and he ended with an outrageously funny parody of Henley's central position, showing how easily it could be stretched to make the final test of a writer's merit the acceptability of his views on Irish Home Rule or the Licensing Laws.

My father was at first inclined to side with Henley and against Wilde. In 1894, when he was still in a state of innocence and able to believe that the argument was about writing, he had written an ephemeral piece in which he teased Wilde with an imaginary chef who had adopted the aesthetic position and come out for cuisine for art's sake. This kitchen aesthete thought of his meals as Nocturnes, Fantasias, and Etudes, and believed absolutely in letting the chips fall where they might: "If I needed a flavour of almonds and had nothing else to hand, I would use prussic acid. Do right, I say, as your instinct demands, and take no heed of the consequences. Our function is to make the beautiful gastronomic thing . . ." One of his Nocturnes was to be eaten in almost complete darkness, "in a starlight of small scattered candles." It was to have a velvety black theme, and was to center upon truffles, grilled meat well seared, black pudding, Carlsbad plums, and stout. The tone is playful, and the piece doesn't come within a mile of hinting at either knowledge or disapproval of Wilde's secret life.

I think that my father was still entirely in the dark on that subject at the beginning of the following year. On its second day he had a telegram from Harry Cust asking him to come down to the offices of *The Pall Mall Gazette* as soon as he possibly could. When he got there he was told that the paper's dramatic critic had resigned at short notice, and asked if he would care to have the job. If he did, his first assignment would be to write about the new play by Oscar Wilde that was to open on the following night.

My father wanted to say snap to this exciting proposition, but before he could honourably do so he felt obliged to warn Cust that up to that point he had only been to a proper theatre twice in his life. Cust affably brushed this aside by saying that his inexperience would be a positive asset, guaranteeing that he would have a really fresh outlook. He was, however, rather more shaken when my father asked him if he would be expected to wear evening dress? He might have been even more surprised if he had known that the question was disingenuous, and that my father was still so much a stranger to his world as not to possess evening clothes of any description. He hadn't quite realised how very fresh his new dramatic critic's outlook might turn out to be. My father was able to solve the practical problem with the help of an obliging tailor called Millar who had a shop in Charles Street down by the Strand—when the curtain went up on Wilde's new play he was in his place in the stalls in the full glory of the mandatory uniform of his new profession. The play was a success, and my father enjoyed his evening.

Two nights later he had an experience of a very different kind. He felt a sympathetic nausea as he watched a carefully produced new play foundering in a sea of aimless chat in its second act, and later witnessed the humiliation of an affronted and perplexed Henry James, who hadn't realised that he had failed and had been hooted off when he was ill-advised enough to take an author's call after the final curtain. As he left the stricken field on which *Guy Domville* had met its fate, he fell in with a red-bearded and white-faced man, of just about his own age, who introduced himself as George Bernard Shaw and the critic for Frank Harris' paper. Shaw was then living in North London, as my father was, so they walked homewards together, talking over the fiasco as they went along, and as the hansoms and the growlers clip-clopped past them. When my father gave it as his opinion that James had asked for his nasty experience by writing a play that didn't move, Shaw maintained that the beauty of its language more than made up for its lack of dramatic action. My father wasn't convinced, by Shaw or by his argument. He felt that his new acquaintance was a *farceur*, and took it that he was being deliberately perverse in order to dazzle someone he had sized up as a greenhorn. He said as much, and Shaw replied by launching into a comparison between Wilde and James as playwrights—the former, according to him, being wholly irresponsible as an artist and so able to do anything for the sake of dramatic effect, and the latter so entirely serious about his art as to be incapable of learning even the first thing about the theatre. Shaw failed to make my father believe that *Guy Domville*, which struck him as a tissue of absurdities, was serious in some way that *An Ideal Husband* was not, but he did leave him with a lively sense that he had entered a new world of discourse. He had never met such a brilliant talker before.

In the next few months, during which my father's life was undergoing the transformation that I have described at the end of my last chapter, Wilde was being undone stage by stage. The insultingly addressed message that lured him into his fatal libel action was handed in at the Albermarle Club in mid-February; *The Time Machine* began to run as a serial just before he went on trial, and Dent and Methuen respectively bought *The Wonderful Visit* and *The Island of Dr. Moreau* in the month that saw him convicted and sent off to prison. My father, who had not forgotten Wilde's kindness in urging Frank Harris to give him a chance when he was starting to write, couldn't understand why Henley was so delighted by this outcome. He asked him why it gave him pleasure to see a fine writer brought down by a personal weakness: wasn't Wilde's ruin a tragedy, and something to be regretted? Henley referred him coarsely to *The Picture of Dorian*

Gray, telling him he ought to read it if he wanted to know what a nasty piece of work the slimy bugger really was—when he'd been through that, he'd be able to see that the man who wrote it had to be rotten through and through, and that he'd gloried in his uncleanness.

My father read the novel in question soon afterwards, and was enthralled by it. He was appalled both by its content and by what Henley had made of it. The point of the thing, as he saw it, was not that it glorified perversion or a vicious way of life, but that it was an act of self-destruction. My father had never come across anything quite like it before, and he found it of breath-taking interest. Here was a writer, trapped in a pattern of behaviour that was bound to ruin him sooner or later, sitting down to describe his losing battle with the element in himself that he feared but couldn't control, and giving his self-examination the form of a novel that would of necessity complete his defeat and make it irretrievable. My father could see that the evidence given at Wilde's trial had increased the novel's transparency, but he could not believe that it had ever been obscure. From the time of its publication its secret had been an open one, and from then on it had only been a matter of when its forecast of ruin and exposure would be realised. Beyond that, my father was impressed by the novel's immediacy. He had never before come across a piece of English fiction in which the writer was so vividly present in the work, or in which there was such direct communication between writer and reader about a matter of importance to them both—in this case the discrepancy between a man's knowledge of what his society would like him to be and of what his animal nature has made him . . .

Some will see all this as a justification of Wilde's contention that a work of literary art is a glass in which each reader will find the reflection of his own interests and obsessions. But my father was sure that he had understood the book as Wilde had intended him to; he argued the case for it with Henley and was shocked by his reaction. He found himself being subjected to the kind of steam-rolling that Yeats was to complain of in his memoirs—Henley did not like his writers to stand up to him when he had laid down the law. As they argued, my father found that he was being asked to believe that Wilde had been pursuing his mentor with his malice long before the appearance of Whibley's review. There was proof of this in Wilde's habit of dropping sour digs at "Caliban" into his essays and criticisms—the pretence was that he was getting at the average, vulgarly philistine man-in-the-street, when he did this, but Henley knew that it wasn't so—all Wilde's references to Caliban were covert sneers at him and his infirmities. My father's confidence in the value of the friendly monster's advice and counsel began to ebb away. He was growing as he entered his new world.

Some of the growing up that my father did in the summer following Wilde's trial was stimulated by visits to his parents, in the course of which he went over to Uppark with my grandfather on a number of occasions, walking there from Nyewood. They would amble along companionably on the kindly surfaces of the still unmetaled country lanes linking the two places, talking as they went. They would pass Turkey Island and Down Place before cutting across the South Down Way between Harting and Tower Hill, to come out onto the grass track that ran along beside the paling fence that marked the boundary of the old deer park and of the plantation of beech trees just inside it that had been planted there even before old Sir Harry's time to shelter the house from northerly winds. They would follow the grass track until it brought them to a point where the palings were down and they could enter the park to go to a spot which gave them a view across a valley of close-cropped turf to the now empty house. Nobody, in the aristocratic sense of the word, had been living there since Frances Bullock's death at the beginning of the year; it was still waiting for the estate to be settled and for the new owners to bring their own pattern of life to it. The chapter in its history that had begun when old Sir Harry had plucked the older Bullock girl out of his model dairy had come to an end at last, and the new one had still to begin.

Both my father and my grandfather could see Uppark with new eyes now that their connections with it had become part of the record of the dead past. My grandfather considered it with a tranquil wonder, as the place where he had been when he had made the biggest mistake of his life for reasons that were no longer either clear or important to him. He would have mourned had there been any profit in crying over spilt milk, but there was none, so he contented himself with wondering how he could have been such a fool. My father's reactions were of another kind. He was surprised to find that he no longer hated the place, that he rather admired it, that it was, well, a beautiful thing, a marvel. And how could it be?

When my father had first seen Uppark it had been an ogre's castle —the hated other place into which his mother had withdrawn when she broke up the family household in Bromley. Soon after he first saw it he had discovered the Housekeeper's Room, the seat of empire for which she had forsaken him and his father. The room was buried deeply in the ground, over there, at the southeast corner of the building. There was, as he very well knew, no way of looking out of that semisubterranean chamber into the miles and miles of gloriously open upland in which they were sitting unless one first climbed onto a chair or mounted a stepladder. The windows that faced the abundance of light, space, and beauty that lay outside were set high up in the walls, of the room, and gave onto narrow ventilation pits that sheltered hart's-tongue ferns and mosses, and were always shadowed and damp. Only the last few inches of their uppermost panes were on a level with the close-cropped lawns outside, and as a result the Housekeeper's Room was a sombre, almost lightless, and heavily airless space. The whole basement floor shared its qualities, as did the huge underground kitchen buried beneath a shrubbery at some distance from the main building, and connected with it by a tunnel—a long passage dimly lit in the daytime by light from overhead skylights made secure by prison-like metal gratings.

My father's initial response to his discovery of this nether world of underprivilege below Uppark had been one of blind rage. This was because it had been my grandmother's most persistent complaint against my grandfather that his lack of consideration for her condemned her to spend the greater part of her day every day below ground level in the basement kitchen of Atlas House, a room that borrowed its light from a pit covered by a metal grating set into the pavement of Bromley's High Street. It had infuriated my father to find that his mother had tried to destroy all his hopes, and to condemn him to be something less than a lackey, on the pretext that she was seizing her last chance of escape from her underground servitude, when it had been her intention, all along, to instal herself in this larger version of the same thing. His bottled-up feelings on this score, mingled with others, even more powerful, concerning the fundamentals of the relationship between his parents, had finally burst out into the open in his descriptions of the loathly caverns inhabited by the light-fearing Morlocks in *The Time Machine.* That purgative release, followed up as it had been by the news that Fanny Bullock was dead, had defused all the menace that Uppark had once held for him. He was able, that summer, to make a cool appraisal of the place for the first time.

There could be no doubt about it, although Humphrey Repton had laid a heavy hand on its north front, its other three faces, the unaltered work of William Talman, its original architect, justified its inclusion in any listing of the outstanding houses of the late seventeenth century still standing in England. Talman's designs made the happiest possible use of the architectural language of balance, harmony, and restraint then in vogue in northern Europe. His façades proclaimed his intention of making a habitation that would stand through the centuries as worthy accommodation for a race of rational, humane, and polished beings. And yet there, behind those serene faces that the house so sweetly presented to the east, south, and west, only a few feet below the elegant apartments on the *piano nobile,* it was—the squalid internal slum. How could a designer who knew so much about harmony and beauty have built that contradiction into his scheme? How could he have been so blind to the genuinely degrading function of those ill-lit and ill-ventilated quarters?

With my mind's eye I can see my father of nearly ninety years ago staring at Talman's masterpiece on the far side of that sunbaked downland combe—a tiny, eager, still very young young man with the look of birdlike fragility that he is to lose in the next few years, sitting beside the solid ruin of my grandfather on a huge fallen limb torn from one of the beeches by a winter storm. He has been giving less than half an ear to what the older man has been saying—sticking to a habit of tuning out the grumbling note he has known too well for too long. His mind is fixed on the aesthetic riddle presented to him by that thing over there—drowsing softly, rosily, in the stillness of the late summer day. It is at once an abomination, a monument to callousness and indifference, and, in some final and absolute sense, cellars or no cellars, an addition to the human heritage of enduringly fine things. The meaning of what my grandfather is saying suddenly becomes clear to him. The old man is passionately recalling the torture of his last months in service, the violence of his desire to be his own man, his loathing of the life he was living, his certainty that Sarah Neal shared his feelings, the horror of his discovery that she did not, that she had no inkling of what he felt or why, the misery of finding that she had loved above anything the life of the big house, of being a part of it, of being borne along by its routines, that she had liked nothing better than being at the beck and call of her ladies. He had tried to bring her round, but he could not reach her, had not known how to begin. My father is taking in what he is saying and realising what it means for the first time: it is what he has known in his blood all along but has never been able to bring himself to face or admit. The marriage had been torture for them both from the very beginning, each had poisoned the air the other breathed from the very start, and it had gone on like that year after year, and was still going on. They had found no way out. My father was being given his first glimpse of the desolate landscapes that he was to become more familiar with when he came into possession of his mother's diaries after her death.

But my father was not at that time, concentrating his whole being upon the problems that he might have to face if he should prove to have it in him to be a serious writer. He was also getting on with life as it seemed to have been given to him to live it—cheerfulness kept breaking in upon him. Earlier in the year he and Amy-Catherine had moved out of London and into the sandy and gravelly stretch of country, characterised by heather and silver birches, southwest of London. They had found themselves a house with a garden in Woking, and they had taken up cycling. It was the hour of the bicycle. Lightened by the introduction of light alloys and the tubular diamond frame, and transformed as a ride by the coming of the pneumatic tire, the bicycle had suddenly become hugely popular. The members of the first cycling generation, my father and Amy-Catherine among them, rejoiced to find themselves gliding almost silently along the uncrowded country roads, tasting a new freedom. They could now go easily and swiftly anywhere they wanted, without having to hire or borrow a gig or a trap, and without having to contemplate the backside of a jogging horse by the hour. And above all, when it wasn't in actual use this biddable appliance didn't need fodder, or stabling, or any of horse coping's endless chores—it would stay undemandingly where it was put away until it was wanted for another ride. And it was fast, too; for a while the fastest thing on the road. My father and Jane —as he was now beginning to call Amy-Catherine—plunged into this new form of recreation with enthusiasm. They spent a good deal of their time that summer on their machine, exploring the byways of Surrey and Sussex.

That use of the singular is not a slip—they were riding tandem on a curious model that had been made to my father's order by the Humber people. It had the peculiarity that its handlebars were placed amidships, between the two riders, so that the steering was done by the partially unsighted occupant of the second saddle. When I first saw photographs of this oddity I thought that they were telling me something about my father. It seemed to me that he had gone to an extreme to see that he retained executive control while resigning the front seat. Much later I learned that there was nothing unique about the arrangement; it had even been quite common at one stage in cycling history. When the "penny farthing" went out of favour a number of makers had experimented with tandems steered from behind the occupant of a front seat; they had mostly been perambulator-like tricycles and four-wheelers. Why my father revived this obsolete form I don't know, but I have come to believe that male chauvinism wasn't a part of it: I think that he was quite simply trying to arrange things so that Jane, then a beginner, could come with him on his expeditions without being condemned to spend hours with her nose pressed into the back of his belted norfolk jacket. Be that as it may, the tandem was retired at the end of their second season, and thereafter they rode two conventional bicycles, skimming along side by side as they explored most of southern England. They were married on Thursday, October, 27 1895, at the end of their first cycling autumn.

All manner of absurd things were happening in the literary world while Jane and my father were getting accustomed to each other. Henry Harland's annual *The Yellow Book* had to cease publication. It had become too scandalous for any publisher to touch it—because Wilde was said to have had a copy of its latest issue under his arm when the police had taken him away from the Cadogan Hotel after his arrest. Aubrey Beardsley, as the designer of *The Yellow Book*'s cover and layout, had, of course, been unemployable since that rumour had gone into circulation; his work had given the publication its identity. He became a catalyst for the absurdities of the great panic. Towards its end, the promoters of a new magazine—*The Savoy*—defied fate by taking him on as their designer. George Moore, who was to have a story in its first issue, was horrified when he received a copy of its prospectus and saw that Beardsley's dread hand had been laid upon it. That man was capable of anything! Moore got no further than the front cover of the brochure. There he found a drawing of John Bull in riding britches, and at a point on Bull's lower abdomen where no bulge should properly have been, a cluster of wrinkles that could only mean one thing. In haste Moore convened as many of his fellow contributors-to-be as he could reach at short notice in Edgar Jepson's chambers in The Temple, round the corner from *The Savoy*'s offices in the Strand. When all concerned had arrived, Moore displayed the prospectus and interpreted the wrinkles: Beardsley, he claimed, had given John Bull an erection. He warned the company that their good names were at stake and urged them to join him in self-protective action. And so, presently, after the formal election of a six-man delegation, one member of which happened to be no less a person than George Bernard Shaw, Moore led the way to *The Savoy*'s offices, where he demanded the withdrawal of all the eighty thousand copies of the offending brochure. It was while the hysteria that produced this episode was still at its height, early in 1896, that *The Island of Dr. Moreau* made its appearance at last.

Although my father had foreseen that his book might run into some adverse comment in the prevailing climate of opinion, he was upset when the opening blast came. It was the unexpected quarter from which it originated that took him by surprise. The hostile review was written by Peter Chalmers Mitchell, a man who had been a fellow student at South Kensington, and whom he had thought of as an understanding friend. It shook him further that it had appeared in what he had thought of as a friendly publication, *The Saturday Review*, whose editor, Frank Harris, had never been accused of being a prude. The line taken by Chalmers Mitchell was that the book seemed to have been written for horror's sake, that it was purely obsessive in its resort to physically unpleasant detail, and that it was excessively suggestive. My father was able to soothe his wounded feelings for the moment by telling himself that he must have touched on some sore spot of Chalmers Mitchell's connected with the large number of dissections he was required to do in his line of work as an up-and-coming zoologist. But this comfort didn't hold for long. A week later he was being given a drubbing in the columns of *The Speaker* for having written a book about sex. The reviewer in this case insinuated that the obvious next step for any experimenter who succeeded in giving an animal the outward semblance of a human being would be to have sexual relations with it—having brought this subject up from the depths of his unconscious the reviewer than flinched delicately away from the notion while making my father responsible for it: "We need not go further into this delectable theme. Mr. Wells, as we have said, has talent, but he employs it here for a purpose which is absolutely degrading." The next weekly to be heard from was *The Athenaeum,* which asked its readers how far it was legitimate to create feelings of disgust in a work of art as a preliminary to saying that even if it were, my father had in this case exceeded all permissible bounds. The pack was now in full cry, and a little while later *The Guardian,* then the leading Church of England weekly, was asserting that the novel could only have been written for nastiness' sake.

In later life my father discovered that he had been thinking of deeper meanings when he wrote the *The Island of Dr. Moreau,* and that he had meant it to be his personal tribute to Swift. He told me on one occasion that its starting point had been the idea of putting the Old Testament God in complete charge of the evolutionary process, and showing him to be fighting a losing battle to turn the brute creation he had fashioned from the common clay into something closer to the angels. He liked to attach fictions of this kind to another, that *The Guardian*'s reviewer had been the only one among the book's earlier critics who had managed to say anything about it indicating a degree of understanding of his intentions. Resort to the review itself shows that this suggestion is hung arbitrarily on a single sentence in which the critic raises, only in order to dismiss, the possibility that the novel had been meant to "parody the work of the creator of the human race, and cast contempt upon the dealings of God with his creatures." He goes on from there to make the assertion that I have already quoted, that nastiness was all that my father was after.

I think that my father was grateful to *The Guardian*'s reviewer for having credited him, even if only momentarily, for having had a leading idea when he wrote the book. The ways of his mother's dreadful God with man might very well have been what the book had been *about,* if it had been organised in that way. He adopted the explanation as it came by him on the wing because he knew that books were supposed to be hung on that kind of idea, the relationship qualified them for serious consideration. But he was a visualiser, and the truth was that *The Island of Dr. Moreau* had lived a life of its own while it was being written, having moved on from one intensely visualized situation to the next in accord with a logic of plausibility and consistency until it had run its course. He had begun by meaning to do something in the manner of Conrad, and had "seen" the open boat with a lost man in it, all by himself, out in the wastes of the Pacific, and had gone on from image to image from that starting point. And he had become aware soon after the story had started to move that it was being fed with details that came unbidden from the darker corners of his mind and owed nothing to the requirements of a coherent scheme. His sense that there was something loose in it that he didn't altogether understand or care for was what had led him to expect trouble with *The Island* before publication—the same element in *The Time Machine* had alerted its critics to be on the watch for something odd in its successor. They had found what they were looking for.

The reception given to *The Island of Dr. Moreau,* coming on top of Henley's friendly warning that he wasn't giving enough thought to what he was doing, gave my father pause. He was driven to reconsider his approach to the means of getting by that had so startlingly taken possession of him, and was now announcing itself to be his profession. He couldn't allow himself the luxury of a cooling-off period in which he could think his problem out—he couldn't afford that. His float of ready cash wasn't big enough to allow for layoffs; he had to keep producing if he wasn't to let his little army of dependents down, he simply had to go on earning money.

He was getting some help in this quarter. James Brand Pinker, one of the first literary agents to go into business, had approached him at the beginning of 1896, and they had come to an agreement soon afterwards. But good as Pinker was at nosing out buyers and getting the best possible price for a story or a novel, he still had to be given something to sell. The pressure started to build up. The house in Woking began to seem very small indeed as my father toiled away, doing his writing on a table in the dining room that had to be cleared for each meal. And he became rather more conscious than he had been at first of the noise from the passing trains—Lynton was almost too close to Woking Station. Yet in the eighteen months that he spent in that house he managed to get *The Wheels of Chance, The War of the Worlds,* and *The Invisible Man* off the dining-room table, along with a draft for the opening chapters of *Love and Mr. Lewisham.*

The astonishing thing about this performance is that it was combined with a considerable development in his approach to what he was doing. The first of the three novels begun and finished at Lynton was an unregenerate potboiler, produced in response to the pressure that I have described on the foundation of the Barrie formula for bringing in the odd guinea. In it my father scrambled his knowledge of cycling and of the highways and byways of southern England with a light comedy plot, and slapped the mix down on paper as fast as he could. It represented no forward progress whatever, but the two novels that followed were rather different. The seed idea for *The War of the Worlds* is to be found in *The Time Machine,* in the passage that describes the fears that crowded in on the Time Traveller as he hurtled on into the future: suppose that, in the enormous interval between the *now* of his departure and that of his arrival, some eight hundred thousand years further on, mankind had undergone substantial evolutionary changes and had "developed into something inhuman, unsympathetic, and overwhelmingly powerful? I might seem some old-world savage animal, only the more dreadful and disgusting for our common likeness—a foul creature to be incontinently slain . . ."

My father took this thought and married it to a fresh element. Suppose that living creatures were to come to earth from another planet—from Mars, say—beings so far ahead of earthlings technologically and in every other way as to make it impossible for them to think of us as fellow creatures? And suppose that they were to treat the earthlings as Europeans had treated the backward peoples that they had come upon in the earth's far corners—the Tasmanians had been run off their native grounds and exterminated in fifty years; the Belgians were doing something of the same kind in the Congo; and the Zulu nation had been treated almost as vilely. Suppose these Martians had our racial arrogance and had come to clear our planet for colonisation, as Tasmania had been cleared? Suppose that their advance parties were already on their way? That their first rocketload—they would be coming in big rockets—was to make its landing, right here, in Woking, tonight?

> I was at home at that hour and writing in my study; and although my French windows face towards Ottershaw and the blind was up . . . I saw nothing of it. Yet this strangest of all things that ever came to earth from outer space must have fallen while I was sitting there . . .

Given his habit of visualisation, and his gift for spinning a yarn, it was as easy for him to carry on with this naturalistic faking as it was for him to keep breathing—but this time the text does not write itself. Its content is determined by the central idea, and the details of the imagery come from the probabilities of what is being proposed, not from those dark corners where his secret fears did their painting. It is a much more deliberately considered piece of work than anything that he had so far written, but it still has a glaring basic defect: it is a speculation that doesn't trench on its author's or on any other human being's experience, and it consequently calls on a large measure of conscious fraud. The tone, that of the privileged eyewitness keeping his little circle of intimates or fellow club members enthralled, is that which undermines so much of Conrad's writing; it labours the authenticity, and achieves falsehood.

The Invisible Man begins with a leap forward; its very first words accept themselves:

> The stranger came early in February, one wintry day, through a biting wind and a driving snow, the last snowfall of the year, over the down, walking as it seemed from Bramblehurst railway station and carrying a little black portmanteau in his thickly gloved hand.

My father is moving on from pretence—the simulated reporting of what has not happened and cannot happen in the nature of things—to something more genuinely creative. He is no longer having his reader on, but is making him a consenting partner in his imagining. He cannot, however, keep this up through the book, which before long falls foul of the fundamental flaw that G. K. Chesterton was quick to point out soon after its original publication. The title proves to be misleading: the story does not deal with an invisible man's interaction with the world we know, but with what befalls an invisible madman, a person impenetrably concealed within his own special frame of private references, resentments, obsessions, and compulsions, and altogether set apart from the generality of mankind. When my father had done with the story he was aware that he had come very close to a complete success in the realm of the *tour de force,* but he had not convinced himself, and he was well aware of the extent to which the shadow of the arbitrary lay across his fiction. He had made his readers follow him into a region of his choice outside the common ground of possible experience—but he had not come within a mile of any of the things that press on people of flesh and blood as they live out their lives.

It was in the light of this realisation that he roughed out a scheme for the opening chapters of *Love and Mr. Lewisham,* the story of a very ordinary young man's slow slide into a self-destructive marriage. This last product of the Lynton dining-room table was to be the first of the long string of novels in which he was to use his own recent experience, and his reactions to it, as a quarry for material. It is also the first of his novels which deals openly with sexuality. The novel is not straightforwardly autobiographical—none of my father's novels were to be that. He does not allow young Lewisham his own good fortune, but he assigns to him the fate that he had only narrowly escaped after his failure at South Kensington. His Lewisham is a born loser, a better-than-average but still not a brilliant student, without means, who throws away his chances of an academic career and a decent life because he is hagridden by his need for a sexual relationship. The educational powers that be who have given him his scholarship have offered him a devil's bargain: he can have everything he wants from them on the one condition that, on his part, he must live against the grain of his physical being for a term of years. Mr. Lewisham cannot do it, and motivated solely by his desire to have a bedfellow, he sells himself short by plunging into a marriage that is fatal to all his prospects.

My father had come at last to see what his union with his cousin had been all about, and to the realisation that if he could get the essence of that experience into a novel he would have something that would really tell with the thousands upon thousands of his contemporaries who had condemned themselves to lifetimes of frustration and unhappiness in the same way. And so he stepped forward onto the stage of his own pages, in his own person, without pretending to be someone else wiser, more mature, and more experienced, to tell the story of what might very well have happened to him if things between him and Isabel had come to their logical and typical conclusion:

> The opening chapter does not concern itself with Love—indeed that antagonist does not certainly appear until the third —and Mr. Lewisham is seen at his studies. It was ten years ago, and in those days he was assistant master in the Whortley Proprietary School, Whortley, Sussex, and his wages were forty pounds a year, out of which he had to afford fifteen shillings a week during term time to lodge with Mrs. Munday at the little shop in West Street. He was called "Mr." to distinguish him from the bigger boys, whose duty it was to learn, and it was a matter of stringent regulation that he should be addressed as "Sir."

The intentions that my father had in mind when he wrote the first draft of this novel's opening chapters were to be modified again and again before it was finished. At times the book seemed to be actively resisting his attempts to bring it to a conclusion, and at one point the stress of battling with it brought on a physical collapse that lasted for several weeks. His trouble was that his rapidly increasing knowledge of the world and its ways kept forcing him to revise his original assessments of the meanings of the personal experiences he was drawing on, he kept running into stone walls that could not be broken through until he had come to recognise that he now knew better than he had when he had conceived an episode, his expanded awareness had made the original conception ring false. In the four years that it finally took him to solve all the problems that were embedded in his outline it gradually became evident to him that in setting out to describe his personal ordeal he had stumbled on a theme of major importance. He did not see the nature of the issue as plainly then as he was to fifteen years later, when he wrote *The New Machiavelli,* but as he fought his way through to the end of *Love and Mr. Lewisham* it did begin to dawn upon him that the something that had been terribly wrong with his upbringing was a something that was terribly wrong with the prevailing ethos of his society. It was not simply that he had been allowed to grow up in a state of the densest ignorance of all sexual matters, and indoctrinated with the belief that everything connected with the subject had to be shameful and degrading, unmentionable in public and before women; it was, more importantly, that he had been taught to think of what was biologically the central element in his life, his sexuality, as something marginal and almost irrelevant to the serious business of living. Once he had seen his essential experience in that light, and had recognised to what extent it had been typical, he was compelled as a rational being to go on to recognise the necessity for a revolution in the realm of sexual mores —no society that required the majority of its citizens to live at odds with the terms of their nature throughout their lives could be either sane or prosperous. In its writing, *Love and Mr. Lewisham* became my father's declaration of intent to do all that he could to bring on that revolution. It was to be the first of a series of novels, making up the greater part of his fiction, devoted to describing the ways in which the prevailing mores frustrated and stultified the young, and to encouraging them to demand the freedom to find their own ways to happiness. This may sound as if I am saying that that my father had made up his mind to be a crusader against marriage and the family, but that is not what he was doing. He was setting out to to do away with the sort of marriage that was a life sentence passed upon two people who hardly knew each other, and with the kind of family that was only too often the product of such a union. He had nothing against the ideals that these two institutions represent, but he detested the reality of the suffering to which their unthinking worship condemned millions of men and women, and their children. As time went by, and as his experience widened, bringing him insight into other lives than his own, he became more and more convinced that he was right to pursue this issue, and that it was a vital one.

Chapter XIII

I was sensible of amazing gaps. . . . All sorts of
things that a man of twenty eight would not dream
of hiding from a coeval he had hidden from me. For
some days I had to remain in his house, I had to go
through his papers, handle all those intimate personal things that accumulate around a human being
year by year—letters, yellowing scraps of newspaper, tokens, relics kept, accidental vestiges, significant litter. I learnt many things I had never dreamt
of. At times I doubted whether I was not prying,
whether I ought not to risk the loss of those legal
facts I sought, and burn these papers unread.

THE PASSIONATE FRIENDS

G EORGE GISSING, A FELLOW WRITER
who was not quite ten years my fa-
ther's senior, played a larger part in awakening him to the importance
of the sexual revolution than he was willing to admit in his autobiography. The two men first met in the summer of 1896, after Clement
Shorter had persuaded my father to join a dining club in which he
took an interest. Shorter was fascinated by writers and writing, and
would have loved to be one, but as he had no spark of the creative in
him he had to get into literature by the back door. He did it by
producing studies of the lives of dead writers, and by editing periodi-
cals. In 1896 he was on the crest of his wave, being simultaneously
editor of *The Illustrated London News*, *The English Illustrated Magazine*,
and *The Sketch*, and the published author of *Charlotte Brontë and Her
Circle*. His book had created something of a stir, and its anticipation
of modern standards of documentation led to his being described by
one critic as the sort of man "who would print a sufficiently famous
writer's blotting pad in a limited edition if he could get hold of it."
The dig contained in this jibe, that Shorter loved to bask in the
reflected glory from established reputations, was to a considerable
extent justified. But he more than made up for this weakness by always

238

keeping a sharp eye out for new talent and opening what doors he could for the promising newcomer. He couldn't claim to have discovered my father, who belonged incontestably to Henley's stable of finds, but in that age in which who you knew was a large part of getting on, he could do something just as important as finding him, he could put the feller into the swim—and that was what Shorter's dining club was all about. It was called The Omar Khayyam Club, and ostensibly it existed to do honour to the Persian poet and his gently eccentric translator Edward FitzGerald, but its quarterly dinners were the thing, and being good fellows of the right sort. When Shorter urged my father to join the club in his twangy, adenoidal voice he didn't say anything to him about the *Rubaiyat,* his point was, quite simply, that the dinners were the greatest possible fun.

When my father first sat down to take a meal with his fellow Omarians, at Frascati's Restaurant, on a Tuesday late in November 1896, Gissing had already been a member of the club for over a year. The occasion of his entry provides another instance of Shorter's brand of kindness. He had, early in 1895, put his head together with that of his friend Edward Clodd, the crusading rationalist who was presently to second the proposal that my father should be elected to the club, and they had hatched a little conspiracy. They were in agreement that George Gissing stood far lower in the world's regard than was right —he was so nearly very good, and he did try so very hard. It would surely put some wind into his sails if he were to be made a member of the club, and if his introduction to the club were to be made memorable.

What the two avuncular operators contrived was ostensibly a dinner to honour the ancient George Meredith. As he was very frail, and had almost given up going out, this had to be laid on at the Burford Bridge Inn, virtually on the old man's doorstep in the shadow of Box Hill. This made it possible for Meredith to eat quietly at home before walking over to the inn to take coffee with the members and their guests. Edward Clodd arranged everything with the great man, and Edmund Gosse won Thomas Hardy's promise to be there. Close on forty Omarians took the double bait and pledged attendance, so that the success of the dinner was as good as assured in advance. And nobody had been disappointed. Meredith's late entry had proved very effective. Before he had taken his seat beside the chairman at the head of the table he had made a little progress round the room pressing hands as he went. He had paused before Gissing and had beamingly announced that he was especially gratified to find him there. This moment had given Shorter and Clodd as much pleasure as it had given Gissing—it was an incontestable literary event, and it had taken place on hallowed ground. The Omarians knew to a man that Keats had put the finishing touches to *Endymion* while staying at the Burford Bridge Inn—and they had seen dear old Meredith, backed up by Hardy, welcoming Gissing aboard in that very same place. If it wasn't actually literary history that they had been making, it was at least a very jolly little footnote to it.

Time has darkened the Omarian picture; only those who have immersed themselves in the lore of the period will realise how entirely right Shorter had been to say that it would be well worth my father's while to join the circle. J. M. Barrie, who never wasted a minute, was a member, and so were such men as H. W. Massingham, E. T. Cook, Robertson Scott, and Harry Cust. Their names are now without resonance, but they were then considerable—and worth knowing—as the editors, respectively, of *The Daily Chronicle, The Westminster Gazette, The British Weekly,* and *The Pall Mall Gazette.* They were powers in the market place that no free-lance writer could afford to ignore. Less immediately useful, but in their ways more enduringly influential as shapers of the general literary consensus as to who counted and who did not, were those Omarians who actually wrote, and who straddled the fence between criticism and creative writing. That grouping included such men as the man who was, in public, the stout and splendidly bearded critic and literary biographer William Sharp, and Theodore Watts-Dunton, the lawyer and first-string critic for *The Examiner* and *The Atheneum,* who laboured to be a poet. Sharp's secret was that behind his beard he was a woman. Dressed in the height of fashion, bejewelled, corseted, and bustled, he sat down whenever he could to write the romantic novels of swordplay and passion in the Glens that he published over the signature of Fiona Macleod. Theodore Watts-Dunton had no secret, but the center of his life was something that he had no inclination to talk about. He had been acting as companion-cum-jailer in charge of the living remains of the poet Swinburne since 1879. In that year Watts-Dunton had decided to spare his friend, who had ceased to be competent to care for himself, the horrors of a private asylum, and had taken him into his own home. When my father met him among the Omarians he had served only seventeen years of the thirty-year term to which he had unwittingly sentenced himself. Signs of strain were beginning to show, but he was still far from being the dim and comically boring figure of fun that Max Beerbohm was to turn him into after his death. It was in this forgotten world of celebrity and success that my father had won himself a place with the éclat achieved by *The Time Machine* and *The Island of Dr. Moreau.*

It may tell one something about my father that the man out of all the Omarians who were present at Frascati's that night who appealed to him most was George Gissing. He was struck by Gissing's fine head, by his great charm, and by his ebullient cheerfulness. He sized him up as a man whose natural mode was to enjoy life: "to laugh, jest, enjoy, and stride along with the wind." He had wanted to see a lot more of this refreshingly sane individual at once and wrote to him on the morning after the dinner to tell him so. He wanted, he said, to have a real talk, without interruptions, and with that in view suggested that they should get together as soon as possible, either at his place or at Gissing's. The reply my father got to his overture gave him his first inkling that his new acquaintance might be a little more complicated than he looked. In it Gissing allowed that he did in fact maintain an establishment at the address he was writing from, but: ". . . the less said about it the better. One must have a local habitation, and here, somehow or other, I live; but I have never yet asked mortal to come and see me here—and probably never shall, for which let my friends be grateful."

My father saw quite a lot of Gissing that winter, but he learned no more about what was supposed to be so badly wrong with his new friend's Epsom household until the following spring, when he and Jane cycled down into Devon to meet him, by arrangement, in the neighborhood of Budleigh-Salterton. He was evasive and uncommunicative for the first few days of their visit, until my father realised that he was dying to talk but couldn't let himself go in Jane's presence. She had a diplomatic indisposition on the following day, and when the two men went for a walk by themselves, the story of Gissing's troubles came pouring out.

Gissing's home life was becoming unendurable. He was married to a dreadful creature who was making him miserable. It was his own fault. A few years earlier he had come to the conclusion that he was never going to be able to earn much more than four hundred a year from his writing, and that he had no right to ask any educated woman to face the squalor of married life on such an income. As he couldn't live without a woman at his side he'd resolved to try his luck with some girl who had known real poverty from birth. And almost at once he'd run into just such a person—the daughter of a day labourer. When he married her his one fear had been that it might be hard to live with someone who was barely literate, but in the outcome his bride's lack of book learning had proved the least of her defects. According to Gissing, she had hardly been turned into his wife before she had revealed herself to be foolish, disobedient, ill-tempered, and a scold. Later on she had begun to drink, and since then her behaviour had become so perverse, and so unpredictable, that he was beginning to wonder if she was still altogether sane.

Gissing had so candid a manner, and looked so honest, that it never crossed my father's mind that there might be another side to this story than the one that he had been given. He passed it on to Jane as it had come to him, and she, too, took it at face value. Between them they made Gissing their project, determining to do all they could to help him to endure his hateful situation until some way out of it could be found. By the time that their month in Devon was over, they were deeply committed to his cause.

For the rest of that summer Gissing was one of the more frequent visitors to Heatherlea, coming down from London by the late-afternoon train to dine and spend the night more or less whenever he felt inclined. Gissing was always responsive to people who accepted him on his own terms, and by the time that he began to make preparations to take himself off to Italy that autumn, he felt sure enough of the two tiny people who had fallen so completely under his spell as to suggest that they should come out to join him there—the best time, he told them, would be when the weather began to open out after the new year, he'd like nothing better that to show them the wonders of Rome in the spring! My father jumped at the lure, and so did Jane. She knew how hard my father had been driving himself in the five years that had rushed by since the breakup of his first marriage, and she knew how well he had been doing. He was earning more than a thousand a year by this time. He was entitled to a celebration. And more than that, he had never yet been abroad. She felt that it was high time that he took the plunge into a wider world.

The Rome that my father went to in the spring of 1898 is no longer there to be visited. It had begun to change in the two previous decades, but in that year it was still very substantially the city of churches, palaces, and gardens that had grown up between 1400 and 1800 among the earthquake-torn remains of the city of the Roman

Emperors and their Gothic successors. My father was bowled over by its beauties and its delights, and awed by the sheer magnificence of its architectural and historic legacies. Although it was the scene, even then, of the dismal breakdown of a parliamentary democracy, the relics of its days of unchallengeable greatness spoke to him thrillingly of the human animal's almost unlimited capacity for rising above itself to imagine great things and to execute noble projects. He saw all about him the visible evidence for the titanic scale of the sustained effort that had gone into making the city credibly the seat of a system of orderly government for the Western world. The Romans had tried to achieve their aim for universal power by physical force, the international church by imposing an ideological tyranny, and both had stooped again and again, under the stress of the exorbitant undertaking, to the use of contemptible and often loathsome means. But it was still, in spite of everything, on this ground, impregnated with the blood of countless cruelly tortured and wickedly butchered victims, and among these buildings, which had witnessed every vileness, that the basic conceptions of the just society, of the common cause of humanity, and of a world order, had been worked out.

The revelation was a crucial one. As a provincial, and, a Protestant, my father had gone to Rome with a certain inner queasiness. He had learned the language of nonconformist polemic at his devout mother's knee, and he had been raised to think of the church synonymous with the city as The Scarlet Woman, and of its Pope as Antichrist, or even as The Beast of the Revelation. He had rejected that line of thinking with the concepts that produced it during his growing up. But the associated biases had returned to his mind in his student days under the cloak of the not altogether untenable thesis that the prosecution of Galileo had made the church the fountainhead of all anti-scientific obscurantism. So far as it was the city of the Papacy, Rome was always to figure in my father's imagination as an enemy fortress, but he was to love it to the end of his days as he had seen it in that first springtime vision, as the mother city of the culture of the Renaissance and the capital of the invisible Republic, of reason and the intelligence, that he had made his country.

There was, however, a flaw in the crystal of this experience. While he was immersed in it the comic muse that intervened so often when he was on the brink of grandeur to remind him that he was more an Art Kipps or a Mr. Polly than a Newton or a Darwin struck at him with her slapstick. Before Gissing had turned his back on the Italy of the

Goths and Vandals to move south to keep his Roman rendezvous with Jane and my father, he had made a stay in Siena. He had made friends there. A little group had formed round him consisting of Brian Boru Dunne, a good-looking young American who was travelling with a guitar, and who sang to it; Arthur Conan Doyle, who had already invented Sherlock Holmes; and E. W. Hornung, Conan Doyle's eupeptic and hearty brother-in-law, who was soon to invent Raffles, the amateur cracksman. They had done Siena *en bande,* and they came on to Rome as a jolly bunch of inseparables. It would have been one thing for my father to "do" Rome with his friend, but it was quite another for him to have to explore it in the company of a pack of chance acquaintances—particularily of such very large acquaintances. A photograph, possibly taken by Dunne, tells the story. It shows Gissing, abashedly pretending not to be there, standing with Hornung, Conan Doyle, and my father, in a Roman street. These were the days in which the homburg with its braided brim was the one socially acceptable form of soft hat, and my father's braid-accentuated hat brim, his hat being set squarely on his head, falls into line with the collarbones of his companions. He is, in that faded sepia souvenir, visibly the "wee, fantastic, Wells" of Rupert Brooke's first impression —a tiny being certain to be sized up instantly by the average middle-class philistine of the day as an undersized and underbred little nobody.

My father did not enjoy finding himself in situations in which he could be seen too readily in that light, and always felt a degree of discomfort in such line-ups. He fairly radiates his feelings on this occasion. Gissing, sweating it out at the other end of the line, has a twofold cause for his uneasiness, my father's, which he detects but doesn't fully understand, and his own, which is a matter of longing for another soul-baring closed session with my father's credulity. He knows that with these two, and the Brian Boru Dunne of the simplicities and the enthusiasms, sticking like glue, he isn't likely to get it.

Nor did he. All through their time in Rome the two men were never alone together for long enough to allow Gissing to get the full flow of creative pseudo-revelation going. At the end of it, all that my father had been told was that Edith Gissing was getting madder than ever, and that Gissing was now haunted by the fear that she might harm, or even kill, his son Walter and her baby boy if she were to be left alone with them.

My father's enlightenment as to the nature of these fears began later in the year. After going on from Rome to Naples, Capri, and Pompeii, on their own, the Wellses had returned to England by way of Florence, Bologna, Milan, and Switzerland. My father had hoped to settle down to work with renewed zest once he was back at home, but when he sat down to his desk to face the now cold and inert mass of *Love and Mr. Lewisham* he found that he simply couldn't get into it. Although he knew perfectly well where it had to go, he found it impossible to bring it to the right ending. When July came round, to find him just as badly stuck as ever, he decided, characteristically, that what was wrong was Heatherlea. He had turned against the innocent little villa, the suburban atmosphere, and the lack of sweep to the heathery, piney, silver-birchy, gravel-based, and closed-in landscape of the neighbourhood. What he needed, he was quite sure, was a change. He needed an open sky, and the generous roll and sweep of chalk downs under his feet.

And so, on July 29, 1898, he set out on what was to have been a leisurely bicycle ride down to the south coast with Jane. They had booked rooms at Seaford, where they planned to spend three or four weeks with the open skies of the Channel over them and the Downs behind them. By the end of their holiday *Love and Mr. Lewisham* was to be finished, and my father was to be a new man. But that was not to be the way that things were to turn out. The cyclists were caught in a sudden shower and soaked before they reached their destination, and by the time that they got there my father was already running an alarmingly high temperature. Over the next few days it became clear that he was suffering from something much worse than a mere chill: he was having severe spasmodic kidney pains and feeling very sorry for himself indeed. At the end of a week of it they decided to leave Seaford for New Romney, where a doctor who was a friend of Gissing's was in practice. Gissing had recommended him to them as an excellent physician who was a kindred spirit. One of his virtues was that he had a big house, and that he kept several rooms in it for the use of such of his patients as might be likely to benefit from a complete rest and some building up. He was, Gissing had assured them, a very pleasant man to live with.

After exchanging telegrams with Henry Hick, my father and Jane set out for New Romney on August 9th. Although the distance to be covered was minute by modern standards, the actual journey was a tedious one involving three changes of trains and much waiting about. As the hours wore on, my father began to feel more and more uncomfortable, and his visits to the various station toilets at length began to give him bloody reasons for thinking that he was even worse off than he had feared. Late in the afternoon a rather frightened Jane handed him over to Dr. Hick, who had no trouble at all in making a diagnosis. My father had an abscess on the kidney, which he had damaged while playing football in his schoolmastering days; he was in for a course of treatment that would keep him on his back and under Hick's roof for the best part of a month.

When my father had been put to bed and settled down, Dr. Hick did his best to reassure Jane, and to make her feel at home. It was, he told her over the teacups, quite a coincidence that, as friends of George Gissing's, they should have come down on him at the particular moment, since Gissing's older boy, young Walter, had just come to spend a few weeks with him. And a day or so later Gissing himself wrote to wish my father a speedy recovery, and to express the hope that the Wellses would see something of his son while they were with Hick.

My father wasn't in shape to reply to this note, or didn't feel like it, so it was Jane who wrote for him: she'd seen young Walter, she said, and found him in good spirits. She hoped that things were going better in Gissing's home, and that Edith wasn't being too difficult. Gissing's response to this was almost jaunty: ". . . you delight me with your description of Walter. If only the other little boy could be with him! I can get no news of the state of things in London, but it is pretty certain that the child's life is endangered whilst it remains with that mad woman. I told H.G.—did I not—that she had attacked her landlady with a stick, and was taken from the house with the help of a policeman?—she is now in I know not what lodgings . . ."

As Gissing had not previously said anything at all about this episode to either Jane or my father, this reference puzzled them, and led them to ask Hick what was in fact going on. The doctor was inclined to be evasive at first, but when he saw that they were genuinely concerned for Gissing's well-being he decided to tell them at least something of what he knew.

Dr. Hick had known a great deal about Gissing's private affairs for a long time, and had, indeed, inherited a protective interest in him from his father, who had given the poor fellow a helping hand in a dark hour back in the seventies when he had been going through some kind of late adolescent crisis. The doctor had learned quite a lot about that, but he didn't propose to go into ancient history. He limited

FROM BEATRICE WEBB'S DIARIES FRONTISPIECE VOL. 1924–1932. COURTESY OF THE AUTHOR'S PRIVATE COLLECTION

Towards the end of the Fabian Road: Sidney and
Beatrice Webb take afternoon tea in the garden of
Passfield Corner. The photograph dates from the later
thirties, after Sidney had been elevated to the peerage as
Baron Passfield, and the pair had become enthusiastic
admirers of Stalin and Stalinism.

AUTHOR'S PRIVATE COLLECTION

Cicily Isabel Fairfield in just such a mood as that in
which she adopted the name of one of Ibsen's more
inexplicably motivated and unattractive characters at the
start of her writing career in 1911.

AUTHOR'S PRIVATE COLLECTION

Rebecca West and the author, 1916

COURTESY OF THE BBC HULTON PICTURE LIBRARY

Violet Hunt

Ford Madox Ford and Violet Hunt were among Rebecca West's closest friends in the early years of World War I. My father liked Violet but didn't get on with Ford.

Ford Madox Ford

COURTESY OF THE BBC HULTON PICTURE LIBRARY

This photograph captures the authoritarian and
dictatorial side of Henry James that most Jamesians like
to forget; it was his literary politicking with such as
Edmund Gosse that irritated my father into producing
his *Boon.*

PICTORIAL PARADE

Lord Beaverbrook

AUTHOR'S PRIVATE COLLECTION

My father having a moment of self-doubt in the sunken
garden at Easton Glebe as he passes through the dead
ground between the success of *Mr. Britling Sees It Through*
and his departure in a new direction with
The Outline of History.

PICTORIAL PARADE

Gorky with Lenin in Petrograd in July 1920.

himself to filling my father in on Gissing's current situation. The writer had come to him for a stay early in the summer of 1897. He had said that he wanted a rest cure after passing through something in the nature of a nervous breakdown, but Hick divined that his real need was to talk. He had his own ideas about the connections, between worry and illness, and he had developed a technique of helping his patients by listening to whatever they might have to say. He made it a rule never to let himself show that he was shocked or antagonised by what they said, and he had noticed that they often did themselves a great deal of good by getting their concerns off their chests. He had soon seen that Gissing had come to him to be told that it would be the right thing for him to do to break off his relationship with his wife.

Hick had never met Edith Gissing, and had no idea of what she was really like, so that he could not tell whether Gissing's case for leaving her was sound or not. Gissing had spent a good deal of time giving him his reasons for thinking that Edith had now definitely crossed the boundary between sanity and madness, but he had gone on from that topic to propose the terms of a possible settlement of their affairs that did not seem compatible with this belief. It was to be based on a proposition which consisted in essence of the too simple suggestion that she should sell Gissing her interest in their two sons. She was to agree to drop out of his life and theirs, in exchange for an allowance of twenty-five shillings a week.

Hick had been positively alarmed to discover that Gissing's powers of self-deception had become so great that in the course of outlining this far from generous proposal he had managed to persuade himself that the idea hadn't originated with him, and that Hick had suggested it to him as a possible solution to his problem. He had even devised a fantastic scenario that assumed Edith's acceptance. They were to make a truce, and then they were to spend a last summer holiday together at Castle Bolton in Yorkshire. At the end of it Edith was to go her way, with her new life on twenty-five shillings a week before her, and he was to go his, with the children. He had never actually made the offer to her, although they had gone so far as to set out for Castle Bolton together with the children. In the course of the long train journey Edith had become suspicious, and had started to nag him. What was all this friendliness about? What was he really up to? She was quite sure that he was going to try something on her, but what was it? Why could he never be honest with her?

Gissing could not endure having his motives questioned even at the best of times, and now, when his intentions were anything but straightforward, he found Edith's interrogation particularily hard to bear. He took refuge in the mutism that he had always found to be his most effective weapon against her, and she was soon in one of the furies that he used as a basis for his charge that she was as good as mad. Long before they had reached their destination, he had given up all idea of coming to any kind of agreement with her. When he left England for Italy that autumn he was running away from the unresolved problem.

He had not improved his chances of making a reasonable settlement with Edith by what he had done before his departure. He had split up his family: leaving the baby Alfred Charles with Edith in a London lodging house, and entrusting the older child, Walter, to the care of his brother, who lived up in Worcestershire. As Edith had obviously no intention of giving up either child, he had resorted to a trick to get Walter away from her, telling her that he was taking her son out for an airing in the park, when he was in fact taking him to the station. With Walter at any rate out of harm's way he left for Italy without making any further attempt to communicate with Edith, who still had no idea where Walter was or of what had happened to him at the time when Gissing was showing my father round Rome. When he came back to England she was still in the dark. After his return he even went to the length of feeding her false information in the hope of breaking her will to resist before he reopened negotiations with her. This led to the incident of her attack on her landlady, so jauntily reported in Gissing's letter to Jane. As soon as Walter had been removed from his temporary home in Worcestershire and was safely boarded out elsewhere, Edith was given Gissing's brother's address and told that she might find the missing boy there. When she appeared on his doorstep Algernon Gissing assured her that her son had never been with him, and that he knew nothing of his brother's recent movements. The row with her landlady had followed when she made her way back to her London lodgings, perplexed and exhausted, to find that she and the baby were to be denied shelter until she had come up with a week's board in advance. Since then the poor woman had been drifting from one dingy rooming house to the next, living as best she could on a tiny allowance paid to her by Gissing through a friend of his who was a social worker. She still hadn't been told where Walter was. The boy was being moved from place to place without rhyme or reason on the pretext that he had to be shielded from his mother's murderous impulses. It was all very pitiful, and Hick found it impossible to say that he could foresee any happy outcome.

While Jane and my father were digesting this information Gissing was not letting the grass grow under his feet. Not long before they had set out on their unlucky journey to Seaford, Gissing had asked my father to do him a favour: a Frenchwoman had approached him who had made it her ambition to translate certain of his novels and to be his agent in France. She claimed to have good connections with several French publishers, and she had asked him to see her. That was his problem, he had no home to which he could invite her. It would be a very great kindness if the Wellses were to ask them both to Heatherlea for lunch.

The Wellses had been delighted to do their friend this service, and so Mlle. Gabrielle Fleury had come into their lives. My father had liked her enthusiasm for Gissing's work, which she seemed to know well, but he had otherwise been unimpressed. He had found her commonplace, pretentious, and inclined to be coy. He doubted if her standing in the French publishing world was as high as she made out, and he was afraid that she might be deluding his friend with false hopes. When she left he had not expected to hear more of her, and he was surprised when her name began to come, with increasing frequency and warmth, into the letters that Gissing wrote to him to cheer him up as he lay on his sickbed in New Romney. "Mlle Fleury," he was told in one of them, "has a mind of rare delicacy, emotional without emotionalism, sensitive to every appeal of art, and rich in womanly perceptiveness. . . . she is the very best kind of Frenchwoman, uniting their fine intellectuality with the domestic sense which it is common to think peculiarly English."

When Jane read these puffs for Gissing's new acquaintance aloud to my father, they were both dismayed. It was only too easy to see what was sure to follow. And sure enough, even before my father was up and about, the predictable letter arrived. Gissing was in seventh heaven, he had come to an understanding with Mlle. Fleury, and a new chapter in his life story was about to begin.

The letter in which Gissing gave my father this piece of news has unfortunately been lost, so that there is no way of telling what precisely it was in it that touched off my father's indignation. He was well enough to be handling his correspondence for himself by the time that it came, and he let Gissing have it hot and strong by return of post. What on earth did Gissing think that he was about—was he just going to turn his back on the mess he was already in, to waltz off into the blue with this woman he hardly knew? Had he given a moment's thought to what it would cost to run two households—he was having enough trouble to keep going as things were, did he begin to understand what he was letting himself in for? What *was* to happen to the wretched Edith and the two little boys if he ran out of money? Wasn't it his duty to provide for them before he took on further responsibilities?

Gissing replied in a tone of pained nobility only slightly marred by an attempt to pull his seniority:

> Well, my dear boy, this is candour with a vengeance! But you are too severe. My error has been in bearing so long with a woman who has used me so unmercifully. Of course I did it for the children's sake. And remember that, if I gave her the opportunity of getting a divorce (an opportunity she would not use) I should run the the risk of having the children removed from my control. To them is my first responsibility, and I shall always recognise it . . .

My father's exasperation with Gissing did not last. The illogic of this letter, demonstrating the degree of stress that his friend was under, along with the man's strange invertebrate charm, and the pathos of his blindness to his folly, all played their parts in calming him down. The falling-out was put behind them and a degree of intimacy restored. But things had changed. Gissing now knew that my father was thinking his own thoughts about his proceedings, and Jane and my father knew that he was beyond aid. He was determined to bury himself in trouble, and was not to be saved from himself. It was no surprise to them that his affair with Gabrielle did not prosper, or that, later on, when Edith Gissing had sunk into a crippling depression and her two boys had been put into their father's care, he made not the slightest effort to make a home for them. His reaction to the news that his wife had at last been placed in an asylum was a rather special one:

> I need not tell you that, on the whole, I regard this as a good thing for the woman herself, who was merely leading a brutal life, causing everybody connected with her a great deal of trouble. She will now be taken care of in a proper way, at less expense to me than before. Little Alfred . . . is to be sent to a farmhouse in Cornwall. . . . My mind, on that score, is enor-

mously relieved. I have always felt myself guilty of a crime in abandoning the poor little fellow. He will now have his chance to grow up in healthy and decent circumstances. I cannot tell you how greatly I am relieved. Indeed I believe that this event is already having a good effect upon my health.

The next thing to be expected after this would be the news that Gissing was making some sort of effort to make a home for the two boys. But Gissing went on from there to say that he and Gabrielle were thinking of moving on from the Gironde to one of the smaller resort towns behind Biarritz on the French slopes of the Pyrenees. He was aware that this would entail certain inconveniences, but he did not seem to reckon that distancing himself still further from his children would be among them. "It is a grave decision to settle so far from England," he wrote, "where I can get no books without buying them."

My father was to follow the successive stages of the decay of the Gissing-Fleury relationship with an affectionate concern tempered by exasperation. Gabrielle had come from that desperate lower level of French petty bourgeois society in which the keeping up of appearances was the be all and end all of existence. Her family's claim, as with untold thousands of such families, was to have "semi-aristocratic" connections, and to be in comfortable circumstances. She liked to pretend that her father had been an administrative officer in the Customs House of the Port of Marseilles, and a minor dignitary in the bureaucracy, but he had in fact been the cashier to a private firm of warehousemen. At the beginning of their liaison this worthy had still been alive, but he had been forced into early retirement by ill health and was to die in January 1899. The family Fleury had been struggling along on his savings, and on the tiny income produced by Madame Fleury's ironclad marriage-settlement trust. It was the classic shabby genteel situation, requiring the most rigorous balance between public ostentation and private parsimony. Delicious meals would be served when there was a guest to impress, but in the normal course of events the family squeaked along on the edge of malnutrition. Gabrielle had been brought up in the shadow of the knowledge that she must marry well, and must be seen to do so. After a school career devoted to coming out at the top of her class, she had decided to combine prudence with a means for satisfying her desire for distinction by marrying a literary man who had means. The route she had taken to this end was charming in its directness. She had adopted the practice of calling unchaperoned on literary lions with the expressed intention of asking them for their autographs. Persistence with this implausible line of approach over a period of years had very nearly paid off. Gabrielle had been able to believe for a few exciting weeks that she had landed the plump, oldish, but undoubtedly monied Sully Prudhomme. But a flying wedge of his relatives had broken that up when they learned how pitifully inadequate her dowry was going to be. That setback had befallen Gabrielle when she was twenty-nine, and very much aware that time was beginning to run out on her. It was then that she had approached Gissing.

What had followed had been a tragicomedy of errors. Gabrielle had believed that Gissing held a position in society that would have been accorded to a writer of equivalent literary standing in France, while he had believed that she had the place in the French scheme of things to which she laid claim. He had in particular accepted her view of herself as a member of a literary circle. It is true that she had literary acquaintances of a kind: She knew the seventy-nine-year-old Madame Lardin whose brother, Alfred de Musset, had been dead for forty-two years, and she also knew the eighty-year-old Emma Herwegh, widow of the German Romantic poet who had been a figure in the brave days of '48, but who had been dead for twenty-three years. Her link with the German writer Sacher-Masoch was, however, through a very much younger person who had actually written something on her own account. She was an industrious authoress of pulp fiction who had altered her first name to Wanda after her divorce from Sacher-Masoch, rightly concluding that it would do her sales no harm if she were to be identified with the heroine of her ex-husband's *Venus in Furs.*

It had taken Gissing a little more than eighteen months to realise how thoroughly he had been fooled. By then Monsieur Fleury had died, and Madame Fleury had dropped into the vacant slot of family invalid, a tactical move that allowed her, or so it seemed to Gissing, to absorb virtually all of Gabrielle's time and energy. It had become clear to him at last that the two women had very little money between them, and that it had never been in Gabrielle's power to win him the recognition in France that England had denied him. He had put himself in a box, and all for nothing. He had also become aware that an avenue of unappetising and possibly humiliating experiences lay ahead of him. The Fleury ace in the hole was an apartment in Paris that entitled them to think of themselves as *Parisians.* But they could not afford to live in it, they had to sublet the place furnished and use the rent they received to eke out their tiny income while they played out their dismal farce of being property owners in a variety of third-tier resorts and spas in provincial backwaters. Gissing had not expatriated himself in order to learn the art of benefiting from the off-season rates charged in such places, but he had never been the man to admit to having made a mistake, and he was not about to do so now. He decided that he was in trouble again because Gabrielle was weak and her mother was mean. A new fantasy of female wickedness began to take shape in his mind. Madame Fleury, bedridden though she affected to be, still kept an iron hand on the family budget. She was using her fiscal power to starve him to death, he was never allowed a proper breakfast. How could anyone expect him to write when he was hungry? If he could only start the day properly with a really nourishing meal.

My father hadn't shared Gissing's French experiences, and when his friend turned up in England again, looking gaunt and haggard, he was easily convinced by the story of hardship that he was told to account for his rundown appearance. Dr. Hick was also worried by Gissing's emaciation when he saw him, but he was even more concerned by some ugly eruptions that were breaking out on his face. He did not tell my father his real reasons for worrying about them, but told him that in his view Gissing would be most unwise to return to France until he had been put through a course of treatment and given a complete rest. It took the combined efforts of Hick, Jane, and my father, and a pliable specialist who had been brought into the plot to back them up, to persuade Gabrielle, who had only agreed to come to England on the understanding that it was to be the briefest of visits, that this was so. In due course she gave in to the very considerable pressure that was being put on her, and went home alone to look after her mother. After spending a week being pampered by Jane in the dashingly modern new house at Sandgate that my father had just had built for him by Dr. Hick's extremely gifted architect brother-in-law, Charles Voysey, Gissing was packed off to Norfolk to be fattened more expertly at a sanitarium run by a woman doctor. There he was given what she disarmingly called her "open air and over-feeding cure," and waited upon hand and foot. The idea that a man's health might be improved by getting him to put on a lot of weight in a hurry is not the only thing to emerge from this episode to point up the differences between those not very far-off times and our own. It was while he was in this lady's care that Gissing was at last persuaded that it was not actually dangerous to sleep through the night in a room with an open window . . .

How ill Gissing really was at this juncture, and what he was truly up against, were matters that my father then knew very little about. He believed, as did most of Gissing's friends, that it was a question of lung trouble, a phrase that could cover anything from a liability to bronchitis to tuberculosis, but in this case was supposed to mean the latter. My father thought that Gissing was tubercular, and that he had been a sufferer from the complaint since his adolescence, because that was what his friend had told him. Gabrielle Fleury, however, took his trouble to be what would now be called a psychosomatic disorder—she saw it as something that Gissing had unwittingly fostered as an excuse for his repeated failures of will. She had rather shrewdly reached the conclusion that his current collapse was a product of an uncertainty as to his next move, and that it had overwhelmed him in England so that he would be able to stay there for as long as he wanted without having to make a decision about where he wanted to live, or with whom, that would commit him to a particular future. Gabrielle had also concluded that the link between my father and the man on whom she had no legally enforceable claims (he was still Edith's husband in the eyes of the law) was a close one, and that she would be better off with him as her friend than her enemy. My father consequently received a series of letters aimed at proving to him that she really was the right woman for Gissing, and that whatever he might say about the minor irritations of the life that they had been forced to live together by the successive illnesses of her father and her mother, he had the first call on her natural affections, and would always have her devoted support.

These letters, written in a style that mirrored the almost saccharine sweetness of her overmodulated and calculatedly musical speech, contributed largely to the final hardening of my father's heart against poor Gabrielle. He came to dread their arrival, and presently, with a savagery that I find it hard to excuse, wrote to her to tell her that to spare himself further aggravation, he was handing the correspondence over to Jane. This manoeuvre, however, failed of its purpose. Gabrielle went on writing at him through Jane; she had guessed, quite rightly, that whatever she said would be passed on. My father could never, in the end, bring himself to forgive her, not for having had the hardihood to claim that her understanding of his friend was better than his own, but for having been right in thinking so. At the time, nothing could persuade him to the contrary, he had been absolutely certain that no woman could understand Gissing as he understood him.

The devoted Jane, who had still a great deal to learn about my father, agreed with him about this, and I think that they were both very much surprised when Gissing, saved from the immediate threat of starvation at the hands of Madame Fleury, and restored to a comfortable plumpness, slipped away from them, and from Dr. Hick, in order to go back to Gabrielle. They saw him only once between September 1901 and December 1903. It was when they were passing through Paris on their way back from a holiday in Italy. They both thought that Gissing looked seedy and uneasy, and that he eyed them with a mute appeal, as if he was regretting his mistake. The Wellses were doing very well and enjoying their life, and Gissing was not. A gulf was opening between them. Gissing's letters were becoming progressively more guarded and restrained, and on his side my father was beginning to wonder how he had ever had quite such warm feelings for a man who could really believe that the case for thinking of Bacon as the man who wrote Shakespeare's stuff for him needed answering; describe Carlyle's stupefying *Sartor Resartus* as one of the most important books of the century; and, worst of all, speak of Ruskin—yes, John Ruskin—as "the last of England's really great men."

That they were growing apart might have accounted of itself for this drop in the temperature. My father had moved on from the jolly smallness of the Omarian circle in which they had first met, and had become somebody much more like his later self. The book that he had published in 1901 called *Anticipations,* or, to give it its full, and very Wellsian, title, *Anticipations of the Reaction of Mechanical and Scientific Progress upon Human Life and Thought,* had been taken seriously, and had led such very different people as Winston Churchill and Beatrice and Sidney Webb to write to him to take up points he had raised, and to open relations with a manifestly considerable arrival. Its success had marked my father as a coming man, someone whose career was going to go on for some time—and in that, above all, had distanced him from his cornered and desperate friend, who was only too obviously firmly aground in the old century. In his approach to the novel as a form, in his style, in his habits of mind, and even in his personal appearance, Gissing had begun to date, and date badly. It wasn't so much that he gave the impression of an old-fashioned writer, he began to look like a common or garden loser. And then, to push the two men further apart, these were the years in which Jane bore my father two sons, and he went through a developmental crisis that troubled him very much indeed.

The crisis was originally touched off by a letter written to him by his first wife in June 1898. It contained an appeal for help. She was up against the difficulty that all unsuccessful poultry farmers see as the root of their problems—she was undercapitalised. Could he let her have the trifling sum, two hundred pounds would be ample, that was all she needed to push her struggling little business over the hump and into profitability. Isabel's letter had touched some chord in his being, and just as soon as he was able, he had cycled over to spend the day with her at her small holding at Twyford in Berkshire. His account of what happened when he got there, written close on thirty-five years after the event, constitutes one of the more touching episodes in his *Experiment in Autobiography*, but moving as I find it, I am not at all sure that it has any very close relationship to the reality of the experience. I am not doubting that he went off to spend the day with his ex-wife after he had read her letter, or that he was disturbed to find that she still attracted him physically when he saw her, but I am quite unable to believe either that he tried to persuade her to become his mistress during the visit or that she rejected his proposition in the gently motherly way that he suggests. The meeting and the parting that he describes fall too patly into the line of a vein of fantasy that runs through his least admirable fiction to be credible to me. I suspect that something much more like the truth about the actual happening is to be found in *The History of Mr. Polly,* a book written ten years after it took place, and published in 1910. In its relevant passages, a man who is very like my father in spirit and physique is seen inspecting the theatre of an ex-wife's disorganised efforts to make a go of running a teashop. When faced with the place, and later with the woman, he feels an immense relief at being free of the muddles, ineptitudes, and smallnesses that had given their life together its characteristic flavour. As my father was aiming at broad comedy when he wrote the book, he left out the important part of the experience in this account of it—there was no fictional point in troubling his Mr. Polly with the stab in the back of sexual desire for his abandoned wife that had hit him in real life. But that he had found himself wanting Isabel for the moment was the point that had hit him hardest at the time, and was to stay with him to give rise to the revised version, at once more and less honest, given in the autobiography. I believe that his sudden surge of inappropriate feeling for Isabel on this occasion left its enduring mark on my father's imagination because it took the lesson he had learned from his first infidelity to her, his brief coupling with the young retoucher of photographic negatives, a stage further. It was as if he had caught himself out in the enactment of an alternative ending to *Love and Mr. Lewisham*—one in which the hero, having wriggled out of his mesalliance, and having married the woman of character and intelligence who was clearly the right partner for him, was driven by something animal in him to go back to the other woman, who had nothing but her sexual responsiveness to recommend her. His discovery, it amounted to that, that the neat little applecart in which he was bowling along so successfully with Jane could be upset at any moment, just as soon as he should hit it off with an accessible woman who was in tune with him physically, alarmed him. He believed that he had escaped from all that when he had broken up with the placidly unresponsive Isabel. His perturbation on finding that he hadn't, and that he was as vulnerable as ever, had played no small part in producing the collapse that had forced him to take refuge with Hick that August, and in generating his explosive reaction to Gissing's naïve disclosure of his simple plan to ditch Edith Underwood in order to take up with Gabrielle Fleury.

The reader will have noticed that one of my father's more strongly urged objections to that plan had been that it too casually ignored any provision for Gissing's two boys, who obviously weren't going to find places in the Fleury household. It is striking to me that my father should have built himself a house and started a family as soon as he did after his discovery of the undiminished strength of his tendency towards philandering and the episode of Gissing's breakout. The architect he chose to employ was a man who notoriously aimed at an impression of solidity and weight, even in his smallest houses, and it appears to me that the choice must echo the adumbration in some recess of his mind of a strategy for anchoring himself and his marriage to the ground. Even if he wasn't fully aware of it, he was, by building and breeding, creating a situation that would make it unconscionable for him to bolt, and almost impossible for Jane to follow Isabel's example by giving him his marching orders in a crisis. That he needed all the anchoring he could get was demonstrated by his immediate response to the challenge of fatherhood. Almost as soon as his first son, George Philip, had been born, on July 17, 1901, he took off into the blue on his bicycle. He was to be gone for just over two months, and for the first few weeks of his fugue-like performance Jane had no idea where he was, or what he intended by his absence.

In the initial phase of his reappearance my father was in touch with Jane, intermittently and unpredictably, by telephone and through the mail, but in spite of these contacts she was not to know what his plans were, or have the assurance of a sight of him, until he surfaced at Ramsgate in the second half of September. Where he had been, and what he had done, in the interval is still far from clear. At an early stage he had spent a few days with his parents in the little house that he had bought for them at Liss, but there his track disappears. He seems to have cycled off without any plan, following his nose and going wherever his fancy took him next, as if he were a child acting out some dream of tasting the freedom that adulthood will bring. The period of waiting for him to reappear must have tested Jane's commitment to him to the utmost, but it stood the strain. As soon as she had been given an address to write to she let him know that she was neither hurt nor angry, that she blamed herself for having driven him away from her side by being overpossessive, that she wanted him to know that she understood his needs, and that he was to realise that he would always be free to come and go as he pleased—just because he was married to her he wasn't to think of himself as being tied to her apron strings.

The language in which this rather crucial declaration is couched is interesting. From a very early stage in their relationship Jane and my father had made all their most intimate communications to each other in a private language, a form of baby talk that might well have been invented for the express purpose of ruling out any possibility of an inadvertent lapse into importance or maturity. The earliest transactions in which it was used suggest two children playing house, but its later use, beginning here, in what both parties must surely have recognised as being in the nature of a moment of truth, brings to mind an exchange between mother and child. Something really serious has happened at last, but Jane assures him, in her maternal role, that nothing has changed, and that, no matter what, she will always love him, and be there to play whatever game he wants her to take part in. To prove it she says it to him in the established language of their happiest game. Although he has in fact become the daddyman, he can still go on being her playmate, for as long as he wants.

In the twelvemonth that followed, a period in which my father remained uncertain of what exactly Jane had been offering him in this remarkable letter, he wrote his least Wellsian book, *The Sea Lady*. It begins as comedy, a joke based on the idea that it would be fun to know what observant mermen and mermaids would make of human affairs, if there really were such creatures and they were intelligent. The tone is light-hearted in the book's opening chapters, in which an extremely worldly establishment figure, a very cool player of the English parliamentary game, is seen coping with the considerable practical difficulty involved in the business of making a place in his life of conventions and hypocrisies for a real mermaid with the tail of a fish. But in the end the comedy of manners turns in my father's hand to become something oddly strained and haunted. The mortal smoothie is no match for the mermaid, who has magic on her side, is immortal, and cold-blooded. She persuades him that she is the embodiment of a life-enriching sensuality, and having converted him to the view that sexual fulfillment comes before everything that he has valued in his life of calculation, takes him down with her into the depths in which he can only drown. My suspicion, I can't pretend that it is anything more, is that my father wrote this book to get something off his chest that he had not been able to admit to himself or to discuss with Jane in the further negotiation of their private treaty. What he was being given was the right to have any sexual adventures that he wanted, so long as love was kept out of it. This might suit him, and might suit Jane, but it could have hidden costs.

The Sea Lady had been finished, and the treaty brought close to its final form, when Jane became pregnant for a second time. My father's reaction to this development was less extreme than it had been when his first trial of fatherhood was in question. He was, nonetheless, laid up through Jane's seventh month, flattened by one of the disabling physical collapses that had been his stock response to stress throughout his early years. When he had recovered from this breakdown he left Jane to wait for her time alone and went abroad to recuperate. He was absent, walking in the Swiss Alps with his friend Graham Wallas, for the whole of Jane's eighth month.

In the Jura my father behaved like a boy who has unexpectedly been let out of school. He frisked and gamboled, and soon earned himself a somewhat stately rebuke from Wallas for trying his luck too openly and too eagerly with various young women they met with on their line of march. Wallas let him know that he didn't think it an appropriate moment for my father to be getting himself involved with new women, and had difficulty understanding him when he replied by saying that no involvement was in question—all he had in mind was going to bed with attractive girls who had given him signals that could only mean that they were ready for a little fun if he felt like it; they knew as well as he did that nothing serious was intended, and that they would in all probability never meet again after they'd had their little fling and parted. That was, indeed, the point, these little affairs on the road were in time out, play off the record that wasn't meant to count. How could there be any harm in that? Wasn't that sort of thing a natural part of being young, and happy, and on holiday?

Wallas had objected that, if nothing else, it wasn't altogether fair to Jane, to do things behind her back that he wouldn't be able to do in her presence, and was unconvinced when my father insisted that it was no more unfair for him to enjoy a tumble with a pretty girl who came to hand when he was away from home than it was for him to eat a good lunch, go to a concert, or look at a fine view with someone else when she wasn't able to be with him. Wallas countered this by saying that he didn't think that Jane would like it if she were to hear of it, and was incredulous when my father said that he had no secrets from her. When the terms of their compact were then explained to him, Wallas said that he was interested to learn that two people had got that far in practice as well as in theory, but he went on to warn my father that he didn't think that it was going to be as easy to combine the roles of paterfamilias and libertine as he seemed to suppose. The two men were still friends at the end of the trip, and were to remain so until Wallas died in 1932. I do not mean to suggest that Wallas, who was a man of acute intelligence, swallowed my father whole: his attitude was more that of an affectionate Wells watcher—he was genuinely fond of him, but the focus of his attention was on the question of what sort of trouble the dear man was going to find himself in next.

My father returned from the Jura calmed and refreshed. He did not bolt when his second son put in his appearance on the last day of October, and by the time the Christmas holiday came round it seemed as if the occasion for anything like the postpartum breakout of 1901 had passed by. The inner tensions created by the event were, however, still to be released, and when a telegram from Gabrielle Fleury was brought to him on December 22, his balance disintegrated immediately. The message he had received was the product of desperation, Gabrielle had found herself alone in a situation with which she was quite unable to cope. She did not say this in so many words, but it was easy to read it into her message, which said simply that Gissing was *in extremis,* and that my father would have to come at once if he wished to see his friend alive. It had been handed in at the post office in St. Jean Pied-de-Port near Biarritz early that morning. While he was wondering what he should do in the circumstances, he thought of Morley Roberts, a fellow Omarian who had known Gissing since their student days, and got in touch with him. Roberts had received a similar message, but there was nothing he could do about it for the moment—he was in bed shaking off an attack of influenza and it would be another forty-eight hours, at best, before he could face the long journey to southwestern France.

My father decided that he had no alternative but to go to Gabrielle's rescue himself, and accordingly left England and his family on the morning of December 24. He reached his destination in the middle of the afternoon on Christmas Day, to find that Gabrielle had not overstated the case: all hope for Gissing's recovery had been given up four days earlier. His friend was running a high fever, was hallucinating and altogether inaccessible. He was talking incessantly, but not making any sense, his flow of words having partly to do with fantasies of remote involvements based on the material he had accumulated for use in his historical novel, and partly with a renewal of his earlier dreams of escaping from Gabrielle's penny-pinching regime to an England of rude Dickensian plenty, of huge steak-and-kidney pies, suet rolls, plum puddings, and platefuls of buttered toast.

Gabrielle herself was in a bad way. She had been nursing Gissing to save the expense of professional help, and she had miscalculated her powers. She had believed that she had learned all she needed to know about sickbeds while her father had been dying, and while she had been looking after her querulous mother. But Gissing was dying hard, and demandingly. He was not slipping out of life but fighting death, inch by grudging inch. He had worn Gabrielle out before my father arrived, and she had lost touch with the realities of her case. She was full of a sense that she had made great sacrifices, and had suffered. She behaved as if she was being ill-treated by fate, and that she had claims on my father's sympathies at least as strong as those of the dying man.

My father was exhausted by his journey and distressed by the state in which he found his friend. He had no previous experience of dementia, and was shaken by the sick man's chantings that seemed to have meaning, but did not. He was edgy, too, because an inner voice was telling him more and more insistently that he had been a fool to come. He should have known that there would be nothing he could do. The only function open to him was one that he had no appetite for: he might have done something for Gabrielle, and made her wait for Gissing's end easier to endure. But the way in which she seemed to be bidding for the centre of the stage grated on his nerves and exasperated him. She was carrying on as if the poor chap were already dead. It was intolerable. He joined her in her denial of the realities of the situation, and decided to make a fight of it. He took charge of the sickroom with a high hand, expelling the widow-to-be from the death chamber on the ground that she was in need of a good sleep, and setting everything and everybody at odds. He brought in a nun from a nursing order to give Gissing proper care until a trained nurse he had wired for should come out from England, and for the sake of doing something positive meanwhile, boldly reversed the dietary instructions of the French doctor in attendance, starting to feed the dying man cups of broth and quantities of whole milk. They soon had their effect, and Gissing's temperature shot up. An altercation broke out, in which Gabrielle swore that the angry doctor had warned her that this overfeeding would be fatal to Gissing's last chances of recovery.

While the two rivals for his love were hissing tensely at each other in whispers, Gissing was staring straight up through the ceiling into Gothic Ravenna and holding muttered conversations with its notables.

My father's nerve broke. He was lonely, utterly out of his depth, and scared. It could just be that he had blundered appallingly with Gissing's diet. He had no sort of claim to medical knowledge. What on earth was he doing in this godforsaken spot, bickering lethally with this frantically unhappy woman? On the day after Christmas he abruptly reached the conclusion that he had had enough, and he sent Morley Roberts a telegram saying that he would be forced to leave on the following day. He fled the scene on the 27th, even though he had not received an answer to his telegram. Roberts left his home on the same day, spent the night in Bayonne, and reached St. Jean Pied-de-Port in the afternoon of the 28th, only to learn that Gissing had died during the morning.

That my father was well aware that he had not come up to scratch on this occasion, and that he had let himself down, is demonstrated by the use he made of the episode in the novel *Tono-Bungay.* In that work, published five years after the event, the narrator's Uncle Ponderevo is made to die Gissing's death all over again in the very setting in which it took place. My father, present in the narrator's person, behaves very well this time around. He is cooly competent in his organisation of the dying man's sickroom, and he stays with him to be a pillar of support and comfort until he has drawn his last breath.

But in the end it was to be the sequel to Gissing's death rather than the manner of his taking off that was to have the more profound effect upon my father. Soon after his return to London, in the earliest days of the new year, he was approached by Edmund Gosse, who needed briefing on the arcana of Gissing's private life. As Librarian of the House of Lords, Gosse had the duty of mediating between the government of the day and the worlds of art and culture, and one of his functions was to advise the Prime Minister as to who was, and who was not, entitled to aid from the Royal Literary Fund, which existed to bring relief to artists and writers, and their dependents, who had fallen upon hard times. Gosse had been told that Gissing had left a wife and two children virtually unprovided for. The dead man's estate, as he understood it, consisted of nothing much more than an interest in some copyrights that were of little value; and while it sounded like an ironclad case for the Fund, he wanted to be sure that there had been nothing scandalous about the relationship—the Fund was not supposed to intervene in situations that arose from vicious or Bohemian behaviour. Had Gissing been all right?

My father let Gosse have an answer by return of post which began by saying that Gissing had been "a most amiable decent man" and went on to deal with some of the consequences of the disastrous error of judgment that had resulted in his marriage to Edith Underwood. He ended his letter with the observation that in his view the best line for Gosse to take with Prime Minister Arthur Balfour, who was an extremely understanding man, would be to let him have the facts. This would have been the right thing for my father to have said had all that Gissing had told him about himself been true, but in the course of the next eighteen months or so he was to learn how very little he had been told was true, and how much of it that had been true had been either substantially or wholly misrepresented.

My father's enlightenment came by way of his remorse. He wished to atone for having failed Gissing in his last hours, and it seemed to him that he might go some way towards doing so if he were to volunteer his services as literary executor to the dead man's estate. In that office he proposed the early publication of the uncompleted historical novel that Gissing had left on his desk, with an introduction that he undertook to provide. It was to include a brief biographical sketch and a critical assessment of the body of Gissing's work making much of the merits of his earlier novels, most of which had been allowed to go out of print. My father hoped by this strategy to give a little boost to the value of their copyrights. Before he settled to his task he received a teasing letter from Frederic Harrison that began by saying darkly that he was perhaps the only living person who really knew Gissing's story, and having hinted at horrors in this way, went on to draw a protrait of him utterly at variance with everything that my father had seen of him. Filled with a natural curiosity, and a certain apprehension, since Harrison had made a point of letting him know how glad he was that the story would never be told, my father pursued the issue, finally getting his informant to tell him what he wasn't willing to put onto paper.

Harrison, who had been born in 1831, was a Victorian of the Victorians: a jurist who had founded and edited *The Positivist Review,* had become an outspoken Radical and a prolific author after passing through his fiftieth year, and had functioned as a highly effective leader of the opposition to the South-African War as he left his sixties behind him. He had been almost professionally upright throughout his long life. When he told my father all that he knew of Gissing's early years he was, at seventy-three, still producing his book a year, and almost as formidable as ever. He was just beginning to be a little crotchety and censorious. He had liked Gissing very much at first, he said, and had trusted him absolutely because he had so very much the look of an honest man. They had met back in 1880 because the twenty-three-year-old Gissing had then sent him a copy of his first novel, *Workers in the Dawn,* in the hope that he might review it. Harrison had been impressed by the book, even though he had not enjoyed reading it, or been able to agree with the ideas that it had expressed. He felt sure that Gissing was a writer who deserved encouragement, but at the same time he did not feel able to give him a favourable review, or even to tell him that he had liked what he had done. He felt that he owed Gissing a precise explanation of his attitude. He accordingly asked him to come to see him at his home. When Gissing appeared before him, seedily dressed and manifestly in want, he decided instantly that emergency measures were called for. Before Gissing was allowed to leave the house he had been hired as a private tutor for

Harrison's two growing sons. The two boys liked Gissing, Mrs. Harrison liked him, Harrison liked him; he was soon a friend of the family and spending much more time with these pleasant people than his job required him to. All went swimmingly until, one day, chance brought a young man to the house who had been a fellow student of Gissing's five years earlier when they had both been attending Owens College in Manchester. The newcomer recognised Gissing at once, and at the first opportunity told his host that the man he had engaged as a tutor for his sons had a criminal record. While at the college, Gissing had been caught stealing money from his fellow students, brought before the magistrates, and sentenced to a prison term as a common thief.

Harrison presently asked Gissing if this story could possibly be true, and on being told that it was, had gone on to ask how he had come to do such a very foolish thing. Gissing had then told him a romantic though squalid story. When he was in his seventeenth year, he had said, he had fallen in love with a light-hearted girl very close to his own age who had allowed him to pick her up in the street. It had not taken him long to realise that this was not her first such adventure, and that she had innocently embarked on a course that could only become a steady drift into outright prostitution if someone didn't take charge of her. He had liked her too well to find the prospect bearable, and had set out to save her from it by taking her into his own keeping—he hadn't had the wit or the experience to know that the allowance that his widowed mother was giving him, though generous enough in relation to the needs of a bachelor student living in digs on his own, was nothing like enough for a couple to live on—especially if one of the pair liked to drink and enjoyed having a good time. He hadn't realised until late in the day, that the girl liked drink more than she liked men, and when he did come to that understanding he was already in deep trouble because love had come into the picture. He hadn't wanted to face the truth about the girl or about his situation, or to admit to himself that it was beyond his power to break with her. He had done his best to pretend that things might come out all right if he could, somehow or other, just keep going for a few more weeks, or a few more days. Under that pathetic illusion he'd resorted to the desperate shift of stealing. He'd begun by lifting anything pawnable that he could find lying about the college looking ownerless, and had ended by dipping into the pockets of clothes left hanging in the changing rooms in the hope of finding money. The college authorities were soon told that a thief was working the place, a trap was set by the police at their request, and Gissing was caught. Although he had no previous record, the magistrates before whom he had to plead were merciless, and he was sentenced to a month's imprisonment at hard labour. On his release Dr. Hick's father had found him work as a clerk in a Liverpool office, but he hadn't liked that, and had soon cleared out, to go to the United States to try his luck there. His luck hadn't been good, and after eighteen months of swimming against the tide he had borrowed the fare home from his brother Algernon and returned. It had really been the girl that he had been returning to, he hadn't been able to bear the thought of what might be happening to her. He had sought her out and married her.

Gissing had been disingenuous in his account of what had followed. With an air of generosity he told Harrison that none of it had been the girl's fault. It could not be said that she had been bad, it was simply that she had been ignorant, foolish, wilful, and disobedient. And she was a drunk—once she started drinking there was no way of controlling her, and if she was denied money with which to buy liquor when the fit was on her, she would go back to the street. She would do anything, no matter what, to get the drink that she had to have. And when her bout was over she would become herself again, to tell him remorsefully that he had seen her drunk for the last time, and beg him to give her another chance. He knew, even as he forgave her, that it was not in her power to keep any such promise, but he could not bring himself to turn her off, and each time he would forgive her. The worst of it all was that she didn't really like him very much. He was the wrong sort for her, and she took what little pleasure she had from life in keeping low, boisterous company. He knew what he should do in common prudence, but he had married her, and he couldn't bring himself to turn his back on someone he had promised to love and cherish.

The Harrisons had taken this at its face value and had believed that Gissing was doing his innocent best to save a dreadful woman from herself. They decided to help him so far as they could by showing him that their regard for him was unshaken, and that he could count on their affectionate support. Their protégé had rewarded them by keeping them abreast of the developing story of the marriage. But he had made sure that they never met his wife. Before long he was telling them that she had taken to brawling in public places when "under the influence," and, not much later, that he had been forced to have her shut up in a home for inebriates in Battersea.

The storyline up to that point had been simplicity itself, but it now took an incomprehensible turn. Gissing told the Harrisons that his wife had escaped from the home, and had come back to him. She had talked him into a resumption of marital relations. Gissing saw that the Harrisons had found it difficult to swallow this one, and seemed to realise that he had gone too far. But his interest in his game with them had begun to flag, and his next instalment was slackly invented: he had lost touch with his wife, he told them, she had taken herself off and he had no idea where she had gone.

He left the running story at that for a year, and then brought his wife up again. This time the story was that a police inspector had sought him out in order to tell him that she had been involved in a closing-time brawl outside a public house, and that she was now known to the force as a common prostitute. In the circumstances, the friendly officer had said, he would be well advised to take divorce proceedings: the magistrates were apt to come down very hard on men who had come under suspicion of living on the immoral earnings of their wives. Grateful for this chilling hint, Gissing had, or so he said, hired a private detective to watch his wife for a two-week period. He had not been able to move further in the direction of the divorce courts, however, because the detective had seen nothing that could by any stretch of the imagination have been interpreted as evidence of misconduct. It was this small point that had made Harrison, whose confidence in Gissing had been slowly oozing away, lose faith in his veracity altogether. The detective's report was simply unbelievable if the woman was really earning her living as a streetwalker. Gissing had apparently sensed a change in the attitude of his patron, and he now dropped the subject of his marriage for a three-year period. When he took it up again it was only to tie off the loose end he had left dangling —he gave the Harrisons the news that his wife was dead, and that he had saved her from the disgrace of being being buried in a communal grave as a pauper by having her put away at his own expense.

Between 1887 and 1890 the Harrisons had heard no more of Gissing's private life. They were then abruptly readmitted to its dark landscapes after they had sent him an invitation to a formal dinner. Gissing's reply informed them that he had given up attending that kind of function. He was no longer living in London, and he was systematically breaking off all his links with educated and monied people—he had realised that he wasn't destined to be a popular writer, and that he was never going to be rich enough to keep his end up in the polite society in which such people as the Harrisons were at home. In the future he was going to limit his frequentations to the lower social level on which he belonged. He had found a girl of the artisanal class who was willing to face life with him on the sort of money that was all that he seemed able to earn, and he had been married to her for some months. The Harrisons might think him foolish, but the course was one that he had been compelled to follow —the truth of the matter was that he couldn't endure to live alone.

Frederic Harrison had disregarded Gissing's economic argument as a rationalisation, and had interpreted the letter as his young protégé's confession that he had a perverted appetite for women who were his social and intellectual inferiors. His wife had read the communication in the same sense. The episode brought an end to the Harrisons' warm feelings for Gissing as a man, and although their developed sense of justice required them to go on admiring what was admirable in his work, and to give him critical support, they discharged these duties with cool detachment and with minds averted so far as possible from the question of how he chose to live.

When he had said this much about Gissing, Frederic Harrison had closed down on the subject. He had not wanted to go into what else he had learned of either of Gissing's marriages. He had not met the women concerned. He believed, though he could not say so with any certainty, that the second Mrs. Gissing had been a girl of fourteen when the marriage took place. He did not, however, want to discuss the matter. For information about that side of Gissing's life, my father would have to turn to Morley Roberts. He, or so Harrison understood, knew everything that there was to know, or almost everything, in that department. He might even be able to explain the apparently incomprehensible severity with which Gissing had been treated by the magistrates when he had appeared before them at the beginning of the whole dreadful history. My father did as Harrison had suggested, and dashed off a note to Morley Roberts: "What is all this stuff that Harrison has given me about Gissing's first marriage?" he asked. He had opened a door on a world that he had known nothing about, just as Henley had done with his naïve question "What is this 'dreadful scandal' about Oscar Wilde?"

To say that my father was upset by what Roberts presently told him about the first marriage and its origins is to put the matter mildly. There was no way in which he could extract a romantic story from the information he was given, and the crassness of its broad outlines as well as of its detail was abrasive. Gissing had not been an innocent wandering out of his depth when he formed the connection. He had already been going to prostitutes for some time when he came across Mary Ann in the front parlour brothel run by a procuress known to him as "Mother B." The encounter was not an accident. A fellow student at Owens College, John George Black, with whom he was in the habit of exchanging such tips, had told him that if he were to go to Mother B's, he would find a beginner there who was hot stuff. This tip had been fatal to Gissing for two reasons: it had been given him, incredibly enough, in a letter, and he had kept it, as he had kept all Black's letters to him. He undoubtedly earned himself his prison sentence by this foolish mistake. When he came under suspicion of thieving, the college authorities had searched his locker, and there the letters were. The college authorities had passed them on to the police, who had passed them on to the prosecution. Before the case came on, they were slipped to the clerk of the court to be shown to the magistrates as background information bearing on the real character of the accused too disgusting to be put forward in evidence. After reading them, the magistrates had no hesitation about treating Gissing as a bad lot in spite of his official standing as a first offender with a clean record.

The letter that had done Gissing the most damage had been written at a later stage in this Dostoevskyan affair. In it Black had apologised for reacting with manifest incredulity on the previous day when Gissing had told him that he meant to marry Mary Ann as soon as he could do so, with or without parental consent. Black had begun by saying that he was fonder of Gissing than of any other man he knew, and that he was the last person in the world he would wish to offend, but all the same it was hard for him to take the idea of this marriage seriously. He'd found himself at loose ends forty-eight hours earlier, and he'd gone to Mother B's feeling as good as certain that he'd find Gissing there. He hadn't wanted to leave the place without seeing him, and Mother B had finally had to show him into the room behind the ground floor parlour where the big bed was to prove to him that there was nobody there. Looking into its emptiness, and knowing that if Mary Ann wasn't with a customer she would be on call downstairs in the basement kitchen, Black had asked Mother B to send her up to him. When she appeared she was evidently glad to see him and they had made love. He had felt awkward about it at the time, and so had she. She had become tearful, and had begged him to promise not to say anything about it to Gissing; she had made it difficult for him to leave her. When he had come to the end of his confession, Black had gone on to raise another subject bearing on his inability to take Gissing's plan seriously. He was afraid that he had picked up an unpleasant disease. Any doubt of what he was hinting at had been cleared up by a subsequent letter in which he gave Gissing a vivid description of the untoward state of his penis, and asked him if he had been afflicted in a similar fashion when he had been caught. Could Gissing give him the address of the man he had gone to for treatment?

My father found it desolating to think of this man, in whom he had seen so great a capacity for laughter and enjoyment, becoming engulfed by the ugly and the sordid so early. He asked Roberts if he understood how this Mary Ann had managed to get such a hold on Gissing, and was given no clear answer. Roberts was not at all sure that it had been like that. He doubted if the girl had been the agent in the disaster. He thought that her role could have been a purely passive one. He couldn't really say, however, because he had never known her. He had sometimes been with Gissing when she was in the same house or flat with them, and as close as the next room, but he had never spoken to her, and he had not seen her until after her death. Gissing had sent for him one day in February 1888, asking him to come to his lodgings. When he got there he had found Gissing in a wildly excited condition. He had received a telegram telling him that Mary Ann was lying dead in a house in Lambeth, and asking him to go there at once to make the necessary arrangements for the disposal of her body and her things. He couldn't altogether believe it, and was afraid that it might be the bait to some kind of trap. He begged Roberts to go to the address given ahead of him to find out how the land lay—he couldn't bring himself to go near the place until he had the word of somebody he trusted that the woman was really dead.

Roberts had found a corpse in the house in Lambeth. Whatever chronic ailments the dead woman might have been suffering from, the actual cause of death had been starvation. The body was terribly wasted. The only trace of food in her room, carefully put away in a bureau drawer where the mice wouldn't be able to get at it, was a dried-up piece of buttered bread from which a single bite had been taken. A collection of pawn tickets in a pudding bowl showed where almost all the dead woman's bedding and clothing had gone.

The scene had been a pitiful and disturbing one, but what struck

Roberts was the number of elements in it that were discordant with Gissing's account of the woman as a drunken virago, lost to all sense of decency, who had hated him. In the bowl along with the pawn tickets Roberts had found a number of temperance pledge cards signed at the prescribed monthly intervals, evidence that Mary Ann had been fighting against her worst failing to the last. Other things did not jibe with the specification. She had kept every letter she had ever had from her perplexing husband, and along with those letters, his photograph, and two engraved reproductions of portraits of the poets he had idolised in his youth, Byron and Tennyson. It was the presence of these things that had made it possible for him to make a positive identification of the body. There had been nothing about the thing itself to relate it to the lively-looking young animal of sixteen or seventeen, with her mass of glossy hair tumbling down her back, whose photograph Gissing had shown him to give him an idea of what she had been like. Gissing himself was faced with the same difficulty when he had at last been convinced that he could safely come into the room. The mummy-like cadaver, so small, so slight, had not reminded him of anyone—but there were his letters, and that was his photo-graph—and he recognised the engravings. The body, or so it seemed, had to be hers. In the course of this macabre recognition scene, Roberts' suspicion that however great a disaster his first marriage might have been for Gissing, it had been an even greater misfortune for poor Mary Ann, became a certainty.

When my father compared what Frederic Harrison and Roberts had been able to tell him of Gissing's first marriage with what he had himself learned, directly or through Roberts, of the second of his ventures, he was impressed by how much they had in common. In each case Gissing's choice had fallen upon someone who might have been specified as hopelessly wrong for him, and in each case he had started to treat the girl as if she had done him some monstrous wrong by becoming his wife as soon as the knot had been tied. To avenge it he had inflicted a kind of social death on each partner, keeping her out of sight of the world at large and of his intimates. He had spoken of his wives to some of his closest friends, but it had only been to complain of them, and of their behaviour. For Roberts, who had come closer to them than most, they had remained nothing more than presences in an adjoining room, or the putative origins of voices raised in anger or despair in a more distant part of the house. He had once, and only once, been in the same room with one of Gissing's wives, his second. She had been lying in a drunken stupor behind a screen while the two men had talked.

Gissing had developed a formula that provided, in his eyes, a perfectly reasonable explanation for his extraordinary treatment of these unlucky women. Unpresentable as they had been to start with, they had become very much more so after he had married them. The trouble hadn't had its origins in their obvious defects, indeed it might have given rise to some of them. It wasn't just that he had picked on ill-bred, uneducated, and uncouth young women to marry or that they had both been drunks—they could easily have overcome these handicaps once he had lifted them from the squalid surroundings in which they had been brought up if they had wanted to—the horrifying truth was that it had been his misfortune to be married, twice, to women who were teetering on the brink of madness . . .

My father's feeling that there was something suspicious, if not altogether unlikely, about this case of lightning striking in the same place twice was in the back of his mind as he immersed himself in the body of Gissing's writings before settling down to the task of writing the introduction to *Veranilda*. He was surprised to find how much plainly sadistic and paranoid fantasy had been blended in with the sober realism of most of his work.

The chain of thought provoked by my father's discovery of the darker aspects of Gissing's imaginings, and of his life, was stimulated further when he came to check over the notes he had made in preparation for writing his biographical memoir. He was depressed to find that most of the information that had come his way was less useful than it had seemed to be in the gathering, even when it came directly from informants who had been close to Gissing. In the space of the relatively brief period in which he had been at work, my father had been told with assurance that Gissing's original meeting with his second wife had taken place in the Marylebone Road, in Oxford Street, and in a tea shop. This small point bothered him, since he had a perfectly clear recollection of having been told, and by Gissing himself, that the encounter had taken place in Regent's Park. It was also tiresome to find that, although Gissing had described his second wife's father as a sculptor when speaking to the Registrar of Births, Deaths, and Marriages on the occasion of their wedding, he had told other people at other times that his father-in-law had been a farm worker, a shopkeeper, a plasterer, and a bootmaker. These discrepancies, while unimportant in themselves, added up, little by little, to a startling total. In the end my father found himself confronted by two largely unrelated characters—one of them the candid, good-natured, and thoroughly likeable man he had known, and the other a veiled and secretive fraud who had, for whatever reason, been virtually incapable of telling anyone the truth about anything more important than the state of the weather. The Gissing he had known had, for instance, always been firmly on the right side on the increasingly important woman question. He had recognised that women were potentially men's peers, and that their appearance of being something a good deal less than that was a product of their gross abuse by the law and the mores of Victorian society. He had written with sympathy and understanding of their disadvantages. It was difficult to relate the Gissing who argued on this side of the great question with the man who took pride in having learned, in the course of breaking in two wives, that a man who found himself short of a cane when he wanted to give a woman a good thrashing need never be at a loss in a house with a carpeted staircase in it—there was nothing to equal a stair rod for that purpose. The Gissing who had made this discovery had also been capable of passing the tip on to a friend as one that any married man would be sure to find useful.

My father began to feel that the sane and healthy Gissing of his first impressions had been an invention of his own. It had been Gabrielle Fleury's great offence that she had tried to tell him so. In more than one of those enfuriatingly mannered letters that he had dreaded, she had done her best to make him see the darker reality. "I know how impossible it is to feel absolutely sure and safe with him," she had said in one of them, "on account of . . . an extraordinary, terrible, and perhaps morbid unstability [*sic*] in mind, views, decision [and] feelings." My father had rejected all such formulations out of hand at the time, assuming that they rose from nothing more to be reckoned with than an emotional woman's tendency to make the most of trifles. All that she had truly been aware of, he had thought, had been an absolute incompatibility of temperament. He could now see that she had been on the right track. His new-found knowledge of the coldly considered cruelties that had been the staple of so large a part of Gissing's transactions with his women, put beside the latent sadism of so many of his imaginings, had brought my father a desolating sense that his friend had been badly damaged somewhere along the line of his development—the eagerly and joyously sensual being that he could so easily have been had been crippled and transformed into something devious and crabbed, a man who could only deal with a woman who was at a disadvantage, and who was compelled, even then, to teach her, by the most brutal possible means, that he was not to be counted upon for anything.

The usurpation of his mind by this new image of Gissing made it difficult for my father to write the wholeheartedly enthusiastic tribute to the man and his work that he had intended the introduction to *Veranilda* to be. He did his best to be tactful and to avoid all mention of Gissing's darker secrets, but the burden of his knowledge could not be cast off, and the essay came out as an apologia for a gifted writer whose promise and potential had never been fully realised. This was not at all to the liking of Gissing's family, whose members were united in their expectation of a eulogy. They had wanted my father to describe the career of a finished artist whose splendid achievements had never been given their due recognition. They were provincials who lived in a provincial backwater, and although they were shrewd and hard headed enough in living their Yorkshire lives, they were paranoid in their relationship with the larger world in which their maverick had lost his way and gone wrong. Gissing had never been able to tell them of his liaison with Gabrielle, and they had not enjoyed hearing of it after his death. They had known of his earlier involvements, and they had hoped that he had learned his lesson from them. It shocked them deeply to find that he had not, and that he had gone to live in France to cohabit with a Frenchwoman. As all foreign women, and especially French ones, were morally suspect until proved the contrary in the shopkeeping circles in Wakefield to which they belonged, they assumed that his association with Gabrielle was another chapter in the same old story. Because they had very precise ideas about what they did not wish to have said about their prodigal, my father's memoir seemed to them to be full of transparent hints pointing directly to what they most wanted to suppress. They refused to allow what they read as an indictment to be attached to the book, and eased their feelings about it by burning the copy that had been submitted to them.

Gabrielle Fleury was also upset by the memoir, even though she was never to read it. Gissing had been as selectively secretive with her as with his family, though about different things. He had never told her of his expulsion from Owens College, or what had occasioned it, for an instance. When a version of the memoir, purged, as he thought, of everything that had offended the Gissings, at length appeared in

The Monthly Review, someone was kind enough to tell her that it was still loaded with transparent references to such matters. It was then that she declared that she would never be able to bring herself to read anything that my father might write about either her husband, as she was still firm in calling him, or his work. He had, she said, told her, not just once but several times, that he had never thought much of my father as a critic, or believed that he had understood what his literary intentions had been.

My father had foreseen these reactions, but he was surprised when he found that he had given grievous offence in another quarter altogether. When Dr. Hick saw the revised preface in *The Monthly Review,* he blew up. He read its references to Gissing's persistent ill health in the light of his own intimate knowledge of the case, and took it that anyone else who came across it would be able to do the same—the article would then be as good as a public announcement that Gissing had been a syphilitic. He had gone on from that assumption to the further conclusion that it had pilloried him by implication as the sort of gabby practitioner who would be capable of sharing his patients' medical secrets with any journalist who was willing to spend a little time in chatting him up. His fury knew no bounds, and under its influence he not only denied ever having said that Gissing had become infected by the disease but even went so far as to deny the fact. His surviving correspondence with Gissing shows that he was not in a position to do so, and my feeling is that the violence of his anger stemmed in part, though only in part, from guilty knowledge—he had indeed been indiscreet in talking of Gissing's private affairs to my father. Another cause for his overreaction can be ascribed to his loyalty to the social code—it was not the done thing for one man who was supposed to be a gentleman to expose another to the sneers either of those who might look down on him from above or of those in a lower station of life who were required to look up to him with respect.

My father had liked Dr. Hick, and was much wounded by some of the things that he felt called upon to say in his anger. He was particularly hurt by the doctor's observation that the memoir was just about what he should have expected from a man with my father's background. The tone of this rebuke was one that he was beginning to be familiar with at this stage in his career. This was at the start of the age of the manufacture of celebrities by advertising, and his name was too much in the papers, too often on the hoardings and the sandwich boards, for some people to stomach. The publicity was bad enough in itself, it was worse that he was making his success with a new reading public that had come up from below with him, the readers of the cheap new mass-circulation papers and magazines that were coming off the steam-powered rotary presses by the tens of thousands. The members of the more genteel public that read the literary monthlies and quarterlies and liked its novels to come to them in hard covers from either a proper book shop or one of the old-style lending libraries, like Mudie's, thought of him as a self-advertising boomster and the embodiment of all those tendencies in literature and society that they cared for least. Hate mail started to come his way as early as 1900, and he was more or less used to the idea of getting nasty letters long before he fell foul of Dr. Hick. But what he was hardened to was the ill will of the comfortably well-off idlers and second raters who wrote to him from such places as country rectories, the service clubs in the West End, and the obscurer colleges of the older universities. Such correspondence was easily brushed aside. My father had caricatured such people as its producers often enough in his writings, and turnabout was fair play. By 1902 the funnier and more violently abusive letters were being pasted into a hate-mail album, and a practice had been established that was to be kept up until Easton Glebe was sold at the end of the twenties. But the contempt of my father's natural enemies was one thing, and abuse from a man he had liked and respected something else again. My father had come to think of Dr. Hick as a friend, and it was no fun at all to be rounded on by such a person and told that he should have stayed below stairs, where he belonged, if he wasn't willing to try to behave like a gentleman. They had been talking in confidence behind closed doors, and my father should have realised that he had no right to treat what he had learned in such circumstances as copy. Dr. Hick was never to recognise that my father had written as he did of Gissing's affairs with serious intentions, and they were not to be reconciled.

My father's falling-out with Hick was the first experience of this kind that had come his way, but he was embarking on courses that would soon bring him many more. In his middle forties he was to become the subject of so much scandal that he was to be ostracised by a great many people who had once been his friends.

Chapter XIV

I envisaged that reconditioned Fabian Society as becoming, by means of vigorous propaganda, mainly carried on by young people, the directive element of a reorganised socialist party. . . . If I were to recount the comings and goings of that petty, dusty conflict beginning with my paper *The Faults of the Fabian* (February 1906) and ending with my resignation in September 1908, the reader would be intolerably bored. Fortunately for him it would bore me far more to disinter the documents, fight my battles over again and write it all down. And nobody else will ever do it.

—Experiment in Autobiography

My FATHER'S PLUNGE INTO THE INTERnal politics of the Fabian Society three years after he had joined it in 1903 is often treated as an inexplicable aberration on his part. But the mistake he made, that of accepting the Society at its own valuation as an important sounding board for new political ideas, was an easy one for a man with his background to make. Although he had been calling himself a socialist for years, he had little knowledge of political theory, and none of practical politics. He had started saying that he was a socialist when he was still not much more than a rough draft for the prickly young misfit who serves as the eponymous hero of *Love and Mr. Lewisham.* He hadn't at that stage any idea of what socialism was, beyond that it required a man to go about looking fierce, running down the system, and wearing a red tie. When called on to defend his position, he hadn't been able to do much more than sick up some scrambled stuff that he'd got from a random sampling of the literature of dissent. He had retained what caught his attention or what had fired his imagination, and let the dull bits go. It was in the hope of finding a shortcut to a fuller understanding of what he was committing himself to that he began to attend the gatherings that were taking place every Sunday evening through the winter months of the middle eighties in William Morris' boathouse beside the Thames just above Hammersmith Bridge. These gatherings were intended to bring the saving light of socialist doctrine to the benighted British workingman, but while my father caught an occasional glimpse of someone who looked like a worker there, the real thing wasn't often to be seen sitting at Morris' feet. What my father got from the sessions was a sense that socialism was something coming from abroad that was mixed up with a great deal of locally generated stuff about getting back to an England of happy peasants and contented craftsmen in which each had worked for weal of all, and nobody had been too pushing or too greedy. Morris hadn't struck him as much more impressive than the boathouse message— he had seemed, in fact, to be short-tempered and something of a bully. When he took the chair at the meetings he used to silence speakers whose general drift he didn't care for by drowning them out with the clanging of a hand bell that he kept beside him for that purpose. This didn't seem quite the democratic thing to my father. It wasn't long before he found himself going to the boathouse because it was heated and the show was free: he hadn't seen much of the well-to-do middle class until then, and he was fascinated by the games that these liberated members of it were playing.

Most of the regulars at the boathouse meetings were nice people with a nice bit of money who were going in for being arty to ease the pain of living on dividends in a hard-working society. As most of them lacked any kind of creative gift, they concentrated their activities in the grey area of handcrafts. They were collectively great cutters of wood-cuts, operators of hand presses, weavers on hand looms, binders of books, and relentless art potters, and they relieved their horror of the aesthetic brutalities of the industrial age they happened to be living in by making quantities of coarsely conceived and hideously ugly parodies of medieval and Elizabethan household articles that only very rich collectors could afford to buy. A few of them, the theorists of the movement, neither delved nor spun, but were content to think in order that a brighter day might eventually dawn. One of the boat-house ideologues who was always to be remembered with affection, if not exactly with respect, by my father was Belfort Bax. His reputa-tion in the boathouse circle rested firmly on the belief that he had actually read the whole of Marx's masterwork, *Das Kapital*. It was his passionate attachment to the principle of the equality between the sexes that made it impossible for him to support the agitation for female suffrage. It would, he said, be wrong to give women the vote because the census showed that there were more women than men of voting age. It followed from this statistic that the enfranchisement of women would merely substitute one form of sexual tyranny for another.

Some may feel that Bax cannot have been typical of the middle-class socialists of the day, but it must be said that the eighties were not the finest years in the intellectual history of English socialism. In the middle of the decade another boathouse regular, Sydney Olivier, who was later to become my father's friend, was advising Marjorie Davidson, another member of the coterie, on a delicate point. She was thinking of marriage (her choice of a man had fallen on a certain Edward Pease, another boathouse regular, later to become secretary to the Fabian Society, and my father's dedicated enemy), but one thing gave her pause. If she were to burden herself with wifely cares, she might prejudice her social utility as a trained schoolteacher. She knew that this problem would not arise if she were to hire a maid— *but could a socialist woman employ a servant in good conscience?* Deeply perplexed, Marjorie Davidson had sent a circular letter to all the socialists she knew of, to ask them what they felt about this issue. Most of her respondents fobbed her off with courteous evasions, but Olivier had done his level best to be helpful. She could, he had said, duck the question altogether by moving into furnished rooms in which the landlady would hire the help; or she could persuade some unmarried female relative to live in and do the chores in exchange for free bed and board. But since there was something that smacked of equivocation about both these solutions, the best thing of all might be to cast about for a genuinely congenial member of the servant class and to hire her, not as a *maidservant,* but as a *helper* or *assistant,* and on the understanding that she was to eat with her employers and to take part in their mealtime conversation. If they were to treat her as a *human being* from the outset, no ethical question could arise.

Green though my father was, he could hardly believe the evidence of his own senses when he heard William Morris preaching, with a great air of one having his feet on the ground and his head well screwed on, the imminence of a popular rising to audiences of people who were capable of treating such problems as matters of real substance. What seemed especially disconcerting to him was that Morris apparently took it for granted that when the hour struck, the working-classes would be turning to him, and to people like him, for leader-

ship. My father had just about come to the conclusion that socialism
—or at any rate the English version of that commodity—was so much
playacting on the part of a privileged set of people who had never
quite grown up, when the modestly dreadful events that took place in
and around Trafalgar Square in the autumn of 1887 came along to
put a seal on his disillusionment.

These events had their origin in something real and sufficiently
serious, an acute regional crisis of unemployment affecting London's
East End. Demonstrations supporting the presentation of petitions
from discharged workmen to the House of Commons that had been
taking place sporadically throughout the early eighties became weekly
events in '86, and almost daily affairs in the first few months of '87.
When the House rose for the summer recess at the end of May that
year, with nothing done for the London poor, and no sign given to
indicate an awareness of the problem, the scene changed. Up to that
time the demonstrations had been made by operatives in particular
trades who had been put out onto the street by the closings of specific
workshops. But in the summer of that year they became episodes in
a coordinated campaign carried on by the unemployed as such to
demand recognition of their situation as a national problem. Although the country as a whole was prospering, and inclined to ignore
gloomier matters in favour of making the most of Queen Victoria's
Jubilee celebrations, the government became deeply concerned by
this development. Its fears were fostered by the Metropolitan Police,
who showered the Home Secretary with reports from their informants
stating that the focus of the consolidated campaign had become Trafalgar Square rather than Parliament. A ban on the use of the square
for political purposes had been imposed at the beginning of the year,
and the organisers of the campaign appeared to have adopted the
thesis that if they could break through the police lines and take possession of the forbidden ground for long enough to hold a meeting, they
would make an impression on the whole country that would force the
government to recognise the existence of the problem and to do
something about it. If this was their belief, as the Home Secretary had
good reason to suppose, the matter at issue was no longer one of what
should or should not be done to relieve the sufferings of the unemployed, but a constitutional question of who should govern. It was not
possible for any government that wished the parliamentary system to
endure to allow a sectional interest to force its hand by resort to
extralegal means. Foreign experience had made it perfectly clear that

governmental surrenders to mobs of demonstrators led to coups d'é-
tat and the installation of dictatorships. The rot would have to be
stopped before it went any further. There were no circumstances in
which a mob from the East End could be permitted to take over the
square.

Undeterred by the government's declarations of its intent to en-
force the ban, the organisers of the campaign did their level best to
march crowds of East Enders into the West End by way of the Square
on successive Sundays between mid-September and early November.
Such enthusiastic supporters of the campaign as Morris cheered the
marchers on with reiterations of the glib assurance that when the
police, and the foot soldiers and cavalrymen who were at hand to back
them up, saw how many they were, and how determined, they would
simply fade away. It was a considerable surprise to both the demonstrators and their sympathisers to find that the opposition became
more rigid and more determined as the size of the mobs increased.
The collisions between the contending groups began as scuffles, built
in scale and in violence from week to week, and reached their climax
in two honest-to-god riots in November.

Morris was in both the November clashes, and although he had only
lately been appealing to the members of the Socialist League to prepare for grim events in his worst verse-for-the-workers style: Hear a
word, a word in season, / For the day is drawing nigh, / When the
cause will call upon us, / Some to live and some to die, he was utterly
horrified to find himself part of a crowd that was being taken seriously
as menace to the existing social order by the police. He ran, like
everybody else, from the swinging batons. It had made no difference
to the outcome that the crowds had been enormous and the numbers
of the police very small. Morris was back in the approaches to the
square on the day of the second riot, and once again amazed to see
thousands running from hundreds. He experienced a flash of hope,
however, when he learned that the police had killed a man in one of
the clashes. The blood of martyrs was supposed to be just what such
movements as this needed to get them off the ground. It appeared
that a man he knew by name—and had, indeed, *met* somewhere, had
been knocked down by a mounted policeman's horse, trampled, and
killed. There was something not quite right about the story, but no
matter. The man had died, and in the square. His death could be
crafted into instant mythology. The vision of a broadsheet presented
itself to Morris' inward eye—the sort of thing that used to be bound

into the old chapbooks. It would feature a rousing ballad about the dire event, a woodcut illustrating it, a lavish show of type flowers, and a few bars of music giving the air. Morris churned out the engaged ballad that very night, and in the course of the following morning his friend Malcolm Lawson carpentered up a singable tune to go with it, as Walter Crane was cutting the woodblock and designing the layout. The hand-printed sheets were ready for distribution to the mourners as they came in at the cemetery gates on the day of the burial.

The interment, as was only to be expected, came as something of an anticlimax at the end of a day of marches and speeches. It was nearly teatime, and the light was going, when the demonstrators reached the graveside at last. As Stewart Headlam, a liberal church-man who thrived upon such occasions, began to read the burial ser-vice, the steady drizzle that had been falling for some time gave way to a downpour. Hundreds of umbrellas, kept furled until then "out of respect," began to open on every side. The sound of the rain drumming on their shining surfaces was soon mingled with that of untrained voices having a go at Morris' *Socialist Battle Hymn:*

> We asked them for a life of toilsome earning,
> They bade us bide their leisure for our bread.
> We craved to speak to tell our woeful learning,
> We came back speechless, bearing back our dead.
> Not one, not one, nor thousands, must they slay
> But one and all if they would dusk the day.
>
> They will not learn, they have no ears to hearken,
> They turn their faces from the eyes of fate;
> Their gay-lit halls shut out the skies that darken,
> But lo! This dead man knocking at the gate.
> Not one, not one, nor thousands, must they slay,
> But one and all if they would dusk the day.

When this string of bogus archaisms and mock heroics was done with, Morris was heard to mutter a defensive "Well, I like ceremony" as he gloomily joined the crowd making for the cemetery exits through the drenching rain. In his own address, made earlier in the day, Morris had rather strangely spoken of this happening as a "most successful celebration." He had, no doubt, been thinking of it in terms of the gate—which had been astonishingly large. But just what had they been celebrating? As Morris very well knew—he had been forced to own to it in his eulogy—the Alfred Linnell they had gathered to mourn hadn't been the Linnell he had once met, and the poor chap hadn't gone to the square to prove anything, or even to make a gesture, he had been there out of idle curiosity. He had just wanted to see what was going on. And, what was worse, he hadn't been killed by a policeman's horse while in the thick of the action. He had died of a heart attack as he watched a clash between the police and a body of the marchers at a considerable distance from him on the far side of the square. His death in that place and at that time had been no more than an irrelevant accident.

Over the Christmas holidays Morris had seemed to be in less than his usual grumpy good spirits, and on the approach of spring he had taken himself off to his sixteenth-century manor house at Kelmscott, beside the upper Thames on the far side of Oxfordshire. From that retreat he presently wrote to a friend to say that he would be putting rather less of himself into agitation in the immediate future. He had a topping idea for a book, and writing it was going to keep him fully occupied for a while.

The topping idea was for a prose romance, *The House of the Volsungs*. It was to illustrate "the melting of the individual into the society of the tribes" back in those healthy, pre-capitalist, and happily under-documented times around six or seven hundred A.D. when Nordics, at any rate, still possessed a sound social instinct that had made it natural for them to recognise and respect those among them who had been born to be their leaders . . .

It was in this comic mask that Socialism had first presented itself to my father. The effect of the encounter was made all the greater by an accident. Just after the finally disillusioning farce of the anti-martyr Linnell's funeral had taken place, a recurrence of his lung trouble had driven him to take shelter under his mother's wing at Uppark. It was then, when he had been set up to appreciate it by his disappointment with the Hammersmith brand of left-wingery, that he at last discovered what there was in Old Sir Harry's library. He fell under the spell of France's eighteenth-century leap forward, the intellectual adventure of the Enlightenment, and of its most characteristic product, Diderot's splendid idea for The Great Encyclopedia, which was to have been a grand assize of human knowledge. After the backward-looking dream stuff of Morrisite fantasies, and the semi-mystical conjurations of Marx and his hypnotised devotees, there was a wonderful practicality about the determination of the French *savants* to establish how much they knew about their world before they set out to remake it. Their belief had been that once men were given a clear picture of the extent of their capabilities, and of the possibilities open to them, they would become united in amity by a common desire to make the most of their opportunities for improving the quality of their lives. In the vast educational enterprise of the Encyclopedists my father recognised the concept of a true revolution. When he had first made his way to the boathouse he had thought of it as a time for the paying off of old scores, of taking vengeance, and turning out the greedy rascals who had been on top in some exhilarating explosion of justifiable wrath, just as Morris had. But he now saw that it could have nothing to do with the idiotic business of whipping up the envious spite of the ill used and ignorant, much less with posturings and heroics on barricades before a backdrop of burning buildings, or with the calculated brutalities of mass executions. The underdogs were to be liberated from their disabilities because it was in the public interest to liberate them, and the new order was to come in, like the tide, inch by inch, propelled by the irresistible force of the case for demonstrably better ways of doing things. It was to be a revolution by consent, and as different from the revolution of the guillotine, born of hunger and rage, as chalk is from cheese. My father's love affair with this sane educational revolution, that began so thrillingly for him as he was recovering from his illness and his disillusionment at Uppark in the winter of 1887–1888, was to last for the rest of his life. It was to have a fundamental effect upon his thinking. Though he was to go on calling himself a socialist, and defending his commitment to socialism, it was the rationalism of eighteenth-century France's intellectual elite that was to command his loyalties from then on.

That is not to say that his thinking about the strategy of the constructive revolution was to remain the same until he died. When he went to Uppark that winter he was still a very naïve young man, sure that what was the root of all social evils was the inequitable distribution of wealth and the waste of human resources involved in the workings of the class system. But as he grew older it seemed to him that other things might do more to determine whether life was worth living. He saw that while it was in general true that poverty made for misery, some of the very poor were not at all unhappy, and many of those who were miserably unhappy were not at all poor, particularily if they were women. He had also been surprised to find how often natural gifts—particularly where women were concerned—went unrecognised and undeveloped among the children of the upper classes. It struck him that privilege could be as much of a trap as the lack of even a fair shake, and, particularly after his immersion in the murky detail of Gissing's life, that the conventional order of revolutionary priorities might very well be all wrong. It could be that the first order of business in any truly radical transformation of society for the common good ought not to be a matter of either wealth or class. It could be that an end to the subjection of women would be the thing that might most certainly and most rapidly enlarge everybody's chance of happiness. It could be done by recognising them as the legal equals of men, and setting them free to become their rivals or partners, as they might choose, in whatever field they elected to enter. It could be done without killings or expropriations, and it would bring a rapid end to the appalling waste of brain and ability involved in restricting half the population to the menial tasks reserved for the uneducated. Above all, it would do away with the chief cause of the desperate unhappiness characteristic of Victorian family life, by making marriage a contract between equals. The brute facts of biology had not escaped my father, and he had the common sense to see that all legislation aimed at the liberation of women would be futile if they were to be disregarded. By 1903–1904 he had convinced himself that the most effective solution to the problem that they posed lay in taking money from the general tax fund to subsidise motherhood: he felt sure that once it was generally accepted that a woman was entitled to state support through pregnancy and the early years of her child's life, the back of it would have been broken.

It was only natural that his habit of thinking about such questions, and of thinking along such lines, should have turned his mind towards political action for the purpose of influencing or introducing progressive legislation. That much was obvious to even his least attentive readers as early as the turn of the century. He was delighted when Beatrice Webb wrote to him in 1900 to say how interesting she had found some of the points he had made in his recently published *Anticipations.* This was his first book of serious speculation about the directions in which modern societies were likely to move in the future, and her reading of it led Mrs. Webb to ask him if he might care to join a dining club that she and her husband, Sidney Webb, were organising. It was to be called The Co-efficients, and it was intended to bring a selection of the big guns in party politics into regular contact with some of the brightest people outside them who had ideas about social questions that were becoming the burning issues of the day.

My father decided that if he were to become a Co-efficient it would give him just the sort of entry into the political world that he was looking for. He joined, and soon found himself dining regularily with a group that included Arthur Balfour, a former Home Secretary who was soon to be Prime Minister; Richard Haldane, who was to be Minister for War and Lord Chancellor; Sir Edward Grey, a future Foreign Secretary; the right-wing Conservatives Leo Amery and Lord Milner; the establishment poet Sir Henry Newbolt; and the Radical-Whig philosopher Bertrand Russell. The group also included a man who had been Minister for Justice in New Zealand, and who had lately come to London to discharge the quasi-ambassadorial function of the Dominion's Agent-General, a certain William Pember Reeves, whose wife was an ardent Feminist, and whose daughter, Amber, was on the brink of growing up.

My father enjoyed himself among the Co-efficients and was a success with them. At the end of his first year as a member Beatrice Webb thought he might make a useful recruit for The Fabian Society and told him that he ought to think of joining it—he was just, she said kindly, the sort of intellectually adventurous generalist it needed to jolt it out of its tendency to stick to the narrow path determined by the special interests of the more domineering members. But she was sure that even if he simply came to look and listen he would find a great deal that was stimulating and challenging in their debates, which often reached a really high level when such members as Shaw and Graham Wallas were in form. My father hesitated for a while before falling in with her suggestion. He had heard a certain amount about the Society from Wallas and Olivier, and not all that he had heard had been to its credit. He had gathered the impression that it was a sort of court that the Webbs had made for themselves, a little mutual-admiration society that had strong affinities with the socialist cell in Morris' boathouse, where that detestable handbell had drowned out all dissent. Still, there was the outside chance that if he went into it, he would be gaining access to the sort of audience that might prove responsive to his ideas about the importance of making an end to the subjection of women part of any effective program for social reform. After much hesitation he joined the Fabian Society in February 1903.

My father's first performance in front of a Fabian audience was not a success. Although he was the best of company when he was among friends because he could talk so well, he had none of the capabilities that make a good public speaker. He had learned this the hard way, by failing to hold his own in undergraduate debates in his student days. He came before the Fabians for the first time feeling more or less certain that he was going to fail again. It cannot be said that he lost his audience, because he never took it by the collar. Knowing that he was going to start piping if he tried to force his voice, he began, and went on, in a low mumble, addressing himself to an invisible presence a few inches below the notes spread out before him. He later retrieved something from this wreck by taking the idea that had constituted the core of his presentation and transforming it into the germ for his sociological fantasy *The Food of the Gods.* It describes with a great deal of verve the reduction of the turn-of-the-century world to chaos by the physical consequences of the accidental release of an enormously powerful stimulus to growth which makes young things of every kind permanently larger than their parents. When the story ends, a new race of giants who have outgrown their fathers are seen to be girding themselves for the task of creating a substitute for the world of little things that they have become too large to inhabit. What my father was saying in this parable was that the consequences of the industrial revolution, the overall increases in population, the huge growth of the towns, the vast increases in the volume of trade and the scale of industrial operations, and above all the appearance of titanic accumulations of wealth in the hands of the new Trusts and Corporations, had brought new forces into being that the politician who intended to be a social architect could no longer afford to ignore. Had the Fabians who had attended the meeting at which the original presentation was made been able to hear what my father had been saying, they might possibly have understood why he had put his chosen topic before them. What he had left it to them to infer was that he had come to the conclusion that a body limiting itself to a membership of seven hundred, and clinging to the intimate format of a private club, could not hope to be an effective agent of social change in the context of an industrialised state, and that the Society's first step, if it really wanted to achieve its larger aims, had to be its own transformation into a national organisation with a marching strength that would give it political credibility.

Although he went to a number of their meetings in the interval to listen to what was going on, the Fabians heard nothing more from my father until just over a year had gone by. What happened then—in March 1904—was that he wrote to the organisation's secretary, Ed-

ward Pease, to tell him that he was thinking of resigning his membership. He gave as his reason his sympathy with his friend Graham
Wallas, who had himself resigned a short while before to protest
against the adoption of a piece of nonsense from Shaw as the Fabian
position on the issue of Free Trade versus Tariff Reform.

Some writers have suggested that my father waved this threat at
Pease, not because he supported Wallas' views, but because he wasn't
sufficiently grown-up to find a situation endurable in which he was
required to own to being wrong about any subject on which he had
a positive opinion. To back this up they quote from the letter in which
Pease, having my father's threat to resign before him, tries to get him
to withdraw it by breaking it to him, as if he were a backward child,
that it wasn't the done thing for members of democratically constituted bodies to flounce out of them whenever they found themselves voting with a minority on a policy issue. My father had already
begun to resent Pease's habit of condescending to him as one of lowly
origins, and since he knew very well that Graham Wallas hadn't
earned himself any such educational lecturings by *his* resignation, the
secretary's persuasions had the usual negative effect upon him on this
occasion. Stroking by Shaw and the Webbs, however, proved more
effective in bringing him back into the fold. The Webbs went so far
as to commit themselves to a whole weekend to soothing him; they
ran down to spend two days with him in his brandnew house looking
out over the Channel from its site at the end of the Folkstone Leas.
They rounded out the good work by giving him one of their little
dinners on their return to town—the Shaws were there, so was the
Bishop of Stepney, and the exasperatingly admirable Arthur Balfour,
now actually Prime Minister. My father, who could never resist Balfour's enormous private charm, had a very good time, and presently
relieved his feelings of guilt about allowing himself to be manipulated
by such flattering attentions by writing a tart letter to Pease withdrawing his threat of resignation. In it he made his position absolutely
clear. "I highly disapprove of the Fabian Society," he said, and went
on to explain that he was staying on only in order to turn it upside
down. With that declaration of intent off his chest and in the record
—Pease had never in his life thrown away anything that could be put
on file—nobody would ever be able to say that he had remained a
member on false pretences. But it was not until eighteen months later
that he came out into the open to let the membership in general know
that he intended to change the Society beyond all recognition.

It is perhaps necessary at this point to remind the reader that my father's first year as a Fabian was also that which had ended so painfully and so strangely for him with his Christmas journey to St. Jean-Pied-de-Port, and his humiliating failure of nerve beside poor Gissing's deathbed. That disquieting experience had been followed by his even more upsetting immersion in the morass of his friend's pathetic secrets, and that in turn by a personal setback of another kind: he found that he couldn't finish the book he had been working on for over two years as he wanted to. He was only able to bring it to a conclusion by cutting thirty thousand words out of the text and dropping an important character from the story that he had intended to tell. As the scrapped portions of the book have survived to prove that they really had to go before *Kipps* became publishable, and as it is still thought of by many as one of his more effectively organised novels, it may be hard for the non-literary reader to understand why my father felt so badly about doing what had to be done to save it— but to think along those lines is to ignore the dismay that any writer is bound to feel when he is made to see that he hasn't been in control of his own work for a space of weeks or months. In this instance the effect upon my usually mercurial father was to throw him into a slump from which it took him two months to recover. He very characteristically worked himself out of it by having a fight with something else that was bothering him at the time—the question of the actual terms of his private treaty with Jane. He took his doubts about what they had actually agreed to and worried their substance into a book—*A Modern Utopia*.

In this work he took as his starting point his walking tour through the Jura with Graham Wallas, turned himself and his companion into characters, and then had them step through the boundaries between the dimensions into another world existing in parallel to our own. Before long they met their counterpart selves in the counterpart Jura they had entered, and learned from them, among much else, that not only were such private arrangements as he had made with Jane the normal thing there, but also that the powers in control had already adopted the principle that motherhood and child care should be funded by the state. My father was, in fact, taking a look in fantasy at a polity in which his humane sexual revolution had already taken place. In the course of his wrestle with his doubts about his compact with Jane he had found a way of constructing a trial balloon that would give him some indication of how his ideas about what was then known as "Free love" were likely to go down, inside the Fabian society, and out of it, before he came into the open with them as the basis for a program of social engineering. When *A Modern Utopia* appeared, he was agreeably surprised by its reception, and positively delighted by the number of Fabians who wrote to him to say how much they liked what he had to say on the subject of sexual mores and the possibility of improving upon them. They liked him for saying without circumlocution that his Utopian authorities were right to take no interest in what went on between adults who were not married, no matter who they were, or what they did, provided only that these activities remained private, and without consequences. This hands-off approach was especially appealing to those younger Fabians who were lawyers, and who had strong feelings about the misuse of the criminal courts as courts of morals. Others of them, who were for the most part women, liked it because they felt that the passage from child to adult would become almost infinitely easier for both boys and girls in a society as tolerant of experiment as that which he had proposed in the book.

One of these younger Fabian women was the no longer all that young wife of Pember Reeves, the Australian-born feminist Maud Reeves. She had joined the Fabian Society at my father's suggestion, partly because she was eager to get back into politics, and partly because she didn't like the idea of being made into a mere social appendage to her husband as a result of his posting to London. When she realised that my father had committed himself to the principle of making women full citizens, she made made herself not only his ally but also his coach. She knew her business in this field, having played a leading role in a successful campaign to get New Zealand's women the vote before leaving the Dominion. By becoming my father's political tutor in matters of tactics and organisation she transformed his chances of moving the Fabian Society into new courses overnight. She knew the world of the committee rooms backwards and forwards, and she had the energy and the persistence needed to carry organisational work through to its completion. She very soon saw that my father was never going to be very good at that side of the great game, and concentrated thereafter on teaching her arts to Jane, who had loyally followed my father into the Fabian ranks as soon as her younger son had been weaned. The two women were soon working harmoniously together, and by the middle of 1905 they had done more than enough to give his hitherto nebulous plans for turning the Society "inside out" real credibility. The next step was to get a formal challenge to the existing Executive Committee onto the agenda for the next General Meeting, due to take place at the start of the new year. My father accordingly drafted a motion calling for an enquiry into the effectiveness of the Society's current policies, and passed it on to the secretary in due course. The way seemed to be open to a straight fight about the aims and objectives of the Society, but that was not what it was to be.

My father's subsequent troubles among the Fabians were in large part due to the fact that by addressing himself directly to the Feminist issue he had won the support of too many of the Fabian wives. One of the first of them to rally to his banner after he had submitted his draft motion to Edward Pease was, improbably enough, that worthy's wife, the former Marjorie Davidson. When she had read *A Modern Utopia* she wrote to Jane to say that the more she thought about my father's proposals for the reform of the Society, the more she liked them. She foresaw a new era for Fabianism—"if only everyone will be sensible and broadminded." She had come to think of the Society as a narrowly exclusive "Baptist Chapel dominated by Deacon Webb," she went on, adding that "my socialism . . . is much more democratic and comprehensive."

And, as if unsatisfied with this ideological abduction of the wife of the Society's secretary, my father had also taken over the life partner of no less a person than Hubert Bland, a founding member who had been its treasurer since its very first meeting. He was an extraordinary figure whose waking hours, and possibly even dreams, were devoted to a cluster of impersonations. He owed his position in the Society to one of them. At that faraway first meeting a collection had been taken up to provide Pease, as the secretary, with a float of petty cash that would enable him to buy such stationery and stamps as he would be needing if he was to keep in touch with the membership. The whip-round yielded, from the fourteen persons present, the sum of thirteen shillings and ninepence (three dollars and twenty five cents, more or less, as things were then). Bland was made treasurer and entrusted with the money on the ground that he was the only businessman there. His claim to that title rested on very little. While he did read the city column of his daily paper every morning, he was without substance, and his experience of affairs was limited to having failed to make a go of running a small brush factory. By the end of his Fabian days he had become in his own mind a city man with a unique knowledge of public finance.

Another of Bland's impersonations was that of a born soldier whose instinctive grasp of military matters made him an expert on questions of Imperial Defence. He dressed this part, and by dint of plastering his hair with pomade, parting it in the middle, waxing his mustache and twisting its ends, glaring out at the world through a monocle, and encasing his torso in a waisted frock coat (that may well have concealed a corset) at all times, made himself appear to be every inch the heavy military swell. There was no more behind this act than a childhood spent in the garrison town of Woolwich. His parents had owned a house a few streets from the Headquarters of the Royal Artillery Regiment and only a little farther from the famous Arsenal. That was as close to military realities as he had ever been. His most closely guarded secret—that his grandfather had been a working plumber and house painter—lay buried beneath another of his forged identities, that of "The Old Catholic," one of the few survivors of a family of north country recusants whose fanatical attachment to the religion of their forefathers had cost them their lands, their houses, and their personal treasures. The part was one of Bland's favourites, and strangely, and rather touchingly, he had done his best to legitimise this boldest of his fabrications by actually becoming a convert to Roman Catholicism in his last years, as if he had been toying with some wild hope of rising from the grave to pass in at heaven's gate under false colours.

It was Bland who assumed the leadership of the opposition when the liberal Fabians proposed to make the reform of the divorce laws one of the Society's objectives. While doing so he had told fascinated audiences that he was utterly against committing the Society to any such objective, on the grounds that to make divorces easier or cheaper to get would do irreparable damage to the quality of English family life and lead to a tragic collapse of moral standards. While Blanderies of this kind amused some Fabians, and astounded others, as revelations of what might be going on in the heads of the older members, they came as an even greater surprise to those who knew him well enough to have encountered him on convivial occasions when there were no ladies present. When he was at a stag dinner and it came to the mellowing stage at which the cigars were lit, and the decanters of port, brandy, and whiskey were being passed about, Bland would become talkative, and, if the subject of women was raised, anecdotal. He tackled the topic in the person of a psychologist who had done field work, and he would describe "purely for purposes of illustration" one curious experience after another that had come his way, thus revealing, as if in the interests of science, and quite inadvertently, that he was a tireless and extremely successful amorist.

My father detested him, but very quickly became very fond of his wife, Edith Nesbit. Bland had first met this complicated and gifted woman in 1877 when she was nineteen years old, he was twenty-two (and my father a child of ten). The Blands were married three years later, when Edith Nesbit was in the seventh month of her first pregnancy. Her child proved to be a boy. Bland's second son of record was born two years later, in 1882. But although Edith was to pay for this child's upbringing it was not hers. Bland had his mind on more important things than mere money grubbing by this time, and he was leaving it to his wife to deal with the grossly material side of life. She was in fact keeping them both, and such children as came along, by writing romantic potboilers for the new pulp magazines. While pursuing this arduous trade she met and made friends with one Alice Hoatson, a young woman who was not very happily employed in the office of *Sylvia's Home Journal.* She was drawing a miserable salary as a reader of manuscripts and doing all the work that the male fiction editor was being paid relatively well to undertake. When Edith became pregnant for a second time, at the end of 1884, she persuaded this new friend to become a part of the Bland household as a combination secretary, mother's helper, and companion. Edith gave birth to this child, another boy, in 1885, and found herself pregnant again within the year. While she was getting used to the idea, Alice Hoatson had to tell her that she, too, was carrying a child. Edith's baby was born dead early in the spring of 1856, much to her distress, and Alice Hoatson gave birth to a living daughter a little later. Bland came to Edith some weeks after Alice's delivery to tell her that it distressed him to see her grieving for the baby she had lost. He suggested that she might at once ease her pain, and help her friend Alice out of the spot she was in as an unmarried mother, by adopting the little girl and bringing her up as her own. Edith liked the idea, and so her friend's child presently became Rosamund Bland in the eyes of the law.

It took Edith all of six months to realise that her husband was Rosamund's father, and that Alice was still his mistress. She was briefly furious with herself for having been so gullible, and as angry with Bland for having deceived her, but before anything irretrievable had been said or done she calmed down and decided that she might as well live with the arrangement. She had never quite believed that she had it in her stars to be happy, and she enjoyed living interestingly, so she might as well carry on with her husband.

The Blands were still living interestingly, but rather differently, when my father came to know them fifteen years later. Edith was no longer writing for the pulps, having become an outstandingly successful writer of children's books. Her chronicles of the doings of the Bastable children sold, and sold, and sold. There was no more scraping for the odd guinea—but there was no certainty in anything either. Edith was keeping Bland in a style that he could never have aspired to on his own, having installed him in Well Hall, a delightful moated house with a lovely garden deep in the Kent countryside but with very good rail connections with town. The Blands lived there expansively and generously, and never seemed to turn a friend away. The money that flowed in from the children's books was spent as fast as it came in, and sometimes faster than that, but the continuous house party went on as if it could go on for ever. Bland himself was still bringing off his successes with women, but he was beginning to look more like a baggy and debauched Matthew Arnold than a heavy swell, and his victims were being kind to him more often than they were being swept off their feet. As for Edith, she hardly seemed to care who the latest girl was, or whether she was in trouble or not. These things seemed, one way or another, to get themselves sorted out, and there weren't too many variations to the standard script. She wasn't finding Bland and his affairs as interesting as all that anymore, and she had become more concerned with her own intense platonic friendships, and the ongoing group life. Was she going to have enough empty beds to hold all the people who would be running down from town on the late-afternoon and early-evening trains? Was there enough food in the house to feed them all? And would they all get on.

My father, as I have said, became very fond of Edith Nesbit, but he found Bland third-rate and incredible and did his best to ignore him. Bland never cared for men who treated him as a mere passenger on his wife's ark, and his distaste for my father became a positive enmity when he saw that Edith was taking up the Wellsian cause in his back yard. He was the last person to accept the idea that the Fabian Society was an institution ripe for drastic reforms and enlargement. His service to the Society, as treasurer and a member of the Executive, gave him his only real claim to be the *somebody* of his fantasies and impersonations, and it was only to be expected that he should look on my father's proposals as a menace to his happiness, and that he should make up his mind to frustrate them if he could. It was as natural that he should forget his recent quarrels with his ancient ally and former friend Pease and alert him to the necessity of doing something to stop my father in his tracks before he did "their" society irreparable harm. Alerted, Pease, already of the same mind, settled down to do his obstructive best, so that at the end of a full year the motion that my father had drafted with Maud Reeves's help was no closer to presentation to the Society's General Meeting than it had ever been.

At the beginning of 1905 Maud Reeves saw, and made my father see it too, that if he really wanted to put his mark on the Society, he would have to show that he could lead as well as intrigue. He would soon have to get up on his feet and demonstrate that he had it in him to dominate a meeting. She told him that no politician could hope to succeed who had a horror of the platform, and that he was overrating the importance of his physical deficiencies. Having a big voice and a presence wasn't everything—if he kept cool, spoke slowly, and didn't start gabbling and swallowing his words, he would be heard and listened to, she had no doubt of that. She gave him the courage to put the memory of his initial setback behind him, and to test himself by facing Fabian audiences at two open meetings soon after the new year had begun. He was billed to speak on the controversial subject of *The Faults of the Fabian* on January 12, but the Executive didn't think that self-criticism would be altogether the thing on the eve of a General Election, and asked him to substitute another topic. He was, luckily, ready with a light essay on the realities of poverty, a subject that he felt that the average Fabian knew very little about, and so this naïve attempt to throw him off balance didn't succeed. *This Misery of Boots* doesn't read very well today but its first hearers were won by its freshness and directness. Because he had done well then, an expectant audience was waiting for him on February 9, when he was able to get *The Faults of the Fabian* off his chest at last. Maud Reeves had persuaded all the younger members that she could reach to turn out, promising them something good, and inspired by the warmth of his welcome he handled himself well. He had his listeners laughing with him from the first as he parodied the melange of private references and family jokes that invariably formed part of any address from a Fabian regular. He had gone on to argue seriously that the accepted Fabian mode was symptomatic of coterie thinking, and that its very existence had to be a sign that the Society was too ingrown and clubby to be capable of carrying out its declared mission—that of preparing the ground for a radical reconstruction of the social order.

For all the funning, *The Faults of the Fabian* was a tougher, cooler, and more effective presentation of the case for the enlargement of the Society that he had failed to put across three years earlier. And this time he had put himself in business. When he finished he had the sense of the meeting with him. A majority of those in the hall saw that a real challenge had been offered to the Executive, and were glad of it.

The Fabian Old Guard, the members of the Executive who had been in the Society since the early eighties, declined to admit that my father had become any sort of a threat to them. They persisted in regarding him as a transient phenomenon, a self-advertising boom-ster who had come into their domain to see what publicity he could get for himself by ruffling a few feathers and kicking up a rumpus. Their feeling was that he had no principles and no serious intentions. Whether he succeeded or failed was all one, either way he would soon drop his game of the moment and move on. The right thing to do about him was to stick to the policy that Pease and Bland had already adopted—they should tie him up in a web of procedural obstruction and wear out his patience.

Shaw was the only member of the Executive who disagreed with this view. He told Pease and Bland that they were wrong to underestimate my father, and warned them that the challenge was a genuine one, and that it could only be turned back by defeating him in an open trial of intellectual strength. Sidney Webb, who liked to lecture but did not relish debate, was inclined to hold back in Olympian fashion while my father finished himself off, until he suddenly saw that yet another Fabian wife was in danger of going over to the interloper's side—this time his own.

Beatrice Webb's diaries for this period show how right Sidney was to be concerned. Between one entry and the next she moves from admiration to contempt, from the feeling that my father's presence in the Society is beneficial and stimulating, to an even stronger one that he is a danger to be resisted. She does not often let her writing give away the extent to which she was affected by the profound snobbery that so frequently afflicts the children of new money, and I find it revealing that her encounters with both Jane and my father were liable to bring on especially violent bouts of it. They testify, I believe, to the strength of her conscious determination not to let herself surrender to my father's influence, and to the real shrewdness shown by her husband in recognising what a hold he had already established on her imagination and her sympathy. The possession of this insight did not make Sidney Webb any the fonder of my father, and it galvanised him into action. He abruptly assumed the leadership of the Stop Wells movement, and became its most active member.

Webb began by giving my father a surprise. He euchred my father's proposal that there should be an enquiry into the effectiveness of the Executive's management of the Society by simply conceding the point. This move took the initiative out of my father's hands, and deprived him of any chance of delivering an indictment of the Executive in a speech proposing such an enquiry at the next General Meeting. It did more than that. Because the enquiry was being instituted by the Executive itself, the power to appoint the investigative body, and to define the terms of its mandate, stayed in its hands. To my father's intense vexation he found himself a *spectator ab extra* to the selection of something that was invariably referred to with ironic courtesy as "The Wells Committee." His aggravation was presently increased when he became aware that "his" committee would hold no open hearings and would not even be reporting to the membership at large. It was to present its findings to the Executive, which might then, or, again, might not, lay any recommendations for remedial action that they included before the membership as a basis for further discussion.

When my father realised how ably and how completely he had been outmanoeuvred he saw that the only course open to him, other than that of meekly accepting total defeat, was to try to find some way of side-stepping the worst consequences of the disaster. He hoped to do this by introducing a motion at the now impending General Meeting calling for a revision of the so-called Basis, the statement of Fabian goals that all members had to commit themselves to on joining the group. He accordingly sat down to draft a revised Basis that would commit the Society to a sexual as well as to an economic revolution.

Edward Pease summarised my father's draft Basis in his account of these events. It called, he said, for the Society's members to work for a reconstruction of the social order that was to involve three things: the transfer of land and capital to the state; the recognition of equal citizenship of men and women; and "the substitution of public for private authority in the education and support of the young." He goes on from there to observe with heavy irony that "what the last clause meant has never been disclosed." Its content can only have remained mysterious to those who were determined to ignore what my father was telling everyone who was willing to listen to him, that he was trying to get the Society behind his proposal for the introduction of a system of maternity and child-care benefits that would shield women in general from the chief of their economic disabilities.

My father may or may not have made a mistake in taking up this particular cause at that particular time. It was obvious that opinion in the country as a whole was not yet ready to see such a program put into place. But the essence of leadership is being innovative, and the Society was supposed to have an educational and directive function. Advocacy of such a scheme might have put the Society too far ahead of the crowd, but it has to be remembered that the English poor lived in a barbaric state in those days in which pregnancy often amounted to a sentence to prostitution. There was a great deal to be said for a program that would have kept an untold number of young mothers off the streets, and done a great deal to save a multitude of children from being killed slowly or crippled for life by malnutrition. If there was one thing that could be said with absolute certainty of unsubsidised motherhood with things as they then were, it was that it was providing the nation with an unfailing supply of badly damaged human beings. The issue was not, however, to be debated on its merits. What my father had said and done outside the Society was to prove to be his undoing within it, and in the arena of politics.

My grandmother had died at the beginning of June in 1905. She had drifted out of life after a longish period of deepening senility in which all but the memory of her stubborn and upright character had perished. The essence of the final state of her relationship with my father is conveyed by a photograph of them both taken by Jane on the lawn of Spade House sometime in the previous summer. In it my father is to be seen in the midst of an attempt to get through to the old lady, almost as if he was a medium courting a shy apparition. He obviously wants to let her know that everything is, yes, really, *all right.* That brand-new house behind them is really his, there are no process servers or bailiff's men in wait in the kitchen or round the corner. My grandmother looks wonderingly away from him, her face a mask of confusion and dismay. She clearly has in mind those terrible days at the New Inn, in which her mother had lain dying while the airy fabric of her father's shams and pretences had collapsed all round them. It could not be right that her shiftless boy, who could not stick at anything, had hired his own architect to design and build a house for his family to live in; it was not his place to do such a thing. Only gentlefolk, and men who had succeeded in respectable trades, had the right to build. Her son was flying too high, and his wife and child would be the ones who would presently have to pay for it all. When the truth came out that Bertie was a nobody, with nothing behind him, his fairweather friends would all abandon him, and Jane and her boys would be put out of doors. What my father is telling her doesn't reach her, all she can hear in his voice is the remote echo of her own father's shiftless optimism. She had never been able to to believe in his arrival, or to tell him that she admired him for doing what he had done.

And then, suddenly, she was gone. My father's interest in photography was at its height when she died, and after she had been laid out he hung over her coffin for hours trying to capture something of her with his boxy camera before she vanished from his sight forever. The faded sepia prints of the photographs he took then are now to be seen in the library of the strangely remote university in the heart of middle America where the bulk of his private papers eventually came to rest. They show that death had lifted the softness and weakness of old age from her face, and had restored to it that look of granite that had made her such a terrible adversary when my father had been fighting her for what had seemed to be his right to live. He had hardly been able to bear what he had seen in that implacable visage, and in the developed photographs, and he was unable to forget the sight. He was to recur to that image in novel after novel over the next several years. And her death had not closed the book on the worst of the relationship—it had begun a new chapter in its history. It gave him access to that appalling fabricated diary, with its revelation of the devoutly cherished hatred that had been the hard core of her marriage, and of the deadly wager to which he owed his existence. As he read it he looked back across forty years to that terrible first moment after his delivery from her enclosing flesh in which she had been made to face the fact that she had resumed her physical connection with her detested husband to no purpose, and that the slippery, bloodied *thing* that the midwife was washing as if it were precious was another boy. She had not been given the girl that she had prayed and prayed for, to make up for the loss of her beloved Possy.

My father's reaction to the tremendous walloping that he had been given by his reading and re-reading of that atrocious document was typical of the kind of man, and the kind of writer, that he was. He tried to find relief from his discomfort in fantasy, imagining a state of things in which nobody could find themselves trapped in such a nightmare as that ghastly marriage. He was keeping up with the scientific news of the day in which there was much talk of comets. Encke's comet was due to be back in 1906, Halley's in 1910. The technique of spectrographic analysis had just come in, and lively discussions were in progress about the meaning of the information that it was producing about the chemistry of the traditionally fiery tails of such bodies. It was a new discovery that quantities of the gases that formed the greater part of these plumes could be stripped from them unburned when they passed through the gravitational fields of the larger heavenly bodies. Such detached clouds had been seen to disperse in the void after lesser comets had been exposed to the pull of the earth's mass. Encke's comet was a short period member of the family that took two and a half hours less time to complete each of its three-and-a-half-year circuits of the sun. Calculations suggested that this meant that every circuit was bringing it a little closer to the earth—if that were so, then it could be that one day in the foreseeable future the comet might pass close enough to our planet to be stripped of the greater part of the gas cloud that it was dragging along behind it. The gas would then become part of the earth's atmosphere. Now suppose, just suppose, that one of the chemical components of that gas cloud happened to be a mind-bending substance. Suppose it were to nullify all the promptings of instinct and emotion that gave rise to irrational behaviour. Suppose that after the comet had passed, reason itself was in the air we breathed. Its passage could mean the beginning of a new era. My father had his book, *In the Days of the Comet.*

There is a large element of innocence in this invention, and if the conclusion to the story that my father built upon it shares that quality, there is no hint of it in the tale it tells of the bad old times before the chemically induced change in human nature took place. That part of the story makes the most of my father's feelings about the moral ugliness that degrades and corrupts mean lives meanly lived in the push-and-shove societies in which everything has a price and women are treated as an especially desirable form of property. While it is concerned with the nineteenth-century social picture, it has an almost Swiftian mordancy. But the general line of the novel was self-defeating. Its happy ending, not the burden of its argument, was what was found unendurable. Its original readers could not bear to be told that when its four leading characters had been cured of their jealousy and possessiveness by the inhalation of comet gases, they should be able to put their rancorous past behind them and settle down in a friendly hugger-mugger in which each man was involved with both women, and each woman with both men. Given the prevailing climate of opinion, my father could not say this in so many words, but he managed to make himself plain enough. His narrator, who had been within a hair's-breadth of doing murder in a jealous rage when the great change came, describes its effect guardedly but without ambiguity: "We four from that time were very close, you understand. We were friends, helpers, personal lovers in a world of lovers."

My father had done with *In the Days of the Comet* long before he sat down to rough out his draft for the revised version of the Fabian Basis. Macmillan had accepted it, and had given it a place on their autumn list. He consequently made no connection between the happy ending of the completed novel and his proposed goals for the revitalised Fabian Society. The revised Basis was a thing apart for him. He discussed it with his friends and allies in the Society, who liked it pretty well, and in the middle of February he put it into the hands of Edward Pease for submission to the Executive. He enclosed a brief personal note for Pease along with his draft, telling the secretary that he would be leaving for the United States at the end of March, and that he would be glad to know before he left if he was to be allowed to bring the matter up at the next General Meeting. Pease let my father have a reply to this note after a short interval, informing him that the Executive had agreed to give it a place on the agenda, and that on their instructions the draft itself was to be circulated to all members in the forthcoming issue of *The Fabian Newsletter.* He left for America with a pleasant sense that he had everything in hand.

On his return to England my father found a further letter from Pease waiting for him. This was to tell him that since his draft for the revised Basis was put to the membership he had been snowed under with questions about the precise meaning of its second and third clauses. How far was recognition of the equality of the sexes to go— beyond the issue of the franchise? Or not? Were all children to be state-supported, or only those born in wedlock? If all children were to benefit from his proposed maternity allowances, how was he going to answer to the charge that he was proposing to subsidise immorality? The secretary was holding a mid-October speaking date open for his use in the hope that he would like to avail himself of an opportunity to deal with the host of such queries that had been raised. Would my father let him know as soon as might be if he was minded to face his questioners at that time?

My father was happy to tell Pease that he most certainly would like to defend his proposal before such a meeting. It apparently never entered his head that by nibbling on Pease's attractive bait, he was undertaking to discuss these matters at an open meeting just about a month after the date set for the publication of *In the Days of the Comet.* If that novel's obscurely phrased but absolutely unmistakable endorsement of Free Love were to stir up any sort of a row, it would be just about at its peak when the time for him to keep that mid-October speaking engagement came round.

Nothing was to alert my father to the possibilities for trouble inherent in his arrangement with Pease in the course of the next few months. This was because summer was a season in which nothing much could happen in the Fabian world of those days. The Fabians left town in a body as strawberry time came in, and they were in and out of each other's country cottages and farmhouses, rented or owned, until the second crop of raspberries had come and gone, and the red admirals were in clouds among the rain-battered Michaelmas Daisies and the first windfall apples. The Fabian summer of 1906 had rolled along as peacefully as any other until well into September without giving any of the Old Guard cause for alarm, but then Shaw, back from a refreshing break in Ireland, threw them into something close to a panic. Following the dictates of his essentially treacherous nature, and wishing to cover every eventuality by appearing to be everybody's friend, he had checked in with his contacts among the younger Fabians, and had soon learned that something had, after all, been going on through the holiday season. Maud Reeves and Jane, assisted by a group of volunteers, had been at work in all of June, July, and August, building up my father's voting strength among the rank and file of the membership. They had succeeded beyond their expectations, having come within a measurable distance of creating a block large enough to swing a floor vote at a General Meeting. As a little spice to this bad news for the Old Guard, Shaw was able to add to it the news that the split in Hubert Bland's extended family had widened —his daughter Rosamund's name could now be listed along with that of his wife on the roster of my father's adherents. Maud Reeves was finding her most useful as an aide.

It abruptly became clear to the Webbs and their allies that far from irrationally "breaking out," as Beatrice Webb had scornfully put it a little while before, my father was most effectively breaking in, and that their twenty-year control of their hobbyhorse might be drawing to an end. But late in September, when their gathering dismay had put them in a mood to clutch at straws a loaded weapon, with instructions for its use, was unexpectedly put into their hands. *In the Days of the Comet* had been published at last, and a review of it had appeared in *The Times Literary Supplement.* "Socialistic men's wives," the *Times*'s reviewer wrote, "are, no less than their goods, to be held in common. Free Love, according to Mr Wells, is to be the essence of the new Social Contract. One wonders how far he will insist upon this in the tracts which he is understood to desire to write for the Fabian Society, and what the other Fabians will say."

As soon as Shaw had read his presentation copy of the novel he leapt to the conclusion that my father had dealt his opponents a hand with four aces in it. He saw no reason to go on hedging his bets, and celebrated his deliverance from fear by writing my father a letter advising him to drop his campaign to secure control of the Executive before Bland and Webb combined forces to drive him out of the Society altogether. My father hadn't had time to reply to this communication before Shaw wrote to him again—having by then read the review in the *Literary Supplement.* The tone of this second letter was openly gloating. In it Shaw let my father know just how the Free Love issue was going to be exploited in the coming power struggle by making the ironic suggestion that the Shaws and Wellses should join together in a foursome of the kind proposed at the end of the novel. He went on from there to give a rough outline of the minimum terms on which the Old Guard might agree to bring an end to the row without forcing my father to undergo a public humiliation.

Shaw had foreseen, correctly, that the London dailies and the provincial papers would be quick to take up the lead offered to them by the *Literary Supplement*'s attack, but he had calculated quite wrongly when he had reached the conclusion that my father would not be man enough to stand his ground in the face of a storm of public abuse combined with a well-run campaign of private harassment. He had felt sure that my father would cave in sooner rather than later if the matter was to be pressed, and he had looked forward to having some fun while he was pressing it.

My father was, however, committed to that mid-October discussion of the two cryptic clauses in his draft for a new Basis, and he had no intention of being jockeyed into funking it. The pressure that was being put on him behind the scenes angered him, and he came before the Fabians on the night with his dander up. Nothing would stop him from making his position clear. When he came out onto the platform with his notes for an address that had been unpromisingly advertised as *Socialism and the Middle Classes,* he found himself in front of the largest audience that had up to then come together to listen to a Fabian speaker, and he hadn't been facing it for more than a split second before he was made pleasantly aware that the gathering was overwhelmingly friendly. Buoyed up by the warmth of the welcome he had been given, he spoke with assurance, and shook the Old Guard and their supporters by making a lucid and convincing case for the detoxification of marriage and the liberation of women as socialist goals of prime importance.

To the dismay of his adversaries his listeners seemed to like him even more when he had done than they had when he started. They had swallowed marriage as a civil contract terminable by mutual consent eagerly; they had gobbled up full political equality between the sexes; and they hadn't boggled at a hint of sexual freedom for women. But worst of all, they had been positively enthusiastic for the idea that the time had come for a reorganisation of the tiny and exclusive society as the cadre of a national political party open to anyone who might wish to take part in its work. The sole criterion for entry was to be a willingness to subscribe to the Basis. It did not make things any better that my father had been able to serve up his program without faltering or hesitation—he had come on like a winner.

When the cheering was over, and the horrors of the occasion were being recollected in tranquillity, the various members of the Old Guard had settled down to comfort each other. The thing had been an illusion—the disproportionate amount of noise made by my father's young followers had made it almost impossible to tell how the thoughtful element in the audience had taken his address. Hubert Bland was quite certain that a great deal of silent disapproval had been drowned out, and after reflecting on the matter for forty-eight hours, he wrote to Pease to tell him so: "I am afraid that Mr Wells' lecture did no sort of good to the propaganda. Judging by what I heard afterwards a lot of people were quite upset." But some advantage might come from my father's risk taking: "I am inclined to think one might do worse than force this 'sex and child' question to an issue amongst us Fabians. We had to do that with the Anarchists and we may have to do that with the Free Lovers." Beatrice Webb evidently sensed that the atmosphere in the Society was turning nasty. Four days after Bland had written to Pease in this strain she made this suggestive entry in her diary:

> H. G. Wells is, I believe, merely gambling with the idea of Free Love—throwing it out to see what sort of reception it gets —without responsibility for its effect on the character of his hearers. It is this recklessness that makes Sidney dislike him. I think it is important not to dislike him: he is going through an ugly time, and we must stand by him for his own sake and for the good of the cause of collectivism.

I take it that Beatrice Webb's phrase "an ugly time" refers to the continuing fuss about *In the Days of the Comet,* which she had not, at that time, read. She was finally to do so at the end of October—with what her husband and her friends among the Old Guard can only have seen as appalling results. She had never until then had any use at all for the feminist movement, and had even spoken out against the agitation for votes for women in scathing terms. *In the Days of the Comet* turned her right round. As soon as she had finished the novel she dashed off a note to my father to tell him so, and within the hour she had written a more formal letter to Dame Millicent Fawcett, the leader of the largist group of Feminists who couldn't go along with Mrs. Pankhurst about the use of violence, to let her know the good news, that she had changed her mind about the franchise. It would have been hard enough for the male insiders among the Old Guard to take this *volte face* calmly even if it had remained a private matter—but Beatrice Webb had given Mrs. Fawcett leave to send her letter on to *The Times* for publication. So, on November 5, there it was, in the centre-page correspondence column of that then uniquely important newspaper for everybody in England who was anybody to see.

The three active leaders of the Stop Wells group on the Executive, Pease, Bland, and Sidney Webb, now had to face the fact that they were in trouble. If the behaviour of their wives was to be taken as an indication, a real swing in my father's direction had to be taking place among the women in the Society. Something had to be done, quickly, to undermine his credibility as a proponent of the feminist cause. Bland was sure that he knew just what would do the trick. A little scandal-mongering would show the women that Wells's so-called

Feminism wasn't in the least disinterested, and that what he was peddling was a lecher's charter. Women were down-to-earth creatures, and you could always get them to see reason by giving them a case in point. If he was to tell a few of the Fabian women what he knew about Wells, it would be all through the Society in no time. He had something pretty ripe to tell them about Wells and the wife of a chap called Bowkett, a man who'd been the little cad's best friend since their schooldays; and he could make something pretty good out of the story of the lengths he'd been forced to go to, to keep his own daughter out of that rotter's clutches. It wasn't going to be a nice business. But the world wasn't a nice place, and they had to take the long view of what was at stake—the social utility of the Society. When all was said and done, it was the national interest that they would be protecting.

At this juncture my father showed his weakness as a politician by letting an idea for a new book seize his imagination. It was to be a big thing, one of those state-of-the-nation novels that Dickens used to have such fun with—it was to turn on the career of a wonderful character, the embodiment of innocent rapacity, who was to be a blend of Whitaker Wright, a large-scale operator who had lately gone bust; Horatio Bottomley, a charming rogue still on the way up who had every gift except the ability to tell right from wrong; and his utterly delightful and hopelessly bent second cousin by marriage, the Alfred Williams who had landed him in the soup down in Somerset back in his days as a pupil-teacher. With the aid of this hybrid he was going to have a tremendous lark caricaturing the business world of boom today and bust tomorrow that was taking shape. He felt sure that he could rough out a negotiable outline inside three weeks if he could just get down to it, that would be time enough if he were to go off somewhere stimulating where he would be free from interruptions —say, Venice. So off he went, and there he was beside the Adriatic, completely out of touch with things English, for the greater part of November. He returned to England on December 1, and very soon learned what Bland had been up to while he had been giving his mind to the delights of Venice and the draft outline for what would presently become *Tono-Bungay*. The General Meeting of the Society, at which he was to make his formal challenge to the Executive was slated to take place on December 7.

The situation that Bland had created for my father was not made any easier for him to handle by the fact that he had indeed enjoyed both the women named. Nell de Boer, Sidney Bowkett's wife, had found my father useful to her in a way that many unhappily married people, before and since, have found an only marginally important but sympathetic and agreeable friend helpful. She had wanted to put a man she liked between her husband and herself to make the coming break a less earth-shaking wrench. My father had served her purposes, and she had soon passed on to a more serious attachment. Rosamund Bland, on the other hand, had been, quite simply, anxious to be grown-up. Her anxiety to make a beginning was something that the undercurrent of erotic tension that was never very far below the surface of things at Well Hall might have been designed to foster, and there had been an element of inevitability about the affair. In it both parties had been able to give the other exactly what was wanted—the physical experience as such, for its own sweet self and friendship's sake. My father's difficulty with Bland's gossip was that the facts alleged could not be denied. The only thing that he could possibly say in his defence, that no seduction had been required, and no wrong done, in either case, was in the prevailing climate of feeling in such matters unsayable. Had my father stood his ground, and said plainly that both women had been free agents who were as ready to lie with him as he had been to pleasure them, he would have been demonstrating that he was willing to destroy any woman's reputation to get himself out of a tight corner. This would have justified the worst, and most insistently pressed, of Bland's charges, that he was a cad who was not fit to associate with decent people.

The Class system, and its conventions, are no longer what they were, and *cad* is now an evasively defined word that has lost much of its sting. A cad used to be a jumped-up member of the lower classes who was guilty of behaving as if he didn't know that his lowly origin made him unfit to have sexual relationships with well-bred women. The line Bland had taken while spreading his scandals about my father had been that what made "the little bounder's" behaviour so outrageous was that he had been messing about with the wives and daughters of "people like us." It was stuff that could, in itself, be counted upon to infuriate a man who had come up the social ladder very fast, and who was inwardly haunted by the sense that his appearance and physique told the story of his early poverty. But it was almost unendurable to be expected to take it from such a man as Bland— Bland of the confessional anecdotes, of the myriad adventures with shop girls and pretty little milliners—Bland, the plumber's grandson!

In his anger my father became infected with the paranoia that often afflicts the persecuted. He could not believe that Bland had been acting on his own. He was sure that he must have had the backing of Webb and the inner circle of the Old Guard. He had a point, but he underestimated Sidney Webb's natural caution. Once Webb had realised what Bland had intended to do in the way of character assassination, he had gone to considerable lengths to insulate himself from any knowledge of what was actually being done. When my father bearded him in a fury, he was unable to turn his enemy's carefully prepared position. Webb looked him in the eye and said, with some hauteur, that he very much regretted that anything might have been said or implied by any member of the Executive to upset my father, but that he had no idea what it could have been. Would my father care to tell him what it was that had struck him as so offensive? No doubt there would be some quite simple explanation for whatever it was that had been the cause of the misunderstanding. It was always a mistake, in his experience, to put any faith in third- and fourth-hand reports of things that people had said.

My father saw that he was to be led up the garden path. He declined to be side-tracked. He had come to Webb, he said, to give his slimy friends on the Executive fair warning. If they wanted a dirty fight they could have one. It would give him real pleasure to break up their game of "superior persons." He would love to show them up for the hypocrites that they were. If Bland, or any other member of the group, was to make further use of a knowledge of his private life against him, there would be the devil to pay. He knew as much about Bland and his way of life as Webb himself did, and if any more dirt was to be thrown at him from that quarter, he would make sure that every member of the Society learned of it too. Webb falteringly repeated his claim not to know what it could be that my father was complaining about, and was told brusquely that what he was saying was unbelievable. The interview came to an abrupt end.

My father came away from this encounter in even more of a rage than he had been at its outset. He was still furious when he went down to Essex Hall to address the General Meeting of the Society on December 7. But he was no longer angry with Webb and the Old Guard, he was disgusted with himself. How could he have been fool enough to go off to Venice like that? And how could he have made the mistake of blundering into that confrontation with Webb? He had made a mess of everything. Because he was thinking ill of himself he assumed the hostility of the house when he came before the assembled Fabians. He forgot everything that Maud Reeves had taught him about public speaking. He clung in desperation to the speaker's desk, talked down into his notes, swallowed his words, and forced his voice so that it became thin and piping. On top of all that he lost his thread from time to time, to the confusion of his supporters and to the delight of his opponents. A total disaster was averted by a mere chance: he had come on late in the proceedings, and he had rambled on for so long that when he was done there was no time left for the formal business of putting a motion to the house and voting upon it. The meeting stood adjourned.

Shaw was exceedingly busy in the week that followed, putting his best efforts into making sure that when the meeting reconvened, the issue would not be the proposed changes to the Basis, but one of confidence in the Executive. He accordingly sent every Fabian a printed flyer announcing that the members of that body would resign *en masse* if things went my father's way when the vote was finally taken. He was sure that this would give the incumbents the edge. It was his experience that old friends always came out ahead of a leap into the dark.

But Shaw was never the man to put all his eggs in one basket. He also set about the task of undermining my father's position as the hope of the Feminists. He sensed a slackening in the intensity of Maud Reeves' support for him, and thinking that, unlikely though it seemed, Bland's nasty stories might have got through to her, he decided to work on her. He went to her to tell her that her cause might have other, more reliable, friends than my father. He alleged that Beatrice Webb's change of front on the issue of the suffrage had brought several of the men on the Executive round—he could promise her that if it were to fall to the incumbents to carry out the revision of the Basis in the coming year a commitment to the Franchise would certainly be part of their program. She should consider that a probable conse-quence of a victory for my father would be the break up of the Society. As things were, the Fabian endorsement of any given social or eco-nomic proposal counted for something. The Feminists might be doing their cause a mischief over the long haul if they were to drive the existing Executive from office.

Maud Reeves was in a very difficult position. She had no desire to pull out of my father's campaign. She was only doing so for her husband's sake because he couldn't bear having it said all over town that his wife was working hand-in-glove with an advocate of Free Love and a sexual revolution. He lived in dread of hearing that word of what she was about had got back to New Zealand and was being used against him in the Dominion's Tory press. Maud Reeves was torn between her concern for her husband's peace of mind and her liking for my father and his ideas. She didn't, in particular, want to seem to be responding to my father's first serious check since the start of their association by stabbing him in the back. What Shaw was telling her seemed to suggest that the Executive might be moving in my father's direction, and she decided to have a try at a statesmanlike evasion. She told Shaw that if she would be taking any line at all at the forthcoming meeting, she would be coming out for the wisdom of a compromise. This was a long way from the outright defection that Shaw had been angling for, but it was enough to build on. His intuition had been right —Maud Reeves was, for whatever reason, backing off. He settled down to devise a scenario for the actual debate, in which he would be playing the leading role, and my father would be without the active support of his most effective ally.

My father was not greatly upset by Maud Reeves's retirement from the thick of the fray. He understood her position, and felt able to live with it. He may also have been unable to appreciate how valuable her services as floor manager had been to him during the run-up to his December 7 fiasco. However that was, the loss of her active support gave him no nightmares, and he had, in fact, recovered a good deal of his self-confidence before the critical December 14 meeting took place. When he came into Essex Hall that night he felt that he had excellent chances of winning back all the lost ground, and was quite sure that his case for shaking up the Society and revising the Basis was stronger than anything that the supporters of the old order could possibly put forward. He was consequently very much surprised when an opening statement from Maud Reeves, containing little that he hadn't expected, was immediately followed by a bravura performance from Shaw at his most clownish in which virtually nothing was said about the real issues, and everything was reduced to triviality by being presented in terms of a clash of personalities—between the serious, hard-working, consistent, and conscientious members of the Executive and the puckish, volatile, and whimsical intruder into their domain. Shaw committed the debate to that topic, and kept it there with consummate artistry, until the point was reached that he could put it to the gathering that: "There is nothing for it now but the annihilation

COURTESY OF MARTIN J. WELLS

Moura Budberg with Gorky and my father in Petrograd
in September 1920.

BUST BY BARBARA PHILLIPS PERLE. COLLECTION OF COMMUNITY CHURCH OF NEW YORK

This bronze portrait bust by Barbara Phillips Perle
captures Margaret Sanger's vitality and charm as no
photograph ever did.

UNIVERSITY OF ILLINOIS AT URBANA-CHAMPAIGN

Jane Wells in her last years, in which my father's life became divided between England and France.

My father with Odette Keun at Lou Pidou, the farmhouse outside Grasse that he built for her in 1927, the year of Jane's death.

AUTHOR'S PRIVATE COLLECTION

UNIVERSITY OF ILLINOIS AT URBANA-CHAMPAIGN

My father at the peak of his career as a
publicist; he is the H.G. Wells of the Stalin and Roosevelt
interviews of 1934.

COURTESY OF MARTIN J. WELLS

The cover of the *New Statesman* pamphlet in which the
text of his interview with Stalin was reprinted.

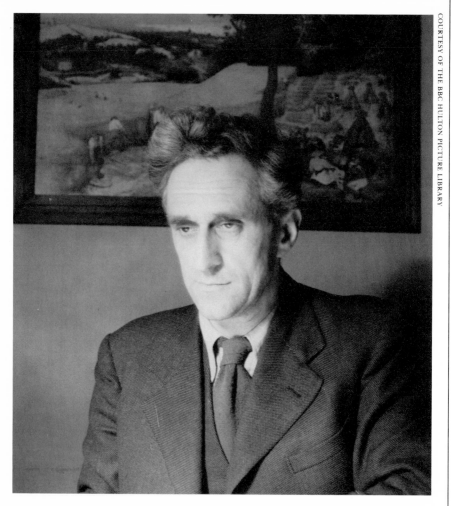

COURTESY OF THE BBC HULTON PICTURE LIBRARY

Kingsley Martin, the editor of the *New Statesman*,
who turned my father's greatest journalistic coup into
a clown show.

PICTORIAL PARADE

The diminished and defeated Gorky my father
encountered in Russia in 1934. His old friend's condition
had as much to do with Wells's final rejection of the
Soviet path as anything Stalin said to him.

COURTESY OF MARTIN J. WELLS

My father has an agreeable meeting in Australia in 1939.
He is chowdling a duck-billed platypus. This was the
year in which he had a hard knock from pneumonia and
began to age.

of the present Executive or the unconditional surrender of Mr. Wells." The vote was taken after that, and with a good half of those present thinking that they were choosing between old friends and a new broom, and forgetting all about equality under the laws, maternity benefits, and the rest of my father's package, the incumbents won handily.

When the dust began to settle, my father was not alone in thinking that Shaw had been more than devious on this occasion. Graham Wallas, who had been present, wrote to say how much he had "loathed the mixture of gerrymandering, bluffing, browbeating, quibbling, baiting and playing to the gallery" that had carried the day, and a member of the Executive resigned out of hand in protest against the abuse of orderly procedures that had been involved. Even Beatrice Webb characterised Shaw's operation as "an altogether horrid business" but she went on, with typical obtuseness, to observe that the odd thing about it all was that if my father had been content to push for his own policy without attacking the Old Guard, he would have succeeded in getting his own way.

My father had not, in fact, been as decisively checked as he for the moment supposed, and as accounts of the episode written for the record by partisans of the Webbs and the Old Guard are apt to suggest. His friends and counsellors, Sydney Olivier and the indefatigable young giant Leslie Haden-Guest, were soon telling him that the last had not been heard of his revised Basis. His suggestions for what the Society's goals should be were to be discussed at a series of meetings that had been scheduled to take place in the course of the first three months of the new year. There was no way in which the Executive could either call them off or change their annouced agendas. Since he still commanded the loyalties of a great many of the Fabian women—who made up approximately a quarter of the membership—and those of at least a third of the Fabian men, it seemed plain to these two that they had fighting chances of getting some of my father's planks accepted without too much watering down. Olivier, who was at his best as a committee man and a negotiator, and Haden-Guest, who loved a fight, looked forward to the prospect. My father did not. He was a writer, and he had become used to converting his imaginings into realities by dint of sitting down at his desk and organising them on paper—fighting them through committees and into the report of a hostile secretary just wasn't his game. He showed signs of backing out, and Haden-Guest became rather short with him. He

buckled down, even though it meant taking his mind off *Tono-Bungay.*
After all, it would be a job well done if they were to succeed in
transforming the tiny private talking shop into a real political force.

Both sides came away from the first meeting of the series, that of
January 11, 1906, well pleased. What happened on that occasion was
that the Executive paid off, to the precise extent that the majority of
its members had a mind to, on the assurance that Shaw had given to
the Feminists through Maud Reeves. The meeting had adjourned
after a vote had been taken on a carefully worded motion that committed the Society to the principle that women should have the franchise,
but not to the initiation of any steps in the direction of giving it to
them. Both parties were jubilant as the meeting broke up, the Old
Guard telling themselves that their opponents had swallowed it, and
the Wellsians that they'd actually got what they wanted. In the cold
light of the morning after, the Wellsians saw that they had been
fobbed off, and that the Old Guard did not mean to let them have
anything that could be kept from them by finagling or fraud. They
were consequently a great deal more watchful when they came to the
second of these meetings a week later.

This had been set up as another blocking play. The motion under
consideration called for the abolition of the rule in the Society's
constitution limiting the membership to seven hundred persons. The
Old Guard had put this forward in the hope that my father would
accept it as their commitment to his proposals for the enlargement of
the Society preparatory to its transformation into a parliamentary
party. They made this gesture with every confidence in their belief
that there would be no inrush of new members if nothing were to be
done to launch a recruiting campaign, or to widen the scope of the
Society's activities. It was to be a second meaningless gesture. Sydney
Olivier did not agree, and he drew my father's attention to possibilities inherent in the motion. It would offer the Wellsians an opportunity to change the balance of power within the Society. They could
recruit a following of their own in the outside world, and bring it into
the society to beef up their support. If they were to make themselves
sufficiently active in such places as Universities and Polytechnics, and
wherever constituencies of young and youngish progressives were to
be found, they could expect to turn their minority vote at the General
Meetings into a majority in from one to three years. When they had
done that, they would be able to elect their own Executive and proceed with the transformation of the Society in line with my father's

ideas. There could be no harm in giving the manoeuvre a try. The Wellsian insiders had accordingly shown up at the January 18 meeting with simulated calm but considerable inner excitement. They had been delighted when the Executive's motion had gone through as a matter of routine. Edward Pease learned of Olivier's calculation in the course of the third meeting in the series, at which the question of Fabian participation in a serious effort to form a national parliamentary party of the left, to oppose the Liberal and Conservative parties in the Socialist interest, had been raised only to be dismissed without formality of a vote. Pease had not been disturbed. He knew, he was absolutely convinced of it, that no matter how far my father's supporters went in searching for them, they simply weren't going to find any hitherto undiscovered coverts with hundreds of potential Fabians lurking in them. He had no doubt but that Olivier's plan would come to nothing.

The contending groups were thus able to come to the Society's General Meeting on February 22 in a relaxed and even genial frame of mind. Providing for the revision of the Basis was the purported business of the evening, but what the Old Guard were preparing for was my father's final extinction as a menace to their peace and quiet. After some discussion of the details of its mandate, a four-man committee, consisting of George Bernard Shaw, Sidney Webb, a certain Sidney Ball, of Oxford, and my father, was entrusted with the task.

The strategic concept behind the institution of this quadrumvirate was obvious; there could be no way in which my father could get anything out of that committee that Shaw and Webb didn't like. Having set it up, the meeting proceeded to the next order of business, the election of a new Executive. Twelve of the twenty-one seats went to insiders of the Old Guard, and the remainder to members of the Society at large, about eight of whom were committed Wellsians. The Webbs and their faction did not look beyond the obvious fact of their complete success, but my father and his closer associates considered the totals of the votes cast for winners and losers, and found the margins between victory and defeat reassuringly narrow in most cases. They saw that they would not have to bring in nearly as many new members of the right sort as they had thought in order to turn the existing majority into a minority. Their chances for success in the long term looked good.

My father now made a partial withdrawal from the Society's affairs, giving out that he was rundown, and that he was forced by financial necessity to put what energy he had into writing his new novel. He was in reality leaving his supporters on the Executive to mind the Fabian store for him while he went out into the highways and byways in the hope of confounding Pease by finding those recruits to the progressive cause. His efforts paid off. The figures show that whereas there had been sixty-seven applications for membership in 1904, and one hundred and sixty in 1905, there were four hundred and fifty-five in 1906, and eight hundred and seventeen in 1907. His campaigning, for that is what it essentially was, took him constantly into the company of the young and the enthusiastic, and gave him the exhilarating sensations that come to a surfer who has found his wave. He particularily enjoyed his contacts with the Cambridge Fabians.

The history of this Fabian group began in King's with the foundation of a very private society called "I Carbonari" that had only two members at the start of 1906. These founders were Rupert Brooke, the almost excessively pretty poet, and Hugh Dalton, a young man with a monumental presence and an unusually resonant and solemn speaking voice who was already on the upward path, from one poker-faced solemnity to the next, that was to make him a figure in the first Labour Cabinet to take office. These two freshmen at King's were presently taken over by a third-year man at Trinity, Ben Keeling, who mocked them for their romantic devotion to the revolutionary spirit of 1848 and for their enthusiasm for the poetry of Swinburne, Henley, and Belloc, and made them converts to his own cult for my father's version of Fabian Socialism. It was because he had accepted my father's thesis that female suffrage had to be an integral part of any truly socialist program that he insisted upon bringing in students from the women's colleges, Girton and Newnham, when he got his friends to agree to the transformation of the tiny I Carbonari into the Cambridge University Fabian Society in 1907. When my father went to give a lift to the new organisation's first membership drive he consequently found himself among friends. Maud Reeves's daughter Amber was the society's treasurer, and Sydney Olivier's daughters Margery and Brynhild were members. He got on famously with Brooke and Ben Keeling, and enjoyed teasing the labrador-like Dalton. Cambridge became an agreeable part of a new life for him. On a typical visit, in mid-February 1908, Geoffrey Keynes, Maynard's younger brother, asked him to give a talk on socialism to a private group that met in his rooms in Pembroke, and a few nights later he was the opening speaker in a debate on The Future of the Family that took place in Rupert Brooke's rooms in King's. The people who were present on that occasion included Goldsworthy Lowes Dickinson of *The Greek Way of Life,* and a certain Arthur Schloss, who would in due course become the Arthur Waley of the superb translations of Chinese and Japanese classics. Ben Keeling was his host later that year, at a May Week dinner for twenty in his rooms under the leads at the top of one of the turrets overlooking Trinity Great Court. Olivier, now Sir Sydney, and home for a short leave from Jamaica, where he had recently begun to serve a term as Governor, was the centre of attraction on this occasion, and my father, who had come in late, after the chairs had run out, had to eat his meal from a plate on his knees as he roosted in a window seat. He came back into the picture at coffee time, after Olivier had made a short speech and the gathering had broken up to reassemble in Francis Cornford's rooms. There my father was good-naturedly set upon for having endorsed a forbidden candidate in a recent by-election. Although a resolution calling for the expulsion of any member who was found to have worked against a socialist candidate in a parliamentary election had been passed at a Fabian Society meeting not long before, my father had shamelessly come out for Winston Churchill, who was in a three-cornered fight with a Tory blockhead called William Joynson-Hicks, and Dan Irving, a decent but colourless socialist nonentity. Of Dan Irving he had known nothing good or bad but that he was sure not to win. Of Churchill he knew that he was open-minded and educable, and that he had lately bolted the Tory Party to join the Liberals because he supported their relatively progressive social programs. He was thought to have a chance of scraping home if he could make sure of every loose vote that was going. Joynson-Hicks, on the other hand, was a Tory diehard of the old school who had been going for him, personally, as a writer of indecent novels and an advocate of Free Love, for nearly two years. What could he do but sin against the letter of the resolution in such a situation? Brooke enjoyed my father's performance in his own defence. "He argued," he wrote to tell his mother, "in his thin little voice for a long time, in a very delightful manner."

The Cambridge of that scene was the educational institution of my father's youthful dreams, it was bliss to him to have even this marginal connection with it—and it had added to his buoyancy when he got back to London after that May Week visit to learn that Macmillan was ready to give him his price for the English rights to the completed

Tono-Bungay. He was to have an advance of fifteen hundred pounds and royalties, and with the other three thousand that he had coming to him from *The War in the Air,* a book he had thrown off in his spare time since the beginning of the year, he could feel that he hadn't a thing in the world to worry about. He didn't, but Jane did. She was beginning to know him. She had spotted that he was developing a habit of replenishing his fund of of experience and fresh ideas when he had emptied himself into a novel by embarking on an affair with a new woman. Jane knew that *Tono-Bungay* had become a very big book in the writing, and that it had taken a lot out of him. She knew, too, exactly what Cambridge meant to him. He was forty-two, an age at which a great many men whose lives haven't given them just what they would have liked begin to think how nice it would be if they could, somehow or other, go back to start all over again, this time with hindsight. Since there was no way of doing that, there was the temptation of the next best thing, a new departure with someone very young. Amber Reeves was youth itself. She was Cambridge, and Cambridge was all that he had been denied in his youth. Like an experienced sailor, Jane read the signs and prepared herself for a spell of heavy weather.

Though there was a certain inevitability in the outcome, my father remained quite blind to the risks that he was running. His mind was full of other things. All through March and April of that year he had been devoting a large part of his time and energy to a prolonged teasing of Webb and Shaw. Its pretext had been a simulated effort to get that committee charged with the revision of the Basis together to at least go through the motions of getting on with the job. It had never met, and Pease had long since let him know, with a glint of pleasure in his eye, how very unlikely it was that it ever would meet. My father took his revenge by playing the part of dupe up to the hilt. He showered Webb and Shaw with suggestions for the best ways of proceeding, and with reminders that they really owed it to the membership to do the work quickly and well; it was, he said, the general good that they should be thinking of.

By the time that my father had nettled Shaw into giving him a stately rebuke for not treating Webb as one of his betters he had begun to tire of this pastime. The English political scene was changing. Ramsay MacDonald had done wonders, and there were Labour Party members sitting in the House of Commons as portents of things to come. To waken the Old Guard Fabians to what this could mean to the

Society, he took the provocative step of dropping an apparently inno-cent enquiry onto the desk of his old enemy Pease. What had hap-pened, he asked the secretary, to the ten thousand pounds left to the Fabians fourteen years earlier to finance their propaganda?

My father knew exactly what he was about when he blew on the coals of this old Fabian scandal, having had the story of how the legacy had been disposed of from Ramsay MacDonald on the one hand, and from Graham Wallas and Sydney Olivier on the other. Olivier had been able to tell him how the whole thing had begun. He had been a guest, along with George Bernard Shaw, of the Webbs in the farm-house near Godalming that they had rented for the summer holidays of 1894. All four had been together at teatime one day when a letter from the lawyer of a certain Henry Hutchinson, deceased, came in by the afternoon post. Addressed to Webb, it told him of the Society's windfall: the money was to be held by a trust, to be administered by a board, of which he was to be chairman, and it was to be used to finance the "propaganda and other purposes of the Society." Webb read the letter aloud, and his wife and his two guests rejoiced over its contents with him.

Shaw and Olivier were given a surprise at breakfast the following morning when the Webbs told them that they had decided on the best use for the money. London had no equivalent to the wonderful Pari-sian Ecole Libre des Sciences Politiques; they would capitalise a simi-lar institution with the bequest. They had even hit on the perfect name for their institution. It would be called The London School of Eco-nomics and Political Science.

An astonished Shaw pointed out that they couldn't even begin to think of making decisions until they had a board of trustees to consult, and Olivier followed this up by saying that he knew of no Fabian document declaring that the creation of educational institutions was among the Society's purposes. It seemed to both men that the Webbs were thinking of the legacy as a personal gift that they would be able to use in any way they fancied, and that under that illusion they were evidently contemplating something very close to fraudulent conver-sion. After Webb had been sticking to his guns for over a year, insist-ing that he could do anything he wanted to with the money, so long as his trustees approved it, Shaw was finally to spell it out to him that malversation was the name of the game he seemed determined to play, and that it was a felony where the conduct of trust fund was concerned.

A compromise was then arrived at, by which the money was to be divided between the Society's direct and indirect propaganda. The London School of Economics was to be considered an organ of indirect propaganda, since its concern would be with the ideology on which the direct propaganda would be based. Shaw agreed to this without dreaming that Webb intended to let the new institution have nine pounds for every one that went to spreading the socialist message. When he belatedly realised what was being done, Shaw exploded with anger; and when Graham Wallas heard of it, after Webb had persuaded him to accept the position of the new school's Director, he immediately resigned the office. But things were beyond recall by then, and the money almost spent. The episode had left Olivier with doubts about Webb's integrity that were never to be dispelled.

It may be difficult for the reader to understand why, with the money so long gone, my father troubled to raise this matter in 1906. What he intended was not to bicker about the use of the Hutchinson Fund, but to remind the Old Guard of one of the greater opportunities that their ingrained habit of thinking small had caused them to miss. In the course of 1896, when very little of the fund had been dissipated, a rumour that the Society had been presented with a war chest reached Ramsay MacDonald. He had just joined forces with Keir Hardie, the leader of the Independent Labour Party, and with a number of Trades Union leaders and heads of workingmen's associations in order to make a major effort to put a third party on the map whenever the next General Election should take place. MacDonald was sure that the Fabians ought to make at least some of the Hutchinson money available to him to help finance this attempt to launch a Parliamentary Labour Party. The Webbs had turned MacDonald down flat, on the ground that the English system was a two-party affair, and that no ad hoc socialist grouping was ever going to have the width of appeal or the strength to move in on the territories that had been pre-empted by the Liberal and Conservative parties respectively. So far as they were concerned, MacDonald was about to repeat the mistakes that had been made by William Morris' Socialist League, and before that by the Social Democratic Federation. They might just as well pour their money down a rat hole as let him have it.

And in the event, their decision had seemed to be justified: MacDonald had failed to elect a single one of his twenty-eight candidates when the next General Election took place, and they had only been able to attract forty-five thousand votes between them, nationwide.

The Fabians had plumed themselves on their wisdom for staying out of it, and had been moved to pity when MacDonald and Hardie had stood up on the stricken field to assert that a beginning had been made, and that more would soon be heard of the Parliamentary Labour Party.

In the end it had been the Fabians who had been proved wrong. In the General Election of 1906 the Labour Party had won thirty seats in the House of Commons, and the third party had been put on the map beyond any questioning. It was this incontestable arrival that had made my father bring up the long-dead issue of Hutchinson's bequest. He did not give a damn about what had actually happened to the money. He wanted to remind the older Fabians that they had missed the boat in 1896, and that they were showing every sign of doing the same thing all over again. The Society was, as he saw it, being left behind by events and rapidly losing its never very impressive claim to represent the advancing front of English Socialism. After their rebuff by the Fabians in '96 the Labour Party's leadership had gone to work to build themselves a power base in the country by talking bread-and-butter socialism on the shop floor, at the factory gates, and in the Union Chapels. They had created a party of the working-class interest from the ground up. They were beholden for little or nothing to the Fabians, and only a thin pretence of comradeship now linked the virtually unrelated bodies. The possibility was in a fair way to becoming a probability that the Fabians were going to be left out in the cold, and that England, for good or ill, was going to have the first European national working-class party that had no place in it for intellectuals of the left and no use for socialist theory. If that were to happen, the Parliamentary Labour Party might be fated never to rise above sectional issues and class interests to take part in the socialist mission of creating a new kind of just and open society in which life would be better for everybody.

It was in the light of this foreboding that my father had dashed off his note to Pease. He should have known by that time that the secretary was not the man to look for a hidden meaning in such a communication, and that he would take it literally as the query it seemed to be. Pease read the note, sent my father the briefest possible reply, informing him that the fund had been exhausted, and its books closed. By the same post he sent Webb an urgent warning: my father was about to raise the dormant scandal. Sidney passed the message on to Beatrice: there were, he said, disturbing indications that my father might be thinking of "breaking out again." From then on these two were watching his every move, and it was not long before they became aware of the frequency and depth of his contacts with the young Fabians at Cambridge.

This was the summer, of 1908, in which Amber Reeves won her double first in the Moral Science Tripos, and began to come into her own as the charming and considerable person she had always promised to become. She was *en fleur.* She had been keen on my father for four years, and he had liked her a little more each time they met. They came under Beatrice Webb's cold eye as a pair that September, and inspired a patronising and venomous entry in her diary:

> Amber is an amazingly vital person, and I suppose very clever, but a terrible little pagan—vain, egotistical, and careless of other people's happiness. This may be a phase, for she is a mere precocious child, but the phase is not promising. . . . A somewhat dangerous friendship is springing up between her and H. G. Wells. I think they are both too soundly self-interested to do more than cause poor Jane Wells some fearful feelings—but if Amber were my child I should be anxious.

The occasion for making a scandal of the liaison seemed to have been removed, however, on the day after Beatrice Webb wrote these words. When Pease came into the Society's offices that morning he found a letter from my father on his desk. It told him that my father had become filled with a sense that his efforts to bring about a revision of the Basis and the regeneration of the Society were futile; that he'd been especially cast down by his failure to win the Executive over to his ideas about maternity benefits; and he believed more than ever that any scheme for social reform that left things in that department as they were would be a miserable perversion of socialism. Thinking as he did on these issues, he could only feel that he no longer belonged in the Society. Pease brought the letter to the attention of the Executive, and it was printed in full in *The Fabian Newsletter* not long afterwards, beneath a curt announcement that the proffered resignation had been accepted.

This should have marked the end of my father's tussle with the Webbs as leaders of the Fabian Old Guard, but it did not. There were two reasons for this, both questions of personality. The first was that like all born intriguers, the Webbs had the greatest difficulty in believing that anybody could be safely credited with straightforward intentions. They saw that Jane Wells had neither followed her husband out of the Society, nor moved to resign her seat on its Executive. It was natural for them to assume that she was staying on for a purpose, and that she would be holding the pro-Wells minority inside the organisation together while he continued his campaign against its leadership from outside it. As the external leader of an internal opposition my father would be unfettered by even the pretence that he was their collaborator. They saw that he might be about to cause them more trouble and annoyance than ever, and they followed his every move with alert suspicion.

The second reason for the prolongation of the conflict lay in the character of Maud Reeves's husband, who had been under an increasing strain ever since his wife had made herself my father's ally in the first stages of his fight for the revision of the Basis. His unstated feelings became too much for him to suppress any longer when, in the course of April 1909, Amber Reeves found it necessary to tell her parents that she was pregnant, and that the man responsible was my father.

The two men had first met nearly ten years before, as members of the Webbs's private dining club, and even though my father had always found the older man a little heavy in the hand, he had been content to count him as a friend for the lively-minded and energetic Maud Reeves's sake. But he had been dead wrong about the husband in one essential matter—he took him to be a modestly successful man who had been given most of what he had wanted from life in the way of recognition and reward when he had been chosen by the New Zealand government to be its Agent-General in London, a post that gave him a rank equivalent to that of an Ambassador. He had never realised that in Pember Reeves he was dealing with a disappointed and embittered man.

Reeves had been in politics in New Zealand, and with the money of his apparently wealthy and successful father behind him, he had got off to a brilliant start. When he was taken into the Cabinet as Minister for Education and Justice in the last days of his thirty-fourth year he was widely talked of as being next in line of succession to his party's aged leader, and almost a certainty as the Dominion's next Prime Minister. But within weeks of his taking office his fortunes were abruptly transformed. His father was briefly ill, and very soon dead, and he left nothing but debt and scandal behind him. The scandals involved a wide circle of of the dead man's cronies, and a formidable list of offences against company law, some of them no more than technical, but many of them fraudulent and criminal. Although it was never to be alleged that the young Minister of Justice had taken part in the wrongdoings of his father's set, it was whispered everywhere that he must have known what had been going on under his nose unless he was an utter fool.

Between January and April of that bitter year Reeves had ceased to be one of his party's assets and became a liability it could not afford. He fought against acceptance of the realities of his situation from the end of 1891 through into the beginning of 1895, when his will suddenly collapsed. He had eaten a great deal more than the proverbial peck of dirt in resisting his fate, and he could take no more. He allowed the men who were bent on excluding him from the party's leadership to kick him upstairs by making him Agent-General and packing him off to London.

When Reeves arrived in England nobody seemed to care whether he was there or not, and when he went to pay official calls at the various ministries with which he had to do business, he rarely got beyond the under-under-secretaries. But the word slowly spread that the new man wasn't at all what the words "a colonial politician" were usually taken to imply: he was, really, quite the presentable article. Doors began to open to him, and he eventually achieved the ultimate certification as a somebody when Max Beerbohm made him the subject of a caricature. Borne up by this illusory success, the snobbish foundation of which he never properly understood, Reeves began to believe that he was living down the scandal unleashed by his father's shipwreck, and that he might soon be able to go back to the Colony to take up his interrupted career where it had been broken off, with the added prestige of having had a personal success in diplomacy. It was when the Glorious Reign had come to its end, after he had been in London for five years, that he was at last made to see that his success had indeed been a personal one, and that the post he was filling had no standing in the world of diplomacy whatever. He had been doing his career no good at all. When coronation time came round he was not seated in the Abbey in the company of the Ambassadors of the Foreign Powers or anywhere near the centre of interest. He had been given a place down at the far end of the nave from which he could hear little and see less, behind and above the rows of seats

allotted to the provincial mayors and their wives. He should, he realised, never have come to England.

Reeves's black moment in the Abbey had come to him in 1901, and
by 1906, when the scandal of my father's book *In the Days of the Comet*
had erupted, long brooding over his irretrievable blunder had taken
the stuffing out of him. The row over the novel had made him uneasy
because it had given Bland the idea of hawking it about that Maud
Reeves had been helping my father to make advocacy of Free Love
one of the Society's platform principles. Reeves had been given a taste
of that sort of thing. In his youth he had written a series of articles
for his father's paper, *The Lyttleton Times,* in which he had summarised
the philosophies and aims of various left-wing thinkers and organisations. One of them had dealt with the early Fabians, who at that time
still had Annie Besant in their fold. Reeves's essay on this subject had
dwelt at length on her belief in state aid for farming and industrial
cooperatives. Years later, when Reeves's enemies were out to finish
him off, this article was resurrected and used against him. What he
had actually said didn't matter; the thing was that Annie Besant had
been mentioned, and everyone knew all about her—she had lived in
sin with Charles Bradlaugh, and she had been in favour of letting
women learn all they wanted to know about birth control. By writing
about her, they argued, Reeves had identified himself as a Free Love
advocate and an Enemy of the Family. They had plugged this line
against Reeves all through his downhill slide, and flung it at him
nastily when it was at last announced that he had accepted his ticket
to oblivion: what was the Prime Minister about, they asked, sending
a believer in Free Love with a whiff of old financial scandals about him
to represent the Colony at the Court of St. James's? It is not hard to
imagine how Reeves must have felt when he saw the direction in which
my father was leading his wife. As soon as he saw my father's draft for
the revision of the Basis it was clear to him that when its second clause
spoke of equality of the sexes under the law, sexual freedom was part
of the package. He hated that concept. Although he was intellectually
a liberal and a progressive, he was at heart a conventional male chau-
vinist with very firm ideas about what constituted appropriately femi-
nine behaviour. He was, for instance, firmly of the opinion that no
woman should allow herself to smoke in public, since to do so was to
admit to low moral standards. He hated the idea of Maternity Benefits
just as much; they undermined the very foundations of all decency.

Reeves was having a hard time holding his feelings in check all through 1906, and the strain of it was wearing him out. A New Zealand friend who had been close to him in the Colony but who had not seen him for a decade came into England towards the end of the year and was shocked to find his man looking, and evidently feeling, elderly. He had just turned forty-nine. Beatrice Webb had been worrying about him for some time: she'd noted in her diary that he seemed to be "settling down to a certain plaintive dullness of spirit and aim" as early as 1904. Maud Reeves hadn't seen it then, she'd been too busy with Fabian affairs and the feminist cause, but his reaction to the row over *In the Days of the Comet* awakened her to his changed state.

It is my belief that Maud Reeves's concern for him had been responsible for her sudden decision to give in to his appeals to her to become less active in my father's support just as the fight for the revised Basis was coming to a crisis. He went on behaving as if he was a broken man through most of 1907, but in the following year he made an effort to break his links with his brutally disappointing past. He had resigned his post as Agent-General in order to set himself free to accept that of Director of the London School of Economics, offered to him as a pick-me-up by Sidney Webb. He had been on the job for six months, and was beginning to realise that he was a figurehead, fronting for the Webbs, when the terrible day came in which his wife had to tell him that their daughter was pregnant and that the man responsible for her condition was no thoughtless Cambridge stripling, golden with promise, but their friend, my married, middle-aged, and already scandalous father.

This final blow released all the rage, resentment, and bitterness at the sheer unfairness of all the checks and disappointments that had come his way since his father's death stored up in Pember Reeves's heart. In his fury he wanted someone, anyone, to be made to pay for all he had been through. His daughter and her lover were at hand as scapegoats, and he wanted them to sweat for being the latest contributors to his mass of wounds. He wanted them punished, no matter that it might cost him, or them, or anyone else. To make sure that things should go hard with them, he spread the word of the abominable way in which the guilty parties had repaid him for his love and trust. He went round the circle of his acquaintance pouring out the tale of his sorrows to anyone who would listen to him, with the consequences that I have described in an earlier chapter. He made the private scandal a public matter.

My father had his say about his Fabian fiasco in two of his books: in *The New Machiavelli,* a novel which has the sour tone of something written in anger to offset its considerable virtues; and in his *Experiment in Autobiography,* in which he had the conflicting aims of telling the truth and closing the books on much that he had come to regret. In the novel he had been bent on giving the group of people who had lately been doing their best to ruin him what he felt they deserved, and in the autobiography he was doing his best to kill any lingering interest in his Fabian adventure that might have survived by owning that he had been hasty, inconsiderate, ill-mannered, and ill-tempered throughout its course. What he produced was an obvious cover-up, but what he wished to conceal, at any rate for the time being, was the matter of his relationship with Amber Reeves and her family. He had come to look upon that as the biggest personal failure of his life, regretting about equally his weakness in letting himself be drawn into the affair; his failure to keep it within the bounds of the reasonable; the distress he had inflicted upon Maud Reeves, who had been a dear friend; and, not least, the misery he had brought into the life of the amiable, decent, profoundly unhappy, and more than sufficiently unlucky Pember Reeves. There was one other thing left over from this affair that made him reluctant to rake over its ashes—the agreement that Rivers Blanco White had forced upon him after the publication of *Ann Veronica* was still binding upon him at that time, and under its constraint he had neither seen nor spoken to his daughter since the day on which he had signed his name to it. She had grown up, he had heard, to be a brilliant young woman, and he was regretting her absence from his life more and more.

These were the things that made up the real substance of the Fabian episode as it had affected him, and when they were omitted from the story he felt that there was nothing much left but the record of an ill-considered plunge into a very small pond that he should never have gone into. Some will feel that my father's views of the Fabians and Fabianism were self-serving, but there was a tremendous difference between the habits of mind on the two sides of the fence. The width of the gap between the two mental worlds is exemplified for me by the serenity with which Hubert Bland was able to patronise my father when it fell to his lot to write a review of *Tono-Bungay* for *The Daily Chronicle* in February 1909. Adopting an easy, avuncular tone, Bland accused my father of developing a taste for the irrelevant that was threatening to make an inferior Sterne of him. Backing up his case,

Bland drew the attention of his readers to "an episode that hinders rather than helps the progression of the story, and does nothing whatever towards the development of any of the characters, an episode that had much better have been given as a short story." Bland had unerringly put his finger on one of those truly brilliant things that come up again and again in my father's writing, often when they are least expected, to convince one that he was an authentic genius. The Quap episode in *Tono-Bungay* is one of those pieces of expository writing that bring something altogether new forward from the realm of the recondite and into that of the general consciousness. It marks the opening of a new horizon.

I've already described the typically Wellsian route by which Uncle Ponderevo of *Tono-Bungay* came into fictional existence. After he'd gone bankrupt as a retail chemist of the old-fashioned sort, he had moved on to the new field of proprietary drugs, where he hit pay dirt in the way of a formula for an absolutely valueless and only slightly harmful tonic consisting of tap water, a little colouring, a touch of sugar, something to give it flavour, and a little mildly habit-forming touch of something else that makes it a stimulant. With the aid of some wholly irresponsible and dishonest advertising it becomes a huge seller, and in no time at all it starts to bring in a seemingly inexhaustible flow of ready cash. This washes him along until he becomes the owner of a controlling interest in half a dozen substantial concerns and a major power in the business world. To his original belief that profit is everything he now adds another, that so long as you keep expanding you're going to be all right. When his cardhouse of flotations and mergers grows too big for him to manage, and the earnings from his sales of the tonic cease to be of significance in the face of his ever-growing cash-flow problems, Quap comes into the picture.

As advertised by its discoverer and promoter, the new substance sounds like a marvel—a natural substance from which it should be possible to make the perfect filament for an electric light bulb—in the prevailing state of the art the exploiter of Quap should be able to corner the light-bulb market in the whole of the Western world. It offers an irresistible temptation to Ponderevo. More money has to come from somewhere, and with ruin round the next turn of the road, and no other options, Quap has to be worth a try. And the promoter is very persuasive. According to him, the stuff is lying out in the open on a bar that has built up on the end of an island in the mouth of a

West African river—it's not only going to be easy to get at, it's also going to be easy to work—it's soft, almost a slurry, so that all that will be needed on the site in the first instance will be a few shovels, a windlass, and a bucket on a dragline. So Ponderevo's clean-cut nephew, the narrator of the whole story, goes out to look the place over to see if this wildcat last chance can possibly be for real, and to bring home a trial load if he can. And so we are taken at last to have a look at something that is truly remarkable—the Western world's first premonition of what a radiation-blasted landscape will look like.

What the younger Ponderevo is confronted with when he gets to the sinister mud bar that is his destination is less immediately impressive than the state of its surroundings. For some miles on all sides of the the bar every living thing appears to be sick or dying. Before he left London young Ponderevo had been told that the inhabitants of the region were in awe of the place, and that they looked on the bar as a thing accursed. He begins to share their feelings before very long, but, being a reasonable man, he conceives the idea that he is dealing with a piece of ground that is suffering from some kind of disease of matter. But business is business, and he has not come three thousand miles to indulge in speculation. He is there to load Quap. So he fills his chartered schooner with the lethal goo, and sets sail for home. Within a few days the men of his ship's company, who had already begun to break out with sores while they were handling the Quap aboard, start falling sick and dying, and presently the ship itself begins to come apart. Just before it founders, Ponderevo and the surviving seamen scramble off it into a rotten gig that barely holds together until they are picked up.

I can see that it is possible to take this as a piece of storytelling for its own sake, but I can't help feeling that it takes a large measure of intellectual arrogance to disregard the combination of logic, prescience, and cogency that gives it its position in the fabric of which it forms an integral part. I find myself surprised every time I reread this section of the book by its startling prevision of the let's-have-a-go spirit of the Gadarene rush into the exploitation of atomic energy as a power source that followed on the heels of the wartime achievement of uncontrolled nuclear fission. But that almost clairvoyant anticipation is not the main point. What my father intended his allegory to demonstrate was the inevitability of the progression from peddling the mildly harmful to the exploitation of the wholly lethal that had to follow on the general acceptance of the principle doctrine of marketplace capital that profit justified all things. He had recognised, as soon as he had reached an understanding of what his young acquaintance Frederick Soddy, a man just eleven years younger than himself, was telling him about the very strange properties of radioactive substances, that no questions of prudence or ethics would prevent the speculators from crowding into the field just as soon as the exploitation of the new knowledge began to look like becoming a practical proposition. The operators would have their gamble with the future of the species the minute that they saw an outside chance of raising the money to stake on it. The idea that speculators were becoming more and more irresponsible as their power to do social damage increased was not in any way original with my father. The first Roosevelt had, in fact, already fought a campaign in which he had made much of the issue, and the need for some degree of control and regulation of flotations had been discerned as early as the eighteen-forties. But most people who considered the topic before my father's day did so with the thought of finding remedies for minor defects in a fundamentally healthy social structure. The focus was on the individual victim, and even those who saw that damage was being done to society as a whole were inclined to think of the trouble as something that could be put right relatively easily by piecemeal legislation and without resort to radical measures of reform. My father was, I believe, bringing something new into consideration when he described the wild growth and proliferation of the new super-businesses and conglomerates as being comparable to the spread of cancer through a living body. He had made a beginning with the idea in *When the Sleeper Wakes* of 1899, a novel in which a single giant conglomerate gobbles up the economic power of the entire Western world, taken it up again in *The Food of the Gods* in 1904, and brought it to its full development in *Tono-Bungay*. He does not want anyone to miss the point of what he is saying about Quap:

> ... there is something—the only word that comes near it is *cancerous* ... about ... Quap. ... to my mind radioactivity is a real disease of matter ... a contagious disease. It spreads. You bring these debased and crumbling atoms near others and those too presently catch the trick of swinging themselves out of coherent existence. It is in matter exactly what the decay of our old culture is in society ... I think of these inexplicable dissolvent centers ... [and] I am haunted by a grotesque fancy

of the ultimate eating away and dry-rotting and dispersal of all
our world . . . Suppose, indeed, that is to be the end of our
planet; no splendid climax and finale, no towering accumula-
tion of achievements but just—atomic decay!

My father is speaking here in the person of young Ponderevo,
whose only motive for trying to launch the enterprise that might have
spread this infection round the world was that its success might, just
possibly, have delayed his uncle's bankruptcy by two or three years.
There is an unexpected extra dimension to the episode: the stuff
involved is demoralising in its effect upon those who have to handle
it, just as greed is demoralising to those who give way to it. The
narrator of my father's story has not sought the permission of the local
authorities to lift Quap from their territory, and when he starts loading his vessel he is entering on a new career as a thief or pirate. (Not
that he *means* any harm, it is just that there isn't any time to go through
the correct procedures of getting export licences, and so on . . .) He
goes on from theft to murder, as pirates are apt to do. His hope is that
his operation will go through undetected, and to keep it alive he
shoots a fellow creature in cold blood. The man, some kind of beach-
comber or deadbeat and a *native,* has come to a spot almost within
sight of the schooner when the narrator runs across him—what more
natural than to let him have a bullet in the back and to bury him where
he falls?

The incident may sound extravagantly arbitrary, and perhaps even
superfluous, when detached from its context as it is here. But in its
place in the novel the vile act comes as something almost overdue, an
inevitable consequence of being in that place to meddle with that
stuff. There is a progressive drop in the moral tone of the adventure
as it proceeds, just as there was around the Manhattan Project as the
nature of the work being done became steadily less escapable. I don't
wish to overload this parallel, but that guiltless intruder does get shot,
and it is the *good* narrator who does the shooting. However far my
father may have been from any knowledge of the technology of the
enterprise that made Oppenheimer utter his dark saying that "we
have known sin" in the hour of his success, I still can't find it possible
to doubt that his intuitions had given him a similar awareness back
there between 1906 and 1908. But when my father has been given full
credit for his foresight it isn't his prescient grasp of the horrid possibilities lying dormant in the discoveries of the first generation of

atomic physicists that makes the book interesting and important. The measure of its virtue is that it looks through and beyond the venality of the exploiters and speculators it entertainingly caricatures to the fatal human habit of always plumping for the course that offers the immediate return, no matter how trifling the obvious gain, or how certain that it will have to be paid for in full in the long run. The book delivers, in a very powerful and original way, the ancient message of the story about the forbidden fruit, that man is his own ultimate enemy. It is no accident that young Ponderevo's uncle ends up on Gissing's deathbed, the novel incorporates all that my father had learned about self-destructive compulsions from his postmortem immersion in the detail of that unhappy being's secret history.

But I must turn back from my contemplation of the content of what has solid claims to be my father's most successful novel to round out the matter of his involvement with the Fabians. The extent to which he didn't belong among them is encapsulated in the last two sentences of the ineffable Bland's criticism of the book: "But to do Mr. Wells justice, he did not set out with a view to keeping to the point; on the contrary, he rather boasts and glories in not keeping to the point. He zigzags." This cheap shot at a big man's big book, fired off by a critic who had only escaped being a seedy nonentity because he had lucked into marriage with an industrious and gifted woman willing to keep him, catches the condescending tone of Fabian discourse to perfection. It is something I cannot hear without regretting that my father wasted so much of himself in trying to make himself master of that tiny little stage. Some of his biographers have it that he made the greatest mistake of his life when he turned his back on it, but the facts do not support that view. The history of the Society falls into two sections, and when my father resigned from it, the Webbs were about to bring the first of them to an end with a dazzling display of political ineptitude.

The occasion for their demonstration was produced when the work of a House of Commons committee enquiring into the defects of the existing Poor Laws reached the report stage. The committee split into a Majority and a Minority over the matter of recommendations; and while the Majority Report was responsive to popular feeling throughout the country in proposing bold steps in the direction of humanised Welfare Services, the Minority Report, to which the Webbs put their signatures, went no further than the proposal of a mass of cost-conscious administrative reforms, improving the in-house efficiency of the old machinery while leaving its character largely untouched. When the Webbs realised the extent of their blunder they abandoned the stricken scene and went off on a trip round the world, leaving Lloyd George to go ahead with the work of laying the foundations of England's system of unemployment and health insurance schemes. They were out of things altogether for a year, in which the Society began to fall apart. The steep rise in the intake of new members that had taken place in the years of my father's drive to bring new life into the organisation started to dwindle away, and the numbers of those who were willing to let their memberships lapse began to increase. The Society was only saved from extinction in 1916 when it was remade in a new image by G. D. H. Cole and others of his kidney. Its main function since that time has been to serve as a left-wing think tank, providing the necessary facts and figures to justify whatever socialist dogmas may be in vogue at the moment. Its influence on the policies of the Parliamentary Labour Party has never been as great as its apologists have liked to make out, and it has never had any in other quarters.

As for the Webbs, socialists who loathed and despised the un-washed masses only a little less than the democratic process that required their desires and ambitions to be taken into account, they were to end up, naturally enough, alongside George Bernard Shaw in the ranks of the more fervent defenders of Stalinism at its ugly worst. At the end of their days, when they had come to believe that the Soviet State as it was represented the complete fulfillment of the Fabian ideal, they were listening nightly to the English-language broadcasts from Moscow in order to make sure that their opinions of what was going on in the world owed nothing to a source of news that could be tainted by propaganda.

The truth is that the Webbs were an easy pair to quarrel with. They had a very high opinion of themselves, and a very poor one of the generality of mankind. She was an extremely arrogant woman of limited intelligence, while he, as his complete failure as a Cabinet Minister was to demonstrate beyond doubt, had the fatal combination of self-satisfaction with a complete lack of common sense. It was admittedly no sinecure that came his way when he was pitched into the Colonial Office, then responsible for Palestine, just as Jewish immigration was becoming the crucial issue. But all the same, the Webbs managed to bring something all their own to the problem. As things were warming up after Jabotinsky's Wailing Wall riot had taken place, Beatrice raised a singular question in her diary: "From whom were descended those Russian and Polish Jews?" She came to her remarkable answer to this query a year later:

> What interests me about all this ferment over Palestine is the absence from first to last of any consideration of Palestine as the cradle of the Christian creed . . . imagine the awful shock of the mediaeval crusaders if they had foreseen the Christian Kingdoms of England, France, and Italy withdrawing Jerusalem from Islam in order to hand it over to those who crucified Jesus of Nazareth and have continued, down all the ages, to deny that He is the son of God. . . . The Christian tradition of the infamy of the Crucifixion is ignored. An additional touch of irony to this ill-doomed episode lies in the fact that the Jewish immigrants are Slavs and Mongols and not semites, and the vast majority are not followers of Moses and the prophets, but of Karl Marx and the Soviet Republic . . .

The Webbs met my father over a luncheon table at about the time that Beatrice confided these profundities to her diary, by so doing bringing an end to a complete breach in their relations that had endured for seven years. He found them entertainingly wrong-headed on all major questions, and had occasional difficulty in concealing his amusement. Beatrice did not like that, and accordingly noted how fat and pleased with himself he had become. It was interesting to her that while most English people tended to look like one breed of *dog* or another in age, he was beginning to look more and more *piglike.*

The great mistake that my father had made back in 1909 had not been walking out of the Fabian Society, but losing control of his private life and exposing himself to that unrelenting spite. Nothing else in his adult experience, with the possible exceptions of his reading of my grandmother's doctored diary and his discovery of Moura Budberg's duplicity, was to affect him more deeply than the public scandal that was made of his affair with Amber Reeves. Everything that could be done to make a man think ill of himself was done to him while it was at its height, and for another two years after it he was to be showered with gratuitous slights and insults. They were visited on him by an extraordinary variety of people, most of them complete strangers to him, but some men and women he had come to think of as his friends. It was to take him a full ten years to recover his belief in his own value, and to get his professional life back on course. And his recovery as a writer was only to be accomplished by a change of field—he never altogether regained the nerve to run the risk of self-exposure that is an inherent part of writing fiction, and when he made his comeback it was with *The Outline of History.* From then on he was publicist, ideas man, and propagandist first and foremost, and only incidentally the novelist. The marvellous directness of his early work —the absence in it, once he had been through his preliminary warming-up exercises, of any distance between him and his reader—had vanished for ever. And fallout from his ordeal was to burn him from time to time for a much longer period.

It was, for instance, in 1932, after he had delivered his *mea culpa* in his *Experiment in Autobiography,* and after Pember Reeves had died, that he put out a feeler in Rivers Blanco White's direction through E. S. P. Haynes, suggesting that the time had surely run out on the ban that had kept him from having any kind of contact with his daughter by Amber. Blanco White agreed that the time had perhaps come for Anna-Jane to be told who her real father was, and given a chance to meet him and to get to know him, if she so desired. She had grown up in the belief that Rivers Blanco White was her real father, and it was one of the foundation stones of the emotional structure from which she was making her attack on life. She did not like having it pulled out from under her. At twenty-three she was very fond of Rivers, who was a very nice man in whom she had learned to place an absolute trust. When she was brought face to face with my father she found herself with a stranger. She knew that she was expected to like him, but she was not able to do so. It was some time before my father was able to come to terms with this hard fact. He did not handle the situation at all well. A part of the trouble was that he was going through a phase in which he was feeling a need to revise certain aspects of his past. He did not like it that his children had grown up to be strangers to one another. He was anxious to bring them together and to get some sort of family life going before he died. In his hurry he rushed things. He introduced me to Anna-Jane before he had established any kind of rapport with her. He arranged a tea party at which we were to meet within days of his telling me of her existence over a lunch at Scott's. It took place in the drawing room of his uninspiring apartment in Chiltern Court, the big block of flats that sits on top of Baker Street Tube Station. She was already in the room when I arrived, and the jumble of vibes that she was emitting rather powerfully suggested to me that he might have asked her to come early so that he would have a chance to explain me to her as she had previously been explained to me. I imagined that I understood her feelings, but I couldn't think of anything to say to her, and after we had exchanged strangled how-d'you-dos we both found ourselves incapable of further utterance. My father gave us tea and made conversation as if he were someone afraid of animals who was trying to win the confidence of two large ones who were known to bite. It was not an occasion that Rivers Blanco White could either have arranged or have made such a mess of if he had. I have always thought that it did a lot to make up Anna-Jane's mind about her feelings towards my father and to bring him to a realisation of what they were going to be. The blow, when he finally had to admit to himself that she didn't like him, was one that he wasn't able to take lightly.

It was my marginal participation in one or two more experiences of this kind that brought home to me the full weight of the tremendous beating that my father had been given between 1908 and 1916. His awareness that he had let himself in for the organised social persecution that he endured in those years had not made it any easier for him to live with it, and I believe that it was this that led to the development of the tendency to overrespond to personal criticism which became part of his character in his later fifties. I won't pretend that he didn't, in those later years, raise the explosive outburst to the level of an art form, but a thin skin is something to expect in a man who has survived a flaying. The more I learn of what my father had to go through in the immediate aftermath of his Fabian involvement and as its long-term consequences, the easier I find it to understand and to forgive the short fuse and the violent outbursts.

Chapter XV

If I have much more of this bloody steamship, I
shall begin to write like Dorothy Richardson.

—LETTER WRITTEN ABOARD THE S.S. ADRIATIC

BETWEEN NOVEMBER 1906 AND APRIL
of the following year, while my fa-
ther's Fabian battle was at its height, he managed to find the time for
one of the strangest and most revealing of his affairs. It was with
Dorothy Richardson, a woman he had known since his Worcester Park
days. When I first met her as an adult, thirty years later, she made a
very strong impression upon me as at once the most conceited and
the least sensuous person of either sex that I had up to that time
encountered. She carried herself and wore her clothes with a peculiar
stiffness that suggested a dressmaker's dummy or one of the human
figures from an old-fashioned Noah's Ark set. It was hard for me to
believe that she could ever have been to bed with so lively a man as
my father, but there it was—she had written an account of her traffick-
ings with him, only thinly disguised as fiction, into her endless autobiographical stream-of-consciousness novel *Pilgrimage,* and he had
never denied that the affair had taken place.

When she was a girl, Dorothy Richardson had been at school with
Amy-Catherine Robbins. The two had been drawn together by fellow
feeling. Both their young lives had been shadowed by a sense of
coming trouble, and with reason: something had been going terribly

335

wrong with the affairs of their fathers. Mr. Richardson's troubles were typical of the period. They sprang from his passion to climb up the social ladder to a point at which he would be accepted as a gentleman. He was the only son of a prosperous small-town grocer, and his first act on inheriting his father's business had been to sell out. This gave him thirteen thousand pounds, and with that much in his poke he settled down to live the life of a man of property while playing the stock market. Although he was technically underfinanced, he was comparatively lucky, and he managed to keep clear of the bankruptcy court for nearly twenty years. Being what he was, a typical family man of his epoch, he had never discussed money matters with his women-folk, and his slow slide towards an irretrievable disaster, broken by episodes of illusory success, had been a hell of uncertainty and apprehension for his wife and for his four daughters.

The two older Richardson girls had reached marriageable age as the waters had begun to close over Mr. Richardson's head, and they had just made it to the altar before he went down for the last time. When it came to actually filing a petition, Mrs. Richardson, overwhelmed by the realisation of her worst fears for herself, and for the two girls still unmarried, went clean out of her mind. As the younger of the two was not yet out of school, it fell to Dorothy to become the madwoman's personal nurse and attendant. After some weeks the two sons-in-law clubbed together to send "Mother" to the seaside in Dorothy's care, in the hope that the peace and quiet of Hastings in the off season might calm her and bring her round. The move was futile, since rest was out of the question for Mrs. Richardson. She was deeply into an agitated depression, and she could neither sleep, nor stop talking, nor stay still. At the end of the first five days in their Hastings lodgings the madwoman had worn herself out, and she collapsed onto a bed. Her daughter, nearly as exhausted as she was, seeing her lying there apparently fast asleep at long last, took a gamble and slipped out to snatch some fresh air and a few moments to herself on the sea front. There she committed the folly of sitting down on one of the benches facing the waves, and was lulled to sleep in a moment. An hour later, when she ran back to the house where she had left her mother unwatched, it was to find that the poor troubled lady was dead: she had cut her throat with a bread knife.

Everybody had been very kind to Dorothy, but the general feeling that the dead woman should never have been left alone was inescapable. That nothing was said about it was the worst of condemnations.

In the aftermath to this traumatic breakup of her family, Dorothy moved into central London to start a new life as the receptionist for a Harley Street dental partnership. Her employers were to pay her a pound a week.

As soon as she had settled herself into an attic room in a lodging house within walking distance of the job, she began to take steps to make her new life endurable. Her first move was to look up those of her former schoolmates who were living in and around the city. Before long she found her way to the snug little suburban villa in Worcester Park where Amy-Catherine Robbins was living with my father and undergoing the first stages of her transformation into Jane Wells. Jane had very vivid memories of what she had been through at the time of her own father's suicide, and had no difficulty with entering into her hard-hit friend's feelings. My father also, remembering the shadow that Joseph Wells's back-yard tumble had cast on his youthful spirits, could also sympathise with her readily enough. Between them they made standing by Dorothy a project: she soon became a regular at their gregarious Sunday lunches, and often came out to Worcester Park on Saturdays to spend the night.

Dorothy's biographer, Gloria Fromm, says that she soon won my father's admiration, but I do not believe that this was so. When Jane and my father looked at Dorothy in those Worcester Park days it was to see the same thing, the numbed victim of a run of rotten bad luck. It took a long time for them to learn to see her as anything else because it took her the best part of sixteen years to recover from the shock of her mother's death and to get herself off dead center. My father's ability to understand what was weighing her down was undoubtedly much increased when his mother's death in 1905 put him in possession of the diary in which she had recorded her reactions to the shattering experiences she had undergone at the time when her parents had died one after another in the Inn at Midhurst. The parallels between Sarah Neal's ordeal and Dorothy's weren't that close, but the excess of misfortune that gave them both their tone was the common factor that told. Even so, it will have provided him with grounds for empathy and compassion rather than admiration. Ten years from their first meeting at Worcester Park she was still clinging to that not very dazzling receptionist's job, and her one literary achievement had been getting an unsigned piece into *The Outlook*. There wasn't really too much there for the youngish man who had just published *Kipps,* and who already had twenty novels and three collections of short stories to his name, to be bowled over by—she was, to be blunt, an object of his pity rather than anything else when they embarked on their brief, and dismally unsuccessful, affair in 1906.

The fiasco came about in the following way. When Dorothy began life on her own in London she felt that she was running certain risks. As soon as it was possible for her to do so, she set herself up with a male companion to protect her from the menaces to which she felt that she was exposed as an unattached girl. She didn't have to look far for what she had in mind—providence had placed a certain Benjamin Grad, a young Russian Jew, in a bed-sitter one flight down from her attic room. As he was new to the country and had very little English, she was able to insert herself into his life as a mentor and guide in the simplest and easiest manner, instructing him in his new language and the local customs. Their relationship developed and presently took on another character, becoming a game of perpetual courtship in which neither suitor wished to succeed. To make sure that Grad should never ask her to deliver, Dorothy had told him at an early stage that being a witness to all that had led up to her mother's madness and suicide had turned her against marriage forever, while he, after letting her know that he had spent a year as a patient in an insane asylum before leaving Russia, made it clear that so far as he was concerned, sex without marriage was unthinkable. They would have been able to go on playing this risk-free game ad infinitum but for the arrival on the scene of a young would-be actress, Veronica Leslie-Jones, a runaway from a county family. She broke in on them to declare an unholy passion for Dorothy, who found herself, much to her surprise, responding in kind. She caught herself wondering for the first time if she had not been denying herself something by planning to do without sex. She was half inclined to give her eager new friend what she seemed to want so badly, but hung back from consummation because she could not be sure that the girl's demonstrative lesbianism was more than a performance—a matter of a person's desire to seem dashingly and interestingly corrupt rather than the usual thing in order to impress. And beyond that it wasn't, she rather suspected, Veronica's femininity that she had responded to so much as to her sexuality and her eagerness. She wasn't at all sure that a lesbian affair was what she had found herself wanting. Her difficulty was that she knew nothing, nothing at all, about that side of life. The point was one that only physical experience of the actual thing could clear up.

A man who comes on stage to play the role of instructor to a younger woman in such a situation as this is inevitably suspect. A legacy from the comic tradition of the past associates innocence with youth and experience with age, so that the hint of a transaction between one and the other calls up images of a decrepit dotard slavering after some fresh young thing. The affair between these two is often presented in that light, partly because that tradition exists, and partly because Dorothy's dream self, the heroine of her interminable *Pilgrimage,* aged a good deal more slowly than she did throughout its action. The facts are that when they at length became lovers, my father was thirty-nine and Dorothy was thirty-two. The further suggestion is sometimes made that it was reckless of my father, and perhaps even deliberately cruel of him, to trifle with the affections of a brilliant young writer, all insight and sensitivity, in a way that could have broken her stride and jeopardised her career. It wasn't quite like that. When the affair took place in 1906, Dorothy was more often perceived as being stuck than promising. The stiffness of backbone that had once been almost charming as part of a defiant perkiness in the face of adversity was beginning to suggest the onset of a premature rigidity. My father, and Jane also, who had both begun by going along with her in supporting her claim to be a *somebody* who was quite certain one day to be *something,* out of kindness, couldn't help feeling that she was showing every sign of becoming a very ordinary old maid.

When she began to send my father unmistakable signals indicating the existence of her desire to change her condition, he was glad. He felt sure that she was doing the sensible thing at last. He didn't for a moment flatter himself with the idea that he had moved her deeper passions—he couldn't have entertained the notion even if he had wanted to, because she had made it plain that she was turning to him to find out something about herself. He was happy to oblige her, and not only because he enjoyed the act for its own sake. He hoped that she would find making love enjoyable because he believed that sexual experience was an essential part of growing up and maturing. He didn't think that it was possible to be a complete person without it, and he was sure that a pleasant passage between them would mark the end of her unlucky years and the beginning of a much happier chapter in her life story . . .

When it presently became only too clear that she didn't enjoy going to bed with him, and that he wasn't being any help to her at all, he felt that he had made a mess of things and was contrite. The truth was, as he had to admit to her, that he had done her wrong. He had come to her when he was tired, and with his head full of other things. He had, in truth, though he wasn't so unkind as to say as much, been *fitting her in*. During the six-month stretch in which they had had their seven or eight saddening meetings he had been up to his neck in the most intense phase of his enormously time-consuming and energy-draining tussle with Sidney Webb and the Fabian Old Guard; wrestling *Tono-Bungay* into shape; carrying on an elaborate flirtation with Violet Hunt that had really amused and interested him; and doing much else beside. He hadn't done his best for her. It was all his fault. She wasn't, he told her, to blame herself on any account. Whatever had been wrong between them would almost certainly come right with custom and familiarity. They should give it more time, and when she came to him again it should be with less anxiety, and perhaps with lower expectations—although sex was one of life's great pleasures, and although it was the source of a kind of happiness that irradiated and illuminated everything, it wasn't anything transcendental or sacramental, it was the simplest and most natural of things: she was not to lose heart.

Dorothy was astounded by his lack of comprehension and horrified by his apparent suggestion that they should go on with the affair. It wasn't that there had been some particular thing wrong between them, or any failure of tact or technique on his part. The trouble was, quite simply, that she hadn't been able to endure any aspect of the thing itself—the act had proved to be even more profoundly distasteful to her than she had feared it might. What she had learned in bed with my father had been that she did not want sex with anyone—she wanted to remain untouched and unmoved. All she wanted was to get out, without acquiring the stigma that attaches itself to running away.

She got clear of my father in two stages. She first told him that she was pregnant to give herself an excuse for breaking off the physical relationship, and then that she had suffered a miscarriage. This enabled her to distance herself from him without seeming to be in flight. She took a six-month leave of absence from her miserable job, and went off to hide herself in the then untroubled and remote piece of Sussex countryside behind Eastbourne between Hailsham and Hurstmonceux, saying that she needed a complete rest after the physical ordeal that she had been through.

My father was never able to believe that Dorothy had been pregnant, let alone that she had suffered a miscarriage, and felt that her disengagement procedures involved something in the nature of over-kill. But he made not the slightest effort to resist her decision to break off the meaningless affair. That was, as he saw it, pre-eminently a matter in which she had to be free to do as she pleased. What concerned him most was that she might run into practical difficulties once she had cut the umbilical cord connecting her with the dental partnership's cash box. He had done his best to teach her the Barrie system for cooking up occasional pieces out of nothing at all, but she hadn't the light touch needed to make a success of hack work for the dailies and had a positive nose for the unrewarding outlet, selecting as her markets such publications as *Ye Crank, The Open Road,* and *The Dental Record.* To help her with what he saw as her immediate problem, he came up with the suggestion that she should become his copy editor —he would send her his galley proofs when they were sent to him by the printers, and she would check them out, for the verbal repetitions that were his greatest weakness, and for such errors in style and grammar as had got past him. He had always found reading over his own work with an eye to such things the dullest of dull chores, and he would be endlessly grateful if she would undertake the labour for him. She would be paid, of course.

My feeling is that Dorothy invented her story of her fight to get out of my father's clutches to give some coherence to her picture of her general situation at this time. As a consequence of her series of fiascos with him she was putting a lot behind her, and in a hurry. She was saying goodbye to more than sex, my father, and the dental practice; she was breaking up her settled London life and offloading her old friend Benjamin and her new friend Veronica as well. The tigerish Miss Leslie-Jones was effective in making her accelerate her disengagement. She made an initiative early in June that scared Dorothy half out of her wits by its urgency and its persistence: they were to become lovers without further ado because Veronica had been made miserable by the defection of her male bed companion of the moment. Dorothy held her at bay for a few days and then developed a counter-proposal. She suggested a triangular mystic marriage: all three kindred spirits, Dorothy, Veronica, and Benjamin, should become one on the spiritual plane while Veronica and Benjamin were united legally on the lower level of the physical. They would then be able to cohabit without scandal, and produce the children who would be just as much Dorothy's in spirit as they would be Benjamin's and Veronica's in the flesh . . . When she had planted this seed in their minds—they had neither of them even considered each other until she put her idea to them—Dorothy skedaddled, taking refuge from all pressures by going into retreat in the heart of her new-found Eden in East Sussex. She came back to town briefly in October to attend the marriage she had invented, and then distanced herself from it by going off to Switzerland for a long holiday. When she returned it was not to her familiar world of London digs and bed-sitters, but to this tranquil backwater. She was taken in as a parlour boarder by a Quaker family called Penrose. Mrs. Penrose ran the house, and her two sons ran the small holding as a truck garden. They made Dorothy one of the family and she stayed with them for the next four years.

The reality of this performance was something that she was never to admit to. She told my father that she had gone into her retreat to recover from the consequences of her miscarriage, and she seems to have let the Penroses know that her medical advisor had told her that her only chance of averting a nervous breakdown lay in taking a complete rest in peaceful surroundings. My belief is that the one story is as untrue as the other, and that her use of the two stories gave her a clue to a strategy for avoiding that confrontation indefinitely. She would make up another story, a much longer one, that would show her actions in a completely different light. She would make telling it her life and her livelihood. She would become a novelist like my father, but her novel would not be mere fiction, as his novels were. Her novel would be both her art, and her life in art. It would describe, thought by thought, the development of a dedicated artist whose medium was prose, and it would show how every phase in that unfolding had been, despite all outward seeming, determined by the interactions between a unique sensibility and an irresistible aesthetic imperative.

The leading facts of the professional life that resulted from the adoption of that strategy are impressive: she expanded her essay in self-examination into something in the nature of a super-novel running to twelve volumes. Eleven of these were issued as entities complete in themselves, but the twelfth never saw independent publication as a novel. It made its first appearance as the final section of the fourth volume of the 1938 collected edition. This was said to present the completed work, but that was not the case. *Pilgrimage* never was to be completed. Although she began work on a thirteenth section, she was never able to really get it going. What she had managed to do, in the twelve volumes, and in twenty-four years of writing time, extending from 1912 to 1936, was to cover the sixteen years of her own actual existence between the years 1891 and the end of 1907. The significance of the break-off date hardly has to be underlined. Her eleventh volume, *Clear Horizons,* which centers on a wholly incredible account of the final stages of her affair with my father, comes to a formal conclusion. Credible or no, the thing has a beginning, a middle, and an end. But its successor, *Dimple Hill,* while running to novel length, never looks like going anywhere, and finally just peters out. Dorothy's inability to give it shape and a climax finally exhausted Duckworth's monumental patience. They were happy to hand its indeterminate mass over to Dent, feeling pretty sure that Dorothy never was going to manage to find her way out of it. Dent's editors were confident that they would be able to show her how to solve her problem, but they didn't know their woman. After two years of getting nowhere they seized the hour, announced to her that she had brought her entire project to a triumphant conclusion, and brought down the blade of the guillotine. They wouldn't, they told her, lose any time by giving *Dimple Hill* independent publication, the book would draw much more attention if it came out as what it was obviously intended to be, the final section of the fourth volume of the great work.

Dorothy's objections to this arbitrary proceeding were not spirited, and her complaints to her friends had a *pro forma* ring to them. She may well have been relieved—Dent's editors had, after all, let her off the hook by giving her a perfect excuse for never actually coming to grips with whatever it had been that she was running away from in that far away August. It was, of course, too bad that her stride had been broken just as she was coming to the crux that would have made everything clear, but there it was, that was the sort of thing that inevitably happened now that publishing had become such a crudely commercial business. She had at least one thing to console her—nobody could say that she hadn't tried to make her statement.

When my father saw the first section of the great work, *Pointed Roofs,* in 1915, it filled him with doubts about what was to follow, and what was to become of Dorothy. She had been talking the book throughout the eight years that had gone by since her disappearance into East Sussex, and some of her ideas had been interesting. She was going to address herself to the perfectly valid point that there could only be one character in a novel—or indeed in any piece of fiction that wasn't a collaboration. She was going to face up to the limiting fact, and make an advantage of it, by writing a novel of the interior life of a single character who would have to be herself. The whole of the action would be concerned with the development of her perceptions of the exterior world, and her deepening understanding of them. He had wondered if she was aware that her great discovery was a truism, something that every writer who has ever thought about what he was doing has always known, but he had hoped, against the odds, that the novel she intended to build on it might, nonetheless, work out. And there, after eight years of talk, was *Pointed Roofs*. My father knew what its basis had been. In 1891, when she had been halfway through her eighteenth year, Dorothy had gone out to take up a post as a pupil-teacher in a finishing school for middle-class girls in the German town of Hanover. She had not liked the girls in the school, who had been the children of army men, minor officials, professional people, bankers, and successful businessmen, and she had not been able to get on with her employer. Soon after her arrival it had become apparent that she did not have the right qualifications for the job, and that she had no gift for teaching. Within six months she had been fired and sent home. My father had known what it was to face classes as an untried teacher, and, knowing Dorothy, he could guess at what had actually happened. She would have condescended to her pupils as she was in the habit of condescending to him, treating them as her inferiors in culture and in intelligence, and they would have refused to take it from her. Germany, in the days of which she had been writing, at the beginning of the nineties, had been the most class-conscious and precisely layered society in Europe, and those girls would have gone after her relentlessly until they had succeeded in placing her exactly at her proper level. If she had let fall as much as half a sentence that might have led them back through her father's shell of humbug to that grocer's shop! A bankrupt's daughter! A girl from a shopkeeping family! The mobbing of a white crow would have been nothing to it. And if she had come across with that, she would have had something —but that would have meant facing up to the simple salient fact of the case, that she hadn't, however excusably or understandably, *measured up*. She hadn't been able to bring herself to peel the scar tissue of that old wound, so what she had served up in place of the truth of the experience was a sunny little vignette of the thing as it hadn't quite been. Was the whole *Pilgrimage* going to turn out to be like that—so much consolatory fabulation? He hoped not, for her sake.

He did not have to wait long before Dorothy was to give him further confirmation of his dark view of her literary prospects. Lodgings were her identifying determinants. The rooming houses that constituted her natural habitat shaped her life. Her first lodgings had produced Benjamin Grad for her, and with him, her first intimate relationship with a man. Another, and more important intimacy, followed on the publication of *Pointed Roofs.* It had caused some talk, and it looked as if it was going to earn its advance. It might even bring in as much as twenty pounds more than the thirty pounds she had already received. Emboldened by this prospect she had moved up a notch, from the seven shilling-a-week room in a house on the outskirts of St. John's Wood that she was then occupying, into much nicer accommodation, costing all of sixpence a week more, in Queen's Terrace, just off the Marlborough Road. She was still up under the leads on the attic floor, but to make up for that she wasn't obliged to go out if she wanted a cooked breakfast—the landlady "did" that meal for her lodgers in the basement kitchen. She now started to go down there as a regular thing, and there, almost every morning, she would find the tenant of the big front room on the first floor that the landlady called The Studio, eating his daily kipper and reading his copy of *The Times.*

Alan Odle was very close to going under at this stage, barely surviving on a tiny allowance paid to him weekly by his bank-manager father. He was earning virtually nothing, and, in Robert Ross's phrase, just managing to keep his head under water, by dint of stretching every penny and sticking religiously to a daily routine. Breakfast was his one daily meal, and after he had eaten that kipper, and washed down a couple of slices of toast and marmalade with tea from the landlady's brown pot, he would fast until the evening, spending the long hours of daylight in his room puttering with whatever he might have on his drawing board. Once it was dark he would put on his high-camp artist's rig out and go down to put in an appearance at the Domino Room in the Café Royal, the place that he truly believed to be the nerve center of London's literary and artistic life. He had it firmly in his mind that as long as he maintained a visible presence in that room as a member in good standing of one of its sets, he would be taken seriously as an artist.

Odle's pathetic act was convincing no one. It was only necessary to look at him as he made one of his entrances into the Domino Room to see that he was locked into the worst of all things in the arts, a fly-blown fashion. In his art-school days, when he should have been fighting shy of the exhausted convention of the new that had done for the nineties, he hadn't been looking for anything fresh. He had been slavishly working through Aubrey Beardsley's legacy of images looking for tricks to steal . . . even his personal style had come from Beardsley's prop hamper. It was the old story of the century, a repetition on another level of that of Dorothy Richardson's father. Alan Odle had been determined to be as unlike his hard-driving, hard-working, and relentlessly scrupulous male parent as he could be, and had seen art as the quick road to that end. He had gone in for decadence of the fin du siècle variety to round out the anti-bank performance. He had been able to get away with his wholly unoriginal line while he was all bounce, promise, and beauty, but he had fallen off a shelf in his early twenties—possibly as a result of drinking too much absinthe too often. His faun-like good looks went, virtually overnight, and once they were gone his camping ceased to be amusing. The bills to be paid for his lack of originality and insufficiency of talent rapidly became past due. When Dorothy first came across him as he ate his morning kipper he had been undergoing the painful experience of being dropped for four rather horrible years. He had been given a moment of false hope not long before their encounter, when a man called Henry Savage had asked him to take the post of art editor of a magazine he was starting, *The Gypsy*—but this had proved to be a device for getting some artwork out of him for nothing. He was so near the bottom that some of the false friends of his palmy days were starting to do him small favours out of pity, and he was beginning to be glad of them.

It was the hopelessness of Odle's situation that drew Dorothy to him. He was, like her father, a born loser, and like him, a *fainéant*, pretending to be an artist where her father had pretended to be a gentleman of means, and like her father, he was plummetting downwards in his fall. She could help him because she knew the ropes in the shabby genteel world of the downstart. She had learned every trick in the book about penny pinching and getting by on next to nothing a year. She resolved to help him to adjust to failure. She began with his food, telling him that he could not expect to survive on a diet of tea, kippers, and toast, alone. He was to eat other, more nourishing things from time to time. His health, she warned him, was something he could no longer afford to neglect: to fall ill in lodgings was to be done for. He teased her by sticking to his diet for a time, but she came in on him like the tide and slowly but surely wore down his resistance and made him her dependent.

346

At the end of two years she discovered something about him that told her a great deal: he was living in fear that he was going to be called up. This did not make her think of him as a coward in the conventional sense, but it made her feel almost certain that his camping was largely an act. Had he been your straightforward bread-and-butter homosexual, she decided, he would have no more reason to fear conscription than a bank robber to dread a chance of employment in a bank. The armed forces were by a hallowed tradition the happy hunting grounds of the persuasion. She divined that Odle was in reality just as averse to sexual entanglements with men as with women. She was correct in coming to this conclusion. He had tried swimming in the homosexual mainstream while he still had his looks, but although he had enjoyed peacocking around and being courted, he had always found delivering on the expectations his behaviour had aroused distasteful. He had not enjoyed the physical bit at all, and had ended by wrapping himself up in his poverty as if it were a cloak, shying away from bed with anyone, male or female. They were two of a kind, and might club together without risk.

Dorothy's last lingering doubts that some residue of masculine forcefulness or hunger for domination might be lurking within Alan were finally removed when he went before a medical board in July 1917. After the examining doctor was done with him, he had not only the C3 rating that exempted him from military service but also a note addressed "To whom it might concern" certifying that the condition of his lungs made him unfit for regular work of any kind. This did the trick. If Alan Odle was truly in such a state, he could be no threat to her—the probability was that he would be her dependent for as long as he might last. When they were married, two months after he had undergone that medical examination, she was forty-four, and he had just turned twenty-nine.

When my father met the newly married pair a little later, he saw at once that what Dorothy had obtained by the union was the appearance of the condition without its physical reality. If that was what she wanted, well and good, but the more he thought of it, the more likely it seemed to him that it would be fatal to her declared literary ambition. If she was willing to go that far with counterfeiting in her actual life, her great novel of self-exploration was almost certain to be a sham in which she would be explaining away her inventions and evasions. Time would show whether she had the courage to deal with the actualities of the arrangement she had made, but he did not think that the prospects looked good. He did not believe that Dorothy could afford Alan Odle. She had told him the story of Alan's allowance from his father. The Bank Manager had undertaken to let him have a pound a week for as long as he was willing to send in a weekly letter applying for it. This was the sum total of his regular income. The newlyweds had been in some doubt as to whether the Bank Manager would go on coming across with that pound now that his son was married, and that was why there had been no announcement in *The Times*. They were keeping it from Mr. Odle. My father guessed that it might come to cadging before long. He remembered the way in which Dorothy had invariably refused to listen to him when he gave her tips on how to liven up her hack work—he had told her how she could easily bring in a comfortable three or four hundred a year if she would only learn her trade. But she had told him that she could not bring herself to do it. He knew just what line she would take when the time came—she would beg with the martyred air of someone willing to sacrifice anything, even her pride, in loyalty to her absolute dedication to the highest aesthetic principles.

My father's instinct was sound. Within a few years the Odles had settled down happily to what was essentially an eleemosynary existence. It was migratory in character and hinged on movements between London and Cornwall. They spent their summers in the city and their winters in a seaside holiday place in order to benefit from the off-season rates for accommodation at both ends of the line. Both in town and by the sea they went through the motions of earning their daily bread, but most of their income came from thinly disguised handouts. Alan Odle, whose work was virtually unnegotiable on the open market, sold the odd drawing now and again to an acquaintance or old friend, and he was occasionally given commissions by publishers of borderline erotica who wished to give their so-called luxury editions the look of hard-core pornography without its actionable substance. But these jobs came in the main from bohemian amateurs on the arty fringes of the grubby business as a result of persistent lobbying by Dorothy and her friends, and the pay, if it actually came to that, wasn't as a rule enough to cover the cost of the materials used. Odle had, too, the born loser's nose for a sinking ship. His two major projects in the years between the wars came to nothing when their publishers to be went under, leaving him unpaid. Dorothy herself was not much luckier. Her *Pilgrimage* caused a good deal of talk at the outset, but interest in it in literary circles wasn't sustained there, and never spread beyond them. Few of its volumes sold out their pitifully small first printings, and there was rarely anything to come after the advance, even when Duckworth prudently reduced her advances from fifty to thirty pounds. They would soon have been right out of their depth if it hadn't been for Dorothy's copy-editing fees from my father, and for the more direct subventions that came their way, from 1923 onwards, from a woman writer who was the daughter of England's richest shipowner. Bryher, who was then married to Robert McAlmon and living in Paris, came across the early parts of *Pilgrimage* in Sylvia Beach's book shop, and, possibly because she had herself just been trying to do something very much like it, found it infinitely promising. On her next visit to London she sought Dorothy out to tell her so. When she came to the Odles's rooms in St. John's Wood she was appalled by what she saw, and what she deduced from it—the ambience spoke so clearly not only of the mean shifts they had to resort to, to stay alive, but also of the poverty of their human contacts.

Bryher was not one to appreciate the lodging-house way of life, and knew deprivation when she saw it. She told Odles that they ought to see more of the world, and a few weeks later, when in the ordinary way they would have been disappearing into North Cornwall for the winter, they were off to Paris and Switzerland with money for a six-month's stay. Bryher had given it to them, under the kindly pretence that it was a loan.

In the short run this led to some splendidly comic scenes in which Dorothy tried to impress such friends of Bryher's as Ernest Hemingway with a performance as a major literary figure, and, in the long, to the sort of dependency that my father had seen lying in wait for her as a consequence of her marriage. The loan that had financed the trip had very soon been recognised as the gift it had always been, and before long Dorothy fell into the habit of sending Bryher periodic situation reports that were in fact begging letters. Bryher had money and a warm heart, and she soon taught Dorothy that she could always be counted on to produce a cheque or a banker's order in exchange for a suitably "plucky" account of the latest setback or disappointment that had befallen the poor Odles—Dorothy developed, and with quite remarkable celerity, the arts of the practiced sponger.

Dorothy's experiences of Bryher's generosity led her to take a poor view of my father's performance in this department, and toward the end of 1924 she saw fit to show him how he could bring it into line with her expectations. He received a letter from her which surprised

349

him a good deal. An old friend of Alan Odle's, a poet, was dying in misery. It would be a splendid gesture on my father's part if he were to come up with the "few hundred pounds" that would be all that it would take to give "the old man" a last few months in comfort at some seaside resort such as Brighton or Hove before he died.

My father's reaction to this letter has to be considered in relation to the fact that the poet in question was one of the more noisome in the cast of unsavoury characters who had walking on parts in Wilde's tragedy. He was a latecomer to that affair, the literary con man T. W. H. Crosland, who had attached himself like a leech to Lord Alfred Douglas in its exceedingly unpleasant aftermath. He had not only produced the text of *Oscar Wilde and Myself,* the nauseating vilification of Wilde that Douglas had published as his own, and justified as his way of getting even for what his former lover had said of him in *De Profundis,* he had also masterminded Douglas' bitterly pursued campaign to ruin Wilde's friend, and my father's, the gentle and amiable Robert Ross. This had not been a simple matter of smearing Ross by planting a few nasty stories about him here and there, it had been an elaborate Balzacian scheme involving the forgery of incriminating documents, and the subornation to perjury of two ex-convicts, and it had been designed to force the police to bring Ross into court to face charges very similar to those that had been Wilde's undoing. It had ended in court appearances by Crosland and Douglas, who were charged with publishing criminal libels. My father, who had been brought into that case as a character witness for the prosecutor, Robert Ross, had not enjoyed this experience, and felt that he had owed it largely to Crosland's Iago-like proceedings. It will be seen why Dorothy's letter led him to write a reply of the kind that is sometimes called a stinker. Did it not occur to her, he began, when she was making her suggestion that he should spend a few hundred pounds on making things nice for the dying Crosland, that the pitiful dodderer on whose behalf she was soliciting this outlay was, at the age of fifty-six, two years his junior? Had she never heard that his well-simulated heart attacks had notoriously been part of his standard operating procedure for getting ready cash out of Douglas throughout the period of their connection? Didn't she realise that he'd tried the same dodge on at least a dozen people in recent years? And, finally, hadn't it struck her as a trifle odd that if Crosland had really been dying when she visited him in his rooms in London in August, he could still be in a condition to be moved to Brighton or anywhere else in mid-December? Would she please, please, try not to be quite such an idiot? He had incautiously put a trump into her hand. Crosland, untrustworthy and aggravating to the last, had not been shamming when that August visit to his rooms had taken place. He died very shortly after Dorothy had received my father's angry letter. She took the opportunity he had given her, and wrote to tell him how disgusting she thought it had been. It showed not only that he was heartless, but also that he was no gentleman. Poor Crosland had been Douglas' devoted friend.

It may perhaps tell the reader something about Dorothy Richardson's make-up that she was still fighting this battle, and sticking to her guns, when I went to see her in 1949, twenty-five years later. When she told me her story of this ancient conflict she painted the same picture for me that she was presently to urge upon her American biographer, Gloria Fromm, of a falling-out that was entirely creditable to her, and wholly discreditable to him. It was, she said, revelatory of a mean streak that had unhappily been close under my father's skin. He had behaved, oh, very badly indeed, when she made her appeal to him on poor Crosland's account. She stood up to him and told him what he had to be told, about the things that gave away his lack of breeding. Jane should have done it, but she had never had the nerve to stand up to him, she had been afraid of him. So he had never become used to it. He didn't like it when people faced him. She had been taking a terrible risk when she did so, because she had known that standing up to him might mean the end of her copy-editing—and that would have hurt! It had taken her all her courage . . . and waiting for the axe to fall had been a strain too. He hadn't replied to her letter —she supposed that he had been too ashamed of himself to do so— and she'd been left in doubt for nearly two months before his next manuscript had come to her to be worked on. He had been like that, inconsiderate. He hadn't, she was sorry to have to say, quite possessed the instincts of a gentleman. There had always been, lurking in the background, something of the draper's assistant, something that was not altogether fine. You could never tell what might bring it out . . .

While she was telling me this my mind went back a decade, to the early thirties, and to a dinner party at which we had both been present. It is described, very much from Dorothy's point of view, in Gloria Fromm's sedulous but, in my opinion, uncomprehending biography.

At the end of the summer, she once again came face to face with the "arch-manipulator" of her young life. Just before she and Alan left London for Cornwall, they spent an evening at H. G. Wells's home in Regent's Park. Also present were the Baroness Budberg, who was introduced as Moura, and Wells's son Anthony West. . . . Anthony was something of a shock, she said, "looking tense & glowering far away at the back of himself" where she was sure he had withdrawn to "escape coercion of one sort or another." She hoped his young wife would help to draw him out. At the moment, however, it seemed to Dorothy that he could hardly speak—in her opinion because of the "attempts" that must have been made on his life. She felt she knew at first hand what such attempts were like.

Dorothy had been at her outrageous worst on that occasion. She had begun by treating my wife, who had already been given two "one-man" shows in West End galleries and was well into her professional career, as if she was some dubiously talented miss just out of the schoolroom, and by speaking to me as if I was an idiot child showing encouraging, and quite unexpected, signs of beginning to understand simple sentences and even a few of the longer words. When she'd done her best to put us down, she had settled to an evening of teasing my father for the naïveté of his shallow views on literature and any other subject that came up. Odle didn't have too much to say, but it was clear that he was enjoying the fun. They were both out to show their audience, consisting of Moura, my wife, and myself, that they weren't fooled by my father for a moment, and that they were doing an "amusing" piece of slumming by sitting down to table with the philistine pigmy who thought himself a giant, and who knew all about everything without understanding any of it.

At one of Dorothy's particularily exasperating sallies I found myself compelled to turn to him in incredulity, to see if he was going to let her get away with it. He met my eye, and with a glance told me that he understood my feelings, that he wished me to know that the situation was in his control, and that, despite appearances, everything was as he had expected it to be. To prove to me that it was so, he presently introduced a new subject with an apparently artless inquiry: had Dorothy had any news lately from her American friend, the wizard of Devonshire Place? She took the bait and plunged instantly into a breathless account of a wonder, performed the previous summer by the faith healer William Macmillan, rendered in the classic terms of

the "unsolicited testimonials" in the old-style patent-medicine adver-
tisements. Her man had, it appeared, taken up the case of a poor
paralysed woman who had been through the hands of twelve Scottish
doctors, as many Harley Street specialists, and the great Lord Horder
himself, in the space of six years, only to be told by each and every
one of them, that "medical science" was powerless to help her, and
that her condition was "absolutely incurable." It had taken Macmillan
less than a week to get her back on her feet and walking again.
Dorothy told my father that he could laugh at her story if he liked, but
she knew that her wonder worker was genuine. He had saved her
eyesight for her that winter. She had been sure that it was going, but
he had put the condition right with six weeks of treatment. What
exactly had her trouble been asked Moura. Dorothy wasn't sure. But
your eye man must have told you, prompted my father. She hadn't,
she admitted, consulted an eye doctor, and really couldn't say what
it had been. But Macmillan had known, and he had cured her, and that
was all that she needed to know. Macmillan was a brilliant psychologist, and if he didn't have any of the usual qualifications, he did have
valid intuitions, and that was what counted.

When Moura and the Odles had gone home at last, and my wife had
gone over to "Mr. Mumford's," the mews flat down at the end of the
back garden where we were spending the night, I had asked my father
what the point of Dorothy was. He had considered me for a moment,
and then told me that he thought of her as an extreme example of a
type. With the possible exception of her husband, she was the most
completely de-socialised human being he had come across outside of
a mad-house. She was an exaggerated caricature of solipsism in action. Alan Odle had been made for her—the one was mirror on the
wall to the other, invariably giving the right answer to the one really
important question—and even then it wasn't the extremity of their
self-regard that made them so remarkable, it was their isolation.

My father told me that night that he had been encountering people
of the same breed as the Odles, suffering with varying degrees of
intensity from their disabling conviction of their superiority to the
generality of mankind, ever since the days when he had seen Morris
drowning out the voices he didn't wish to listen to with his hand bell
in his Hammersmith boathouse. It had seemed to him then that what
had ailed Morris and his coterie had been their feeling that they were
doing the rest of the human race a favour merely by being alive. He'd
been studying the patterns of self-flattery and self-delusion of their

like with a fascinated repulsion ever since. The Odles were the speci-
mens of the breed that he was closest to and knew best. He'd come
to think of them as the exemplars of a social pathology—the thing that
had begun with the cult for the compensatory self-worship of Byron,
become epidemic with the propagation of the Goethe myth, and then
endemic as the anemia of the children of middle-class new money,
thinning their blood with the master idea that living without working
and beautifully being one's own very special and lovely self was the
highest human aim. The Odles had never had the feeling that they
owed the community anything, or that they had any reason to take
part in its collective life. They existed in the certainty that they had
been set apart from all common things by their terrible destiny. They
were people of culture, and it was their duty to the sacred cause of
art to stay clear of the degrading vulgarities of the market place, and
to have nothing to do with the mind-coarsening stupidities of the
world of getting and spending. In their eagerness to secure immunity
from such contagions they had embraced ignorance, and in their
dread of being poisoned by received ideas they clung to a world view
conceived entirely in terms of their own limiting preconceptions and
prejudices. They believed devoutly in the venality of the press, in the
mediocrity of all politicians, and the second-rateness of the political
game, in the greed and stupidity of all businessmen and traders, the
deadening influence of science and the scientific outlook, and the
menace of bigness as such. They had a particular horror of everything
to do with the United States, the possibilities of easy money that it
seemed to offer apart, a feeling so far beyond words that it could as
a rule only be expressed by the *visp* of a breath drawn sharply through
closed teeth. All experience but their own, and that of the chosen few
who, as they did, lived for art, was vulgar and without real meaning,
and so was all "mere" action and activity. They were above that sort
of thing, entirely.

I listened to my father's explanation of the Odles with mixed feelings. In it I felt that I could recognise fragments of things that I had
met with before. Most of his state-of-the-nation novels, of which *Tono-
Bungay* and *Kipps* are the types, include somewhere within them
fiercely expressed attacks on the softness and inconsequence of the
privileged children of the small winners in the social lottery, the men
and women who, like Dorothy Richardson's father, had taken the
inherited fruits of the upward struggles of their parents and cashed
them in so that they could live like the gentry, without toiling or

354

spinning, as comfortably as their modest unearned incomes would allow.

As my father had talked on, sticking to the pretence that Dorothy and Alan Odle were his subjects, I found it increasingly obvious that I was going to have to ask him the question *why* sooner or later: what had this most peculiar evening been all about? He surely couldn't have arranged it for his own pleasure or for mine. When I finally nerved myself to put it to him, what came out was my guess at the answer to the riddle, the suggestion that he wanted me to take Dorothy and Alan as a warning of what playing the artist could do to you. He looked at me from under his eyebrows with his head tilted a little forward in a way he had, and for a moment I was afraid that he might be going to lie to me. But if he considered the possibility, he very soon abandoned it.

"Yes," he said, "that's pretty much what I had in mind." This exchange marked the start of an era of frankness and plain speaking between us in which we achieved something like intimacy, and in which I learned a great deal about him that led me to love and respect him even more than I might have been naturally inclined to do. It was not, unhappily, to last for very long, and it ended badly, in the way that I have already described in giving my account of his last illness.

As those who can recall something of that account will be able to appreciate, the situation at the time of our final parting was such as to leave me with a strong feeling that too much had been left unresolved between us. A good deal of what I must own to have been brooding over the matter, in the year between my father's death and its final confirmation by the dispersal of his ashes, led me to the conclusion that the crux of it had been the wilful interpolation of a piece of fiction into the facts of my life. I had been represented to my father, at a time when his critical faculties were at a low ebb, and ebbing fast, as being caught up in something ugly that had no relation to any reality whatever. It occurred to me as I rehearsed the details of this piece of unmotivated malignancy that there was more than a possibility—it was discernible, to me at any rate, as a probability—that large parts of my father's record might soon be enriched and extended by the same simple process. It presented itself to me that it might be necessary for someone conscious of the danger to devote the necessary time and effort required to keeping the record of what my father had been, and of what he had stood for, more or less straight.

Those who did not live through the four or five years of anticlimax

355

that followed the defeat of the Axis powers as adults can have only the sketchiest idea of what they were like—so much was lost and gone, so much to be done, so much to be cleared away before it could be attempted, and so few signs that the necessary energy, resources, spirit, and money would ever be available. It was a time of exhaustion in which many people found my father's ideas of bringing about the transformation of society by getting men of good will together almost repellently irrelevant. In the public mind he stood for everything that the experience of total war and the fascist years had shown to be facile and false in liberal meliorism. The idea that any writer competent to do the job should wish to give up two or three years of his life to the biography of a man who was so obviously a survivor from a bygone time seemed to be in the nature of an absurdity. His standing had never been so low, and there seemed to be almost universal agreement with Lytton Strachey's verdict, pronounced in Cambridge all those years ago, that Wells simply wouldn't do. My passions, my interest, and my sense of justice told me otherwise. It seemed to me that my father was still very much alive in the thoughts of the more steadfast, and more realistic, section of the public that was then active in the implementation of the Marshall Plan, the conversion of the victorious military alliance into a greatly improved League of Nations, and the drive in the direction of a federalisation of Europe represented by the Common Market. It occurred to me that if nobody else was prepared to state the case for thinking of him as one of the more influential ancestors of the truly progressive outlook of today, doing that might be a pleasant way of paying my debts to him. I could try to show how much more to him there had been than the novelist who had lacked the patience to learn his business properly of the critical legend, and I might be able to justify Bertrand Russell's conclusion that he had been an important liberator of thought and imagination, and the stimulator of a sane and constructive approach to the consideration of social reform and the ethics of personal relations. In that frame of mind I entered on the course that has at last produced this book.

I began work on the project in 1948, and in the following year, when chance took me into the neighbourhood of her Cornish home for the summer, I looked up Dorothy Richardson in the hope that she might be inclined to either modify or add something to the unflattering portrait of my father as someone silly and obtuse that she had drawn in the latter part of *Pilgrimage*. She was then in her seventy-sixth year, and her age, the austerities of wartime, and the loss of her husband eighteen months earlier had all combined to pull her down. Alan Odle had gone out for a morning stroll one day in the middle of February 1948, a month after keeping his sixtieth birthday, and had dropped dead at the roadside before he had put more than a few hundred yards between him and their front door.

Dorothy had been dumbfounded by the abruptness with which he had been taken off, and still more so to find that she was the one who had been left alone. After a short period, in which she took refuge from the unacceptable fact in silence, she emerged to establish a substitute presence for Alan in her existence by plunging into the task of making an inventory of his drawings and designs. She had always thought of him as a generously creative spirit, and it astonished her to find how little there was to his oeuvre. One portfolio after another that was supposed to hold either a season's or a year's work, or the near realisation of some major undertaking for this private press or that, had proved to have virtually nothing in it. She had no alternative but to conclude that either Alan Odle had been a dedicated idler with a costive talent or the portfolios had been systematically stripped by thieves over the years. Understandably, she preferred to embrace the second of these possibilities, and, as understandably, she dropped the task of putting the disappointing legacy in order. In its place she assumed another, on which she was still theoretically engaged when I sought her out. At the time she was at pains to keep up her pretence that *Pilgrimage* was still a work in progress, and that her writing was leaving her very little free time. I could choose whether I would rather come in to take tea with her or look in for an hour or so after dinner —she never broke into her working rhythms by taking time out of her working hours for social lunches. So it was as we talked over the tea things—in a setting closely resembling that of Adrian Allinson's marvellous double portrait of the Odles as they were in the middle thirties —that she told me that what she had actually been doing for the past several months was to crawl back through *Pilgrimage* as it had been printed up in Dent's collected edition, searching that text for such printer's errors as might have escaped her attention and the eyes of its proofreaders. I do not know in just what spirit I asked if she was finding herself pleased with what she was having to read so closely as a piece of writing, but I was glad that I had done so, since she instantly told me that she was astonished to find how really good it was. "Sometimes," she said, "it just makes me crow with pleasure." She was, she

357

went on, beginning to understand why the novel had been so highly
thought of by so many people when Duckworth first brought it out.
This was something she had not really understood before—she had,
she now realised, created a work of art almost inadvertently as a
consequence of her absolute determination to give an entirely honest
account of the development of a single mind; she didn't believe that
anyone else had come as close as she had to a solution of the problem
of the point of view, not even Proust. My father, she went on, patting
my arm to show that she meant no offence, even though she had to
speak her mind, had never even begun to realise that there was such
a problem. This was because he had believed that there was such a
thing as science, and that it had a voice that he could borrow. He had
known that there was something lacking in his make-up that gave his
own voice a hollow tone. The trouble had been that he did not believe
in himself. That was because he had no proper interior life. He had
not wished to look into himself, and to explore his own being, because
if he did so he would be brought up against the fact of that deficiency.
It was because he knew himself to be a hollow man that he had made
so much of science. He had used scientific knowledge as spirits at
séances used the megaphones provided for them by mediums, to
compensate for the lack of resonance of their voices. It was his awareness that she possessed what he so completely lacked that had made
him so dependent upon her, and so demanding of what she had to
give. He had wanted to live through her, and he would have sucked
her dry if she had not had the courage to break away from him. It had
been a hard thing for her to do, because there had been the pathos
of something half-grown and tender about him. In their most intimate
moments their relationship had been that of mother and child, and it
had been agony for her to turn her back on his pleadings for what was
basically comfort and protection. But she had been forced to do it.
She would not have survived had she weakened. People were apt to
take him for a thinker who was interested in ideas, but he had once
told her that she thought too much and that she was messing up her
mind by entertaining too many new ideas. He had never been as
open-minded or as intellectual as she had, and he had often turned
to her for fuller explanations of concepts that were too difficult for
him in the forms in which he had encountered them. He had once told
her—it had been jokingly, of course, but he often expressed his
deeper feelings in that fashion because he shrank from open displays
of his real emotions—that if he were to be allowed to have only one

of the many women who had figured in his life to share in a rerun of it, she would have to be his choice. He had said this because he knew in his heart that she had understood him, and the irresolvable conflict between his instinctive and emotional real self and his assumed rational identity, better than anyone else.

It occurred to me while I was listening to all this that it was something that she had been through so often in her mind that she had come to believe in it as the reality of that experience of the winter and spring of 1906–1907 in which she had spent some scattered hours with my father trying, and failing, to achieve a few moments of purely physical harmony. I diverted the flow of her recollections and she was soon telling me how appallingly my father had behaved at the time of "poor Crosland's" death, and how she had been forced to stand up to him once again about that. We parted amiably on the understanding that I would come to have tea with her again later in the week.

We met again several times in the course of my holiday, usually over her teacups, but once over one of those ration-stretching meals that she used to take every so often at the small boardinghouse close to her cottage. The experience of getting to know her was a curious one, deeply coloured by the moment. In the European theatre the war had come to a flat end, giving very few people anything like a sense of victory. It was as if it had gone a long way off to die. The letdown was to be felt with a peculiar poignancy in places like that in which Dorothy was living, of which one had an ancient acquaintance. I had known her village as a child, at the age when summers seem to last forever. It forms part of the landscape which provides the background of sensation to John Betjeman's cliff top and beach poems of adolescence. The tide of war had swept over it to leave behind the usual wrack of mysteriously intended enclosures hemmed in by rotting barbed wire, vandalised temporary hutments, and dilapidated pieces of worn-out heavy equipment, such as concrete mixers and earth movers. Through this military slug trail the true spirit of the place manifested itself with haunting insistence, offering one stimulus after another to the recollection of childhood happiness. It was not possible to respond to any one of them without reviving the insistent thought that in those lost years something had gone terribly wrong in the world that must never be allowed to happen to it again. It was not just that so much more had been broken, wasted, and spoiled, this time than last, it was the warning proffered by the manner of its ending, in those two unthinkably destructive explosions, that if there was to be another trial of total war, the increase in the loss of lives and the wastage of laboriously created things would be so much greater that it could mean an end to living and creating as we understood such things. This is, of course, to take a subjective view of what was in the wind in those years, but I believe that it can, nonetheless, fairly be said to reflect the national mood of the time, and the general feeling throughout western Europe, that the world could no longer afford to run the risks entailed in letting a general war happen every so often, and that both men and nations would have to find more sensible ways of living together than those which we had grown up to think of as natural and inescapable.

My teas with Dorothy took me into another mental country. Her flight from the reality of Alan Odle's death into the text of the collected edition of all the volumes of her serial novel constituted more than a mere duplication of her flight into Sussex from the problems of her London life of 1907. This time she was trying to get right out of the world of common experience in order to start life all over again inside her own fantasy.

Dorothy was, though I wasn't aware of it then, going through a period of intense mental activity in which she was suffering from confusions of thought that brought her close to the condition in which her mother had done away with herself. This was a prelude to the lapse into senility that lay not far ahead of her, but that was not obvious. She still seemed to be her immensely and confidently talkative self, and the only hint she offered that anything might be going wrong was given by a heightening of her tendency to end by talking about herself no matter what subject had started her off. It was clear that she had experienced the war, but as clear that she had done so in her own way. Its focal point had been in Ealing while she was there, and in Constantine Bay when she had left London for Cornwall. She was convinced that her Cornish retreat had been the pivot on which the Allied effort had turned in the last year of the fighting in Europe. It had been there, on her doorstep, all around Padstow, that the army of liberation had been concentrated. She was marginally aware that what had been going on had troubled the even flow of a great many lives, and to bring it home to me what extraordinary departures from the normal the general disruption had enforced she told me how, one day towards the end of the conflict, she had gone into a café in Padstow with Alan, and not finding a table free, had taken seats at a table at which a young soldier was sitting alone. *He had turned out to be the son of a couple that she and Alan had known in earlier years but with whom they had long been out of touch!* There had been so many such happenings while the war was going on, occurrences so unlikely as to defy all rational explanation. One was compelled to believe that there had been a temporary lowering of the barriers between the worlds of the normal and the paranormal.

And it had not ended with the war. Her friend Mac, the faith healer, had achieved some of his most remarkable cures in the previous eighteen months, even though he was a tired man. . . . and she could not forget the strangely quizzical and appealing look that Alan had given her just before he left the cottage in which they had then been living for the last time. He had turned in the doorway before he had walked out to his death to ask her, in a peculiarly meaning tone, *if it was not unusually cold.* . . . It was as if he had known something . . . The scientists for all their talk about having the answer to everything had no explanations for such moments when their rules broke down.

As Dorothy maundered on after this fashion I spent part of my time marvelling at what there could have been in my father's make-up that had made it possible for him to put up with her patronising conde-scensions for so long, and the other part in growing almost fond of her and her unerring instinct for the wrong end of any stick. When I left Cornwall at the end of that summer I fully intended to keep in touch with her, but it was my fate to be out of the country for the next several years. When I returned I was sorry to find that she had died while I was away. At the beginning of the fifties her manner towards those she judged to be her inferiors had become too overbearing to be borne with, and she began to run into practical difficulties that made it impossible for her to go on living by herself. Her relatives had felt compelled to uproot her from the Cornish niche in which she felt that she had come to belong, in order to place her in a South London nursing home where they would be able to visit her more easily. She went under protest, and survived the move for little more than three years, for most of which she seems to have been largely inaccessible. It would be hard to say how dotty she actually became, since those who had her in their care had been so poorly briefed for the particular job that they were able to take her claim to have been a novelist for part of a pattern of delusions. When she took to telling her attendants that my father would soon be visiting her, and that she was going to let him know how disrespectfully they were treating her so that he would see to it that she was paid the attention due to her as somebody special, her threatenings were taken for part of the pattern. Poor old thing, they said to each other, on her good days she knows Wells has been dead for donkey's years just as well as the rest of us. When she died, in 1957, she had outlived him by just over a decade.

I have given all this space to someone whose real role in my father's life was that of a personal copy editor rather than a love, or even friend, partly because the relationship illuminates a certain aspect of his character, and partly because her use of it as the basis for a private mythology provides a perfect example of how it is with fabulists—those people who deal with unacceptable truths, by modifying them again and again until they have been transformed into more negotiable material. I wished to make it plain, by showing just what Dorothy did in the way of substituting her daydreams for her experience of life, that what I am saying that my mother did as a matter of settled habit is neither so very unusual nor, given her circumstances, all that hard to understand. The essential differences between the two women are, of course, very marked. But they are differences of scale rather than of kind, on a par with those that distinguish the drawing-room soloist from the primadonna who can fill and dominate the largest opera houses. But just as those two examples have singing in common, so Dorothy and my mother have their compulsion to improve the truth, and to persist in its improvement, between them. I would not for a moment suggest that their both being women has anything whatever to do with it—the transformation of the truth was the name of the game where the self-images of Gissing and Bland were concerned, and my father's *Autocracy of Mr. Parham* is a very direct critique of his own tendencies in the field. My only purpose in stressing the large part that fabulation has played in the lives and works of these two women has been to justify my contention that neither should be accepted as a reliable source for information about my father's character or behaviour. Recent biographers who have done so have been led far astray. It is my experience that neither woman can be trusted absolutely in anything that is in the nature of autobiography, and that both are at their least trustworthy in matters having to do with my father. They reveal themselves in their statements, but little else.

Some readers may feel inclined to dismiss this caution as no more than an invitation to take sides in an ugly family row. At the risk of lending some colour to this view, I must now bring up a piece of my personal history that can only seem on a first showing to be small beer of the meanest brew. In the early spring of 1928 a combination of stress and the normal adolescent crisis pulled me down and I began to waste away. Victorians would have said that I had gone into a decline, and would have accepted it as the sort of thing that happened when young people "outgrew their strength." But in the enlightened twenties, people had begun to expect more from their medical men than that, so first one doctor, and then another, and then a big gun with a title and a Harley Street consulting room came to my Kensington bedside to tap my chest and my back, finger my neck beneath my ears, charm me with a few moments of affable general conversation attuned to my youth and low state, and to withdraw to murmur the bad news to my mother in the downstairs drawing room. It looked like tuberculosis, they said in turn, and in turn said that certainty would have to wait upon sputum tests and x-rays. And in due course, with the tests made, and the photographs taken and developed, the verdict would be delivered.

Of the basic meaning of this diagnosis there was at that time no doubt: a disease for which there was no cure had laid its hands upon me. But that was not to say that my number was up. While tuberculosis was a killer in those days, and the death of thousands, it was also omnipresent, and far from inevitably fatal. Huge as the number of those it actually finished off in a given year might be, that of those it attacked, scarred, and spared was very much greater. And autopsies, which were more often made then than they are now, showed that in many cases those who had given it a lodgement at one stage or another in their lives remained unaware of the fact—for them the potentially deadly complaint had not been even serious. The view of my case taken by the authorities was not a grave one for these reasons. They held that the infection had been caught at an early stage, that it was a matter of a small spot on one lung, and that there was little cause for alarm. A few months of rest, country air, good plain food, and absolute quiet would be almost certain to put me right. It was much too soon to think of Switzerland—the time for that might come, but the contigency was a remote one. The right place for a case like mine was the place run by Dr. Morris at Kelling in Norfolk. Morris had a high success rate with his younger patients, and the probability was that I would be back in circulation before six months were out.

In the face of this situation my mother had two options: she could decide to thank her stars that things were no worse and to keep as calm as possible while Dr. Morris did his best for me, or she could milk it for such drama as could be squeezed out of it. My mother adopted the second course. Before long the atmosphere surrounding me was Spanish in its gloom, and my father had been given to understand that I was beyond hope. The six-month period that had been mentioned by the medical men was transformed into the term of my probable survival.

When this bad news reached my father he was filled with sympathy for my mother and concern for me: he felt that it was too bad that my career was to be cut short in this mouldy way, and thought that it might make it easier for me to bear up in the face of my troubles if I was made aware that I had some family, and that it was behind me. In pursuit of this somewhat confused thought of a beneficial rallying he presently brought my twenty-seven-year-old half-brother, George Philip, to my bedside. As they came into my sickroom I was playing the role of interesting invalid for all it was worth, lying very small and very flat under the covers, barely moving, and concealing to the best of my ability the pleasure I was getting out of being the centre of attention and indulged in every whim.

But my father was not only, as Shaw was later to complain, an irresistible charmer, he was also an energiser. He hadn't been at my bedside for more than ten minutes before he had me sitting up, the better to enjoy his presence. My half-brother, who had been inclined towards solemnity by the terms of the occasion, brightened visibly. Half an hour flashed by, and at the end of it, when my father told me that he was quite sure that I was going to get well in no time at all, I felt that he hd somehow taken charge, and that everything really was going to be all right.

By how much the content of this first moment of man-to-man complicity between us has enlarged itself over the years that have since gone by I can't say, but I remember it that from then on I was conscious that my illness meant one thing to my mother, and another, less dark and appalling, and more negotiable, to my father. I suppose that I might have felt very differently about his conviction that it lay in my power to get well quickly if I would but summon up the spirit to do so had I known how very wrong he had been about Jane's chances at the beginning of the previous year, but I knew nothing of that story then, and his magic was able to do the trick for me. When a big limousine from Daimler Hire in Knightsbridge came to the door a week or so later, to take me off on the long drive up into northern Norfolk, I was completely under his spell. As I climbed into the navy-blue machine, supported from one side by the uniformed and leathergaitered man who was to do the driving, and from the other by my mother, I had no feeling that I was about to be taken off somewhere to be ill. I was quite sure that, wherever the Kelling Sanitarium might be, I was going there to get well. I had no doubt of it, my father had told me so.

The truce of affliction between my parents had begun to break down even before I reached the place. A few days after his session at my bedside my father had written to my mother to reject the dark view of my prospects that she had proposed to him. She had taken marked objection to the implied rebuke, and when her angry rejection of his case for a qualified optimism was met by a somewhat less cautiously worded rebuttal in which my father had come out flatly for my chances of making a quick recovery, her anger, at what she had considered to be his callous—and in some way *selfish*—dismissal of the plain realities of my situation, became outrage. She fairly let him have it. The specialist had told her—and he was one of the best men in the field—that the most that I could hope for would be a life lived out on borrowed time as an invalid. I would have to go to some place abroad with a suitable climate. It was a pitiful thing to have to contemplate, but there it was, and he would have to learn to live with it. The future couldn't be ordered about to suit his book as he seemed to suppose. His reply was short. He'd had a good look at me. I'd looked washed-out and underweight. I might be going to die, but he didn't think it very likely. Nothing was going to stop him from looking forward to my early recovery.

I did very well in Dr. Morris' care, and each time that my mother came up from London to see me, making the journey in one of those ark-like Daimlers, hired, with the driver, for the weekend, she would find me a little less convincingly the dying boy. By the end of my first three Norfolk months it had become only too clear to her that she had painted herself into a corner, and that my father had been right about my prospects all along.

This was not at all to my mother's liking, and very soon after she had realised how things were going with me, the facts of my situation had begun to undergo a process of transformation that was to go on for years. Forty-three years later, when an advanced version of it was made available to a distinguished American academic, the story had been changed almost beyond recognition. It had been my mother who had been the first to see that my chances of recovery were good, and my father who had tardily come round to her view.

At the same time, wrong as the medical men had been when they had mistakenly asserted that my life was threatened by tuberculosis, I had really been in danger. What was ailing me was a highly selective clinical entity that had never been heard of before, and has never been heard of since, "an uncommon type of pneumonia then causing a number of deaths among what the medical journals called 'well nourished children.' "

I think that this fine example of the habitual fabulists fancy footwork was invented to explain why it was that my mother, having seen through the faulty prognosis of the professionals, was still so anxious about my condition as to have found it necessary to keep a deathwatch at the Kelling Sanitarium's gates for the first three months of my stay there. The American academic referred to above believes in this vigil, and he tells the readers of his little monograph on the relationship between my parents not only that it was a "black experience" for her but also that "its only redeeming feature" was that it gave her the courage to break off an affair with a lover whose inconstancy had become distasteful to her. I would have to suppose that she had been forced to summon him up into Norfolk to receive his dismissal if my memories of my first ninety days with Dr. Morris weren't perfectly clear. Through that phase of my cure my mother was coming to see me at intervals of two to three weeks. She would come into the district for the weekend, coming up from London on the Friday, spending three nights at one of the comfortable and club-like Edwardian golf hotels that served the seaside links at Cromer and Sheringham, and leaving for London again on Monday morning. She came and went in one of those big Daimlers every time because the railway journey from town was so inconvenient, and she kept the car and the driver while she was up there because she didn't feel that the local buses and cabs were to be relied upon. I'm not, incidentally, complaining that she wasn't coming to see me often enough. Far from it, I'd been going to boarding schools for most of the previous five years, and had become hardened to seeing very little of her in the longish stretches between holidays. While I was with Dr. Morris I saw more of her than I usually did in term time, and was conscious of being in luck in that respect. Between visits she was, of course, getting on with her normal social and professional life in London. Vigil there was not, but be that as it may, the story that the American academic had from my mother goes on to end as follows:

Finally the Doctor in charge of the sanitarium, alerted by the fact that Anthony had inexplicably been putting on weight and gaining strength, recognised that he had never had tuberculosis. Rebecca then consulted another specialist, the ranking authority of the day, who could also find no signs of present or past tuberculosis. From the case history he was of the opinion that the boy had been the victim of the peculiar type of pneumonia already mentioned.

This is all as pat and circumstantial as can be, and yet every chest x-ray that I have had since Dr. Morris discharged me from his care has borne upon it the unmistakable signature of a once active tubercular lesion. Some may assume, as my mother evidently did, that a scar on an internal organ might be expected to fade away and vanish in there in the warm dark in half a century or so. But that is not what happens with scarred lung tissue. In the case of a tubercular lesion, minute deposits of calcium build up at the boundaries of the regions of damage, defining them more and more sharply as the years go by. The correctness of the original diagnosis of my case is, consequently, a thing that has never been even arguable: since my brush with the complaint I have been walking about with confirmation of its accuracy stamped on my lung.

My opinion is that any attempt to find a motive for this singularly arbitrary piece of fabulation has to begin with another look at that "black experience." I don't think that it is to be disposed of by saying that my mother was an incurable self-dramatiser and leaving it at that. The notion, of a "black experience," has to have a point of crystalisation, however remote, in some experienced reality other than the stated one. The thing named clearly won't do in that role. While it may have been *boring* for my mother to keep on dragging herself all the way across East Anglia on those rides up into Norfolk, the language used seems too strong for the given case: keeping in touch with a child of one's own while it makes an unexpectedly rapid recovery from a potentially dangerous infection can't be deemed to rate very highly on the scale of black experiences. It is also hard to see just why, since the outcome was, conventionally at least, a happy one, the need for investing it with externally derived redeeming features came into the picture. It seems clear to me that transference has taken place, and that one actual experience is being discussed in terms of another that is less negotiable. I feel that a useful clue to this riddle is offered by the gratuitous interpolation of the information about the dismissal of the inconstant lover. Though it is carefully phrased in such a way as to eliminate the possibility that it might refer to my father, I am as good as sure that it does so.

This apparently perverse position is based on the ground that I became ill some six months after Jane Wells's death, at about the time that my mother was at last constrained to admit that the event that she had been praying for since 1917–1918, the removal of the woman at the centre of my father's life, was not going to make any difference to her one way or the other. She had been compelled to face the fact that even though there was now nothing to prevent him from doing so, he had not the slightest intention of asking her to marry him. If anyone was going to fill the place in his life that Jane's death had left vacant, it was going to be Odette Keun. This reading accounts, I think, for the curious evocation of courage as a leading product of the vigil-that-never-was at the sanitarium gates. It does take courage of a sort to own to oneself that one has foolishly given up a term of years to the pursuit of a *fata morgana,* and to cut one's losses before making a new beginning.

That was one thing; but the idea of a vigil, of a long wait for something disagreeable to happen that had not as yet occurred, was another that had to come from somewhere else. I believe that this was a matter of a tactical error she had made in her guerilla war with my father. When she first took me to the Kelling Sanitarium to hand me over to Dr. Morris, she had already sent the corrected galleys of her book of critical essays. *The Strange Necessity,* back to its publishers. It was due to appear in mid-July. She knew that she was in for a serious row with him as soon as he read it because it contained an unkind parody of his style at its worst that was offered to the reader as if it were a direct quotation from one of his novels. The thought of this coming battle had been hanging over her as she had quarrelled with him about how ill I really was in May, June, and the early part of July.

The Strange Necessity was one of those mid-life wagers that the nonacademic literary figure must make in order to achieve recognition as a serious critic. It was intended to convince those who knew her only as a literary journalist and a writer of *Saturday Evening Post* short stories that she had the root of the matter in her. As was more or less inevitable, given the year, and given the aim, the core of her presentation consisted of laudatory considerations of the innovative

fictions of Joyce and Proust. As inevitably, since she had been preco-
cious, and had made her debut as one of Ford Madox Ford's geniuses
in the days before the flood, she also had to begin with some ritual
disavowals of outdated allegiances. To clear herself of any Edwardian
taint she had included derisive put-downs of Shaw, Galsworthy, Arnold Bennett, and my father. It was while putting paid to his account
that she had made her technical mistake.

My mother had wished to finish my father off as quickly as possible
in order not to seem to be taking him over seriously. She had accordingly gone straight for the central defect in his fiction, the poverty of
those scenes in which his men and women had to reveal a developing
emotional interest in each other. My mother had wanted to illustrate
this shortcoming with a quotation from one of his novels, and she had
expected to find exactly what she needed in the pages of his novel
The Passionate Friends. She felt, with cause, that this was in that particular respect the weakest thing he had ever done. She had forgotten that
it was also, without any question, the most diffuse piece of writing to
which he had ever put his name. In the wordy fog she simply couldn't
find the essentially Wellsian man-to-woman exchange that she had
expected to find. But she had a gift for parody, a ready wit, and a sharp
ear, and it was child's play for her to invent a scene more Wellsian
than anything in Wells. In no time at all she had made one of his more
deplorable love scenes jerkily visible by the device, akin to the use of
stroboscopic lighting, of linking a series of ultra-Wellsian phrases
with strings of dots, thus: . . . . It was then that she made her mistake. She enclosed the whole thing in quotation marks. In this way a
legitimate critical *jeu d'espirit* was transformed into a piece of fabricated evidence. Beneath the overt crime, another subliminal one lay
hidden. My mother had given her archetypal Wellsian woman the
name *Queenie.*

To understand the force of this second blunder it is necessary to
remember that both parties to this episode had grown up in the
pre-1914 layered and class-ridden society in which there were even
class names. The first thing that would be settled between a newly
employed maid servant and her mistress in those days, for instance,
would be which of the house's permitted maid's names she was to
answer to—there would be no question of calling her by any of her
given names unless it was one appropriate to her station—menials
had to answer to menial names, identifying them as belonging below
stairs. My father always had a tin ear in this region, and his more

refined admirers often complained of the tiny flaw that allowed him to give his females such *awful* names—poor Weena of *The Time Machine* being a favoured case in point. The defect was brought up against him most frequently in the scandalous years after 1909, when St. Loe Strachey, the Webbs, their man Colegate, and such as Harley Granville Barker, were in full cry after him. It was then said that his use of names gave away the fact that he was no gentleman, and explained why he was incapable of behaving like one. Social change had begun to make that line of attack ridiculous by the end of the twenties, but there was still sting in the use my mother made of it. "Queenie" hadn't even been a servant's hall name—it had come from a still lower social level—it could belong to a sweatshop seamstress, a laundry hand, a popular barmaid, or a boardinghouse slavey who was on cosy terms with the male lodgers, some denizen of the lower depths in which Gissing had found his first two wives. In using it my mother had been playing with fire, her implication had been that he had a cockney imagination, and that he had never been able to rise above its limitations. My belief is that my mother came to realise that she had made these two blunders in some moment of retarded insight after the book had gone to the binders, when it was too late for her to do anything about them. Her black experience was that of waiting for the inevitable row that would dispel her last shadow of a hope that something might still be saved from the wreckage of their relationship.

In due course, in mid-July, the day of reckoning came. Who, my father asked her, was she to condescend to him? He was not impressed by her as a highbrow critic. He did not think that anyone else would be. She had an elaborate, intricate, and allusive style that was admirable for demonstrating her own cleverness—but when she applied herself to first and last things, all that it did was to show her up as a lightweight. It was the story of *The Judge* all over again. She'd been meaning to show the world that she was a second Dostoevsky when she wrote that one, and it hadn't come off. She would have to learn to recognise where she belonged. She had found her level as one of the star turns in Ray Long's stable; she was a storyteller, like Willie Maugham. If she was smart she would build a lasting and prosperous career on the narrative talent that Long had recognised. *The Strange Necessity* was an aberration; all she had proved by it was that she didn't begin to understand what she was really good at.

My father's opening blast was met with a counter blast, and one of the pair's long-drawn-out exercises in mutual exasperation began. The gulf between them widened as the insulting letters that had become their only link flew to and fro. My father was still, the Somme battles and every other human folly notwithstanding, the worshipper of the Great Encyclopedia, and of the Encyclopedists. He was, as he was always to remain, indissolubly wedded to the pursuit of the Enlightenment. He held firmly to the proposition that there was an objective reality out there about which there was a verifiable truth to be ascertained, and that the worst of treasons to the human cause was to pretend that mere prejudices and suppositions were knowledge, and to propagate error by so doing. One of his pet aversions was for Matthew Arnold, whose conceptions of the social responsibilities of the individual he was inclined to admire, but the generality of whose ideas he despised and detested. He took particular exception to Arnold's sustained efforts to make his contemporaries turn their backs on the sciences on the ground that Lucretius and the classical philosophers had known all that mankind needed to know about the nature of things, and that all the sciences had to offer was a mere proliferation of facts. The worst of Arnold's crimes in my father's eyes was his advocacy of the thesis that the truth of things had to be something grander and nobler than any set of qualities and attributes attached to material objects and observable phenomena. For him the really worthwhile research lay not in the exploration of the vast deserts of the tangible and the ascertainable, but in the cultivation of an inner life. My father had no use at all for Arnold's belief that the truth consisted of the sum of insights given to the very best people when they looked into their own hearts.

My mother, when it came right down to it, was of Matthew Arnold's party. Even though she had a violent antipathy to whatever it was in him that had made him the coiner of the vulgarly sentimental slogan *sweetness and light,* she had every sympathy with what she understood him to mean by it—a species of spiritual radiance generated by the culturally and intellectually privileged elite class of an ideally layered society. This was, of course, one in which artists and poets were the unacknowledged legislators, and emotion and intuition the ultimate values. It was Arnold's stance that my mother attempted to adopt in the later stages of the correspondence, but my father wasn't having any. He told her that it wasn't a bit of good for her to come it over him as the complex of finer feelings known as a dedicated artist, or to bring up dear old Henry J's self-serving guff about the primacy and

the singular beauty of the creative process. The place where she liked
to meet her kindred spirits was The Ivy. She knew as well as he did
that the arts had come in with full bellies and spare time, and that
careers devoted to contemplation and the inner life were features of
societies that boasted such institutions as caste, slavery, and invest-
ments. The Greeks with their slave-operated silver mines and the
Indians with their sweepers and their untouchables to do the dir-
tywork were the boys for higher spiritual values. My mother became
rattled when she realised that he simply had no use for anything that
she might have to say about the artist's priestly function as a mediator
between the divine world of instinct and impulse revealed to the
intuitions and the humdrum realm of everyday experience and reason. He seemed to really mean it when he described telling the truth
as the latest and most promising achievement of the human mind, and
to be wholly serious when he went on to posit a new culture based on
the concept of scientific method. Its literature was to be the antithesis
of the existing one of fantasy and make-believe, objective, precise in
statement, absolute in candour, and intolerant of prejudice and falsifi-
cation. My mother recoiled from the deliberate philistinism of it, and
the hint of something personal in the suggestion that one of the things
required of the writer of the future would be an absolute honesty. She
unwisely countered this by introducing the topic of my father's decision to make Odette Keun's home in Provence the new center of his
activities in succession to Easton Glebe. She did this in her own way,
by warning him that his ideas were beginning to sound grotesquely
eccentric, as if he was losing touch with his intellectual peers. He was,
when all was said and done, a considerable person; it would be tragic
if he were to hide himself away in a world of private references in a
provincial backwater. My father, who had been sitting on the issue of
those quotation marks up to this point, now threw them at my mother
with bitterness. Odette, he told her, might be wild, and when she was
wound up she might be a compulsive talker, but at least she was
honest. She would never have found it possible to do what came to
my mother as naturally as breathing. My mother had made something
up, pretended it was his, and used it as supporting evidence when she
wanted to pull down his reputation as a writer. He had never put a
character called Queenie into a book, ever. My mother came back at
him, but not responsively to the issue. He had no right to object to
what she had done. He had always been her enemy professionally. He

had run down the merits of both *The Return of the Soldier* and *The Judge* behind her back, and he had often tried to sabotage her career by turning editors and publishers against her. He gave her a very short answer to these charges. When she brought them forward, she was lying, and she knew it as well as he did. The correspondence was abruptly over. He had sickened of it, and he dropped it.

My mother was outraged when my father turned his back on her in this way. He was quite unaware that he had committed an unpardonable offence by doing so. It was, on the contrary, his impression that he had cleared the air with a timely piece of plain speaking and put an end to a lot of nonsense. When he came up into Norfolk to see me a few weeks later he was in a jolly mood, and obviously of the opinion that a cloud had been lifted from our relationship. I was up and about by that time, and allowed off the sanitarium grounds for as long as four hours at a stretch when I had a visitor who wished to take me out to lunch. This made it possible for him to take me over to Wells-next-the-sea, a place, on beyond Blakney Point, with miles of salt marshes and the cold North Sea on one side of it, and Holkham Park on the other. It was a lark-haunted countryside that he remembered with affection from his cycling days. When we'd had a scratch lunch there under an arbour in a public-house garden we strolled out along the track across the saltings that took us to the Life Boat Station. While we were there he made me take a photograph of him with the Vest Pocket Kodak he had sent me for my birthday back in the beginning of August. He posed himself for it, standing out on the launching ramp in front of the boathouse with the untroubled September sea behind him, and when I'd finished he said, "There you are now, you've got a picture of Wells-next-the-sea at Wells-next-the-sea." In the moment in which he floated off this endearingly flat little jocularity he became an extrapolation of one of his own characters—a Mr. Polly, perhaps, who had been allowed to become a father, or a secure Art Kipps, to whom it had been permitted to live comfortably with himself and his good fortune. I would like to leave him there, in the warmth of those remembered instants of shared affection and laughter in which he was so beguilingly the father of my dreams, but to do that would be to present him in terms of the needs of a lonely and neglected child. In his own person he was so much more than that. The kindly, generous, impatient, but in the main good-natured individual of my mature knowledge who possessed the marvellous imagination, who wrote all the books, who looked so far and so searchingly into the past and into the future, and who cared so profoundly about the present well-being and the future happiness of the whole foolish race of men, transcended his origins and made himself a very big man indeed.

Notes and References

PAGE

5   "*. . . Marriage*" Book review: RW, *The Freewoman,* September 19, 1912.

5   "leave his position in no doubt . . ." Letter: HGW to RW, February 1913.

6   "He broke off the affair . . ." Letter: HGW to RW, June 1913.

6   "Amber Reeves . . ." Oral communication: AR to author.

10   "William Pember Reeves" Oral communications: HGW, ESPH, and others.

10   "Sidney Webb hated . . ." Oral communication: GBS (1948) Diaries BW. 1906–1910: *passim.*

11   ". . . how she intended to proceed . . ." Biography: BW, Kitty Muggeridge and Ruth Adam, 1967.

12   ". . . poor little Amber . . ." *Ibid.*

12   ". . . At this point . . ." Letter: GBS to BW. September 30, 1909.

13   ". . . Sexual irregularity . . ." Muggeridge and Adam, *op. cit.*

16   "Henry James avoided him . . ." Diary: Sidney Waterlow, November 29, 1911.

16   ". . . Blanco White . . ." Oral communication. AR to author.

20   ". . . he wrote to my mother . . ." Letter: HGW to RW, January 1914.

21   "Not long after his return . . ." Article, *N.Y. World,* January 1, 1909.

24   ". . . he had the bad luck . . ." Four counts of criminal libel had been alleged against Douglas, and the hearing, in the Central Criminal Court began on November 19 and ended eight days later. There was a hung jury, and the prosecutor entered a plea of nolle prosequi on December 11. See William Freeman: *Life of Lord Alfred Douglas.* See below note to p. 350.

24   ". . . manchild' . . ." Letters: HGW to RW and to RR, August 1914.

25   ". . . but in surrounding herself with staff . . ." Correspondence: HGW to RW and return, 1914–1920, *passim.*

27   ". . . she *said* he was her Mr. West . . ." The development of this cover story may be followed in a sequence of letters:

HGW to RW, February to October 1914. It is seen "in place" in a letter: HGW to RR, July 1914.

28 "My father did his best . . ." Letter: HGW to RW, April 1915.

29 "The tone of Ford's South Lodge years . . ." Memoir: *Portraits from Life*. Ford. 1937. Like everything else from Ford dealing with the real world, the whole is more or less true but no detail can be relied upon.

30 "Ford was a sweet man . . ." See memoirs: David Garnett, *Golden Echo*; Violet Hunt, *Flurried Years*; Douglas Goldring, South Lodge; and Biography: *FMF*, Arthur Mizener.

32 ". . . Wilma Meikle . . ." All, and rather more than all, that can be said in favour of this marginal figure was well put in a review: WM, *Towards a Sane Feminism,* RW. *Daily News,* November 17, 1916.

32 ". . . wrote dismally to tell an old friend . . ." Letter: RW to SKR, February 4, 1916.

32 ". . . wrote sadly to him . . ." Letter: RW to HGW, September 19, 1916.

36 ". . . she had, on the contrary . . ." Letter: Jane to HGW, August 4, 1914.

38 ". . . but as it happened . . ." Letter: HGW to Jane, mid-April 1915.

41 ". . . poor, unhappy George Gissing . . ." Recorded in Diary: Sydney Waterlow, December 7, 1907. ". . . The irredeemably provincial lout . . ." Letter: HJ to VH, July 4, 1903.

42 ". . . apropos *The Passionate Friends* . . ." Letter: HJ to HGW, September 21, 1913.

42 "He took up his pen . . ." Letter: HGW to HJ, September 21, 1913.

42 ". . . had joined forces with Edmund Gosse . . ." Letter: HJ to HGW, March 20, 1912.

42 ". . . his instant refusal . . ." Letter: HGW to HJ, March 25, 1912.

43 ". . . wouldn't at all do among us . . ." Letter: HJ to EG, March 26, 1912.

46 ". . . a ponderously warm manner . . ." Diary: TH. 1886, quoted in Biography: *The Early Life of TH*, Florence Emily Hardy, 1928.

47 ". . . someone else . . ." This is Mr. Blandish's butler, Mutimer. The name is borrowed from GG's novel *Demos* where, possibly significantly, it is attached to a character

who reads books for what he can get out of them while remaining indifferent to their aesthetic value or lack of it.

47 "... talking very freely about him behind his back ..." It was HJ's unlovable habit to be two-faced in this way. See, for an example, his praise of *Tess* to TH's face, and his denigration of that novel as vile to Robert Louis Stevenson.

48 "... soon to allow him to believe ..." Letter: HJ to WJ and AJ, December 12, 1915.

48 "It is art that makes life ..." Letter: HJ to HGW, July 10, 1915. "I don't clearly understand ..." Letter: HGW to HJ, July 14, 1915.

50 "... the consequences of radical improvement ..." Book: E. B. Ashmore (O.C. Defence of London 1916–1919), *Air Defence* 1929.

50–51 "... soon after he had reached ... his home ..." Letter: HGW to RW, September 13, 1917.

52 "... to make the World State his mistress ..." Letter: HGW to RW, September 18, 1917.

57 "Later in her life ..." The development of this entirely fabricated case may be traced from its first appearance in the letter quoted above, RW to SKR, March 21, 1923; through an intermediate form in *HGW, His Turbulent Life and Times,* biography; Lovat Dickson, Chap 17, p. 292 and onwards; through an expanded and more specific version offered by Norman and Jeanne MacKenzie, *The Time Traveller,* Chap 21, pp. 336–340; and on from there to its final version, accompanied by much highly suspicious documentation (drafts of letters not elsewhere recorded, variously dated memoranda, and alleged extracts from diaries, originals for which may possibly exist) made much of in Gordon Ray, *HGW and RW. Op. cit.*

59 "There was the cook ..." *Ibid.,* p. 61.

59 "... a 'drunken old Major ..." *Ibid.,* p. 108.

59 "... my father's pocket diary ..." HGW's pocket diaries are in the Wells Papers.

60 "The proprietor of the Hotel ..." Ray, *op. cit.,* p. 117.

61 "Finally we settled for the night ..." *Ibid.,* p. 122.

62 "Since 1916 he had been ..." HGW joined The League of Free Nations Association in the year after its foundation by Leonard Woolf and others.

PAGE

63 ". . . a conference with Sir William Tyrrell . . ." Autobiography: HGW, Chap 9, Sec 6.

64 ". . . a biologist's history . . ." HGW's declaration of intent in this matter was printed in the September-October 1918 issue of The League of Nations Union's magazine *Today and Tomorrow.*

66 ". . . making him a rich man . . ." Bank books and working ledgers will be found in the Wells Papers.

67 ". . . Winston Churchill had been right . . ." Letter: WC to HGW, Wells Papers.

68 ". . . outbreak of war between Poland and Russia . . ." Georg von Rauch, *A History of Soviet Russia,* p. 117.

68 ". . . Masaryk told him . . ." Oral communication. HGW to author.

69 ". . . the Russians had won a second major victory . . ." G. von R., *op. cit.,* p. 118.

70 "in August . . ." Wells Papers.

71 "He had been staying with my mother . . ." Oral communication: RW to author.

72 "Guchkov and Miliukov . . ." G. von R., *op. cit.,* p. 40.

72 "My father heard no laughter . . ." Oral communication: HGW to author. See also Nina Berberova *The Italics are Mine,* 1969.

73 "she was still in the nightmarish situation . . ." Oral communication. MB to author.

76 ". . . that Philip Snowden's wife . . ." She was there as a member of the Second International's Delegation which had been sent out to express the Social-Democratic movement's solidarity with the Menshevik regime then in power in Tiflis with the support of the Georgian nationalists. See G. von R., *op. cit.,* p. 122.

77 ". . . but whatever Lenin may or may not have said . . ." Articles: HGW. *The Dreamer in the Kremlin, Petersburg in Collapse, Daily Express,* 1920, and book: *Russia in the Shadows,* same year.

79 "There is, for instance, no doubt . . ." Berberova, *op. cit.,* p. 191, reports an occasion on which Vladislav Khodasevich and Gorky compared notes as to what had happened to them on their separate visits to this hostel.

82 "He gave the book to Churchill for review . . ." Articles: WC reviewing HG, December 15; HGW in rebuttal, December 16, 1920, *Daily Express.*

82 "This convincing proof . . ." Correspondence and contracts relating to these matters will be found in the Wells Papers.

83 ". . . Margaret Sanger . . ." Novel. HGW. *Secret Places of the Heart.* Although this is a work of fiction it gives a quite literal account of the impression that MS made upon HGW, and of his ideal of what a *passade* should be.

91 "a sprawl of a book . . ." Letter: HGW to RW, August 1922. The criticism has merit.

92 "I have tried to leave . . ." Letter: RW to SKR, March 21, 1923.

94 "At that point, in June 1923 . . ." Letter: GPW, March 1976 issue of *Books and Bookmen,* established correct chronology of this episode. Oral communications: HGW, ESP.

95 "My mother saw her . . ." Oral communication: RW to GR, 1971 or 1972, quoted in Ray, *op. cit.*

96 "If I live, write to me . . ." Draft letter: RW to HGW, alleged date, June 1913. Actual date composed, unknown.

100 "The record shows. . ." Pocket diaries: HGW, *op. cit.,* and correspondence, HGW-RW, *passim.*

100–101 "The first letter that he had . . ." Letter, RW to HGW, November 3, 1923. "If, he told her . . ." Letter: HGW to RW, November 19, 1923.

101 "Why in heaven's name . . ." Letter: HGW to RW, November 26, 1923. ". . . that he doesn't exactly . . ." Letter: HGW to RW, November 27, 1923.

102 "What difference could . . . marriage . . ." Letter: HGW to RW, December 15, 1923.

103 "My father was a good friend . . ." My mother's fear of what AB might be recording of HGW's confidences in his diaries apart, RW's intense dislike of him at this time was fueled by the pianist Harriet Cohen's very evident liking for him.

104 ". . . living with Gorky in the Villa Sorrito . . ." Mussolini had given Gorky permission to live anywhere in Italy except Capri, in the spring of 1924, after he had been allowed out of Russia. For life in the villa, see Berberova, *op. cit.,* pp. 192–197.

105 "She appears close to the end of its second volume . . ." Novel: HGW, *The World of William Clissold,* Book IV, Sec 14.

110 "Elizabeth Russell . . ." The last avatar of the former Mary Beauchamp, and one time Elizabeth von Arnim, who had married Bertrand Russell's older brother, the second Earl Russell in 1916. Born in the same year as HGW, she had made a hit with her first novel in 1898, published under the

nom de plume "Elizabeth." She had a long and modestly successful career which was brought to end by the publication of her eleventh novel in 1934. It was unkindly, but probably truthfully, alleged that each of her novels marked the ending of a personal involvement. She was involved with HGW from the autumn of 1911 until the early summer of 1913, and from then on a friend. Pussy would scratch when aggravated, but her line was detached irony and she rarely lost her cool.

113 "When Jane began to die . . ." Oral communications: HGW, GPW, FRW, Peggy Wells, Julian and Juliette Huxley, and others.

120 "Bennett also noted . . ." Journals: AB, Vol. III. Bennett did not approve of my father's way of handling himself at this time, and let him know it. This finally broke the back of their longstanding friendship, already strained by HGW's inability to conceal his belief that AB had made a terrible mistake when he took up with Dorothy Cheston Bennett. It did not make matters easier between the two men when events proved that HGW was right about this. The two men had not been reconciled by the time of AB's death, which was, for that reason, doubly painful for HGW to have to accept.

125 "I shall look to America . . ." For HGW's arguments supporting this opinion see *The World of William Clissold,* 1926, and *After Democracy,* 1932, a pamphlet that expanded an address given to the Liberal Party's summer school in that year.

132 "In the spring of 1934 . . ." Autobiography: HGW, Chap 9, Sec 9.

138 ". . . to be run in the issue following that in which it was to appear . . ." The interview ran in the NS and N for November 10, 1934, Shaw's commentary on November 17, 1934.

141 ". . . in successive issues . . ." *Time and Tide,* October 13, 20 and 27, 1934, under the general title *Wells the Player,* a literal translation of Odette's *Wells le Comedien.*

142 ". . . when Amber Reeves presently told him . . ." Oral communication, AR to author.

142 ". . . Apropos of Dolores . . ." Novel: HGW, 1935.

147 ". . . between 1935 and the end of 1940. . ." HGW was, of course, 69 in 1935.

148 ". . . a modernized version of the Bill of Rights . . ." Letter: HGW to the Editor, the *London Times,* October 23, 1939.

PAGE

155 ". . . my grandfather, Joseph Wells . . ." Autobiography: HGW, Chap 1, Sec 3.

157 ". . . the owner of Redleaf . . ." Though important in this role in the present context, he has a more solid claim to fame as an enthusiastic art collector. He had accumulated three hundred and twenty-eight canvases by living artists by the time of his death, and was the chief backer of the new naturalistic and anti-romantic school of painting of which Sir Edwin Landseer was the leading exponent.

158 ". . . in the summer, directly the day's work . . ." Autobiography: HGW, Chap 1, Sec 3.

159 ". . . had walked into and out of at least three . . ." *Ibid.*

159 ". . . Uppark . . ." The mistaken usage "Up Park" has been copied from book on book on Wells, following the lead given by him in his autobiography. My father was, however, relying on memory when he adopted it, and what was in his mind was the usage of the servants' hall. There is a considerable documentation of Uppark as a property, and as a work in architecture, and this leaves no doubt that Uppark is the correct form. A full account of house is to be found in Nairn and Pevsner, *The Buildings of England,* Sussex, Penguin Books, 1973, pp. 358–360; and a fuller, more aesthetically responsive, treatment of it is to be found in the beautifully illustrated *English Country Houses: Vol II, Mid Georgian, Country Life,* London, 1956, pp. 29–40.

160 ". . . Sarah Neal . . ." Diary: SW. Wells Papers. Unpublished.

165 ". . . my grandfather's new employer . . ." Oral communication: Sir Charles Shuckburgh, present owner of the property.

165 ". . . Sarah Wells, as she now was . . ." Diary: SW. *Op. cit.*

178 "This may sound like a purely fantastic notion . . ." Autobiography: HGW, Chap 1, Sec 4.

179 "My father drops his account of the accident." *Ibid.*, Chap 1, Sec 5.

183 ". . . with Fred gone . . ." *Ibid.*, Chap 3, Sec 1.

187 "He reproduced the letter . . ." Letter: HGW to SW, July 4, 1880.

188 ". . . Tom Pennicott of Surly Hall . . ." Autobiography, HGW, Chap 3, Sec 4. ". . . Alfred Williams . . ." *Ibid.*

188 "It is customary . . ." Biography: *The Time Traveller,* Norman and Jeanne MacKenzie, Chap: *Little Bertie,* pp. 38–39.

189   "Almost as soon as he had moved into Cowap's house . . ."
Autobiography: HGW. Chap 3, Sec 7.

192   "But then, when the start is made . . ." Letter: HGW to SW,
reproduced in facsimile, Autobiography: Chap 4, Sec 3.

199   ". . . when my father went off . . ." *Ibid.*, Chap 5, Sec 6.

201   ". . . Briggs . . ." *Ibid.*, Chap 6, Sec 6.

201   ". . . apologising . . ." Letter: HGW to SW, October 14, 1891.

201   ". . . teaching . . . at the Tutorial College . . ." Letter: T.
Ormerod to Editor, *Manchester Guardian,* August 21, 1946;
in this brief memoir a former pupil shows what a good
teacher HGW had very quickly become.

202   ". . . *The Educational Times . . .*" My father had an inside track
with this publication as a fellow member of Briggs's staff,
Walter Low, who was his best friend in those days, was
editing it in his spare time. Low, whose Jewish parents had
moved from Hungary to London, had a daughter named
Ivy who grew up to be a novelist of merit and wife to that
same Maxim Litvinov who became Chicherin's successor as
Soviet Russia's Commissar for Foreign Affairs. My father
had kept in touch with Walter Low's wife and daughters
after his untimely death in 1895, and his link to Litvinov
through Ivy Low undoubtedly played its part in making
HGW's interview with Stalin the friendly occasion it
was.

203   "It took place in a house in Wandsworth . . ." Autobiography:
HGW, Chap 7, Sec 2.

204   ". . . redolent of shag tobacco . . ." Letter: HGW to Eliz
Healey, Wells Papers, January or February 1888.

204   ". . . my grandmother's Indian summer . . ." Diary. SW. *Op.
cit.*

205   ". . . it still must have been very hard for my grandmother
. . ." My father saw this, and moved the reassembled menage to better quarters not far off in Liss during the winter
of 1895–1896.

205   ". . . he found Fred on his doorstep . . ." Autobiography:
HGW, Chap 6, Sec 6.

207   ". . . honest, sober, decent and pleasant . . ." *Ibid.*

208   ". . . it is true that . . ." *Ibid.*

208   ". . . J.M. Barrie's *When a Man's Single* . . ." *Ibid.*

209   ". . . Not bad is it?" Letter: HGW to FJW, October or November 1893.

PAGE

210 "... Elizabeth Healey..." Letter: EH to HGW, Wells Papers.

211 "... she had persuaded her mother ..." Autobiography, HGW, Chap 7, Sec 1.

212 "... He had a burden of another kind ..." While much that is said of Mrs. Robbins in the following pages is drawn from HGW's autobiography, more is derived from a series of conversations with a cousin and former schoolmate of Jane Wells's who gave me a mass of information about the Robbinses and their reactions to the elopement. Chance had made us neighbours in the Hampshire village in which I was living in the early forties.

212 "But just at that juncture ..." Autobiography: HGW, Chap 8, Sec 1.

213 "When my father was summoned ..." *Ibid.*

215 "The first blow ..." *Ibid.*

216 "Henley came to the rescue ..." Letter: WEH to HGW. July 1894.

216 "Rather!" Letter: WEH to HGW, September 1894.

216 "It was a growth ..." Oral communication: HGW to author.

217 "Henley was delighted ..." Letter: WEH to HGW, September 28, 1894.

219 "He always contended..." Biography: Kennedy Williamson, *W.E. Henley.* 1930.

222 "If I needed a flavour ..." Essay collection: HGW, *Select Conversations with an Uncle,* 1895, *A Misunderstood Artist.*

222 "... on its second day ..." Autobiography: HGW, Chap 8, Sec 1.

223 "... Henley referred him ..." Oral communication: HGW to Author.

224 "... there was proof ..." Biography. Kennedy Williamson, *op. cit.*

225 "... an ogre's castle ..." For the ambivalence of feeling about the great house as an institution see passages *in re Bladesover* in Novel: HGW, *Tono-Bungay, passim.*

228 "made to my father's order ..." Autobiography: HGW, Chap 8, Sec 2.

229 "... John Bull ..." Memoirs: Edgar Jepson recalls this incident in his *Memories of a Victorian,* and for an account of it from GBS see Grant Richards; *Author Hunting.*

230 "We need not go further ..." Review: *The Speaker,* April 18, 1896.

PAGE

230 ". . . The Athenaeum . . ." Review: May 9, 1896.

231 ". . . parody the work of the creator . . ." Review: *The Guardian*, June 3, 1896.

232 ". . . James Brand Pinker . . ." Letter: JBP to HGW, January 13, 1896. Pinker liked driving blood hackneys in tandem, and boasted of having once covered 35 miles in an hour in one of his rigs.

233 ". . . developed into something inhuman . . ." *The Time Machine*, Chap III.

234 "The stranger came . . ." *The Invisible Man*, Chap 1.

234 "The opening chapters . . ." *Love and Mr. Lewisham*, Chap 1, Line 1, Page 1.

238 ". . . The sort of man 'who . . ." Biography: Siegfried Sassoon, *George Meredith*, 1948, p. 230.

239 ". . . Shorter's Dining Club . . ." Biographies and Memoirs: Siegfried Sassoon, *op. cit.*; W. Robertson Nichol, *A Bookman's Letters*; ESPH, *A Lawyer's Notebook* (successive vols); and E. Clodd, *Memories*, along with Jepson, *op. cit.*, and Grant Richards, *op. cit.*, these books open a door on the world of my father's bread and butter masculine associations.

239 ". . . the two avuncular operators . . ." Diary: GG. July 13, 1895. Letter: GG to E. Bertz, August 27, 1895.

241 "a man whose natural mode . . ." Autobiography: HGW, Chap 8, Sec 3. ". . . the less said about it . . ." Letter: GG to HGW, November 27, 1896.

241 "Gissing's home life . . ." *et seq.* Letters: GG to Bertz, August 15, 1890, September 6, 1890, October 23, 1890, January 23, 1891.

244 ". . . the wee, fantastic, Wells . . ." Letter: Rupert Brooke to Hugh Dalton, April 1898.

245 ". . . and so, on July 29 . . ." Autobiography: HGW, Chap 8, Sec 4.

246 ". . . you delight me . . ." Letter: GG to Jane, August 18, 1898.

247 "Hick had been positively . . ." Oral communication: HGW to author.

249 "Gissing had asked . . ." Autobiography: HGW, Chap 8, Sec 3. Diary: GG, July 6, 1898.

249 ". . . 'Mlle Fleury,' . . ." Letter: GG to HGW, July 30, 1898. "The letter in which Gissing gave my father this news . . ." An educated guess at what it was about the letter in which GG gave HGW this news that exasperated the latter

so greatly can be made after reading Letter: GG to Bertz, November 1, 1898, which handles the same topic.

250 "Well, my dear boy . . ." Letter: GG to HGW, August 27, 1898.

250 "The falling out was put behind them . . ." Letter: GG to HGW, September 1, 1898.

250 "I need not tell you that . . ." Letter: GG to Bertz, February 24, 1902.

251 ". . . semi-aristocratic connections . . ." Letter: GG to Morley Roberts, February 6, 1899. ". . . comfortable circumstances . . ." Letter: GG to Bertz, November 1, 1898.

252 ". . . literary acquaintances of a kind . . ." *Ibid.*

252 "It had taken Gissing a little more . . ." See Letters: GG to Clara Collet, HGW, Jane, Morley Roberts, and Gabrielle; and, further, Gabrielle to these correspondents, *passim*, for the progressive decay of GG's belief in the standing of the Fleurys over this period, see, especially, Gabrielle to Jane, July 12, 1901.

253 "It took the combined efforts of . . ." Autobiography: HGW, Chap 8, Sec 3; and Memoir: Henry Hick, *Recollections of George Gissing.*

254 "Gissing was at last persuaded . . ." GG's French medical man, Dr. Chauffard, had told him it was safe to do this earlier, but GG had been unable to take the word of a foreigner on such a point.

254 ". . . a series of letters . . ." A typical example is Letter: Gabrielle to HGW, June 24, 1901.

254 ". . . Gabrielle went on writing at him through Jane . . ." See, for example, Letter: Gabrielle to Jane, July 12, 1901.

258 ". . . in the initial phase of his reappearance . . ." Letters: both parties to this correspondence were almost compulsive as letter keepers (though see foreword) and the greater part of the exchange survives in the Wells Papers.

259 ". . . in the Jura . . ." This incident is referred to obliquely and misleadingly in *The Time Traveller,* Part 3, Chap 11, where it is said to have led to a serious quarrel between the two men. It did not, and they were better friends than ever when their holiday came to an end.

260 ". . . a telegram . . ." Autobiography: HGW, Chap 8, Sec 3. Morley Roberts gives his fictionalised version of these events in *The Private Life of Henry Maitland,* 1912.

262 ". . . Tono-Bungay . . ." The episode based on GG's last days

runs through sections 6 and 7 of the first chapter of Book Four.

263 ". . . let Gosse have an answer by return . . ." Letter: HGW to Edmund Gosse, January 4, 1904.

264 "Before he settled to his task . . ." Letters: F. Harrison to HGW, January 27, 1904, and February 4, 1904.

270 "Gissing had sent for him . . ." Diary: GG, March 1, 1888.

273 ". . . in more than one . . ." Letter: Gabrielle to HGW, June 24, 1907.

274 ". . . introduction to Veranilda . . ." A much modified version of this paper was printed as an in memoriam article in *The Monthly Review* for August 1904.

274 ". . . even though she was never to read it . . ." Letter: Gabrielle to Morley Roberts, September 24, 1904, declares this intention.

275 ". . . my father had liked Doctor Hick . . ." Oral communication: HGW to author. He continued to do so, and regretted the breach.

277 ". . . he began to attend the gatherings . . ." Autobiography: HGW, Chap 5, Sec 4.

278 ". . . Belfort Bax . . ." For a contemporary Marxist's view of BB, see Biography: E.P. Thompson, *William Morris*, 1955, Part III, Chap IV, Section I.

281 "Hear a word . . ." Poem: William Morris, *All For the Cause*, written specially for recitation on the occasion of the Hyndman-Bradlaugh debate, April 17, 1884.

282 "We asked them for a life . . ." Poem: William Morris, original title *Death Song*, first published in *Commonweal*'s worker's songbook, *Chants for Socialists*.

282 "In his own address . . ." Speech: verbatim report, *Commonweal*, December 24, 1887. "Well, I like ceremony . . ." quoted in E. P. Thompson, *op. cit.*

285 ". . . when Beatrice Webb . . ." Autobiography: HGW, Chap 9, Sec 9.

288 ". . . the letter in which Pease . . ." Letter: Pease to HGW, March 29, 1904. ". . . the Webbs went so far . . ." Diary: B. Webb, April 19, 1904. ". . . one of their little dinners . . ." Diary: B. Webb, April 20, 1904.

288 "a tart letter to Pease . . ." Letter: HGW to Pease, April 28, 1904.

289 ". . . he couldn't finish the book . . ." HGW had started *Kipps* as *The Wealth of Mr. Waddy* in the winter of 1898–1899, for

its pre-publication history see Monograph: Harris Wilson, bearing the book's original title.

289 ". . . *A Modern Utopia* . . ." Novel: HGW, 1905. Contains fictionalised account of HGW's walk through the Jura with Graham Wallas, *supra.*

291 ". . . the first of them to rally to his banner . . ." Letter: Marjorie Pease to Jane, March 24, 1906.

291 ". . . He was an extraordinary figure . . ." Autobiography: HGW, Chap 8, Sec 5; and Biography: Doris Langley Moore, *E. Nesbit,* 1933. N. and J. MacKenzie, *The Time Traveller, op. cit.,* were probably the last people to take him at his own valuation as "a catholic, the son of impoverished gentry in the North of England." They had been put onto Langley Moore and others by the time they came to write *The First Fabians,* 1977.

297 ". . . euchred my father's proposal . . ." For the Old Guard's version of these manoeuvres see Memoir: E. Pease, *History of the Fabian Society,* 1925. When I contacted Pease in the late forties I found him as keenly engaged in this power struggle in a teapot as ever.

297 ". . . what the last clause meant . . ." Memoir: E. Pease, *op. cit.*, Chap IX.

301 ". . . we four from that time . . ." Novel: HGW, *In the Days of the Comet,* 1906, Epilogue.

301 ". . . after a short interval . . ." Letter: E. Pease to HGW, February 15, 1906.

303 ". . . in *The Times Literary Supplement* . . ." anonymous review, September 14, 1906.

303 ". . . openly gloating . . ." Letters: GBS to HGW, undated, probably September 14, 1906.

304 ". . . Hubert Bland . . ." Letter: Bland to Pease, October 14, 1906.

305 ". . . four days after . . ." Diary: B. Webb, October 18, 1906.

305 ". . . dashed off a note . . ." Letters: B. Webb to HGW, and to Millicent Fawcett, November 2, 1906.

309 ". . . sent every Fabian . . ." Flyer: document reproduced in facsimile in *Collected Letters of GBS,* Vol 1898–1910, Ed. Dan Laurence, p. 665.

309 ". . . never the man . . ." Oral communication: HGW to author, confirmation, Chap 13, *The First Fabians, op. cit.*

311 ". . . loathed the mixture . . ." Letter: Graham Wallas to HGW, December 10, 1906.

PAGE

311 ". . . the last had not been heard . . ." Letter: GBS to S. Webb, November 25, 1906. In this, Shaw tells Webb that HGW is right on the issue of getting the society into party politics.

311 ". . . Haden Guest became rather short with him . . ." Letter: LHG to HGW, February 6, 1907.

312 ". . . what happened on that occasion . . ." Memoir: E. Pease, *History of the Fabian Society, op. cit.,* Chap IX, and see also Chap X, which begins with the admission that the years 1907–1908, thanks to the numbers and quality of the new members brought in by "HGW's propagandist enthusiasm," were those in which the high-water mark in the prewar history of the society as a forum and an influential body was reached.

314 ". . . sixty-seven applications . . ." This, and the succeeding figures, from Pease, *op. cit.*

314 ". . . 'I Carbonari' . . ." Biography: Christopher Hassall, *Rupert Brooke,* Chap IV.

315 ". . . Keeling was his host later in the year . . ." *Ibid.,* Chap V.

316 "All through March and April . . . a prolonged teasing . . ." Letter: S. Webb to HGW, June 12, 1907, is a reaction to this teasing.

316 ". . . had nettled Shaw . . ." Letter: GBS to HGW, March 22, 1908. ". . . what had happened, he asked . . ." Letter: HGW to Pease, April 30, 1908.

317 "My father knew . . ." A short history of this matter, distributed like the corpse of a certain kind of murder victim, will be found on and between pp. 140 and 351 of N. and J. MacKenzie, *The First Fabians, op. cit.* A franker version of the story is given in Sidney Caine, *History of the Foundation of the London School of Economics,* 1963.

318 ". . . Shaw exploded with anger . . ." Caine, *op. cit.*

318 ". . . MacDonald . . ." Letter: RM to Pease, April 8, 1896.

319 ". . . there were, he said . . ." Diary: B. Webb, April 30, 1908.

320 ". . . an amazingly vital person . . ." Diary: B. Webb, September 15, 1908.

320 "This should have marked the end of my father's tussle . . ." For a great deal of what follows between pp. 320 and 324 I am indebted to Biography: Keith Sinclair, *William Pember Reeves,* 1965. The facts he gives have been freely interpreted in the light of information received in Oral Communications from AR and others.

330 ". . . to which the Webbs put their signatures . . ." Diary: B. Webb, January 17, 1909. This entry records the signing of the minority report. The entry for March 7, 1911 records the virtual dissolution of the original Fabian Society under the weight of the landslide victory of the Liberal Party in the general election of 1910. Legislation based on the recommendations of the Majority Report was introduced in the House of Commons in May 1911. The Webbs left on what was to be a leisurely trip round the world in mid-June 1911.

331 ". . . they were listening nightly . . ." Social history: N. and J. MacKenzie, *The First Fabians.* Epilogue.

332 "From whom were descended . . ." Diary: B. Webb, January 4, 1929.

332 ". . . all this ferment over Palestine . . ." Diary: B. Webb, October 26, 1930.

333 ". . . for instance, in 1932 . . ." Oral communication: AR to author.

335 ". . . a woman he had known since his Worcester Park days . . ." Autobiography: HGW, Chap 8, Sec 3.

336 "Mr. Richardson's troubles . . ." Biography: Gloria Fromm, *Dorothy Richardson,* 1977. Fromm states that Richardson *père* ran through his father's estate in "little more than sixteen years." As he inherited his small fortune in January 1874 and ended up in the bankruptcy court "at the end of the year" in 1893, it seems to me that his run lasted for as near to twenty years as makes no difference.

336 ". . . a hell of uncertainty and apprehension . . ." It was DR's custom to preface her very vivid account of her father's downfall and her mother's last days with a declaration that she was about to disclose something that she had never been able to speak of before. My version of it is based mainly on the story as she gave it to me in 1948, but also takes into consideration slight differences in detail between that and the versions she put to HGW, RW and Gloria Fromm at different times.

337 ". . . her one literary achievement . . ." *The Outlook* issue of October 4, 1902.

341 ". . . such publications as . . ." The first two of these littlest of little magazines were edited and published by their owner, DR's friend Charles Daniels.

342 "The leading facts . . ." The successive volumes of the work appeared in 1915, 1916, 1917, 1919 (two volumes), 1921,

1923, 1925, 1927, 1931, and 1935. The twelfth volume never achieved independent publication, and "came out" as the conclusion to the whole when the complete work was published in four volumes in 1938.

346 "... he was to eat ..." DR's years as a dentist's receptionist had qualified her as an expert on diet in her view, and in this role she was a frequent contributor to a third of Charles Daniels' publications: *The Healthy Life.*

349 "... some splendidly comic scenes ..." Autobiography: Robert McAlmon, *Being Geniuses Together,* 1938.

350 "... prosecutor ..." Many people would expect the word plaintiff to appear here. But this was a case brought under the old order of things in which one private individual accused by another of the kind of criminal act that could lead to his physical punishment (as by being sent to prison) could defend himself from the accusation by laying an information with the police in which he charged his accuser with criminal libel. From the time that he swore to the information that a criminal libel had been committed, until a determination of the validity of his complaint was made by a court, the person laying the information was referred to as the prosecutor in the case. The defence against a charge of criminal libel was to establish the truth of the original accusation.

350 "... his well-simulated heart attacks ..." Biography: William Freeman, *Life of Lord Alfred Douglas, op. cit.*

352 "... William Macmillan ..." Autobiography: WM, *The Reluctant Healer,* 1952. After they had been introduced by DR, the tempestuous Veronica, wife to Benjamin Grad, became Macmillan's secretary and most devoted admirer.

356 "... pronounced in Cambridge ..." At a Sunday breakfast party given by Maynard Keynes: see *JMK,* Biography, R.F. Harrod, 1951.

356 "... Bertrand Russell ..." *Portraits from Memory,* Memoirs, BR. 1956.

357 "... it astonished her to find ..." Oral communication, DR to author.

361 "... when I returned ..." I am indebted to Gloria Fromm for much of the information that follows. GF, Biography: DR. *op. cit.*

Index

About the Author

ANTHONY WEST, born in England on August 5, 1914, emigrated to the United States in 1950. The child of Rebecca West and H. G. Wells, parents who both qualify as hard acts to follow, he spent most of the English part of his life trying to avoid odious comparisons and the profession of letters, first by adopting painting as a career, then by becoming a dairy farmer. His friend Graham Greene took charge of his destiny in the period of confusion and fresh starts that followed World War II by shaking his beginner's novel, *The Vintage,* out of him, and he has been writing ever since. His name was familiar to *New Yorker* readers as the book reviewer throughout the twenty-year period between 1950 and 1970, in which he was also active as a novelist. Since its end he has been fully occupied with the production of this biography, which he decided he had to write sooner or later as long ago as 1948, and which he has had on his mind as his ultimate goal ever since.

LAGRANGE COUNTY LIBRARY

B
/91487

91487

OFFICIAL DISCARD

B
WE
West, Anthony
H.G. Wells: aspects
of a life

DATE			

© THE BAKER & TAYLOR CO.

6 $3.95

W9-DFP-071

Praise for
#1 Blackboard Bestselling Author

FELICIA
MASON

"Mason is a superb storyteller...she creates magic."
—*Publishers Weekly*

"[Mason] places the Christian theme front and center
while also making room for a touching portrait
of human desires and frailties."
—*Booklist*

"Felicia Mason...will make the reader sigh,
cry, then shout for joy at the triumphant,
healing power of true love."
—*Romantic Times*

FELICIA MASON

SWEET DEVOTION

Steeple
Hill®

Published by Steeple Hill Books™

STEEPLE HILL BOOKS

Steeple
Hill®

ISBN 0-7394-4768-8

SWEET DEVOTION

Copyright © 2004 by Felicia L. Mason

All rights reserved. Except for use in any review, the reproduction
or utilization of this work in whole or in part in any form by any
electronic, mechanical or other means, now known or hereafter
invented, including xerography, photocopying and recording, or in
any information storage or retrieval system, is forbidden without
the written permission of the editorial office, Steeple Hill Books,
233 Broadway, New York, NY 10279 U.S.A.

All characters in this book have no existence outside the imagination of
the author and have no relation whatsoever to anyone bearing the same
name or names. They are not even distantly inspired by any individual
known or unknown to the author, and all incidents are pure invention.

This edition published by arrangement with Steeple Hill Books.

® and TM are trademarks of Steeple Hill Books, used under license.
Trademarks indicated with ® are registered in the United States Patent
and Trademark Office, the Canadian Trade Marks Office and in other
countries.

Printed in U.S.A.

This book is for all of the Ambers
who seek shelter, peace and hope.

A portion of the proceeds of this book
is being donated to Transitions Family
Violence Services, an organization
that supports women and children in crisis.

❧ *Chapter One* ❧

Armed with a carving knife, Amber Montgomery took cover as a metal folding chair hurtled her way. The chair crashed against the edge of a white-draped carving table, taking out the end of the serving station where she'd been carving beef at the Wayside Revelers' Annual Dinner Dance.

She watched in horror as eight pounds of beets splattered to the floor sending deep red beet juice splashing up and out like a demented geyser.

She'd known, of course, that taking this catering job carried a certain amount of risk. The Wayside Revelers tended to revel a bit too much at their functions. But after their last fiasco at the VFW hall, Amber thought they'd mellowed and would be on their best behavior tonight.

That, obviously, wasn't the case.

She didn't know how this melée started, but she needed to—

"Watch out!" someone yelled.

Amber ducked just a moment before another chair came within inches of taking *her* out.

This was getting personal!

She jumped up. "Hey, I'm the caterer. Why are you attacking me?"

But no one heard her or paid any attention. They were too busy destroying the hall and themselves—and having a great time doing so. The scene in front of her looked like a barroom brawl in the wild wild West. Except, this wasn't the eighteen-hundreds frontier. It was peaceful little Wayside, Oregon, population 17,800, in the twenty-first century.

Over the commotion, Amber heard what sounded like police sirens. Help was on the way!

Maybe she could salvage the trays of lemon meringue tarts—six hours of work. Amber inched toward the desserts, but someone else spied them at the same time. An elderly man grabbed one in each hand and smiled.

"Don't you have any respect for food?" she demanded.

Unmindful of the scene playing out behind him, the man shook his head, grinned a toothless smile and aimed.

"Don't you dare!" Amber said, holding a hand up in front of her face.

"Lighten up, honey," he said. "It's just a pastry."

And then her own lemon meringue hit her in the face. Amber shrieked and whirled around—

"Hold it right there."

With one hand Amber wiped pie from her face. She cleared her vision enough to see the pie thrower scuttle off to the side and disappear into the crowd. She wiped away more meringue and the shadow in front of her came into focus, the details registering. Tall, with broad shoulders, a slim waist and feet planted apart, he scowled at her. A very big, very threatening cop stood not three feet away.

"You're under arrest, lady."

"Me? What did I do? I'm the one being attacked. Arrest one of them," she demanded, waving the carving knife toward the Revelers now merrily flinging the rest of her lemon tarts at each other.

The cop didn't spare a glance at the havoc being wrought behind him. "Drop the knife now."

Amber tensed at the tone. Then she looked up at the cop. His eyes glinted and she realized that his hand hovered near his revolver.

"What knife?"

He took a menacing step forward, and Amber whimpered. The carving knife she'd forgotten she clutched in her hand clattered to the floor. In the next moment, the cop was all over her. He grabbed her arm, yanking it around her back.

"You're hurting me."

He didn't answer. Instead, she felt the cold steel of handcuffs clamp on her wrist.

Something snapped in her then, and Amber fought. A

fragment of the self-defense she'd been taught flickered through her. She kicked out at him. "No! You can't do this. I won't let you do this..."

One of her kicks connected and she heard his intake of breath. Her small victory, however, was short-lived. He held her tightly and secured the other wrist.

"Lady, if you don't settle down," he said, his voice a deceptively calm growl, "I'm going to add resisting arrest to your charges."

It wasn't so much what he said as the way the words sounded that got to her. They held a rumbled warning of coming pain. She knew that tone, knew what would happen to her if she defied him again. She'd tried to fight. She'd tried to remember she didn't have to be a victim. She'd also tried to remember how to defend herself.

But he had the physical advantage of height and weight and strength. Resistance *was* futile, she realized. Why did it always have to be this way?

Amber closed her eyes and surrendered to the inevitable.

The handcuffed woman went limp, and Paul had to move fast to catch her before she hit the floor.

Police Chief Paul Evans commanded a force of forty sworn officers and a full complement of dispatchers, secretaries and other civilians whose job it was to maintain the peace in Wayside. He'd been warned that the Wayside Revelers had a tendency to get out of hand at their events. So he'd been on patrol in the vicinity of the community center.

When he heard first a shout and then breaking glass, he'd called for backup and rushed in, just in time to have a small, blond beauty threaten him with a wicked-looking blade.

Even now, with the hellion subdued at his side, his officers swarmed the building rounding up rabble-rousers.

He turned to call one of the officers—

Thwack!

A mound of potatoes au gratin hit his forehead. Paul spotted the culprit, a little old man who quickly ditched the serving spoon he'd used as a missile launcher. The man then snatched up a serving tray lid and used it as a shield against the lemon tarts hurled his way.

"Jones!" Paul bellowed.

The cop sprinted forward.

"You there," Paul ordered the old man. "Stop it."

The devilish gleam in the elderly man's eyes was replaced by an expression of innocence and fake senility. "Me?"

"Yeah, you."

Dragging along a remarkably subdued knife wielder, Paul unlocked a second pair of cuffs.

"You're arresting me?"

"That's right, sir."

"Hot diggity!" The little man stepped quickly to don the cuffs, showing pretty amazing dexterity for someone his age. Paul put him at close to eighty.

"Take these two out to my squad car," he said to the young officer. "I'll go round up some more of them." He wiped his brow, shook potato goo from his hand and glared at the old man who was still grinning at him.

"Assaulting an officer could earn you some jail time, sir."

"As long as you have cable, that's fine by me. I like to watch wrestling."

"I'll just bet you do," Paul muttered, walking away and stepping around a huge puddle of beets. The whole place was a wreck.

In the police car, Amber stared out the window, her face an expressionless mask.

"Isn't this fun?" the little man asked.

It took a moment for the question to sink in and for Amber to comprehend that the pain hadn't kicked in yet. She turned toward the voice, expecting to see her tormentor. Instead, she came eye-to-eye with an elf. Her eyes widened and her mouth, a thin line, began to tremble.

The man looked alarmed. "Aw, please don't be mad. It was just a little pastry. It didn't hurt, did it?"

Amber opened her mouth but no words came forth. Her tongue felt like sandpaper. She blinked once. Then again. And then the tears she'd hoped to hold back started to fall.

The man moved as if to comfort her, then, too late, remembered his hands were cuffed. He almost toppled into her lap. Amber squealed and pressed her back to the door. The little man righted himself.

"Oh, honey. It's not that bad. Really. They'll just take us down, do some fingerprints and then give us a good lecture. I missed last year's dinner-dance, but that's what I'm told happened."

Amber just moaned.

To the casual observer, the Main Street district of Wayside, Oregon, might look a whole lot like Mayberry, R.F.D., but the police bureau was a reminder that crime happened in the town just like it did in every other American locality.

Once inside the large oak and cherry doors of the police bureau, it was apparent to any visitor that despite Wayside's size, it had a state-of-the-art police department, fully equipped to handle any twenty-first century criminal activity and to protect the town's citizens from such.

A long line of Revelers was herded past the intake desk and into lockup.

Amber stood in the midst of about thirty-five food-stained wretches, most of them incredibly self-satisfied over this bonus extension of their night's festivities.

"My name's Silas," someone said.

Amber looked beside her. There stood her pie thrower, the little man from the police car. Having recovered enough to speak, Amber opened her mouth to give him what-for. But a voice boomed out over the general hubbub, drowning out her first words.

"Listen up, people."

Amber's skin prickled at the voice. She turned toward

the voice and got another jolt when she looked at the man who'd cuffed and arrested her.

"My name's Paul Evans and I'm the police chief here."

"Hi, Chief Evans." A couple of the Revelers called out the cheery greeting.

"Welcome to Wayside," the little man at Amber's side hollered.

Amber watched the big cop shake his head in bemusement. She rubbed her wrists. Though the handcuffs had been removed she still felt the weight of the shackles on her spirit. Taking a much-needed deep breath, Amber fought for the calm she knew she could find if she just took it slow. *Keep it light,* she coached herself. One breath at a time.

"We'll be processing each one of you. After that, you're free to go until your court date."

"What about the lecture about being responsible citizens?" one of the Revelers asked.

The cop folded his arms across his chest. Amber watched muscles bunch and constrict, the blue fabric of his uniform pulled taut. Her study of the man missed no detail. From the black hiking boots at his feet, to the gleaming hardware on his gun belt.

His face matched the rest of him. Clean-shaven, angular. She paused at his eyes. Something wasn't right about his eyes. A deep, almost piercing blue, they fit his face, but... Amber tilted her head a fraction, getting another view. At just that second, his gaze connected with hers.

She caught her breath.

He watched her for a moment, then turned his attention back to the group. "You want a lecture about acting like six-year-olds? The community center is completely trashed thanks to your food fight. Who's in charge of you people?"

The crowd in lockup parted. Amber edged forward so she was near the front.

"I don't belong in here," she said. "You've made a mistake."

Paul's eyes narrowed in on her.

"About you, lady, there was no mistake."

"I'm the grand marshal," a man said, stepping forward and poking his chest out.

If it hadn't been for the meringue in his hair, the potatoes on his tie and a missing shoe, he might have passed for "grand."

Chuckling at the assembly, a couple of cops walked up behind the police chief, surveying the mass in lockup.

"What are you doing here, Amber?" Sergeant Caleb Jenkins asked.

"Caleb. Thank God." Relief poured through Amber. "That's the same thing I've been trying to find out. That lug head you call a police chief hauled me in here."

People behind her snickered.

A muscle flickered angrily in Paul's jaw. Though locked bars separated them, Amber stepped back.

"Lug head?"

"Uh," Caleb started. "I, uh... He's not a..." The sergeant didn't meet her gaze, focusing instead on something on his boots.

"There's been some kind of mix-up, Chief," the sergeant said, marshaling his vocabulary and coming to her defense. "This is Amber Montgomery. She's not a Reveler. She's a caterer."

Paul didn't look convinced of her innocence. "You threatened me with a knife."

Amber glared up at him, not letting the physical disparity of their heights dissuade her. "I am a *caterer.* If you'd done any kind of police work, you'd know that that was a carving knife. But how could you do any real police work—you were too busy shoving me around."

Amber thrust her wrists in front of him. "Look." Two bruises marred her pale skin.

Paul looked horrified. "What happened to you? Did somebody in the cage do that to you?"

"No, *Chief* Evans. You did. And you better believe that I'm filing a formal complaint."

She whirled back toward Caleb. "Who hires the police chief?"

"Uh." He looked from Amber to Paul. "Uh..."

"The mayor," Paul supplied.

Just then a commotion in the hallway interrupted them. The main doors burst open. Wayside's mayor strode in, followed by a reporter and a photographer from the *Wayside Gazette* and a frantic-looking Haley Brandon-Dumaine.

"Amber!"

"Paul," the mayor bellowed. "What is going on in here?"

It took a good ten minutes to sort through what had happened.

"I'm pretty disappointed with you, Randall," the mayor told the Revelers' grand marshal. "I thought you all learned your lesson the last time."

The Revelers' last dinner-dance had resulted in a lifetime ban from the VFW hall.

"Some of us weren't there then," Silas called out.

It took a while, but on the mayor's word and that of several longtime police officers, Amber was released from lockup. Haley stood with Amber as she signed the requisite forms.

"Ms. Montgomery, I'm truly sorry. It was an honest mistake," Paul said, approaching them.

Amber's derisive snort clearly said she wasn't buying it.

"Will you let me formally apologize?"

Amber spun around. "You've got a lot of nerve, mister. First you yank me around like I'm some kind of rag doll. Now you think you can just make nice and I'll forget about the way you treated me. Never again," she said. "You'll be hearing from my lawyer."

Those were fine words coming from someone who didn't even know a lawyer, let alone have one.

Amber's dramatic exit from the police station sapped the rest of her energy. By the time they got to Haley's car, Amber felt like a rag doll that had not only been yanked around and dragged across the ground but also run through a washing machine.

"Are you all right?" Haley asked.

Amber nodded, but she stared out the passenger-side window of Haley's car. "I need to get my stuff. My van is still at the community center."

Haley winced. "I don't think you'll be able to get it. At least not tonight. Chief Evans isn't letting anyone near there until they get photos of all the damage. When I drove by, your van was inside the crime scene tape."

"Great, just great. How am I supposed to make my deliveries tomorrow?"

"You can take my car if you need it. I'll have Matt drop me off at school." Haley stopped at a red light and reached a hand out to her cousin. "Amber, I'm worried about you."

Amber didn't meet her concerned gaze. "I'm fine," she said, trying to convince herself. "And I'm not going to have a breakdown, if that's what you're worried about."

The two women rode in silence for a moment. Then Amber, in a voice that was steady and strong, said, "The only thing on my mind is making that cop pay for what he did to me."

Haley glanced at her. "Which cop, Amber? The one here, or the one who hurt you in L.A.?"

❧ Chapter Two ❧

Paul Evans pulled into his driveway after a long shift. In his three months in Wayside, this had been the first time he'd experienced any rowdiness in the small town.

And he'd take what amounted to a massive food fight over the rough and tumble of the place he'd come from. Wayside, Oregon, was a world and a culture away from Los Angeles.

He'd been given a heads-up about the Wayside Revelers, so he'd been expecting a need to cruise by their dinner-dance during his patrol shift.

The Revelers were all supposed to be retirees, or at least card-carrying members of the AARP. One in particular, however, didn't fit that profile. Paul hadn't been prepared for the fiery beauty who stood up to him brandishing a knife.

How was he supposed to have known she was the

caterer? Her eyes flashed and she looked as if she were out for blood—his in particular. In the evidence room, he'd taken a look at that knife again. Carving knife or not, it could have done some damage had it truly been used as a weapon.

On the drive home, just one thing stuck with Paul, though, nicking his conscious, pestering his peace of mind, making him doubt what he'd seen with his own two eyes: How could he have grabbed her so hard that he'd left a bruise?

That ate at him like nothing else—even the fact that she kept saying "again." He searched his memory, but couldn't recall arresting her in L.A. Granted, he'd arrested a lot of people in his ten years as a cop on the street there. Maybe she'd been in the number. But surely he'd remember someone who looked like Amber Montgomery—like summer and cornfields and blue skies.

She'd caught his eye, all right.

Not remembering her as a suspect in L.A., however, didn't bother him as much as that bruise on her arm.

The other Revelers tossed food around. Messy, yes. But not necessarily deadly. The knife wielded by Amber Montgomery, well, that piece of business was another story altogether. Despite her objection, the weapon had been bagged, tagged and put into an evidence locker at the police station.

He thought he'd let go of at least some of the wariness and care that had served him well on the LAPD. But apparently, he'd not yet gotten acclimated to Wayside and its considerably lower crime rate.

If a geriatric food fight ranked as serious crime here—serious enough to roust the mayor and get him to police headquarters—Paul had definitely settled in the right place. In a city the size of Los Angeles, only crimes like mass rioting, terrorism or a high-profile celebrity slaying ranked severe enough for top public officials to make an unscheduled appearance at police headquarters.

Yeah, he'd take a food fight any day over what he'd left behind.

Drawing a deep breath, Paul shed the cares of the job in exchange for the role that brought him the greatest sense of satisfaction.

"Hi, Eunice," he said, walking in his front door. He un-buckled his gun belt, locked both the revolver and the belt in a closet, then tucked the key away on the chain he always wore around his neck.

"Well, howdy, Chief. Busy night, huh? I heard the Rev-elers got out of control again."

He nodded. "You could say that. Thanks for staying with the kids."

She wrapped up the knitting she'd been doing, placed yarn and needles in a large quilted bag at her side. "Not a problem. Sutton and Jonathan are fast asleep, bless their little hearts. You have two fine children there, Chief."

Paul thought so, too. "I hope they didn't wear you out too much."

Eunice pooh-poohed that. "If anything, it's the other way around," she said on a chuckle. "We had fun."

He pulled out his wallet.

"If you hand me any money, Paul Evans, I'm going to be mighty insulted."

"Eunice, I can't let you do this and not pay you."

"You're new to Wayside," she said, patting his hand. "You'll get the hang of the place soon. I left a plate of cookies for you. We made gingerbread men."

Paul smiled. Having Eunice Gallagher living right across the street was a godsend, one of many he'd encountered in Wayside. She was the secretary at Community Christian Church, where he'd transferred his membership shortly after arriving in Wayside. A native of Wayside, she'd all but adopted him and his kids.

He helped her with her coat.

"Eunice, do you know a woman by the name of Amber Montgomery?"

The older lady beamed. "Of course! Everybody knows Amber. Don't tell me you haven't had one of her honey pecan rolls yet."

"Honey pecan rolls?"

Eunice laughed. "Goodness, how in the world have you lived here for three months and not had one of those yet? Tell you what, I'll swing by the inn tomorrow and get you some if they're not sold out by the time I get there. You're in for a treat."

He was still trying to understand. "Wait, so she's the town baker?"

Eunice picked up her knitting bag. "No. She's a gourmet chef. She runs a catering business called Appetizers & More, but most people know her for the honey pecan rolls and her lemon meringue tarts." Eunice smacked her lips. "Talk about delicious."

Since he'd been hit with potatoes and not tarts, Paul couldn't agree or disagree. He thought back to Amber's earlier behavior, though, if she hadn't looked so dazed, he'd have sworn she'd played a tactic used by nonviolent protesters. That going limp bit had been used for decades.

"Shock," he surmised. She had to have been in shock. Law-abiding citizens could be counted on to react in one of two ways—outrage or polite pacifism—while they waited patiently or impatiently—for things to get sorted out.

He'd spent so many years working the violent streets of South-Central L.A. that he'd forgotten about law-abiding citizens. Tonight wasn't the first time he'd had a knife in his face. But it probably was the first time in his law enforcement career that the brandisher hadn't tried to slice him with it.

Paul felt bad—really, really bad—about the bruise he'd put on her arm.

After he watched Eunice cross the street, open her door then flick her front porch light, Paul looked in on his sleeping children. Sutton, whose teddy bear Bentley and rag doll Angel cuddled close to her, looked like an angel herself. Her blond curls spread out over the pillow.

She looked a lot like her mom. Paul's heart constricted at the thought.

He stood watching her for a while. Then he placed a kiss on her head and whispered "I love you" to the sleeping child.

A bathroom connected the two bedrooms, and the doors always remained open. On the countertop sat Wally, another of Sutton's stuffed toys—this one a rainbow fish.

With a small chuckle, Paul greeted Wally. "So you're on the night watch this evening."

Paul walked through to Jonathan's room where lights blazed overhead and at the boy's desk. Sprawled on his twin bed with its cartoon-character sheets, Jonathan had, as usual, kicked all the covers off. Paul tugged the sheet and light blanket up.

The boy stirred. "Izzat you, Unca Pa?"

Paul smiled, easily translating the sleep talk. "Yeah, sport. It's me. I'm home. Go back to sleep."

Jonathan sat up, bleary eyed. "Tried to stay awake. Protect the women."

"I know, sport."

His heart went out to the child. Paul hugged him close, then settled him down and tucked him in. "I'll take over the watch now. All right?"

Jonathan murmured his assent and closed his eyes. Paul leaned down, pressed a kiss to the boy's head, then turned off the lights in the bedroom.

The bathroom lights stayed on at night. Always. They helped chase the bad guys away.

* * *

Amber didn't have an answer to Haley's question. No doubt about it, she'd flashed to Raymond Alvarez tonight, at some point confusing the two men, the two situations. Miles away from her former terror, she thought she'd put it all behind her. Until tonight.

The height, the uniform, the eyes...

She shook her head, again thinking of Paul Evans's eyes. Were they the same deep Mediterranean blue as Raymond Alvarez's? She couldn't remember, but the police chief's were somehow different. Kinder maybe?

No, not kinder, she decided. Compassionate. Though he wore the uniform and carried the gun, Paul Evans's eyes had regarded her with warmth. Raymond's eyes, like his soul, were hollow, devoid of any human warmth or consideration. He was a heartless snake in the grass, and it had taken a long time for her to realize that. Too long.

"Would you like me to stay with you tonight?" Haley asked.

Amber shook her head. If there were any ghosts that needed exorcising, she'd do it alone. "No."

"How about staying over with me and Matt? The bed in the guest room is mucho comfy."

That got a small smile, but Amber shook her head again. "I'm all right." And she truly believed she was. She rubbed her upper arm where the cop had gripped her.

"Maybe we should swing by the hospital and have that looked at."

"It's just a bruise, Haley," Amber said. "I've survived much worse."

There was nothing Haley could say to that.

After Haley dropped her off, Amber let herself into her apartment.

Once before she'd been a victim. Never, ever again. Anger still propelling her, and before the fear kicked in, she drafted a letter demanding an investigation into the unnecessary force used by the police chief of Wayside, Oregon. It felt good, too, to lambaste him in writing for the way he'd manhandled her.

In the morning, she'd mail copies to the mayor, the town council, the editor of the *Wayside Gazette* and the news department at the radio station she listened to. Amber knew that letting off steam in the letter was healthy—a much better response than when she used to pretend that nothing was wrong, that her feelings or her body hadn't been physically violated.

Surveying her handiwork, she nodded, satisfied, then put the letters in envelopes and stamped them. Then, with every light on in her house, Amber sat in a deep chair, arms curled around her legs.

Eventually she fell into a fitful sleep.

Morning came quickly. She ran five miles to get the kinks out of her body and to chase away the shadows of the previous evening. The fresh air of an early Oregon morning did wonders in restoring her self-confidence.

She'd face down this day and whatever it delivered with a new determination, a new purpose.

The lesson of last night, Amber decided, was a test of her commitment to rebuilding her life post-Raymond. It had taken three years—three long, liberating years—to get where she was today. Amber had no intention of letting one bullying police chief bring her down again.

After returning from her run, she showered and tried to shrug off the vestiges of the previous night's trauma. Next to running, which she did at every opportunity, Amber's all-time favorite stress reliever was working in her kitchen. Today she got to do something fun, something she enjoyed. She mixed up the basic dough for sugar cookies and chocolate chip cookies.

Using a light frosting, she decorated the sugar cookies once they were baked, with whimsical designs. It was time to pack up the cookies that were ready. She lined a large basket with a red-and-white gingham cloth and alternated layers of chocolate chip and sugar cookies.

She pulled a clean apron with the logo of her Appetizers & More company out of a drawer. She added a miniature version of it to the stack of stuff she'd need. Then, with basket in hand, she headed outside. That's when she remembered her van wasn't out back where it was supposed to be, but still at the community center. She couldn't very well make deliveries on her bicycle.

Frustrated, Amber returned to her apartment and called Caleb, told him where the extra key was hidden under the tire carrier, and listened to a lecture about leaving a spare key where any common criminal could get it.

"Like we have common criminals in Wayside," she muttered.

"Amber, there *are* criminals here."

"And one of them wears a badge that says 'Police Chief,'" she retorted. "Are you going to get my van or not?"

"Yeah," he mumbled. "I'll get it."

She wasn't about to tell him that, during the bad time, she'd taken up the practice of keeping a key hidden on her vehicle, never knowing if she might have to escape with just the clothes on her back, that spare key her only route to freedom.

It *had* come to that.

Thanks to Police Chief Paul Evans, those memories, ones she'd managed to suppress in order to make it through each day, now lay right on the surface, taunting her again. Reminding her that a woman was never truly safe.

Fifteen minutes later, Caleb drove up in her van, a Wayside squad car behind him. Amber couldn't see who sat behind the wheel.

"Sorry about the inconvenience, Amber."

He smiled a shy smile and handed her the key. "Where you headed today?"

"Over to Sunshine and Rainbows," she told him. "Hold on a sec, I'll be right back." Amber dashed back to her apartment, tucked a couple of cookies in a small waxed paper sleeve, sealed it with one of her company stickers and picked up her cookie basket.

Back downstairs, she handed Caleb the cookie bag.

A big grin split his face. "Thanks, Amber." He glanced back at the squad car. "Do I have to share?"

"These," she said holding up the basket, "are one way for the kids to learn about sharing. So the answer to you is yes."

The cop groaned and Amber laughed. "Thanks for bringing the van over."

"Not a problem. The chief's really sorry about—"

Amber held up a hand. "Don't even mention him in my presence."

Shaking his head, Caleb glanced back at the squad car. "But, Amber, he's a good guy. Really."

She slid open the side door and tucked the cookie basket inside. "If you really want to show me that *you're* a good guy," she said, "you'll help me load up the rest of the van."

Looking over his shoulder again, Caleb shrugged.

Not waiting for an answer from him, she headed back inside to get the two additional deliveries she had to make: one to the Wayside Inn Bed & Breakfast, and the other, a special order, to the Train Depot.

A few minutes later, Caleb slid the tray for the inn into the specially designed rack in the van. "Amber, I really think you should reconsider about Chief Evans."

She faced him, her expression serious. "Caleb, if you want to remain friends, and I hope you do, you'll not mention the police chief or your unfortunate choice of occupation in my presence. Comprende?"

The cop nodded.

"All right, then. I'll see you around."

She left him standing in front of the house where she rented a second-floor apartment.

Caleb went back to the waiting squad car and got in the passenger seat.

"She's still pretty steamed at you, Chief."

"I gathered as much from your frantic waving. What's she doing?"

"Making deliveries. I can't believe you've been here for three months and you haven't had one of her honey pecan rolls." The cop smacked his lips together. "Delicious."

"So I've heard." Paul pulled onto the street to head back to the station. "She shouldn't leave spare keys on her vehicle. That's just inviting trouble."

Caleb broke the sticker seal on his treat and counted his cookies. Two. He glanced at the chief sitting next to him.

"What?" asked Paul.

"I only got two."

"Two what?"

"Cookies. She said I had to share."

"Cookies?" In a flash, Paul knew just where one of her deliveries would be made. For the last month, Sutton and Jonathan had been raving about the Cookie Lady at their after-school program. She came once a week.

From their description—soft and funny, and "she smells good"—that from Jonathan—he'd come to the conclusion that the Cookie Lady was a sixtyish grandmother who spent her retirement baking cookies for the town's kids.

If, as he suddenly suspected, Amber Montgomery was the Cookie Lady...Jonathan was partly right. Paul could claim firsthand knowledge of the soft part. But the Amber he'd met smelled like beets, beef and lemon meringue. And there'd been nothing funny or entertaining about last night.

Breaking off a teeny, tiny bit of chocolate chip cookie from the large treat, Caleb offered it to Paul.

"What's this?"

"Well, she said I had to share. But if she knew you were the person in this car, I don't think she'd want you to have any."

Paul snorted. "You're probably right." He glanced at the sliver. "This is your idea of sharing?"

Caleb bit a piece of his much larger cookie, closed his eyes and moaned. "I'd marry that woman in a heartbeat if she were interested."

That comment earned him a quizzical look.

"She doesn't date."

Paul grinned. "Maybe you're not her type."

Caleb smiled back. "That may be so." He waved the last bite of the first cookie at Paul, then popped it in his mouth. "But I'm the one with the cookies."

❧ Chapter Three ❧

Amber's trademark honey pecan rolls went to the inn, then she dropped off a baker's box filled with miniature versions of the sweet rolls to the Train Depot, a gallery in town that showcased model trains and railroad memorabilia.

Amber's little business was growing. Soon it would be time to consider expanding, maybe finding a space to rent or building a Web site. But she liked being a small, one-woman operation. That way, she didn't have to depend on anyone else. Self-sufficient. That's how she described herself.

And that fit in more ways than one.

Appetizers & More by Amber didn't have any employees. But Amber did have two faithful college students who, for a flat fee and a meal, helped her out with some of the larger events.

"Oh, no!" She'd forgotten to check on Dana last night. She couldn't recall seeing her at the police station. So maybe she'd gotten away before the police roundup.

If she got caught in the dragnet, Dana probably got as much of a kick out of it as that little man Silas.

Amber didn't like or trust cops. The only reason she tolerated Caleb Jenkins was that she'd gotten to know him first as a fellow runner and then as the instructor in a karate class she'd taken shortly after moving to Wayside. It had been almost six months before she found out what he actually did for a living. By then, she'd learned to trust him. A little.

That thought led her right back to Paul Evans, and her mood soured.

The Cookie Lady couldn't greet the kids at Sunshine and Rainbows looking or acting like Oscar the Grouch. So she deliberately forced out of her head all thoughts of a tall, broad cop with steely blue eyes.

At least, that's what she told herself.

But she did make a quick cell call to check on Dana.

"Wasn't that a riot? Those old folks really tore up the place. Hey, what happened to you?"

Amber quickly explained about getting caught in the roundup.

"Well, I'm glad you're okay. I gathered up all the serving utensils and your knife kit. A knife is missing, though. I looked everywhere."

Amber rolled her eyes. Her best—translation, "most expensive"—carving knife was safe and sound...in police custody. "Don't worry. I know where it is."

"Whew, that's a relief. That's the one thing they teach us to guard like Fort Knox."

Amber made a note to get Dana a good wrap the next time she went to her favorite cook's supply store in Portland. Just like barbers and beauticians, every professional chef traveled with a personal kit that carried the tools of the trade. Amber had seen it all used, from heavy-duty toolboxes purchased at hardware stores to carryall bags that looked like sling packs. She preferred wraps that had slots for every knife and easily rolled up.

Of course, that numbskull police chief wouldn't know anything about what a chef needed to do her job. He just made assumptions, and probably would have snatched her kit as evidence if Dana hadn't rescued it. Amber assured Dana she'd swing by the college, pick up her knife kit and give Dana her pay.

"And I'll add a little something extra," she told the young woman. "When I asked you to help, I didn't know I needed to provide combat-duty pay."

Dana laughed. "Hey, I'm not gonna turn it down. I'm a starving college student."

"Starving, eh?"

The plump Dana, who always complained that she gained three pounds every time she worked for Amber, chuckled. "Well, you know. Amber, I can't thank you enough for this opportunity," the college student gushed. "I have a blast when I work for you."

Amber grunted. Seeing her food thrown around like garbage, then being arrested didn't exactly rank in her book of top ten ways to have fun. "Different strokes for different folks, I guess."

On the short drive to Sunshine and Rainbows After-School and After-Care Center, Amber did some deep breathing exercises, trying to center herself again. It didn't work. But when she walked through the doors of the kids' center, her spirit soared.

Delighted squeals and children racing each other to clamp themselves around her legs could do that to a woman.

"Well, hello there! With that kind of welcome maybe I'll have to come here more often."

One child, while clearly excited, hung back from the others. Amber smiled at her. "Hi, Sutton."

The girl beamed, but didn't say anything.

"Come on, you guys, let the Cookie Lady through." Marnie Shepherd shooed kids away. "Why don't you go get your mats and show the Cookie Lady how good little boys and girls greet guests?"

The kids raced off, and Amber laughed. Sutton glanced over her shoulder at Amber. She sent the little girl a three-finger wave.

"You do have a way with them," Amber said to Marnie.

Shaking her head, Marnie smiled. "You'd think they'd never had cookies before. It's good to see you again, Amber."

The two women headed to the area where once a week Amber sat in a rocking chair, read a story to the kids, then passed out cookies from her basket. She took pleasure in the activity and always suspected that she got more out of it than the kids did.

"Hey, I have all but three permission slips back for next week. And," Marnie added, pleased with herself, "there are four parent volunteers to make sure things stay under control."

"I'm impressed," Amber said. "But remember, we're not really baking. The no-bake cookies are pretty easy. It's mostly just mixing ingredients. We won't need that much help."

"Oh, yes, we will."

Amber shrugged. What did she know about kids? "If you say so."

She paused at the aquarium, mesmerized as the fish in the huge tank swam by. Watching tropical fish could be the most calming thing.

A little boy approached. "Come on, Cookie Lady. We're all ready."

"Well then, let's get started."

Amber followed her young escort to the section of the room designated with a colorful banner proclaiming it Story Corner.

Some of the children tried to put their mats in front of others to claim a seat closer to the rocker where she'd sit. Amber smiled as one of the aides got them all settled, assuring everyone that they would be able to both see and hear the story. Looking over them, Amber's gaze fell on Sutton.

She liked Sutton. The quiet little girl with the strawberry-blond curls reminded Amber of herself at that age. All pigtails and wide eyes, Sutton never said a lot, but Amber could tell she was bright; the child's eyes never missed a thing and she'd unselfconsciously laugh at a joke until someone noticed her, then hide her face. The girl's older brother always hovered near, keeping her in sight like a miniature bodyguard.

Amber smiled, wryly this time, for that, too, was a familiar scene. Her own older brother had always assumed the role of champion and protector—whether she had wanted him to or not. When she'd really needed a protector, however, Kyle had been half a world away. She'd neither seen nor heard from him in about five, maybe six years, and since she remained incommunicado with her parents, who probably knew his whereabouts, there existed little chance of finding him.

As she watched the boy—she believed Jonathan was his name—bend over and tie the little girl's shoes, Amber realized just how much she missed Kyle. Moisture filled her eyes and she blinked rapidly to dispel the tears that threatened.

"Amber?"

"Huh?" She wiped at her eyes and glanced over at Marnie.

"Are you all right?"

Amber nodded, then forced a grin. "Fit as a fiddle and feeling fine."

After placing the cookie basket on a low table, Amber took her seat in the rocker and addressed the children. It was an effort to dispel thoughts of Kyle, but she put a real smile on her face and in her voice.

"Today, Miss Shepherd tells me that my helper will be from the five-year-old class. All the five-year-olds, raise your hands."

About eight little arms shot up in the air.

"Oh, my. I'm the lucky one today. So who will it be?"

"Me! Me!"

Marnie stepped up with a paper bag. "Have a seat, Junior. You know the rules."

Each time the Cookie Lady—or any special guest—paid a visit, one child got to be the helper. The special role rotated among the age groups. All the children wanted to be the helper when the Cookie Lady came. Being her assistant meant getting to wear a special apron as well as receiving an extra cookie.

Marnie shook the bag with the five-year-olds' names in it. Then, with her eyes squeezed shut, Amber stuck her hand in the bag and pulled out a slip of paper. She read out the name written in blue crayon: "Sutton."

The little girl's eyes widened. Then, suddenly unsure, she scuttled back. Her brother was right there.

"It's okay, Sutton. You get to be the helper today."

Amber held out a hand. "I have the Cookie Lady apron for you to wear. Would you like that?"

The girl nodded.

Amber held it out. Sutton got up and put her hand in Amber's. The two smiled at each other as they donned their aprons.

Sometimes in addition to passing out cookies, the helper turned pages in the storybook. Amber whispered something to Sutton, who nodded and whispered something back. Then Amber started reading the story.

Today's tale came straight from the barnyard and required a lot of animal sound effects.

Paul dropped Caleb off at the police station, then continued his patrol of the town. Even though he served as chief of police, a job largely administrative in a town the size of Wayside, Paul had put himself in the patrol shift rotation after he got acclimated to the day-to-day job as chief. He wanted to get better acquainted with the Wayside community and its residents, and there was no better way to do that than work patrol. And in East Wayside, a section more prone to crime, he walked a beat, getting to know people.

Today, though, since the center was near his patrol area, he decided to swing by to see if Caleb's cookie lady was indeed the Amber he'd met last night. Sutton and Jonathan raved about the Cookie Lady. Paul wanted to see for himself. Maybe last night had been an aberration.

Where his kids were concerned, Paul had to admit to being an overly protective and cautious parent. He'd checked out several programs before choosing Sunshine and Rainbows. Three different people, including Eunice, had recommended it. It was going well, so far. He'd even signed up to be a parent volunteer when they had a cooking lesson next week.

Paul strode into Sunshine and Rainbows and greeted the aide who manned the front desk.

"Hi, Chief Evans. Did you come to check on the kids?"

Paul took off the Wayside Police Bureau cap he wore and tucked it in a pocket. "I was just in the area," he said, feeling a little guilty since he'd deliberately put himself in the area. "Thought I'd stop by. How's everything going?"

"Just fine," she said with a grin. "The Cookie Lady is here."

Paul bit back a smile. This grown woman sounded as delighted about that as Sutton and Jonathan had been the last time this infamous Cookie Lady put in an appearance.

"Everybody's in the activities room," she told him. "She just started reading not too long ago. If you hurry, you'll get to hear some of the story."

"I think I will," Paul said.

He headed to the center of the U-shaped building. Classrooms and nap rooms ringed the perimeter, but the center of activity was the core of the horseshoe, a large room subdivided by a hundred-gallon aquarium to the right and a bunny cage to the left.

The fish usually caught his eye and gave him a reason to pause. But not today. His gaze zeroed in on the story corner.

What he saw floored him.

Like peacocks showing off their plumes, Amber Montgomery and his daughter strutted around, clucking and fluttering their arms. The children sitting on mats on the floor giggled, some of them rolling over on the floor laughing.

The sight of Amber and Sutton stopped Paul cold for two reasons. Sutton never, ever opened up like that. And the two of them together had to be the most adorable sight he'd seen in a long time.

❧ *Chapter Four* ❧

After finishing their clucking, Amber and Sutton turned back to the storybook. Amber read a page of the barnyard tale. Sutton, lifting the book high so everyone could see the pictures, spotted him.

"Daddy!"

Amber looked up.

Paul knew the exact moment when Sutton's greeting registered with Amber and she recognized him.

Her eyes shuttered and the light so evident a moment ago disappeared. She swallowed, and he watched as a shudder seemed to move through her. She held his gaze—almost defiantly, Paul decided—then deliberately turned her attention back to the children and the book.

"Hi there, sweetheart," he said to Sutton.

"I'm the helper today."

"Is that a fact?"

Sutton smiled and nodded, her pigtails bobbing. Paul's heart wrenched. It had been so long since he'd seen her animated—or talkative. And the woman who'd made it so was the very one who even now surreptitiously inched away from the girl. But was it really away from Sutton, or was it away from him? Paul was afraid he knew the answer.

Some people just didn't like cops. He needed to apologize to her again, and today was his opportunity. After she passed out the cookies, he'd have a word with her. But Paul watched her withdrawal and wondered what she was hiding—and why he took her rebuff personally.

"Cookie Lady, are you going to finish the story?"

Amber jerked as if she'd been pinched. "I... I... Yes."

She reached for the book Sutton held and tried to see beyond the police chief, who suddenly stood much closer than she liked. She stuck her head in the book, anxious to finish the tale so she could escape. But her skin grew clammy and she lost her grip on the book.

Sutton caught it and glanced at her. "We still have three more pages, Cookie Lady."

Amber gave the girl what she hoped was a smile, then quickly read the remaining pages of the book. She closed it and hopped up while the children applauded. Rubbing her hands against her apron she asked, "Who'd like a cookie now?"

Every child's hand shot straight up. Amber lifted the napkin from the basket and carefully handed the cookie basket to Sutton. "Do you know what to do?"

Sutton nodded. "Everybody gets one cookie. At the end, I get two."

"That's right," Amber said. Taking the little girl's hand in her own, Amber led her to the front row of children eagerly awaiting the treat. Then she excused herself.

"Amber?"

"Miss Montgomery?"

Amber ignored both Marnie and the police chief. She headed straight to the rest room, a place to which she knew he wouldn't follow her.

She closed herself behind a stall and leaned her head against the door.

Breathe, she coached herself. *Breathe.*

Her pulse pounded. She felt as if she'd been dumped into the middle of a marathon.

She tried to convince herself that she was in no physical danger from him, that she'd simply overreacted. But she couldn't get her heartbeat to slow down, or her fear to subside.

A knock on the stall door made her jump. "Who is it?"

"Amber, are you okay?" Marnie asked through the door. "What happened?"

"I'm...fine," she said, a hitch in her voice.

"You don't sound fine," Marnie persisted. "And you looked like you were about to faint out there. Would you like some water?"

"No, thank you."

For several minutes, the only sound in the rest room

was Amber's breathing. Amber's feet hadn't moved from the edge of the door where she stood.

"Amber, are you okay? Come out. Please."

"I will." But she made no move to unlatch the door.

Marnie knocked again. "Amber?"

Amber closed her eyes and tried to remember everything she'd been taught, tried to recall some of the deepbreathing exercises she'd learned.

"Amber, you're scaring me."

She forced herself to face her fear, and slid the lock free.

Marnie reached for her hands and clasped them in her own. "You're freezing."

Amber tried to tug her hands free. "I'm fine. Really. I just..." She shrugged, unable to finish the explanation, sure that Marnie with her perfect life and perfect job wouldn't be able to understand her problem, let alone identify with it.

Marnie pulled Amber toward the sink. She ran cool water and made a compress from paper towels that she then pressed on Amber's forehead. Then she ran warm water and plunged Amber's hands under the steady stream. She rubbed Amber's hands, getting the blood circulating again.

"Does that feel better?"

Amber nodded, and Marnie handed her a paper towel to dry her hands.

"You want to tell me what's going on? You ran out of there like something was on fire."

"Nothing's wrong," Amber said automatically.

If she kept telling herself that, maybe she'd eventually believe it.

For a moment, it seemed as if Marnie would let it go....

"I want you to know I care about you, Amber. You do good work here with the kids. I'd hate to lose you."

"What makes you think I'm going somewhere?"

Marnie stilled her hands and stared at Amber. "I see it in your eyes. You look scared and ready to bolt." Then their gazes connected in the mirror above the sink. "What can I do to help you?"

Amber shook her head. "Nothing."

"I think I know what's wrong."

"I doubt it," Amber said.

"Yes, Amber. You see, it takes one to know one."

"Is the Cookie Lady coming back?"

Paul glanced at one of the aides who'd stepped in after both Amber and Marnie Shepherd disappeared.

"I'm sure she will," he told the child.

"Hey, Chief Evans, can I take a ride in your police car?"

"Maybe next time, Max." He bit back a smile at the boy's excited grin.

"Tomorrow?"

"Maybe not that soon."

"Okay," the boy said, confident that the promise extracted from the police chief would eventually be fulfilled.

Sutton finished passing out the cookies and brought the basket to the front of the Story Corner. She placed her two cookies on a paper napkin, then carefully folded the two cloth napkins, bringing as much care to the job as Amber would have, as she placed them inside the basket. She then put the basket on the table next to Amber's rocker.

"I was the helper today, Daddy."

Paul squatted down and gave her a hug. "And it looks to me like you did a terrific job."

"I get two cookies." She offered him one. "Would you like this one?"

Paul took a bite and munched on it, savoring every bite.

Wow. No wonder Caleb was so opposed to sharing. He glanced in the direction of the rest rooms.

His radio squawked. Paul pressed the speaker button at his shoulder unit. "Go ahead."

"Chief, we've got a domestic in progress on Patterson in East Wayside."

"On the way," Paul answered.

"Daddy, what's a domestic?"

"Domestic disturbance. Right, Chief?" Max piped up. "Somebody's hitting somebody."

Had it been any other kid, Paul would have been disturbed at the child's knowledge. But Max Young came from a long line of law enforcement officers. "Right, Max."

With a final glance toward the place Amber had skittered off to, Paul said farewell to the children and to the aide. He hugged Sutton and placed a hand on Jonathan's shoulder. "I'll see you guys soon, okay?"

Jonathan, who didn't care for public displays of affection, edged closer to Paul. "You'll catch 'em, right?"

"Catch who?"

Jonathan motioned for Paul to get closer. He leaned down and watched the boy look to his right and left. "The domestic disturbance. You'll get the bad man, won't you?"

Paul blinked, sudden moisture in his eyes. He wrapped an arm around his son's shoulders and pulled him close for a hug. "I'll get 'em, Jon."

Marnie peeked out the bathroom door. "He's gone."

"I'm not afraid of him."

"Uh-huh," Marnie said. "That's why we've been in here ten minutes."

"I need to go."

Marnie stopped Amber with a hand on her arm. "Whatever's going on, Amber, I'm here for you and so is the Lord. I'm keeping you in my prayers."

Amber opened her mouth to say something, thought better of it, then slipped from the rest room. Her Cookie Lady persona cloaked around her again, she bid farewell to the children, thanked Sutton for her help and got a huge hug in return.

Startled, Amber didn't quite know what to do. Then she wrapped her arms around the girl, fusing both of them in the much-needed embrace. "You take good care now, okay?"

The little girl nodded. "I love you, Cookie Lady," Sutton whispered in her ear.

Astounded, Amber blinked. When was the last time she'd gotten unconditional love? Swallowing hard, she smiled at the girl, tugged on a pigtail and hightailed it out of Sunshine and Rainbows.

Who knew delivering cookies and reading a story could be just as dangerous to her state of mind as catering a Wayside Revelers' event?

When she got home, two messages awaited her.

She pressed the button on her answering machine, then tucked away the cookie basket and put the aprons in a laundry bin.

"Hi, Amber." Haley's voice rang out. "I was just checking in. I'll try to catch you later. Wanted to ask you something."

"More like checking up on me," Amber said, as the machine beeped and forwarded to the next message.

"It's me again," Haley said. "Can you join us for dinner tonight? Matt's going to grill."

Amber's mouth watered at the thought. She was a whiz in the kitchen, but Matt Brandon-Dumaine worked wonders on a barbecue grill. She could hear his voice in the background. Then Haley laughed on the recorder.

"Matt says to tell you if you come over he might, emphasis on the word *might,* share one of his secret barbecue sauce recipes with you. Steaks and chicken go on the grill at six. Hope you can make it."

Amber smiled. She had to give it to Haley—her cousin

never stopped trying to get her to live a little, to do some socializing in Wayside.

But Amber had no interest in developing any close ties beyond those she needed to make and maintain her catering company. She'd learned the hard way that friends and even family—Haley excepted, of course—couldn't be counted on to be there in a pinch.

Just one person had Amber's best interests at heart: Amber.

She could tolerate having dinner with Haley and Matt or a cup of coffee with Kara Spencer, her longtime friend and sometime therapist. Beyond that, Amber wasn't interested. She couldn't afford to be.

On her arrival at the barbecue, her eyebrows rose as she noted the number of cars in front of Matt and Haley's large house. And the moment she walked into the living room, Amber realized she'd been set up. Not only that, but it was a setup operating on two fronts.

"Hi, Amber!"

Trapped.

Too late to turn and head back out the door.

"Hello, Caleb," Amber greeted. "Funny seeing you here."

She cast her eyes toward her cousin, who merely smiled sweetly as she presented a tray of almost depleted hors d'oeuvres to Cliff Baines, *Reverend* Cliff Baines, pastor of Haley's church.

A single guy and the preacher. Great, Amber thought.

Just great. Maybe instead of eating dessert, they could just get married.

"Why don't you replenish that," Amber suggested, as Haley came around with the tray. "I'll help you," Amber said, lacing her voice with sweetness.

Haley wasn't fooled, though, as she followed Amber into her kitchen.

"You wouldn't hurt a pregnant lady," Haley said, as the swinging door closed behind the two of them. Outside on the deck, under an awning that protected him from the rain starting to fall, Matt waved.

Amber waved at Matt, but glared at her cousin. "I'm deciding," she said. She glanced at Haley's stomach. "You're not even showing yet."

Haley lifted her hands to frame her face. "But Matt says I have a glow."

"You're glowing, all right. This was no spur-of-the-moment cookout, Haley. You know I hate setups."

"What setup? It's just a few friends."

"Uh-huh," Amber said. "Your pastor and his wife to hound me about not going to church, and that puppy-dog-eyed policeman."

"Cliff and Nancy are friends. They aren't going to hound you or anybody else. And I'd hardly call Caleb puppy-dog-eyed."

Amber reached for and munched on a celery stick filled with cream cheese and pimento. "He reminds me of the Ebb character from Classic TV."

Haley shook her head. "You *do* need to get out more.

Satellite TV is addling your brain. And for the record, Caleb is also a friend. You're family. What's wrong with having friends and family over for dinner?"

Amber knew she wouldn't win this round with Haley, but she had a trump card. "When you're eight months pregnant and craving a lemon tart or a honey pecan roll, I'm going to be all sold out."

"That's mean," Haley said, but she laughed.

Matt came in, greeted Amber with a "Hey, cuz" as he leaned in to buss her on the cheek, then carried a bowl of something to the dining room.

Haley moved to follow him. "Come on. Let's get these out to everyone."

The doorbell rang as they reentered the living room.

"I'll get it," Matt said.

A moment later he opened the door to Paul Evans and Marnie Shepherd.

Amber saw the pair and let out a shaky breath. Is that what Marnie had meant in the rest room at Sunshine and Rainbows? That Amber didn't have to fear Paul because Marnie knew him to be an honorable man. *Her* man? They'd never really talked about personal stuff, so Amber had no way of knowing whether Marnie was seeing the police chief.

"Did you make these?" Caleb asked.

"Huh?"

Amber took her eyes off the pair at the door, turning her attention to Caleb, who was enjoying a corn fritter. "No. Haley did. Or maybe Matt."

"They're probably not as good as yours."

Amber looked at Caleb as if seeing him for the first time. "Excuse me." She fled to the kitchen.

Caleb looked from her retreating back to his boss at the front door.

"He followed me home, can I keep him?" Marnie said with a smile, indicating the police chief.

"Come on in," Matt invited.

She knew it was a little crazy but Amber had to talk to someone right now. From the wall phone in the kitchen, she called Kara—and got an answering machine.

She slammed the phone down, then tried a little deep breathing. If she kept jumping at shadows like this she'd be a basket case, not to mention right back where she'd been three years ago when she first came home to Wayside.

Leaning against the sink, she considered her options. She could escape out the sliding glass doors and go home, or she could face her fears and walk out into that living room.

The choice, to some degree, was taken away from her when the kitchen door swung open and in walked Wayside, Oregon's Police Chief Paul Evans.

Amber gripped the edge of the sink behind her. She assessed all of him. Tonight he didn't wear the uniform that marked him as an officer of the law. Gone also were the gun, club and cuffs. He stood at the door in jeans, work boots and a chambray shirt. He looked more like a cow-boy than a cop.

He's just a man, Amber coached herself. *You're in a safe place. He's just a man.*

"Hello, Miss Montgomery. I waited at the day care the other day to have a word with you, but I got a call and had to leave."

She didn't say anything.

He took three steps forward. Amber forced herself not to flinch.

He must have noticed something because his eyes narrowed a bit, and the smile on his mouth fell a notch, not enough that any casual observer would even notice. But Amber wasn't a casual observer. Fight-or-flight kicked in. Since he now blocked both exits, it would have to be fight.

"I don't see how that concerns me." She deliberately aimed for belligerent and defensive.

"I want to apologize," he said, glancing at her arm. "About the other night. I didn't mean to grab you or to leave a bruise."

"The complaint letters are already mailed." That wasn't true, but he didn't have to know it.

"I mistook you for one of the Revelers."

"So I look seventy years old?"

A smile tilted the corners of his mouth and a dimple showed. "Hardly, Miss Montgomery."

She told herself she wasn't going to be charmed by that smile, that her guard would remain up. But she did allow her body to loosen. She'd been holding herself so erect that she'd need a masseuse to get the knots out.

"Please let me finish. I also want to thank you for something," he said.

"Thank me? For what?"

"For bringing a smile again to my daughter's face."

Chapter Five

"She's a sweet girl."

"But she's been through a lot. It's not very often I see her smile and giggle and act like the five-year-old she is."

"What's wrong with her?" The question was out before the impertinence of it dawned on Amber. She'd always been one to speak her mind first and worry about the consequences later. The cloud that shadowed his face told her without words that she'd done it again. "Never mind," she added. "Don't answer that. Your apology's accepted, Chief Evans. Now, if you'll excuse me."

She gave him a wide berth as she moved toward the door leading back to the living room and the safety and comfort of other people.

Paul watched her retreat. He didn't feel a need to bolster his own defense mechanisms in response to her anger; to his utter amazement, what he was feeling was a surge of protectiveness. But everything about Amber Montgomery said "woman with a past—avoid like the plague."

He couldn't determine if she didn't like cops in general or if it was him in particular. Whatever the case, Amber brought out in him an interest that extended beyond the professional.

Since it clearly wasn't reciprocated, he'd have to move on.

He hadn't believed anyone existed who could draw the kids out of the shells in which they'd lived these past few years. But Amber Montgomery, the Cookie Lady, had done just that, not only for Sutton and Jonathan, but for him, as well.

Moving to Oregon, this little town in particular, had facilitated the healing process for the three of them. Paul hadn't expected to find love in Wayside. But he'd hoped to find a woman with whom he was compatible, someone who could open her heart and accept not only him, but the two children he was now raising as his own.

Meanwhile, as another consideration, Marnie Shepherd was great with the kids. They liked her and the time they spent at Sunshine and Rainbows. Of course, no one would ever replace their mother, but Jonathan and Sutton still needed mothering. Every child did.

"Come on out here, Chief. The reverend is going to say grace, then we'll eat."

Paul joined the others in the living room where Cliff Baines waited to lead the dinner guests in prayer.

Looking around the assembled group, Paul realized just what Haley and Matt Brandon-Dumaine were up to. Their little soiree included two married couples and four singles who looked likely to be matched up. And if the episode with the cookies in the squad car served as an indicator, Caleb was well and truly infatuated with Amber Montgomery.

That meant Matt and Haley had paired him with Marnie for the evening. Paul wasn't opposed to that. He enjoyed speaking with her at church. With her pretty smile, bubbly personality and her way with children, Marnie was an attractive woman. He'd never believed in love at first sight or any of that romantic nonsense. People got together because they were compatible. And Marnie got along well with Jonathan and Sutton. That was a good place to begin.

He moved into the small circle they'd formed for grace and looked at Marnie again. She smiled as she leaned over, telling Haley something. Paul nodded to himself, silently agreeing with the not-so-subtle matchmaking.

Maybe he would ask Marnie out to dinner and a movie. For some reason, though, Paul's eye kept wandering to the aloof blonde with the haunted eyes. On the pretense of moving a chair, he shifted his position toward her.

Amber had been standing next to Matt, but when she bowed her head, a strong hand clasped hers. Her gaze flew to her right. Paul Evans stood there, tall, strong, his head bowed in prayer, his hand holding hers. Warmth suffused her.

She cleared her throat and tried to ease her hand from his. But he held on as the minister started to pray.

"Thank you, Lord, for bringing good friends together to share good times and good food. Amen."

Amber opened one eye to peer at Cliff. That was it? That was his idea of grace? What about blessing the hands that prepared the meal, and three minutes of other supplications and prayer-time clichés? She knew them all.

"Amber?"

She glanced up at Paul. "Yes?" she said, surprised that he didn't know you weren't supposed to talk during a prayer or moment of silence.

"You can let my hand go now."

Her gaze swept the room. The others, already having broken away from the prayer circle, headed toward the dining room. Amber's face flamed. She dropped Paul's hand and hastened a safe distance away.

"Steaks are ready!" Matt called out from the kitchen before she could think of a good reason to leave the dinner party.

Rain may have chased the cookout indoors, but it didn't dampen the enthusiasm inside. Since the evening was supposed to be informal, everyone grabbed a plate and helped themselves from the feast Matt had laid out on the dining room table. Instead of settling there, Haley led the way back to the living room, where the guests spread out wherever they felt comfortable.

For Nancy Baines and Marnie, that meant the floor with the coffee table pressed into service.

Caleb perched on the edge of a chair near them. "I'll grab some napkins for you ladies."

When Paul and Cliff claimed two of the TV trays, Amber moved hers a bit away.

Matt got his wife situated and kissed her.

"Hey, none of that," Amber said.

"Yeah," Marnie added, laughing. "You'll make the rest of us jealous."

"I still have six months to go, but he acts as if delivery is imminent."

"It is," Matt said. "The time's going to fly by."

While Marnie and Nancy asked about baby names and nursery colors, Amber watched the byplay between Haley and Matt. A lot of love flowed between them. In their soft gazes swelling with shared affection and regard it was there for all the world to see.

Once upon a time she'd loved like that—or so she'd thought at the time. The love hadn't flowed both ways, though, and Amber found out the hard way just how much she'd pay for that.

She supposed that some people truly were happy. But for her, love was a lie she'd learned to reject. She'd learned to simply live, day to day. And that suited her just fine.

Again and again, however, her gaze slipped to her cousin, and something akin to jealousy snipped at her, surprising her.

Keep it light, she coached herself. If she allowed what-if thoughts to intrude, she'd never make it through the evening.

For a few minutes, the four couples ate in companionable silence, the only accompaniment to their meal an instrumental CD playing in the background.

"I've got to hand it to you, Matt," Caleb said. "You have grilling skills."

"He's supposed to reveal the sauce recipe," Amber said. "The promise of that is the only thing that lured me here tonight."

"Ah," Caleb said. "And here I thought it was the thrill of seeing me again."

"In your dreams, Jenkins," she said.

Caleb chuckled at that.

This she could handle, keeping it casual. The easy camaraderie in the room masked the awkwardness Amber felt around Paul.

Over a glass of cider, she studied the police chief. Without the uniform, he didn't look nearly as intimidating as he had previously. Of course, he was still tall and broad-shouldered, but that made him look solid, the sort you could depend on in a crisis.

Like Kyle.

His gaze connected with hers. Caught staring, Amber blushed and averted her eyes. She cut a piece of steak, making careful work of slicing the meat just so. When she dared, she glanced up.

He was still looking at her. He smiled.

Amber's pulse rate leaped.

"Anyone want more potatoes?" She hopped up from her seat.

"I do," Paul said. "I'll help you."

"I'm closest," Marnie said. "Sit down, both of you."

Before either could object, Marnie disappeared and came back from the dining room with a tray of skewered roasted potatoes with red and green bell peppers. She offered the tray to everyone, sending—at least it seemed so to Amber—a brighter, longer smile in Chief Evans's direction.

"So, what's going on over at Community Christian these days?" Caleb asked.

"Camp. Camp and more camp," Nancy said. "Forty-five kids this year. We have a good crop of seniors who've been with us and will serve as the teen counselors, but still I worry."

"Don't mind my wife," Cliff said. "She's the overall coordinator of our annual fall jamboree and things are just a little stressful right now."

"That's because it's less than a week away, and I still have two weeks' worth of work to do."

Cliff placed a hand on her shoulder as he passed by with a refill from the dining room. "It all comes together beautifully each year. This year won't be an exception."

"We're really blessed to have so many volunteers," Haley said. "Everyone from the church pitches in and helps in some way. And with that community grant Kara got for us this year, we're able to do a lot more."

Amber let the conversation flow around her. She had nothing to say and wondered just how soon she could make her escape without seeming too obvious.

If, for some silly reason, she felt another nip or two from the green-eyed monster as she looked at Matt and Haley, and even at Cliff and Nancy Baines, the preacher and his wife, she let it slide. They looked so...happy.

It didn't matter. She didn't go to Community Christian or any other church—and had no intention of starting anytime soon. Plus, through the years she'd had enough church camp to last her not one or two, but several lifetimes.

Amber couldn't remember the last time she could count herself truly happy. And she now knew she'd never really been in love. Not the way the Baineses were in love. She'd been part of a couple once. And all she had to say for the experience was good riddance.

"So, how are you finding Wayside?"

The question, directed to Paul from Nancy Baines, made Amber look up from her plate.

Paul swallowed a bite of food. "Just fine, Mrs. Baines. It's a lot different from L.A."

Amber's throat constricted. "You're from Los Angeles?"

He nodded. "I needed to get Sutton and Jon out of the big city environment." He shook his head. "It wasn't healthy for any of us. And, where I lived and how I used to work didn't lend itself to fatherhood. At least, not the way they needed."

"The children are just adorable," Nancy said. "I have Sutton in my Sunday school class."

"Yes, she really enjoys that," Paul said. "I'm glad I found Community Christian. That was one thing I thought I might miss about Los Angeles. Even though I worked crazy hours, I had a church family that was devoted to the gospel and family values, both incongruous notions in L.A."

Caleb helped himself to another kabob. "The chief here was on the LAPD for—what?—about twelve years, right Chief?"

Amber gasped. Her eyes widened and her fork clattered to her plate. She stood up so fast she almost lost her balance. "Excuse me." And she left the room.

Matt and Haley shared a look.

Cliff put his plate down. "Maybe I should..."

Haley got up. "She'll be all right. I'll go check on her," she said as she headed toward the kitchen.

"Was it something I said?" Paul asked.

"Uh, don't worry about it. I'm sure it's just something to do with setting out dessert," Matt said, but his look was hardly reassuring.

Spending an evening with a room full of church people, even ones she knew, wasn't Amber's idea of a great time, but she'd found herself laughing at the byplay among Cliff, Nancy Baines, and even Caleb, and actually enjoying herself...until just now.

He was one of *them*.

"Amber, are you all right?"

She shook her head. "I have to leave."

Haley wrapped an arm around her cousin's shoulders. "I know. I'm sorry, Amber. I didn't realize he was—"

"It's not your fault." Amber stopped her. "This is my bugaboo. I have to learn to live with it."

Amber headed to the sliding glass doors that led to the deck and yard of Matt and Haley's home.

"It's still raining outside," Haley said. "Let me get you an umbrella."

"I'll be fine. Sorry to break up your party."

And then she escaped into the dark night—a night a lot like one she'd tried for a long time to banish from her memory.

"I think tonight was supposed to be a setup," Marnie told Caleb Jenkins later.

He laughed. "So it wasn't just me getting that vibe."

"I think now that she's happily married and starting a family, Haley has decided to play town matchmaker."

Caleb held the door for Marnie, who'd been dropped off at Haley and Matt's by a co-worker.

"The thing I'm trying to figure out," he said, "is who was supposed to be with whom."

"I think I was supposed to be with Chief Evans. Did you see that pleased look on Haley's face when I appeared at the door with him?"

"How did that come about? Happenstance?"

She waited until he came around and settled behind the wheel. "Something like that. He drove up at the same time I was dashing through the rain for the front door.

So if Haley planned for me to get cozy with Chief Evans, that means she has her eye on you and Amber as a pair."

"Amber is a friend."

Marnie smiled. "Mm-hmm."

Caleb started the car. "Have you ever thought about selling the house?"

She gave him a knowing look, but didn't call him on the abrupt change of subject. "Yes." The single word came out slow and long. Marnie shifted in her seat.

He glanced at her, but didn't follow up with the next obvious question.

"It's a lot of house," she said. "Selling it makes sense."

Caleb nodded, but not because he agreed with her or particularly liked the direction of the conversation and what selling that house might mean. It just seemed the right thing to do at the moment. But instead of following that thread of their touch-and-go conversation, he asked another question that had been on his mind for a while.

"So, how have you been? Really been, I mean?"

Marnie chuckled softly, relieving the sudden tension in the car. The history between them didn't get discussed very often. "I'll answer that if you admit you have a secret thing for Amber Montgomery."

Caleb raised an eyebrow. He knew that to deny it again would be protesting too much.

So they drove the rest of the way to her home in silence.

Caleb didn't regret asking the question about how she

was really doing. He still wanted an answer, but maybe it was still too soon for her. Maybe it would never be the right time. He worried about Marnie. On the outside, everything looked okay, but they never talked about the thing that stood between them—the element that connected them. By not talking about Roy, they could pretend everything was just fine.

He pulled into the driveway, careful to skirt the thick tree trunk that pushed through the gravel. He knew Marnie would rather cut off one of her own limbs than cut the tree down, so at some point the driveway would have to be realigned and rerouted around the ancient oak, the only non-maple tree on Maple Street.

He came around and opened the passenger-side door, an old-fashioned habit he'd been taught as a child. Some women liked it, others made fun of him for doing it. Marnie, he knew, was in the first group.

"For the record," he said as if they'd never stopped talking, "Amber bakes a mean cookie, but I don't have a thing for her. And anyway, she's not interested."

Marnie opened her mouth to say something, then apparently changed her mind. "Thanks for the ride, Caleb."

He nodded. "Anytime."

He meant it, too, but didn't know how to go further— to say the important things that stood between them.

So he saw her to the door and waited until she let herself into the house. She turned in the doorway, looking soft and vulnerable and painfully beautiful.

"Do you want to come in for a cup of coffee?"

Yes.

But he knew the way he was feeling right now, it was best if he went on his way. "No, it's kind of late. I'll just head on home."

She hesitated. "All right, then. You take care. Thanks for the lift." She turned to go, then paused. "Caleb?"

"Yes?"

She raised a hand and stepped forward. "I... I just thought you could use a hug."

Caleb closed his eyes.

No. No. No. *Yes.*

She wrapped her arms around him and hugged him close. Caleb stored up every moment of the brief embrace.

"Thanks again for giving me a lift. And, Caleb, if you like her, you should tell her. Amber's a nice girl. You take care, okay?"

When he nodded, she waved from the door and then closed it.

Caleb Jenkins stood there for a while, watching lights go on as Marnie made her way through her home, a big house made for the family she very much deserved but didn't have.

Marnie had always been a special woman, blessed with a gift for making people feel exceptional, wanted, loved. That's why she was such an asset to Sunshine and Rainbows. The children blossomed under her care.

There were so many things he wanted to say to her. He wished he could explain. To open up with her the way he'd always wanted to. But he didn't have the right—had never had the right to hope for anything more than polite friendliness with Marnie. Especially now.

Making light of his social life, or lack thereof, came easy to Caleb. He dated now and then, and flirted with a few women like Amber just to keep the loneliness at bay, but nothing serious.

How *could* he get serious about any other woman? His heart had always belonged to Marnie Shepherd—his brother's wife.

❧ Chapter Six ❧

Hours later, Amber pulled into the drive and parked behind Kara's car. Even though Kara was engaged to a multi-millionaire, recording artist Marcus Ambrose, she still drove the same car she always had. A For Sale sign in the front yard was the only indication that any change was in the works in her life. Soon Kara would move to a new home outside Los Angeles.

Just the name of the city brought a shudder.

She didn't have many friends and the thought of losing one of them hurt, particularly since visits to L.A. were completely out of the question. The City of Angels might be large, but not large enough for Amber to escape the memories of her years there. When she'd left, she'd vowed never to set foot there again.

She glanced up at the second-floor windows. Dark. Maybe she should have called first.

But before she chickened out, Amber went to the back door and rang the bell. Then she leaned on it.

A few moments later, a light flicked on in the kitchen. "Who's there?"

"It's me, Kara. Amber."

The back porch light clicked on, bathing Amber in its glow. Then she heard the dead bolt slide.

To her credit, Kara didn't exclaim about the lateness of the hour or ask why Amber was standing on her porch in the rain. She just opened her arms and let the troubled woman in.

Fifteen minutes later, dried off and with a cup of chamomile tea to warm her inside and out, Amber sat in one of the comfy chairs in Kara's sunroom.

"Do you want to talk about it?"

Amber stared into her mug for a bit, then she blinked back tears. "You've been very patient with me."

Kara, a psychologist by profession—though she primarily did community block grant work these days— never balked when Amber showed up at her door, a honey pecan roll in hand and things on her mind. Kara knew some of what had happened to Amber in L.A., but Amber had never told anyone—not even Haley—the whole story.

"I thought it was all behind me," she said. "But it's back again and I don't know what to do."

"What's back, Amber?"

"It's like a hole inside me, a hole that's eating away at my insides. It was all patched up and doing okay.

None of the bad stuff was leaking out. Then he showed up."

"Wait, what? Who is 'he'?"

"The cop."

Kara tread carefully here. "Your former boyfriend?"

Amber lifted wide hollow eyes to her friend. Trust didn't come easily, but Kara had proven herself to be a friend, someone who could be relied on.

"It's the police chief," Amber finally said. "Chief Evans."

Though she tried to hide it, Kara's surprise came through in her voice. "Chief Evans hurt you?"

Amber shook her head. "No. Not in the way you mean."

Kara leaned back in her chair, waiting for Amber to gather her thoughts and open up. This time, Kara instinctively knew, Amber wouldn't run when the memories and the pain closed in. She could see it in the other woman's eyes—the determination to move on, to heal.

To face the monster from her past.

Paul spent a frustrating couple of days trying to figure out just what was with Amber Montgomery. Everything he said, every move he made, seemed to spook her. She responded to him as if she were guilty of a crime still undiscovered.

Paul considered himself a pretty good judge of character, yet all of his instincts went on alert around Amber. His first thought was to run her name through NCIC. The

National Crime Information Center had data on every known and wanted criminal. Amber didn't look like a criminal, but fugitives from the law came in all shapes and sizes.

The only problem with his instincts when it came to this particular woman was that for the first time in his law enforcement career, he found himself having a difficult time ascertaining if the gut feeling that had never let him down before was professional or personal. Amber intrigued him, mainly because she evoked in him so many conflicting emotions: wariness, desire, the urge to protect, the need to unravel her mysteries.

And that's the part that the cop in him wouldn't let go. Wayside, Oregon, his new home, the place he'd sworn to protect and serve, was just the sort of town that would make a good hideout for someone who wanted to disappear. Its population of 17,800—well, now with him and the kids, 17,803—was just big enough for newcomers to blend in if they didn't make any waves, and just small enough to provide a sense of comfort. That's why *he'd* chosen it. And the good Lord knew he'd needed a place to be renewed.

Amber Montgomery was an enigma. A well-protected enigma. He'd tried to find out from his hosts, Matt and Haley Brandon-Dumaine, just what had been said or done that spooked Amber. They'd been polite, but close-mouthed. Ditto for Pastor Cliff.

Paul had another source available to him, though.

Caleb liked Amber, which meant he could probably answer some questions.

Even though Wayside was small-town America at its best, the community never missed out on any federal money that the police bureau knew of. So in addition to the state-of-the-art headquarters building, the Wayside Police Bureau boasted not one, but two community policing branches, one of which was in East Wayside, a particularly crime-ridden area. He convinced himself it was a public safety issue and not a personal concern that made him corner his patrol chief near the command desk at the police station.

"What's up with Amber Montgomery?"

Caleb grinned. "I wondered how long it would take you to ask."

Paul narrowed his eyes, but Caleb held up a hand to stave off the potential irritation.

"Before I answer, I need to know who's asking. Paul the man who is my friend, or Police Chief Evans, my boss?"

In his few months in Wayside, Paul had made a few friends. He counted Caleb Jenkins among them. He didn't, however, want to admit that he found himself attracted to Amber. "The police chief."

Caleb folded his arms across his chest. "Really? Well, in that case, *Chief* Evans, Ms. Montgomery is one of our upstanding citizens, a small-business owner."

With a jerk of his head, Paul steered Caleb away from listening ears. They walked a few feet to a snack-machine area. "All right, *I* want to know. What did I say that sent her flying out the door the other night?"

"I don't know."

Paul's patience, already frayed, didn't improve with that answer. "What do you mean, you don't know?"

Caleb shrugged. "I don't know. Honest. I met Amber a few years ago. She'd enrolled in a self-defense class I was teaching over at the college. You should have seen her then, Chief. Hollow-eyed. She was incredibly thin. She looked like a refugee from a war zone."

Something crossed Caleb's face then. "I—" He shrugged again. "I felt responsible somehow, even though I'd just met her. I wanted to protect her, keep her safe."

Paul could identify with that. He felt the same—unreasonable—way about her. Though he'd never admit as much to his patrol sergeant. Maybe there was nothing extraordinary about Amber except that the fragile blonde brought out the protectiveness trait in some men. The Amber he'd met bore no resemblance to the hollow-eyed woman Caleb described. Paul's Amber was vibrant, active, and great with kids. His kids.

"She started baking one day," Caleb said. "She made some honey pecan rolls for a booth during Wayside Market Days. They sold out in no time. Then someone, probably Haley, talked her into preparing a basket for the picnic basket auction."

"Picnic basket auction?"

Caleb quickly explained about the annual event that

was a part of Wayside Market Days. "Amber always makes up a lunch basket filled with good stuff that goes for a pretty penny during a public auction over at the gazebo. But Matt Brandon-Dumaine holds the record for the most money bid on a single basket. Haley's, of course."

"And what does this have to do with anything?"

"You wanted to know about Amber, so I'm telling you," Caleb said. "You do want a complete snapshot. Right?"

When Paul nodded, Caleb continued. "Everybody likes her—those honey pecan rolls of hers transcended her privateness. They were the beginning of her relationship with Wayside. She's responsible for a lot of memberships at the gym."

"Because she has a bakery shop near the gym?"

Caleb chuckled. "Nope. Because folks have to work off the pounds that creep up as a result of too many of Amber's honey pecan rolls."

"I'm going to have to get one of those things," Paul muttered.

"Thanks for agreeing to do this," Marnie told Amber on Wednesday. Along with one of the Sunshine and Rainbows assistants, they'd set up the cooking demonstration area. Big plastic mixing bowls and wooden spoons were at the ready, along with measuring utensils and ingredients just waiting for little hands to create yummy masterpieces. "The kids are so excited."

Amber looked around. "Where is everybody?"

"In their classrooms. Since they're going to be so keyed up with you here, we thought a quiet period beforehand made sense."

Twenty minutes later, the center room bustled with kids, parent volunteers, and Amber, who was in her element.

"What's the first thing you should do before you start cooking?" she asked the kids.

"Wash your hands!" several of them yelled.

"That's right. Who remembered to do that?"

"I did, Cookie Lady."

Amber looked at the soft-spoken girl in the front row. Her brother and two other girls were her table partners. "Good job, Sutton," Amber said.

She was grateful that their father hadn't put in an appearance. Marnie said he'd been delayed. That was fine by Amber. With any luck, they'd be finished by the time he completed his police duties. The three other parent volunteers and one of the center's assistants could easily handle the job of monitoring the children's progress.

Over the next ten minutes, she taught the children about measuring dry ingredients. The no-bake cookies included oatmeal, chocolate chips, crisped rice cereal and mini chocolate candies. The sugar high alone would keep them all bouncing off the walls for a while.

Amber walked along the rows of tables that had been converted into kitchen workstations. She paused at the back of the room to show a girl how to use her spoon to level off a cup of oatmeal.

"Is this too much?" Max Young asked as he dumped half of a five-pound bag of flour into his bowl. White powder poofed up. Max waved his arms, trying vainly to lessen the damage.

"Just a little," Amber said.

She reached for a towel to clean up some of the mess, Max helping. And her hand connected with a much larger, warmer one.

Tingles shot up her spine. She knew who it was without even turning around.

Paul chuckled. "I think that's way more than you need, Max."

"Hi, Chief Evans!" exclaimed Max.

"Hi, Max. Hello, Amber."

"Good afternoon, Chief Evans."

"Please, call me Paul."

Amber was saved from having to agree to that when one of the other parents asked a question. "I'll be right there," she called. "Excuse me," she said to Paul.

Marnie stood watching the parry and retreat between Amber and Paul. She doubted they even realized what was happening between them, all darting eyes and uneasy contact. From her vantage point, they presented an intriguing pair. But, Marnie knew, Amber had a lot to overcome before she'd allow herself to trust a man like Paul Evans.

It wasn't Paul. He had a lot going for him. Plus, he looked like a walking dream. About six feet tall, he had the lean look of a tennis player, and the muscle tone of a man who regularly worked out. In the dictionary next to the entry "all-American boy next door" would be a picture of Paul Evans, his blue eyes sparkling.

Marnie realized her brother-in-law also fit that general description. Sometimes it amazed Marnie that Caleb and his brother Roy had actually come from the same womb. They were different in every way. If she'd met Caleb before meeting Roy...

She smiled, self-deprecating. That didn't even warrant a completed thought. She'd made her choices and there was no going backward hollering, *"I changed my mind. I want Bachelor Number Two."*

Shuddering through the thin turtleneck and pullover sweater, she rubbed her upper arms. She took a deep, calming breath and focused on the children. If she were even remotely interested in another relationship, Marnie might consider Paul. But right now, all she wanted to do was enjoy her hard-won freedom.

Her gaze slid to Amber, who now knelt at a child's side. Marnie knew Amber had been sent into her life for a reason. Marnie could make a pretty educated guess as to why. With the exception of one thing, nothing remarkable had ever happened to Marnie. Amber, Sunshine and Rainbows' beloved Cookie Lady, had been in her prayers for a while and Marnie was in the right place to reach out to her.

"Hi, Daddy!"

"Hey there, pumpkin," Paul said. He swung the girl up for a hug. "Did you make some good cookies?"

Sutton nodded. "But they're not as good as the Cookie Lady's."

He put her down, and reached for one of the brown blobs on her sheet of waxed paper and sampled it. "I disagree," he said. "Yours are way better."

Sutton beamed at him, and then sent a smile Amber's way.

Amber returned the smile, then bent to help another child.

Amber did her best to avoid Paul for the remainder of the kids' cooking class. He put her nerves on edge in ways she didn't want to consider. So instead, she focused on the kids and their questions, and found herself inordinately relieved when the whole thing ended and Paul Evans left, promising to pick up his children at their appointed departure time.

Having finished the last no-bake cookie, the kids thanked Amber and headed back to their classrooms. Amber helped Marnie with the cleanup, then the two women sat in Marnie's office.

"That was fun."

"Yeah," Amber said. "It was." She looked at the day care director. Amber's circle of friends was small, very small—like, all of two—Haley and Kara. Maybe if she put forth a little effort she could turn a close acquaintance into a friend. Marnie seemed like a good bet. And she'd said something that had been nagging at Amber for days now.

"Can I ask you something?"

Marnie leaned back, closed her eyes and rolled the kinks out of her shoulders. "Sure. What's up?"

"The other day when we were talking in the bathroom here, you said 'it takes one to know one.' What did you mean by that?"

Marnie slowly sat up. "You were so upset that day, I didn't think you even heard me." She looked intently at Amber, apparently weighing her words. "We all have secrets, Amber. Some are best kept locked up tight. Others need the light of day to break their bonds."

Trying to keep it light, Amber waggled her brows and lowered her voice to mimic a television announcer's. "What deep, dark secrets could she be hiding?"

Marnie smiled, but she wasn't going to let Amber off, not on something this important. Not when her own spirit was crying out to her that this woman needed her. She said a silent prayer, asking how to say what needed to be said at this particular moment.

"I have scars, Amber. Physical ones that will be with me for a long time, maybe forever. And I have emotional ones. Those, however, I've worked to banish."

Amber scuffed her sneaker on the floor. "What are you talking about?"

Marnie reached a hand out and clasped Amber's. "I think you know."

Pulling away, Amber rose. "I think I don't want to talk about this."

"Amber, being a battered or abused woman is nothing to be ashamed of. That's in your past."

"Who said I was battered?"

"Just a guess," Marnie said with a sad smile. She stood. "Like I said, it takes one to know one, Amber."

The next morning, Eunice Gallagher, known as Mrs. G around Community Christian, greeted Haley and Kara with a smile, glasses of fresh-squeezed orange juice and bad news.

"We have a slight problem."

"So what else is new?" Kara asked. "Let me guess, Sunday school?"

"Thanks," Haley said on a dry note. Since Haley directed the church's Christian education department, any problems in the Sunday school would fall under her purview.

"Nope," Eunice said. "It's not the Sunday school. Or the choir. Or Reverend Baines or the church board."

Kara and Haley exchanged a look. At this time of year, just one big project loomed. "Please tell us it's not the camp."

Eunice winced. "It's the camp."

The two younger women groaned, then headed to the conference room.

"If it's any consolation," Eunice told them, "I called and ordered some honey pecan rolls to help you mull over possible solutions."

Kara pulled out the box containing the student registrations. Every September, Community Christian sponsored a jamboree for the church's youth. This year, however, with Haley's outreach vision in play and Kara's grant-proposal writing skills at work, the camp was being expanded to include fifteen at-risk youth from the community. Several older and experienced teens from Community Christian, including Adam Richardson and Cindy Worthington, would serve as counselors.

Everything was in place for the three-day, two-night camp—from food to activities to adult volunteers. The setup would begin tomorrow night.

"This can't be good," Haley said. "If she has to butter us up with Amber's rolls."

"I was just thinking the same thing," Kara said as she pulled out a chair and sat.

"Okay. We're ready now," Kara said, squeezing her eyes shut really tight. "Tell us the bad news."

Eunice laughed. "It's not *that* bad."

Kara peeked out of one eye. "Really?"

Eunice nodded.

The other two women breathed a sigh of relief and Haley sat down as well. "So all we have to oversee now is loading equipment tomorrow. The kids will start to arrive after four o'clock Friday."

"Well, there's equipment and...one more thing."

Haley and Kara, best friends, shared another look, then each closed one eye and peered at Eunice through the open one.

"Okay. Spill it, Eunice."

"Jocelyn can't come. Her mother is sick down in Salem, and she had to leave."

For a minute, the import didn't sink in. Then Haley and Kara gasped simultaneously.

"What are we going to do with forty-five kids and no cook for three days? Camp starts the day after tomorrow. Jocelyn was supposed to spend tomorrow setting up everything in the kitchen—"

"Yoo-hoo, anybody here?"

"We're back this way, Amber," Eunice called. She got up to greet the chef with the sweet treats.

Haley and Kara turned as Amber appeared in the door, a white baker's box in one hand.

"Amber," they said in silky sweet unison.

Amber eyed them. "Whatever the two of you are thinking, the answer is no."

"Cousin." Haley came around and greeted her. "So nice to see you." She took the box from Amber's hand and placed it on the table. "We've got a wonderful opportunity for you that would also be a tremendous favor to us." They proceeded to explain.

"No," Amber said a few minutes later. "Absolutely not."

"But it's just for a few days."

"Appetizers & More is a gourmet catering company," Amber said. "And despite the fiasco that was the Revelers' dinner dance, I haven't sunk to beans and franks and s'mores, or bug juice."

"What's bug juice?" Eunice asked.

"That icky-sweet orange drink that is a staple at church camps. It draws bugs. Ants and gnats and who knows what else. They always end up in the drinks."

Eunice frowned. "That's nasty. Thankfully we don't serve orange drink at Camp Spirit Fire."

"Please, Amber, we need you," Kara implored. "We're desperate."

Amber eyed them. "How desperate?"

As it turned out, quite so. To pinch-hit, Haley and Kara offered Amber double the rate the camp cook was going to get. Knowing they were on a tight budget and would never agree to it, Amber asked for triple. She smiled smugly at the women's stricken expressions.

Haley and Kara glanced at each other, then, as one, turned to Amber. "Deal."

❧ Chapter Seven ❧

"Deal? What do you mean 'deal'?" She'd been so sure they'd never agree to that much money.

"We'll pay you triple rate," Haley said, restating the deal. "It's fairly easy money for just four days. You'll have some free time to do whatever you'd like. And you'll even have an assistant or two." She nudged Kara, who flipped through a page on top of the registration forms.

Kara ran a manicured finger down a list. "Two assistants," Kara confirmed. "Leanne and Kirsten. They're both very dependable."

She *could* use the money. But that wasn't at all the issue. Amber had had her fill of religious campsites with know-it-all holier-than-thou's. When she'd left home years ago, the one thing she'd promised herself was that she'd never set foot in a mission site again, particularly ones in remote corners of the globe.

"I don't like church camp," she said.

"You won't be attending," Kara said. "Just cooking the meals for the campers."

"I don't like being out in the woods."

"Great!" Haley said a bit too cheerfully. "Camp Spirit·Fire is on a private lake. And there are some dorms. You don't even have to go into the woods if you don't want to."

Amber groaned. "I really don't want to do this."

"Please," Haley said. "It's not at all like you think."

"Pretty please," Kara added. "We're desperate."

Eunice rose. "As much as I'd like to listen to the rest of this begging session, I do have some work to do," the church clerk said. "I'll be in my office. Tell me how this all works out."

"Draw up a contract for Amber," Haley called to Eunice's back.

"If I do this, you guys are gonna owe me big," said Amber.

"We're paying you triple scale!" Haley said.

"That's business," Amber said. "This is personal."

"Okay, we'll owe you one," Kara said.

"Two," Amber countered.

"All right," Kara said. "We'll both owe you a big favor."

"And I plan to collect on it," Amber said. She turned to her cousin. "You *know* I really despise church camp."

"This is nothing like that," Haley said. "I promise."

"Humph," Amber said as she stomped out of the conference room muttering, "I knew I shouldn't have agreed to bring an order over here."

"So she's going to do it?" Kara asked.

Sure that once her cousin committed to a deal she'd follow through, Haley nodded. "She'll do it," Haley said with confidence. Then she bit her nail, thinking about Amber's aversion to church, its rituals and its members in general. "Well," she amended, not quite so certain anymore. "I *hope* she'll do it."

"What's the deal with her and church camp?"

"Well, you know my aunt and uncle were missionaries?"

Kara nodded.

"They spent a lot of time in developing countries," Haley said. "Mostly in Central America, primarily Guatemala and Honduras. I think church camp reminds Amber of all those places she and Kyle grew up in. I got to visit with them once before her parents retired from missionary work. I loved it, but Amber hated it. A lot. She wanted a normal life, regular parents."

"Hated it enough to renege on our deal after she thinks about it?"

Haley nodded. "'Fraid so."

"Well, Camp Spirit Fire is hardly the same as a Central American jungle."

"That's not what has me worried."

"What, then?"

Haley pulled out the registrations and pointed to two names: Jonathan and Sutton Evans. "Has she talked to you at all about him?" She left the who of the him unsaid. They were both well aware of Amber's aversion to police officers.

"A little, but..."

"I know, client confidentiality and all that. I'm just worried about her."

"Amber is a friend, not a client," Kara said.

"If she'd just talk about what happened to her in L.A. I think she'd be able to move on."

"What she went through isn't something a person can easily move on from. It takes time."

Haley tapped the registration form for Paul's children. "I just worry that her run-in with Chief Evans at the Revelers' has begun to bring everything back out in the open."

By the time she got to the campsite, Amber knew she should have stuck to her guns. Driving through a rustic gate welcoming people to Community Christian Church's Camp Spirit Fire, Amber's thoughts roamed back through the years to a similar sign over a similar camp.

It had taken two days by a camp truck on an almost nonexistent road and then a five-mile hike to get to the site the Montgomery family would call home for nine months. Amber didn't like the way the trees looked or the things she saw hanging from branches and scurrying off in the underbrush.

She held tight to her brother's hand, wishing they didn't have the parents they did. Normal parents didn't make their kids tote Bibles in their backpacks or sleep on folding cots inches above a ground teeming with creepy crawlies.

Her skin itched from mosquito bites, but she didn't let Kyle's hand go.

"It'll be all right, Amber," he'd assured her. "I'm here for you. It'll be all right, you'll see."

And she had believed him. Always.

Except, it wasn't. Not then. And definitely not now.

Sniffling and banishing from her mind thoughts of that last painful missionary assignment, Amber followed the pickup truck in front of her. Her first impression of Community Christian Church's camp was that it was pristine—tranquil even. It looked more like a state park than the missionary sites she'd grown up in. Five large buildings—the middle and biggest one of them including a front porch and probably a lodge—were to the right. Picnic tables positioned under large pines were scattered about the area. A small pond, not really big enough for anything but a view, was to the immediate left. And off to the far left, she saw several paths leading to a copse of trees.

The pickup pulled in front of the large building where Nancy Baines waited. She waved and came to greet Amber.

"I'm so glad you were able to do this."

Wish I could say the same, she thought. "Not a problem," Amber said out loud. "I brought some gear with me, just in case."

"Oh, good. Just let me know if you need anything. Mess hall's over there," Nancy said, pointing toward the other buildings. "The last one."

"Thanks," Amber said. "I'll go take a look around."

"Manuel will help you get everything set up. He's our groundskeeper. He's around here somewhere."

"Right-o," Amber said.

No stranger to hard work, Amber figured she'd be on her own setting up the kitchen. Now all she had to do was find it.

"I don't want to sleep in the woods by myself," Sutton told Paul.

"You won't be by yourself, pumpkin. There'll be lots of people from the church and from your Sunday school class."

"What if they don't have a night-light like we have here at home?"

"I've packed one in your bag, with extra batteries. You can keep it next to your pillow."

Sutton didn't look at all appeased by the concessions.

Truth be known, neither was Paul. This camping trip was the first time he'd be away from the children since that angry, ugly night that brought them all together almost three years ago. The counselor he'd worked with in Los Angeles had said the first time would be tough. Paul just hadn't expected to feel as if he were abandoning them.

He poured milk for the kids and had started to put the carton away when he decided to have a glass for himself. He'd made meat loaf and mashed potatoes for dinner.

"How's that salad coming, champ?"

"Almost done," Jonathan reported. He plopped cherry tomatoes around the salad bowl, then admired his handiwork. "It looks too good to eat."

Paul chuckled. "Nice try, Jon, but you're eating it."

"I like salad," Sutton said from her perch on the counter.

"I know you do. Jon does, too. Right?"

The boy wrinkled his nose. "I hope they don't have lettuce at the camp."

Paul lifted Sutton up. "Don't forget the napkins."

"I already put them by each plate," the girl reported.

"Good job."

The small family sat at the table in the dining room of the house Paul bought in Wayside. Here, he'd been able to afford a real home with a backyard, the right sort of environment in which to raise his niece and nephew. In L.A., he'd been lucky to find a dump of an apartment to rent for the same price.

They held hands and Paul said grace. Over the meal, he again reviewed the rules about the camping trip.

The younger kids would be in a dorm, so he didn't worry about that. A list of what-ifs plagued him, though: What if Sutton had one of her nightmares? What if Jon started wetting the bed again? What if a snake bit? Or one of them got injured in a fall?

Get a grip, he told himself. He had done a site visit, had looked all around and deemed the camp a safe environment, just the sort of place he wished he'd had available while growing up.

"Let's run through the safety procedures one final time," he said. "What happens if somebody gets sick?"

"Find Mrs. Baines," the kids echoed.

"What if..."

"What if the boogeyman comes?" Jon said, a grin splitting his face.

Paul sucked in his breath, struck by how much Jon looked like his father had at that age, full of fun and mischief and big dreams for the future. But Mikey's future had been cut short.

"Daddy?" Sutton's voice was shaky.

"Don't tease your sister," Paul said, almost automatically. "And eat your salad, Jon."

"Why can't you come, too, Daddy?"

He'd been asking himself the same question. But Paul knew the answer. He couldn't baby them forever. This trip would be just as good for him as it was for them. While they made new friends and did arts and crafts, maybe Paul could practice using his own rusty social skills. The evening at Haley and Matt's house was the first time since moving to Wayside that he'd done anything with adults other than work. His heart wasn't in it, but maybe he'd call Marnie Shepherd and invite her to dinner or a movie or something.

"It's a camp for kids," he said, realizing how lame that sounded. "It's time for you to make some more friends."

"We'll make friends at school," Jon pointed out.

Paul had enrolled them in Wayside Preparatory, the private elementary school where Haley Brandon-Dumaine taught. School would start there the week after the camping trip.

"You won't hear Bible stories or sing around a bonfire at school. And remember," he said, "I'll be there family night. You can show me what you've learned."

"It'll be all right, Sutton," Jon said. "If something happens, I can call on the cell phone. Right?"

Paul tapped fists with the boy. "Right."

Sutton eyed the men. "Are you sure?"

Jon nodded, looking much older than his seven years. "Absolutely."

She didn't want to be here, but she'd given Haley and Kara her word. So Amber determined to make the best of a bad situation. She'd whip up some fabulous dishes and avoid all contact with the camp's program activities. She was here to do a job, not participate.

"Keep your mind on the job...and the money," she said.

One good thing that could be said about the mess hall at Camp Spirit Fire was that Community Christian Church didn't skimp on the cookware. She paused and took in the large kitchen with its large copper pots. Designed for a cook's easy movement and access to essentials, Amber couldn't fault it one bit. The mess hall's kitchen, fully equipped, met her picky standards. She ran a hand over the cool surface of a pan, and then the gleaming metal of an oven door. Everything she'd need was right here.

If she set up a cot over by door, she'd never even have to go outside. The mess hall at Camp Spirit Fire was set up for comfort in a pastoral setting. The outside of the building looked rustic, but the inside had serious amenities, right down to something that looked suspiciously like a satellite dish television connection in a little office off the kitchen. From what she'd seen so far—and that wasn't much since she hadn't taken any time at all to look around the place, and didn't plan to—it appeared to be a far cry from the backwoods campsites and cook fires she remembered from her youth—places with outdoor pits dug in the ground for stoves and no running water or indoor plumbing.

She found fault with just one thing here. Amber cast an unkind glance at industrial-sized cans of pork and beans. With *a lot* of doctoring she could make that edible—maybe.

"We're sure glad you were able to help out," said a voice behind a dolly filled with boxes. "Where would you like me to put these?"

"Are you Manuel?"

He poked his head around the load. "In the flesh."

"What is all that?"

"Fruit. Canned and fresh. I have a couple more loads. Oatmeal, breads. The milk, juice, eggs and stuff will come this afternoon."

Amber sighed. "Over there," she said, pointing toward a pantry. "Do you know when the mess hall volunteers arrive? I was told there'd be two people helping me."

"Sorry, don't know anything about that. Mrs. Baines has the volunteer list, though." He wheeled the dolly into the large pantry. "If you catch her, she'll probably be able to tell you. She's checking the tent sites."

"Tents?"

Hadn't Haley said something about dormitories? Amber had seen several buildings.

"Sure," Manuel said. "But only the senior kids are allowed to camp outside. Those who are going to graduate from high school in the spring do it as a tradition. You know, a last hurrah before college and jobs."

Amber nodded, relieved.

At first she'd planned to sleep in her own bed every night, then realized she hadn't given the logistics of this job much thought. To drive up here every morning to have breakfast ready, she'd have to leave home at three in the morning. It would be a long drive home at night, only to start the process over again before dawn.

Maybe she should have demanded quadruple rate.

Community Christian's annual youth camping trip was a tradition that the church's young people looked forward to each year. Held in early September, it was part revival and part final farewell to summer before buckling down seriously to a new academic year.

The church usually had about thirty children between the ages of five and eighteen participate in the weekend event that started with a Friday night jamboree and welcome. This year, however, Amber would be cooking for

fifteen more kids, whom Kara Spencer's grant had enabled the church to include from various mentoring and
outreach programs the church ran.

"Is Marcus going to be able to make it up this weekend?" Haley asked.

She and Kara were in the lodge in the back of the gathering room. Just as soon as a few stragglers got checked
in, Cliff would open the weekend with prayer and a mo-
tivational message.

"Nope. He's really been putting in a lot of hours trying to get all of Patrice's tracks done for her CD. She's
so excited."

"Being able to record like that has to be a dream come
true for her."

Kara nodded. "It is. We're all so proud of her. My baby
sister is going to be a gospel star. She's done all right for
herself—"

"Excuse me."

They edged out of the way as Amber and Manuel
pushed a large cooler in. "Popcorn and bug juice for the
snack tonight," Amber said. "Real food in the morning."

Just as soon as they got the cooler situated, Amber
wiped her hands on her jeans.

"Thanks again for agreeing to do this," Kara said. "I
know you could have said no."

Amber grinned. Spending time in a kitchen always
lifted her spirits. "What mortal could resist dual salvos
from the dynamo twins?"

Haley and Kara shared a smile. Best friends for years,

the two women were not physically similar: Haley a tall, well-rounded blonde, and Kara a petite black woman with crimped hair and always-perfect makeup. Haley and Matt and Kara and Marcus looked like people who belonged on the covers of magazines. Heck, Marcus *was* on the cover of magazines! And as the R & B superstar's fiancée, Kara had been, too.

Next to Haley and Kara, Amber felt like a slouch. Though she and Haley had the same coloring and hair, her idea of a hairstyle was pulling her shoulder-length blond curls into a ponytail. She rarely, if ever, wore makeup. And while Haley always looked like she'd stepped straight out of a magazine ad, Amber had never met a pair of jeans that didn't speak to her. Even her work clothes for her catering business tended toward the practical—cleaned and pressed khakis with polo shirts that carried the Appetizers & More logo. If she had to dress up, she exchanged the pullover for a crisp white shirt with black slacks.

For the camping weekend, she'd opted for jeans, hiking boots, and chambray shirts and sweaters that could easily be worn in layers when the days and nights got cool.

At least this is easy money, Amber thought. And as long as she didn't let anything interfere with that, all would be well.

Nancy Baines, looking smartly efficient with clipboard in one hand and a pencil tucked over her ear, came up and hugged them all. Kara and Haley threw themselves into the embrace, while Amber leaned in awkwardly. She didn't like people touching her, but Nancy Baines reminded her a lot of her mom.

"Did you find Jocelyn's notebook?" Nancy asked. "She said she left it in the office so her replacement could find some of the recipes."

"I saw it," Amber said. "But I don't need it. I'm using my own recipes."

"Well, uh..." Kara started. "Remember, these are kids. They aren't expecting or looking for anything fancy."

With a wink and a smile Amber waved away the concern. "I have everything under control," she assured them. As a matter of fact, she'd already mapped out menus for the next two days.

Nancy patted her arm. "I'm sure you do. If you're missing anything, need anything, please," she said, "don't hesitate to ask." Then, turning to Haley and Kara, she asked, "Are you ladies staying overnight?"

"Can't," Haley said. "But we'll be back."

"I'm looking forward to my rap sessions with the kids this year," Kara said. "It's hard to believe some of them are graduating already."

Nancy nodded. "I see someone I need to speak with." She reached for Amber's hand and gently squeezed it. "Amber, I'm so glad you were able to help us out. You're truly a God-sent blessing."

Amber didn't like thinking of herself in those terms, so she quipped, "I was coerced," sending a grin toward Haley and Kara.

"Well, the Lord knew we needed you here," Nancy said. "Don't stay holed up in that kitchen all weekend. There's lots of free time. Join in on some of the activities."

"I love white-water rafting," Haley said. She placed a hand on her stomach. "But Matt won't let me do anything fun."

"I guess we won't be rock-climbing together this year," Kara said.

"Don't think so."

Nancy chuckled. "Don't let these two fool you with their tall tales," she said. "One of them—I won't name any names—decided last year that an outdoor excursion meant a sun chair and a novel over at the lake."

Kara laughed out loud. "I was exhausted from running after little kids that year."

Nancy nudged Amber and both women grinned. "See, she told on herself. I wasn't going to say which one—"

"Mrs. Baines?" A voice floated over.

"On the way," she called. "Seriously, though, Amber, please, join us for the campfire chats, any of the outdoor excursions, the Bible study. Whatever you feel led to do. Okay?"

Amber nodded. She was pretty sure, however, that she wouldn't feel "led to do" anything except the job she'd been hired to perform.

Twenty minutes later, lanterns lit the evening as Amber and all of the others stood or sat around the front pond. Cliff Baines welcomed everyone and then talked about finding yourself and helping others.

"Everyone attending this weekend gathering is here as a result of God moving in your life," the preacher said. "There are no coincidences." He leaned toward the younger children. "That means nothing happens by accident. Over the next few days, we're going to have some fun. We'll enjoy this beautiful camp area, eat some great food, enjoy the water and hiking trails, and then, when it's time to go home, we'll all leave refreshed and renewed. Ready to seriously hit the books," he added with a mischievous grin.

That last comment earned him plenty of groans.

"Let us enjoy the weekend without thinking about that," Adam said.

Chuckling, Cliff opened his Bible. "All right. It's a deal. Let me share this Scripture text with you. It'll be our focus for this weekend."

As he read a familiar passage from Proverbs, a chill shimmered through Amber. She tried to shut out his words—the words she knew so well.

A long time ago she used to trust in the Lord with all her heart. Until he let her down. Now, the only path she walked was the one she could see. Believing that God would see her out had almost killed her. Faith was not a concept she could count on or believe in.

"Hi, Cookie Lady."

She looked down to see Sutton Evans, and smiled. "Well, hi there to you, too. What are you doing here?"

"Camping!" The girl grinned. "You, too?"

"I'm the camp chef. I'll be cooking all your meals."

Sutton's eyes widened. "Cookies every day?"

Amber chuckled. "Maybe cookies on one day."

"Two days," the girl shyly bargained.

"We'll see."

When a group of teens with tambourines and a guitar stood up and started singing, a tiny hand found its way into Amber's. For a moment she was startled. She looked down at Sutton, whose eyes didn't miss a thing going on around her. But the little girl held on tight, as if she were afraid Amber might disappear.

If it weren't for Sutton, she just might. As she listened to the foot-tapping melodies that reminded her too much of similar nights in Central America, Amber tried to focus on the triple rate that would add to her bank balance, rather than the fact that once upon a time, Proverbs 3:5-6, the passage Cliff had just read to the campers, had been her favorite Scripture.

❧ Chapter Eight ❧

The youngest children, housed in King Solomon's Palace—each building had a biblical name—slept eight to a room on bunk beds. Sutton Evans didn't like the idea of being separated from Jonathan, who was across the hall. Jonathan's skills as a negotiator ultimately prevailed when he talked Mrs. Simmons, the dorm mom, into letting him sleep in the bunk closest to the door in the boy's room with Sutton in the corresponding spot in the girl's room. That way, just a little more space than what divided their bedrooms existed between them.

The hall light blazed, giving each child an extra measure of comfort.

"Do you have the phone?" Sutton double-checked—for the fifth time.

"It's right here," Jonathan assured her, patting his

robe. "When I get in bed, I'll put it under my pillow. It'll be okay, Sutton."

She bit her bottom lip, nodded. Later, as she padded to her own lower bunk, she still worried. Only five girls between five and eleven years old were at the camp, so they got to spread out a little in the room. And no one slept on the top bunk of Mrs. Simmons's bed.

Normally, all the boys were in two dorms and the girls in the other two. But the addition of the scholarship teens changed the makeup of the camp. With additional chaperones on duty and an adult in each room, Nancy and the camp board had decided to house the campers by age this year. If it didn't work out, they'd switch back next year.

While the other children settled in their beds, Sutton got on her knees to say her prayers. She could see Jonathan doing the same thing across the hall.

"Dear God, help me not be afraid to be in here by myself. And keep Daddy safe. Amen from Sutton."

Mrs. Simmons smiled. "That was a good prayer, Sutton. I'll tuck you in now."

Sutton looked at her but didn't say anything. She simply scampered into bed and pulled the cover up over herself and Wally, a stuffed plush fish with bug eyes and fuzzy rainbow fur.

"All comfy?"

Sutton nodded.

"Everybody settled?" Mrs. Simmons asked the room.

When she got affirmative answers from the girls, she said "Good night" and turned out the light.

Sutton flipped over on her stomach and looked toward Jonathan. He waved at her. Sure that everything was safe, considering that her daddy wasn't there, Sutton closed her eyes and fell asleep.

Amber did as much prep work as she could for the morning meal. She planned to serve waffles with peaches and a cream sauce for breakfast. She wasn't too happy that the peaches were canned and not fresh, but, given the season, she'd have to make do with a few substitutions. For lunch the next day, she'd decided on a bacon-and-cheese topped casserole that would at least get rid of some of the pork and beans in the pantry.

Her two assistants—high school students Kirsten and Leanne, both members of Community Christian—proved to be eager helpers. The girls were planning to study culinary arts after graduation, and by asking lots of questions they showed an interest in learning all they could from Amber over the weekend.

Confident that her meal plan included a variety of appetizing choices—with the exception of the pork-and-beans abomination—Amber finally made her way to the adult dorm, the one set aside for grown-ups who didn't have chaperoning duties.

As she walked across the compound, she could hear laughter and voices drifting on the quiet night. Though the hour was late, the teens and older kids who opted to sleep in tents or under the stars were apparently having a late-night gab session. She paused for a moment to listen to the snatches of conversation and laughter she heard, but couldn't quite make out what they were saying from this far away.

The sounds put her in mind of the natives whispering among themselves when the missionaries showed up with big smiles, open hearts and backpacks full of Bibles. Over time, she'd learned the languages and dialects, but in the beginning it had all been so foreign and frightening and seemingly pointless.

Growing up, Amber hadn't had many friends. Often, the local girls, wary of outsiders with a salvation agenda, ignored her attempts to make friends. In all her years, she'd been close to just two of the people at the missionary campsites. Ben who'd drowned while trying to save a puppy in a hurricane, and Angeline.

With a start, Amber realized she hadn't thought of her old friend in many, many years.

When her parents first got the Honduras assignment, they insisted that Amber and Kyle learn Spanish so that they could read and speak it fluently. The Spanish was the only good thing that lingered from those early years. It served her well, too well in fact, because speaking the language was how she'd met Raymond Alvarez.

Shaking off the melancholy brought on by lost years, forgotten friendships and continuing nightmares, Amber moved on.

The teens camping out apparently still had plenty of energy to burn. Amber couldn't say the same. All she wanted was a hot shower and then a bed that wasn't on the ground. On her shoulders she carried a sturdy back-pack designed for rugged wear. One of the few things she'd kept from her missionary days, the pack had a bedroll attached, just in case. If nothing else, Amber knew how to prepare for the worst.

Checking her locker key and room assignment, Amber entered Joshua House. The thought of that hot shower propelling her, Amber found her room, one she'd share with three others. But four people were already sprawled across the beds. With duffel bags open and toiletry kits out, the four women looked as if they belonged there.

"Uh." Amber looked at her key and assignment again. "Hi."

"Hey, Amber," one of the women said in greeting. "What's going on?"

Amber glanced at them, all fresh-faced and energetic. She felt old, well beyond her twenty-nine years.

"I was trying to find my place— I mean my bed," she said. "This says Joshua House, Room 4, Bed 2."

"Oh, they didn't tell you?" One of the women scram-bled up and reached for a tote bag. "I'm Jen, by the way."

Amber had a bad feeling about that breezy "didn't they tell you" comment. Though prepared for the con-tingency, the last thing she was of a mind to do was spend a cool Oregon night sleeping on the ground.

The others introduced themselves, including Betsy, a woman Amber remembered from earlier in the day. She'd let Amber know about a peanut allergy.

"There were some reassignments," she said. "We're the praise-and-worship team, so Mrs. Baines put us all together so we could practice a bit and go over what we need to do.

Jen came back with a sheet of paper. "This says you're in King Solomon's Palace. That's Building 5."

"Thanks," Amber said.

She trudged back outside, but stopped short on the front steps. She hadn't been paying too much attention while her chef assistants chattered in the kitchen, but she did recall that name. Wasn't King Solomon's Palace a kids' dorm?

Sleeping on the ground in the woods would be preferable to sharing sleeping space with children she didn't know how to relate to. The Cookie Lady persona she donned for an hour on Wednesdays was one thing; trying to maintain it for three straight days up here was another beast altogether.

When she got to the room Betsy and Jen had indicated, it was filled with four bunk beds.

"Hi, Amber. I wondered when you'd find your way over here."

Amber turned at the voice.

"I'm Harriet. We met earlier."

"Isn't this a kids' dorm?"

Harriet nodded, a smile on her face. "They're a good bunch. Most of them fell asleep about half an hour ago. Come on, I'll show you where we are."

She led Amber into the room filled with bunk beds,

unlike the accommodations for the adults. "Sorry there's no lower bunk available," Harriet said on a whisper. "I parked my stuff here, but I can move up if you'd prefer the bottom."

"It's not a problem," Amber said, but she was already counting the hours until she could get back to the security and comfort of her own apartment.

The only good thing was that she'd be up and out before the children really stirred. After a tepid shower, she climbed into the bed that was hers for the next few days.

Amber fell into a fitful sleep, dreams of Kyle and Guatemala, Honduras and hurricanes filtering through her. They ran through the underbrush, a headless man chasing them. She stumbled and fell, screamed when she landed on top of a snake.

The screaming continued. On and on.

Amber sat up, blinked and realized that the terrified sound, much like that of a trapped animal, hadn't been part of her dream at all. It was one of the girls.

She jumped down from her bunk.

"What? What?" Mrs. Simmons tossed her covers off, and several of the girls bolted upright and also started hollering, more from confusion than anything else.

But Amber was already there—at Sutton's side.

The child was having a nightmare, one that gripped her and wouldn't let go. She thrashed from side to side as if doing battle with something or someone.

"Daddy, don't let them shoot me. Don't let them take me."

"Sutton, wake up. Wake up."

Sutton's eyes opened, but she stared vacantly as if trying to figure out where she was and what had happened.

Amber lifted the girl into her lap, rocking her, soothing her any way she could think of. She knew what it was like to wake up in a strange place surrounded by strange people.

Barefoot and with his flashlight and cell phone in hand, Jonathan came running into the room. "What did you do to my sister?"

Sutton saw her brother and burst into tears, but she clung to Amber.

The phone rang and Paul snatched it up, rolling out of bed at the same time. "Hello? Jon? Sutton?"

"Sutton had a nightmare. A bad one. She says she wants to go home."

"I'll be right there."

Paul broke the speed limits he normally enforced, but got to Camp Spirit Fire in record time. The kids were supposed to be in the same bunkhouse, so he headed there first. But he couldn't find them.

Panic shot through him. He whirled around, ready to wake up everybody in the place.

"Chief Evans. Over here." A woman beckoned. "Hi, I'm Harriet Simmons, dorm mom and room 3 chaperone. Your kids are over in the kiva with Amber."

Paul blinked. With Amber?

He followed the woman to a common room. And

there, on a deep sofa, sat Amber with Sutton in her lap and Jonathan hovering nearby. Protecting the women.

Paul rushed forward. "Jon? Sutton? What happened?"

Amber cast wide eyes up at him, a tremulous smile on her face. "Just a bad dream— Right, honey?"

Sutton nodded.

"Your dad's here," she told the girl in a quiet tone.

Sutton didn't let go of Amber, but she held a hand out to Paul. "Amber made the monsters go away."

"Oh, baby. I'm sorry I wasn't here."

Sutton bit her lip. Paul held his arms out to her and the girl went into them.

He wrapped an arm around Jonathan, and hugged his two precious charges close. "I won't leave you alone again. I promise."

Caleb Jenkins drove by Marnie's house. The lights were on upstairs. He wondered what she might be doing and whether she would welcome her brother-in-law's company for a bit. His foot hovered over the brake pedal as he cruised the street.

An upstairs light blinked out. The two front rooms, he knew, were bedrooms.

Caleb didn't let his mind go there. Instead, he pressed the gas and hightailed it from the danger zone. That's what he'd come to think of Marnie as. As much as he loved her, he could never let her know. She'd been married to his brother—was still married to his brother as far as Caleb could figure. For a woman like her to remain shackled to a man like Roy could mean just one thing: she still loved him.

Roy didn't deserve any love. What he needed to be was dead. Just like all those kids he killed.

Conviction hit Caleb hard then. As a man of God, it wasn't his place to sit in judgment. But as a law enforcement officer, he knew his brother hadn't got nearly what he deserved.

"I'm sorry," he said, talking out loud to God. "It's how I feel. I can't make how I feel go away."

Yes, you can. The quiet conviction came from a place deep within.

He whipped his head around in the patrol car. No one was there, of course. No one at all. His windows were up. The AM/FM radio off. There hadn't been so much as a peep from his police radio in thirty minutes.

Caleb.

He heard the summons as clearly as if someone were in the vehicle with him. Caleb swallowed, and then sighed wearily. The old saying "You can run, but you can't hide" came to his mind.

Caleb pulled the squad car over. He left it running but cut the lights. Then he carefully placed both hands on the top of the steering wheel.

With his eyes closed and his head bowed, Caleb answered the summons. "Yes, Lord."

When he finished praying and meditating, he knew he'd be called to minister to a certain group of people—even though he didn't feel qualified.

* * *

Marnie stepped away from the window. The first time she'd seen the police car go down her quiet street, she hadn't thought anything of it. But the second time, and then the third time, she started to pay attention. Wayside wasn't all that big, and her street, a quiet established one, rarely saw traffic except for the people who lived there, let alone a police presence.

At first she'd thought someone had had a break-in. But the block's neighborhood watch system would have kicked in under that circumstance and she'd have gotten at least a phone call.

Then, this latest police car had paused. Right in front of her house. And she'd seen him. Caleb.

Marnie smiled. It was nice of him to check up on her like that. But Caleb needn't worry. Marnie knew how to take care of herself.

She turned out the light in the spare bedroom where she'd pulled out an overnight bag, then went to her own room.

Marnie had some decisions to make about her life. She loved her work at Sunshine and Rainbows, but had come to realize that she couldn't do that forever. She'd started working with kids as a way to give back what Roy took. But it was time to live her own life the way God meant for her to do. Marnie's faith was strong, but quiet—a hard-earned faith, tried and tested, that at times was all she'd had to cling to.

In the overnight bag she tucked the few things she'd

need for her two days and nights volunteering at Camp Spirit Fire. She planned to enjoy the weekend, since it could very well be her last at Community Christian's church camp. A new church family and experience awaited her. All she had to do was say yes to the opportunity she'd been given.

From her nightstand, she picked up the newspaper from Coos Bay, a town near the coast, about two hundred miles away.

This weekend she'd give some thought to the job offer. She'd give some *serious* thought to it. Her divorce from Roy was final, the decree on the way in the mail from her attorney in Portland. She'd even started using her maiden name again. All that tied her to Roy was the house they'd shared. She could sell it—had planned to do so anyway—and begin her life anew.

Coos Bay, Oregon, would be a nice place to start over.

✺ Chapter Nine ✺

Amber zapped water in the microwave and made cocoa for the children. Then, as unobtrusively as possible, she tried to slip away. It was going on one in the morning and she'd barely get four hours of sleep before it would be time to get up to start breakfast for the campers, counselors and chaperones.

"Miss Montgomery— Amber, would you wait?" Paul asked. "I want to have a word with you."

Her reluctance must have been evident, because he added "please" to the request.

"Let me get them back to bed, and I'll be right back," he said.

She nodded. While Paul saw to his children, Amber reached for a packet of cocoa, then filled another cup with water and put it in the microwave.

It took him longer than a minute. She'd moved outside, the temptation of that comfy sofa a lure she needed to resist if she were to stay awake while waiting for him.

The door opened behind her, and she turned. The police chief's powerful physique took her breath away. But for the first time, it wasn't in fear. Amber wondered what it might be like to be truly loved by a man like Paul. Paul Evans doted on his kids. He'd probably been the same way with their mother, Amber figured. The way Cliff and Nancy acted with each other. They'd been married for forever, but still acted as if they were dating.

He joined her at the railing where she'd been staring out at nothing while thinking complex thoughts that left her mind reeling. The portion of Cliff Baines's message that she'd heard tonight ran through her head, tormenting her with its upbeat sincerity and hope. Then there was Sutton. Why had the girl latched on to her the way she had?

"Thanks for what you did with the kids," Paul said. "I know it can't be every day that you have a hysterical five-year-old on your hands."

"She wasn't hysterical. Just a little scared after a bad dream."

"She has nightmares sometimes," Paul explained. "I had hoped they'd stopped. I think the excitement of the day and the new surroundings probably prompted this one."

"I know how that can be." Amber stared at the night sky for a bit, her mind still on the fireside message she'd heard earlier. "In his opening remarks, Reverend Baines said everything happens for a reason. Do you believe there's a divine order to the universe? That everything *really* happens for a reason?"

He nodded. "I do. Think what might have happened here tonight if we hadn't met at that crazy dinner-dance."

"Nothing would be different."

"Not true," Paul said, hitching a boot along one of the rails. "If we hadn't met that night, you'd be a stranger to me. I'd have been kind of freaked out to find my niece clutching some strange woman. But I knew you from that night. And Sutton and Jonathan, well, they know and trust the Cookie Lady. Before I even met her, I liked the Cookie Lady because she made my kids smile."

"That was before you thought she was holding a knife on you." Amber didn't dare touch the *I liked the Cookie Lady* part. Surely he meant it in a generic sort of way. So she ventured to other, safer territory that didn't involve her own life.

"Sutton's your niece? I didn't know that. What happened to them in L.A.? Jonathan started to explain, then said he'd better not."

Paul expelled a long breath.

"If you'd rather not get into it..." Though he looked pained, inside Amber was just dying to know what was up with those two kids.

"No, that's not it," he said. "It's such a long story."

"So give me the microwave version. Less time, less fat."

He smiled and leaned back, his hands behind him. "I was a cop in L.A. for many years, quickly moving up the ranks. I made a lot of collars—" he glanced at her "—that's arrests—of some pretty bad people."

Knowing the lingo, she nodded.

"The brother of one of them had been gunning for me for taking his gang leadership down," Paul said. "He took it personally and laid an ambush for me. But instead of taking me out, the hit he ordered killed my brother and his wife."

Aghast at what he related in such clinical terms, Amber stared at him. The anguish on his face told her, though, that the hurt still ran deep in him. She reached for his hand.

"I'm sorry. I know that sounds lame, but I don't know what else to say."

He sighed again.

"What happened?" Amber's question seemed loud in the quiet night, embers from the dying bonfire providing light and the occasional snap of wood.

"Mike and Sarah were staying at my place while their house was getting painted. Sarah was pregnant and they didn't want her exposed to the fumes. Somebody kicked the door a couple of times. They thought it was me with an armful of groceries.

"Mikey opened the door and got two bullets straight in the heart. Sarah came running and they took her out, too."

Amber gripped his arm. "Where were Sutton and Jonathan?"

"In the next room. They hid when they heard the shots. Jonathan is the one who called 9-1-1. He was holding Sutton and clutching the phone." Paul closed his eyes, his voice hollow, weary. "That's how the first units at the house found him. Sutton crying and screaming and trying to get to her mom, and Jonathan clutching the phone and Sutton."

She reached for his hand. "Oh, God. Those poor babies."

She closed her eyes, trying to imagine the horror of that day, sure that her worst imagining paled compared to what actually happened. Two innocent children witnessing the brutal slaying of their parents. How did they ever recover from that? Could they ever recover?

At least she now knew why Jonathan was so protective of Sutton. She hoped he'd always be there for his sister, unlike her own brother. Without even realizing she did it, she said a little prayer of comfort for the children.

"I was their only family," Paul said. "And it was my fault. Sometimes I don't know how we got through that first year. Jon had horrible nightmares. The sound of a car backfiring would make him grab Sutton and duck. And I was blaming myself. If their parents hadn't been staying at my house, they'd be alive today."

"You don't blame yourself anymore?"

"Oh, yeah. I do. But I've learned how to handle it a little better than I did that first year."

"Whatever happened to the guy?"

Paul gave a smile, but it wasn't a pleasant one. Amber

realized again just how intimidating he could be. The look on his face right now told her that vengeance—and maybe even revenge—had been exacted.

"He's right where he belongs," Paul answered. "On death row."

Later, back in bed, Amber thought about what Paul had told her. They had more in common than she'd initially believed. They had L.A. in common. The City of Angels hadn't been kind to either of them and they'd both sought solace in Wayside, a world away from everything that was California.

Amber woke up tired and cranky, but working on the meals for the day lifted her spirits considerably. She took special care whipping a vanilla cream sauce, and she taught her two eager assistants a few tricks to shorten preparation time in the kitchen.

Proud of their hard work, Amber wasn't prepared for the hit when the first group of hungry campers came in for breakfast.

"Ew! What's this white stuff on my waffle?"

She heard it so many times that she knew she was in trouble. She, Kirsten and Leanne had already made all but the last batch of waffles with peaches and the cream sauce.

The adults raved, but the kids and teenagers were having serious qualms. One in particular, a Daphne with unruly red hair and freckles, led the revolt. "Where's the scrambled eggs and sausage?" she demanded.

Many of the others quickly took up the chant, hollering for real food, for scrambled eggs and sausage.

Mrs. Baines hustled to the kitchen where Amber stood in the middle of the floor trying to regroup. "Amber, there's mutiny in the dining hall."

Amber paced. "I know. I know."

"We've been telling them that lunch will be more to their liking. Didn't Jocelyn leave the menu book for you?" Nancy hurried to the office, where she found the big three-ring binder and brought it out and put it on the prep table.

"Yes, I saw it," Amber said. "I told Haley and Kara this wasn't going to work," she muttered.

A chant swelled up from the dining hall. "We want sausage! We want sausage!"

"I'm not a short-order cook."

"Oh, dear," Nancy said. "I think I'd better page Cliff. Do you think lunch can be more...normal? I thought the waffles were great, but I'm not a kid. And this weekend is really about the children."

Amber nodded. When Nancy dashed back to calm the mutinous little scamps, Amber plopped onto a chair. "Maybe I should go home right now."

"You can't do that," Kirsten said. "What'll everybody eat?"

"Apparently, not my cooking."

Leanne, the other would-be chef, joined them. "This is my fifth year coming up here. We always kinda eat the same stuff. It's tradition."

Beaten in spirit, Amber sighed. "Hand me that binder."

She spent the next hour trying to convince herself that beans and franks, gruel and s'mores were good eating. At least none of her regular Appetizers & More clients were here to witness her humiliation.

By lunchtime, she'd just resigned herself to the task at hand, never mind her bruised ego or the meals she knew to be both delicious and nutritious. Forget the vegetable omelettes with applesauce-and-almond muffins, or the mixed grill with chicken and chutney. No honey pecan rolls for this undeserving crew. On a white board in front of the mess hall she wrote out the menus for the rest of the day.

Lunch: corn dogs, pork and beans, and French fries, pudding, and milk

Dinner: corn chowder and chicken strips, applesauce, and milk

Late-night snack: marshmallows, popcorn, juice

For her own lunch, Amber made a small fruit and chicken salad, garnished it with a few peaches and brewed a pot of coffee.

"So what do I have to do to get a plate like that?"

She looked up.

Paul Evans stood in front of her.

"I thought you went home."

"I did, but I came back up for lunch only to find I'd missed the kids' mealtime. Sutton's in an art class and Jon is getting a canoeing safety lecture. So I figured I'd try to find you."

She cocked her head. "Why?"

He held out a little blue gift bag. Blue and white polka-dot tissue paper peeked over the top. "I wanted to say thank-you formally for last night."

"You didn't have to buy me anything."

"I know. I wanted to." He offered the bag again. "I saw this in the window at one of the stores on Main Street and thought of you."

Amber tugged out the tissue paper and found inside a ceramic "cooking" angel with wire wings. The small piece of folk art featured a mini rolling pin in the angel's arm. Amber smiled. She'd seen and admired the piece at World Emporium, a specialty shop on Main Street.

"Thank you." She was so touched she didn't know what else to say.

"The sign out there says beans and fries for lunch," he said, indicating the entryway to the dining room. "But that looks really good. Not like any camp food I've ever had."

"That, apparently, was the problem," she muttered. Hours later she still smarted at the reaction to her breakfast.

"What was that?"

"Nothing." She glanced at her meal. "I can share."

He smiled. "I'm not going to take the food from your mouth."

"You're not. Have a seat. I'll make you a plate. Would you like some coffee?"

"Sounds great."

She didn't know why she suddenly felt so charitable toward him. Maybe it had something to do with the vulnerability she'd seen in him last night. Or maybe it was because he'd done something nice for her, knowing instinctively that the cooking angel in the store window might be something she'd like.

A few minutes later, Amber returned from the kitchen with chicken salad and peaches for Paul and a carafe of coffee. She picked up her fork, but paused when he started saying grace. Amber felt chastised at her lapse, but bowed her head.

"Thank you, Father, for bringing Amber into our lives. She's been a blessing, and I pray you'll continue to bless her heart and her hands. Amen."

Amber stared at him.

Paul smiled at her and picked up his fork. "I heard there was a revolt here earlier. I hope Sutton and Jonathan weren't a part of it."

She shook her head. "No. I think it was just a couple of people, but they were loud and vocal. The others just rode the tide to have me tarred, feathered and run out of camp."

"They're just kids," he said. "I'm sure they didn't mean any real harm."

Amber disagreed, but didn't say anything. She concentrated on the chunks of chicken in her salad.

"Will you answer a question for me?"

She glanced at him. "Maybe."

"How'd you get Sutton to talk to you?"

Amber blinked. She wasn't expecting that. She shrugged. "I don't know. I didn't do anything special."

"Yes," he said, reaching for her hand. "You did."

A little uncomfortable with his praise and his touch, Amber pulled her hand away and tried to change the subject.

He didn't let go, though. "Sutton doesn't talk very much, and rarely to people she doesn't know well. Yet, last night she was all over you."

"She just knows me from the day care center."

"Hmm" was all Paul said as he lifted his fork.

"Are you staying up here the whole weekend?"

Caught in the middle of a bite, he chewed and swallowed first. "This is really good," he said, indicating the salad. "I have a patrol shift, but I'll be back tonight and then I'll stay the rest of the time."

"Since when does someone at chief rank work patrol shifts?"

"You sound like you're familiar with the police hierarchy."

"Unfortunately," she mumbled under her breath as she bit into a slice of peach.

He looked curious.

She shook her head. "Nothing. Listen, I hate to eat and run on you, Chief. But I promised Marnie I'd go hiking with her today. I don't have a lot of free time here and I'd hate to waste the little I do have."

He nodded, conceding that she viewed being with him as a waste of time.

"I didn't mean to delay you. Don't worry about me," he said. "I'll clean up after myself."

She picked up the gift bag with the kitchen angel. "Thanks again. See ya." Amber rose, took her plate and mug and disappeared.

He waited, but she didn't come back through the dining area. Paul figured she'd slipped out a back door, much like she'd slipped out of the conversation when it turned to policing.

This time he would run a check on her. If for no other reason, he needed, as Wayside's police chief, to ensure that the elusive Amber Montgomery wasn't up here hiding from the law, and possibly putting the church's young charges—including his own children—at risk.

"I'm ready to talk now," Amber said. "But I don't want to hear any of that Jesus stuff. I'm not into that."

"Why?" Marnie asked.

The two women stood on a high bluff overlooking the valley. They'd hiked up one of the faint trails, chatting along the way and now stood at a lookout point. Though they were safe where they were, jagged cliffs and outcroppings reminded them of the danger below. Small brush and the beginnings of what might later be large Douglas firs grew out of the side of the hill.

"Because I got an earful of it growing up. Because Jesus wasn't there for me when I needed him."

"I meant, why do you want to talk now?"

"Oh." Expecting the evening to grow cool, Amber

had thrown a sweater about her shoulders. Now she twisted the ends of the sweater arms, tying and untying them. "I just meant... Look, this isn't easy for me."

Marnie sat on two logs lashed together to form a bench at the lookout point. "Do you know what the hardest part was for me?"

Amber didn't answer.

Not dissuaded by her silence Marnie continued. "For me it was feeling like I'd somehow failed the test of being a human being. That I couldn't even handle the basics of being a woman."

Amber stared out at the view. The only sounds between the two women were the late-afternoon creatures coming alive in the brush, chirping, croaking and hooting. "So, like, what happened to you?"

Marnie rubbed her hands on her jeans. "I was married to Caleb's brother, Roy."

Amber turned at that revelation.

"He had a drinking problem." After a moment, Marnie shook her head, editing that description. "No, he was an alcoholic and a mean one to boot." She smiled sadly. "When he wasn't drunk he was a terrific guy. But after the third or fourth or tenth beer he turned into a different man, one who was vicious and cruel, who cared only about his own needs. The world was supposed to revolve around Roy."

"You said you have scars. You mean emotional ones?"

Marnie nodded. "Those, too." She shrugged out of her jacket, then lifted her sweater and T-shirt to reveal several small round scars on her stomach and side. Amber stepped closer to peer at them.

She reached a hand out, but didn't touch Marnie's skin. "What is that?" she asked gently.

Pulling her clothes down, Marnie said, "When he got drunk, I was Roy's human ashtray. I have some on my arm as well."

Horrified, Amber just stood there. No words formed in her brain as she struggled to process what she'd just seen and heard.

"Why'd you stay?" She asked Marnie the same question she'd asked herself over and over.

"I didn't have anywhere else to go. I thought it was my fault that he was the way he was."

Amber considered that. "Why didn't you tell Caleb? He seems like a decent enough sort."

"Tell him what?" Marnie countered. "That his adored big brother used me as a punching bag? That I was a failure as a wife? That I couldn't manage my own household and affairs? A part of me believed it was my fault. That if only I were a better housekeeper, a better cook, a better lover, maybe my husband would love me enough to stop hurting me."

"So, do you still think those things?"

"No," Marnie said. "But I did for a long, long time."

Amber stared at Marnie, then carefully asked, "What made you see things differently?"

"Three things. A good counselor, someone who specialized in domestic violence issues. A shelter where I met other women like me. And the love of a man who gave His all for me."

"Caleb?" Amber asked.

Marnie shook her head. "No, Amber, it was Jesus who gave His all for me."

A day ago, even a week ago, Amber might have bristled at Marnie's answers. But today she soaked them in, thinking about what she'd said. Kara had given her the name of a counselor who could be trusted. Amber still had the little piece of paper on which the telephone number had been written.

She'd never used the services of an emergency shelter, though now, looking back, she realized she should have. She had even known of one near where she lived in L.A. A neighbor had slipped her their brochure one day in the laundry room.

Amber blinked rapidly and her heart swelled. She'd been sent a message that long-ago day. The woman had tried, in the only way she knew how, to help. But Amber hadn't recognized the Lord's hand in the woman's gesture. Instead she'd just angrily tossed the brochure in the trash, had told the woman to mind her own business and had gone back upstairs—where Raymond beat her that night for forgetting to bring the stain remover upstairs from the laundry room. Though she'd run downstairs to get it, he claimed a stain had already set in his uniform and that it was all Amber's fault.

"I'm sorry," she said.

"There's no need to be sorry," Marnie said.

Surprised for a moment to even see Marnie there, Amber just looked at her friend. Her thoughts had been back in L.A., in that apartment complex—the apology meant for the neighbor who'd only tried to help.

Amber faced the lookout point again. "What happened to him? Your husband?"

"An accident. His fault, of course," Marnie said. "He was drunk and hit a van filled with children from Corvallis coming home from a band competition."

Amber faced her again, standing in front of a boulder next to Marnie. If she'd had any softness in her she'd have put her arm around the other woman's shoulders. But Amber didn't know how to do that.

"They died, didn't they?"

Marnie nodded. She blinked several times and tried to wipe the side of her eyes without Amber seeing the moisture there. "Everybody but Roy. I've lived my life since that day in service to children. In a way, doing penance for Roy's mistakes."

Amber turned her back on Marnie. "If Jesus was your Savior, where was He when your husband was putting his cigarettes out on your stomach?"

Marnie didn't take offense at the belligerent tone. She simply smiled. "I'm here today, Amber. That's testimony to the fact that His love kept me, even through the worst of it. Many, many nights I thought about just killing myself. Swallowing a whole bottle or two of the painkillers I hoarded for the burns."

Amber shook her head, not getting it. "Why didn't

you just...you know, end it all?" She'd sure considered that on more than one occasion while she lived with Raymond.

"Because I had so much more to live for. So much more to do."

Amber thought about that. Was the Lord's hand even in that? *Could Marnie have been spared just so she could be on this Oregon mountain today to talk to me?* The very notion seemed incredible. Yet Amber couldn't deny the possibility.

"You're still married?"

Marnie shook her head. "Not now. But it didn't seem right to divorce him right after the accident. I was his wife. He needed help. But I eventually needed some closure, some way to reclaim my own sanity."

"How can you stand it?"

"Which part?"

"All of it."

"I'm at peace with my past, Amber. I've forgiven Roy for what he did to me, what he stole from me."

"But how?"

"I found a Savior," Marnie said. "He was my lawyer, my comforter and my provider."

"Caleb?"

Marnie shook her head. "Jesus, Amber. Jesus saved me from the misery of my life."

Amber stood up again and walked to the very edge of the lookout. "I'm not into the Jesus thing." But this time, the words didn't carry quite as much conviction as before.

Marnie stood. "Amber, please be careful over there. Rock slides aren't unheard of around here. If you lose your footing, it's a long way down."

Amber stared out at the valley and the rushing river way below. "Yeah, I know." She glanced over her shoulder at Marnie. "But there is a way back up."

The corners of Marnie's mouth tilted, and Amber knew Marnie realized she hadn't been referring to the mountain.

Caleb Jenkins wrestled with the call that had been put on his spirit the night before. He'd sat in his patrol car for a long time struggling with the mandate he'd been given. His heart still had a hard time embracing the idea, but Caleb had run from God before, only to discover that everywhere he went, God was there, too.

The calling placed on him now seemed counter to everything he knew, everything he wanted in his life. But he didn't doubt, not for even a single moment, that his summons had been a divine one.

He drove out to the minimum-security facility where his brother Roy would be housed for the next twenty years.

In the beginning, while awaiting trial, Caleb visited his brother on a regular basis. Then he found out what Roy had done to Marnie. He'd found out by accident. She'd been having a heated discussion with Roy's lawyer in the courthouse. Caleb, waiting for the jury to return, overheard just enough to make him angry.

But when Caleb confronted Roy in his jail cell, Roy denied everything that Marnie had said. Marnie offered Caleb no explanation, simply saying that some things were between a husband and wife.

He'd never got up the nerve to ask her again about what he'd overheard her say to the lawyer. Caleb had his suspicions, though. And he knew enough to want to kill his brother for hurting Marnie. Even now, though what he felt toward Roy didn't qualify as homicidal, his feelings did make the new calling on his life all the more difficult to embrace.

Caleb believed the Lord wanted him to minister to the incarcerated. He knew he'd need to return to school for chaplaincy training, but doubted there'd be a class to deal with his particular issue. Prison chaplains weren't supposed to harbor ill will against the incarcerated. He just didn't think he'd be able to get beyond what his own brother had done.

If he followed through on the path he'd been called to walk, this could be his last opportunity to talk to his brother, to find out what happened, and maybe to reconcile with the brother he cherished as a child—the one who'd killed four kids and two adults but didn't walk away from the accident that took their lives.

Before long, he was sitting across from Roy. "How are you?"

Roy scowled. "How the hell do you think I am?"

Caleb prayed for some patience. He knew it wasn't easy for Roy. Being a convict had its own stresses, and

Roy had added ones on top of the normal prison pressure. But he was housed in a facility that could see to his needs.

"I just wanted to come check on you."

Roy eyed his brother, then said something profane. "What'd you really come up here for? Did Marnie send you?"

Caleb shook his head. "I'd like an explanation. You owe me at least that, Roy. Just tell me why you hurt her. What'd she ever do to you?"

"I knew she sent you up here. I don't owe you squat, little brother. Why'd you even come?"

"I came because I need some answers," Caleb said.

"Well, I ain't your teacher, so go get your answers somewhere else."

Caleb looked at the man he'd worshiped for so long. For most of their lives they'd been as close as brothers could be. Then things changed. Roy started hanging out with a different crowd. Somewhere along the way he'd met and married Marnie. Things were going well—or at least it seemed that way from the outside. They'd moved home to Wayside, bought the big house on Maple, and everything seemed great. They'd even joined a church, though Roy frequently found reasons not to go to services.

The change was so gradual Caleb didn't notice at first. Then one day he looked up and the vibrant, pretty Marnie he'd danced with on her wedding day was a woman who shrank into shadows and wouldn't accept hugs. On some level, he'd suspected then, but couldn't make himself believe that Roy, his idolized brother, was thumping on Marnie.

He'd asked her once, and she'd laughed it off, the old sparkle again in her eyes. He'd let it go then, because he didn't want to believe it could be true. Then came the accident. Then the trial. Then the words spoken in privilege to Roy's lawyer. His brother came crashing down from the pedestal upon which Caleb had placed him, shattered pieces all that remained.

Roy had killed innocent people and he'd tried to kill the spirit of the woman Caleb loved.

Caleb despised Roy for everything he'd done, everything he'd allowed himself to become. But Caleb couldn't deny blood. So he did his family duty by visiting Roy. Caleb, however, couldn't help wondering how they'd come to this pass—brothers who were strangers with nothing between them except harsh words.

"I miss the old Roy," Caleb said.

"Yeah? Well so do I."

"Why'd you do it, Roy? Why'd you hurt Marnie?"

Roy stared him down, his eyes cold and unfeeling. Just like his heart.

"Go to hell, Caleb." He twisted around and yelled for the prison attendant, who pulled his wheelchair away from the visitation table.

Caleb watched as the man who used to be his brother was wheeled away. Maybe he'd never truly understand what motivated Roy. All Caleb could do was pray for him, pray that one day Roy would face what he'd done and repent his sins.

Roy, Caleb knew, didn't think he was particularly lucky. But he was. He was still alive. Six people lost their lives in the drunken driving accident he'd caused. Roy Jenkins had survived, but without his arms or legs.

✒ Chapter Ten ✒

Marnie and Amber arrived back at base camp in time to see two girls pushing and shoving each other.

"Uh-oh," Marnie said.

"That doesn't look like fun and games to me," Amber said as they approached the lodge.

Then one of the girls threw a punch that knocked the other to the ground.

Amber and Marnie started running, as did two other counselors coming from the opposite direction, one on a walkie-talkie. Some of the children, the younger-age group that had been headed to the pond for fishing lessons, crowded around to see.

"Hey, break it up."

Adam Richardson grabbed the puncher, while Amber and Marnie helped the downed girl up.

"What's going on here?" Adam asked.

"She started it!"

"Did not!" Daphne hollered back.

"Did, too!"

The girls scrambled for each other, but were held back.

"Knock it off, guys," Adam said. He motioned for some help from Cindy, who'd herded the little ones together.

"She's just trying to ruin it for all of us!" Tanita, one of the girls, hollered.

"All right. That's enough," Cliff said, approaching with Nancy. "What happened here?"

"I was just minding my own business—"

"Were not. You said my tennis shoes had holes in them."

"They do."

The girls tried to scuffle again, but Adam held tight, as did Amber and Marnie. It took several minutes to sort out just what had happened between the girls, mostly a string of juvenile insults.

"I'm disappointed in both of you," Cliff said. "You two, come with me."

Nancy directed her attention to the children with fishing poles who'd witnessed the tussle. Some looked interested while others looked either shocked or frightened. One little girl was crying. Nancy went to her and knelt down, putting an arm around her while addressing all the others.

"What just happened here is not how we settle differences. Let's all go sit by the pond and talk about this."

"I want to go home," the girl said.

"All right," Nancy told her. "Let's go talk and then we'll see if you still want to leave. Okay?"

When the girl nodded, Nancy turned to lead the group of children, who'd started to mutter among themselves, to the lake.

The sound of sirens pierced the air and everyone turned to look. A moment later, two Wayside squad cars and an ambulance spit gravel and dirt as they flew up the road leading to the camp.

"Now look what you did!" one of the girls yelled, as she struggled to get to the other. "They're gonna send us to jail."

Cliff looked around. "Who called the police?"

The little crowd in front of the lodge stared open-mouthed at the five police officers and EMTs running toward them, Chief Evans leading the way.

He assessed the scene quickly. "What happened? Who's hurt?"

Seeing nothing truly amiss except two girls being restrained, Paul turned to Cliff, but scanned the group of children around Nancy. "What's wrong?"

Cliff motioned for another of the adult counselors to take the two girls to the camp office. Amber released the girl and stepped aside.

"Chief Evans, no one's injured," Cliff said. "There was a disagreement between a couple of the girls." The minister looked around and again asked, "Who called the police?"

"I did" came a quiet voice.

All eyes turned to the porch of the lodge.

Jonathan stepped out from behind a rocking chair, Sutton next to him. The two were holding hands, both children's eyes wide and frightened.

"They were fighting," Jonathan said. "I dialed 9-1-1."

Tears welled in Amber's eyes. "Oh, Jon."

She ran up to them and enveloped the two kids in her arms.

Paul felt the knot in his gut loosen. It had twisted his stomach the entire interminable time it took to get to the camp. That 9-1-1 call from Jon's cell phone had taken ten years off his life.

"You guys can head on back," he told the officers and paramedics. "May I have a word with you, Cliff?"

The minister nodded.

Amber brought Sutton and Jonathan to him. As they followed Cliff Baines, Amber heard Paul's words to his son.

"We need to have a talk about that phone, sport."

"Yes, sir."

After a conversation with Cliff in one of the rooms near the office, Paul brought Sutton and Jonathan in for a sit-down.

"You can't keep calling the emergency number, Jon."

"But it looked like they were going to hurt each other."

Paul struggled to find the right words. On the one hand, he wanted Jon to be proactive, to not allow himself to become a victim. On the other hand, there were limits that needed to be established.

"Nine-one-one is for emergencies," Paul said. "For when you need help. A car accident, a fire, a shooting." Both children shuddered at that example, but Paul forged ahead. "Help was here. Adam and Pastor Cliff and Mrs. Baines were handling the situation, weren't they?"

Jonathan nodded.

"What if there were a real emergency in town and the police were all up here? The people who really needed help might get it too late."

"I don't want that to happen," Jon said.

"Then, only use the emergency number when there's a true emergency, all right?"

Jonathan nodded. Sutton did, too.

Paul didn't want to do what he knew needed to be done next. He held out his hand. "I need the phone, Jon."

The boy's lips trembled. "But..."

"Campers here aren't even supposed to have them," he said. "I asked Pastor Cliff for a special exception for you after last night. But I can't justify that again, not when it's against the rules to begin with."

"I won't do it again."

"I know, sport. But I'm still going to hold on to it until the jamboree is over. Okay?"

With shaking hands, as if he were saying farewell to his best friend, Jonathan handed over the cell phone.

"What if there's an *emergency?*" Sutton said, accenting the last big word. She put her arm around her brother.

"I trust that Pastor Cliff and Mrs. Baines will be able to handle anything that comes up."

The kids gave him looks that said they weren't so sure about that.

Before dinner, Nancy called a meeting at the lodge of all the teen counselors, advising them of what Reverend Baines planned to do at the campfire chat that night and how to then answer questions that might come up in the dorms that evening. After the teens dispersed to go eat, she asked the adults and Adam to stay behind.

"The additional children this year have presented us with a unique problem," she said. "Something we didn't anticipate, but should have. We just opened our doors without considering that some of our scholarship children might have development needs. We did something we shouldn't have done."

"What was that?" a parent asked.

"We assumed they'd all know and adhere to the common courtesies we take for granted. If we do this again next year," Nancy said, "we'll look at possibly having a daylong pre-camp orientation instead of just the one-hour welcome tour."

"I think it was the right call to let both Daphne and Tanita stay," Adam said.

"Why is that?" someone asked. "Troublemakers are troublemakers."

Unsure for a moment, Adam glanced at Nancy. "Go

on," she encouraged him. "I asked you to stay because I wanted to get your perspective as the lead teen counselor."

"When we do outreach ministry in East Wayside," Adam said, "sometimes we come up against people who don't dislike us just because we're there to talk about church and Jesus. They don't care what we're saying—they don't like us simply because they don't know us. We're strangers speaking what, for some, is a completely foreign language. They've never been exposed to church. All they know is what they already know."

He paced the area in front of the large stone fireplace. "I talked to the girls," he said. "Tanita Jackson and her sister have never had an opportunity like this. They're both excited to be here. Those twins have never been to a camp like this. They've never been anywhere. What happened between them and the others, I think, grew out of fear."

"What's to fear?"

"Everything," Marnie said, from where she sat on the arm of a crate chair. "I remember the first time I went camping. I was with my parents, but the woods were scary. Add a bunch of strangers and forced activities." She shrugged. "It might be pretty scary to a thirteen-year-old, especially if she's already insecure about fitting in."

"And that's why Daphne Gregory picked a fight with Tanita," Adam said. "I think Miss Shepherd is right. It's a fear factor."

Nancy nodded. "Well, keep an eye out," she told them.

"Every year presents an issue. Let's hope that this one was ours for the weekend and that everything from here on out will be smooth sailing."

"Remember that time when the talent show team forgot that Jody was zipped up in that sleeping bag and he was jumping around like a cricket?"

The group started laughing at the recalled incident.

"Or when the skunk sprayed Pastor Cliff?"

Everyone groaned and then laughed at that.

"Pastor Cliff didn't think it was funny," Nancy said, but amusement laced her voice. "I made him sleep in the guest room for two nights until the stench completely faded." Nancy checked her clipboard to make sure she hadn't forgotten to tell them anything. "You guys go get some dinner. I'll join you shortly."

Still chuckling and talking about previous camping trips, the group dispersed.

Nancy went in search of Cliff and found him in the little office he claimed as a study while in residence at Camp Spirit Fire.

"Did we do the right thing?"

Cliff nodded. "I had a talk with both girls. I think everything will be all right between them now."

Nancy rubbed his shoulders and back, working the kinks out. "Then, why are you still so tense?"

"It's not them I'm worried about," he said. "It's Jonathan and Sutton Evans."

"What's wrong with them? Sutton is such a sweet little girl. She doesn't say much, but she has a gentle spirit."

"Too quiet and gentle for a five-year-old."

Nancy paused in her massage. "What are you saying?"

"I talked to Chief Evans," Cliff told her. "He's going to stay up here for the remainder of the weekend. This is the first time he's ever left them alone since the shooting." When Paul joined Community Christian Church, he told his new pastor about his own background as well as the children's. Cliff had kept the small family in his prayers ever since.

"Those poor babies. What they need is a mom. Someone to love them and give them hugs all the time."

Cliff glanced over his shoulder at Nancy. "Funny you say that. I was just thinking the same thing."

"Haley paired him with Marnie."

Cliff, a matchmaker in denial, shook his head. "I think it's Amber."

"Amber Montgomery?" Nancy's tone carried incredulity. "I don't see that. Amber is so...well, Amber."

"What's wrong with her? She's pretty. A great cook. And did you see the way those kids cling to her?"

Nancy had to concede that point. "She just doesn't seem like the hearth-and-home type, despite the baking."

"You're just comparing her to Haley, who is all of those things."

"True," Nancy said. "But you know she doesn't like men like Paul. He's a police officer, and the chief of police at that."

"Love has a way of overcoming those things," Cliff

said. "Since he'll be staying here, you'll get to see something I've seen."

"What do you mean?"

Cliff just smiled. "Check out the way they look at each other when they think no one's watching."

Amber had them ready, but no marshmallows would be roasted around the fire tonight. Snacks would be served in each of the kivas or at the tents. With Kirsten and Leanne, Amber made fast work of distributing bags of the sweet treat along with juice boxes to each of the sites. The teens then hurried to the campfire, where Pastor Cliff had just started his message. Amber followed.

"About eight years ago, my wife and I moved to Wayside. We'd been here before because we owned a little land not far from here, though we'd never spent a lot of vacation time in the area. We came up from Salem when the Lord called us to minister in Wayside."

With Bible in hand, he encompassed the entire group of children, teenagers and adults with his gesture. "We didn't have friends in Wayside because we didn't know anyone. But over time, we developed friendships, and we work at maintaining those relationships. It takes time and effort to have and keep your friends."

He looked out over the group. "You may wonder why I bring all of that up. It's because I wanted to illustrate to you that everyone, at some point, starts out as the newcomer—the person nobody knows."

Amber looked at her toes.

"Over time, Mrs. Baines and I met people, made friends and became a part of the community. And in this sense, I mean the Wayside community as well as the family of Community Christian Church. That's what we are, you see, a family. All of us here are a part of a large family."

He motioned for Nancy to join him. She did, and the two held hands. "Sometimes the two of us disagree."

"That's the truth," Nancy said to chuckles in the crowd.

"But that doesn't mean we ever stop loving each other."

"That, too, is true," she said.

Cliff kissed his wife's cheek. When she moved to sit, he continued to hold her hand.

"When Mrs. Baines and I have differences, we don't slug it out with each other. We sit down and talk about how we feel, how we can work out a solution to whatever the problem is. And we also pray together, as a couple and as individuals."

He released her hand then, and Nancy slipped back to her seat. "When we go to God in prayer, we turn to another family member, our Father. How many of you know 'The Lord's Prayer'?"

Hands shot up all around the camp. Cliff nodded. "Excellent," he said. "Excellent."

Opening his Bible, he turned to a passage in the New Testament. "The directions on how to say that prayer are in the Bible. You can find it at Matthew 6:9-13. Through His word, the Lord told us—in other words He taught us—how we should properly pray. Instruction isn't rebuke." He leaned toward the youngest children and asked, "Does anyone here know what *rebuke* means?"

A few heads nodded. "Max, stand up and tell us."

Max Young jumped up. "To rebuke means to fuss at."

Cliff nodded, and several of the adults smiled. "Yes, I suppose so. Good job, Max."

The boy beamed and sat back on the ground.

"We begin 'The Lord's Prayer' by saying 'Our Father...' Right?" More nods. "Well, if we say that, and mean what we're saying, we're acknowledging a Father in heaven who we report to. Just like you have to report to your moms, your dads, your grandparents or other adults in your household, as well as your teachers at school.

"As a family, we've been coming to Camp Spirit Fire for five years. When you're here, you are family no matter what other family you have back at the place you call home. Everyone here has equal access, to the facilities and the food. Equal access to all the activities because we provide for your needs while you're here."

He looked around, his gaze pausing on each of the young people who'd come to the camp as a result of the grant proposal Kara Spencer had written. "And each member of the family has equal access to both acceptance and forgiveness. But forgiveness doesn't just come out of the blue. You have to do something to get it. Does anyone know what that is?"

Several kids, including Max, raised their hands high. Cliff spotted Jonathan Evans among them and called on the quiet boy. "Tell us, Jon."

Jonathan stood up. "You have to say you're sorry and mean it," he said.

Cliff put an arm around the boy's shoulders. "Exactly. Jon is exactly right. So tonight, before lights-out in the dorms and at the tent camp, I hope you'll all have some conversations about family acceptance and forgiveness."

Amber stood listening to Cliff, marveling at the way he talked about what they had done to her and about the incident with the girls, but without making anyone feel singled out.

She watched as Jonathan tugged on the pastor's sleeve. When Cliff bent down, Jonathan told him something. Amber had a pretty good idea that it was probably an apology about the phone. When the two hugged, she smiled.

And she thought about her own family—not just Kyle whom she'd lost contact with and missed desperately, but the parents she refused to see or speak to. They had done what they thought was best.

Maybe it was time for her to ask their forgiveness.

❧ *Chapter Eleven* ❧

The last thing Amber wanted to do was open her heart again. The last time she'd done so, it had almost cost her her life. But she'd listened to Pastor Cliff, and pondered his words long after all of the others left. For the first time in many years, Amber began to consider that maybe God hadn't forsaken her back in L.A.

She felt Paul approach from behind. She didn't need to turn around to confirm it was him. Something in her spirit recognized him.

"May I join you?"

She waved a hand over the free bench. The campers, counselors and chaperones had all returned to their dorms or camp areas. But Amber still sat near the bonfire, enjoying the warmth cast by its dying embers.

"A penny for your thoughts."

"A penny doesn't get you anything these days," Amber said.

He dug in his pocket. "Well, how about a Camp Spirit Fire 'buck.' Sutton gave it to me and told me to buy myself a treat."

Amber smiled. "Keep your money, Chief. I understand you'll need that if you want extra goodies at the talent show Sunday. How are Sutton and Jonathan?"

"Wiped out." He settled on the far end of the bench where Amber sat, and rested his elbows on his thighs as he, too, stared at the burning wood. "I confiscated Jon's phone."

"The kids aren't supposed to have cells and pagers up here," Amber said. "The focus is supposed to be on God and nature. I heard them tell all the teens to keep them packed up. It probably never crossed anyone's mind to check with the little kids, too."

They remained quiet for a moment. Amber never shied away from asking the questions on her mind. In that regard, she might have made a halfway decent journalist. So she asked Paul the question that, to her, seemed obvious. "Why does a seven-year-old boy have a phone in the first place?"

Paul sighed. "I suppose it's my fault," he said. "Jon has some protection and safety issues that linger from the shooting. For him, having a phone at the ready means help is always available. I'd hoped this weekend would be the beginning of a little independence for them, especially Jon. Maybe I rushed things a bit."

Paul wasn't sure why he was telling her all of this. Despite her standoffishness where he was concerned, Amber seemed open and nonjudgmental when it came to children, his in particular.

She glanced his way. "It must have been hard for you."

"What?"

"Going from single guy to single dad with two kids."

He shrugged. "The Lord doesn't give us more than we can bear."

"Hmm." Amber stared at the fire, then glanced at him. "Something tells me you went through a lot before you could say that."

His steady gaze seemed to bore into her. He opened his mouth as if to say something, closed it, then just shook his head. No one else had ever sensed that in him. With a start, Paul realized that the pretty but skittish woman, who was so quiet about her own life, knew more about him than most people.

"You'd be right," he said, finally answering her.

They were quiet for a few moments.

She glanced at him. In jeans, hiking boots and a sweater, he didn't look nearly as intimidating as he did when he had on the blues and the holster that marked his profession.

"You changed. What happened to your cop gear?"

"Manuel ran me home to get some clothes and my truck."

"So you're staying up here?"

Paul nodded. "Manuel's going to put me to work. He said he can use another pair of hands."

He would be at the camp the rest of the weekend. Amber processed that information, and couldn't decide if that gave her comfort or made her nervous.

"Jon and Sutton will be glad to have you around."

"I'm going to try to give them some space. Instead of being just a cell call away, I'll be within hollering distance."

Amber smiled. "Did you really confiscate the phone?"

"It's in the back of my SUV."

She sighed, taking in the night. "He reminds me of my brother Kyle. We used to be close like that."

"Used to be?"

Amber shrugged. "We grew up and went our separate ways. The last time I saw him was..." She paused, trying to remember. Then, shaking her head, she said, "It's been about five or six years. The last I heard he was somewhere in Asia, following in my father's footsteps."

"Teaching?"

Amber laughed, but the sound carried a sardonic tone. "Preaching."

"You're a preacher's kid?"

She glanced over at him. "Don't go getting any ideas about PKs. I'm not that kind. My parents were missionaries."

"That must have been pretty cool."

She huffed. "Only if you like getting eaten alive by mosquitoes and other creatures or never knowing whether your bed will be the ground or a hammock high up in a tree. I didn't want to come up here for exactly that reason."

Paul peered up at the nearby trees, including some towering Douglas firs that had weathered many a Pacific Northwest storm. "I don't think they make anyone sleep in the trees here."

Amber chuckled, in true amusement. "No. But everything else is the same. Well," she added, "almost everything. The kitchen and mess hall are pretty spectacular. I'm a last-minute replacement and was expecting to have to cook over an open fire or a pit in the ground."

"I admire you," he said.

She turned questioning eyes toward him. "For what?"

"For agreeing to come up here not even knowing what the conditions would be like. If you were ready to cook meals for all these people over a campfire, you must be pretty resourceful."

Amber was quiet for a moment, bemused by the compliment. She'd never thought of herself as resourceful. She simply lived her life day by day, just trying to survive, trying to maintain some semblance of control over what happened to her.

But things weren't always in her control. She'd learned that lesson the hard way.

"Did you hear the campfire message Reverend Baines gave tonight?"

"Not all of it," Paul said.

Amber glanced at him, then reached for a twig and twirled the edge of it in the dirt at her feet. "Do you believe that stuff?"

"Which part?"

"About family and acceptance?"

"I have to," Paul said. "Otherwise, everything that I do, everything that I am is invalid."

She studied his profile in an attempt to figure out where he was coming from.

Amber, neither naive nor inexperienced, knew when a man was interested in her. Until now, none of the interest sent her way by the single men in Wayside had been reciprocated on her part. This cop's reluctant but apparent attraction both baffled and frightened her— even while it intrigued her.

Too many thoughts crowded her head: Paul, who was not only a cop but also the town's top cop. Her parents who'd treated her like a pariah. The brother who'd abandoned her, gone off seeking his own destiny. And Paul's children, Sutton and Jonathan, clinging to her today.

Too many emotions, too much to sort through. Amber didn't like complications. *Keep it light,* that's how she preferred it. Too many quandaries lurked below the surface.

Between Pastor Cliff's message that sent her out here to think and Paul's questions that rustled up the past, Amber figured she'd done way more than enough deep diving for one weekend.

"Reverend Baines decided not to expel the girls who were fighting," Paul said, breaking into her thoughts. "But they aren't in the same bunkhouse anymore."

"That's probably smart."

Amber stood up. "Listen, a friend of mine will be up here tomorrow. Well, actually, she's my cousin Haley's best friend. But, anyway, you might want to let her talk to Jonathan and Sutton."

"Why would I do that?"

"She's a shrink. No, they're the ones with the medical degrees, right? Kara is a Ph.D." Amber shrugged. "But even if she wasn't, she's good to talk to."

He caught her hand before she disappeared. "So are you."

Amber's breath hitched, and she immediately tried to pull away, but his words halted her. "I..."

"Thank you," he said. "For being there for Jon and Sutton today. And for sharing your time with me tonight."

"I...I need to go." Amber made fast her escape.

Paul remained on the bench a while longer. His thoughts were in disarray, tumbling over each other. But ultimately they returned to the scene he'd witnessed that afternoon: Amber running to Sutton and Jon and them throwing themselves into her arms...much the way they'd seek solace from a mother.

It seemed they, too, responded to the gentle spirit Amber Montgomery tried to keep hidden.

When Amber arrived at the camp kitchen the next morning, three messages tacked to the door awaited her. As she pulled them down, she wondered who'd gotten up before her. No one had stirred in her dorm or on the compound when she'd slipped out at four-thirty to get showered and dressed. She glanced at her watch. In a mere two hours a hungry throng crowding the dining hall would again trash her cooking.

But Amber—a fast learner in every regard except the one that mattered most—had already figured out how to forestall that backlash and whining: stick to the program. Instead of the stuffed French toast with strawberries and cream that she'd initially planned, she'd find something else. She reached for the binder and Jocelyn's breakfast menus.

She started a pot of coffee, then slit open the first message, folded over three times.

I loved the cream sauce and waffles yesterday. If, by chance you're going to whip up some adult food after you prepare the kids' meals, I'd love to get some.

The note was signed *Harriet.*

Amber smiled. At least somebody appreciated her efforts.

She opened the next message.

Kirsten and Leanne told me about that great salad you made for lunch. Any leftovers available?

It was signed *Nancy Baines.*

Laughing, Amber reached for the third missive.

Her breath caught and the smile fell from her face.

She stared at the words, hardly believing what she saw on the small sheet of paper.

* * *

When Caleb found himself at loose ends on Saturday morning he decided to work out a bit. His visits with Roy always left him in a funk that no amount of prayer or Bible study or meditation ever lifted. It almost seemed as if his brother sapped from him every ounce of energy he had in his body. Caleb didn't like visiting the prison, but he felt he owed Roy some kind of allegiance.

This last visit had proved otherwise.

Maybe.

If he followed through on what had been laid on his heart, he'd be spending a lot more time in jails and prisons. The thought didn't sit well with him.

Before the accident Roy had been a firm but fair man—at least, that's how Caleb knew his brother. The Roy that Marnie married, however, was a different man, a hard-drinking man who seemed to suck all of the life and joy out of her.

She'd blossomed in the time since Roy's conviction.

Caleb paused in the middle of a repetition with the free weights and gave that some thought. He'd heard whispers about Roy, about things he'd supposedly said and done. Cops talked like that. But who was he supposed to believe—his own flesh and blood or unsubstantiated rumors?

He put the weights down and headed to the locker room. The only place he wanted to be at the moment was with Marnie, and since she was up at Community

Christian's camp, that meant he couldn't sort of drop by Sunshine and Rainbows the way he tended to do during the week.

When his cell rang, Caleb was glad for the interruption. "Jenkins here."

"Hey, Caleb. How busy are you?"

"Depends on what you're calling about," he told Paul. "Do you need me to pull a shift?"

"Nope. I was wondering if you could run something up here for me."

"Where are you?"

"At Camp Spirit Fire."

A slow smile split Caleb's face. "Oh, yeah? What is it you need?"

Amber found Paul splitting wood for the campfire. She watched muscles bunch and flex under the white T-shirt he wore. He'd removed his pullover sweater for the task; it lay on a stump not far from the growing pile of wood. He hefted the ax and brought it down right in the center of a big chunk. The wood pieces fell to either side.

"If you keep looking at me like that, I'm liable to damage something."

Amber averted her eyes, embarrassed to have been caught. "I..." She quickly gathered her scrambled thoughts. "It's not every day you see somebody doing the lumberjack thing. Where'd you learn to do that?"

Paul grinned and wiped his brow with the back of his

forearm. "Manuel showed me about twenty minutes ago. Did you get my note?"

"I did. That's why I came up here. You shouldn't have said that."

"It's true."

Amber folded her arms. "True or not, you can't run around leaving notes like that on doors."

"I left one note, for one woman. So, will you?"

Amber blinked. Tried to get her bearings. Tried to understand what was behind his interest.

The note he'd tacked to the door for her that morning was an invitation. White-water rafting. With him. A sort-of date, by Amber's estimation.

Several teams were going out. Her kitchen duties were done. The midday meal consisted of bag lunches she and the girls had prepared right after breakfast. Everyone would be out doing sporting activities today. Some had opted for hiking, others were either rock-climbing or canoeing on the placid man-made lake. The more adventurous souls would attempt to tame the rapids.

She'd always wanted to try that, but hadn't had the nerve to throw herself into a hollowed-out log several years ago and go barreling down a river when Angeline and Ben tried to talk her into trying the sport in Honduras.

"I'm not a very good swimmer."

Paul smiled. "I am. You'll wear a life vest and we'll have a great time."

"What about Sutton and Jonathan?"

He set up another large block of wood to cut. Then he brought the ax down, splitting the block in two. "Sutton is on a hike and Jonathan is with the other boys, learning how to rappel."

"Isn't that dangerous?"

"I took a look at the wall. It's very sturdy. He'll be fine. So how about it? Will you go white-water rafting with me?"

Amber studied him. If she planned to get over her aversion to police anytime soon, she may as well start with Paul.

"Okay."

About an hour or so later she regretted that easy acquiescence.

The teams, all outfitted and ready to brave the rapids, stood around eagerly awaiting their turn to board the rafts. But Amber was having serious second thoughts. The boat looked too small and that water seemed awfully cold and deep.

It might be deceptively calm on the surface, but what lurked below and beyond? Amber identified with the water, cool and calm on the outside, with a churning, raging mass hiding beneath the depths. She stared at it as she waited to be called forward for her group's safety lesson and rafting demonstration.

"You ready?" Paul asked.

"I don't think so."

"You'll be fine," he assured her.

Marnie and four others completed their demonstration

and joined their river guide at their boat. With everybody strapped into life vests, they all looked to Amber like mini-blimps about to float above the Macy's Thanksgiving Day Parade.

"I don't know how to swim," she said when their river guide asked if anyone had any questions. "What if I fall in?"

"Falling in can be the best part," the enthusiastic guide said. When Amber frowned, he quickly added, "But that's why I'm here. And," he said, slapping Paul on the back, "you've got not only a life vest, but one of the best wild-river riders in the region right here."

"You've done this before?" she asked Paul.

He nodded.

"He's being modest," insisted the guide. "When we end our run, I'll tell you about a Class V river we've both run. Everybody ready?"

Amber settled into position in their raft and, without even realizing it, said a quick prayer.

"Hold on," the guide said. "Here we go!"

The raft barreled into the middle of the river. About one hundred yards out, they turned a bend and water sprayed up and around them. Amber let out a whoop that had Paul and the others laughing.

"Whoo-ee!"

The rush, glorious and liberating, pulsed through her like life-giving energy. "This is better than a roller coaster!" she hollered, enjoying the thirty-five minute ride.

Amber held her position, working the river with

gusto, wondering why she'd put off this great experience until now. Taking this wild ride was like nothing she'd ever done.

"Left, left!" Paul said, as the boat hurtled over a particularly rough patch.

"Easy now, everybody," the guide directed. "Easy. We're almost home."

The five river runners could see the end of the route. Waving, the others waited on shore to welcome them after the triumphant run. Amber, thinking about taking another ride down the river, took her attention off the water.

"Look out!" the guide yelled.

Out of nowhere, the rocks came at her. She'd taken her eyes off the river for a moment, just a moment. Amber lost her paddle and floundered, reaching for it. A rush of voices, everyone yelling. Then the tumble. And the water.

Shocking.

Cold.

Surrounding her.

"Help me, Lord. I can't swim. Help me, Lord."

Chapter Twelve

Icy fear clawed her insides, making her want to scream. But Amber knew how to deal with pain. And she knew not to cry out. That only brought more pain.

Things were somehow different this time.

He'd never tried to smother her.

Also different: This time she wanted to live. Not to cower or die like an abused animal. She wanted to live!

Strong arms clamped around her waist. She wouldn't let him win this time. She could fight. For herself. For her life.

The arms tightened, and Amber swung her arm out, aiming for any part of her attacker. She kicked and scraped and felt water rush down her throat.

Waves of blackness, of a forever nothing rippled through her.

He was taking her down, but Amber refused to go. She

kicked and broke the surface, sputtering and coughing, trying to take deep life-giving breaths.

And then the hands again, grasping at her. Tugging. Pulling at her hair. He was screaming her name.

This time the neighbors would surely hear. They'd come to her rescue. Surely.

But no one came to help. She slipped under again, looking for that peaceful place she sometimes found during the worst of it. Her lungs were filled with fire, heat pushing in all directions looking for an outlet.

Amber flailed. Refusing to give in.

Not again.

Not this time. If she died this time, at least she'd go out fighting.

Paul dove after her again. He'd had a good hold and had been kicking them to shore when she'd twisted and socked him with a punch that carried a wallop. She fought him like an alley cat, hampering his efforts to get her above the surface and pulled to shore. Though she wore a life vest, her panic could do her in.

The water wasn't that deep here, maybe seven or eight feet, but it wouldn't take that much to drown them both, the way Amber flailed about.

He wrapped his arms around her and kicked for the surface. They broke it, gasping.

"Here, man. I've got you." The river guide tugged on Paul, getting them closer to safety.

"No!" Amber screamed.

She lashed out, twisting with everything in her. Breath rushed from him and he couldn't hold on.

Paul saw the guide dive after her. Treading water, he shook his head, took a deep gulp of air and plunged under the surface again. This time, the current fought against him. There! A flash of blond hair. He shot his hand out, but came up empty. A moment later though...there!

He reached Amber at the same time as the guide. Together they hauled her, swimming for shore and the hands that reached out to pull them all out of the river.

Embarrassment quickly replaced fear. She felt vaguely silly having struggled against Paul, but Amber still didn't like the added attention, people scrutinizing her every breath. Not when she was dripping wet and looking like a drowned kitten. Her teeth chattered.

"Here, let me get another blanket to put around your shoulders," Paul said. He came back with a thermal survival blanket.

She looked at him, really looked at him. "Why are you being so nice to me?"

"You had a scare out there," he said. "I'm worried about you." Then, possibly sensing that there was more to her question, he paused mid-tuck. "I care about you, Amber—"

Her breath caught.

"I care about every person here," he finished.

She exhaled slowly. He spoke in generalizations, not specifics. Getting to know him in this setting was different, but the bottom line would always be that he was a cop. Doing a job. Some of them apparently took seriously their oaths to serve and protect. If serving meant rescuing a panicked woman in the middle of a domestic violence flashback while treading water in a raging river, so be it.

"Did I do that?"

He fingered his bandaged forehead, a cut near his eyebrow. "Yeah. But I'm okay."

A part of Amber wanted to apologize. But the words wouldn't come. She'd spent too many years apologizing for things that weren't her fault. The Anaheim Angels losing a game. Putting the wrong brand of mayo on Raymond's roast beef sandwich. The laundry service adding too much starch to his uniform.

Amber swallowed, then took a deep breath. Raymond Alvarez wasn't here. Paul Evans was the man with the bandage. The man who'd helped save her from drowning.

They were both cops. Cops with deep blue eyes. But Paul's eyes were different. There was warmth and concern in his. Not the ice and indifference she'd learned to recognize as the precursor of what would be a bad night in the apartment she shared with Raymond.

"Are you warm enough?"

She nodded.

"An ambulance is coming."

"I don't need an ambulance," Amber said. "I'm fine. Really."

"I'm worried about you, Amber. You took in a lot of water."

She tried a smile, but knew it looked pathetic. "I'm fine. Just a little cold."

She gathered the second blanket closer to her body. "When you worked in L.A. with the police..."

He glanced over at her, an air of expectancy in his expression, almost as if he held his breath awaiting her question.

"Did you know a Raymond Alvarez?"

He thought about it for a moment, then shook his head. "The name doesn't ring any bells. But the LAPD is huge, really huge. It's not anything like the Wayside Police Bureau where everybody knows everybody and their families, too."

Amber nodded. She was trying to get a handle on this man, on why, without even trying, he seemed to be breaking through all of the defenses she'd carefully erected over the past few years. The last thing she wanted in her life was another complication. Being friends with a cop—Caleb Jenkins excluded because she'd met him in a different setting—was not in the game plan.

Neither was hanging out at a church camp.

She didn't like the thoughts that lingered in her mind. Years ago when she still believed in redemption and devoting a lifetime of work to God, she never made a move without being sure of the next step, confident in her ability to distinguish God's will from her own. But those inner voices had been silenced. And Amber had no intention of heeding it at this point in her life.

"How many bad cops work in Los Angeles?"

Paul seemed surprised by the question. "I'd say a lot. A force the size of the one in L.A. has a percentage of cops who go bad. The sheer numbers account for that. But the majority of a police department's employees, here as well as there, choose this line of work because they come from cop families, or maybe they have something to prove to themselves. A lot of people become cops simply because they want to help people."

"Help them what?"

Paul chuckled. "It'll sound hokey, but the answer is, help people live in a just society. People should be confident that laws exist to shield society from anarchy. Law enforcement officers exist to shield the public—"

"Here's a cup of coffee, Amber," a teenager interrupted. "Maybe it'll warm you up."

"Thanks," she said, taking a sip from the paper cup. The teen went to check on the others who'd been in Amber's boat. "Isn't that a rather rose-colored view of the world?"

"What?" Paul asked. "That people simply obey the law?"

Amber shrugged. "Yeah. You know they aren't going to. Doesn't that make what you do," she shrugged again, adding, "pointless? Don't you ever get tired of going through the same motions over and over?"

"I'm sworn to protect and serve the public," he told

her. "I took a solemn oath in L.A. and one here in Wayside, giving my word that I'd lay down my life to protect the public. We each have callings on our lives. I've always known that mine was to uphold man's law in God's world."

Amber smirked, not buying or understanding that kind of commitment. "Yeah. Okay."

Paul folded his arms. "Is it the law part or the God part that you don't believe in?"

She looked up at him. Not liking the vantage point of him towering above her, she scrambled to her feet, shrugging off his assistance as the blanket fell from her shoulders.

Amber knew he waited for an answer, but the look in his eyes, something that seemed a hybrid of curiosity, pity and pique, irritated her.

She reached for and shrouded herself in the warmth of the survival blanket. She had to get away from him, away from those startling blue eyes that cut so sharp, those eyes that didn't miss a thing. From her own peripheral vision, she saw the river guide approach.

"Excuse me," she said.

"Hey, how ya doing?" the other man asked as he draped an arm around Amber's blanketed shoulders. "That was quite a tumble you took. How are you feeling?"

They walked off, leaving Paul standing there, his unanswered question hovering in the air like an abandoned child—or a lost dream.

He had other questions for Amber Montgomery. Like

what had happened to her in L.A.? And just who was Raymond Alvarez?

She'd fought him in the water, fought as if her very life depended on it. He'd seen the terror in her eyes. It wasn't fear of the water, even though she couldn't swim.

Tumbles from rafts weren't uncommon. Everyone else had laughed it off and waded to shore. Amber, though, she'd panicked, and in the process almost got them both killed.

What troubled Paul was the knowledge that it hadn't been the river that caused her distress. *He'd* been the cause of it. Somehow, and again.

"I'd like to talk with you about Amber Montgomery," Paul told Cliff later that day.

In his time in Wayside, Paul had come to count Cliff Baines as more than a pastor and a wise man; he considered the man a friend. And in this regard, he needed to speak to a friend.

"What about her?" Cliff asked. He closed the laptop and pushed it aside.

Cliff claimed a small room off the common lounge in the lodge as his office. While the kids cleaned up after their excursion, Paul found Cliff there. The pastor's camp study included a rough-hewn table that served as his desk. It was made of the same wood as the furniture in the lodge. A lamp, a file cabinet and a plaid love seat that had seen better days completed the room's decor. The only item that interrupted the rustic feel of the space was a computer monitor and docking station for the laptop that at the moment lay on top of a file of manila folders.

Since the walls, covered with framed photos of groups of campers, seemed to close in on Paul, he stood, facing one of the pictures but not seeing anything in it.

"I was just wondering," he said as nonchalantly as he could, "if there was anything I should know about her."

"Know? Like what?"

The minister wasn't making this easy. It would help, Paul figured, if he had a better handle on just what it was he was asking the preacher.

"We've had a couple of run-ins," he said. "She seems to shut down. To disengage."

Cliff nodded. "That would be Amber. She pretty much stays to herself, always has in the years I've known her. You do know that she and Haley Brandon-Dumaine are cousins."

Paul nodded. He'd gathered that from the cookout. "I guess I just wondered if she was prickly around men in general, or if it was just me."

Cliff raised an eyebrow. He settled back in his chair, folded his hands over his stomach and tried to bite back a small triumphant smile. "I thought you were interested in Marnie Shepherd."

Paul faced the preacher. "I..." He paused. Then he perched on the edge of the love seat. "I'll make no secret of it, Pastor. It may sound old-fashioned, but I need a wife.

The Lord led me here not just for a job and a good place to raise my niece and nephew, but to find a spouse."

"We have an active singles ministry," Cliff said.

But Paul shook his head. "I'm not interested in parading women through my house or my life with Jon and Sutton. Stability is what I'm seeking."

"And you think you'll find it in Amber?"

"No," he said. "I'm not interested in her that way." But even as Paul said the words he wondered about their veracity. "Amber discounts faith. She doesn't want any part of any of the religious activities here or anywhere else."

Cliff sighed. "That's true."

"The woman I settle down with will have to love the Lord with all her heart and mind and spirit. I was just asking about Amber because of what happened today."

The minister sat up. "What happened today?"

Paul related the white-water rafting incident and Amber's response in the water.

Leaning forward, Cliff braced his elbows on the desktop and steepled his hands. "From what I know of Amber, and it's not a lot," he said, "she had a rough time before she arrived here in Wayside. Her parents live not far from here, but I don't think she has any contact with them."

"Why?"

Cliff shrugged. "What I do know is that Amber Montgomery, like everyone else including you, is here at Camp Spirit Fire for a reason. The Lord got her here via a need in the kitchen, but there's something else here for her. Maybe that something else is you."

Paul actually laughed at that. "I don't think so, Pastor. I don't believe in being unequally yoked."

"Hmm" was all Cliff said to that.

After the police chief left and Cliff returned to his notes for that evening's fireside message, he thought about Amber Montgomery. The woman was a dynamic cook, but she did have a troubled spirit.

He reached for his Bible and opened it to the third book of Proverbs. "In all thy ways acknowledge him and he shall direct your paths."

Cliff considered the Scripture for a moment, then opened the laptop and deleted the sermon he'd started. Tonight he'd speak about letting the river, like God's love, flow in its own direction.

"Hey, Marnie."

Caleb approached the table where Marnie was setting out craft supplies. Two plastic milk crates were filled with items soon to become works of art.

A smile blossomed across Marnie's face. "What are you doing here?"

"I had to bring the chief some paperwork, but I came with the ambulance."

She dropped a box of wooden craft sticks and rushed toward him. "Ambulance? What's wrong? What happened?"

"Whoa," Caleb said, steadying her with hands at her waist.

He brushed hair from her face and desperately tried not to think about how good it felt to hold her, even in this innocent way. Before his thoughts got out of control, he released her and bent to retrieve some of the wooden sticks that had fallen to the ground.

"False alarm. Again," he said.

"What happened?"

Caleb related what he knew of the struggle in the river.

"Amber must have been terrified."

He shrugged. "She's all right. Just a little shaken up was all. People get disoriented in the water."

Lost in thought, Marnie started placing the craft items at intervals on each of the picnic tables. Caleb watched her for a moment, then fell in and helped.

"And you said Chief Evans is the one who rescued her?"

"Yeah," Caleb said, peering into a box. "Are these bottles of paste supposed to go out, as well?"

"Two on each table."

Though Haley's matchmaking had a different goal, Marnie had seen what the others hadn't on the evening of the barbecue. Neither Amber nor Chief Evans realized that their gazes were constantly sliding off of each other. And after Amber's disappearing act, the police chief had gotten quiet, really quiet.

If Marnie had been in the market for companionship, she'd have been put out that night by the handsome police chief's obvious lack of interest. But since she'd walked the same path as Amber, Marnie knew the other woman could still be struggling with whatever had happened to her in Los Angeles. She offered up a prayer for guidance on how she could help Amber—and Paul—if need be.

"Marnie?"

She blinked. "Yes?"

"I was asking if you'd have dinner with me tonight."

She grinned at Caleb. "Sure. You really want to stay up here and hang out with a bunch of little kids?"

"It'll be fun," he said, giving her a smile in return. "I've never been to church camp."

"Well, this is a good day to visit," she said, turning back to the box of supplies. "It's the only night that Pastor Cliff actually delivers a message. Usually in the evenings after he or Nancy leads a short chat, we sit around the campfire singing, roasting marshmallows, that sort of thing."

"I wish my church did something like this."

"You can always join us at Community Christian."

Caleb put the last glue pot on a table, then gazed at Marnie. Had she been looking in his direction, she would have seen his heart in his eyes. "I'll give that some thought."

Paul's goal for the weekend was to give Sutton and Jonathan a bit of independence, to let them interact with other people without him constantly hovering nearby. Jonathan had yet to return from his morning excursion, and Sutton was in the dorm with the other girls, changing into messy clothes for arts and crafts.

With time to spare, Paul thought he'd take a walk around the camp, just to explore. He just hadn't bargained on having a follower dog his footsteps. Since returning from the white-water rafting excursion, he'd developed a shadow.

"I wanna be a policeman when I grow up," Max Young announced.

"I know that, Max."

The little boy's legs pumped hard to keep up with Paul's longer strides. Paul wasn't trying to ditch the child, he just felt compelled to check on Amber. A group of about seven teenagers sat under a tree talking. They waved as Paul and Max went by.

"Do you watch the police shows on TV?"

"Some of them."

"Jon says you're the best policeman ever. That you always catch bad guys. He said that you put bad men in jail for a long, long time."

That stopped Paul. His heart gave a little lurch. He paused and stooped down so he could look Max in the eye. "Does Jon talk about that a lot?"

The boy shrugged. "Sometimes. He told me that it's his job to watch out for his little sister. She has pretty hair."

Paul smiled. He ruffled Max's hair. "Yes, Sutton has pretty hair."

A car pulled into the drive and made its way up to the front of the lodge. The teens jumped up and ran over to greet the woman getting out.

"She has pretty hair, too," Max said.

Paul smiled down at Max, who was apparently a ladies' man in training. Looking up again, he recognized Kara Spencer. He'd met her once in town, and saw her occasionally at church, but hadn't spent any time with her. She was the psychologist that Amber had suggested he speak with about the kids.

In the beginning, Paul had resisted counseling, for himself or for the children. Then his captain had referred him to a group therapy program and his outlook had changed dramatically. There he'd met other men and women just like himself—cops who'd lost their loved ones to violence.

He'd learned the power of letting go of emotions that remained bottled up inside. He'd learned how to harness his anger and turn it into productive activity. And with a single-minded determination, he'd hunted down the people responsible for Mikey's and Sarah's brutal slayings and had seen them brought to justice.

The children rarely, if ever, talked about that time—at least, around him. The therapists said Sutton was too young to remember much of what actually happened that night. But her older brother's fear and descriptions fed her own, so much so that Paul had gotten help for both of them. But now, apparently, Jon had brought it up with his friend Max. Paul wondered if with the move to Wayside he'd done the right thing in removing them from all connections to their dead parents.

The counselor in L.A. advised that he just wait and see

how things went in Oregon. If the children showed any signs of mental distress or if anything happened to remind them of the trauma they'd suffered, time with a good therapist in Oregon would be in order.

"Hello there," Kara Spencer called out.

"Hey, Chief," Max said. "It's time for my class. I gotta go now, okay?"

Paul smiled at the boy. "All right, Max. I'll see you later."

Kara stuck out a hand as they watched Max scurry toward the tables where Marnie talked to his patrol sergeant. "I see you've made a new friend. You probably don't remember me. I'm Kara Spencer. Welcome to Wayside."

"I remember you, Dr. Kara."

She rolled her eyes. "Please, just Kara. Are you doing a workshop, too? Mine starts at three."

"Workshop?"

"I have two groups this time—our scholarship kids and the senior level counselors, mostly high school juniors and seniors. I'll bet your session will be jammed if you're talking about careers in law enforcement."

"So this afternoon is like career day?"

"Something like that." She hefted her satchel onto her shoulder and started walking toward the lodge. Paul fell into step beside her, much the way Max had done with him.

"I understand you're a therapist."

She nodded. "My practice has evolved over the years."

"You work with children primarily?"

Kara stopped walking. She faced him, giving him her full attention. "Not specifically or exclusively. Would you like a recommendation for someone in town or in Portland? You have what, a son and a daughter?"

"I'd just been giving it some thought."

"I'll jot down a couple of names for you."

"I'd appreciate it, Doc. Maybe we can talk before you leave today?"

Her steady gaze met his. "Sure, Chief."

Cliff Baines's hands hovered over the keyboard, not quite sure where to land. Trying to make sense of all the highlights he wanted to hit tonight didn't help one bit when the dominant image was a river, a fast-moving river.

Intellectually he knew that hearing about the white-water rafting incident was what had set the river image so firmly in his mind. But now he couldn't get his mind off of it.

"Like a tree planted by the river," he wrote.

The cursor blinked at him. Cliff stared at the words on the monitor, stared as if the answer to world peace had been laid on his doorstep. He realized he didn't need a prepared message to speak to his youth congregation gathered at Camp Spirit Fire. They came up here every year for friendship and fellowship, to get in touch with nature and to get a little closer to God.

He balled up the sheet of paper and made a jump shot into the trash can.

He didn't need notes for what he'd speak about tonight. He'd preach from the heart. But he might need a spiritual interpreter, someone who wanted to and didn't mind giving a testimony about the goodness of the Lord.

Cliff had just the person in mind.

❧ Chapter Thirteen ❧

The dispute started over a candy bar and who had first dibs on it.

"Give it back," Sarita yelled.

Her twin, Tanita, one of the girls who'd been involved in the earlier dispute, stood to the side. "Let it go, Ree. It ain't worth it."

"Yeah, listen to your sister, Ree-Ree," taunted the girl who'd snatched up the last chocolate bar, the very one that Sarita had been reaching for. Daphne ripped open the chocolate and took a big bite out of the bar.

Sarita swiped at the candy. But Daphne tossed it to a friend, who sneered at the twins before taking a bite herself. "And your shoes *do* have holes in them."

Daphne's friend tossed the bar to a boy who was standing nearby. The five, all eighth graders at Wayside Middle School, didn't get along in school and carried that bad blood with them throughout the summer and into the new school year.

Part of the church's outreach ministry, they and ten others were attending Community Christian's fall jamboree on scholarships.

Sarita lunged for the candy bar, but the boy, Kevin, took a bite and held the remaining portion high over his head.

Daphne and her friend laughed at the girl's effort to get the candy, and her sister's equally strong efforts to pull her away from the fray.

"Come on, Ree. Forget them. We came up here to have some fun, not mess around with knuckleheads."

"Who you calling a knucklehead?" Daphne said, pushing up into Tanita's face.

"You."

The shoving commenced.

"What's going on here?" Adam demanded, approaching the girls who were mere seconds away from physical blows. He looked at Tanita. "I thought we had a talk already today."

"I ain't doing nothing! You need to be talking to that thing over there."

Sarita shoved at her, but Adam intervened. "This might be how you settle disputes at home, but it isn't the Community Christian way."

Daphne jerked her arm free. "I didn't even want to be at this stupid camp—"

"Well, that can easily be remedied."

The thirteen-year-olds cast apprehensive eyes up at the big man who'd come over.

"Adam, I think our friends here would like a little education on what happens to young people who cause trouble here and in town."

Adam regarded the police chief with as much wariness as the squabbling middle schoolers who'd all grown quiet. "I'll set up a time with Mrs. Baines so you can have a group."

"Thanks," he said. Paul sent the five a not-quite-friendly smile, one reserved for recalcitrant prisoners who thought they'd gotten away with a jailhouse violation.

He met each teenager's eyes, then nodded at Adam and sauntered away.

"Just remember," Sarita said, "payback is a—"

Tanita tugged on her twin and whispered, "We at church, girl. Watch your mouth. Plus, you heard that cop."

Still angry and fussing under her breath, Sarita let her more levelheaded twin lead her away. She turned back, though, just in time to see Leslie give her the finger.

Tonight, Daphne mouthed, promising yet another altercation.

From the sidelines, Amber had watched the run-in and she had watched the way the police chief asserted his authority without diminishing Adam's. Paul walked a fine line. She wondered if he handled other aspects of his life with such aplomb.

While all of the other young people were headed toward the lodge, Amber saw one girl slip away, heading toward the hiking trails.

Curious, Amber followed her.

Marnie planned to use part of the time at the jamboree to slip away and think about the job offer in Coos Bay. But she found it difficult to get her thoughts settled enough to do anything except complete her volunteer work. She loved working with kids. That's why she'd accepted the position at Sunshine and Rainbows, and why she could always be counted on to put in at least one day of volunteer effort at the church camp.

But lately, Marnie had found her original inspiration for wanting to work with youth diminished.

She believed that each person was called to a certain work in the kingdom. But what she didn't know and couldn't assess is whether she'd embraced her own calling...or run from it.

A tug on the hem of her blouse drew her attention back to the moment.

"Mine doesn't look like yours."

Marnie smiled at the girl. Sutton Evans had blossomed in the past few weeks. Marnie had heard more words out of the girl in two weeks than she had in the previous three months. If anything, Marnie pinpointed it to the day Amber came to the center and Sutton was chosen as the Cookie Lady's helper.

"That's because art is individual. That's what makes it special. All of them are one-of-a-kind masterpieces."

Sutton studied her sticky mountain of wooden craft sticks and then a sample Marnie had placed on each table.

"It's supposed to be our church."

"And it's a fine church."

Sutton's lower lip trembled. She sat on the bench and blinked back tears.

"Sweetheart, it's okay. Every piece is supposed to be different."

"But I want my house to be perfect."

The words struck a chord with Marnie. She'd wanted her own house with Roy to be perfect. *From the mouths of babes*, she thought.

She wiped Sutton's eyes with a tissue and thought about shedding a few tears herself. "Would you like to start over?"

The little girl nodded.

Marnie placed the box of craft sticks within reach and handed Sutton two to start. Instead of immediately reaching for glue and other sticks, the child studied her first effort, looked at the sample and then sat there for a moment.

The child's concentration as she carefully considered her next move floored Marnie. It was as if a figurative lightbulb flashed over her head.

Instead of carefully considering her situation, Marnie had run headlong into the first opportunity to heal her wounded pride. Her husband hadn't valued her as a person, so she'd found the love and affirmation she craved in the smiles of children. Their messy artwork and sticky hands and big hearts soothed the ache fostered by Roy. Though she hadn't caused his accident or killed all those children, she bore the guilt as if she had.

So she found a niche in the day care center work. It was good work, honorable service, and to Marnie's thinking a form of payback, though small, for what Roy had done.

But she couldn't live her life trying to right Roy's wrongs. She enjoyed her life now. Now that Roy was locked up, paying penance for those deaths...and for abusing her all those years?

Marnie swallowed a lump in her throat.

Was it wrong to think that?

"I like this one better," Sutton said.

Marnie smiled at the girl. Sutton had a lot of words to share today.

Just like Sutton, she'd wanted her own house—her marriage—to be perfect. But when it didn't turn out the way she'd planned, instead of inspecting the base to ensure a sound foundation, she'd retreated.

At the time it had seemed the only option. But now she knew better.

Angela McReady hiked up to the bluff and looked out over the edge. It was a long way down, the terrain pocked by brush and trees growing out of the side of the mountain and between the jagged rocks.

The teenager sat on the ground and edged close to the rim. She kicked a few loose stones and listened to hear them land. No sound returned.

"It's pretty up here, isn't it."

Startled, Angela yelped, then scrambled back a few feet to relative safety. "Uh, yeah."

"Do you mind if I join you?"

The girl looked Amber over. Sensing no threat, she nodded.

Amber settled on the ground, crossing her legs and staring out at the horizon.

After several minutes passed and the young woman said nothing at all, Angela turned to her. "Well?"

Amber leaned back, her hands behind her, her face to the sun. "Well, what?"

"Aren't you going to start telling me about Jesus?"

Amber's laugh echoed around them. "Hardly. I'm not one of them. I'm just the cook."

"Your food wasn't so bad the other day. I kind of liked it."

Amber glanced at her. "Thanks."

And that was all that was said between them.

A bird circled overhead, then swooped down, somewhere below the promontory, in search of small prey. They sat there, listening to the sound of the day, letting the sun's rays warm them.

"Maybe this whole grant thing wasn't such a good idea," Kara said. She had about thirty minutes before she met with her group, and had caught up with Nancy in the lodge.

"Don't say that, Kara," Nancy told her. "If you hadn't written that grant proposal for us, we wouldn't have been able to reach out to so many children in the community. Yes, there have been a few problems and a couple of kids aren't adjusting so well, but there are always wrinkles to iron out during the jamboree. And it's just a weekend, after all." Nancy picked up a miniature box of raisins from a bowl on the table in the middle of the sofa grouping.

"Wrinkles we can handle. Kids who are constantly at each other's throats is something else altogether." Kara tucked her hands in her pockets and paced the area in front of the big fireplace. "I guess I'm just concerned that our kids, the members of Community Christian, will be influenced by the things they see the others doing and getting away with."

"No one's gotten away with anything," Nancy assured her. "And if any influencing is going on, I think it'll be the other way around."

She consulted her clipboard and flipped through several sheets. "I've already done some rearranging among the groups for the talent show. I separated the Jackson twins, as well as Daphne Gregory and her two pals. Instead of ganging up on each other, they'll be in different talent groups."

Kara nodded. "The teamwork should do them some good."

"I think so, too. By the way, Cliff, Adam and I met with the girls. And Adam says Chief Evans handled that last little squabble with finesse."

Kara smiled. "I'm sure Adam was more help than he realizes."

"You're probably right. We're really going to miss him when he heads off to college next year."

Nancy offered Kara the box of raisins. Accepting a few, Kara sat on the edge of one of the sofas and reached for her notebook. "Anything in particular you want me to focus on? I have the high schoolers."

"Nothing that I can think of. But if you have a moment and can find them, it might be a good idea to speak with Sutton and Jonathan Evans."

"The chief's kids?"

Nancy nodded. She told Kara what had transpired during the night and then that afternoon.

"I spoke with Chief Evans when I arrived." Something was going on with those kids. First Amber suggesting a chat with them, then the chief's not-so-subtle questions, now Nancy's comment. And if even Amber, someone who actively avoided anything that even hinted at traditional counseling, could recognize a problem, there must truly be an issue that needed to be addressed.

"Who has the group with the younger kids?"

Nancy smiled and waggled her fingers.

Kara grinned. "Well, that's convenient. What time would you like me to take your session?"

"You're sure?"

"It's not a problem." And it would give her an opportunity to meet the Evans kids.

"So, how's Marcus?" Nancy asked, after Kara scribbled the time and place into her notebook.

Kara's smile grew. "He's just fine. I heard from him this morning. He has two sold-out shows in Atlanta, then he's flying home."

"What's it like having a famous fiancé?"

Kara shrugged. "Since he's the only one I've ever had, I can't compare it to anything else. But guess what?"

"What?"

"Patrice is home for the weekend. And she said she'll make it up here tomorrow for the closing program. You should see her, Nancy. She is so jazzed about this whole record deal. That's what Marcus has to do when he gets back to L.A. There's some post-production work on her CD."

"Well, it's not every day a famous singer shows up in Wayside, sweeps off her feet one of our most beautiful and brightest, then drops a million-dollar record deal in her sister's lap."

Kara laughed. "You make it all sound so simple. The good Lord knows it wasn't."

Nancy winked. "But it was fun. You're in love and I'm very happy for you both."

Her answering smile told Kara's side of the story. She glanced at her watch and jumped up. "Gotta go."

"Have fun."

Twenty minutes later, Kara wondered if *fun* was the right word for the rap session. Instead of being energized like they usually were, the teens all seemed to be in a mood—a bad one.

"All right," she said. "We've been doing this for a while now. You guys know me. What's up? Why is everybody so mopey?"

Adam and Cindy glanced at each other, then glanced in Angela's direction. A few others shuffled their feet, looking at anything and everything except the quiet girl in the corner.

Kara remembered Angela. Her mother had died about a year ago. Cliff and Matt had asked if she'd do some counseling with her. They'd gotten together twice, and then Angela had simply stopped coming. Kara's efforts to find her were fruitless; it was as if she'd disappeared. And truth be told, with all the other craziness in her life, Kara hadn't followed through the way she would have liked to.

Kara nodded at Adam, then decided to try a different approach with the teen group. With luck, the activity might draw all of them out of their shells.

"I don't wanna sing any dumb old songs," Daphne announced to her team.

The assignments for the talent review had been an-nounced during dinner. The teams had an hour or so to meet before the evening worship and campfire.

"We're just tossing out ideas right now," the captain said.

Each small group had seven members. The objective was to create a three- to five-minute sketch for presentation during the Sunday-afternoon closing program. To keep ringers and advance planning to a minimum, the teams were put together by the camp director, the head teen counselor—this year Adam Richardson—and one adult volunteer, all sworn to secrecy.

The teams had only the resources available to them at the camp to use for their skits, although some of the longtime campers had brought along in their luggage possible props, including clothing that could be converted into costumes.

"Well, if you don't like that idea, what suggestions do you have?" Max asked.

Daphne plopped into her chair and flipped the bill around on the baseball cap that covered her short red hair. "Here's a suggestion—how about if we all go home."

"You know," one of the older kids said, "your attitude this whole weekend has stunk."

Daphne swung her leg over the chair. "What's it to you? This whole place is dumb."

Cindy, the senior person in the room, decided it was time to intervene. "Let's go outside to talk, Daphne."

The recalcitrant teen rolled her eyes. "And what are you going to do, Little Mary Sunshine?"

"Don't pick on her!" one of the little girls said. "You're just being a bully."

Daphne jumped up, pushing her chair aside. It clattered to the floor behind her.

Suddenly, a wall of children faced her, all lined up in front of the little girl who'd called Daphne a bully.

"I think you should leave," Cindy said.

"Forget you," Daphne said, flinging at them the sheet with the team's rules printed on it. "Forget all of you Jesus freaks."

She clomped from the room, slamming the door behind her.

"I don't like her very much," Max said.

Cindy reached for the walkie-talkie and radioed Mrs. Baines. A few minutes later, the glum-looking group told Nancy and Paul what had happened.

"Do you know where she went?" Paul asked.

The team members shook their heads. "I hope she went home."

"Well, it's a long way to walk from here." He smiled at the children, giving them the reassurance they seemed to need. "Mrs. Baines, I'll look for her. Why don't you stay and get this group started on their skits."

"Chief Evans?" said Max.

"Yes."

"Do you need a description of the suspect?"

Paul tried hard not to laugh out loud. "I think we know what she looks like," he said. "But thanks for keeping your observation skills honed."

"Hey," someone said. "That's what our skit can be about."

"Yeah," another child said. "Max can be the investigator."

Paul snapped his fingers and pointed to Max. "See you later, Detective Young."

Max beamed at the praise from his hero.

Outside, Paul stood on the porch studying the layout of the camp.

Amber, carrying a large basket, approached. *Keep it light,* she coached herself. "Getting some air, Chief Evans?"

He smiled. "Call me Paul, please. And no," he said as Amber reached the porch. "So, are you Little Red Riding Hood?"

"Huh?" Then she looked at herself and chuckled. She'd donned a red windbreaker in case the evening turned cool before she finished her rounds. "Not quite. More like the Cookie Lady incognito."

He perked up at that and peered at the basket. "You have cookies in there?"

Amber laughed. "You're worse than the kids." But she reached in around the bags that had been packed to hold individual cookies and handed him two of her signature chocolate chip treats. "The kids here don't care for my cooking, but I know the cookies will be a hit."

Paul took a bite of one and moaned his delight. "This is almost enough to get my mind off the problem at hand."

"What's the problem?"

"If you were an angry thirteen-year-old girl who'd

just been run out of your youth group and you were essentially too far from home to walk, where would you go?"

"Well, first, when I was thirteen, the only place to hide was the back of a hut. Second, I was never in a youth group, so I don't know how I'd feel about being run out of one."

"Hypothetically, then."

"And the only place to hide is here?"

Paul nodded.

"Well, the bathroom, for one. I might just go to my bed or tent. But you know the best place I've found so far since I've been here?"

"What?"

"The boathouse. It's where they keep the canoes and fishing gear."

"Where is this boathouse?"

Amber pointed across the pond.

Paul finished off one cookie and started on the second one. "Too close and obvious," he said. "But I will check it out."

Amber glanced at him. He really was just a man. And as she watched his obvious enjoyment of her baking, a sense of pride and pleasure washed through her.

Then, before she chickened out, she said, "Would you like some company? On your search, I mean? You probably shouldn't go traipsing through the girls' dorm or tents by yourself."

"You're on."

She held the basket up. "I need to get these late-night treats to all the sites. It'll only take a minute."

"I'll be right here waiting."

He eyed the basket with a longing that tickled Amber. "Here, you big baby." She handed him two more cookies.

Paul grinned and bit into one. "Thanks."

It wasn't until Amber returned with the empty basket and placed it on a low table inside the lodge, that it dawned on Paul. He'd been the one to get the cookies this time.

So there, Caleb, he thought to himself. Then, he looked at the pretty blonde beside him, aware for the first time that his feelings had indeed changed where she was concerned.

He couldn't deny the fact to himself anymore.

He was interested in Amber Montgomery. Not so much in her past anymore. Just very, very...interested.

❦ Chapter Fourteen ❧

They searched all of the obvious places and a few not-so-obvious ones. Then, concerned that maybe the girl had indeed decided to walk home, Paul told Cliff that he was going to drive along the direct route to see if he could find Daphne or someone who may have seen her.

"Need a navigator?" the minister asked.

"Nope. I've put myself in the patrol shift since I've been here, so I know much of the town and surrounding area. I'll alert the on-duty units to be on the lookout, just in case."

"I guess I'll leave now."

Paul looked at Amber. He held her gaze until Cliff cleared his throat. "Uh, thanks for your help, Amber."

The three shared an awkward little moment, then Paul headed out. Amber got up to leave.

"Can I have a word with you?" Cliff asked.

She sat back down. "Sure. What's up?"

"I've heard nothing but rave reviews about your cooking."

Amber pursed her lips. "You obviously haven't talked to any of the kids at this camp."

"Not from the kids, from the adults. I understand you've been making dual meals. Camp grub for the youth, and serious food for the grown-ups."

Amber shifted in her seat. "Uh, well, I can pay you back if I used too much of your rations."

"No, no, no," Cliff said, coming around the desk and perching a hip on the edge. "I'm just wondering why no one invited me."

Still chuckling about Pastor Cliff, Amber thought about her mother's words: *"A hardworking man will serve up a hard-eating appetite."*

The smile fell from her face slowly as she made her way to the kitchen. She'd thought more about her parents in the past three days than she had in the past year.

She remembered one of the sermons her father had delivered on the mission field. They were in the compound where Ben and Angeline lived. In the soothing tenor that had lulled her to sleep on many a night, he'd sung a hymn about grace, then preached from John 10:10 about abundant life. "The thief comes to kill, steal and destroy, but I come that you might have life more abundantly." Amazingly, she remembered the verse, too. Maybe not word for word, but the essence of it.

With a song in his heart and a smile in his voice, her dad had held his Bible high, exhorting the villagers to embrace the love and peace of the Good Shepherd. In that moment, she'd loved the Lord more than ever, had rededicated her own life to Christ and vowed that she would walk in her parents' footsteps as an ambassador for the Lord.

Now Amber snorted. "Yeah, right."

But her derision faded in the face of what she'd seen so far at Community Christian Church's camp. Weren't they doing the same thing, except the mission field here was a domestic one instead of a remote overseas one?

She pulled out the key to the mess hall as she approached. Her father's sermon wasn't the only element she recalled of that long-ago night. It was the first time Ben had ever kissed her. Not full on the lips the way she'd seen some of the village couples kiss, but on the cheek, nice and sweet.

She smiled, remembering the gentle boy who, along with his sister, befriended a lonely little American girl. She missed Ben so much. Some of the grief she'd felt the night he died came back to haunt her now. He'd died trying to save not just any old dog, but the puppy she'd adopted.

Swallowing hard, Amber stuck the key in the mess hall door, but it swung open.

Her entire attention riveted to the door. It definitely had been locked.

She glanced around, suddenly wishing Paul was around.

She stepped into the mess hall and quickly flicked the switch near the door. The room suddenly flooded with light. And there, at a table near the kitchen, sat the missing Daphne, a five-gallon container of ice cream in front of her.

Amber and the teenager stared at each other for a moment, neither saying anything. Then Amber made her way to the table where Daphne sat. She didn't ask any of the obvious questions, the ones grown-ups always used to make her answer.

As a matter of fact, Amber didn't speak. Still holding the girl's gaze, Amber went to the racks holding flatware. She pulled out a tablespoon and returned to the table.

She peered into the container. "Neapolitan. I like strawberry." She stuck her spoon in and scooped up some ice cream. "Mmm, this is good."

Daphne just stared at her. "What are you doing?"

"Eating some ice cream."

"Why?"

"Because it tastes good," Amber said.

Daphne gave her a cross-eyed look. "What's with you?"

"What do you mean?"

"Aren't you going to ask me how I got in here?"

"Nope." Amber licked her lips, then stuck her spoon in for another spoonful, this time chocolate. "Want some strawberry?"

"How come?"

Amber glanced at her. "Because the strawberry is just as yummy as the others."

Daphne expelled a breath that made the freckles across her nose more pronounced. "How come you're not gonna ask me how I got in here or what I'm doing?"

"Duh," Amber said. "It's pretty obvious. You broke in the front door, went to the freezer and got some ice cream. Eating ice cream always helps me when I have things on my mind, too."

"What makes you think I have things on my mind?"

Amber just gave her a look.

"So, now what?" the girl asked.

"Now what, what?"

Daphne narrowed her eyes at Amber. "You're making fun of me."

"How am I doing that?"

She jumped up, fists balled, ready to brawl. "By... By... I don't know how. But you did."

"I was scared the first time I went to a church camp. Not here, of course—somewhere else. I didn't know anybody, didn't know how to make friends. I was miserable for days. And then something happened."

"What happened?"

"I had a bowl of ice cream with a girl at the camp. Well, not ice cream exactly, but the closest thing they had to it. This camp was pretty far away. Her name was Angeline."

Daphne reached for her spoon and scooped a generous portion of strawberry ice cream. "What'd you and this Angeline talk about?"

Amber shrugged. "Girl stuff. Not fitting in with the others. Boys and whether any of them would ever like us. You know, just talking."

"Uh-huh." Daphne settled in her chair again. "There's nobody to talk to here. They all think they're better than everybody else."

"Maybe. Sometimes other people are just as scared as you and me. They just hide it differently."

"I don't like to sing songs."

"So don't."

Not at all sure what to make of this odd adult, Daphne just stared for a full minute. "You make it sound so easy."

"It is easy," Amber said. "Do what you want to do. But realize you have to take responsibility for your actions. There are consequences for everything."

The wariness returned. "Whaddya mean 'consequences'?"

"Well, here's an example," Amber said, and she stuck her spoon into the ice cream container for another taste. "We're sitting here eating this good ice cream, right?"

Daphne nodded and helped herself to some more chocolate.

"But we're eating it straight out of the container that was for everybody."

"So?"

"So that means when we're done, we either have to have eaten it all, or the rest gets thrown away."

"We can't eat this much ice cream."

"Sanitary rules," Amber said. "Since we can't use this

container for the ice cream social tomorrow, that means one of two things."

"What?"

"I'll have to see if I can get another five-gallon bin, or we don't have enough ice cream for everybody."

"So get another one."

"I'll have to pay for it, probably out of my own money."

Daphne looked at her. "Your money?"

Amber nodded. "I'm responsible for the kitchen and all the meals here. Since something happened on my watch, I have to deal with it." She wasn't exactly sure if that was the case, but she'd have to find out. "The only other option would be to tell people we ran out."

"You could pretend like you didn't know what happened to the ice cream."

"True," Amber conceded. "But we'd both know. And that's one of the seven deadlies."

"Deadlies?"

"You know, the seven things God *really* doesn't like."

Daphne looked up, as if she expected something to happen to her for lying. "That other lady said there were ten rules."

Amber nodded. "That's a different list."

Daphne put her spoon down. "This isn't as much fun as I thought it'd be."

"The ice cream or the jamboree?"

"Both." She pushed her chair back. "I gotta go."

Amber licked the remaining ice cream on her spoon. "Okay."

"Are you gonna rat on me?"

Amber met the girl's hostile glare. "What do you think?"

"What do you mean, he's gone?" Sutton asked Jonathan. "Daddy wouldn't just leave us."

"The truck is gone," Jonathan pointed out.

Sutton chewed on that for a bit. "Maybe he went to the store."

"You stick by me," Jon told her.

"Okay." Sutton put her hand in her older brother's. Together they followed Cindy to the evening worship area. Jonathan assessed the seating options. "If we sit right here we can't see the road."

"I wanna see."

"Okay." He led her to a spot where they could see both the road and Pastor Cliff.

"You guys doing all right?" Cindy asked.

Jonathan nodded. Sutton looked at the ground. Other children filed in beside them.

Nancy made a few announcements before Cliff got up to speak. She consulted her ever-present clipboard, then beamed out at the group.

"Just a reminder, everyone, breakfast is at nine tomorrow. We start a little later because some teams like to get in an early morning practice. There'll be a meeting for all adult volunteers who can attend at eight o'clock in the dining hall."

Her smile encompassed everyone, from the youngest child to the seasoned veterans. "Anyone have any questions?"

A couple of hands shot up. After answering a question about the closing time, and assuring Max that, yes, he'd still have a chance to try the rock wall, Nancy glanced at Cliff.

"Well, as Pastor Cliff comes up, I have one more announcement," she said.

"Uh-oh," Cliff said. "That sounds like a setup. What'd I do now?" Cliff took his wife's hand in his.

Several people chuckled at the byplay between the two.

Amber, watching from the sidelines, marveled again at how open and easy their relationship appeared.

"It's not about you," Nancy assured him. "We'll have a special guest tomorrow for our closing. Some of you know Patrice Spencer from our concert after the film and music festival. Well, she's back home in Wayside now. She just finished recording her first gospel music CD. We're all very excited for her. She and Reverend Matt will give us a soul-stirring send-off to our fall jamboree."

Whoops followed that announcement. Cliff kissed Nancy, then took center stage.

"Well, my wife is always a hard act to follow," he said. "At least I wasn't in trouble this time."

"You're never in trouble, Pastor," somebody yelled out.

"Tell that to the boss," he said, indicating Nancy, who'd settled next to the Jackson twins.

Amber saw Daphne slink into an open space in the back. The girl didn't look happy, but at least she was there—

"Hey."

Amber jumped, her hand clutching her throat. "You scared me to death."

Paul grinned. Amber realized just how much she liked seeing him smile. When Paul Evans smiled, so did his eyes. Unlike her ex's, Paul's eyes held gentleness and warmth.

Spying him, Sutton waved furiously from where she and Jonathan sat near Cindy. Paul waved back.

"Want to come join us?" he asked.

Amber shook her head. "I'm not going to stay long. You go ahead. Looks like Sutton's saved a place for you."

"I'll see you later, then?"

His gaze connected with hers, and Amber's heart raced. The words, innocent enough, seemed to carry another message altogether. His eyes, a clear blue like a summer day or a chambray shirt, held no malice, no hidden agenda.

So was she hearing things, inferring inflection where none existed?

He reached for her hand and squeezed it gently. Then he turned away.

She watched him walk toward the place where Sutton and Jonathan waited. Even his walk was confident, his steps sure. Raymond had walked with a swagger, a calculated movement meant to convey his position and to intimidate both friend and foe. Paul, on the other hand, walked like a man with nothing to hide. Amber blinked back sudden tears.

"Way too much thinking and remembering this weekend," she muttered.

Tuning in to what Pastor Cliff was saying rather than where her thoughts led, Amber folded her arms and leaned against the tree trunk.

"As I was preparing my notes for tonight's message I realized that it wasn't a sermon I needed to preach this evening," the minister said. "I thought I'd start by telling you a story."

Cliff faced the campers, counselors, parents and volunteers. "We've been coming up here for several years, and each fall when we arrive for the youth jamboree, I'm struck by the beauty of the area. When we're at home, we don't often pause to appreciate the things that God put on this earth for us to enjoy. And here, where the air is clean, the water clear and where we fellowship in fun and friendliness, we have the opportunity not only to challenge our bodies—I have a couple of scrapes to prove just how much," he added, showing off his hands and elbows. "But to get closer to God."

Not in the mood for a quasi-sermon, Amber turned to leave.

"We had some people run the river today," said the pastor. "And I understand one of the boats took a tumble. Everyone's okay, but when I was told about that, it reminded me of just how much we depend on God."

Amber paused, wondering where he might be headed with his comments about her fall and near drowning. She leaned back against the tree, and could see Paul a few yards away. Sutton was in his lap, Jonathan at his father's right side.

"Sometimes in life we have to stumble, to fall. Maybe we rock the boat a little or even a lot. And sometimes we fall overboard. Without a life preserver."

Several people chuckled at that.

"But our help, even then, comes from the Lord," Cliff said. "Close your eyes for a moment and think about the worst day or time of your life. Bring it to the forefront of your thoughts."

Amber swallowed hard. She didn't close her eyes because she didn't want to think about that day, the worst one ever. As a matter of fact, she'd spent a lot of energy and time trying to banish it from her memory.

She watched Cliff Baines walk among his camp congregation.

"I know it hurts," he said. "Were you crying on that day or during that time? Did it seem like no one, not even God, could understand your problems, let alone help you?"

Amber saw several heads nodding. She folded her arms and quickly blinked back the moisture that had somehow found its way to her eyes.

"Take the hand of the person sitting next to you," the pastor said.

Amber wanted to leave, to run like she'd never run before. To run like she'd run *that* night. But her feet were planted to the ground. *"Like a tree, planted by the water."* The line rushed through her head, a forgotten vestige of her former life, and her former faith.

"Even with your eyes closed you can feel the person's hand in yours, can't you?" Cliff said.

Amber started.

Pastor Cliff was standing right there beside her. She hadn't even heard his approach, but now his hand took hold of hers.

"Jesus loves you," Cliff said.

Though his voice carried over all of the assembly, it seemed to Amber that he spoke the words quietly in her ear, only for her edification.

"He was there for you during that worst time ever and he's here for you now. All you have to do is open your heart and let him in."

"It's not that easy," Amber said, her face contorting. "It's not that easy." She wrenched her hand from Cliff's and stumbled away.

Paul heard her cry out, and turned in time to see Amber rushing away. He looked to Cindy to ask her to watch the children, but he saw Kara Spencer and Nancy Baines get up and follow Amber.

"Daddy, why are people crying?"

He hugged Sutton close. "Because sometimes they have burdens too heavy to carry."

"And crying makes it better?"

"No, pumpkin. Jesus makes it better."

❧ Chapter Fifteen ❧

It was late, close to eleven. The evening snacks had been consumed, the late-night talent-show rehearsals were over. Lights had gone out in the dorms almost an hour ago, but Amber, still keyed up, couldn't sleep.

Every time she closed her eyes, it seemed as if a wall of water crushed in around her, stealing her oxygen and her orientation. Is that what a near-death experience was like? This sense of stepping a safe distance away from the abyss.

She pulled a pair of sweatpants over her pajamas and tugged a Wayside College sweatshirt over her head. She hadn't been running in all the days she'd been at the jamboree. Edgy and irritable served as good descriptions of how she'd been feeling the past few days.

For a moment, Amber allowed herself to indulge in self-pity. But the party didn't last long. That was one of the things she'd learned in that counseling session, the one that ended with Amber getting a two-year-old headache. Maybe her body was just sending a message that it didn't like going cold-turkey off its regular exercise regimen.

She could run down to the camp road and maybe up the highway a bit. That might make two miles. She figured she could run it twice.

She stuffed into her pockets a compass and her driver's license, then snatched up the red windbreaker and headed outside.

But instead of heading toward the road, her feet seemed to move in another direction. Too tired to argue or to even consider that she again heeded not her own desires but some higher prompting, she just walked to the lake and sat on the ground, her legs crossed, the lake surface a mirror to her stillness. She sat that way for a long time, for so long that her legs cramped, for so long that a chill in the air made her shiver.

That's when she realized she wasn't alone—physically or spiritually.

"How long have you been standing there?" she asked him.

"Long enough to know not to disturb someone who is meditating."

"What makes you think I was meditating?"

He stepped toward her. "Where I come from, people who stare into a river are generally meditating, praying or doing some sort of ritual sacrifice."

She wrinkled her nose. "Where are you from?"

"Cajun country," he said. "I was born in Louisiana, but my parents moved to California when I was ten."

"Haley's husband is from Louisiana. He grew up there."

Paul smiled and shrugged. "I've been a few places, but not east or south. I may have been born in the South, but I'm Southern-California raised, and sometimes it shows."

"What's wrong with Southern California?"

"Why don't you tell me," he said. "You don't seem to like L.A. very much. Each time it comes up, you get tense."

Amber turned back to the still water, willing her shoulders to relax, disturbed that she had a reaction to Los Angeles that showed. "I prefer small towns."

"I'm finding I do, too."

"I don't understand you."

He held his arms wide. "What's to understand? I'm pretty open. I see things in black and white. There's very little gray area for me."

"Then, you miss a lot," she said.

"Why do you always fight me, Amber?"

"I don't know what you're talking about."

The response, instinctive and defensive, made Amber feel small. "I don't mean to," she told him. She shrugged. "I think I'm just not used to cops being genuinely nice."

"I'm more than a cop, Amber. I'm a man, first. Do you mind if I join you?"

She started to say something smart in response, then

just edged over, inviting him to sit without actually putting voice to the invitation.

"It's beautiful up here," he said. "It makes you forget that there's a world beyond the rising and setting of the sun."

"Are you a closet poet?"

He shook his head. "Nope. I've just learned how to appreciate natural beauty."

But as he said the words, his gaze lingered on Amber, not on the dark lake that shimmered quietly in the moonlight and on the surrounding trees.

"You know," she said, "in one of the places where I grew up, if a man and a woman talked together at the riverside, it meant they were agreeing to court."

"Hmm, maybe I should visit that place where you grew up."

"You wouldn't like it," she said. "Southern California is an asphalt jungle. The places where I was raised were just jungle, period."

But what he'd said—and the implications of that—sunk in a moment later. Amber looked at him then, really looked at him. "What were you saying, Paul? Just then, I mean?"

He reached for her hand, covered it in his much larger one. His hands were like the rest of him. Warm, comforting. Amber didn't pull away, and this time she didn't mind him holding her hand. It felt good. The way she supposed a normal woman felt when a man she liked held her hand.

A man she liked!

Amber's eyes widened and she snatched her hand away from him. Who was this man and why was he making her feel things?

"It means that I'm interested in you, Amber Montgomery. I've tried not to be."

"Gee, thanks. You really know how to flatter a girl."

"I think you know what I mean," he said. "There's something between us. Something that's been there from the moment we met."

"Well, let me tell you this," Amber said. "If your idea of wooing me is bringing up that night when you had me handcuffed and arrested, your approach needs some work."

"I'm sorry about that night, Amber."

She got up and skipped a pebble out along the smooth lake surface. It bounced several times as it skimmed along, then eventually sank.

"You're very good at that."

"I spent a lot of time at the riverside waiting," she said. "Waiting for someone to come join me."

"And how many times did that happen?"

"Once," she said. She turned to him. "Just now."

His gaze met hers, then dipped to her mouth. "I'd like to kiss you, Amber Montgomery."

He reached for her hand again and waited for her response. But Amber just continued to stand there, her gaze focused on something he couldn't see.

She didn't pull her hand away this time, but he felt her retreat.

"I'm not good at this," she said.

"Good at what?"

"Intimacy. Quiet moments with the opposite sex. There's something you need to know about me. I'm sure it will color the way you think you feel."

"We all have pasts."

She shook her head. "It's not that— Well, it is that. You're a police chief and I'm..."

"You're a beautiful woman who intrigues this single dad and cop."

"You sound like a personals ad." She tugged her hand away from him and got up.

Paul watched her. "That's it, isn't it. The kids? I'm a package deal, Amber."

"It's not your children. Sutton and Jon are wonderful. As a matter of fact, they're about the only kids I really understand."

"Let me help you."

She faced him, taking umbrage at the notion that a woman needed a man to rescue her. In Amber's experience, it was just the opposite. Women needed to be rescued *from* men.

"Excuse me? Help me? What makes you think I need help?"

He stood, too, tried to take her hand. "It's an educated guess."

Amber's own fear of the conversation and where it might be leading, what he might want of her, made her reckless. Instead of taking his words for what they were, she lashed out angrily. "I see the way you are with your kids, *Chief Evans*. I'm not a child. I don't need to be protected and shielded from the big bad world." She poked a finger in his chest. "I'm some kind of experiment for you, is that it?"

"What are you talking about?"

"I'm not something you can put under a microscope and study to see how I respond to different stimuli. I'm a living and breathing woman."

Everything had been going along fine, just fine. And then, just like Raymond used to do, Paul pointed out her flaws—all the things that needed fixing. By him. He reached for her, but Amber pulled away. "I have feelings," she said, tears starting to mix in with the words. "Feelings that nobody cares about."

She'd been trying to separate them. She knew intellectually that the blue-eyed cop who beat up on her wasn't the same blue-eyed police chief she'd been getting to know this weekend. But with what Paul said, the edges were starting to blur again.

"Amber?"

He reached a hand out to her, to steady her, but Amber was too worked up to see the danger of the large rock behind her. When he approached, she stepped back.

"Amber, look out!"

But too late, she stumbled over the rock.

Quick on his feet, Paul caught her before she fell, hit her head or landed in the lake.

They tumbled to the ground, Paul taking the brunt of

the fall. For a moment, Amber lay sprawled over him. Then she shuddered and scrambled away.

He knew Amber had nothing to fear from him.

The look in her eyes, however, said she believed otherwise.

"Amber?"

She'd curled into a ball, her hands shielding her face. "I'm sorry. I didn't mean to run away from you. Please don't hurt me."

Paul cursed himself a thousand times the fool. Suddenly it all made sense. The way she'd gone limp that first night, and then her attempts to fight for herself. The wavering bravado that was probably the only defense mechanism she claimed.

And he remembered the bruise he'd accidentally left on her arm the night they'd met. The way she'd lashed out at him in the water...

How could he have been so blind? The signs were all there. He'd been trained to watch for them. Yet, with this fragile woman, one he cared for like no other, he'd been oblivious to the pain that *he* caused her.

Amber wasn't a fugitive from justice or a woman on the run or one of the legion who just didn't like cops. She'd been abused by someone. Probably someone who looked or acted a lot like he did.

Other pieces of the puzzle fell into place then. Her reaction when she'd found out he'd been with the LAPD. Later, her questions about a specific L.A. cop. He groaned, realizing too late what all the pieces meant.

"Oh, Amber. I'm so sorry." He reached for her, to comfort her, but he stayed his hand.

Lord, give me the words. Guide my hands and my heart.

"Amber, it's me. Paul Evans." Despite the rage he felt toward the man who'd turned her into a woman living in fear, Paul kept his voice low, soothing. And he didn't touch her.

"I'm not going to hurt you. Can you hear me, Amber? It's Paul."

He looked around for help, but they remained alone at the lake. Nothing but the night surrounded them. He wanted to hold her, to tell her it would all be okay, but he didn't want to frighten her any more.

I need some help, Lord. Please.

Nancy and Cliff Baines sat up talking. Usually they slept apart during the fall camping trip because they were needed as chaperones in the dorms or tent sites. But this year, they'd had more than enough volunteers—too many, really. But at least each child got individual attention.

"I've noticed an interesting dynamic this weekend," Cliff said.

"What's that?" Nancy massaged her husband's shoulders as they talked.

"Have you looked at Paul Evans and Amber?"

"What do you mean, looked at them? I see them. Chief Evans decided to stay here after his children got spooked that first night."

"Not that. I mean the way they look at each other when they think no one's watching."

Nancy leaned over his shoulder. "Are you still playing matchmaker?"

"Me?"

The innocent question brought a smile to Nancy's face. "Yes, you, dear sweet husband of mine." She kissed his cheek.

Cliff turned his head and captured a real kiss before Nancy went back to kneading the muscles along his shoulders and back.

A moment later they switched positions and he worked the kinks out of her neck, shoulders and back.

"This is different," Cliff said. "Not like Haley and Matt, where everybody except the two of them could see they were made for each other."

"What, then?"

"I don't know. I do know Amber has a wounded spirit."

"Were you talking to her tonight?"

Cliff nodded. "I hadn't planned to. I was going to call on Kara to give her testimony, but something led me to Amber Montgomery instead. She's been on my mind and spirit the entire weekend."

"Mine, too. I've kept her in prayer, but I've been so busy putting out fires that I haven't had a chance to talk to her. *Really* talk to her."

"She's a very private person."

Nancy nodded. "And the police chief is very public,

very open. He loves those kids to distraction. But I'm worried about them, too."

"I talked to the Jackson twins after the service tonight."

"And?"

"And I think we won't have any more trouble out of them. As a matter of fact, Sarita wants to join the church," Cliff said. "She said she didn't come forward during the invitation tonight because she didn't want people to make fun of her, Daphne in particular." Cliff sighed. "Ah, young Miss Gregory. What other mischief has she been up to? Besides having Chief Evans out searching for her?"

"Nothing else that I know of, thank the Lord," Nancy said. "Everywhere that child goes, trouble is close behind. She eventually showed up, but didn't say where she'd been."

"Who spoke with her?"

"I did, but she'd never look me in the eye. So the Lord only knows what she'd been up to."

He expelled another breath. "Maybe next year we should screen the scholarship applicants a little better."

"Don't be discouraged," Nancy said. "This is just the first year of opening the camp to people who aren't members of Community Christian. Just because we have a few problems with a couple of kids isn't reason to shut down the whole program. Besides," she added, "this weekend may be their only exposure to the Gospel."

Cliff took her hand. "Have I told you lately how much I love you?"

Nancy smiled. "Yes, but I always like hearing it again."

"I love you, Nancy Baines."

"I love you, too, Pastor Cliff."

"I think there's some work that needs to be done. Join me?"

"Always," she said as she bowed her head, her fingers entwined with her husband's.

Cliff then began an intercessory prayer, lifting up all of the participants at Camp Spirit Fire, in particular the small group of young people, Amber Montgomery included, who still weighed heavily on his heart.

"Father God, we thank you this evening—"

A scream rent the night air, shattering the illusion of safety at the church camp.

It was a girl's long, terrified scream for help.

❧ Chapter Sixteen ❧

Paul's head whipped up at the sound of a woman's cry. "What now?" he exclaimed.

A thought raced through his mind. Sutton? But the voice was too mature to belong to his daughter.

The cop in him wanted to secure the other location, but the man in him knew that other people were there to handle whatever that situation might be. He couldn't leave Amber, not the way she was at the moment, curled up, crying and shaking, locked in a nightmare and terrified of him.

His place, for now, was at the side of this woman who hurt so very much.

"Amber?" He touched her shoulder, lightly. "Amber, you're safe with me," he said.

Even as he said the words, he wondered how many times Amber and women just like her heard those words from their tormentors, from fathers, brothers, boyfriends, pastors and deacons. How many remained locked in an abused state of mind long after the physical torment ended?

He stroked Amber's back, trying to get a handle on what to say and do, since divine providence didn't seem to be raining down on him.

Or was it?

Paul sat on the ground, pulled her into his arms and rocked her until her cries became whimpers, until her whimpers turned to hiccups, and until she turned her wide-eyed but clear gaze directly on him.

She sniffled and ran a hand over her nose. "I'm sorry."

"There's nothing to apologize for."

"I didn't mean to... I mean, I'm sorry you had to witness that. I... Sometimes I forget and it seems like..."

She tried to pull away. Paul offered no resistance.

"You didn't hit me."

Taken aback at her incredulity, he just shook his head. "I don't hit women, Amber. I never have and never will."

Amber said, "I just thought, well, because of, you know...your..."

She blushed furiously. Sitting there with her in the moonlight, Paul found it enchanting that she could blush, given everything she'd been through and the state she'd been in just a few moments ago.

"Whenever Raymond, my old boyfriend, got aroused he used to..."

Fury radiated through Paul at the man who'd so carelessly used this fragile woman, but he held it in for Amber's sake—for his own sake.

"Real men don't beat up on women or anyone else," he said. "And they know how to control their urges."

Amber frowned. "What's that noise?"

Paul glanced back at the dorms where lights were now blazing and kids spilled out on the porches, everyone talking at once. "Something's going on at the camp."

"At—" Amber glanced at her wrist, then remembered she hadn't put her watch on for her run. "What time is it?"

"After midnight, I think," Paul said. "There are plenty of people who can handle what's going on over there. I'm concerned about what's going on right here."

She pushed completely away from him then. "Part of me thinks I owe you an explanation. The other part says, run as fast as you can."

He waited for her decision.

"I..." She glanced toward the main camp compound. "Maybe you're needed back there."

"I'm needed here more," he said quietly.

She rewarded him with a tentative smile. "Thank you."

In that moment, Paul knew that all the things he'd sought were right here in front of him. Not necessarily in the package he'd hoped to receive, but presented to him nonetheless as a gift from God.

Few, if any, gray areas existed for him. People were either law-abiders or law-breakers, believers or unbelievers, honest or dishonest. So it surprised him that when it came to Amber, he realized a gray area did exist. Amber lived in it.

From what she'd told him so far, Amber at one time had had a very deep and abiding devotion to the Lord. The circumstances of her life had changed that outlook, but maybe the reason she was brought here to Camp Spirit Fire this weekend was to reclaim the faith she had once known.

As if her thoughts were attuned to his, she said, "For a while, I grew up wanting to be a missionary like my parents. Then I discovered the true value of an American dollar, and I never wanted to go back to Central America again.

"My brother Kyle—he's a few years older than me—always talked about going to the Far East to teach English and minister there. But my own dreams never quite seemed to jell into anything that resembled a lifetime career of doing the same thing over and over."

"So what'd you do?" Paul asked. He'd settled on the ground, one arm propped on his knee.

Amber smiled, swiftly and then with a touch of lingering sadness. "I did what every American kid daydreams about, but rarely finds—the perfect way to play hooky. I ran away from home."

"You're kidding?"

Shaking her head, she added, "I meant, in a sense. I did everything I was big enough and bad enough to do."

"How old were you then?"

"Two weeks shy of my twentieth birthday. I thought

I knew it all, too. My parents planned for me to go to finish a degree at their Bible-college alma mater. But I backpacked around Mexico for a while, then crossed the border. Hung out in San Diego, then hitchhiked my way to L.A."

"That's very dangerous."

Nodding, she agreed. "And stupid. And childish. So when I met up with a cop who seemed to have it all together—career, faith, finances—I was, like, 'well, see Mom and Pop, I didn't do so bad.'" A shadow crossed her face. "I was twenty-three and everything was right with my world."

When she fell silent, he asked, "Then what happened?"

Amber shrugged. "I found out that looks can be deceiving. I learned that trust isn't something that you can take for granted, that faith without the works to back it up is just a lie. And I found out how many ways you can hurt and not have the pain show."

Loud voices carried from the lodge. They both turned in that direction. Paul was about to ask her what, exactly, she meant, when the sound of a police siren filled the air.

"That's not good. Come on," Paul said, offering a hand to Amber. A moment later, several squad cars filled the compound.

At almost a dead run they sprinted back to the lodge area.

The scene at the teen girls' dorm was a circus. Crying, yelling and name-calling reigned.

An unrepentant-looking Daphne Gregory smirked at the other teens. "Can't you all take a little joke?"

"What you did was dangerous and stupid," somebody yelled, lingering fear making the words sharp. "You could have killed somebody!"

A crowd of campers in various degrees of dress spilled off the porch and into the front yard of the dorm, while others, stragglers who'd heard the sirens and got up to see what the commotion was all about, edged closer.

Inside, the Jackson twins huddled together on a sofa, eyes shooting daggers at Daphne, while the others surrounded them, the young people representing what looked like a united front against Daphne and her cohorts.

"What happened here?" Paul said at the same time as Caleb.

Everyone started talking at once.

"One at a time," Paul said. He didn't know who the dorm parent was, but he saw two people he knew. "Adam? Cindy?"

"Apparently the dispute among these three and the twins wasn't over," the lead counselor explained.

"Daphne and her friends snuck into the room where the twins were and set off firecrackers near their beds," Adam said.

Quick action by Cindy and another counselor had prevented a fire. But they'd called 9-1-1 when Tanita Jackson said she'd been burned and one of the other girls in the room was having trouble breathing.

While the EMTs checked the two girls out, Nancy left to call the parents of the children involved in the fracas. After a nod from Paul, Caleb led Daphne to a squad car.

"Is she going to jail where she belongs?" Tanita demanded hotly.

"We'll let Chief Evans and his officers worry about that," Cliff said.

Nancy returned with a purse and her clipboard. She spoke to Tanita as well as to a girl the EMTs had hooked up to oxygen, just in case. The EMTs cleared them both, declaring fright as the chief problem. Tanita had no visible burns or injuries, but Nancy insisted both girls be looked at further. Their parents would meet them at the hospital.

After a word with Caleb and Paul, Nancy got in the squad car with Daphne. Two parent volunteers rode with the other three girls, the twins clinging to each other.

"It's late," Cliff said, rounding up campers. "I know we all have an early start in the morning, but I'd like to have a word with you."

Suddenly exhausted and still feeling a little raw around the edges, Amber watched Cliff address this latest incident. After a prayer, he dismissed them all.

As the campers headed back to their dorms, Paul turned to Amber. "You're awfully quiet."

"We'd talked earlier," Amber said, her eyes still looking toward the place where the taillights of the emergency vehicles faded away. "I thought things were cool." Sitting in the back of the police car, Daphne didn't look nearly as cocky as she'd been earlier. She'd looked like a scared thirteen-year-old. "What's going to happen to her?"

"Her aunt and uncle—I believe that's who Nancy said were responsible for her—will pick her up at the police station."

"There's always one in the bunch, no matter the place or time. One person who can spoil it for everybody."

Paul heard her, but he wondered if Amber was referring to the incident at the camp, or her own life situation.

As Wayside's police chief, Paul felt duty bound to be at the station to speak with Daphne's guardians and then to check on Tanita and the other girl at the hospital. But first, he'd look in on Jonathan and Sutton. The youngest kids' dorm chaperone stood out front, having kept them all in their bunkhouse.

"Hi there, Chief," Harriet Simmons said. "I should tell you that our little camp is normally very quiet. The biggest thing that's ever happened here was a pack of hot dogs getting burned to a crisp once in a campfire."

"Well, this weekend has certainly been lively."

He climbed the three steps to the porch.

"Did you come to check on the kids? They're sound asleep. Only a couple of them woke up. I remember what it was like to sleep like that."

Paul smiled. "Mind if I peek in on them?"

"Not at all."

A few minutes later, Paul rushed back outside. "They're gone. Jon and Sutton are gone."

"What do you mean *gone?*"

Paul's gaze darted around, looking for likely places where his children might be. "As in, not in their bunks. What happened here, Harriet?"

She clutched her robe tighter. "Nothing. They were... No one left the building. I'd have seen them. Did you check the bathroom? The lounge?"

"They're not in there!"

Harriet stumbled back at the force of his anger and fear.

Paul swiped a hand over his eyes. "I'm sorry. I didn't mean to snap at you."

"What's wrong?" Amber said, pausing in front of the dorm on her way inside.

"Jon and Sutton. They're missing."

"Missing?" Amber grabbed Paul's arm and felt the strength of muscles bunched and tension coiled. "What happened to them?"

"I don't know," Paul said. Running a hand through his hair, he tried to think, tried to figure out what might have spooked them. He slapped his forehead. "Fireworks!"

"What?" Harriet and Amber said at the same time.

"Fireworks going off probably sounded like gunfire to them."

The anguish-filled words, ripped from him, tore at Amber's heart. "We'll find them, Paul. We'll find them. Maybe they just went over to the lodge or to the girls' dorm to see what all the fuss was about."

Harriet dashed inside to look for the siblings herself.

When she returned, she held a walkie-talkie and looked grim. "Their backpacks are gone."

She radioed Cliff and turned to Paul. But he and Amber had already taken off, searching the camp lodge and compound for the two missing children.

"Jon, I'm scared," Sutton said.

"It's safe in here," the boy assured her. "Nobody saw us leave. The bad man won't find us here."

From outside, voices could be heard.

"Shh," Jon said. He held his sister close as the two clutched each other, hiding from the person who'd been shooting up the camp dorm the same way their house in Los Angeles been shot up.

This time it was a real emergency. The police cars they'd heard proved it.

They remained quiet until the voices moved on.

"What if Daddy got shot?"

Jonathan bit his lower lip. He had to be brave. He had to protect his sister. As older brother, that was his job. His mom had told him so.

"He won't," Jon said. But his insides felt trembly and afraid, just like they had *that* night.

"I'm going to search the mess hall," Amber said. "That's where Daphne went to hide."

For the first time since she'd met him, Paul Evans looked truly vulnerable and uncertain. As a man who carried great responsibility not just for himself and his family, but for the entire town, his quick thinking and coolness under fire were attributes that made him a good cop, and an excellent police chief. But the man standing before her now wasn't a cop. He was a father who had just one priority: his children.

"Paul?"

He glanced down as her, his expression grim. "I can't lose them, Amber. Those kids are all I've got left in the world."

Without a word, Amber slipped her hand into his. They stared into each other's eyes for a moment, both realizing the import of what she'd done. Not since Raymond Alvarez had taught her to mistrust all men, particularly men in uniform, had Amber freely given her trust to another human being.

Once he had it, Paul seemed reluctant to let her hand go, as if she, too, might disappear from beneath his nose the way the children had.

"Father God, please keep them safe from hurt, harm and danger."

Paul's prayer, quick and earnest, moved Amber. Her throat constricted.

Cliff and Adam met them in the middle of the compound. Cliff had his walkie-talkie, Adam had a first-aid kit strapped to his waist.

"What's wrong now?" Cliff said. "Harriet said some kids are gone."

"Mine. Sutton and Jonathan. They're not in the dorm."

Adam groaned. "They could be anywhere out here in the dark."

Paul sent a glare in Adam's direction. Amber watched expressions flit across his face before he shut them down, turning into the police chief on an investigation and assignment, rather than a desperate father on a mission.

"They're going to be somewhere where it's safe," he said. "A cave or cubby where they can't be seen."

"That could be a number of places," Adam noted.

"Then, we don't need to waste any more time. Cliff, take the north side. Adam, the south. We'll head in an easterly direction."

"We can cover more ground if I go alone," Amber said. "I'll search that way," she said, indicating the west.

"I don't want to lose you, too." He bent his head, kissed her full and hard on the lips.

Stunned, Amber stood there.

Despite their concern, Cliff and Adam exchanged a smile. "I'll radio for some backup," Cliff said. "Do we need to call your officers again?"

The father in him wanted to yell "yes!" But the police chief knew that a preliminary search needed to be made first. "No," Paul said. "Not yet." He glanced at his watch. "If they're not found in thirty minutes, we'll take the next step."

Watches synchronized, the searchers fanned out.

It took very little in the imagination department for Amber to know just what fear tasted like. Its acrid flavor lingered in her memory. As a child, she'd known fear—of the unknown, of new places, of losing a friend.

As an adult, she'd found new reasons to be afraid. She'd discovered that she gladly would have swapped the fears she'd known as a child for the ones she had been forced to confront as a grown woman.

While the others commenced their segment searches by calling out for Jonathan and Sutton, Amber just stood where she was, revisiting the past.

Once in Guatemala, she'd steered off the trail and found herself lost in lush vegetation so high she couldn't see over it. The night sky, thickly obscured by trees, couldn't help lead her back to camp. She couldn't see the stars. Standing there, she'd felt as if she were quite possibly the only person on Earth. Loneliness almost overwhelmed her eleven-year-old spirit.

She had tried to remember the signs she'd been taught. Moss growing. Brush bent this way or that. But the fear had clawed at her, beating down the survival tactics her parents had insisted she know.

And so she'd sat down, right where she was, in the middle of the jungle. She'd sat down and cried her eyes out.

Now, slowly, Amber opened her eyes and turned around in a slow circle.

Sutton and Jonathan hadn't gone far. She knew it. But just as she'd been well and truly hidden from the search party out looking for her in the jungle, the two children would be hidden in plain view.

She didn't have a watch, but it seemed like maybe five minutes had passed since Paul, Adam and Cliff had started searching. "I know you guys are still here," she said. "Where are you?"

Turning again in a circle in the middle of the compound, she faced two of the camp's outbuildings. Unsure of what was housed in one, Amber headed off in that direction.

Amber's instinct had been right on target. The first building was empty, but in the second one, the boathouse, she'd heard whispering that abruptly stopped.

She passed rows of canoes, stands of oars and footlockers containing life vests. And there, in a corner, sitting between a stack of life preservers, she found two little children.

"May I join you?"

Sutton scrambled up and threw her arms around Amber. "How'd you find us?"

Giving the girl a hug, Amber said, "If I were running away, this would be a pretty good hideout."

Sutton frowned up at Amber, then turned to Jonathan. "We weren't running away. Were we?"

Instead of answering, Jonathan scuffed his tennis shoe on the floor of the boathouse. "You're not my mom."

Taken aback by the comment, Amber shook her head. "No. I'm not. That doesn't mean I don't care about what happens to you."

"Why?" the boy asked.

"Why are you being so mean?" Sutton said, confronting her brother before Amber could answer.

Jonathan got up and stomped away. "All I was trying to do was protect you. Uncle Paul wasn't here. It's my job to protect you."

Amber approached the brave boy who was spoiling for a fight. She placed her hands on his shoulders, felt the tension there, as well as the vulnerability. "You've done a fine job protecting your sister. Tell me, though, Jon, who gets to protect *you?*"

"That's my job," Paul said from the door.

He entered the boathouse, extinguished the flashlight and opened his arms to his children, who propelled themselves straight into his embrace.

"I'm going to need two weeks to recover from this little weekend camping trip," Nancy said later that night.

The Evans children had fallen asleep on the sofa in the common room, their father between them. Amber had excused herself to go bake—what she did best when stressed. So a big batch of honey pecan rolls would probably greet them all in a few hours.

"Maybe I'll treat you to a full day at that spa you love in Portland," said Cliff.

In their room, Nancy smiled at her husband. "That sounds wonderful right about now. This entire weekend has been a disaster from the word go."

"It's not your fault," he said. "You're just focusing on the bad. What about the good?"

In the minister's mind, he counted as good seeing the change in Amber Montgomery. She along with a couple of others remained on his daily prayer list.

"The police have been here—what is it now, three times? Instead of being ambassadors for Christ, we're going to end up with a reputation like the Revelers."

He rubbed her arms, thinking about the switch in perspective. All along, Nancy had been the stalwart, maintaining a cheerful countenance in the midst of all the stress of this year's jamboree. But this latest incident had spooked her well and good.

"I think you're exaggerating just a bit, dear."

Nancy blew out a breath and gave him an exasperated look. "You know what I mean."

He nodded. "Listen, we have just one more day. We'll all eat a hearty breakfast in a few hours. The kids will rehearse their skits. Then we'll have the annual amateur production and go home."

Nancy didn't look as convinced as her husband sounded. "Look at what's gone wrong in just two days. I'm halfway afraid to face tomorrow."

"It's already here," he said. "You have no choice."

"Gee, thanks. Seriously, Cliff. The board needs to discuss this when we get back. Maybe this is a sign that we shouldn't have the jamboree anymore. Maybe we've gotten so focused on doing everything one way that..."

Cliff wrapped his arms around his wife's waist and pulled her close. "Why don't you leave the worrying to the One who has everything under control?"

❧ Chapter Seventeen ❧

Caleb wanted to tell Marnie about the decision that had been placed on his heart. He wanted to hear her ideas about his new venture. He'd yet to figure out how any of this would play in his real life, but for now, at least, after the incident that he liked to refer to as "wrestling with angels until they blessed him," Caleb tried to act nonchalant.

But his heart was beating about seventy miles a minute, just as it had when he was sixteen and asking a girl out for the very first time.

He hadn't known then how to approach Mary Anne Harshont, and now, more than a decade later, he still had no idea how to approach a woman. He loved Marnie with the kind of love that grew deeper by the day—as opposed to the puppy love that he'd felt toward Mary Anne, who grew up to marry a doctor from Bend who knew all the pretty words that seemed to make Caleb tongue-tied. As long as a woman remained his friend, he didn't have any problems talking to her, teasing or even flirting a little. Like he did with Amber.

But when it came to Marnie, Caleb was just a bona fide mess. With Marnie it was all too much, he had too much to say, too much history with Roy, too many things he didn't know...too much that he did know.

And so he suffered in silence.

Maybe Sunday, after church, he figured. He'd go to her house, flowers in hand, and tell her he loved her, tell her how the Lord had laid it on his heart to be a prison chaplain, to minister to incarcerated men and women.

Then, after she kicked him out for reminding her of Roy, he'd go home and lick his wounds and try to mend his broken heart.

The skits went off without a hitch, with only two of the youngest children forgetting their parts. But their teammates helped them out and the Spirit Fire trophy went to the creative effort of a team depicting how faith as small as a mustard seed—portrayed by the silent Sutton Evans holding up a tiny pebble no one could even see—moves mountains.

The one part about the annual jamboree that Nancy Baines didn't like was saying goodbye to everyone. On the one hand, the end of the long weekend meant she could finally breathe and take a well-deserved rest. She planned to hold Cliff to that promise of a day at the spa. Truth be told, though, she anticipated a long soak in a warm tub at home. But before that, she had to bid farewell to all of her charges, the regulars whom they'd expect to see at the same time next year, as well as the scholarship students who'd brought new life, energy, expectations and trouble to the camp.

Now, Nancy watched as the children moved along the closing hug reception line.

"Are you seeing what I'm seeing?" Cliff leaned over and whispered.

All of the camper kids and teens were on one side of the modified receiving line, and all of the parents, volunteers and staff were on the other. From the happy chatter and laughter filling the air as hugs were passed along the line, no one would guess they'd all had a late night. Even the three girls who'd gone to the hospital were among those in the line.

What caught Cliff's attention, and Nancy's, too, was that Chief Evans and Amber had somehow wound up together as they moved through the gauntlet of well-wishers and farewell sayers. Sutton and Jonathan were right in front of them, grinning, jumping to the music that played from a boom box and having a great time.

"I do," Nancy answered her husband. "But I wonder if they see what's so evident to everyone else."

By the time Amber and Paul got to the end of the line where Nancy and Cliff waited to give and receive their own hugs and farewells, Amber's face was flush with laughter.

"Okay, Reverend Baines," she said. "I'll admit this part was fun."

"But not anything else?" Cliff asked, a smile in his voice.

Amber shrugged. "I'll get back to you with that assessment. But for now, just put it this way. The next time Haley and Kara need a backup chef at camp, I'll be busy."

Cliff laughed and gave her a hug anyway.

While Paul shook hands with Cliff, and Sutton and Jonathan got a big hug from Nancy, Amber stepped aside.

She hadn't had fun in the traditional sense this weekend. It seemed she'd been tested the entire time. Physically tested by taking a scary tumble in the water, an incident that now seemed as if it had happened weeks ago instead of in the last forty-eight hours—and tested by faith. She'd taken in a lot this weekend; she'd heard more and considered more than she'd been willing to think about over the past three years.

"You guys ready to load up the truck?"

"And move to Beverly," Amber hummed, finishing the line from one of the television classics she watched on a regular basis.

"I don't wanna leave, Daddy. Can't we stay another day?"

"Yeah, Dad. Let's stay another day," Jonathan concurred. "We can go rock climbing."

Paul crouched down. He smoothed Sutton's hair that had come loose of the band she wore. "The jamboree is over, honey. But, tell you guys what..."

"What?" both kids asked.

"How about on Saturday we go hiking?"

Whoops of joy followed that suggestion. Paul grinned. Yeah, he thought, moving to Oregon was just what they'd all needed.

"Go grab your backpacks and we'll be on our way."

When the kids raced off to claim their gear, Amber was talking to one of the teenagers. Paul watched her and marveled at how much he'd come to enjoy her company.

He wasn't fooled into believing that the intimacy they'd shared in this environment could be replicated once they got home, but he did wonder if Amber would be willing to see him again. He wanted to see her, even as a part of him realized her anger at God and her disdain of the Gospel were obstacles that couldn't be overlooked.

What Paul didn't know was just how much Amber had changed over the weekend. As she hugged Kirsten and then Leanne, promising to keep in touch with the budding chefs, she felt him watching her. His steady gaze, intent and rather disconcerting, seemed focused entirely on her. Amber met his gaze and, for a moment, the air between crackled with an electricity that they neither expected nor knew how to deal with.

"Thanks so much for everything!" Leanne gushed.

Amber blinked, and the moment with Paul was lost.

He cocked his head to the side, looking just as bemused as she felt.

Amber hugged Leanne again.

"I'll see you at church Sunday?" the teenager said.

"Uh..."

Amber saw Paul lean forward, waiting to hear her answer.

"I probably won't make it," Amber said.

She saw Paul's shoulders slump, and felt remorse at something intangible that she seemed to have lost in just that instant.

Two Community Christian Church vans rolled up along with two full-size vans and stopped in front of the lodge. The drivers got out, as did Eunice Gallagher.

"All aboard," she hollered.

As kids started loading into the vans, Eunice walked over and joined Nancy and Cliff.

"Eunice, aren't you a sight for sore eyes," Nancy said.

"I hear it's been lively up there. I missed all the action," the church secretary said.

"How'd the morning services go?" Cliff asked.

"Just fine. That Reverend Henderson kept everybody laughing as he talked about the first time he went fishing. His topic was about being fishers of men."

Cliff nodded. Every fifth Sunday, during the jamboree weekends, and when he and Nancy were on vacation, Community Christian's lead associate minister led the services.

Jonathan and Sutton ran back with their backpacks and duffel bags. "Hi, Mrs. G!" Jonathan called.

"Well, look who's here. Did you two have fun at your first jamboree?"

Both kids nodded.

"Are you going back with me or with your dad?"

Before they could answer, a girl came shrieking out of the woods from one of the trail paths.

All eyes turned in her direction.

"Help me! Help me! I need some help."

On the run, Nancy, Cliff and Paul, along with several of the adults, met her halfway. "Leslie, what's wrong?"

Out of breath, the girl stopped in front of Nancy and Paul, she clutched her side as she bent over. "Daphne. She's gonna jump. You...you gotta h-help her."

A collective gasp filled the air.

Leslie's words and her breathing came out in erratic puffs. "Please. Please. Kevin's trying to make her come down, but...but, sh-she's gonna jump. I just know it."

"Daphne? What is she doing back here?" Nancy said. "I saw her to her house in town. I spoke to her uncle."

"She ran away, caught a ride or something," Leslie said, crying and hiccuping. Tears streamed down the girl's cheeks.

Cliff and Paul stepped into the breach.

"Okay, Leslie," Paul said, bending over the girl. "I want you to catch your breath, okay? You understand?"

The girl nodded.

"We're going to need your help locating Daphne. Do you remember where she is?"

Leslie nodded again.

"All right," Paul said. "That's good. You have to show me just where she is. Do you think you can do that?"

Another nod.

Cliff waved for the van drivers to leave. "Eunice, would you oversee getting all the kids home?"

"Done," the ever-efficient church clerk said.

"D-daddy?" Fear laced Sutton's voice.

Paul paused and turned back to his children. "Dad's going to go to work now, just like I do every day. You guys go home with Mrs. G, and I'll see you soon, okay?"

He looked up at Eunice, who nodded and put her arms around the children's shoulders. "Come along. I'm sure everything here will be just fine. After all, look who's in charge."

She led the children to a van, but they kept turning back to Paul. He was hunched down, listening to Leslie describe where she'd left her friend. Eunice hustled the other children along.

Paul and Cliff quickly determined how they'd handle the situation.

"How did she get back up here?" Nancy asked.

"We can figure that out later," Paul said. "Right now we just need to find her."

"I'll go, too," Amber said.

"Maybe you should..."

"I've talked with Daphne a bit this weekend. Maybe I can talk to her now."

Paul studied her for a quiet moment, then nodded. "Let me grab some stuff from the truck."

He came back from his SUV a moment later with rope, clamps, a first-aid kit and water that he stuffed in a small backpack and shouldered. A braided cord draped across his shoulder and midsection. He handed Nancy a walkie-talkie and jammed a portable police radio in a pocket, then tugged on a pair of scuffed but sturdy gloves.

"We'll call as soon as we can. If it looks like we need more help, I'll tell you what to do."

Nancy nodded. "Be careful."

They huddled for a quick but earnest prayer, and then Paul, Cliff and Amber took off, following Leslie.

Chapter Eighteen

It took almost twenty minutes of hiking to get to the site. Amber recognized the lookout bluff where she and Marnie had talked the other day. Marnie had been concerned about her safety, and Amber was a grown woman who regularly worked out. About fifty yards beyond that point, through a break in the trees, they spied a flash of color.

"There they are," Leslie said. She ran ahead, calling for Kevin.

"I came up here the other day," Amber said. "There's a ledge right off the side of the cliff. You can easily get to it, but coming back up might be tricky."

"How wide?" Paul asked.

"About four feet."

He said something under his breath that she couldn't make out.

A few moments later, they reached the spot. Kevin,

lying on the ground, dangled his hand over the edge of a precipice.

"Oh, boy," Cliff said.

Surveying the area, Paul had to agree with the bleak assessment. If a path existed, he couldn't see it. The area, narrow and scrabbly, didn't offer much room to maneuver. He shrugged off the backpack.

Kevin glanced back at them. Concern etched the boy's face. None of the earlier cockiness the three children had displayed while scuffling with the other campers showed. The boy was scared.

"She's down there," he said.

"Who are you talking to?" Daphne demanded, her voice small but still laced with vehement disdain.

"Uh, it's that preacher. And the cop."

"Cop!" The girl swore. "Go away. I don't want you here. I got nothing to say to you."

"All right, Daphne," Paul said.

He unzipped the pack and pulled out the rope, testing its tensile strength and length. He looked around, but none of the trees in this area looked sturdy enough to serve as an anchor.

"Daphne, we came up to see about you," Cliff said.

"There ain't nothing to see," the girl said. "You kicked me out."

Amber, Paul and Cliff shared a look.

"Daph, you're scaring me," Leslie said. She'd sat cross-legged on the ground near Kevin, who continued at his prone post at the edge. "Why are you doing this?"

"Shut up, Leslie," Daphne said.

Leslie jumped up. "Fine. I don't care what you do. Jump. Go ahead and jump. Nobody cares."

"That's not true," Amber said, her voice quiet but filled with conviction. "Leslie, leave us alone for a minute."

Leslie stormed off down the mountainside, kicking up stones and brush in her wake.

"Who's that?" Daphne demanded.

Paul motioned for Amber to get closer, to talk to the girl.

"It's me," Amber said. "Amber Montgomery, the cook."

"Jesus, what'd Leslie do? Bring the whole camp up here?"

Kevin rolled over to give Amber some room, then scrambled up. He went straight to Cliff, who had his arms open wide to accept the boy whose face was streaked with dirt and tears.

Paul wrapped the rope around his waist and tied a knot. Then he used one of the clamps to secure it to the end of the cording he'd draped over his neck and shoulder.

"Leslie's gone," Amber said. "It's just me and some people who want to help you."

"I don't need any help," the girl said.

But a trickle of pebbles tumbled down and what sounded like a whimper floated up toward Amber.

"I used to think that, too," Amber said.

She looked over her shoulder at Cliff and Paul. Cliff was tending to scratches and scrapes on the boy's hands and knees, while Paul had edged into the thicket, the radio at his mouth as he tried to get a message through to the camp without alerting Daphne.

Amber faced the edge again, then got down on the ground, prone the way Kevin had been. "I used to think nobody cared about me."

"I don't think it, I know it," Daphne said. "Nobody wants me."

"I bet that's not true," Amber said, even as she prayed it wasn't. With a start she realized she'd been praying from the moment Leslie burst into the compound saying Daphne was in trouble. As a matter of fact, she'd been praying all weekend.

Lord, give me the words to help her. Keep her safe, please.

"Nobody likes me at school. And nobody likes me at this stupid camp."

"Did I tell on you when you were in the kitchen?" Amber asked. "Did I turn you in?"

Silence greeted those questions.

"Friends look out for each other," Amber said. "Kevin and Leslie were concerned enough about you to call for some help. We don't want to see anything happen to you, Daphne. Especially me."

"Why?" The question was small and wary.

Amber had been through the same things as this young girl. She'd found herself in an unbearable situation with Raymond, and the only way out had been to take herself out of the game, to declare defeat and just end it all.

Then, like now, Amber wasn't quite sure where her strength came from, but she knew this troubled young teenager needed to hear that others carried burdens, if not identical to her own, just as heavy.

"Because I was once just like you," Amber said. "I was a little older, but I was considering doing the same thing you're considering."

"You were gonna jump off a mountain?"

"No," Amber said. "I was going to shoot myself in the head with my boyfriend's gun."

Paul's head whipped up. Cliff dropped the antiseptic spray he was holding.

But all of Amber's concentration was on the thirteen-year-old with the grown-up problems.

"How come you were gonna do that?"

"The guy I was seeing then, my boyfriend, he beat me up all the time," Amber said.

Daphne sniffled. "My uncle hits me, too."

"It hurts, doesn't it," Amber said.

"Yeah." But the word was clouded by snuffles indicating Daphne was crying. "I hate living there. He makes me do things. In the dark. He tried last night and I ran away."

Amber's heart went out to the girl. Instinctively, though, she knew not to say any of the platitudes that people usually offered up. "It's not your fault, Daphne," she said simply. "And you don't have to take it anymore."

Amber realized that what she said was true, not just for Daphne, but for herself as well.

"He curses at me and hits me, then he..." Daphne started crying in earnest then, the sound pitiful.

Amber's own tears fell. *Lord, tell me what to do.*

"It's going to be all right, Daphne. The Lord loves you, and so do I. You're gonna get through today, and then tomorrow and the next day and the next. And every day is going to be better than the one before. I promise."

The words came from a place Amber didn't even know existed. She didn't know how or why she said what she did, but in her heart of hearts, she knew that it would work out for Daphne.

And if she did nothing else, she'd make sure that that man paid for what he'd done to the girl, just like Raymond Alvarez was paying for what he'd done to Amber.

Amber started when Paul tapped her on the shoulder. She looked back and up. He stood with the ropes, a lasso made to haul Daphne up.

"Daphne?"

No answer.

Amber peered over the edge. Loose stones fell.

A whimper sounded from below.

"Daphne?"

"Uh-huh?"

"I'm going to send down a rope for you. Will you take it so I can get you up?"

"No."

Amber cast stricken eyes up at Paul. He moved his hands in a rolling motion for Amber to keep talking.

"We can talk better up here."

"I'm not going back there."

"And nobody's going to make you," Amber said.

"They did before."

"It won't happen again," Amber insisted. "I'm going to see to it myself."

"Leslie said that big cop was up there. He wants to take me to jail."

"You're not going to jail," Paul said, his voice as level and soothing as if he were tucking a sleepy Sutton into bed. "Why would we take you to jail? We're going to get you some help."

"I don't believe you. Cops lie."

"Yeah," Amber said, her attention back on the girl. "Some of them do. The boyfriend who used to beat me up all the time was a cop. He thought he could get away with it because of his position. But what he did to me was wrong, just like what your uncle is doing to you is wrong. We can put a stop to it, Daphne. But you've got to help."

"How?"

"Well, first we've got to get you up from there."

A piece of the ledge gave way, and Daphne screamed.

Paul tossed the rope to Cliff. "We've got to hurry. I radioed for a helicopter, but it'll take at least another forty minutes to get here from Portland. We don't have that much time."

"Show me what to do," Cliff said.

"Hold on, Daph. I'm coming for you," Amber said.

"Argh!" came up from where Daphne was trapped.

Amber leaned over, and more rocks tumbled. Paul pulled her back.

"I can't have you falling, too." He tugged on the rope, then made a lasso. "Daphne, I'm going to send a rope to you. I want you to put it over your head, settle it under your arms and tug it."

"I can't."

"What do you mean, you can't."

Amber pushed at him. "She's already scared enough. You're gonna freak her out." To Daphne she said, "It's okay. I know you can do it."

She turned to Paul. "Let me. I'll go down there, get her secured, and you and Cliff can pull us both up."

Paul mentally weighed the risks. It was too dangerous to lower Amber to the ledge that was already showing signs of strain.

"It's not safe," he said.

"What can I do?" Kevin said.

Paul had forgotten about the boy. "Mrs. Baines is directing the rescue workers up here. Can you go meet them? Show them where we are?"

Kevin nodded, earnest in his mission. "Daphne, it's gonna be okay," he called out. "We're all gonna get you."

"Okay" came a small, scared voice. "I think you better hurry."

Kevin tore off through the brush down the mountain.

Amber figured she knew just as much if not more than

Paul about wilderness survival. And this sure looked like a survival mission.

"Lower me down and I'll pull her back up."

Paul shook his head. "It's too dangerous."

"I weigh a lot less than you do," she pointed out. "It'll work."

Paul knew she was right, but he didn't like it. Not one bit.

He took the rope from around his waist and put it over Amber's head and shoulders. After securing it, he kissed her hard and fast. "Be careful."

"I will."

With Paul and Cliff acting as anchors, she got on the ground and edged over the side of the cliff.

With Amber dangling over the side of the mountain, rocks and grasses broke away.

Daphne shrieked in terror.

Amber tossed the lasso she carried with her over the girl's head. She could see the crack in the ledge as the ground began to break away. "Pull it down, Daphne, pull it down around you."

Daphne reached for the rope.

The ledge gave way.

✂ Chapter Nineteen ✂

Amber didn't know who yelled louder in that instant—she, Daphne, Cliff or Paul. She'd been scared before, but never, ever, like that. In one agonizingly long moment, she thought she'd lost Daphne, that she herself was also tumbling head over heels down the jagged cliff side and into the raging waters below.

But Cliff and Paul dug in, holding fast.

After the rescue, no one talked during the trip down the mountain, with Daphne on a stretcher that had been hauled up by the EMTs. When they emerged through the trees, a crowd waited at the camp. Word had gotten out in town, and Community Christian Church members, teenagers and worried parents flocked to the camp. A hospital helicopter whirred in a clearing.

A cheer went up when Paul said no one had life-threatening injuries. Daphne had suffered a gash on her leg from a root that scraped her as they'd hauled her up. Cliff had rope burns on his hands. And all four of them bore myriad scrapes and scratches. But they were all safe.

Amber and Paul, both obstinate, insisted they were fine and didn't need to go to the hospital. But despite Cliff's objections, an anxious Nancy insisted he get his hands checked.

While a reporter and photographer from the *Wayside Gazette* snapped pictures and asked questions of some of the teens, Amber slipped away. Spying her, Paul followed.

Even now, safe and secure at the compound, Amber felt adrenaline racing through her veins. She walked in circles, flexing her hands. She wanted to run, to scream, to hit something.

"Walk it off," Paul said.

She whirled around. "Huh?"

"Come on," he said, grabbing her hand. "Walk it off. I can see the pent-up energy pulsing in you. It's like that with near-death experiences."

"I need to run."

"Let's go, then." And so they took off, silent but together. By mutual but unspoken agreement, they headed toward the entrance of the camp rather than the acreage so thoroughly explored over the long weekend. After the third mile, Amber was starting to feel better—and a little silly.

"Thank you," she said, as they jogged along the roadside.

Sparse traffic traveled along the road leading to the camp on this mid-afternoon in early fall. The rest of the day promised to be cool but comfortable.

They eventually slowed to a walk as they again approached the camp entrance. "This has been one long three-and-a-half-day weekend. It seems like we've been up here at least a month."

Paul chuckled. "Time is like that, especially when a lot is going on." They were quiet for a moment. Then, he said, "Amber, I realize now that what happened in the water and the other day while we were hiking together... Well, I want to apologize for my behavior."

"You have nothing to apologize for," she said.

"From the moment we met, all I've done is manhandle you in some way, shape or form," he said. "I see now that I could have managed every one of those situations in a better way."

"I don't usually talk about what happened to me in L.A.," Amber told him. "The life I had there is stuff I want to banish from my memory banks. It's just taken me a little longer than I would have expected or liked."

"What you told Daphne on that mountain saved her life."

"You and Cliff Baines saved her life," Amber said. "You two were the ones pulling. If you hadn't been pulling like crazy, we'd all be dead or seriously injured right now."

Paul shook his head, disagreeing with her as she discounted her own efforts to save Daphne. "I don't think there are any coincidences in this life, Amber. Everything on this earth happens for a reason. Even if we can't see or touch or even know the reason or discover the impact, there's still a reason."

"Like me meeting Jon and Sutton at Sunshine and Rainbows?"

He nodded. "You were meant to be here today, to help that girl. I couldn't have talked her down. Neither could Cliff. We had nothing to offer her." He ran a hand through his hair. "Shoot, if it had just been us up there, she probably would have jumped. Your experience is what she could relate to. You gave her hope."

Not comfortable with the praise, Amber didn't say anything.

"I wish I could get my hands on that cop who hurt you," he said.

"He's probably out of prison and beating up somebody else now."

"But you're here," Paul said. "Don't you think God had a hand in that?"

Amber shrugged, not willing to confess to him that she'd been having the same thoughts.

The God she'd believed abandoned her in Los Angeles had always been there, sheltering her, preparing her. If not for this day and that young girl, for a greater purpose that he had yet to reveal for her life.

She glanced at the man next to her. Over the past few days, she'd come to think of him as more than a lug-head cop. As more than just another man who had the potential to hurt her. Not every police officer was like Raymond Alvarez.

She'd borne witness to the fact that there were, indeed, Christian men who were strong believers, who lived their faith, walked it and talked it even while going about their normal lives.

Growing up, she'd thought of her parents, particularly her father, as a Bible thumper, but she now realized that the particular calling on her parents' lives meant they had to be bold in their faith.

Amber didn't know if she was ready to be bold, but she was ready to make a new commitment to walk in the light. To trust God the way she used to. She looked at her feet, the hiking boots. "Trust in the Lord with all your heart, And lean not on your own understanding; In all your ways acknowledge Him, And He shall direct your paths." He'd surely directed their paths today.

Considering Paul's words, Amber realized that everything so far in her life *had* been leading to this moment, this day. What part did the man next to her have in it all?

"You kissed me back there."

He nodded. "I did."

"Actually, that was the second time this weekend."

The first time, when they'd gone in search of the missing Jonathan and Sutton, she'd been too stunned to think about what that might mean. And up on that mountain, she hadn't had time to process anything except the crisis at hand.

"Why?"

It was Paul's turn to contemplate his feet. "Why did I kiss you?"

He was stalling for time because, in all honesty, he didn't know. "I... Amber, to level with you, I don't know. I didn't plan to either time." He shrugged. "What made me do it? Maybe it had something to do with the adrenaline factor of both situations."

She studied his face. Those Mediterranean-blue eyes were filled with questions, many of the same ones that she herself had. She checked her pulse, then reached for his arm and checked his.

Paul smiled. "What are you doing?"

"The adrenaline factor isn't an issue right now. My heartbeat is back to normal. Yours, too."

He nodded. "And?"

"And I just wanted to make sure that there was nothing going on that this could be blamed on."

He opened his mouth to ask what she was talking about, but Amber placed an open palm on his chest and leaned forward. She didn't let herself think beyond this moment, this single irrational act. All Amber knew was that she wanted to kiss Paul, to have him hold her for just a moment, to be able to believe, if only for this snapshot in time, that she had worth and value and beauty to share.

She pressed her lips to his and felt his arm encircle her waist.

She quivered at the sweet tenderness of his touch.

Marveled at how she felt like a flower blossoming after days without the sun or rain.

And then, she stepped away.

"I need to go."

"But..."

Amber didn't give him a chance to say anything else. She dashed up the drive, leaving Paul standing at the entrance to Camp Spirit Fire, cherishing the precious, precious gift he'd just been given.

For the last time, Amber glanced back at the Community Christian Church camp. She'd taken the job to help Haley and Kara out, as well as to boost her business's bottom line. But over the course of the long weekend, she'd found something far more valuable than an hourly wage payable at triple rate.

She'd found the way home.

Wise words from the Old Testament came to mind: "Train up a child in the way he should go and when he is old, he won't depart from them." After years of running, years of believing that God didn't care a whit about her, Amber realized that He'd never stopped caring, never stopped loving her, even though she'd turned her back on Him.

"Forgive me, Lord," she said out loud.

And instantly, she was delivered, set free and made whole.

Her voice seemed to echo in the van, but Amber sat focused on the joy bubbling up through her spirit and soul. Tears streamed down her face. "Thank you, Lord. Thank you."

She wasn't sure just how long she sat there. Maybe until her tears dried. Maybe until her spirit was completely renewed.

As she reached for the keys to start the ignition, a knock sounded at the window.

Paul stood there, concern on his face. "Are you okay? Do you need a jump?"

Amber looked at him, a grin slowly spreading on her face. Then she opened her door and jumped out. "I'm better than okay," she said. "I'm fabulous!" She threw her arms around his neck.

Laughing, caught up in her enthusiasm, Paul smiled as he clasped her about the waist to avoid them both taking a tumble to the ground.

Amber, laughing and crying at the same time, tried to tell him. Tried to get all the words out. But there was too much. Too much joy. Too much relief that she was once again in the safe arms of the Lord.

She pressed a kiss to his cheek and hugged him close. "Thank you!"

Paul hugged her back. "For what?"

She spread her arms wide. "For this."

Paul's brows creased. "I know it's been a pretty traumatic day. Is this your celebration that it's all over?"

She cupped his cheek with the palm of her hand and gazed into his kind blue eyes. "Yes. And no."

She grabbed his hand, shook it as if he were a stranger

she'd just met, then turned to her van. "There's something I have to do."

A bemused Paul just stared at her.

A moment later, she gunned the engine and sped down the drive. About fifteen minutes after that, the enormity of what she was about to do hit her. She eased up on the gas as she turned onto the familiar street—one she'd studiously avoided for three years.

Everything looked the same, and it all looked different. The grass somehow seemed greener, but the houses smaller. With a start, Amber realized that she'd never really viewed this street—one house in particular— through adult eyes. She wondered if everything about the house and the yard would also be just as it was in her memory.

Her bedroom in the house featured wallpaper with little pink and green flowers, a desk under the window. A straw doll, given by Angeline as a farewell gift, would be on her pillow. That doll was the one thing she'd missed having with her all these years.

In the time since she'd returned to Wayside, Amber had actively avoided her parents. Helen Montgomery had made overtures, had attempted to bridge the divide that separated them, but Amber had rebuffed every attempt at reconciliation. Even so, every year on her birthday and at Christmas, a card arrived, signed by both her parents. Each one carried two things: a familiar Bible verse, and a message from them—*We love you, Amber.*

If she hadn't known better, she'd have been willing to

bet real money that Helen and Richard Montgomery arranged with Pastor Cliff to use Proverbs 3:5-6 as a Scripture text at the camp.

"In all your ways acknowledge Him, And He shall direct your paths."

He shall direct your path. Amber laughed nervously at that. When she'd awakened this morning, it hadn't been with the intention that she'd stop a girl from jumping off a cliff, or reunite with her parents.

Rededicating her life to the Lord was one thing. Showing up on Helen and Richard Montgomery's front doorstep was another altogether.

She hesitated. Then, climbing out of the van and heading up the walk before she completely lost her nerve, she muttered, "What do you have to lose?"

Reaching out a tentative hand, Amber glanced back at her van. She could be out of here and they'd never even know she'd stopped by.

Her heart was racing as if she'd been running.

She was struck by the realization that she had, indeed, been running. All of her life. Running away from unpleasant truths, running away from Raymond Alvarez, running away from her own fears.

It was time to face all of those fears head-on. As long as she kept them bottled inside, instead of dissipating, they grew into out-of-control monsters that threatened to consume her.

Taking a deep, cleansing breath, Amber pressed the doorbell.

* * *

Caleb figured it was now or never.

At some point a man had to face the unpleasant truth. He had to tell Marnie how he felt. Even if she spurned him, even if she said he was despicable for loving his brother's wife and told him she never wanted to see him again, he had to take this next step. If he didn't, he thought he just might explode.

He'd been too embarrassed to talk to his pastor or any of his friends about Marnie. And he sure wasn't about to bring it up with Roy.

Caleb pulled his pickup truck into the drive, skirting the tree trunk. Marnie's grass was a little higher than normal. He made a mental note to swing by later and mow the lawn for her.

Clearing his throat and ignoring the knot in his gut, he knocked at the front door.

A moment later, she opened it, her smile growing wide when she saw him.

"Hi, Caleb. Come on in. I was just thinking about you."

His hopes soared. "You were?"

He followed her into the house.

And stopped cold when he saw the boxes in the living room. Plastic bubble wrap and newspapers were stacked at the ready in the easy chair.

"What's going on?"

"I'm leaving."

His heart slammed into his chest. "What do you mean leaving?"

She went to the sofa and sat down, patting the cushion beside her. Photo albums lay open on the coffee table in front of the couch. Caleb glanced at a picture of the three of them—himself, Marnie and Roy—at a basketball game in Portland. He remembered the night well: the Trailblazers won the game and he'd acknowledged that his feelings for Marnie went much deeper than appropriate given the fact that she and Roy were married.

Marnie tucked a leg under her on the cushion and faced him, excitement racing over her features. "I'm going to Coos Bay," she told him. "I've been offered a job and I've given it a lot of thought. I'm going to take it."

"Coos Bay? That's three or four hours from here."

She nodded, reached for his hands. "Caleb, I'm so excited. I realized this weekend that there's nothing holding me here. Nothing except bad memories. I'm going to go down there and start over."

But I'm here, he wanted to say. *We can start good memories together. Just the two of us.*

But he didn't say the words. Instead, he bit back bitter disappointment. Maybe they just weren't meant to be.

"You deserve that," he told her. "You deserve every happiness."

Marnie leaned back in the sofa cushions and closed her eyes. "I can't believe I'm doing this," she said. She sat up again and grinned. "But it feels so good. Of course, I have to give notice at Sunshine and Rainbows. And find a place to live down there, and get my stuff shipped. But, oh, Caleb, I'm so happy."

She threw her arms around him, and Caleb closed his eyes, savoring the closeness, the light citrus scent of her perfume, her soft curves, the texture of her hair. He inhaled it all, delighting in the moment, storing up the memories that he'd need to get him through the days, weeks and months without her near.

"I'm happy for you, too, Marnie."

But Caleb closed his eyes and prayed he wouldn't start crying.

❧ Chapter Twenty ❧

"Is Amber going to be our mommy?"

Sutton and Jonathan were in Sutton's room, sitting on her bed. It had been a week since they'd returned from jamboree, and the day after a cool hiking trip, but they were still talking about the church camp weekend, Amber in particular.

"She can't be," Jonathan told his sister. "We already have a mommy."

"But I don't remember her," Sutton said. "I want a mom like everybody else. Susie's mom bakes her cookies that look like her doll. And Kenyatta's mom braids her hair." Sutton fingered her ponytail—all Paul could manage by way of styling a five-year-old's hair. "If I had a mommy, she'd braid my hair."

Jonathan pouted. "What do you need a mom for?"

Sutton looked at her brother as if he'd just sprouted two heads. "For just about everything," she said.

Paul stood at the door of Sutton's bedroom. He'd been about to roust them out and downstairs for breakfast, but their conversation stopped him cold. He paused, not quite sure how to approach the children.

He liked Amber—a lot. In the week since they'd been home, he'd thought of little else but the woman who'd placed a hand over his heart and pressed her lips to his.

He'd seen Amber in that week. She'd followed through on her promise to Daphne. The girl and her younger brother were both in the care of a loving foster family, one that Cliff Baines recommended and knew. The circumstances of the children's home life with their aunt and uncle was the stuff of case studies. But with an outraged Amber as an advocate, and both Paul and Reverend Baines as witnesses to what a frightened Daphne said on that mountain, justice would be served on behalf of the girl and her brother.

But each time he'd seen Amber in public, she had acted as if he were nothing but the town's police chief. He'd tried to see her, had even stopped by her place a couple of times, but Amber was either busy with catering orders or on the way to her parents' house.

He knew that what had happened at Camp Spirit Fire had been an aberration, a moment out of time that had no bearing on the reality they all lived. Still, all week, Paul's thoughts had been on Amber.

His prayers for guidance seemed to go unheeded, and now, here sat Jonathan and Sutton dissecting his life—their lives.

Any woman who became a part of his life would also become part of his children's lives. That's why he'd all but stopped dating after Mikey and Sarah died—that and the grief...compounded with the guilt.

Through the group counseling sponsored by the police department, he'd finally been able to accept that he wasn't to blame for their deaths. If it hadn't been Mikey and Sarah, it would have been someone else. But a part of him never let go of the fact that it *was* his fault.

He loved these two children more than anything in the world and he wouldn't risk their already fragile emotional well-being just because he wanted some companionship. The women he had met and dated before the shooting weren't the type interested in a ready-made family. And the ones he'd met afterward—mostly in grief counseling—had had just as much mental baggage as he did. The last thing he needed was somebody else's drama and crisis points while he still worked through his own.

So he'd just skipped the whole dating thing and any thought of it. Until now. He'd moved to Wayside in part to find a woman with godly values who could accept him and the children with love. Instead of finding a morph of housewife stereotypes, though, he'd fallen for a skittish caterer who had just as many issues as he did—maybe more. Despite what he'd thought he wanted, the Lord had had another vision.

Except that now it looked like maybe Amber *wasn't* the one.

Granted, he knew very little about Amber Montgomery, and the part he did know was enough to send a sane man running in the opposite direction. He'd checked up on Raymond Alvarez, and what he'd found still made his blood boil. But Paul wanted to get to know Amber, to go out on a normal date—one that didn't involve half drowning in a raging river or clinging to the side of a collapsing cliff.

It had just been a week, and a busy one at that, but he could take a hint. She'd kissed him with sweet tenderness up at Camp Spirit Fire, but that kiss, he now realized, had been a rite of passage for her, not a declaration of intent or desire for more.

"Hey, guys," he said in greeting.

The children looked up, guilty expressions on their faces as if they'd been caught doing something wrong.

"Hi, Daddy."

"What are you guys talking about? You're looking awfully serious and glum for a cheery Sunday morning."

"Nothing, Daddy," Sutton said, but she cast a quick glance at Jonathan.

"Nothing, Uncle Paul."

Paul raised a brow at that. He doubted that Jonathan even realized that the only time he referred to Paul as "uncle" was when he was sleepy or angry. Since the children were both fully dressed and wide awake, Paul knew he had an issue to deal with. One that couldn't wait.

"Nothing, huh?" he said, entering the room and settling on the edge of Sutton's bed. The girl climbed into his lap. "I heard you guys talking about Amber."

Sutton looked at Jonathan, and then at Paul. "I want Amber to be my mommy, but Jon says she can't 'cause we already have a mom."

"Yes," Paul said. "You do have a mom. But she's in heaven with Jesus, looking out for you."

Sutton gave Jon a "so-there" tongue poke.

Paul tapped her leg. "None of that."

"Are you gonna marry Amber?" Jon asked the question with a belligerent tone, his chin poked out.

Paul realized he needed to be totally honest with them on this. Any decision he made would also have an impact on their lives.

"It's crossed my mind," he told them. "But when and if—and that's a big if—I ever get married, whomever marries me, marries you, too. We're a team. A package deal, and nobody's ever going to change that."

Sutton raised a hand and brushed at the corner of his eyes. "Daddy, you look sad."

Was the girl clairvoyant as well? "We had a long weekend and it's been a busy week. Plus, you wore me out yesterday on that trail."

She stared at him for a bit, as if willing the truth from him. Then, like the five-year-old she was, her attention wandered. "Jon says he didn't like the camp."

"I didn't say that."

"Yes, you did."

"I didn't," the boy said in his own defense. "What I said was, I didn't like the way we had to hurry up and eat. Nobody got to savor their meals."

Paul's brow wrinkled. "Savor their meals? Where'd you hear that?"

"Amber says that's what people should do when they eat," Sutton reported.

Paul grinned. "Well, she's right. How would you guys like to savor some spaghetti after church?"

Their cheers told him he'd picked a winner for dinner. But Paul felt a lingering need to explain about Amber.

"If I ever decide to get serious about someone, she'll have to meet with your approval. You're more important to me than anyone else."

Sutton frowned. "But we don't want someone else. We want Amber!"

Paul looked at Jonathan, who nodded his agreement.

Paul wanted Amber, too. But he was afraid that Amber didn't want him.

The eleven o'clock service at Community Christian Church was jammed. Extra chairs were brought out and placed along the back row. The Sunday after the jamboree was always packed. Kids went home, told their parents and friends about the camping weekend, and both services had an overflowing congregation. But the end of this year's jamboree had been anything but normal.

The *Wayside Gazette* had done three articles about the

mountain rescue of Daphne Gregory and the heroic effort to save her by the pastor, the police chief and the Cookie Lady. Young Kevin even had his picture in the paper showing how he'd led the EMTs to the spot.

During the weekend, several young people had come forward during the campfire invitations, and this was their first exposure to the formal church. So they and all their families were also in attendance.

Matt Brandon-Dumaine led the inspirational choir through two hand-clapping selections. Then Cliff got up. Today he wore a robe, instead of the jeans and light sweaters he'd donned in the woods.

"Welcome to Family and Friends Day at Community Christian," he said. "We're delighted to have all of you with us this morning. And let me just tell you this, we are *truly glad* to be here!"

A cheer went up among the congregation.

He asked all of the people who had spent the weekend at jamboree and those who had helped prepare for the camp to stand. Applause, loud and long, sounded out in the sanctuary.

Near the back, in the only place they'd been able to find seats, Paul and the children clapped with the others and then settled again in their pew.

Sutton motioned for Paul. As he leaned down so she could whisper in his ear, someone slipped into the seat next to him.

"We have many things to thank God for this day," Cliff said. "At this time I'd like everyone to take a few moments to reflect on the goodness of the Lord. As you take the hand of your neighbor, bow your heads and close your eyes for a moment of individual thanks."

Jonathan took Sutton's hand. On Paul's left, Sutton put her small hand in her dad's. And Paul extended his right to the person next to him. He glanced over and his eyes widened.

Amber.

Their gazes held, and then she smiled.

"Hey," she said.

"Hey."

This day had been a long time coming, but Amber had no doubt she'd made the right decision. In private she'd rededicated her life to the Lord. Now, by coming to church again, she'd make the public profession of faith. And maybe, just maybe, she'd step into the light of a new relationship with a man who loved the Lord as much as she did.

As Cliff began a congregational prayer of thanks, Amber put her hand in Paul's. Then, her gaze holding his eyes, she laced her fingers with his.

When he gently squeezed and lifted their joined hands to press a kiss to the back of her hand, Amber knew she had yet another thing to be thankful for.

What would happen next between them would be revealed as time passed and they got to know each other. For now, though, Amber's spirit overflowed with joy.

Sweet peace filled her. The Lord had brought her

through the trials in L.A., and the danger of this week-end, all the while keeping her safe.

He'd seen her reunited with her parents, and now with Paul, He'd provided the potential of something more, something she welcomed because she'd never thought she'd have it in her life: the sweet devotion of a God-fearing man and the love of two beautiful children.

Thanking God for all His many blessings, Amber smiled and bowed her head in prayer.

✎ Author Note ✎

In the time since my first Love Inspired novel was published, I've received many, many letters asking about Amber, who was introduced in *Sweet Accord*. What happened to her? Did she ever find hope and healing? Will she have her own story? Amber did find her way home, literally and spiritually. I hope you enjoyed reading about her journey.

In addition to spiritual guidance, Amber needed a physical guide, someone she could trust who would understand her fears without judging her. In *Sweet Devotion*, Marnie Shepherd served in that role for Amber. But real-life women who are in crisis need a friend as well.

If you or someone who know or love is in need of a friend, a listening ear, there is help available. Domestic violence takes many forms. It can be physical, emotional, verbal or sexual. If you're not sure whether what you're seeing or experiencing is domestic violence, there are organizations across the country that can answer your questions. They cater especially to women who have been abused.

If you'd like more information for yourself or someone you know, call the National Domestic Violence Hotline at 1-800-799-SAFE (1-800-799-7233). It's a toll-free call, and someone is available twenty-four hours a day to offer crisis intervention, referrals to local agencies and help in finding resources. You can also log on to www.ndvh.org for more information.

Thank you for reading *Sweet Devotion*. I enjoy hearing from readers, so if you'd like to write, I can be reached at P.O. Box 1438, Dept. LI, Yorktown, VA 23692. If you are able, please enclose a self-addressed stamped envelope for a prompt reply.

May God's blessings and peace shine on you.